ACCLAIM FOR

The KENNEDYS: AFTER CAMELOT

"An ambitious chronicle...full of delicious inside stories...If you can't get enough of the Kennedys, this book is for you."

—*Minneapolis Star Tribune*

"Thoroughly engrossing...a fascinating tell-all."   —*Birmingham Times*

"Meticulous multilayered details breathe life into remarkable recreations of family gatherings throughout this superb 'fly on the wall' survey of the Camelot clan."   —*Publishers Weekly* (starred review)

"He keeps readers deeply engaged with a comfortable, almost novelistic style...will appeal both to those long fascinated with the Kennedys and those new to following them."   —*Library Journal*

"A revealing glimpse at the ongoing saga of this extraordinary family."

—*Booklist*

"A page-turning, emotionally riveting saga."   —*BookPage*

"Taraborrelli celebrates the enduring appeal of America's royal family... [He] gathers every luscious detail of the scandals, arrests, affairs, over-doses and bad-boy antics that have marked the post-Camelot years. It's all here...The author reveals the family's most intimate details...A big, juicy read for Kennedy fans."   —*Kirkus Reviews*

ALSO BY J. RANDY TARABORRELLI

JACKIE, ETHEL, JOAN:
Women of Camelot

ONCE UPON A TIME:
*Behind the Fairy Tale of Princess Grace and
Prince Rainier*

Elizabeth

The Secret Life of Marilyn Monroe

MICHAEL JACKSON:
The Magic, the Madness, the Whole Story (1958–2009)

THE HILTONS:
The True Story of an American Dynasty

SINATRA:
Behind the Legend

BECOMING BEYONCÉ:
The Untold Story

J. RANDY TARABORRELLI

The
KENNEDYS
AFTER CAMELOT

*A Personal History
of the Kennedy Family
1968 to the Present*

GRAND CENTRAL
PUBLISHING

New York   Boston   Nashville

Grand Central Publishing
Hachette Book Group
1290 Avenue of the Americas
New York, NY 10104

grandcentralpublishing.com
twitter.com/grandcentralpub

Printed in the United States of America

LSC-C

Originally published in hardcover by Grand Central Publishing.

First media tie-in trade edition: March 2017
10 9 8 7 6 5 4 3 2 1

Grand Central Publishing is a division of Hachette Book Group, Inc.
The Grand Central Publishing name and logo is a trademark of Hachette Book Group, Inc.

The Hachette Speakers Bureau provides a wide range of authors for speaking events. To find out more, go to www.hachettespeakersbureau.com or call (866) 376-6591.

The publisher is not responsible for websites (or their content) that are not owned by the publisher.

The Library of Congress has cataloged the hardcover edition as follows:
Taraborrelli, J. Randy.
    After Camelot : an intimate history of the Kennedy family, 1968 to the present /
J. Randy Taraborrelli. — 1st ed.
        p. cm.
    Includes bibliographical references and index.
    ISBN 978-0-446-55390-2 (alk. paper)
    1. Kennedy family.   I. Title.
    E843.T37 2012
    973.922092'2—dc23
    [B]
                                                                    2011029518

ISBN 978-1-538-74433-8 (mti)

For Rocco and Rose Marie Taraborrelli

When I sit at a family gathering, with literally dozens of children and grandchildren, nieces and nephews surrounding me, tears come to my eyes. I marvel at their talents, their articulateness, their devotion to justice and their grace. I am reminded once again that family shapes us all, and that to be held in the arms of a loving family redeems even the most numbing pain.
—Ted Kennedy, Senate prayer, October 6, 1999

To whom much has been given, much is required.
Luke 12:48

CONTENTS

A NOTE FROM THE AUTHOR

If it could ever be said that America had a "royal family," it would be the Kennedys of Massachusetts. For more than half a century, we as a nation have been captivated by their compelling story, a saga that encompasses as much tragedy as triumph, as much heartbreak as joy. In a sense, we are their loyal subjects, consumed with their mystique, mesmerized by their charisma. That the Kennedys always seemed to have an almost pathological aversion to the media only made the reports of their comings and goings all the more interesting. With the passing of the years, we've wanted to know all there was to know about this powerful family, and monitoring their behavior as reported on television or in newspapers and magazines was almost like being there. Of course, there are any number of reasons for our enduring fascination with their lives—not the least of which has been the curse of tragedy that has seemingly haunted them for decades. Still, the singular, most compelling aspect of their story has been its sheer and utter...humanity.

I am reminded of the first time I met Jackie Kennedy Onassis. It was in 1985 in New York City, when she was an editor at Doubleday and I was about to write my first book, a biography of Diana Ross, for that publishing company. A chance meeting in an elevator later led to a spirited conversation in her office about pop culture, which of course I will never forget. As she spoke, I looked into her dark, inquisitive eyes and couldn't help but wonder: Who is she, really? And what does she make of her place in history as a woman whose private tragedies became the public spectacle of an entire generation? After everything she endured—with a life at once so opulent and blessed, and at the same time shattered and cursed— what was the source from which she drew her fortitude, her confidence and self-determination? As we talked, I couldn't help but think about her place in American lore and how trauma and loss had come to define it.

I thought about President Kennedy. Dallas, 1963. Bobby Kennedy. Los Angeles, 1968. Ted Kennedy. Chappaquiddick, 1969. All of these events were entwined with my childhood, all of it my story just as it is every American's. And there she was, standing in front of me, a woman who had actually *been* there, who knew it all. Who had lived it. Go ahead, I thought, my ever-curious mind kicking in for an instant. Ask her something about it. Ask her *anything*. But there was something about her, and about that time with her, that made the idea of asking even a single probing question about her life seem inappropriate. She was so charming, so warm and friendly. So accessible. She was so everyday in her humanity that only the most callous person would ever dream of asking her a personal question that might revive any trauma, any pain.

I think it was on that day as I spoke to Jackie that I began to understand a true secret to the Kennedys' enduring celebrity: There is no wall. True, on the national stage, these people are and would always be ferociously private. But out in the real world, many of them are just as approachable as anyone else you might meet in an elevator. For her part, Jackie—an editor whose office didn't even have windows—certainly wasn't living as though she were larger than life, like most celebrities do: in an ivory tower, detached from the everyday. She was, to put it simply, a very nice lady, and in many ways just like the rest of us. She'd had her ups and downs in life. She'd made the best of the cards she'd been dealt, and now, widowed twice, she was in New York City, starting over at a job that paid her just $200 a week, writing a new chapter of her own story. Not for the sake of the public, or for the history books, or for a young writer she might happen to meet in an elevator on the way to work. She was doing it for herself, living her life *despite* her worldwide fame. That was her secret and, I have come to believe, one of the secrets of the entire Kennedy family: Though celebrated, they are not really "celebrities." At the risk of seeming reductive of such iconic figures who have often appeared larger than life, in many ways they are simply people who have been through tough times and have somehow learned, as a family, to get on with the business of living, all the while maintaining a determined optimism.

Certainly when I first met Senator Ted Kennedy (and his wife, Victoria Reggie) in October 1996 at a symposium on the legacy of the Kennedy women at the John F. Kennedy Library in Boston, I was struck by his congenial, "everyman" attitude. "Yes, we have had some hard knocks," he told me in what was obviously a great understatement, "but we as a family have survived because we have heart. And heart matters." That evening, I also met and had the opportunity to ask questions of three of Ethel's daughters, Rory, Kerry, and Kathleen. What most stands out in my mind about them all these years later is their obvious closeness. It was almost like talking to one woman, the way they began and finished each other's sentences. "It's difficult when your most private moments are also your most public moments," Kerry told me when speaking of the tragedies the family has faced. "But it's interesting, too, because we have never really felt alone in any of it. We have always felt at one with the American public, and I think they have felt the same dynamic with us." With the passing of the years, I would also meet John Kennedy Jr. several times, and without fail be impressed not only by his accessible nature but also his hopeful outlook on life. "While we Kennedys as a family have certainly known death," he told me at the press conference to announce the publication of his own magazine, *George*, "we choose to focus on life. And, I guess, that's how we deal with death."

Doubtless, the Kennedy mystique really took hold of this country when President John Fitzgerald Kennedy was brutally assassinated in November 1963. It was such a shock that this young president would meet a grisly death that there seemed no way to reconcile it then, and even now. The country wept not only for its slain president but also for its First Lady, Jackie, so youthful and beautiful in her black mourning dress and mantilla, walking head held high behind JFK's horse-drawn catafalque down Pennsylvania Avenue from the White House to St. Matthew's Cathedral, giving Americans strength just by her example on the day of the funeral. Little did the country know that she was falling apart inside, that—by her own later admission—she would never really recover from the horror of sitting next to her husband as his head was shattered by gunfire.

When Lyndon Baines Johnson assumed the presidency, he was determined to put into place JFK's legislative agenda, prioritizing his predecessor's promises to reduce taxes and guarantee civil rights. The Civil Rights Act, introduced by JFK and shepherded through Congress and into law by LBJ, was the most important piece of legislation of its kind enacted since Reconstruction. However, with the force of the Johnson juggernaut and his concept of the Great Society, Jackie Kennedy was fearful that her husband's New Frontier—articulated in his 1960 presidential nomination

acceptance speech as "not a set of promises, but a set of challenges...
not what I intend to offer the American people, but what I intend to
ask of them"—would be all but lost when the history of this period was
written. Determined that this not happen, she set about mythologizing
the JFK administration by likening it to the idealized version of the King
Arthur legend as recalled in the Broadway musical *Camelot*. The memorable lyric of the title song reads, "Don't let it be forgot that for one brief
shining moment there was Camelot." Indeed, Jackie was fascinated with
the notion that not only should her husband not be forgotten, but that he
should also be remembered in a heroic light. As it happened, in the days
after the assassination, Jackie became aware of an article that Theodore
White was writing about the national tragedy for *Life* magazine. Since
White was an author JFK had admired, Jackie let it be known that it was
with him that she wanted to share her feelings about her husband. Thus
it would be in the pages of *Life*, read by millions, that the myth of a Kennedy Camelot was first created. "History is what made Jack," she said. "He
was a simple man; he was so complex, too. He had that idealistic side,
but then he had that other side, the pragmatic side. There will be great
presidents again—and the Johnsons are wonderful, they've been wonderful to me—but there'll never be another Camelot," Jackie told Theodore
White.

Lost in Jackie's romantic view of her husband's presidency is how badly
the actual Camelot story played out—with infidelities, betrayals, murders, and even the death of King Arthur himself. Was it possible that she
was unwittingly casting a dark, ominous cloud over the decades following
Camelot's "one brief shining moment"? Was there to be a Camelot curse?
A Kennedy curse?

Curse or not, the Kennedy family had already been stricken with bad
luck for years, all the way back to the 1940s with the institutionalization
of sister Rosemary Kennedy and the deaths of Joe Jr. in a World War II
airplane explosion and Kathleen (nicknamed "Kick") in a plane crash in
1948. But after JFK's death in 1963, another Kennedy scion would meet
his fate in the exact same way—by an assassin's bullet. This time it would
be Bobby, murdered in 1968. It had been thought that the former attorney general would carry on the tradition of Camelot, so young and charismatic in personality, with a wife, Ethel, very different from Jackie and in
many ways much more accessible. Ethel was full of spit-and-vinegar, and

she had ten children—and an eleventh on the way—an American family of hope and promise that mirrored those of so many at the time. In a strange but maybe not so surprising way, Bobby's death just added more allure to the Kennedy image. The mix of youth and vitality with tragedy and despair was a sort of soap opera much of the country could not resist. Then, as Jackie Kennedy went on to marry the billionaire shipping mogul Aristotle Onassis and seemingly scandalize the entire country in the process, the sense of misadventure that now characterized the Kennedy mystique exerted an even greater hold.

In the years after the deaths of Jack and Bobby—the years after Camelot, which are the primary ones examined in this book—the Kennedys as a family tried to hold on to the sense of hope, promise, and national service that had been so integral to the public personas of their fallen heroes. But it was difficult. During many of those intervening years there seemed no way for the Kennedys to live up to the impossibly high standards in part set by Jack and Bobby but maybe in greater part foisted upon them by an America longing for heroic characters. In death, the deceased president and his late brother would take on a kind of saintly aura that would sometimes be impossible to match and would provide years of frustration for any who tried to emulate it. In some respects, the Kennedys knew as much and even privately discussed it among themselves. However, they also knew that the public would accept nothing less of them but to carry on the ideal of Camelot—somehow.

In 2000, more than fifteen years after I first met Jackie Kennedy Onassis, I wrote *Jackie, Ethel, Joan: Women of Camelot*—a book that focused on the lives of the three women who had married into the family as wives to brothers Jack, Bobby, and Ted Kennedy. That work followed its principal characters, including their husbands, primarily from 1960 to 1969, with some references to the years that followed. Consider this book—*After Camelot*—the rest of the story. It is a more than forty-year journey through the family's epic history, spanning from 1968 to the present—the years following Jackie's idealized Camelot. In these pages you will read about and, it is my hope, come to a deeper understanding of certain touchstone moments in our history, such as Ted Kennedy's disastrous weekend in Chappaquiddick, which, it could be argued, forever ruined his chances for the presidency. You will also read about the many challenges Bobby's children faced as they grew into young adulthood—the next generation of Kennedys, two of whom would meet early and untimely deaths. Obviously, there has been no shortage of catastrophic misfortune in the Kennedys' history, and the sudden death of JFK's only son, John Kennedy Jr., is also told in these pages—a loss keenly felt even to this day. But you will also read stories of triumph and achievement, as in the telling of Eunice Kennedy Shriver's world-changing devotion to furthering the understanding of mental retardation in this country with Camp Shriver and the Special Olympics, and her husband Sargent's cofounding of the Peace Corps. You will, I believe, also find inspiration in the way Caroline Kennedy Schlossberg has lived her life with such firm resolve and quiet dignity in the face of so much heartbreak—very much like her mother, Jackie. Through it all, you will find that those who survived Jack and Bobby always managed to pull together as a family just when they needed to, and that, united, they would somehow find the strength to persevere during times most might find insurmountable.

When I first met Eunice Kennedy Shriver in 2002, it was to interview her for a story I was writing about her role in the Special Olympics. I must admit that she, more than any other Kennedy I had ever encountered, at first seemed quite redoubtable. The authoritative manner in which she carried herself and the way her eyes sized me up as she spoke in the distinct, New England–clipped accent that is so Kennedy-like was more than a little daunting. As we talked, though, I soon felt as if I were speaking with an old, familiar friend, especially when she pulled dog-eared photos of her five children—including her daughter, Maria Shriver—from her wallet and began to brag about their many achievements. I also sensed the dedication she had to the organization she had founded so many years earlier, the Special Olympics. Eagerly, she told me about its humble origins, which happened to be in the home she shared with Sargent in Maryland, the same one in which she had raised her family.

"I was just a woman who couldn't believe there were no summer camps for the mentally retarded anywhere in this entire country," Eunice told me. "So what did I do? Why, I started my own. In my own backyard! We called it Camp Shriver. And I found high school teachers and students and friends and anyone else who was willing to be of service, and I made them all camp counselors. It grew and grew and grew over the years and, by God, it was the right thing to do, wasn't it?" she observed, laughing. Here was a remarkable woman, I thought, who not only recognized a need in this country but wanted more than anything to fill it, not so that she might bask in the refracted glory of achievement but because she knew she could use her tenacious nature and her family's considerable power to get the job done—and because she knew it was the right thing to do. And therein lies another Kennedy secret: They have always believed that there is no limit to the amount of service they could do for their fellow man—indeed, their country. "We as a family are so blessed," Eunice told me. "How dare we not be of service? How dare we not at least *try*? That's how I raised my children. You can ask any one of them and they will tell you that not a day went by in their lives that they didn't have Mummy pestering them to be of service to someone else—big or small—just do something!"

Later, when she introduced me to her husband, Sargent Shriver, he repeated what sounded to me like the family's mantra. "The world is full of people in need," he declared. "Be present for them. That's what Jack, Bobby, Eunice, I, and so many of us have tried to do over the years." (On an unrelated note, I can't leave the memory of this day with the Shrivers without first adding that I'd never met a politician more affable than Sargent. "My dad always believed you would have made a great president," I told him. "Him and me both," he said with a hearty laugh.)

During my time with her, Eunice Kennedy Shriver mentioned not only that she had read my first book about her family, *Jackie, Ethel, Joan: Women of Camelot*, but that she had seen some of the television miniseries upon which it was based. Did she approve? Speaking with caution, she said she couldn't vouch for its accuracy, "because I certainly didn't live Jackie's life, nor did I live Ethel's, nor did I live Joan's." But then, after a beat, she added thoughtfully, "I have to say, though, that even I was struck by the universality of some of the themes. So, in a sense, I guess you could say it's not just their story, is it? It's a story we all share. And not just we Kennedys, either. All of us."

I couldn't have agreed more.

J. Randy Taraborrelli
Winter 2011

PROLOGUE

An Unthinkable Tragedy

It was a gray, dreary, and unremarkable Saturday afternoon in Hyannis Port. Out on a stretch of pebble-covered sand and facing a dark, restless ocean stood an elderly woman wearing a black baseball cap. As she took in the endless vista, she bent down to pick up a seashell. She rolled it in the palm of her hand and then flung it into the sea. Appearing lost in thought, she pulled her white down jacket close in order to keep the chill of the Nantucket Sound at bay. To see her walk just a few steps, it was clear that she had a slight limp. Meanwhile, a young lady in a starched white maid's uniform approached and stood directly behind her. After a few moments of hesitation, she tapped her on the shoulder. "Mrs. Kennedy," she said, "the priest will be here at five o'clock to say Mass. He's asked if you had any particular scripture in mind for the reading?" Ethel Kennedy turned to face the woman. With eyes reddened and face drawn, she seemed even older than her seventy-one years. Her frame was slight, shoulders slim and slightly hunched forward.

"How well I remember my own wedding," Ethel said wistfully, not responding to the woman's question. "We Kennedys are known for our great weddings, as you know," she added. "Mine and Bobby's was so beautiful." According to the maid's later recollection, Ethel then spoke of the formal white satin gown she wore on that special day so many years earlier when she and Robert Kennedy were wed. She also spoke of the long, diaphanous veil trimmed with delicate orange blossoms. And the elegant, dainty gloves. "But we called them mitts in those days," she remembered. "They were satin and had pearls on them," she added. "People don't wear gloves so much anymore," she mused as she reached into her pocket and pulled out large black sunglasses. She put them on. "I wonder why that is," she continued, seeming distracted. "Gloves are so nice. Don't you agree?" Her maid nodded.

Over the years, Kennedy weddings have been more than mere events, they've been the subject of national curiosity all the way back to the family patriarch Joseph's, who wed Rose in 1914, through to Bobby and Ethel's in 1950, Eunice's to Sargent Shriver in 1953, and Jack's to Jackie Bouvier, also in 1953. And there were so many more—Kennedy sisters Pat's to actor Peter Lawford in 1954 and Jean's to Stephen Smith two years later. Then there was Ted's to Joan Bennett in 1958 . . . The list goes on and on, especially as the next generation took their own spouses. Who could forget the elegant wedding of Jackie's daughter, Caroline, to Ed Schlossberg in 1986? Wedding guest Robert Rauschenberg once said it felt as if there had been "seventy-five thousand Kennedys present." It probably felt to those in attendance that there were at least that many. But then Caroline's brother, John Fitzgerald Kennedy Jr.—only son of the slain President Kennedy—broke the tradition of big family weddings with a more intimate affair when he married the lovely Carolyn Bessette in 1996. It was a surprise not only to the media but also to many of Kennedy's friends and even family members. How he was ever able to pull it off remained a mystery to many, but John wed Carolyn privately on Cumberland Island, Georgia, with just a few close friends and relatives present. Unfortunately, the wedding ceremony planned for this day—Saturday, July 17, 1999— between Ethel's daughter Rory and her beau Mark Bailey now hung in the balance because John Kennedy Jr., his wife Carolyn Bessette, and her sister Lauren were missing.

John and Carolyn had been on their way from Essex County Airport in Fairfield, New Jersey, to Hyannis Airport on Cape Cod in order to attend Rory's wedding at the Kennedy compound. Although the houses that comprised the compound were summer homes for the Kennedys, the Hyannis Port residences seemed to symbolize their unity, serving as headquarters for observances and celebrations, for funerals and wakes, for auspicious announcements, commemorative rites, and family holidays like the Fourth of July, Thanksgiving, and Christmas. First, though, John and Carolyn were scheduled to stop at Martha's Vineyard to drop off Lauren, a vice president at Morgan Stanley Dean Witter. However, something apparently happened to their plane. The small, single-engine, red-and-white Piper Saratoga hadn't been seen on radar since 9:30 p.m. Friday night, half an hour before it should have landed on Martha's Vineyard. There was nothing anyone could do except to pray.

"Will the Mass be served at my house or at Senator Kennedy's?" Ethel asked. She attended Mass almost every single day, either at her Catholic church or, quite often, in her own home where a priest would come to perform it. Of course, she would also walk out if the sermon hit her the wrong way, or if she didn't like the priest. But everyone knew that about Ethel.

"Whichever you prefer," answered Ethel's maid.

"I think maybe my house would be best," Ethel decided. "Yes, we'll have it on my porch. And will Father O'Byrne say Mass?" she asked.

"Yes."

Ethel shook her head sadly. "He married John and Carolyn just a few years ago," she recalled. "And now here we are today. Oh, my poor Johnny," she added, looking out at the gray sea and merging skyline. She hadn't used the pet name since John was a tot, at least not that anyone could remember. "Oh, dear Lord," she said, as if just hit with a revelation. "If Jackie was alive, I don't know how she would handle this. In fact, I don't think she could bear it. Do you?"

Ethel's maid didn't comment.

"I love all my boys," Ethel continued. "You know I love my girls, too. But my boys, they have given me the most trouble, and for some reason, I just love my boys so much. And Johnny, I always thought of him as one of my own," she concluded sadly.

It had been just before midnight on Friday night—not long after the family and guests retired after the rehearsal dinner—that Senator Ted Kennedy learned of John's missing plane. He wasn't that concerned, at least not at first. After all, John was nothing if not unpredictable. Perhaps he had changed his plans, Ted reasoned, and just hadn't informed anyone. However, after a few calls, Ted began to fear the worst. He spent the rest of the night on the telephone talking to the FAA and the Coast Guard, as well as to any of John's friends he knew to find out if they had any information. Finally, at about 5 a.m., he had no choice but to telephone Ethel to tell her the gut-wrenching news that John's plane had gone missing. He and Ethel—whom he lovingly called "Ethie"—had been through so much over the years that this seemed like just one more awful moment they would have to share. After speaking to Ted, Ethel tearfully gathered those family members present in the house to tell them what was going on. The rest of the day would be a waiting game. Even though it was obvious that the plane had gone down somewhere, no one in the family was willing to give up hope, least of all Ethel Kennedy. "I don't give up easily," she said, "at least not on something I believe in. I have no doubts," she said. "Not a one." It would be just like her nephew, she said, to simply show up a day later than planned and have the most wildly entertaining story to tell about his delay.

The phone hadn't stopped ringing at Ethel's all morning. She would jump every time it rang, hoping it was good news. One of the calls was from Holly Safford, whose company was catering Rory's wedding. She had just heard on television that John was missing. "I am so sorry, Mrs. Kennedy," she said, according to her memory of the conversation. "This is just so devastating. I don't know what to say."

"Holly, my dear, there is no need to be sorry, because they are going to find him," Ethel said, her tone strong and reassuring. "We are going to have a wedding today, I guarantee it."

"Is there anything I can do for you, Mrs. Kennedy?"

"Yes," she answered, "please tell your staff to stand by and wait for further instructions. The wedding is not canceled. They will find John, I know it."

Three long hours passed, and still no word. As Ethel made her way back to her home from the shoreline, two of her grandchildren—Kate and Kerry Kennedy—joined her. She held their hands, and as they passed a flagpole with an American flag flapping in the wind, the three stopped for a second and looked up at it. It was not at half-mast. Not yet, anyway. "Go, go, go!" Ethel was then heard calling out to the children. "Run! Run! Run! It's a beautiful day. Go have fun!" With that, the two children raced across the white sand beach and down to the shore.

Ethel continued walking, still limping and showing signs of the hip replacement surgery she'd undergone earlier in the year. Slowly, she made her way past billowing white tents that had just been erected for the wedding ceremony and subsequent party. The site was bustling with activity as people carried elaborate flower arrangements onto the property— roses, for the most part, of every size, every variety, and, it seemed, most every color under the sun. Meanwhile, caterers with large trays of desserts unloaded their goods from a massive truck in Ethel's driveway. One caterer almost tripped as she tried to navigate over a tangle of power cords while carrying a towering tray of cookies. "Careful," Ethel said, laughing. "Don't hurt yourself!"

Also scurrying about the premises were reporters and photographers from *People* magazine who had somehow gotten into the Kennedy compound. "Inform them that Mrs. Kennedy said they are not allowed on these premises," Ethel was overheard telling one of the many uniformed policemen patrolling the property. "There should be no press here at all," she said, now seeming quite annoyed. In her hand was a white linen napkin, folded and tied at the top with a delicate gold ribbon. "This is our home," Ethel declared, "it is not a park." She then looked at the napkin in her hands and untied the ribbon around it. It had Rory's initials on it, and Mark's. Then—who knows why she did it, whether it was because of some deeply buried sense of the inevitable—she crumpled the napkin and tossed it into a nearby trash can.

Eventually, Ethel walked up the floral-lined pathway to her house. An empty hammock swung on the porch, and the home's windows were shuttered like those of all of the other white clapboard homes in the compound. Standing on her porch and looking out at the waves crashing on the beach in the distance, she tilted her head and allowed the ocean breeze to cool her face. She seemed to be trying to ignore the bedlam swirling around her when, out of the corner of her eye, she must have seen Ted Kennedy approaching from the direction of his own home in the compound. Family members, household staff, and those responsible for the wedding preparations looked on as Ethel extended her arms to the oft-troubled man she'd always considered more a brother than just a brother-in-law. He'd been in the hospital delivery room holding her hand in place of his deceased brother when she gave birth to Rory. How could she ever forget that?

Unfortunately, Ted had bad news for Ethel. He'd just heard from the Coast Guard that a person standing on the shore near Gay Head— less than a mile from Jackie's vacation home—had spotted something black floating in the water. She'd thought it was a trash bag. But then one of her friends jumped into the surf to investigate and moments later returned with a suitcase. The two beachgoers gazed at the luggage for a long moment before finally lifting the identification flap. There they found a business card from Morgan Stanley. On it was the name "Lauren Bessette—Vice President." It would get worse. A prescription bottle made out to Carolyn Bessette would emerge from the waves; a bag of kayaking gear; a piece of an airplane seat; a headrest; an aircraft wheel—all stomach-turning flotsam of a flight gone deadly wrong, now washing ashore and seeming to seal forever the fate of its passengers. Ted had said he didn't know how he would tell Ethel such terrible news, but he knew that it should come from him.

While the visibly shaken senator relayed the news to her, Ethel Kennedy nodded solemnly as if trying to take it in, as if trying to fathom the unfathomable. When he finished speaking, she seemed stunned as she stood in place, just staring at him in disbelief. She'd been so strong all day, as was usually her fashion in times of crisis. But this was just too much to take. This was more than even she could bear. She began to cry. And as she did so, she seemed to become unsteady on her feet. So he reached out for her and held her close. For a long time, he held her close.

PART ONE

Jackie

Trying to Let Go of the Past

*H*ad it all been just a terrible dream? Was he really gone?

Certainly there were moments, though fleeting, when it felt as if it had never happened. She would awaken in the morning and, for just a few seconds, everything in her life seemed fine. But then a bleakness would begin to set in, and in no time it would all come back to her: Yes, it had happened. He was dead. Why him? Why not her? Was there anything she could have done, should have done? And then she would cry, sometimes just a few tears, but often racking sobs. It had been that way for years, and she feared it would remain so for as long as she would draw breath. Of course, sometimes she would have good days, but the bad days were just awful. She wasn't even thirty-nine yet. Was this to be her fate? Would she ever recover? Indeed, these thoughts still consumed Jacqueline Kennedy Onassis in 1968, almost five years after the murder of her husband, John Fitzgerald Kennedy, the thirty-fifth president of the United States.

She was born Jacqueline Lee Bouvier in Southhampton, New York, on July 28, 1929, to Janet Lee and John Vernou Bouvier III. If not to the manor born, Jackie was certainly never lacking in the accommodations that the very wealthy people of her time took for granted: socially prominent parents, a private school education, instruction in the equestrian arts, ballet lessons, travel abroad. When one considers photographs of the twenty-something Jacqueline Bouvier, a number of descriptive words and phrases spring to mind—uncommon grace, flawless taste, culture, great style, unerring charm, a sense of serenity, refinement that comes with excellent breeding.

By the standards of today, perhaps she would not have been considered a great beauty. Her thin lips when stretched into a smile revealed teeth that were anything but perfectly aligned. Her eyes appeared a bit too wide apart. She was definitely the daughter of aristocratic Black Jack Bouvier, as her features attested, and while her father was considered rakishly handsome, Jackie would have to wait for the allure of falling in love with Jack Kennedy for her beauty to come into full force. By contrast, Jackie's younger sister (by four years) Lee inherited the looks of her mother's family, the Lees: aquiline nose, porcelain skin, high cheekbones, fair hair and eyes. Jackie even acknowledged this and was quoted as saying of her younger sister, "Lee was the pretty one. So I guess I had to be the intelligent one."

Arguably, the most famous years of the Kennedy dynasty started with JFK and Jackie's fabled time in the White House. It had been in November 1960 that Democratic nominee John Fitzgerald Kennedy was narrowly elected to the office of the president over the Republican Richard M. Nixon, ushering in a new and exciting era of promise and hope for the country. In many ways, JFK's victory may have had less to do with his political platform than with his star quality and his youth—at forty-three, the youngest man ever elected president and the second youngest to hold that office, that distinction belonging to Ted Roosevelt, the vice president who at forty-two became president after William McKinley was assassinated. It was Jackie Bouvier Kennedy's great good fortune—and ours—that she would become First Lady and one of America's most memorable, echoing the tenure of Dolley Madison some 150 years previously. Like twenty-four-year-old Dolley, Jackie was, at thirty-one, one of the youngest of presidential wives. The public was quickly captivated by her charm and grace and, yes, her beauty. Indeed, with the addition of two lively, photogenic children, Caroline and "John-John," the First Family became everyone's ideal and captured the hearts of all Americans. But then tragedy struck in November 1963 when President Kennedy was brutally assassinated in Dallas. "Take your glasses off, Jackie," he had said to his wife, referring to her large shades, "they want to see your face." It would be his last request of her. Soon after, he would be shot dead at her side, his blood and brains splattered all over her lovely pink dress suit. She would find the loss impossible to reconcile, even after leaving the White House and moving to New York City with her children. Crushed and disillusioned, in November 1964—the one-year anniversary of the assassination—Jackie wrote of Jack, "I should have known that he was magic...I should have guessed it could not last. I should have known that it was asking too much to dream that I might have grown old with him and see our children grow up together. So now he is a legend when he would have preferred to be a man." All around her, life continued to unfold after Jack's death, but certainly not in ways that would help ease her grief, because it just seemed like one calamity after another.

For instance, Jack's youngest brother, Ted, broke his back in a plane crash in 1964, causing some in the family to wonder if perhaps there was a Kennedy curse hanging over them, especially given that two of Ted's siblings—Joe and Kathleen—had also been killed in plane crashes. Then, unbelievably enough, another Kennedy brother was murdered—this time Bobby, on June 6, 1968. Jackie was determined to continue to live her life, though, if only for the sake of her children—and she had decided that she was going to do it with a new man at her side, Aristotle Onassis.

Onassis was a bona fide force of nature born not in Greece but in what is now Turkey, in 1906, the same year as another force of nature, the San Francisco earthquake. The proverbial spoon with which he was born was not silver. It was platinum: His father, Socrates, was a prosperous shipping owner with ten ships in his fleet and extensive real estate holdings, enabling him to provide Ari with a classical education at prestigious schools.

Though there would always be questions about Aristotle Onassis's business modus operandi, they seemed to do little to hurt his reputation as a globetrotting bon vivant. He would entertain potentates in politics and consort with criminal figures with equal vigor and with no apparent damage to his standing in either community. He continued to grow his worldwide shipping business by a method he once described as OPM (other people's money), forging simultaneous long-term alliances at fixed prices with such competing oil companies as Mobil, Socony, and Texaco. Sailing under the duty-free flag of Panama, he turned a profit even as he charged the lowest prices in the merchant marine market. As his coffers grew, so did his holdings—shares that guaranteed his control of ninety-five multinational businesses on five continents: gold processing, airlines, and real estate investments in South America; a chemical company in Persia; a castle, apartments, a skyscraper in Manhattan; Olympic Airways, the airline he founded; ownership of Greek islands in the Aegean, such as his prized isle of Skorpios; the luxury yacht *Christina*; and seventeen banks throughout the world. There was one acquisition he had not yet attained, however, but he was fully determined to do so. That was America's onetime First Lady.

Aristotle Onassis came into the Kennedys' lives when he met Jackie and Jack at a dinner party in Georgetown in 1955, back when Jack was a senator. Shortly thereafter, Jackie and Jack visited Onassis on his famous 325-foot yacht, the *Christina*—named after his only daughter, born in 1954—while it was docked at Monte Carlo and the Kennedys were in the south of France visiting Rose and Joseph. "There's something damned willful about her, there's something provocative about that lady. She's got a carnal soul," Onassis said at the time. It was certainly an odd statement to make about a woman who, at least from all outward appearances, seemed anything but carnal, but that was Onassis—always provocative, always defying expectations.

In 1963, Jackie and Jack suffered the tragic loss of an infant, Patrick. In order to help Jackie recover from the ordeal, her sister, Lee Radziwill, suggested that she join her and a group of friends on a cruise with Onassis. Not surprisingly, the trip garnered worldwide media attention, with an avalanche of pictures being published of Jackie and Ari touring the Blue Mosque in Istanbul and walking about in ancient Smyrna. They also visited Ithaca, Odysseus's island kingdom, as well as Onassis's private and lush island of Skorpios. Onassis had just recently bought Skorpios, a small, barren, waterless island in the Ionian Sea, which he magically transformed into an earthly paradise by planting thousands of trees and other vegetation and building large estates and quaint guesthouses throughout. "Jackie told me she had such a wonderful time, she wished the vacation would never end," said Oleg Cassini, who designed much of her wardrobe during the White House days. "Ever since that cruise, she had a soft spot in her heart for Aristotle Onassis. He had been so warm to her and so understanding of her grief, she would never forget him. Then, in early 1968, the two began to date. It was a surprise. When she told me about it, my first thought was, 'Really, Jackie? That is so odd.' However, what came tumbling from my mouth was, 'Really, Jackie? That is so nice!'"

When Aristotle Onassis first proposed marriage to Jackie Kennedy in the spring of 1968, she seriously considered it. She loved him—though it would probably be overstating it to say she was in love with him—she had a good time when she was with him, and he seemed to care about her and her children. She was tired of being alone. She wanted to move forward with her life and simply didn't want to spend the rest of it being cast as the nation's most celebrated widow. However, at Bobby's behest, her sisters-in-law Ethel—Bobby's wife—and Joan—Ted's—visited Jackie at her home in New York City one afternoon to discourage her from being too hasty with Onassis. They feared that the union might jeopardize Bobby's chances of making it into the White House. As Ethel put it at the time, "For heaven's sake, don't marry him. Don't do this to Bobby. Or to me!" Moved by their pleas, Jackie agreed to put off the wedding, at least until after the election. However, after Bobby was assassinated, she became more concerned than ever about her own safety and welfare, and especially that of her children—and that's when she famously said, "If they're killing Kennedys, my children are targets." Therefore, frightened, alone, and still traumatized by what she'd gone through in Dallas, she'd pretty much decided by her thirty-ninth birthday that she wanted to marry Aristotle Onassis as soon as possible. "You have done all the mourning that anyone can humanly expect of you," he had told her. "The dead are dead. You are living." She had to agree.

Still, bringing a man of such great controversy back to the so-called Kennedy compound was a big deal for Jackie Kennedy. In fact, it could have been argued that bringing any man who wasn't a Kennedy onto such hallowed ground would constitute a true act of bravery. After all, this was a place of rich if often troubled family history, the sanctuary to which Kennedys always retreated not only after tragedies but after victories as well. It was a place where they could completely be themselves, away from media scrutiny—unless they invited the media in themselves—surrounded by their many children and loved ones.

Actually, it wasn't a "compound" per se, just a cluster of large homes, each a sprawling white-frame clapboard structure. The only actual waterfront property was Rose and Joseph's, which they purchased back in 1928. This was called the Big House by family members because, with fourteen rooms and nine baths, it was the largest one in the compound. The house also boasted a movie theater, a boat dock, swimming pool, tennis court, wine cellar, and several large stretches of lawn perfect for impromptu games of touch football, as was always the Kennedys' way. Ethel's house was next door and Jack and Jackie's nearby. Eunice and Sargent and Jean and Stephen Smith also had homes in the compound, and Ted and Joan had a house on nearby Squaw Island, which was about a mile and a half away.

Jackie had enjoyed so many important family milestones with the family on this sandy stretch of Cape Cod land—Jack's election, the birth of her children, the birthdays of relatives, and, of course, the sharing of great grief over Jack's death and then over Bobby's—that it felt almost sacrilegious to bring a stranger onto the property, let alone one with such a shady past. After all, she had always been a woman concerned with appearances, with what was and was not fitting, especially in social situations. This was more than just a matter of appropriateness, though. Indeed, the deeper meaning of bringing someone back to the compound did not escape Jackie, nor, she knew, would it escape anyone else. She realized that not only would such a move on her part signal that she was finally ready to move on, but perhaps it would also be a not so subtle sign to the Kennedys that maybe *they* should move on, too—from JFK's death as well as from Bobby's. "My taking Ari there is loaded with so much symbolism," was how Jackie put it at the time, "I'm not even sure how I'll react to it, it's so emotional for me! It's facing the future and letting go of the past, which is frightening. I'm so worried that the family will be upset or offended." Indeed, no matter what twists and turns her life had taken since that fateful day in November 1963 when America lost a president and she a husband, Jackie was still a Kennedy at heart and she still cared a great deal about them. So what to do?

An Invitation from Rose

About a month before Jackie Kennedy's scheduled visit to the Cape to celebrate her thirty-ninth birthday, she was at her Fifth Avenue home in New York with her dear friend Roswell Gilpatric. Gilpatric had served in Jack's cabinet as deputy secretary of defense and had briefly dated Jackie in 1967. Over dinner, Jackie explained her dilemma about bringing Onassis to the compound. "I have mixed emotions," she told Roswell, according to his distinct memory of the conversation. "I know I'm being silly. I feel so stupid."

"Nonsense," Roswell told her. "You mustn't feel that way. It's completely understandable after all you've gone through. But you know how Rose is. She would want to see you. And she would want you to bring Ari."

Jackie wasn't so sure. "I wonder..." she began, looking at Roswell with questioning eyes. "Would you call her to ask?" He was reluctant. "I don't think it's my place, Jackie..." he said. However, he changed his mind in midsentence, knowing full well that he could never refuse a request of hers. "Okay, I'll do it," he told her. "In fact, I'll do it right now."

Jackie's eyes widened. "Now?" she asked. "But I meant when I wasn't in the room, Ros!" She then scurried out of the parlor, saying she couldn't bear to listen, as Roswell walked over to the telephone on a nearby end table and began to dial. It was always interesting to people who knew her well that while Jackie was ever the sophisticate in public—especially as First Lady—paradoxically she had another side to her, one that was very girlish and even incredibly shy. Ten minutes later, Roswell called out to Jackie. "Okay, you can come out now," he said, laughing. "It's safe." Jackie peeked around the corner into the living room. "I spoke to Rose," he told her, "and she was very upset."

"Oh no," Jackie said, coming back into the living room. "You see, Ross, I told you she would be cross…"

"No," he said, cutting her off. "She's only upset because she couldn't understand why I was calling instead of you. Yes, she wants you to come to the Cape for your birthday. And she wants you to bring Ari. In fact, she's even invited me. Here," he said, handing her the telephone. "Now, call your mother-in-law."

Thus it came to pass that on the afternoon of July 28, 1968, her thirty-ninth birthday and just seven weeks after Bobby Kennedy's death, Jackie Kennedy found herself in the most unlikely of scenarios—back home with her family in Hyannis Port, sitting on the same porch of the Big House and in the same white Adirondack chairs in which she and Jack once sat while enjoying many a golden sunset. Only now a new man was in Jack's place, Aristotle Onassis. Of course, there were awkward moments. It was only natural. "But everyone was at least *trying* to make it work," recalled Barbara Gibson, Rose's secretary, who was present that weekend. "Onassis didn't look like someone Jackie would end up with, so it was jarring when she walked through the door with him. He was much older, he wasn't really very handsome, though I must say he made up for it in sheer charisma. Compared to Jack, who had always been so stunning and elegant, well, it was like night and day. But Rose Kennedy pulled me into the kitchen and said something to me that made a great deal of sense. 'If he was young and good-looking, would that make it any better?' she asked. 'No,' she said. 'In fact, it might make it worse. As it is, he is so very different, I think it will somehow be easier to accept him into our lives.'"

Certainly, if one ponders the raison d'être at the heart of the Kennedy saga, one has to conclude that it was Rose Fitzgerald Kennedy who established the family's moral compass and the model for their purpose-driven lives. Her enduring faith, rooted in her unfaltering devotion to her Roman Catholic heritage, which she passed on to her nine children, was like something out of the scriptures, unassailable, fervent, and about which she reminded her offspring with such passion and frequency that it became her mantra: "God never gives us more sorrow, more burdens, more troubles than we can endure." Her husband, Joseph Patrick Kennedy, had ruled the family with an iron fist, strategizing the campaigns of three sons, which saw one elected president, another become attorney general, and a third a senator, all at the same time. He was as ruthless as he was savvy, amassing a fortune over the years as a stock market and commodity investor. But now, rendered speechless and paralyzed after a debilitating stroke in 1961, all he could do was sit in a wheelchair and stare off into the distance. It was very difficult being in his presence and accepting that the man he once was no longer existed. Still, he was "Dad," or "Grandpa," and an important part of the family. Jackie, in particular, loved him dearly and would spend hours at his side, reading to him, talking to him, and just wiling away the time.

Also present that weekend were two of the Kennedy sisters—Jean and her husband, Stephen Smith (who was the family's business manager), and Pat, who was now separated from her husband, actor Peter Lawford. Ted Kennedy, the only surviving brother and the senator from Massachusetts, was also home for the weekend, along with his wife, Joan, known as "the Dish" because of her striking good looks. There were several other relatives present for the festivities as well, such as cousin Joe Gargan, whose late mother, Mary Agnes, was Rose's sister and who, along with his two younger sisters, had been raised on this same property by Rose and Joseph. Also present were close friends such as Lem Billings, JFK's prep school roommate; Senator George Smathers, JFK's best friend, and his wife, heiress Rosemary Townley Smathers; and, of course, Roswell Gilpatric, who had arrived with Jackie. Eunice Kennedy, Rose and Joseph's oldest child, was not present, as her husband, Sargent Shriver, was now ambassador to France under President Lyndon Johnson's administration and the couple was living for the most part in Paris with their four children.

In the midst of these Kennedys and their close circle of friends was one of the richest men in the world, Aristotle Onassis, doing his best to fit in—and not doing a bad job of it, either. His Old World charm was truly hard to resist. Rose seemed captivated as he smoked a cigar and spoke grandly of his global travels and of Skorpios. "It would be my great pleasure to take you sailing on my yacht, the *Christina*," he told Rose as the family sat on her porch chatting. "Oh my," Rose said, acting impressed. "That sounds marvelous."

"Though she acted as if she'd never been on a yacht before, of course, that wasn't at all true," said Barbara Gibson. "However, she seemed swept away by Onassis and couldn't help but enjoy a flirtatious moment or two with him. 'Why, I simply wouldn't know what to do out there all by myself,' she said, being very coquettish. 'Oh, but I'll be with you, my dear,' Onassis told her as he reached over to touch her hand. 'You don't have to worry about that!' Later, she said to me, 'If Jackie doesn't want him, I just may!' It was all in good fun, though. But it does suggest that Onassis made a great impression on her."

"I'm sorry, but I don't know what to make of him," Ethel Kennedy had said before Ari's arrival, deciding to feign a bad cold and stay in her home rather than participate in the family gathering. (However, her children—at least eight of the eleven of them—were running all over Rose's house, causing chaos in their wake.) Ethel knew that Bobby didn't trust Aristotle Onassis—the feeling of animus had been mutual between them—and that he would never have approved of Jackie's dating him. ("I've known that bastard for years," Bobby once said of the shipping magnate. "He was a snake then and he's still a snake. Other than his bankroll, I don't understand what Jackie sees in him.") Therefore, Ethel couldn't understand how the rest of the family could be so welcoming of him.

"I remember the weekend very well," said Larry Newman, who lived across the street from the Kennedys with his wife, Mary Francis, known as Sancy. "I often saw Ari and Jackie walking along the beach, holding hands and looking very romantic. It was clear that there was a strong attraction, but also clear that Jackie was trying to move on. It was as if bringing him to this place the Kennedys considered hallowed ground was somehow cathartic for her, and maybe for the Kennedys, too."

Newman also recalled seeing Jackie and Ari dancing on the street in front of his house as if they didn't have a care in the world. "No music, of course, just the two of them in each other's arms," he recalled, "and I thought, okay, I think maybe I get it now. She had been so unhappy after the assassinations, this man brought romance back into her life. And, yes, maybe he wasn't that attractive and, yes, maybe he had a checkered past, but it was what it was, and it was apparently working for her. You would see them kissing openly and you'd think, well, this is definitely a different kind of homecoming. I certainly never saw her do that in public with Jack.

"Jack was very much a Kennedy, a little uptight, not demonstrative with his feelings, at least publicly, and so was Jackie. But Onassis was very emotional and he brought something out in her. When you saw the two of them kissing you felt that there was something strong between them. I think, in the end, everyone wanted happiness for Jackie, and that weekend a lot of us saw that she was, once again, happy. When I saw her that weekend I told her, 'You look happy, Jackie. Are you?' And she smiled and said, 'Yes, I truly think I am.' And I believed her. But it was sad, just the same. Not easy at all. I remember thinking, Camelot is over. Long live the King…"

Ted Kennedy felt the same way, at least according to what he told George Smathers that weekend in Hyannis. That very day, Smathers had informed Ted that he'd decided not to run for Senate again at the end of the year; he had been the United States senator from Florida since 1951. Ted hated to see him go; the two had been great friends for a very long time. They were catching up on each other's lives while sitting on rocking chairs on the expansive porch and taking in the magnificent seaside view when Ted suddenly observed, "Having that guy here, it's hard, isn't it?"

"Onassis?" Smathers asked.

"Yeah," Ted said. "He's a crook, you know? Bob hated him."

Smathers, according to his memory of the conversation, agreed. "Bob would hate this whole goddamn thing, wouldn't he?" he asked.

"Are you kidding me?" Ted said. "If Robby was here," he added using his pet nickname for his brother, "he'd sneak into Onassis's room tonight and strangle the bastard in his sleep."

The two men shared a good laugh.

After reminiscing a bit more about Bobby, they let the subject turn to Jack and then to Jackie. As they talked, it became clear to them that what was really bothering them wasn't Onassis's background. It was simply the idea of handing their beloved Jackie over to him. After all, Jackie had been a member of the family since Jack took her as his bride fifteen years earlier in 1953. She was such a vital link to Jack and to the family's memory of him that, as Ted noted, "I don't want to let her go. It's like saying goodbye to Jack all over again."

George Smathers understood. After all, as one of Jack's very best friends, he had been a proud groomsman at his and Jackie's wedding and even spoke on behalf of Jack at the wedding's rehearsal dinner and at the reception. (He'd also been one of the co–best men at Bobby's wedding to Ethel.) He told Ted that while he was sincerely trying to cope with the rapidly developing situation involving Jackie and Ari, "I have to admit that when I first saw them together earlier, it tore me up inside."

Ted nodded. "So what do you think she'll do?" he asked as he continued rocking slowly and gazing off into the distance.

Smathers thought it over. "Well, to be honest with you, Ted," he said, according to his recollection, "I'm pretty sure she's going to marry him."

Ted stopped rocking and gazed directly at George, a look of astonishment crossing his face. "Holy shit," he exclaimed. "This is unbelievable, isn't it?"

George agreed.

"I guess as long as she was single, she was still Jack's and maybe," Ted said, thoughtfully, "she was still ours. But now..."

"But now she's his," George said, finishing Ted's thought.

"But now she's his," Ted repeated.

There was a long moment of silence as the two men rocked in their chairs, lost in their thoughts.

"We have to move forward, don't we?" Ted finally asked.

"Well, my friend," George responded, "I'm afraid it's starting to look like we have no choice."

"It's not going to be easy," Ted admitted.

"I'll say," George added.

Jackie's Thirty-Ninth

On the night of July 28, 1968, the Kennedys enjoyed a small family dinner party to celebrate Jackie's thirty-ninth birthday at Joseph and Rose's house on the compound. This rather informal gathering was certainly nothing like previous birthdays for the former First Lady on the Cape. For instance, two years earlier for Jackie's thirty-seventh, the party—which would be better described as a "gala"—was hosted by Jackie's friend Paul Mellon, a wealthy banker. The guest list was an impressive who's who of political and entertainment notables, such as Jock Whitney—ambassador to the United Kingdom, publisher of the *New York Herald Tribune*, and one of the wealthiest men in the world—along with his wife, Betsey Roosevelt, former daughter-in-law of President Franklin D. Roosevelt. William Averell Harriman—former governor of New York as well as former ambassador to the Soviet Union and to Great Britain—was also at the Cape that weekend, along with his wife, socialite Marie Norton Whitney. William S. Paley, who founded the Columbia Broadcasting System (CBS), was present as well. Along with people such as Broadway producer Mike Nichols and Jackie's hairdresser Kenneth, there were more than a hundred people present, all of them gathered to wish Jackie a happy birthday while being served the finest of seafoods and spirits. This time around, though, Rose Kennedy decided to keep it simple as family members convened in the huge backyard while busy maids served grilled fish, roasted potatoes, and, for dessert, an apple pie made especially for the occasion not by one of the cooks but by Rose herself. Certainly Rose wasn't at her best in the kitchen, but that she at least tried meant the world to Jackie. "If I had known much farther in advance that Jackie was bringing Onassis to the Cape, do you think I would have had such a simple party?" Rose noted to her secretary, Barbara Gibson. "It's all very pleasant, attractive, and practical, but far from elegant," she said. "However, I think this is a side of the Kennedys he may find charming." After the meal, the family adjourned to the home's private movie theater to watch the Steve McQueen film *The Thomas Crown Affair*. Then more drinks and food were served on the porch as they all enjoyed the warm night air.

Much to everyone's delight, Ethel Kennedy finally changed her mind and decided to join the family on the veranda, marking the first time she would meet Aristotle Onassis. As it happened, Ted went over to "Ethie's" house and talked to her, telling her that he felt strongly that she should join the family. Ethel could never resist Ted. They had a very special relationship and she would pretty much always do exactly what he asked.

As for Ethel and Jackie, there would always be reports that they didn't much care for each other. Why were such reports so persistent? Probably because they were such different kinds of women and likely because it was fun for people to pit them against one another, and also because Ethel *did* like to make fun of Jackie. But definitely not because it was true. After all, these two women shared something that no one else in the family could ever really understand, indeed, that most people couldn't even fathom—they'd been forced to witness the brutal murders of their own husbands. It was a tragic way for fate to have bound them to one another, but bind them it did. They would always have a special relationship, no matter the gossip. "My Ethel," Jackie wrote to her sister-in-law just weeks before this party. "I stayed up till 6:30 last night just thinking and praying for you."

"I know you aren't fond of Onassis," Roswell Gilpatric told Ethel Kennedy when she arrived at the Big House, according to his memory of the night. "That's true," Ethel told him. "But as long as she's happy, right?" she asked, trying to lighten the mood. At that moment, Jackie walked into the room and over to the couple to greet Ethel. According to photos taken that night and housed in the Kennedy Library and Museum, Jackie was wearing a cherry red blouse and black cigarette slacks. Her coal-black hair was pulled back from her face with a scarlet-colored beret. Even when she was dressed casually, there was something special about her. The way she held her head, the graceful way she moved her slender body—it was all very contained and regal, her dark eyes full of enormous power, as always. Yet she was also very feminine, very girly. "Ethel," she exclaimed, "look at you! You got over your cold!" The two sisters-in-law shared a secret look, as if in recognition that not only had Ethel been fibbing, but also that it was all perfectly fine. The two embraced.

When Jackie finally introduced Ethel to Aristotle, the tension in the room was palpable. However, Onassis won Ethel over easily. He somehow found a way to make her laugh even though she had been so unbearably sad of late. Soon the two were getting along and even joking with one another. After this gathering, Ethel rarely had anything negative to say about Aristotle Onassis.

When everyone else had retired for the night, Jackie and Ted went into Rose's living room and talked late into the night in front of a roaring fire, this despite the warm weather outside. It was then that Jackie told her brother-in-law that she had all but made up her mind: She was going to marry Aristotle Onassis. By all accounts, Ted did not try to stop Jackie or even attempt to change her mind. Like the rest of the family, he wanted the best for her, and he also must have known that Jack would have wanted him to be happy for her. Jackie said that she needed Ted's assistance, though. "There's something I need you to do for me," she told him. "Would you help me, Teddy? Please?"

It was Jackie. Of course he would help her.

Some Enchanted Evening

*I*n August 1968 Jackie Kennedy and her children, Caroline and John, and her brother-in-law, Ted Kennedy, arrived on the lush isle of Skorpios. The time had come to negotiate a deal whereby Aristotle Onassis would take Jackie's hand in marriage. Though it may have come as a surprise to outside observers, it was only natural in the world in which Jackie lived that money would have to change hands if such a momentous merger were to take place. Wealthy people like the Kennedys and Onassis were accustomed to monetary transactions in marriages, or even just because a birthday had occurred. (For instance, each of the Kennedy children received $1 million when they turned twenty-one. Onassis gave his two children $5 million each when they turned eighteen.) It was Onassis's idea that he would give Jackie a certain amount of money when they married. She didn't ask for it—that wouldn't have been like her. But she also didn't turn it down—that wouldn't have been like her either. Jackie was raised to appreciate affluence, and her love of luxury was well known. She'd always had money, and as she got older, she naturally became more focused on maintaining a certain lifestyle for herself and her children.

"Did she love Onassis? Yes, I believe she did," her friend Joan Braden said.* "But she was also a practical woman with practical concerns,"

---

* Joan Braden was an aide to Nelson A. Rockefeller and a presidential campaign staff manager for both JFK and RFK. She also worked as special assistant to the undersecretary for economic affairs in the State Department for two years (1976–1978). At Jackie's request of LBJ back in 1964, Joan was named a trustee of the Kennedy Center. "I really can not tackle it without her," Jackie wrote to LBJ.

Braden continued. "She said something to me like, 'The first time you marry it is for love, the second time it is for security.' Obviously, she was one of the most famous women in the world. She told me she was not going to end up with a plumber in New Jersey! Onassis was one of the richest men on the planet, said to be worth more than $500 million. In that respect, he was suitable for her, yes. She loved to spend money, as we all knew. Her mother, Janet Lee Bouvier Auchincloss, who I knew well and interviewed for her [1964] oral history [in the Kennedy Library], placed a premium on wealth, and she passed on to her daughters Jackie and Lee the sense that money mattered a great deal, so Jackie was very extravagant. But she was also pragmatic. She told me, 'Life is all about change. The only constant we can count on is that nothing is constant and you can't depend on anyone but yourself, which,' she told me, 'I have learned the hard way.'

"Jackie said, 'Oh, you don't have to make a financial arrangement,'" recalled Arturo D'Angelo, the attorney representing Creon Broun, Onassis's American money manager.* "And Ari said, 'Yes, I do, my dear.' And she said, 'Oh, no no, no!' And he said, 'Oh, yes, I simply *must*.' And they went back and forth with this kind of silly exchange as if there was ever any question that he was going to give her money when they married. He looked at it as a wedding gift, as did she. Of course, it would be viewed as a cold, mercenary business transaction by most people, but not by the wealthy. What always complicated matters is that once it is established that money will change hands, even as a gift, attorneys and managers and family representatives then become involved, and then it truly does become a business transaction."

The admittedly strange marital negotiations took place on Aristotle Onassis's cruise liner, *Christina*, which was docked in Skorpios. The night before Ted's meeting with Onassis, a Greek reporter named Nikos Mastorakis sneaked aboard the yacht, posing as the manager of an Athens bou-

---

* Creon Broun had been a confidant and employee of Onassis's empire since 1947. He retired in 1990 and continued to serve on the board of directors until 1991. In a 1992 telephone interview with this author, he said, "I will neither confirm nor will I deny the existence of a formal agreement between Mr. Onassis and Jacqueline Kennedy which involved the exchange of money on the occasion of their wedding. I will say, however, that Mr. Onassis loved Mrs. Kennedy very much and there was no limitation to what he would have done for her throughout his lifetime."

zouki band that Onassis had hired for entertainment. Mastorakis recalled Ted as acting like "a laughing cowboy from Texas. All—including Jackie and Telis [a popular nickname for Ari]—seemed pleased with their lives," added Mastorakis. "They ate black caviar and red tomatoes. Ted drank ouzo. Jackie, who was resplendent in a red blouse and long gypsy skirt, preferred the vodka. She leaned close when Telis whispered in her ear. At dinner Onassis ate his lamb like a youth. She ate little and nibbled white grapes. But at 4 a.m. with the moon above, the sweet Mrs. Kennedy sang 'Adios Muchachos' with Telis. I felt they were very close."

It had been an intensely romantic evening, and even though the scenario made for an odd juxtaposition to the business at hand, which concerned the exchange of money for a bride, there was still something beautiful, magical, and even wondrous about it. A full moon glistened over the peaceful waters. The air was cool, everyone's spirits warm. In fact, Jackie would recall it as being one of the loveliest nights of her life. Of course, it couldn't end without Ted breaking out in song, as he often did on special occasions. Weddings, funerals, birthdays, anniversaries, and all sorts of family gatherings tended to find Ted leading a group in song, and tonight would be no exception. The number he selected could not have been more appropriate. To the incongruous strumming accompaniment of one of the bouzouki musicians, he began to sing the song "Some Enchanted Evening." While he certainly didn't have what one might consider a great voice, Ted had such a sincere tone and so much heart that his singing was always hard to resist. As he sang the tune from *South Pacific*, Jackie looked lovingly into the eyes of the man she would soon marry. After a moment, she began to sing along with her brother-in-law, and then, one by one, everyone on deck joined in, until by the time Ted got to the bridge, just about everyone was singing.

Jackie: "The Kennedys Can't Support Me Forever"

The next day, in his meetings with Aristotle Onassis, Ted Kennedy made it clear that Jackie Kennedy was widely considered an American treasure, especially given what she had endured with the president's assassination and the manner in which she had handled herself at his funeral. It would take—as Ted put it, according to most accounts—"a leap of faith" for Americans to accept her as the wife of Onassis. "We love Jackie," Ted said, "and we want the best for her." Onassis agreed— he loved her too, he said. Rather than be insulted by Ted's suggestion that he was not good enough for her, Onassis was bemused, especially when Ted let on that by marrying him she would be forfeiting her $175,000-a-year stipend from the Kennedy family. The shipping magnate couldn't believe that the wealthy Kennedy family was only paying a woman they held in such high esteem a measly $175,000 a year. When Ted pointed out that Jackie would also be losing her $10,000 a year annual widow's pension, Onassis was truly gobsmacked. The figures Ted was using were such small potatoes to the shipping magnate, he was baffled as to why they were even being discussed! He said he would pay Jackie much more to be his wife, and, after some give-and-take, the amount he and Ted eventually settled on was $1.5 million. "I believe that's a fair deal," Ted said. Onassis then said that he wanted the wedding to take place in America, a suggestion at which Ted balked.

Even though Ted wasn't opposed to the marriage, he said he wasn't going to put his family in the position of having to attend a big, well-publicized ceremony. It would be too sad. No one would have been able to get through it. "It also would be completely inappropriate," he said. "I won't be moved on this point." Therefore, Onassis reluctantly agreed that the ceremony could be held in Greece.* With a deal now struck, the two men shook hands. When Ted told Jackie about the terms, she was perfectly happy, saying, "Ari is a very sweet and generous man, and I'm very lucky to have him in my life." Ted then sent a deal memo outlining the terms to Jackie's business manager, Wall Street investment banker André Meyer. It was then that matters got dicey.

French-born André Benoit Meyer was a close friend and business associate of the Kennedy family, first through Sargent Shriver and then as

---

* As it would happen, Jean Kennedy Smith and Pat Kennedy Lawford both attended the wedding in Greece, representing the family.

a business associate of Stephen Smith. He was also a senior partner of Lazard Frères & Co., a preeminent financial institution whose origins dated back to 1848. The firm provided—as Lazard Ltd. today still does—advice on mergers and acquisitions as well as asset management to corporations, partnerships, and individuals. Coincidentally, Meyer and the John Fitzgerald Kennedys were in residence at the Carlyle Hotel in New York in 1961 at the same time, with Meyer in a suite directly below Jack and Jackie. In October 1963, Kennedy named Meyer to a committee that was to investigate ways the country could cut its balance-of-payments deficit. A year later, Stephen Smith, who handled most of the family's business affairs via the Kennedys' company, which was called, innocuously enough, Park Agency, Inc., brought Meyer in to help manage the Kennedys' huge holdings of more than $150 million. An eventual board member of the John F. Kennedy Library, Meyer also managed its $60 million building fund. A well-respected financier called by David Rockefeller "the most creative financial genius of our time in the investment banking world," André Meyer often escorted Jackie to events after JFK's death. Jackie viewed Meyer, thirty years her senior, more as a father figure than a possible romantic partner. That said, his friends all knew that he had a crush on her, as did most men who had anything to do with her. He was certainly as much a sounding board and confidant for her and other members of the Kennedy family as he was a business adviser. He could often be found at Jackie's home in New York, helping John and Caroline with their homework—he was that close to the family. So when he took issue with something having to do with Jackie, it was dealt with seriously.*

Meyer was no fan of Ted Kennedy's—that much was clear to everyone in the Kennedy family. "He felt that JFK and Bobby had the brains and maybe Ted had the good looks, but that was it," said Mona Latham, a close friend of Meyer's who first worked for him as a securities analyst and then as his assistant. "When he got the deal memo from Senator Kennedy relating to the Onassis-Kennedy merger, he hit the roof. He called Jackie, who was still in Greece, and said he needed to see her immediately upon her return. So about two weeks later, he and I met with her at her

---

* Meyer was also a close friend of LBJ's, invited to consult with him at the White House a total of twenty-four times between 1964 and 1968.

home on Fifth Avenue. Or, I should say, I went with him but waited in another room as the two of them met in the study."

According to Mona Latham, when Jackie greeted her and Meyer in early September 1968, she was in a bad mood. "Everything is going wrong today," Jackie said as she stood in the doorway with Latham and Meyer. "I don't think I can take any more bad news today. I'm having budget problems around here, as you know." Jackie then began to explain to Meyer that Stephen Smith had come to visit her earlier in the week to ask her to cut back on her expenses. She said that it was a humiliating conversation, but that she should not have been surprised by it. "The Kennedys can't support me forever," she said, "and Rose has made that very clear. They have even cut Ethel back, and she has all those kids!"

Actually, cutting Ethel Kennedy back was easier said than done, and if Jackie knew how much Ethel spent on food and clothing, she might have been surprised and perhaps even upset. Mona Latham would say, years later, that she was astonished by Jackie's financial situation, as outlined by her and André Meyer that day at Jackie's. Apparently, JFK had left her about $70,000 in cash, plus all of his personal effects. There were two family trusts valued at about $10 million, but due to certain restrictions placed upon them, Jackie wasn't able to access any money from them and was instead living on the annual allowance of $175,000 from the Kennedys. It had originally been $150,000, but Bobby managed to get her another $25,000 a year from the family before he died. Now Rose was pushing for Jackie to cut back on her expenses. "Tell her own mother [Janet Auchincloss] to cash in some of that Auchincloss fortune," Rose had said. "Jackie just doesn't know how to cut corners."

Jackie's household staff included two maids—one responsible only for Jackie's needs—a nanny, a cook, and a governess for the children. Each staff member made $100 a week. Jackie also had a personal assistant, Nancy Tuckerman, who was making roughly $200 a week. The total household budget, including food, wine, liquor, and salaries as well as entertaining, came to $1,600 a month. Meanwhile, Jackie spent money on clothes and jewelry as if she were a very wealthy woman. "And that's where all my money is going, I admit it," she told Meyer, "but I am expected to have nice things, André, and so, yes, I buy nice things, I admit it. What can I tell you? I like nice things!"

"And you should have nice things," Meyer told her. "You deserve nice things."

"Thank you," Jackie said. "I agree with you."

As Jackie spoke, she fumbled while trying to insert a cigarette into a long black cigarette holder. She picked up the interphone. "Olga, would you please come here?" she asked. Today her guests were definitely seeing a more imperious side of Jackie. Though she was usually quite down-to-earth, she did have her moments. Within seconds, a small Greek woman appeared, and without saying a word, the former First Lady handed her the cigarette and the holder. The woman put it all together with nervous hands, and then gave it back to Jackie. Jackie held it in her lips while the servant lit the cigarette. "Thank you," Jackie said as she inhaled. Then, exhaling a puff of white smoke, she turned back to André Meyer and Mona Latham. "So, anyway, I simply have to do something," she said. "When Jack and I were in the White House, I didn't have these problems," she added. She said that the last five years had presented "nothing but headaches for me. And I can tell you this much," she said with a determined look, "I will not live like this, André! I just won't do it!"

"Well, that's why I'm here today," Meyer said, as Jackie took a finger sandwich from a plate someone on staff had arranged on the coffee table. When he said he wanted to talk to her "about the Onassis matter," Jackie slowly placed the sandwich back on the platter and gave him a look. "I would prefer that you not refer to it in that way," she told him. "It is not a *matter*. That is so boorish, André," she said. He explained that he was only trying to be discreet, but Jackie shook her head in the negative. She then stood up and suggested that Mona Latham enjoy the lunch that had been prepared while she and Meyer went into the study to chat. The two left the room.

When Jackie and Meyer returned thirty minutes later, Jackie was clearly still not happy. "So, I'll get back to you, then, okay?" Meyer asked as he went to embrace her. She was stiff in his arms. "Fine, fine, fine," she said, obviously anxious for him to take his leave. "Goodbye, then," she added, the severity of her expression unchanging. She then turned and walked away, leaving her two guests to find their own way out of the apartment.

Negotiating for Jackie

*I*n the taxicab on the way back to their office, Mona Latham asked André Meyer what had occurred between him and Jackie Kennedy that had made the former First Lady so cross with him. "André said that he told her he was very much against the marriage," Latham recalled many decades later. "He said that he knew Onassis quite well and thought he was a crook. 'You are America's First Lady, you can't be seen with this man, let alone marry him,' he told her. As I understand it, Jackie listened because she had respect for André, but she wasn't going to be dissuaded, and, more than that, she was insulted."

Meyer brought up the fact that Onassis—who married his first wife, Athina (Tina), in 1946—was known to have been openly having an affair with the married opera star Maria Callas. It was considered one of the greatest love affairs of twentieth-century pop culture, right alongside that of Richard Burton and Elizabeth Taylor. And it also matched the Burton-Taylor affair as a tabloid-fueled scandal. Jackie was not moved by Meyer's reasoning, though. "Everyone has a past," she told him.

Finally, André said, "Then at least let me work out a better financial arrangement for you." Jackie said she was satisfied with what Ted had come up with and feared that Onassis would perceive their going back to the negotiating table as advantage-taking. "But yes," she decided, "if there's more we can do, I suppose we should try." Finally, she agreed, as long as André could promise that none of these negotiations ever made it into the press. "You must act with great discretion," Jackie said, according to what Meyer later told Mona Latham. "The public images of many people could be hurt by such maneuverings, not the least of which is mine!"

Latham continued, "André said it was all very civil between him and Jackie until he crossed a line with her and said something like, 'Do you really think Jack would approve of such a marriage?' That's when Jackie became upset with him. 'How dare you talk to me in this manner! Who do you think you're talking to?' she demanded. He apologized, but she didn't want to hear anything more from him at that point. He knew he had gone too far. The meeting then ended. He wasn't happy about the way it had gone. He hated disappointing Jackie. All he ever wanted was to protect her. He was being candid with her, but maybe a little too much so."

The next day, Meyer sent Aristotle Onassis a counteroffer: $20 million. Onassis was angry. After all, he and Ted Kennedy had already agreed in principle on an amount that was far less. He immediately arranged to fly to New York, and the two met on September 25, 1968, at Meyer's apartment at the Carlyle. According to someone with knowledge of the meeting, Onassis at first approached Meyer as if he were Jackie's father and he was asking permission to take her hand in marriage. "I love her very much," he told Meyer. "And she's in love with me. So what will it take for me to make her my wife?" What would it take? Meyer repeated the figure: $20 million. Onassis said that he thought the price was ridiculously inflated. "The two of them haggled over it for about two hours," recalled Arturo D'Angelo. "Afterward, Onassis went back to his hotel room at the Pierre Hotel. He was very unhappy. As I understand it, he asked his secretary, Lynn Alpha, for a drink, she pulled out a bottle of Johnnie Walker Black Label and poured him a double. Then he dictated a letter to Creon Broun." That correspondence from Onassis to Broun memorialized the shipping mogul's discussion with André Meyer. However, Jackie was not mentioned by name but was instead referred to as the "person in question." It said, in part: "The sum of twenty [million] indicated in the meeting, as a capital, apart from the fact that in the final analysis it would be futile, due to gift, income and other taxes that it would necessarily entail, apart from being detrimental to the feelings of either party, it might easily lead to the thought of an acquisition instead of a marriage."

When André Meyer went back to Jackie Kennedy with the new deal memo, she wasn't at all pleased with the language. It sounded like a cold business deal to her. Of course, that's what it was, but seeing it in black and white was a little unsettling. Meyer spent a few days trying to convince Jackie that if they pushed a little harder they could probably get $10 million from Onassis. He reminded her she was the one who had been complaining about money in recent years, and suggested that this was her opportunity to straighten out that problem. She had to agree. Still, she was ambivalent. Of course, she had her eye on the financial security she could gain by marrying someone like Aristotle Onassis. However, he was the one who had first offered to give her money upon their marriage. She had her limits in terms of how much she would exploit his generosity.

Actually, Jackie was walking a thin line. On one hand, she seemed to want to appear as if these negotiations repulsed her. But on the other, she did want the money, and she couldn't deny it. "As long as he agrees to pay all of my expenses during the marriage," she said, "I don't see what the problem is. But, yes," she decided, "go back and see if you can get $10 million. But then, that's it, André!" she said, drawing a line.

Meyer came back to Jackie a couple days later with the slightly disappointing news that he could only get the figure up to $3 million. As well as that lump sum, she would receive $30,000 a month tax-free for the duration of the marriage. Also, each of her children would receive $1 million, the annual interest of which would go to Jackie.* Onassis would also pay all of her expenses over the $30,000 she received monthly, which, as he would learn, would be a sizable commitment. However, she also signed a provision that would limit the amount of money she could receive at his death, which probably wasn't the smartest thing to do. "I was surprised that André Meyer agreed to it," recalled Mona Latham. "And so the deal was struck. 'Now that's it,' Jackie said. 'Let's just leave it alone now, before Ari gets the wrong impression.'"

On October 15, 1968, the announcement was made with a headline story in the *Boston Herald*: "John F. Kennedy's Widow and Aristotle Onassis to Wed Soon."

"That morning, I got a phone call from Steve Smith," recalled Pierre Salinger, JFK's former press secretary. "'I'm not sure how we should handle this goddamn thing,' Steve said to me. 'I guess we need to make a statement about it, though.' I asked him, 'So, do you know what you want to say?' And he thought about it for a moment and came back with, 'How about, 'Oh . . . *shit!*'"

Five days later, on October 20, 1968, Jackie took Ari as her husband on Onassis's private Greek island, Skorpios.

Three days after that, the deal Jackie Kennedy made with Aristotle Onassis for her hand in marriage was signed.†

---

* John and Caroline also had in excess of $3 million each in trust funds and inheritances from the Joseph P. Kennedy Sr., JFK, and RFK estates.
† In years to come, other deals with Onassis would be structured that would pay Jackie many more millions of dollars.

PART TWO

Eunice

Eunice Kennedy Shriver

$\mathcal{T}$aking a bird's-eye view of the Kennedy clan—four sons, five daughters—Eunice Shriver, with her barely suppressed nervous energy, her gangly and sometimes rather androgynous appearance, and her predilection for long black cigars and man-tailored slacks, seemed to have had more in common with her brothers than her sisters. Indeed, hers would be a service-driven life fueled by the kind of commitment more in keeping with her male siblings than with her sisters. Even in her choice of husband, Eunice seemed to be guided by instincts quite at odds with her sisters, in that Sargent Shriver matched Eunice in intelligence, in ambition, and in a passionate desire to be of service to his country. He was also a devout Roman Catholic, as are all the Kennedys.

Born on July 10, 1921, in Brookline, Massachusetts—the fifth of nine Kennedy children—Eunice graduated from Manhattanville, a Catholic college in Purchase, New York, after attending a series of exclusive Catholic boarding schools. True to her spirit of individualism, she chose to go to Stanford University rather than the Ivy League of her siblings, graduating with a BS in sociology in 1943. The choice of degree affirmed her commitment to social work. After a short time working in the Special War Problems Division in the U.S. State Department, she moved to the Justice Department as executive secretary for a project dealing with juvenile delinquency, a job that led to a position as staff social worker for the Federal Independent Institute for Women. She accepted an offer in Chicago to join the House of the Good Shepherd women's shelter and the juvenile court. It was a fateful move in that it was here that she became reacquainted with her future husband, Sargent Shriver, whom she had first met in 1946 at a Manhattan cocktail party. She and Sarge married in 1954. Over the next eleven years, they would have five children: Sarge III (also known by his middle name, Bobby), Maria, Timothy, Mark, and Anthony.

As a mother, Eunice could of course be loving and caring. But she was also her own mother's daughter, and as such, she could sometimes appear to be emotionally removed. "If the Shriver children wanted affection and understanding, they generally went to Sargent—just as the Kennedy children had gone to Joseph, not Rose," observed the journalist Helen Thomas. "Sarge always knew how to fill his children with self-confidence. 'When you walk into a room,' he would tell his daughter, Maria, 'everyone there is lucky.' Eunice was more the type to tell Maria what to say—and what not to say—once she got into the room."

This isn't to say that Eunice wasn't a loving mother. She enjoyed nothing more than nurturing her children and gave each of them the one thing she knew they needed most—the freedom to choose. She supported their decisions pretty much always—after great discussion, of course. "Though her five children—Bobby, Maria, Timothy, Mark, and Anthony—knew that she loved them, she was a woman of action, not necessarily sentiment," Thomas added. "She was not a patient person. She didn't suffer fools. Her kids knew to toe the line. If they wanted to be coddled, that's what Sarge is for. If they wanted direction, if they wanted motivation, if they wanted a good shove in the right direction, that was Eunice's place."

Indeed, Eunice wanted her children to work hard, give everything their all, and win at life. When Maria was fifteen, Eunice sent her to Africa to live with a family in Tunis—not unusual in a family where the teens were often sent to far-off places in order to expand their view of the world and do charity work. Maria would call her mom to complain that there was no running water and, in fact, no creature comforts at all. "I don't want to hear one more yip out of you," Eunice would tell her. "Get your job done and don't come back until you're finished."

"She wasn't exactly like any other mother you'd ever seen," Maria Shriver would say in her touching eulogy of Eunice Kennedy Shriver in August 2009. "As a young girl, I didn't actually know how to process her appearance much at the time, because most of the mothers were dressed up and neatly coiffed. Mummy wore men's pants, she smoked Cuban cigars, and she played tackle football. She would come to pick us all up at school in her blue Lincoln convertible, her hair would be flying in the wind, there usually would be some pencils or pens in it. The car would be filled with all these boys and their friends and their animals. She'd have on a cashmere sweater with little notes pinned to it to remind her of what she needed to do when she got home. And more often than not, the sweater would be covering a bathing suit, so she could lose no time jumping into the pool to beat us all in a water polo game. Needless to say, when the nuns would announce her arrival, I would try to run for cover."

There was rarely a quiet day for Eunice and Sarge or their children, who were constantly engulfed by the productive chaos and vibrant energy of their parents. "We were taught to make the most of every day," Maria Shriver has recalled. "Our parents never wasted a single second. Yes, it was exhausting. But they had such a love of life and a passion to serve, it just infused everything they did and, in turn, everything we did, too. 'You will. You must. You can,' they would tell us."

In their marriage, the Shrivers provided a great balance for one another. Sargent was levelheaded and grounded, whereas Eunice could sometimes be scatterbrained, brimming with nervous energy. Though he had many important responsibilities, he was organized and structured and had the ability to focus on one project at a time, give his all, and then move on to the day's next task. Eunice, though, always had at least ten projects going at the same time. Some of them got finished, some of them didn't. *"Oh my God!"* she would exclaim as she raced from one appointment to the next. *"I'm going to be late!"* There just weren't enough hours in the day for Eunice.

"Whereas Sarge might be followed by two officious-looking male assistants taking careful notes and helping him organize his day," Hugh Sidey from *Time* recalled, "Eunice usually had a half-dozen women at her beck and call. They were all equally frazzled with notebooks overflowing with charts and graphs, asking questions, taking orders, and shadowing her every move."

Despite often being ill with the effects of Addison's disease—which also plagued her brother Jack—as well as stomach ulcers and colitis, Eunice still managed to keep an extraordinarily busy schedule. She rarely complained, and thus the bar was raised for her kids in how much illness they should be able to tolerate. For instance, they were never allowed to stay home from school with colds or other childhood maladies. "Get to school and I don't want to hear another yip about it," she would tell them.

That Eunice and Sargent Shriver seemed to have a happy marriage for so many years—fifty-five years in all—suggests the couple had found a way to navigate the often rocky terrain that had to have gone along with Eunice's split loyalties between her family and her husband. That said, as much as he was an acolyte of the Kennedys, Sargent Shriver always sought to maintain his and his family's own identity. A famous story has it that his son Bobby had hurt himself while playing, and though he wanted to cry, he didn't because, as everyone knew, "Kennedys don't cry." Shriver told him, "It's okay. You can cry. You're a Shriver." Bobby Shriver recalled of his father, "He didn't want us always to do exactly what the Kennedys did." Indeed, Bobby, like his father and brother Timothy, went to Yale, not Harvard, the traditional Kennedy college. When asked what it felt like to be Kennedys, the Shriver children would almost always answer, "Shrivers are not Kennedys."

Also vitally important to Eunice and Sarge was their Catholicism; they were very devout. They went to Mass almost every day, says Timothy. He recalls their home being "layered with crucifixes and madonnas and other very Catholic sort of statuary. It was not congregational and stark. It was Catholic."

Besides their sharing a deep religiosity, not a lot was known about the personal relationship between Eunice and Sargent. They were both very private. If they fought, it was never in front of other people; they were rarely demonstrative in front of others. Occasionally, though, something would slip that would give others a bit of a peek as to what their marriage might be like behind closed doors.

For instance, in the early 1970s during the height of the popularity of his talk show, Phil Donahue aired a program focusing on female vulnerability. The topic sparked a conversation at an all-girls luncheon between Eunice, Jackie, Jean, and a few of their friends, including Joan Braden. "The question posed was, when are you most vulnerable?" Jackie said. "My answer would have to be when I'm with Ari," Jackie said. "I think that's when I'm most vulnerable."

"Definitely, when a woman is with her husband," Jean said, "that's when she lets down all of her defenses, isn't it?"

Joan Braden agreed. Eunice, though, just sat silently.

"So, what would you say, Eunice?" Joan asked.

"I don't even understand the question," Eunice said, shrugging. She added that in her opinion, vulnerability suggested weakness. "And I'm never weak," she concluded. "So I don't know what to tell you."

The other women just smiled. That was Eunice.

Camp Shriver at Timberlawn

*F*lash back to July 1964.

"It's amazing, isn't it?" Eunice Kennedy Shriver asked Jackie Kennedy as the two women walked through the parklike grounds of the property known as Timberlawn.

It was a sunny Saturday morning and Jackie, Jean, and an assortment of Kennedy family members and friends had gathered at the sprawling estate of Eunice and Sargent Shriver for the weekend to plan a benefit intended to raise money for one of Eunice's pet projects, Camp Shriver. The Shrivers had moved to Timberlawn back in 1961, a bucolic thirty-acre estate just outside of Bethesda, Maryland. "Ethel and Bobby had Hickory Hill, and you and Sarge have Timberlawn," Joan Braden noted with a smile, according to her memory of the day. Jackie had to laugh. "Well, I don't think even Ethel could handle all of this," she said. Indeed, the project Eunice called Camp Shriver was a lot to take in.

As the small coterie of women walked along one of Timberlawn's well-manicured pathways, they passed a tennis court where Shriver children—Maria, Timothy, and Bobby—and Jackie's children—John and Caroline—were playfully hitting balls around with a half-dozen other youngsters. Eunice had personally talked to the Shriver and Kennedy offspring to explain to them why it was important that they interact with children less fortunate. Timothy, who was just three when the camp began, was paired with a mentally handicapped boy named Wendell. They became inseparable, playing all day long and often even getting into mischief together. Nearby, a group of two dozen apparently handicapped children and teenagers were busy doing calisthenics on one of the lawns. Some of their teachers were inmates from Lorton Reformatory in Fairfax County, Virginia, recruited by Eunice to instruct at Camp Shriver as part of a work furlough program. In the distance could be seen a large Olympic-size swimming pool where special-needs children were learning to swim under the watchful eye of Catholic school teachers from Sacred Heart school Stone Ridge in Bethesda. Eunice had somehow convinced them to also volunteer.

Continuing down the path, the small group soon came to a stable where another gaggle of children was learning to ride horses. Their teachers? Diplomats from the British embassy whom Eunice had heard were excellent equestrians and whom she charmed into volunteering. There were, in all, twenty-six volunteer counselors at Camp Shriver and thirty-four children.

Jackie looked around wondrously and asked, "How in the world do you do it? How do you get these people to volunteer? It's just amazing." Jean answered the question. "You know how Eunice is if she wants you to do something for her," she said to Jackie. "She won't take no for an answer. She will pester you until you will either go mad or do what she asks." The women could only look at Eunice with admiration.

It all started back in the spring of 1962 when a woman from Bethesda contacted Eunice as a last resort to ask her if she knew of any summer camp her child—who was retarded—might attend. It was an interesting question, and when Eunice looked into it, she found that there was no such camp anywhere in the United States. "But how can that be possible?" she wondered.

In the 1950s, those suffering from mental retardation were very often viewed as hopeless individuals who should be locked away, hidden from sight, never to be thought of again. There was nothing that could be done for them, it was thought by many, and so it was therefore better to not have to think about them at all. Not only did society not know what to make of the mentally retarded, but parents who'd had the misfortune of giving birth to such children were also often shunned and ridiculed. Therefore, some parents did everything they could think of to keep the child's problems a secret. Those who did their best to raise their mentally handicapped child at home found it extremely difficult. These problems would often ruin their lives, causing them to become socially ostracized and even to turn against each other as pressures and anxieties contaminated their marriage. More than that, it was almost impossible to find doctors who wanted to care for the mentally retarded. Generally, those in the medical profession only wished to treat patients they could cure, and it was thought that there was nothing that could be done for those suffering from mental retardation, so why bother?

It seems impossible to imagine today, but back in the 1950s and before, the parents of mentally retarded children often felt forced to make the heartbreaking decision to lock their sons and daughters away in horribly unsanitary mental asylums, and then tell family and friends that the child had died. In fact, most doctors very strongly suggested this drastic course of action. It was thought that the inevitable fate of the child would be to spend life in an institution anyway, so better that it should happen immediately rather than later when emotional bonds would be that much more difficult to break. If the child then eventually did pass away in the institution, the parents would then sometimes bury him or her in an unmarked grave and do their best to forget the child.

Just as Eunice was mulling over the first telephone call she received inquiring about a camp for the mentally retarded, another mother contacted her with the same question. To Eunice, it felt like a sign. "Enough," she decided. She sat down with Sargent and, according to what he would later recall, said in typical fashion, "There's a need here, and we have to fill it, Sarge."

"Fine, but where?" Sargent asked. "We'll have to lease space, I suppose. Maybe a park?"

"No," Eunice said, "I want to do it here. We have plenty of room here, Sarge."

"But here, in our home?" Sargent said, just a little flabbergasted.

"Well, you know what they say," Eunice concluded. "Charity begins at home."

Sargent had to laugh. "I know that's what they say," he told his wife, "but I'm not sure they meant quite this."

Now she was on a mission—and Eunice Kennedy Shriver loved nothing more than the challenge of a good mission. She started by contacting hospitals and schools, asking them for the names of special-needs students who might benefit from a summer camp. Then she recruited counselors, at first just students from local high schools and colleges. Once she put them all together in her home, she gave birth to what she called Camp Shriver.

It all sounds a little unusual, but if one considers the way Eunice Kennedy was raised, it's really not. "During summers in Hyannis Port when she was young, she and her siblings would all be expected by their father, Joseph, to report to the beach at 7 a.m. and stand in single file like little soldiers," recalled Sancy Newman, a neighbor of the Kennedys in Hyannis Port. "Then, at their father's behest, they would compete with one another in sports activities, interspersed with vigorous calisthenics. Joseph would split them up into teams and the winning team that day would have his approval, while those on the other team were often shunned as 'losers' for the rest of the day—not just by Joseph but by the kids on the winning team. 'We were taught that coming in second place was not acceptable,' Eunice once told me. 'We competed in everything, against each other, whether we were racing, sailing, playing football—we each felt quite strongly that we had to win.'"

The ethos of intense competition was handed down from Joe to his sons, especially to Bobby. His daughter Kathleen recalled in an interview with *McCall's*, "We had to be first in sailing and skiing races. We had to beat our opponents in tennis and get more runs than the other team in softball. And if we didn't he'd get mad. Very, very mad! It was made clear that we weren't to take these sports halfheartedly. And to make sure we were in condition for athletics, Father had the Green Berets set up an obstacle course on the grounds. Can you believe it? The Green Berets. We climbed ropes, jumped, ran, swung, and we toughened up all right."

Sargent Shriver once said of his wife, "I had never heard of a woman so absolutely hell-bent on beating a man at every sport, no matter what it was. Why, she could find a way to turn recreational horseback riding into a deadly competition. I used to think, 'What is wrong with her?' Then, I got it: She's a Kennedy."

Given the strong history of competition fostered in the Kennedy family, perhaps for Eunice to consider hosting athletic events in her backyard wasn't that much of a stretch. She also firmly believed that physical fitness was vitally important to the well-being of the mentally retarded. For instance, she questioned why so many mentally retarded people seemed out of shape and overweight. Was it because of their mental and emotional limitations, or was it because they had no venue for exercise, no opportunity to be physically fit? Addressing these kinds of issues would, of course, present the catalyst for the creation of the Special Olympics, arguably Eunice's most important contribution to society.

Camp Shriver opened its doors on June 7, 1962, attended mainly by children from the Gales Child Health Center in Washington, D.C. It ended in early July so that Eunice and Sarge could spend the rest of the summer at the Kennedy compound with their kids. It would continue with that schedule for years to come, the only major change being that Eunice discontinued the program that saw prisoners from Lorton Reformatory volunteering for her.

"Half the time, Timberlawn would be filled with the most brilliant minds of the country," Maria Shriver added. "And the other half of the time it would be filled by people banging their heads into trees. There would be a hundred Peace Corps volunteers and a hundred retarded children there at the same time. I look back at it sometimes and I think to myself, 'I can't believe I survived that.'"

Sargent Shriver once recalled, "When I'd come home from the office, there's my wife in the pool, holding this mentally retarded child in the water to see if it's possible for that child to swim. She didn't hire somebody for that. She's a hands-on person. She went into that goddamn pool herself!" Maria Shriver laughs at the memory. "That was Mummy," she said. "Hands-on all the way."

Five years later, in July 1968, Eunice realized what would become her life's work, the Special Olympics. The announcement would be made in conjunction with the opening ceremonies of the first Special Olympics being held in Chicago. Standing before a microphone at Soldier Field, she said, "I wish to formally announce a national Special Olympics training program for all mentally retarded children everywhere. I also announce that in 1969, the Kennedy Foundation will pledge sufficient funds to underwrite five regional Olympic tryouts. Now," she concluded triumphantly, "let us begin the Olympics!"

This was definitely a gratifying moment for Eunice. On hand for the occasion was Anne McGlone Burke, a physical education teacher with the Chicago Parks District, who had the idea for a one-time Olympic-style athletic competition for people with special needs. Burke took her idea to Shriver, head of the Joseph P. Kennedy Jr. Foundation, to fund the event. Shriver encouraged Burke to expand on the idea and the JPK Foundation provided a grant of $25,000. Starting on a small scale with some one thousand athletes from across the United States and Canada participating, it would eventually grow internationally, with more than three million athletes from more than 150 countries participating throughout the world. "Let me win" was, as Eunice pointed out, the athlete's oath. "But if I cannot win, let me be brave in the attempt."

It is worth noting that with the growth of the movement, its validity and importance were achieved, thus assuring its continuation. For example, three years after the Special Olympics inaugural games in Chicago, the U.S. Olympic Committee gave the Special Olympics official approval to use the name "Olympics." Six years later, in 1977, the first International Special Olympics Winter Games were held in February in Steamboat Springs, Colorado. In 1988, the Special Olympics were officially recognized by the International Olympic Committee. In 1997, Healthy Athletes became an official Special Olympics initiative, offering health information and screenings to Special Olympics athletes worldwide.

From a physical education teacher's hopeful idea and a powerful woman's remarkable vision and family resources, the small acorn was planted and is now a giant oak in the form of the International Special Olympics, with every indication that it will continue to grow to even greater heights.

What Happened to Rosemary Kennedy?

*E*unice's Kennedy Shriver's lifelong work to advance the public's understanding of mental retardation and erase the dreadful stigma that had once been attached to it is today the stuff of legend. The Kennedys more than just understood the pain and tragedy people faced in 1940s, 1950s, and 1960s when it came to having a mentally retarded person in the family. In fact, they'd experienced it.

Rose Marie Kennedy—commonly known by the family as Rosemary or Rosie—was the third child born to Rose and Joseph Kennedy, on September 13, 1918. As a baby, she seemed normal. As she grew older, though, she began to experience certain learning and behaviorial difficulties. However, it was thought at the time that she just had a low IQ— or at least that's what doctors at first told Joseph and Rose.

For many years, Rosemary would happily participate in the family's many social functions, was a good athlete—she swam and played tennis— and was full of life and beloved by her brothers and sisters as each was born and began to thrive within the family. However, from all accounts she was also a bit slow and could be moody, though apparently everyone recognized, understood, and accepted her limitations. Rose would later say that her daughter also had a tendency to mix up her letters when writing, which would perhaps suggest that she was dyslexic. (As an adult, Rosemary called Rose's secretary, Barbara, "Arbarb," hinting at such a condition.) Suggesting that there wasn't a great deal of alarm about Rosemary's condition is that when she was nineteen and Eunice sixteen, the two went to Switzerland together without a chaperone. In a family where the mandate was always that the older children take care of the younger, it seems fairly obvious that if Rose trusted Rosemary to be responsible for her younger sister, she must have felt that the young woman could handle it.

"Over the years, a great deal of mythology has been created and then disseminated as fact regarding what happened to Rosemary, and much of it is impossible to interpret because of the passing of so many years," observed the noted author Gore Vidal. Vidal had a long and sometimes contentious relationship with the Kennedys; his mother married a man who was later Jackie's stepfather. "Certain doctors supposedly suggested that Rosemary should be institutionalized. However, according to family legend, Joseph supposedly wouldn't hear of it. 'What can they do for her there that we can't do for her here?' he had purportedly asked. Rose wholeheartedly agreed, or so the story goes." In fact, it does seem to be true that Rose—by her own admission—worked diligently to keep her daughter well read, educated, and able to traffic in the Kennedys' fast-paced world. It appears, at least based on Rose's memoir, *Times to Remember*, that she wanted Rosemary to fit in with the rest of her brothers and sisters, and that Rosemary did just that—for a while, anyway.

It is agreed by all parties that things took a dramatic turn when Rosemary was about twenty. Though no one seemed to understand why, the young woman's condition began to worsen, and from some accounts she became argumentative and even violent. It was thought that she had become frustrated that she couldn't keep up with all of her ambitious and competitive siblings as they began to evolve emotionally and physically. As a result, it was posited, she had begun to resent them—and many of her other relatives as well. When she had a physical altercation with her paternal grandfather, Rose and Joseph supposedly realized they had a problem on their hands that they were unequipped to solve. "Mother took Rosemary to any number of doctors," Eunice Kennedy Shriver would recall many years later. "It was always the same—put her away, lock her up...the family is too competitive...she will never find a place. Of course, families had been told this for generations." Is this true or not? Since it came from Eunice, one has to assume that it likely is true—or that at the very least it's what Eunice was told.

"Eventually, the Kennedys apparently sent Rosemary to a Catholic boarding school, a decision that did little to rectify the situation," recalled

Sancy Newman, who knew Rosemary very well as a youngster. "Unhappy with the sense of confinement, Rosemary supposedly took to sneaking out at night, spending evenings away, and, it was feared, maybe being sexually active as well. What if she were raped? What if she became pregnant? As the legend that's been handed down to the family members has it, fears for Rosemary's safety began to mount, and along with them Joseph's reservations. Looking back on it now all these years later, it seems clear that she had some kind of psychotic break that today would probably have been treated with drugs. Who knows? Perhaps she became bipolar. Or was suffering from depression. But retarded? No. I never thought she was retarded."

Though there are still questions as to what really was going on with her, Rosemary Kennedy was beginning to present a big problem to the family, and as Joseph Kennedy saw it, one that might even have had the potential to interfere with the Kennedys' social status and political ambitions. Of course, most people would view Joseph Kennedy as coldhearted in this regard, others as downright cruel. However, one thing was also true about him: He was practical, a man of action who prided himself on his ability to look at a problem with clear-eyed, unsparing vision and then take care of it expeditiously. Indeed, Kennedy did decide to take matters into his own hands where his daughter Rosemary was concerned, and the stunning decision he would make about her in 1941 would yield results nothing short of disastrous.

Lobotomy

In the late 1930s and early 1940s, a new surgical procedure called a lobotomy was being developed in the United States, ostensibly to treat serious emotional problems such as schizophrenia and severe depression. Its success in extreme cases was being trumpeted in some medical circles, though most conventional wisdom at the time viewed the surgery as being extremely risky.

We now know that the frontal lobes of the brain are involved in motor function, problem solving, spontaneity, memory, language, initiation, judgment, impulse control, and social and sexual behavior. In a sense, it could be said that the frontal lobes are also responsible for a person's imagination, for the part of one's personality that inspires desire and ambitions for the future. It was reasoned back in the 1930s and 1940s that a possible explanation for violence and anger in the personalities of some mentally disturbed people sprang from a sense of extreme frustration that their dreams and aspirations could never actually manifest due to their handicapped nature. Therefore, it was posited, if the frontal lobe of a person's brain were compromised and, thus, the part of the brain that creates hope and motivation also became impaired, certain behavior problems could be eradicated as well. How? Because the patient would then have no unrealistic notions about what he or she could achieve and would blend into society in as well-adjusted a manner as possible.

Today the notion of destroying a vital part of a person's brain sounds barbaric. It's difficult to imagine that once upon a time there were doctors who actually specialized in this field, but in fact there were quite a few in the 1940s. During a lobotomy operation, an ice-pick-like device—in some cases, an actual gold-plated ice pick!—or a device resembling a blunt knife was usually inserted under a patient's eyelid and above the tear duct, then hammered into the brain through the thin bone of the eye socket. With that instrument firmly in place, the doctor then simply swished it about, thereby destroying the brain's frontal lobes. Unfortunately, there were no cameras or other kinds of monitoring devices at the time to determine what was actually happening in or to the patient's brain. Instead, the patient was simply put under a local anesthetic and, as the doctor slowly did his work, asked certain questions. When the answers became vague and the patient seemed more distant and detached than previously, the operation was considered over and successful. Horrifying... yet true.

In 1941, Joseph Kennedy consulted with some of the more avant-garde doctors of the time, who told him that a lobotomy was a new and exciting solution to an old problem of mental illness. Other doctors disagreed, and vehemently so. When Joseph eventually discussed the operation with Rose, she asked her daughter Kathleen to look into it. Kathleen came back and told her mother that it was most certainly not the way to go where Rosemary was concerned. It was by no means a solution to mental retardation and was only used on patients with severe psychiatric or emotional illnesses that could otherwise not be treated, and even then it was far from widely accepted. Only about sixty of these operations had been performed up until that time, and with mixed results. Most of the patients were severely brain damaged, though. There was no getting around it. Rose was satisfied to hear as much and told Joseph what Kathleen had learned. As far as she was concerned, the case was closed.

For Joseph, though, it wasn't closed at all.

While Rose was out of town, Joseph took it upon himself to take his daughter to a hospital to have the terrible operation performed on her—apparently without telling a single person in his family about it.

In Rosemary's case, rather than go through the eye as usual, doctors drilled right through the top of her skull. One doctor then inserted the surgical instrument and moved it around, destroying brain matter in the process. Meanwhile, another doctor asked certain questions of Rosemary: Could she recite certain prayers? Sing certain songs? Count backward from ten? They made an estimate about how far to continue "swishing" based on how she responded. Finally, when Rosemary couldn't make sense of the questions, it was decided that the operation was over. Afterward, everyone agreed that it hadn't gone very well. Maybe not surprisingly, Rosemary Kennedy came out of the surgery completely retarded, with virtually no sign of her former personality left in her. She could barely speak and was for all intents and purposes perhaps no more than five years old in her mind. Her head was tilted, she was incontinent, severely brain damaged, and could no longer speak or reason. At just twenty-three, her life was all but ruined.

By some accounts, Joseph was horrified by what had happened to his daughter. By other accounts, he was, if not wholly pleased, at least somewhat satisfied. Rosemary was at first hospitalized, but then Joseph shipped her off to an institution, where she would spend the next seven years.

"When Rose returned home from her trip, Joseph told her and the rest of the family that while she was gone he had taken Rosemary in for a doctor's examination," said Sancy Newman. "It was decided then and there—or so Joseph had lied, anyway—that it was no longer possible for the family to care for her at home. He maintained that Rosemary—like thousands of others at the time—had to be just locked away. And that was the end of it."

One can only wonder about the psychological impact such an event may have had on the Kennedy siblings. After all, one day they had a sister, and the next day they didn't. Once, Ted Kennedy's longtime friend and former Harvard classmate, the writer Burton Hersh, asked him what he as a youngster thought when his sister suddenly disappeared from sight. Ted mulled the question over for a moment before answering, "I thought that I'd better do what Dad wanted, or the same thing could happen to me."

New information now reveals that Rose Kennedy and some of her children began visiting Rosemary in 1949—eight years after she was committed.

Apparently, the private institution in which Rosemary had first been ensconced was no place Joseph wanted his wife and older siblings to visit. Therefore, at the advice of his close friend Richard Cardinal Cushing of Boston—who would for decades be the spiritual adviser for the entire family—Joseph had Rosemary moved to a Catholic community in Jefferson, Wisconsin, then called St. Coletta School for Exceptional Children, today known simply as St. Coletta's. There, Joseph oversaw the construction of a private home for his daughter on the grounds of the Alverno Nursing Home, a facility that was owned by St. Coletta's, which would become known by the staff as the Kennedy Cottage.* It would be here that Rosemary would spend the next sixty years of her life until her death in 2006 at the age of eighty-six, under the care of St. Coletta's staff, always in the company of two caretakers from that community, both of them sisters of the order of St. Francis of Assisi.

It is certainly difficult to believe that Rose Kennedy and the rest of her family were not aware of Rosemary's lobotomy during all the years that they visited her at St. Coletta's, especially since Rose and Kathleen had once discussed the pros and cons of just such an operation. Could Rose have not put two and two together to figure out what had happened to her daughter? However, the story that's been handed down in the family over the years is that no one knew about the awful operation until well after Joseph was gone and some of the family members began asking questions.

What cannot be disputed is that the Kennedys kept secret the fact that Rosemary was retarded and living in a home, certainly not an unusual thing to hide back in those days. In fact, during JFK's campaign it was said by the family that Rosemary was off leading a private life as a teacher in a convent in Tarrytown, New York. The first time the pub-

---

* The Kennedy family contributed money toward the construction of the indoor pool on the St. Coletta grounds, as well as many other projects. In 1983 the Kennedys donated $1 million in honor of Rosemary and Rose Kennedy, which helped fund an addition to Alverno that allowed St. Coletta's staff to better meet the needs of people with disabilities who are aging.

lic had a clue that something was wrong with her was in the July 1960 issue of *Time* when Joseph was quoted as saying she had been suffering from spinal meningitis and convalescing in a Wisconsin nursing home. "I think it's best to bring these things out into the open," he said.

Two years later, in an essay Eunice Kennedy Shriver wrote for the *Saturday Evening Post* in September 1962, she provided a revisionist version of what had actually occurred—with no mention of the lobotomy, of course:

"In 1941...my mother took Rosemary to psychologists and to dozens of doctors. All of them said her condition would not get better and that she would be far happier in an institution, where competition was far less and where our numerous activities would not endanger her health. It fills me with sadness to think this change might not have been necessary if we'd known then what we know today. My mother found an excellent Catholic institution that specialized in the care of retarded children and adults. Rosemary is there now, living with others of her capacity. She has found peace in a new home where there is no need for 'keeping up,' or for brooding over why she can't join in activities as others do. This, coupled with the understanding of the sisters in charge, makes life agreeable for her. Like diabetes, deafness, polio or any other misfortune, mental retardation can happen in any family. It has happened in the families of the poor and the rich, of governors, senators, Nobel prizewinners, doctors, lawyers, writers, men of genius, presidents of Corporations—the President of the United States."

In 1977, Rose Kennedy's secretary, Barbara Gibson, made a startling discovery in the attic of Rose's home—Rosemary's leather-bound diaries, going all the way back to the late 1930s when she was in England with her family while her father was ambassador there. They are fascinating to read in that Rosemary's words paint a vivid picture of a very normal young girl concerned about her nutrition, her schooling, her interest in fashion and in sporting events, and her social life. "Have a fitting at 10:15 Elizabeth Arden's," reads one entry. "Appointment dress fitting again. Home for lunch. Royal tournament in the afternoon." On board the ship taking the family to England, she wrote, "Up late for breakfast. Had it on the deck. Played ping pong with Ralph's sister, also with another man. Had lunch at 1:15. Walked with Peggy. Also went to horse races with her, and bet and won a dollar and a half. Went to English movie at five. Had dinner at 8:45. Went to the lounge with Miss Cahill and Eunice and retired early."

From Rosemary's writings, she seemed carefree and well-adjusted, not at all troubled. She seemed to have had a learning disability, that much is clear from some of the writings in which she writes of trouble in school, and also she seemed dyslexic in her writing, just as Rose had suggested. These diaries, though, were not written by anyone who was severely retarded— they were too concise, too clear, too specific in nature. Rose Kennedy was not happy about their discovery, however. "More than thirty years had passed since her daughter had been institutionalized and Rose and the rest of the family had long ago settled it in their minds as something they could have done nothing about," observed Barbara Gibson. "They didn't even want to think about how things might have been different if Joseph had not acted on his own to solve what he viewed as a problem. Indeed, as far as they were concerned, all of it was just better left in the past."

"Throw them out," Rose told Gibson of the journals. "We don't need them now. Just get rid of them." Barbara Gibson didn't throw them out, though. She kept them.

Joseph Patrick Kennedy

*W*hat can one make of the fact that Joseph P. Kennedy was so beloved and revered not only by his own children but by their spouses as well, despite his responsibility for what had happened to his daughter Rosemary? It doesn't overstate it to say that Sargent Shriver, for instance, hero-worshipped the man, as did Stephen Smith. And the love that Ethel, Joan, and Jackie felt for him was boundless. "Dear Grandpa, you brought all the joy into my life, more than one should dare hope to have. And because of that—all the pain," Jackie once wrote in what appeared to be musings jotted down for a possible memoir, the pages ultimately being sold at auction. "I will remember you. And I will love you until I die."

Though Joseph could be extremely tough and unyielding, there was a paradoxical loving quality to him that was difficult for his children and their spouses to resist—especially given that Rose was by nature so removed and even icy. Not only was she rarely demonstrative, but she also became extremely uncomfortable when anyone around her displayed raw emotion. For instance, even during the darkest of times when Jackie and

Ethel grieved their slain husbands, Rose—by her own admission—would have preferred they do so in private, not in front of her or any of the other family members. It was Joseph who openly showed the most love—tough love, yes, but love just the same. It was Joseph who made the Kennedys feel they were a family, and so it was he to whom everyone was most loyal.

Admittedly, trying to reconcile Joseph the good father with Joseph the man who did what he did to Rosemary Kennedy presents a conundrum, but grappling with such contradictions is essential when trying to understand him. Before setting his sights on politics, he'd made a fortune in the stock market, a huge impact on the film industry in Hollywood (during which time he famously had an affair with Gloria Swanson). He'd also been ambassador to Great Britain under Roosevelt, a tenure that ended very badly. Eleven days after Kennedy's arrival in Great Britain, Adolf Hitler's Nazi forces pushed their way into Austria. In a shortsighted assessment of the situation based on discussions with Prime Minister Neville Chamberlain, Kennedy maintained that the action in Europe had "no long range implications," quoting Chamberlain as likening Germany to "a boa constrictor that had eaten a great deal and was trying to digest the meal before taking on anything else." This would be the first of many miscalculations for Joseph. His efforts to promote U.S. isolationism and his continued antiwar stance, it now seems, were based in a large measure on his fear that his three older sons—Joe Jr., Jack, and Bobby— would be placed in harm's way, fighting a war that he insisted would be our Armageddon. After making a number of speeches that were at odds with U.S. policy concerning Hitler's aggressive march through Europe, Kennedy was asked by FDR for his resignation in 1940.

It was Joseph's zest for politics and for seeing his sons in powerful government positions that became the focus of his life when he returned from England. His firstborn, Joseph Patrick Jr., had come thirteen months after Joseph's and Rose's wedding. It was quickly decided by Joseph that his namesake would be the tyro who would anchor his dreamed-of political dynasty. Two years later John arrived. More children would follow in quick succession over the next six years: Rosemary; Kathleen, known as "Kick"; Eunice; Pat; Robert; Jean; and, finally, another son, Ted. These children would be brought up with a strict and unflinching code of ethics, determination, and the fiercest of all desires—to win. Their dining room would become a lecture hall with constant discussions about current events and politics. "I don't think much of people who have it in them to be first but who finish second," Joseph told his offspring. It was nothing if not a deeply competitive life for all of the young Kennedys.

When Joe Jr. was killed in the war, Joseph focused on his son Jack, who, while not as immediately sharp and charismatic as Joe, was still the best thing the family had going for them—at least as far as Joseph was concerned. "Joseph wheeled and dealed his way into politics," said Hugh Sidey. "Maybe buying elections, maybe not, but definitely at the forefront of the family's ascension into high government. None of it would have happened if not for Joseph's dogged determination. The family owed everything to Joseph, to the way he pulled strings for them, the way he supported them financially and emotionally, the way he pushed them when, frankly, they didn't want to be pushed. It was all because of Joseph."

In 1961, Joseph Kennedy was felled by a debilitating stroke while golfing in Palm Beach, Florida, leaving him unable to speak and walk. This was just the beginning of another series of tragedies in the family. In another two years the vibrant young president, JFK, would be assassinated in Dallas. Next would be Ted's near loss of his life in a 1964 airplane crash. Then, before the decade was over, Joseph's third son, Bobby, would be killed in Los Angeles following a rousing victory speech made after winning the California Democratic primary for 1968's presidential election.

Either overlooking the tragedy that had befallen Rosemary Kennedy or chalking it up to Joseph having done the best he could in a difficult situation, the Kennedy family firmly maintained then—as they do today—that everything they were in terms of strength and resilience was because of the character and example of their patriarch, Joseph P. Kennedy. They would also always acknowledge that their great wealth and political power were the direct result of his hard work and business acumen. Everything they were, in fact, was connected to who he had been in their lives, even their spirituality, for Joseph was extremely religious and passed on that ideology to his family members, most of whom would also be very devout in their faith.

"Everything we have, we owe to Grandpa," is how Ethel Kennedy would put it to her children before a visit to the Big House. "So when you go in to see him," she would say—and at this time Joseph was an invalid as a result of his stroke—"remember that everything you have, every toy, every pet, the house we live in, *everything* we owe to Grandpa."

PART THREE

Sarge

Sargent Shriver

*P*resident Barack Obama perhaps said it best when, following Sargent Shriver's death in 2011, he referred to him as "one of the brightest lights of the greatest generation." Many historians feel Sargent would have— should have—made a great president, that he would have made a significant impact on this country's landscape in the turbulent 1960s and 1970s had he had the opportunity to do so. Not only did he have the energy, the imagination, the magnetism and sense of purpose and duty, but he also possessed what seemed like an organic need to be of service. He cared about society, and he cared deeply. However, one significant stumbling block kept him from advancing his political career: the ambition of the Kennedy family.

First, though, a little history about the man his friends and family called simply "Sarge":

Robert Sargent Shriver Jr. was born in Westminster, Maryland, in 1915, his German forebears among the early settlers of Baltimore. The Shriver family is descended from David Shriver, who signed the Maryland Constitution and Bill of Rights at Maryland's Constitutional Convention of 1776. Sargent's father, Robert, was a banker who had married his second cousin, Hilda Shriver. The Shrivers were hardworking, though not affluent. Following admission on full scholarship to Canterbury, a private school in New Milford, Connecticut, Sarge graduated in 1934 and spent the next seven years at Yale, where he earned both his undergraduate degree in 1938 and his law degree in 1941. As a member of America First, an antiwar organization, Shriver opposed the country's entrance into World War II. But as a patriotic American, he volunteered anyway, serving in the Navy for five years, rising through the ranks to lieutenant and earning a number of commendations for valor. He later recanted his opposition to the war.

Shriver's first encounter with the Kennedys came in 1946 when family patriarch Joseph recruited him to serve as director of Chicago's Merchandise Mart, a home furnishings enterprise. A year earlier, Joseph had bought the monolithic limestone and terra-cotta landmark in Chicago for $13 million, which, at half of what it cost to build, was a very good investment. "People often ask where the Kennedys' greatest source of income comes from," Sargent Shriver once said while taking a journalist on a tour of the property. "Well, here it is." (Though it was an off-the-record remark, it was published just the same. Shriver would never make such a statement on the record.) In fact, over the years it would be the income generated by the rental of office and exhibit space in Merchandise Mart that financed the public and private lives of all of the Kennedys, from Joseph and Rose down to the second generation and the third and—today—even the fourth and fifth. At the time Joseph hired him, Sargent had been working as a journalist, first at *Time* and then *Newsweek*. He became an official part of the Kennedy family in 1954 when he married Eunice at St. Patrick's Cathedral in New York.

Many people today believe that Sargent Shriver started the Peace Corps. That's not exactly true. It had actually been President John F. Kennedy's idea, but Sarge implemented it.

In JFK's first public utterance following his oath of office on becoming president, his inaugural speech in January 1961, he threw down the gauntlet to the American people, imploring, "Ask not what your country can do for you—ask what you can do for your country." This call to service did not fall trippingly off his tongue; it came together following his anguish over the exact wording of how to elicit the most profound response from an eager public willing to fall loyally into lockstep with the new leader of the free world. President Kennedy later pointed out that the Soviet Union had "hundreds of men and women, scientists, physicists, teachers, engineers, doctors, and nurses...prepared to spend their lives abroad in the service of world communism." The United States had no such program, and Kennedy wanted to involve Americans more actively in the cause of global democracy, peace, development, and freedom. He turned to Sargent Shriver, asking him to organize a Peace Corps Task Force. An executive order dated March 1, 1961, less than two months after Kennedy's inauguration, established the Peace Corps with Sargent Shriver as its first director. After half a century of service, the Peace Corps continues to be vital and to grow. Inspired by JFK's vision, it has become an agency devoted to world peace, with volunteers helping individuals to build better lives for themselves, their family, their community, and their country.

After Sargent Shriver distinguished himself in the administration of JFK, he continued to serve Lyndon Johnson after Kennedy's death, creating for LBJ the Office of Economic Opportunity (later the War on Poverty and eventually the Shriver Center) and serving as its first director. It was through the OEO that Shriver created Head Start, a program of the United States Department of Health and Human Services brilliantly conceived as an early intervention program to provide education and nutrition for low-income children and their families. "It was not primarily an IQ idea," Sargent said of Head Start, "it was an idea of intervening early in their lives to…help them become more capable of going to school, which is normally the first hurdle outside the home a person faces."

Sarge always seemed to recognize that there was more to life than politics, maybe unusual in a family like the Kennedys where, at least for the men, politics often seemed to matter more than anything. To Sarge, his family was paramount. He had a strong moral code and passed it on to his children. "He's the one who taught me it's never worth stabbing someone in the back to get ahead," his daughter, Maria Shriver, would recall. "He said that talent and smarts always wins out, that if you're good, you'll get the great job. He said never let a puffed-up ego make decisions for you."

Another priority for Shriver was his faith. "Wherever he traveled to, the first question off his lips would be, 'Where is the nearest Catholic church?'" his son Mark Shriver observed. "Daddy was joyful till the day he died and I think that joy was deeply rooted in his love affair with God. Daddy loved God and God loved him right back. Daddy let go. God was in control and, oh, what a relationship they had."

"A Very Good Shriver"

Repeatedly over the years, the needs and desires of various Kennedy family members and their advisers would take precedence over what would have been in Sargent Shriver's own best interest. Because he was unfailingly loyal to his wife's family, there was always a sort of glass ceiling to how much Sarge would be able to achieve as a public servant. Not that his accomplishments weren't many and weren't historical in their own right, because they were. However, one has to wonder how much more he might have accomplished if not for the fact that one Kennedy or another was always standing in his way—first in 1959, then in 1964, 1968, 1972, and finally in 1976.

It started in the spring of 1959 when there was scuttlebutt that Shriver might run for governor of Illinois. Because he had strong connections in that state and a solid groundswell of support, he toyed with the idea. He hadn't even made a decision one way or another about it, though, when Joseph Kennedy heard the rumblings. "What's this I hear about you maybe running for governor?" Joseph asked his son-in-law one afternoon at La Guerida, the Palm Beach estate. Sargent said he hadn't made up his mind yet but that, yes, he had been approached and there seemed to be significant interest. "Well, let me help make up your mind," Joseph said. "It can't happen. The whole family is behind Jack for president right now. So forget it. Jack needs your help with his campaign." And that was the end of that—at least for the time being.

"Not only did Joseph ask for Sargent's assistance, Jack also had asked for his help...as did his wife, Eunice," Hugh Sidey recalled. "That was a lot of pressure. There wasn't much Sargent could do but sublimate his own desires for that of the family's, which would, as it would turn out, become a recurring way of life for him."

In temperament and personality, Sarge wasn't as shrewd as JFK or as cunning as Bobby, and everyone knew it. Sarge was thought of not only by some of the Kennedys but also by many of their counselors—men who wielded great influence over members of the family, such as speechwriter Ted Sorensen and Kennedy aide Kenny O'Donnell—as a lightweight, a pretender to the throne. They looked at him as naive, a romanticist who believed too much in the good of people, rarely recognizing man's duplicitous nature. (That was certainly an ironic view of him, especially when one considers that President Kennedy's New Frontier would be built on a platform of idealism.) "They believed Shriver had good ideas and was obviously able to make them work in government, but because he wasn't a real Kennedy, he'd never have the same drive, ambition, and smarts as a real Kennedy," is how veteran White House reporter Helen Thomas put it. Maybe Bobby said it best when once asked what he thought about Sargent Shriver: "He's a very good Shriver," was his response. Ted also felt that way. Surprisingly, so did Stephen Smith, Jean's husband, who was also not a "real" Kennedy but, in his view, at least never tried to act like one.

The next time Sargent Shriver's ambition was thwarted was in 1964. At the time, Lyndon Johnson had been considering possible running mates for the presidential election, and Sargent weighed heavily on his mind. Johnson respected Shriver so much that on the day JFK was shot he promised him that if he could, he would one day show just how much he appreciated him. By 1964, with three years of success with the Peace Corps under his belt (*Time* magazine had reported, "The Peace Corps has captured the public imagination as has no other single act of the Kennedy administration"), Shriver continued to demonstrate the leadership qualities he had shown as an important member of the Johnson cabinet as special assistant to the president. However, Shriver's role within the Johnson administration always found him in a difficult position—stuck in the middle between LBJ and Bobby Kennedy and the Kennedy family.

Johnson wasn't in office very long before Bobby made it clear that he might be interested in running against him in the 1968 election. For that reason, RFK never felt comfortable that Shriver was still a part of LBJ's administration. For his part, Bobby had lasted as attorney general under LBJ for only ten months after his brother's death, before departing to run for, and win, his seat in the Senate representing New York. But Shriver was still working for LBJ. "The fact that LBJ had such a direct pipeline to the Kennedys through one of their own, namely Sargent Shriver, troubled a lot of the family members," said Jack Valenti, who handled press relations for Lyndon Johnson (and went on to become the longtime president of the Motion Picture Association of America). Some even thought that Shriver's being a pipeline to the Kennedys was precisely why LBJ had brought him into his administration in the first place. Others would find this a simplification of LBJ's thinking, though it's difficult to believe that it hadn't at least crossed his mind, especially considering his crafty personality. In fact, Johnson had other reasons for wanting Shriver around.

Of all the Kennedys, LBJ loathed Bobby Kennedy with a burning, searing passion. Everyone knew it—and everyone also knew that Bobby felt the same way about Johnson. Still, because of the memory of JFK, Johnson suspected he would have a clear advantage at the polls if he could at least try to stomach Bobby on the ticket with him. But that was asking a lot—more than LBJ could conceive of, in fact. One way for him to avoid the problem of aligning himself with a running mate he detested was to associate himself with the next best thing in the campaign—a Kennedy brother-in-law and, it could be argued, the best of the bunch: Sargent Shriver. To LBJ, this seemed like a very good strategy. "Most people liked and respected Sargent, and LBJ could put up with him a lot easier than he could any other Kennedy family member, with the possible exception of Jackie," said Jack Valenti. Because it became such a serious consideration for him, word of a possible LBJ-Shriver ticket soon leaked to the press.

Scott Stossel has a very telling story in his excellent book *Sarge: The Life and Times of Sargent Shriver*. One day in the spring of 1964, Sargent Shriver was at the Kennedy compound relaxing when Bobby Kennedy happened by. Shriver and Kennedy had always had a difficult, though usually respectful, relationship. Though they tolerated each other because of Eunice, the two were like oil and water. Whereas Shriver was amiable, good-natured, and diplomatic, Bobby was moody, explosive, and dogmatic.

"What's this I hear about you being on the Johnson ticket as vice president?" Bobby asked his brother-in-law, according to Sargent's later memory of events. The two men faced each other, standing just inches apart. Bobby tended to invade another's "personal space" when he was being confrontational. Shriver would recall feeling immediately uncomfortable.

"Well, nothing has been decided," Shriver said cautiously. "So, I'm not sure what will happen."

Suddenly, in one swift and threatening moment, Bobby reached out and pulled Sargent in by his collar. "Let me make something clear," he said in a tone that could only be described as menacing. "There's not going to be a Kennedy on this ticket," he said. "And if there were, it would be me."

Shriver didn't know how to respond. "Well, like I said," he told Bobby, backing away from him but still standing his ground. "Nothing's been decided."

Bobby sized him up for a moment, then turned and walked away without comment.

Bobby Kennedy

After Joseph Kennedy Jr.'s plane crash death in World War II and JFK's assassination in 1963, it fell upon Joseph's third son, Bobby, to once again fulfill what the ambassador had always considered the family's destiny—the presidency of the United States. Born on November 20, 1925, in Brookline, Massachusetts, the seventh of nine children of Rose Fitzgerald Kennedy and her husband, Joseph, Robert Francis Kennedy inherited not only his maternal grandfather's lack of height but also, as it would happen, his feisty determination. The runt of the litter, he would one day grow into an alpha male, but not before struggling academically with his early education, attending by actual count seven different public and Catholic schools from grades one through twelve. He even repeated the third grade in public school in Bronxville, New York, after his family moved there. He always seemed to be challenged by his older brothers, and, like them, he enlisted in the Naval Reserve before his eighteenth birthday in 1944 and signed up for V12 officer training. Bobby also followed his older brothers to Harvard and, despite his size, made the varsity football team, earning a letter his senior year. Unlike them, though, he chose the University of Virginia for law school, enrolling in 1948 and receiving his degree in 1951, following his marriage a year earlier to Ethel Skakel. He graduated from law school in June 1951, and a month later, in July, his and Ethel's first child, Kathleen, was born. The rest of their brood followed in rapid succession: Joseph in 1952, Robert Jr. in 1954, David in 1955, Mary Courtney in 1956, Michael in 1958, Mary Kerry in 1959, Christopher in 1963, Matthew in 1965, Douglas in 1967, and Rory in 1968, six months after Bobby's death.

Making babies would prove to be a sideline for Bobby Kennedy as he also busied himself with the family's business—politics.

In late 1959, Bobby left the Senate Rackets Committee to run Jack's successful presidential campaign. Proving himself to be an important adviser to the president, Bobby was rewarded by being appointed to head the Justice Department as attorney general. He was dogged in his resolve to rid America of the underworld, to the point that some of his adversaries—and colleagues, for that matter—thought of him as an angry lightweight pugilist, always eager for a good scrap. In fact, no attorney general in history had ever wielded the kind of wide-ranging influence on a president's administration that Bobby did.

Bobby also became a tireless implementer of his brother's civil rights program, going after elected officials and others in authority in the Deep South who would deprive blacks and other minorities of their basic civil rights. At the forefront of great change, he and JFK shared a vision that voting was a means to the solution of racial injustice. Together they introduced the most sweeping piece of civil rights legislation since the Civil War and Reconstruction, the Civil Rights Act of 1964. With strong support from LBJ, it was passed after Jack's death.

If he was hard-hitting in the public arena, Bobby could be just as tough privately. "Incompetence would upset him," said David Burke, Ted's legislative assistant and close friend who went on to become vice president of ABC News in 1977 and president of CBS News ten years later. "Lack of follow-through would upset him," added Burke. "Lack of preparation would upset him: if the speech wasn't absolutely the best. He was not overly generous with his compliments. Yet I know he felt very strongly about his staff, and I suppose you'd always feel with Robert Kennedy that if his staff was ever criticized, he'd defend them savagely. Yet he never gave direct compliments. If you did something for *Edward* Kennedy, if the speech was exceptionally good or the legislation prevailed, he'd be very, very generous in his compliments, and the little notes he'd write you and so on and so forth. It is important to staff people who always feel they're laboring in the bottom of the barrel someplace. I never felt that of Robert Kennedy... it wasn't in his nature."

"For him, the world is divided into black and white hats," Ethel Kennedy once said of Bobby. "The white hats are for us and the black hats are against us. Bobby can only distinguish good men and bad. Good things, in his eyes, are virility, courage, movement, and anger. He has no patience with the weak and the hesitant."

Bobby's family and friends knew a man who was often good-natured, a father whose greatest joy was in playing touch football with his many children on the warm summer sands of Hyannis Port, or pushing them on swings to see just how high they could soar. "Let's set a new record," he would tell them as he pushed them higher and higher. "A Kennedy cannot be scared!" he would exclaim. Not only was his own brood devoted to him, but also all the rest of the third generation of Kennedys. "The whole family revolved around him," his nephew Christopher Lawford recalled. "He was the one who taught us what it meant to be a Kennedy. He organized all the games and trips. Everything flowed from him."

Bobby also had a trenchant wit and a quirky sense of humor, which is what Ethel had always found most attractive about him. Moreover, he was extremely passionate and committed, always true to his convictions about justice and the equality of all men. Also, like all of the Kennedys, he was extremely religious. "His faith meant everything to him and was something else that bonded him and Ethel on a very deep level," said Kennedy historian Doris Kearns Goodwin. "He knew he was flawed. He knew he was given to temptation. He also knew Ethel accepted him for who he was, and that made him love her even more."

Though Bobby loved his wife deeply, he was capable of the occasional indiscretion. Unlike his brothers Jack and Teddy, though, from all accounts he felt very guilty whenever he strayed. Apparently, Ethel chose to look the other way.

"After Jack's death, Bobby was a changed man," recalled his former press secretary, Frank Mankiewicz. "Though he tried to encourage everyone to go on with their lives and offered his support to family members in innumerable ways, he fell into a deep and awful depression."

"I was shocked by his appearance," recalled author William Manchester, who was at the time in talks with Jackie to write a book about Jack's assassination. He had met privately with Bobby in that capacity. "I have never seen a man with less resilience. Much of the time, he seemed to be in a trance, staring off into space, his face a study in grief."

No one could really help Bobby, not even his wife, Ethel. Whereas it would have seemed that Ethel would be the one who could have reached him, this was not the case. He could have long conversations about his brother with his sister-in-law Jackie, but not with Ethel. She was closed off from the pain of losing Jack, and simply couldn't—or wouldn't—discuss it. Her coping mechanism was to avoid sadness because she feared that if she gave in to it, she would fall into a depression so deep she might never emerge. She had long ago learned to live her life as dispassionately as possible when it came to dealing with the deaths of loved ones. Therefore, when she did talk about Jack, it was always in empty platitudes. For instance, one night, according to family history, Bobby was particularly sad at the dinner table. "There will never be anyone like Jack again," he said. Ethel looked at him and said, "Well, don't worry, Bobby, because Jack is in heaven looking after all of us, and everything will be okay." It wasn't what he needed to hear in that moment. He shook his head in dismay. "And those were the words spoken by the wife of the attorney general of the United States," he said, his tone one of disdain.

Bobby tried to go on—and, of course, he would go on—but it was different for him after November 1963. With Lyndon Johnson as president, Bobby's role in government was greatly diminished. He served in LBJ's cabinet for less than a year before resigning over Johnson's escalation of the Vietnam War. He viewed the war as divisive and unwinnable and felt he could best oppose it by becoming a senator from New York in 1964, replacing Senator Kenneth Keating, who was retiring. He also felt that with a half-million troops now overseas, there was little hope that the escalation of the war would end anytime soon. Therefore, he began speaking out against it, and with each speech he felt a bigger groundswell of public support. By 1967, it had become clearer than ever that Bobby Kennedy intended to run against LBJ for the presidency in '68.

Getting Sargent Out of the Way

*T*he possibility that Robert F. Kennedy might enter the presidential race was of great concern to President Lyndon Johnson. Almost as bad for Johnson was the very real possibility that Sargent Shriver might somehow end up a part of the RFK team. After all, at this time—the beginning of 1968—Sarge was still director of the Peace Corps under Johnson and also special assistant to the president. Though Bobby had made it clear that he considered Sarge a threat, Sarge was still his brother-in-law. Therefore, Bobby would likely find a place for him on his campaign, and it was thought that Sargent would probably accept such an appointment. Thus it had become a very real possibility that an important and well-respected person in LBJ's cabinet—Sargent—could end up aligned with one of the president's sworn enemies—Bobby. LBJ wasn't happy about any of it and felt he needed to take decisive action. The next thing everyone knew, he came up with the novel idea of packing Sargent Shriver up and sending him to Europe as ambassador to France.

Obviously, the president wanted Shriver out of the country and as far away from the Kennedys as possible, thus the offer. It wasn't as if there were many in his administration or in the Kennedy family who didn't realize his true motivation. The question was whether or not Sarge and Eunice would go for it. "It wasn't the worst idea in the world for Sargent," recalled George Smathers, "in that it would get him out of a bad situation. He was either going to have to remain loyal to LBJ, as was his duty. Or remain loyal to the Kennedys. The problem was thought to be Eunice. If Bobby was going to run for president, no way was she not going to be in the States to help with the campaign. It seemed pretty black-and-white that Eunice would never go."

Torn Loyalties

*T*hroughout the years, it has repeatedly been theorized that Eunice Kennedy Shriver would unequivocally support her family's interests over her husband's. She was a Kennedy, it has been explained, and as a Kennedy she would naturally place more importance on what her family wanted than on what Sargent wanted. This was simply not the case. In fact, the opposite was usually true. Eunice almost always supported her husband's interests before her family's, and it was well known in the family that this would be her position. She believed Sargent was a great man and always maintained that it did not diminish her brothers or anyone else in the family to recognize Sarge's immense contribution to society and his own political goals and ambitions. Yes, of course, she wanted the best for her Kennedy family. But she was an independent thinker. She didn't just go along with the family's aspirations. She was a Shriver as well as a Kennedy, and she wanted what was best for her husband. Anyone who thought otherwise just didn't know Eunice Kennedy Shriver. This loyalty pull would always be an issue for her, however, sometimes causing her great pain. She simply couldn't understand why her family was so ambivalent about Sarge. Considering all of the good Sargent had done for America, Eunice couldn't fathom how anyone could be so dismissive of him. Her father, Joseph, certainly didn't feel that way. He had made it clear many times that he was a big supporter of Sarge's. Were Bobby and Ted just jealous?

The more she thought about it, the more Eunice was able to trace the family's ambivalence about Sargent back to his decision to stay on with LBJ after JFK was killed. "They were upset about anybody working for President Johnson," Eunice would admit many years later. "But Sarge felt a real loyalty to the programs. I agreed with him. What was the alternative? Sarge has terrific talent and great concern for people who are underdogs. That's not something he came upon when he married me or when he went to work for the Johnson administration. It was part of the very core of his being. If you take that out of somebody's life because you think he's being disloyal to a man who is dead, well, I just didn't think it made sense."

Eunice thought she at least had her mother Rose's support when it came to Sargent, but then in March 1968 something happened that made her question even that. During a visit to Timberlawn, Rose had asked Sarge to take a walk with her after lunch. She told him that she understood that LBJ had offered him the ambassadorship to France and she wondered if he was going to accept the position. He said, according to his later memory of the conversation, that he hadn't made up his mind. She wanted to know why. He was still considering possibly running for office in Illinois, he told her, and also he wanted to make sure he wasn't needed in Washington. Perhaps he was alluding to a position on Bobby's team if Bobby decided to run for president. Rose said, "I want to tell you something, Sarge. Getting offered the opportunity to be ambassador is the best thing that could happen to you and your family. When Joe became ambassador to Great Britain, it was marvelous for our children. You've got an opportunity here to do for your family what Joe was able to do for ours." As they walked along one of the manicured pathways of Timberlawn, Rose continued, saying, "You know, it's quite a compliment the president is paying you by asking you to be ambassador of France." Sargent agreed. "Then why haven't you accepted?" she pressed. "Why haven't you told him you're ready to go?"

When Sargent reported back to Eunice the conversation he'd had with her mother, Eunice wasn't sure what to think. It was obvious to her—as it was to just about everyone else, for that matter—that LBJ just wanted Shriver out of the country to clear out another Kennedy acolyte. LBJ's wishes aside, if Bobby was to run for president, shouldn't Sargent be in America to help with the campaign? He had been invaluable to JFK's campaign, after all. It was as if Rose Kennedy was now another family member who didn't recognize Sargent's true value. Perhaps the Kennedy matriarch wasn't looking at it quite that way and was really just trying to be supportive, but it felt to Eunice that she had aligned herself with Bobby and Ted in their view of Sargent.

"If that's how Mother feels, and that's how Bobby feels, then fine. I say we go," Eunice decided. Of course, there were other reasons to go as well, as Eunice well knew. "She might have been a little annoyed at the time, but she was also eager for new opportunities abroad and realized her husband would excel at his ambassadorship," observed Jack Valenti. "It was an important job and, certainly, peace could not occur in Vietnam without France's involvement. Sargent Shriver was more than qualified, had the diplomatic skills necessary for the job, and could doubtless act as a valuable conduit between French president Charles de Gaulle and the American president—Lyndon Johnson, or whomever would be his successor."

Therefore, in the second week of March 1968, Sargent Shriver accepted President Johnson's offer to be ambassador to France.

Questioning LBJ's Motives

Just a couple days after Sargent Shriver told the president that he would accept the assignment to France, Robert Kennedy announced that he would run for president of the United States. Most people in the Kennedy camp were very enthusiastic about Bobby's plans, but surprisingly, Ted was not. "Ted's position was that it was the wrong time for Bobby to emerge as a presidential candidate," recalled David Burke. "His concern was that, in the end, the election would not be about Vietnam, it would be about the Kennedys, and whether or not the family was hungry for power. He was afraid that Bobby's running would be negatively perceived by many Americans, and that if he then lost the election it would contaminate the terrain for '72. He was worried about the Democratic Party. Ted was very shrewd about politics. In some ways, more shrewd than Bobby, and that was saying a lot. He was afraid the party would end up splintered, and as a result, someone like Richard Nixon could end up president. He turned out to be very prescient. Then, of course, there was the personal issue. He would never say it, but he was afraid of losing Bobby the way he had lost Jack. He would say things like, 'We're not that far from 1963,' which would hint at his true feelings. There was a lot of fear there, which was understandable."

Still, the announcement was made on March 16, 1968, in the Caucus Room of the Old Senate Office Building—the same room where his brother declared his own candidacy eight years earlier. RFK stated, "I do not run for the presidency merely to oppose any man, but to propose new policies. I run because I am convinced that this country is on a perilous course and because I have such strong feelings about what must be done, and I feel that I'm obliged to do all I can."

That same week, Sargent and Eunice Shriver hosted Joan Braden and Jackie Kennedy for dinner at Timberlawn. Over the meal, Jackie brought up Sargent's possible appointment as ambassador. According to what Joan Braden later recalled, Jackie said she thought it was an interesting idea, but she was suspicious of LBJ's motives. "After all," she said, "did you know that he once wanted to name *me* ambassador to Mexico?" Everyone was more than a little surprised by that revelation. Even Sarge didn't know about it.

In fact, back in November 1963, right after JFK's death, LBJ came up with the unusual idea of naming Jackie ambassador to Mexico, replacing the then-present ambassador, Thomas C. Mann, who had been appointed to that position by JFK and was set to retire in December. LBJ discussed the matter with an aide in a taped telephone conversation.

"This is screwy, but can you hold on to your chair?" LBJ asked his aide. "Would it be just terrible to ask Mrs. Kennedy to be ambassador to Mexico?" LBJ laughed nervously when the aide seemed taken aback by the idea. When the aide said he needed to "sleep on" the idea, LBJ continued to push it. Finally, the aide said he was concerned about how Jackie—and the public—might perceive the offer. What would be the effect of that? "There wouldn't be any effect if nobody knew it but the two of us," LBJ argued, "and I wouldn't mention it to anybody but you, and if she didn't

want to [accept] nobody would ever know it but you. And if she did want
to, God, it would electrify the Western Hemisphere," Johnson continued.
"It'd be more than any Alliance for Progress and she could go on and do
as she damn well pleased...she'd just walk out on that balcony and look
down at them and they'd just pee all over themselves every day." When
the aide still seemed hesitant, LBJ asked, "She wouldn't be mad [at the
offer], would she?"

The aide answered, "Oh God, no. Then after an awkward beat, "God,
no." And another beat: "God, no." LBJ continued: "You think they [pre-
sumably the public] would think we're tryin' to use her, or somethin'?"

"I'd really like to think about it," answered the aide.

LBJ then said he had recently talked to Jackie "and she just oohed
and aahed over the phone and she's just the sweetest thing and she was
always nicer to me than anybody in the Kennedy family...she just always
made me feel like a human being, and that's the biggest thing I got [to
offer] and I think it would just revolutionize Latin America." Jackie could
live in Mexico for three weeks, LBJ said, and come back to the States for
a week, if she wanted to, "'cause I don't give a damn what she does," he
said, "but I think she and Tom Mann together would sew up this hemisphere, and I believe that's what she'd want to do. And I think her husband up in heaven would look down and say, by God, he [LBJ] saw she
had it just like I did."

In the end, LBJ decided not to present the offer to Jackie; the job
went to career officer Fulton Freeman. However, Jackie found out about
it anyway—from Ethel, who heard about it from Bobby. Jackie respected
Thomas Mann, had met him when she and Jack visited Mexico during
the Chamizal border conflict, which the president was responsible for settling. She said privately that she would have been embarrassed for Mann
to even know that LBJ had made such a consideration. After all, there
were any number of delicate negotiations going on at the time between
the United States and Latin America, and it seemed completely reductive
of the position to think that Jackie could fill it.

"Looks like he just wanted to use you, Jackie," Sargent opined. "What
do you know about Mexican affairs?" he added with a gentle smile.

"That's exactly my point!" Jackie exclaimed. "And now I think he's
using *you*, Sarge."

Sargent didn't comment on Jackie's theory. Neither did Eunice.

The Decision Is Made

*T*hat Bobby Kennedy had officially announced his intention to run against him was not good news for President Johnson. But at least he had gotten Sargent Shriver out of the picture. "LBJ was tickled that he could hold a Kennedy brother-in-law out of the race," said his aide Joe Califano. "To him, the appointment of Shriver as ambassador to France was made in political heaven."

But then, at the end of March, in what was nothing if not a fast-moving story, a plot twist occurred that few saw coming: Lyndon Johnson decided that he would *not* accept the Democratic nomination for president in the 1968 campaign.

In the end, there were many reasons for LBJ's surprising decision, but the unpopularity of the Vietnam War most certainly topped the list. Throughout his presidency, Johnson had been adamant that America could not lose the war, for if it did the country would appear weak to the world and, he feared, risk making its global interests vulnerable to attack. At the time, it was said that JFK had intended to cut back the number of troops in Vietnam (this theory is up for debate now, with some historians considering it revisionist history), but it became LBJ's mandate to increase those numbers, and as he did, the casualties mounted as well. By 1968, it was a very unpopular war, and most Americans linked it, and the deaths of so many servicemen, to their president. "All of his other achievements—his successful push toward civil rights, for instance, and his [and Sargent Shriver's] War on Poverty—didn't much matter when contrasted against the Vietnam War, at least in the popularity polls of the time," noted Jack Valenti. In fact, Johnson realized that there was practically no way he would be reelected and decided to bow out, stunning the entire country with his now famous words, "I shall not seek, and I will not accept, the nomination of my party for another term as your president." In short order, Vice President Hubert Humphrey announced his own candidacy for president of the United States.

Now that LBJ was officially out of the race, was it really necessary for Sargent Shriver to accept the post he had been offered as ambassador to France? Perhaps not. Certainly, if Bobby had simply appealed to Sargent and told him that he was needed on the campaign, it seemed unlikely that Shriver would have gone to Paris. "But I don't think he ever felt, quite honestly, that it really made a difference to Bobby," Eunice would say in an interview in 1972. "In those three or four months that led up to the decision [for Bobby to run] he [Shriver] was never consulted. He knew Bobby could get along very well without him. When Sarge is told he could make a difference, he doesn't hesitate twenty seconds."

In fact, Bobby asked Eunice to intervene and talk to Sargent about possibly becoming involved in the campaign. However, Eunice felt strongly that if her brother needed Sargent's help, he should be the one to ask for it, again demonstrating her genuine loyalty to Sargent. That Bobby asked her for help and she refused him said a lot. "Bobby, why don't you talk to him?" she pressed, according to her memory. "He'll do anything you want him to do." However, Bobby was nothing if not stubborn, and he still resisted personally calling Sargent. His reluctance just made no sense to Eunice. Certainly, if Sargent needed Bobby's assistance, she reasoned, he would have shown him the respect of picking up the telephone and calling him personally. Now Eunice was starting to get angry.

Finally, in early April, Bobby Kennedy did make an overture to Sargent Shriver—he dispatched an attorney named Donald Dell to meet with him.

Until very recently, Donald Dell had been special assistant to Shriver in the Office of Economic Opportunity. A former professional tennis player and three-time All American, Dell had been a member of the U.S. Davis Cup team and would go on to become one of the nation's first professional sports agents. (In 2009, he was inducted into the International Tennis Hall of Fame.) In 1968 he had just begun working for the RFK campaign. Bobby had been a close friend and frequent tennis partner. According to what Dell recalled many years later, "Bobby obviously knew of my history and close friendship with Sarge, which is why he sent me to meet with him. We sat down in one of the parlors of Timberlawn's main house and talked about Bobby's candidacy. You could really talk to Sarge. Anyone could, really. He was very approachable."

Donald began, "So, Sarge, we were thinking, what are the chances of you not going to Paris and staying here to work for Bobby?"

Shriver seemed to mull it over for a second. Though he didn't say as much, he was perhaps still wondering why Bobby hadn't called him personally. "It does sound interesting," he said. "But I'm not really sure that I'm needed."

"Why, of course you are needed, Sarge," Donald responded, according to his memory of the conversation. "How could you think otherwise? Bobby has the greatest respect for you."

Sarge didn't respond. At just that moment, Eunice walked into the room with her usual briskness. After carefully studying the two for a moment, she said, "And what's going on here?"

The two men just looked at her.

"Well, I think we should leave for dinner now, Sarge," she said, eyeing them with more than a little suspicion. "I have reservations at eight, you know?" She and her husband then shared a secret look. "So, what are you two talking about anyway?" she asked.

"Well, Donald here has an interesting proposition," Sarge answered.

"Oh really?" Eunice asked as she stood before her husband and the visitor. Since the two men were still seated on cushioned chairs, Eunice towered over them in a way that was perhaps a tad intimidating.

"Bobby sent me to talk to Sarge about possibly joining the campaign," Donald said. "We all know Sarge would be invaluable to—"

Eunice cut him off. "Well, that can't happen," she said, her face darkening. "It's not possible now."

"Why is that?" Donald asked.

Looking down at Sargent, Eunice asked in a commanding tone, "Well, you told the president we were going to France, didn't you? Is that not what you said?"

"Yes, I did say that," Sarge answered. "But, you know, I thought that perhaps we could—"

"Well, then, *that's that*," Eunice said, interrupting her husband. "We're going to France to be ambassadors there, just as we promised President Johnson. So it's done. The decision is made," she concluded. "Now, let's go to dinner."

Not Meant to Be

*T*ed Kennedy had an ominous feeling about his brother's decision to run for president. He wasn't the kind of man to verbalize his fears to many people, but it had been clear from the beginning that he was afraid for Bobby's life. He decided to abandon his concerns, however, and do what Kennedys always did at important junctures in their family's history—pull together for the greater good. "I know that he had a difficult time overcoming his fear," said David Burke, Ted's close friend, "but at the time, what could he do? He couldn't just sit around in fear. He couldn't allow himself to be immobilized in that way. To the extent that Bobby believed with all his heart he could be of service, that the party needed him, indeed, the country needed him, Ted had no choice but to be completely supportive. I have to also say, though, that Ted wasn't alone in his concerns. The rest of the family was quite fearful but took the same action as Ted—which was to swallow their fears and hope and pray for the best."

Bobby Kennedy's 1968 campaign for his party's nomination was in high gear almost from the start as he racked up delegates everywhere, attracted as they were by his youthful energy, his pit-bull style, and his liberal agenda. But then, of course, everything changed one awful June night in 1968 when he was gunned down in Los Angeles. It seemed impossible, yet it was true. Another brother, gone. "It was as if everyone had to then reset and try to figure out how to proceed with all of the rules once again changed, just as they had been when Jack was killed," recalled David Burke. "You had a sense that the world had gone mad, that nothing made sense. It was as dark a time as I can remember, a period in our country's history we still have not been able to reconcile. Those of us who were personally involved were, of course, devastated beyond words."

On the political front, who can say what kind of President Bobby Kennedy might have been had he run and won the election that fateful year? "[Bobby] achieved something special in that last campaign," observed Bobby's son Max—who was just three when his father died. "It was the first time Americans in the middle class and the poorest Americans were really brought together. Men and women from all sorts of racial and economic backgrounds joined together in that campaign. I have always found it striking that after June 4, 1968, many of the Americans who supported my father supported George Wallace, not because of the latter's racial views but because he was the voice of the middle- and the lower-middle-class worker. Wallace, however, appealed to the dark side of their hopes. I believe that there is a dark side to every American and it is easier perhaps for politicians to appeal to that darker side, but we are all also receptive to what is best in us. Robert Kennedy chose to appeal to the light."

Of course, Bobby's senseless and tragic death would impact everyone in the Kennedy family in a deep and very personal way. His mother, Rose, would be left wondering how God could take her boys in such a cruel way, and her daughters—Bobby's sisters—would never be able to get over the loss. His devastated wife, Ethel, would be left with eleven children—her cross to bear made even heavier by the troubles her oldest sons would bring into her life. His sister-in-law Jackie would take an unlikely husband, in great part due to her fear that her two children were now in danger. For their parts, Sarge and Eunice would leave for Paris as they had agreed to do, but now with great sadness and regret. Meanwhile, the last surviving brother, Ted, would spend years trying to decide if he was up to the task of accepting his lot in life as the next Kennedy in line for the presidency.

Without Bobby, life would go on for all of the Kennedys, just as it had without Jack. But it would never be the same.

Humphrey-Shriver?

I know there were feelings that we should not have gone," Eunice Kennedy said in 1972, referring to her husband Sargent Shriver's accepting the appointment as French ambassador by President Lyndon Johnson rather than staying in America and campaigning for her brother Bobby. "But Sarge was not what you'd call an inner man on Bobby's campaign. He was never a close friend of Bobby's." Certainly there were people in the Kennedy family who seemed never to have gotten over the Shrivers' decision, not understanding that it sprang, in part, from the feeling that Bobby hadn't had enough respect for Sarge to call him and personally ask for his assistance. "Your daddy didn't come back from France to campaign for our daddy," some of Ethel's children used to chide the Shriver children. Indeed, the sense that Sargent had been disloyal was even passed on to the next generation of Kennedys, none of whom could have been expected to understand the subtle nuances of emotions that had figured into the Shrivers' decision.

The ill will against Sargent Shriver had been subtle up until Bobby's death, but afterward, it bubbled over in a very hurtful way.

Sargent and Eunice had been in Paris on that terrible June day in 1968 when Bobby was killed. It just so happened that Ted's wife, Joan, was there as well, visiting them. They returned immediately upon hearing the news, flying into LaGuardia Airport to rendezvous with family members and aides there. As some of these family members and Kennedy advisers loaded Bobby's casket off the plane, Sargent tried to help. However, they angrily pushed him aside, acting as if he was a traitor. "I think maybe nothing hurt him and Eunice more that that," Pierre Salinger later recalled. "That was an awful way to treat Sarge. I don't think he ever got over it."

It seemed to many that Ethel Kennedy was one of those who had held a grudge against Sargent for his decision. Ethel's feelings about the matter were very complex, though. When, just weeks after Bobby's death in 1968, Hubert Humphrey began floating the idea of asking Sargent to be his Democratic running mate, Ethel wasn't comfortable with the idea at all. It was too soon, she felt, for anyone in the family to try to continue where Bobby had left off. Plus, there was a rule of succession in place, and she wanted the family to stick to it. It wasn't official, but it could not have been more clear: first Jack; then Bobby; then Ted; then, maybe, Sarge. Also, Ethel couldn't help but still question Sarge's loyalty to Bobby when she factored in his decision to go to France. Finally—and this was perhaps the biggest issue for her in her consideration of these matters— she was loyal to Ted at all costs. What he wanted, she wanted—and that was the end of it for her. He was there for her as Bobby's stand-in, and she would be there for him too, always. However, she was still deeply grieving Bobby's death and wasn't up to debating family politics. So she just let it be known that she wasn't supportive of the idea of Sarge taking part in the Humphrey campaign, and then let it sit.

Maybe Eunice Kennedy Shriver didn't catch on to Ethel's signals, though, because she told *Life* magazine in 1972, "I consider Ethel my greatest friend. I've never had any feeling ever from her about disloyalty. And if she didn't want Sarge to do something, I have full one hundred percent confidence that she would call me and say, 'For God's sake, will you say this or say that to Sargent.'"

Be that as it may, the clear word back to Humphrey was that the Kennedy family would not be pleased with the idea of Sargent Shriver as vice president. In fact, Kennedy aide Kenny O'Donnell—who often derisively referred to Shriver as "half a Kennedy"—went so far as to pass a message on to Humphrey that the family would consider his adding Shriver to the ticket "an unfriendly act."

A big reason to bring Sargent Shriver onto the ticket, at least as Hubert Humphrey saw it, was to garner the Kennedys' blessing. "What the Kennedys said and how they felt mattered a great deal to Democrats, and having them support the ticket might go a long way toward ensuring its victory at the polls," explained Hugh Sidey. "However, if the Kennedys were going to just disavow Sargent Shriver—either by leaking negative stories to the press about him or even by just not saying anything at all about him—then what was the point of putting him on the ticket?" Of course, such reasoning totally overlooked Shriver's years of stellar achievement and his obvious qualifications for the job, but as Joseph Kennedy once put it, "Politics presents itself as a nasty bit of business, doesn't it?"

Besides Ethel, there were others in the Kennedy family and connected to it who were not exactly supportive of a Humphrey-Shriver ticket. "The family resents it," Stephen Smith told a politico—off the record—at the time. It was clear that Stephen Smith resented it, anyway, and Smith's feelings could not be overlooked. He was the family's financial analyst and political strategist. Not only was he responsible for much of the money that came in and went out of the Kennedy organization, but his duties also included raising money for all of the campaigns, namely Jack's, Bobby's, and Ted's. He was a powerful person in the family who also kept a low profile. Other than his wife, Jean, and his brother-in-law Ted, he really didn't have close personal relationships with the Kennedys. Put it this way: There aren't a lot of warm family anecdotes about Stephen Smith. But somehow he managed to stay out of the line of fire by just keeping his nose to the grindstone and doing his job. He wasn't politically ambitious, though he toyed with the idea of running for mayor of New York City in 1969. He generally believed that politics was a game better played by the Kennedy brothers, certainly not their in-laws. When he took issue with another person's ambition—such as he did with his brother-in-law Sarge's—people knew it and paid attention to it. "In Stephen Smith's mind, Sargent Shriver was on a par with Peter Lawford," is how Pierre Salinger once put it. "He had little respect for either of them, but at least Peter never tried to run for office."

Siding with Stephen Smith against Sargent Shriver was just about everyone who had ever supported Bobby—including aides Arthur Schlesinger Jr., Ted Sorensen, and Kenny O'Donnell. "Some of us didn't believe Shriver to be intellectually equipped enough to handle the demands of the presidency," Schlesinger once recalled. It was difficult to fathom such criticism considering Shriver's mammoth achievements, but politics does have a way of sometimes making the most reasonable of men act like competitive children in a schoolyard. Another issue had to do with what might happen in 1972. For instance, if the winner of the 1968 race was the Democratic nominee and Shriver was his VP, what would happen should the president decide not to run again in '72? If Ted was interested in running at that time, how would Shriver's presence in office affect things? Or what if the winner was the Democratic nominee and Ted decided he wanted to challenge him by vying for the party's nomination in '72? How would Shriver's presence affect that scenario? As usual, Sargent Shriver found himself in the way of Kennedy ambition.

Still, Shriver decided to take secret meetings in Paris to determine the feasibility of his being added to Humphrey's Democratic ticket. "We need Ted's approval," he finally decided. "That's the only way this thing can work." That was easier said than done, though. After Ted sent word that he definitely wasn't interested in running himself, he agreed to meet with Sarge in Paris to discuss the matter. The much-anticipated meeting was set for the second week of August 1968 at Shriver's home.

Ted Disappoints

*O*ne person who worked for Eunice Shriver as a personal assistant when the Shrivers were in France recalled Sargent Shriver's being locked away in his private study waiting for Ted's arrival that second week in August 1968. He took no calls and spent hours studying certain issues so that he would be able to present his case to Senator Kennedy, recalled the assistant. Shriver's study was enormous and graceful-looking, with a carved pine fireplace, pine-paneled walls, fine antiques all about, and expensive, comfortable furniture with rich colors on chintz fabrics. There was also a great deal of French oil artwork of great value, just as there was all over the ambassador's residence. Of course, there were books everywhere—he was an avid reader. Also in this study—and *only* in this study—Sarge put mementos of his public life. This room was Sargent's private sanctuary in the sense that there were no mementos of his public life anywhere else in the sprawling mansion.

At his homes in the States—both at Timberlawn and at the Kennedy compound—Sarge had his own bedroom that was decorated in much the same way as his study in Paris, and it had the same purpose— as a safe haven from which he could escape the madness of his wife's world. His sons used to love going into his bedroom because, as Bobby put it, "you had a sense that things were different in there, that it was a world apart from the Kennedys—it was the Shrivers' world." Indeed, Sarge had all of his best suits hanging in his closet, his finest coats and hats and other apparel, all orderly and in pristine condition. His bottles of expensive cologne were lined on his bureau along with his gleaming cuff links and shining watches—and there was never any dust on anything. Books about politics, science, and religion were perfectly arranged on shelves. Moreover, all of his stellar achievements were memorialized only in his office in Paris or his bedrooms in Virginia or Massachusetts, nowhere else in the homes. In these special rooms would be found many framed pictures of Sarge with an assortment of political figures such as Lyndon Johnson, Dwight Eisenhower, and other dignitaries—including, of course, Jack, Bobby, and Ted, everyone looking courageous, strong, and determined.

"We'd been told that Mr. Kennedy left the States and was on his way, but that his plane had been delayed," recalled Eunice's former assistant. "After the passing of several hours, Mrs. Shriver came into the house, ran up the stairs and directly to the study. She seemed agitated as she raced by me and burst into the study."

"He hasn't even left America, Sarge," Eunice exclaimed, according to the assistant's memory. Shriver was at first confused. "What are you talking about?" he asked his wife.

"Ted!" Eunice exclaimed. "I just spoke to Joan. Ted is still in the States. He's not coming, Sarge!"

"What?" Sargent responded. "But that's not possible. His office told me he left the States hours ago."

"Well, it's apparently not true," Eunice said. "It's not true!"

As members of the staff congregated in the hallway to see what was going on, Sargent told Eunice that maybe there had been a scheduling conflict and that they should give Ted the benefit of some doubt. However, Eunice said she was certain there was no mistake. She decided that she would call her mother to find out what had happened. Eunice then made a transatlantic call to Rose Kennedy. Apparently, either Rose hung up on her daughter or Eunice decided to terminate the call herself, judging by the way she slammed the phone down after a very brief conversation. "This is *your* time, Sarge," Eunice then said, turning to her husband. "You've worked hard for it. And you deserve it." Noticing the household employees who were now standing in the hall, Eunice turned to face them. "What are you all doing out there?" she demanded. "There is no show here. Nothing is happening in here that concerns any of you. So go about your duties and leave us be." With that, she slammed the door shut.

The Shrivers stayed in the study for another hour. When they emerged, Eunice seemed somewhat calmer. "There, there," Sargent said to her, his arm around her.

"She repeatedly had me place calls to Mr. Kennedy, but he was never available to her," recalled Eunice's former assistant. Later that day, Eunice was seen outside on a patio in the garden, walking back and forth slowly with her beads in her hand, saying the rosary.

Sargent Appeals to Ted

*T*he problem of course was what it always was—Ted Kennedy's selfish nature. He really didn't care about Sargent's Shriver's ambition, he was concerned with his own. He couldn't help it. That's just who he was, and those who knew him well understood that a major part of his—indeed, of any successful politician's—psychology was his ego, his absolute belief that he had the right answers, the solution to important problems. "It comes with the territory," was how Sargent Shriver put it. On August 19, 1968, though, Ted finally buckled under family pressure to telephone Sargent Shriver in Paris.

According to what Sargent would later recall of his conversation with Ted, he started off by reminding Ted that never once had he ever asked him or anyone else in the Kennedy family for any favors. All he had ever asked for was a chance to implement the important projects in which he was interested, all for the good of the country and to the credit of JFK's and LBJ's administrations. Therefore, he could not understand why Stephen Smith or anyone else in the family was so intent on attacking him. Ted conceded that many Kennedy supporters and family members were still angry at Shriver because they felt he could have done more to help with Bobby's campaign. Ted reminded Sarge that his acceptance of LBJ's offer to be ambassador to France at precisely the same time Bobby was getting ready to run for office did not ingratiate him to anyone in the family. Be that as it may, Sargent responded, all he was now asking for was for Ted's neutrality, even though he would have of course preferred Ted's total support of the Humphrey-Shriver ticket. Instead, Sarge was asking him for much less: He simply didn't want Ted to speak out against him. Could Ted offer him at least that much? Maddeningly for Sarge, Ted had to admit that he really wasn't sure. He would have to think about it. He did allow, though, that he would at least talk to Stephen Smith and ask him to stop bad-mouthing Shriver to others. That was pretty much the gist of the conversation Sargent had with Ted on that August night, at least according to Shriver's notes. It was disappointing at best and certainly not much for Sargent to feel good about in terms of Ted's or the Kennedy family's support of his political ambitions.

Three days later, on August 21, Ted gave his first speech since Bobby's death. "There is no safety in hiding," he intoned. "Like my brothers before me, I pick up a fallen standard. Sustained by the memory of our priceless years together, I shall try to carry forward that special commitment to justice, to excellence, and to courage that distinguished their lives." He said that he intended to return to the Senate, but would not run for office. In other words, he had no intention of being Humphrey's vice presidential running mate. "Each of us must take a direct and personal part in solving the great problems of this country," he said. "Each of us must do his individual part to end the suffering, feed the hungry, heal the sick, to strengthen and renew the national spirit."

A week later, on August 29, 1968, Hubert Humphrey made it official. He was going with Maine senator Edmund Muskie as his running mate.

In the end, Humphrey and Muskie would lose the race to Richard Nixon and Spiro Agnew. Ted had been afraid that Nixon might get elected if Bobby ran and lost, and that's exactly what happened even with Bobby's death. To this day, many political pundits believe that Humphrey might have won the presidency had he had Sargent Shriver at his side and the Kennedy family's blessing of the union. If so, who knows how that might have affected history? One can't help but wonder what the world might be like today had there never been a Watergate.

Of course, Sargent and Eunice Shriver were both greatly disappointed by what happened in 1968. Typically, though, Sargent decided to focus on his work and resist the temptation to become bitter.

"In politics," Sargent Shriver—ever the diplomat—concluded, "when men are playing for such stakes, you can't count on personal ties and shouldn't take these things personally." He hoped he would have another chance at political office—though even he had to admit that it seemed that the odds were starting to stack against him. As far as Ted Kennedy was concerned, all of this political melodrama involving his brother-in-law and his sister was just a blip on his radar screen. It didn't seem to matter to him at all. And soon he would have even more reason to be distracted.

PART FOUR

Ted

"Sick with Grief"

*I*t was just after midnight on the morning of July 19, 1969, when Jackie Kennedy Onassis received a collect telephone call from Ted Kennedy. When the call came, she was on the isle of Skorpios with her husband, Aristotle Onassis, her children, and Pat's daughter Victoria Lawford. He was in serious trouble, he told her. He—indeed, the entire family— needed her. He was vague—something about a girl being killed in an automobile accident while he had been driving. The more questions Jackie asked, the more evasive Ted was with his answers. It didn't sound good, though. Jackie believed in Ted. He had always been an ally to her, having been there as a surrogate father for her children, and for Ethel's too. Jackie thought of Ted as dependable, trustworthy. He had also recently negotiated her marital deal with Onassis, and she appreciated it very much. Therefore, when he asked her to come home, of course she could not turn him down.

With Bobby Kennedy gone, the Kennedys had quickly turned to his younger brother, Ted, with the hope that he might be the family's father confessor, the keeper of the flame, the one who would guarantee that the notion of Camelot would somehow endure. But America was no Camelot by the summer of 1969. The country was still reeling from Bobby's senseless death, and also from the assassination of civil rights leader Martin Luther King Jr. In fact, a deep sense of loss and hopelessness was still felt by many people who were trying to deal with the loss of JFK years earlier. The Vietnam War continued unabated; there seemed no end in sight. Truly, it was a calamitous time in the nation's history. It was thought by many Americans that perhaps Edward Moore Kennedy—Ted—might be the man to unify the country. Certainly his recent years in the Senate proved to many that he understood the problems the country faced and that he was willing—even felt obligated—to do something about them. However, he was now in trouble and the entire family was being summoned to meet at the Hyannis Port compound.

Ethel Kennedy had been attending a Special Olympics function at the University of Connecticut when her mother-in-law, Rose, called her on the morning of July 19, 1969. She quickly made it to Hyannis Port, dropped off a box of trophies and T-shirts at her home next door, and then sprinted over to Rose's. "Mother, whatever Teddy has done, I am sure he had a very good reason for it," she told Rose, according to what Rose would later recall to her secretary, Barbara Gibson. "Let's just wait and see what it is. I'm sure it's not so bad." Rose, who was just a couple of days short of her seventy-ninth birthday, didn't know how to respond. All she knew was that Ted had told her not to go to a charity bazaar at her church, St. Francis Xavier, for fear that she would be ambushed there by reporters. He said he would explain everything to her later.

Arriving after Ethel was Ted's wife, Joan, from Boston. Slim and gorgeous, her hair falling in a soft tumble to her shoulders, she seemed somehow unsteady on her feet. Six weeks pregnant, she looked so unwell, in fact, that Rose insisted she sit down immediately. "Do you know what happened?" Rose asked her. Joan said she only knew what Ted had hurriedly told her on the phone. "He said he had been driving a girl somewhere and that he drove off a bridge," Joan said, according to her later recollection. "And he said that the passenger had drowned. He told me, 'I tried to save her, Joansie. But I couldn't. She's dead.'" At that, both Ethel and Rose just stood in place gaping at Joan, not knowing how to respond.

Finally, Ted arrived. "He was so unlike himself, it was hard to believe he was my son," Rose later recalled. "His usual positive attitude, which he displayed so clearly at other times of difficulty, had vanished. He was disturbed, confused and deeply distracted, and sick with grief."

"Where's Dad?" Ted wanted to know. Before he could do or say anything else—even to his own mother—Ted felt he had to see his ailing father. It had always been Joseph's opinion of him that most mattered. Joseph's nurse, Rita Dallas, recalled Ted as having been "drawn and downcast" when he went to his father's bedside upstairs. Sitting next to his dad, he held Joseph's hand and, according to Rita, said, "Dad, I'm in some trouble. There's been an accident and you're going to hear all sorts of things about me from now on. Terrible things. But, Dad, I want you to know that they're not true. It was an accident. I'm telling you the truth, Dad, it was an accident." Ted then told his father what had happened. Paralyzed from a recent stroke, all Joseph could do was nod, squeeze his son's hand, and shed a tear. After he left Joseph's bedside, Ted pulled Rose, Ethel, and Joan into another room. There, he told them a terrible story.

Chappaquiddick

*I*t all started on the evening of July 18, 1969, just as the Apollo crew was about to realize President Kennedy's dream of exploration of the moon. Ted, who was thirty-seven, was taking part in the Edgartown Regatta off Martha's Vineyard. Participating in the event, which was sponsored by the Edgartown Yacht Club, was a longtime tradition, and two Kennedy boats, the *Resolute* and the *Victura*, were entered in these 1969 races. Ted also thought that the weekend's activities would provide a good reason to reunite some of the girls who had worked for Bobby's campaign, affectionately known as the Boiler Room Girls because of the difficult backroom work they did for Kennedy. Therefore, after the Kennedy boats raced in the regatta, a party was held at a cottage near the beach on Chappaquiddick, a small island just off Martha's Vineyard. Kennedy cousin Joe Gargan made all of the arrangements.

At least for part of his childhood, Joe Gargan was raised by Joe and Rose Kennedy after his mother, Rose's sister, died, and he always had one chief responsibility. "I was to look after Ted and make sure he didn't get into trouble," he recalled. Rose Kennedy had decreed it so, that's how it always was, and that's how it remained, even though Joe was now a successful lawyer and also vice president of a Hyannis bank.

Present at the party were Gargan, Ted Kennedy, Paul Markham (a lawyer and former U.S. attorney for Massachusetts), and some other male friends of Ted's. The Boiler Room Girls were all present too—six women in all, including Mary Jo Kopechne. All but one of the men had wives; the women were not married.

At some point after 11 p.m., Ted left the party with twenty-eight-year-old blonde and blue-eyed Mary Jo, a former teacher and more recently a secretary for Senator George Smathers, as well as for Bobby Kennedy. She was also a devout Catholic. Ted later explained that his intention was to give Mary Jo a ride to the ferry headed back to Edgartown, where she was staying. Was there something more to it? Of course, only the two of them would know, but Mary Jo was not necessarily Ted's type. She was plain and wholesome, whereas Ted usually went after the blonde bombshell type. Not only that, but he didn't even know her last name when he offered to drive her to the ferry. Of course, it's likely that Ted had many an assignation with women over the years whose last names were unknown to him, but people who knew him best seem confident that Mary Jo was not one of them. After Ted asked for the keys to a black 1967 Oldsmobile Delmont, he and Mary Jo took off to meet the moment that would forever change both their destinies. Somehow, Ted lost his way. He later said that he made a wrong turn and, before he knew what was happening, had driven off a wooden bridge with no guardrail. The car plunged into the Poucha Pond, seven feet of cold, cloudy water. Ted escaped. Mary Jo was not as lucky.

Ted would later testify that he had dived into the water seven or eight times in hopes of finding Mary Jo, but to no avail. Dazed and disoriented, he then walked back to the cottage where the party had been taking place. Then he, Joe Gargan, and Paul Markham—both attorneys—returned to the scene of the accident. "We got there and I'm standing there looking at this Oldsmobile submerged under the water," Joe Gargan would recall many years later, "and I thought to myself, holy shit! If Mary Jo is in that car, she's dead for sure. And I thought to myself, goddamn it, everything is about to change in this very minute. Kennedy family history is being altered this very second. I was very conscious of it, and very afraid of it, as well. I quickly stripped off all of my clothes and I was standing there naked and shivering and I said to myself, this is it, Joe. You gotta do this. I took a deep breath and dove in. Paul did the same." In fact, the two men dived into the water several times in an effort to rescue Mary Jo, but to no avail. "I couldn't see a thing, it was so dark," said Gargan. "I was feeling my way, holding my breath, just trying to find her down there, but…nothing." By this time, Ted was in tears and hysterical. "I'm diving into the water," Gargan recalled, "and meanwhile I see Ted on the side of the road on his back, his hands behind his head and his knees up, and he's wailing, and crying, 'What's going to happen to me now? What am I going to do now?'" Once out of the water and dressed again, Gargan and Markham insisted that Ted report the accident to the authorities. "You have to report it now," Joe told him. "I mean it, Ted. Right now." Ted hesitated. So much was obviously at stake, it was as if he didn't know how to proceed. "I don't know what to do," he cried in a low voice raw with agony. "This can't be true. None of this can be true."

The three men got into Joe Gargan's car and headed toward the

Edgartown Ferry slip, all the while discussing how to proceed. "It was like we were sleepwalking," Joe Gargan would recall. "It was hard to know how to process it." It was especially hard, one might imagine, with Ted trying to find ways around culpability.

Obviously, a person can react in any number of ways to a situation such as this one. Some would own up to their responsibility, their moral code simply not allowing them to act in any other way. Others might make a different choice and do anything they could think of just to get out of trouble. Of course, the reasons for that choice can't be painted with a wide brushstroke without generalizing. In Ted's particular case, he was a man who had lived a life of privilege and entitlement and was fairly used to things going his way. This rapidly unfolding situation at Chappaquiddick seriously threatened the world he had created for himself. In short, he was terrified of losing everything. Therefore, seeing his life crumbling before him, he went into "fix-it" mode rather than taking responsibility for his action. While it's obvious that this wasn't the best choice, maybe it's understandable in its human fallibility, at least as a first impulse. But then again, Ted Kennedy was never a man easily understood.

Perhaps one of his closest friends, David Burke, put it best when he said, "I saw Ted through his happiest of times and I saw him through his saddest, but to say that even I had his fullest trust would be to overstate our relationship. When one of your brothers was the slain president of the United States and your other brother the slain attorney general and you come from a family with as many eyes on them as the Kennedys, you tend to not be very trusting by nature. You don't always know who is going to be the one to give that interview that will betray you. So you hold back with everyone, which is what I think Ted often did. You don't show your emotions. One memory comes to mind: I went with Ted to Vietnam in 1968. He was on the chair of the subcommittee of refugees and also acting as a sort of minister of Bobby's. It was really a fact-finding mission. A group of us went to all sorts of hospitals, medical facilities, and refugee camps and saw the most horrible things, men who had been terribly, terribly wounded in the war. Children, too. Many children. It was difficult for any of us to keep from crying. But Ted never cried. He would just walk away rather than betray his true feelings. That was Ted. Therefore, for anyone to say he truly understood him or the way his thought process worked would be a leap. In many ways, Ted Kennedy was unknowable, and that was by understandable design."

If Burke's assessment of Ted Kennedy's personality is accurate, and there's little doubt that it is, then it's even more remarkable—and out of character—for Ted to have acted in such a dramatic fashion at the scene of the Chappaquiddick accident. If anything, it would suggest that he truly was in shock and not in his right mind.

"So, look, what if Mary Jo had been driving alone?" Ted posed as a theory to Gargan and Markham. "And what if she just went off the road? No one needs to know I had been in the car. No one saw us drive off, so that could work! We could say that!" Moreover, Ted even came up with the scenario that Gargan and Markham take him back to the party so that he could make an appearance there and tell everyone present that Mary Jo had his car and that he was now going to leave with his cousin, thereby creating an alibi. When the two refused to participate in that charade, Ted asked them to report the accident as if they had come upon it and just not mention that Ted had anything to do with it. The two men flatly refused. Ted had a few other scenarios in mind, but stopped short of asking the men—Joe in particular—to take the blame. "We couldn't have stayed friends if he'd gone that far," Joe Gargan would say years later. Still, Ted was furious with him and Markham for not being more helpful. After all, maybe Markham had an excuse not to be cooperative, but as far as Ted was concerned, Gargan didn't. His mandate had always been to take care of Ted, and now he was failing miserably at that task. "Screw you guys, then," Ted said once the car had reached the slip. "Thanks for nothing. Now, screw you!"

"But Ted, you have to report this thing now," Joe Gargan said. "Promise me that you will call the police, promise me!"

"I'll take care of it," Ted said angrily. "Just don't worry about it. I'll do it."

With that, Ted Kennedy dove, fully clothed—and with his back brace on from his plane crash—right into the cold black water. "Holy shit, Ted!" Paul Markham exclaimed, stunned by his friend's sudden action. Without turning around, Ted then began to swim frantically toward Edgartown. "And I thought to myself, 'You know what? Screw him,'" Joe Gargan would recall years later. "'I hope the son of a bitch drowns, that's what I hope.' That's how mad I was. And I love Ted. I was raised with

Ted. He meant the world to me. But I was just so goddamn mad at him in that moment."

As his friends drove off, Ted Kennedy continued to swim across the five-hundred-foot channel all the way back to Edgartown, where he had been staying at the Shiretown Inn. He later recalled, "I started to swim out into that tide and [I] felt an extraordinary shove...almost pulling me down again, the water pulling me down and suddenly I realized...that I was in a weakened condition, although as I had looked over that distance between the ferry slip and the other side, it seemed to me an inconsequential swim, but the water got colder, the tide began to draw me out, and for the second time that evening, I knew I was going to drown... and after some time, I think it was in the middle of the channel, a little farther than that, the tide was much calmer, gentler, and I began to make some progress and finally was able to reach the other shore." Once ashore, Kennedy walked back to the Shiretown Inn and then to his room. By now totally exhausted, he stripped off his wet clothes and crawled into bed. He spent the night tossing and turning and getting up and pacing and staring into the darkness, all the while hoping against hope that, somehow, none of what had just happened had actually occurred or, at the very least, that Mary Jo had somehow found her way out of the car and was not dead.

The next morning, Joe Gargan and Paul Markham showed up at the inn to find Ted having what seemed like a pleasant conversation with a bunch of people on the porch. Gargan grabbed Ted by the arm and pulled him aside.

"So, what did the police say?" he asked his cousin, according to his memory.

"I didn't report it," Ted said, his judgment obviously still crippled.

"Goddamn it, Ted!" Gargan exclaimed. "What is wrong with you? This thing just got ten times worse than it was last night."

"Look, I've made up my mind," Ted said, not making eye contact with his cousin. "I'm going to say I wasn't there, that Mary Jo was driving alone."

"Holy shit," Gargan said. "Have you lost your mind?" Now Joe was almost at a loss for words. "Why, you can be placed at the scene!" he managed to sputter.

"Only by you guys," Ted countered.

Joe understood where Ted was going with this line of reasoning. "No way," he told his cousin, according to his memory. "I'm not lying for you, Ted. I'm just not doing it."

At that, Joe Gargan and Paul Markham got back into the car and drove off, headed back to Chappaquiddick Island, leaving Ted alone with his plan—one that, as it would happen, he did not implement. At around 8:45 a.m., the car he had been driving was found submerged in Poucha Pond by two amateur fishermen, and Mary Jo's body was extracted from the murky water. Ted heard about it when a year-round resident of the island named Tony Bettencourt approached him and said, "Senator, do you know there's a girl found dead in your car?" It was only then—almost ten hours after the accident—that Kennedy went to the local police station to report what had happened.

Ted Kennedy

*Y*ou can have a serious life or a nonserious life, Ted," Joseph Kennedy had told his thirteen-year-old son. "I'll still love you, whichever choice you make. But if you decide to have a nonserious life, I won't have much time for you. You make up your own mind. There are too many children who are doing things here that are interesting for me to do much with you."

Imagine how it might shape a boy to know that his own father might not have much time for him if he wasn't as ambitious and as productive as his siblings, especially if he believed his dad practically walked on water—the way Ted Kennedy felt about his father, Joseph. After all, it was from Joseph that Ted received the most attention, with him that Ted felt most secure. Imagine how it might have made him feel that perhaps he wasn't worthy of Joseph's love. Ted, the youngest member of the Kennedy family, may have grown up feeling inferior, sensing very strongly that he wasn't worthy of his father's time, that he paled in comparison to his intellectual siblings, especially his brothers, and then pretty much spent his entire life vacillating between proving this thesis true—and trying to prove it wasn't true.

Edward Moore Kennedy was born on February 22, 1932, at St. Margaret's

Hospital in Boston. As the baby of the family, he was at once spoiled by a father who doted on him and usually ignored by a mother who was customarily not expressive of her emotions. He was also constantly challenged by his father to compete with his older brothers, but then again, all of the children were encouraged by Joseph to compete with one another. Ted, though, was always impetuous and a little foolhardy. For instance, with the country at war in Korea, he joined the Army and, in an effort to show his independence, impulsively signed up for a four-year hitch assuming it was for two. His father was furious, yelling at his son, "Don't you ever look at what you're signing?" The enlistment was shortened to two years thanks to Joe, who then arranged for his cushy assignment to the honor guard at SHAPE (Supreme Headquarters Allied Powers Europe) outside Paris. Just after his twenty-first birthday, Ted was discharged as a private first class in March 1953. He then went to Harvard and the University of Virginia Law School, where he would earn his law degree. "He was a good football player on the field for Harvard, but in life Ted was never one to play by the rules," Joe Gargan would observe.

Indeed, in an overzealous desire to be eligible for the varsity squad at Harvard, Ted persuaded a friend to take his Spanish-language final exam. The pair were quickly caught and expelled. However, they were told they could reapply for admission, provided they stayed out of trouble. Having others perform his schoolwork would be repeated in other instances, though, such as when he talked Jackie into writing an art history paper for him, earning him an A and the comment "keen perceptions."

In 1958, Ted Kennedy interrupted his law school studies again to run JFK's campaign for his senatorial reelection. Marshaling his abundance of Irish charm, good looks, and an uncanny ability to connect with Democratic voters in the Bay State, he was able to engineer his brother's record-setting election to reclaim his Senate seat, setting him on the road to fulfill his presidential destiny.

With JFK in the White House by 1960, his Senate seat was vacant. Though Ted felt entitled to it because of his role in securing his brother's election, at twenty-nine he was shy of the thirty-year age minimum for a senator. He would wait out the period serving as an assistant U.S. attorney in Massachusetts, while a Kennedy ally, appointed by the governor, kept the Senate seat warm until a special election was held, which he handily won.

The next eighteen months saw two devastating events in Ted's life—the assassination of his brother, Jack, in Dallas in 1963 and his own near death in a plane crash a year later. The year of his crash also coincided with the end of his term in the Senate. Using a walking cane to steady himself, he returned to the Senate in January 1965 and was sworn in with Bobby, now New York's junior senator.

Despite Ted's seniority in the Senate, Bobby never missed an opportunity to remind his younger brother that he, Bobby, had inherited the mantle of his late brother, not only in the family but politically as well. It was an entitlement Bobby felt was his due by virtue of his longer political career and the reliance placed on him by JFK. "It was always interesting to people who knew the Kennedys that titles mattered to them so much," recalled Helen Thomas, "almost as a way of reminding each other of their stations in life. For instance, Joseph was almost always called 'the ambassador,' even around the house in casual circumstances. 'Have you seen the ambassador?' Rose would ask her children, instead of referring to him as their father. JFK was very often called the president. 'Will the president be joining us for dinner?' Rose would ask. Similarly, Bobby, when he was named to the position, was usually called 'the attorney general,' and Ted was practically always called 'the senator.' In fact, Joan very often called him that all through her marriage when referring to him, even when he was in the room. 'The senator and I are so happy to see you,' she would say to guests when she and Ted would entertain in their home. Even his second wife, Vicki, would usually refer to him as 'the senator.'"

Ted's political course would be stayed. Bobby's would not, unfortunately. What Ted feared most had come to pass, which was Bobby's death in 1968. Who would ever forget Ted's moving eulogy at his brother's funeral? "My brother need not be idealized, or enlarged in death beyond what he was in life, to be remembered simply as a good and decent man, who saw wrong and tried to right it, saw suffering and tried to heal it, saw war and tried to stop it," he said. "Those of us who loved him and who take him to his rest today, pray that what he was to us and what he wished for others will someday come to pass for all the world. As he said many times, in many parts of this nation, to those he touched and who sought to touch him: 'Some men see things as they are and say why. I dream things that never were and say why not.'"

At this time, Ted Kennedy was considered a hero by many people. At the very least, there was a lot of sympathy for him by 1969, the tide of popular opinion strong and moving him in the direction of the White House, pushed along by the media and also much of his constituency. In truth, the die had long ago been cast, and without Jack and Bobby to lead the way, there was little doubt that Ted was a presumptive future president of the United States. In a poll taken in 1968, 79 percent of Americans believed that he would one day be leader of the free world. He didn't know that he wanted the job, though. For her part, Joan was definitely against the idea. In fact, the idea of Ted as president caused her great panic and distress. It didn't matter, though. After the deaths of his brothers, it had become Ted's obligation, indeed his duty, to step into the national political spotlight to fulfill his father's obsessive ambitions and his brothers' legacy. The problem, of course, was that Ted Kennedy came with a lot of baggage—not the least of which was what happened on Chappaquiddick Island.

Joan Kennedy

*J*oan, what in the world has happened?" Webster Janssen wanted to know. He was Joan's second cousin and calling her at her home on Squaw Island after hearing the news reports of Ted's accident.

"I honestly don't know," Joan answered, according to Janssen's memory of the conversation. She sounded absolutely exhausted. "All I know is what you've heard on the news. I guess Ted was in some kind of car accident and...someone died. I guess."

"But how?" Webster asked.

"Again, I don't know," Joan answered.

"Well, have you talked to Ted about it?"

"No," came the response.

"But how is that possible, Joan?"

She sighed loudly. "How is *any* of this possible?" she asked.

Indeed, life for Joan as a Kennedy wife had never been easy, presenting one impossible situation after another. First, a little background.

In 1957, Ted Kennedy began to date Virginia Joan Bennett—known to all as Joan—a beauty queen and part-time model whom he had met while delivering a speech at Manhattanville College where she was a student.

Joan was born on September 9, 1936, in the Riverdale section of the Bronx, New York, to wealthy Irish-American Catholics, Joan Stead and Henry Wiggin Bennett Jr., an advertising executive. After growing up in Bronxville, New York, she attended Manhattanville College in Purchase, New York, as had future sisters-in-law Jean Kennedy Smith and Ethel Skakel Kennedy. She was a knockout: a stunning blonde and product spokesperson on popular network TV programs such as *Coke Time with Eddie Fisher* and *The Perry Como Show* while still in college. She was also a music major with the kind of piano skills that could have earned her a place on the concert stage had she decided to pursue it.

Ted was immediately and totally smitten by the gorgeous coed and after a whirlwind courtship asked for her hand in marriage. But then, the night before his wedding, he got cold feet. He didn't really know this woman, he told himself and his family members. Maybe he should wait to marry her. He still wanted to date, enjoy his sexual conquests. However, his parents were adamant that Joan was a good catch for him. He would probably never do better, Rose told her son. After all, Joan had impeccable provenance as a prospective Kennedy wife—devoutly Roman Catholic, Sacred Heart education, breathtaking beauty, musical accomplishment, enviable social position, wealth, sparkling personality, *Harper's Bazaar* stylishness, and the Kennedy matriarch's anointment and stamp of approval. She seemed to have everything going for her. She was also nice enough not to mind being told what to do when and if the time ever came. "Besides," his brother Jack told him, "you can still date and have sex with women. No one is going to stop you from doing that just because you're married." And so with all of that on Ted's mind and nothing on Joan's but the opportunity to please the man she loved, wedding vows were exchanged on November 29, 1958, at St. Joseph's R.C. Church in Bronxville, presided over by Francis Cardinal Spellman, archbishop of New York. In 1960, the couple welcomed a daughter, Kara, followed by sons Ted Jr. in 1961 and Patrick in 1967.

Putting aside for a moment Joan's glowing list of attributes and accomplishments, when one considers some of the less obvious, darker periods in her formative years—"an overbearing, overprotective, often emotionally abusive, alcoholic mother," as her second cousin Webster Janssen put it, "as well as a father who also suffered from untreated alcoholism"— it becomes clear that the fragile, sensitive twenty-one-year-old woman was ill-prepared for the turbulent Kennedy landscape that she would be expected to negotiate. A big problem for her in her marriage to Ted would be his chronic self-absorption. Because he was the last remaining son, a great deal of attention was paid to the particulars of what he was going to do in politics, how, and when. That focus, combined with the fact that he was very busy all of the time and usually involved in important legislative matters, made him the kind of man who tended to suck up all of the energy in the room. Sometimes, other matters took precedence, but those were usually issues having to do with his or Jackie's or Bobby's children because he felt such a responsibility to his brothers. "In fact, he was much more available to Jackie and to Ethel than he was to his own wife, Joan," said Sancy Newman, the Kennedys' neighbor in Hyannis Port. "Also, he was there for his mom when she needed him. But that was about it, and maybe it could be argued that was a lot, and maybe even enough. But one thing was sure, Ted wasn't there for Joan, and he didn't expect her to be there for him, either."

Soon after marrying Joan, Ted began to see other women. Joan felt there wasn't much she could do about it, though—except to ask her sister-in-law Jackie for advice.

"Forbidden fruit is what is exciting," Jackie would later write to Joan in the summer of 1979. It was a statement that spoke volumes as to how Jackie felt about an unfaithful husband. "It takes much more of a real man to have a deep relationship with the woman he lives with. The routine of married life can become boring. If you married Mootsie & she had a few miscarriages [Joan would have three] & had to go to the movies at the Cape and on the Marlin with the whole family every day—you'd be sneaking off from her too after a while."

Jackie suggested that Joan "take vacations with your friends, not the family." Moreover, she advised her not to be intimidated by the powerful Kennedy sisters or by their mother, Rose. "Make the sisters scared to death of you so they don't walk all over your house and appropriate your husband," Jackie wrote. "He's *your* husband. That's more important than being their brother. Tell Eunice *everything* & be *mad* when you're telling her. Say you'd like to talk to his mother about it.

"Don't explain where you will be, don't speak of yourself as a delicate health problem. Don't ask permission. Be a bit mysterious. Then he can't plan things around your absence," she wrote.

It wasn't so easy for Joan. Ted's philandering whittled away at her already diminished self-esteem, and she began drinking. Then Jack's and Bobby's deaths just added to Joan's despair, causing her to drink even more. Now, with whatever had happened at Chappaquiddick, it was difficult to imagine how her marriage could survive. "There was so much pressure," Joan would recall years later. "I truly didn't know how to handle it except to drink in order to escape it, if even for a moment."

Joan recalled one specific moment of heartbreak at the Kennedy compound during those dark days, an incident that, as she has told it, crystallized for her the reality that even though she was his wife, her place in Ted's life had its limitations. She'd been sequestered in her bedroom, told that she should not be exposed to what was going on because of her emotional fragility and also her pregnancy. But one morning when she picked up the phone to make a call, she heard voices on the line. Someone was talking on an extension. Because she heard what sounded like crying, she listened for a moment. It was Ted. He was confiding his troubles to another woman.

"The End of Camelot"

*T*hey were a family in crisis. It hadn't been the first time, and it certainly would not be the last. The Kennedys would do what they always did in such situations: They would come together.

On July 20, 1969, Eunice and Jean Kennedy arrived in Hyannis Port. Both had been in Europe with their husbands, Jean vacationing with Stephen Smith in Spain and Eunice in Paris where Sargent Shriver was serving as United States ambassador to France. While Stephen would be integral to the Kennedy team as an adviser in trying to figure out how to proceed, Sarge would not. He absented himself on purpose, feeling it would compromise his position as ambassador to fly to Hyannis to help Ted get out of whatever trouble he had gotten himself into. Eunice wasn't sure how she felt about Sarge's decision; she thought Sarge should be present if only to show solidarity. He was already not in good standing for having accepted the ambassadorship from LBJ instead of stumping for Bobby, and his not showing up when Ted was in trouble only promised to make things worse for him. However, in the end, he sent his wife, alone. Pat Kennedy Lawford arrived shortly thereafter from California, where she had been with her four children. Now divorced from actor Peter Lawford, she'd gone to Manhattan to rebuild her life after her marriage fell apart, but maintained a residence in California as well. The next day, July 21, Jackie arrived from Greece. The family had wondered whether Jackie would show up in Hyannis Port, not knowing that Ted had called her. In fact, Jackie was the first person Ted called from a pay phone in Edgartown. The second was a close friend of the family's, the Austrian-born Helga Wagner, with whom, according to many accounts, Ted was romantically involved.* In all, Ted made seventeen calls, including several to attorney Burke Marshall, whom Bobby had appointed assistant attorney general in charge of the Justice Department's civil rights division in the JFK administration. He was now a VP at IBM.

Ted showed up soon after Jackie's arrival. Of course, he was elated to see Jackie, overwhelmed that she had made the long journey so quickly and embarrassed by the circumstances. He appeared as if he were still in shock, his eyes hollow and empty. Swaying slightly and seeming unsteady on his feet, he looked at his former sister-in-law for a long moment. Jackie offered him a warm smile and then drew him into her arms, the two embracing for a long time. It appeared, according to one observer, that Ted was about to collapse in Jackie's arms, but he pulled away and took his leave before that could happen.

After everyone learned about the trouble Ted had found himself in, there were mixed emotions. Of course, the family was horrified that he had almost lost his life. That said, the senator was extremely evasive about

---

* In numerous conversations with Ms. Wagner, and finally in an interview for this book, she would neither confirm nor deny these reports, nor would she speak at all about Ted Kennedy other than to say, "The reason he called me after the incident was to get the phone number to his sister, Jean, and her husband, Stephen Smith, who were in Spain." She further stated, "I do not want to say anything at all about the Kennedys, because I love them. They are my wonderful friends. I care for all of them and I would never want to hurt any of them by saying anything publicly about my relationships with them over the years."

details. His handsome face wiped clean of any expression, he couldn't seem to articulate the full story. Everything he said and did was by rote and automatic. He seemed to be in shock. "The biggest question—or at least one of the most pressing questions—remained unanswered: Why had he waited ten hours to report the accident to the police?" recalled Leo Damore in a 1994 interview; he wrote the definitive book on Chappaquiddick, *Senatorial Privilege*. "After all, perhaps Mary Jo could have been saved if the authorities had been summoned. There were other questions—such as what were he and Mary Jo doing in the car together, and where were they going? Ted said he was taking her back to her hotel so she wouldn't miss the last ferry from Chappaquiddick to Martha's Vineyard. Others would later speculate that the two were on their way to or had just come from a romantic rendezvous. Maybe she wasn't his type, but they were both drinking, so who knew for sure? As it happened, Mary Jo left her handbag at the party. Was it because she intended to return after the rendezvous? With so many unanswered questions, the scenario seemed to point to a lack of truthfulness and dependability in Ted, and maybe worse—perhaps even character and integrity."

For Rose, a big question was: Why was Ted alone in the car with Mary Jo when Joe Gargan was around, as were other men? One cardinal rule of politics, as far as she was concerned, was that no man in office should ever be alone with a woman he doesn't know well. "It was very stupid," she would later tell her son. "You should have known better." She couldn't understand why all the men at the party had allowed Ted to drive off alone with Mary Jo—why not one of them had had what she called "gumption enough" to get in the front passenger seat of the car with Ted, and have Mary Jo in the backseat; but in the end she blamed Joe Gargan. After all, it had always been his responsibility to look after Ted; he had failed miserably at his job, and Rose would never forget it. (In fact, she would proceed to cut him out of her will. But then, a few years later, she would have a change of heart and reinstate him.) Another question for Rose, and another one she would never reconcile, was why Gargan and Markham didn't just report the accident to the police, even if Ted didn't want to do so. She would later say she found it "brutal" that Mary Jo's body was in the water—she even used the word "unforgivable"—and that no one reported the accident; and, of course, her questions would mirror those of most people with the passing of the years.

One of his closest friends who would not speak for attribution recalled a conversation he had with Ted while the two sat in the living room of his parents' home. It was a rare moment, one in which Ted truly revealed himself, which he was usually not inclined to do. "You know, I had a car accident in Florida last winter," Ted said, out of the clear blue. "I was driving back to the [Kennedys' Palm Beach] estate and drove right off the goddamn road."

"Did you report it, Teddy?" asked his friend, knowing the answer.

"No," Ted said. He explained that he was not hurt, that he walked home and the next day his chauffeur, Frank Saunders, went to the accident site and retrieved the damaged automobile.

"Were you drinking?" his friend asked.

Ted nodded solemnly.

"This time, too?" the friend asked. "Were you drinking this time, too?"

Again, Ted nodded. "I'm finished," he added. "I'll never survive this thing. This is manslaughter."

At that, the two men just stared at each other. They then somehow began to discuss Bobby, and Ted's belief that his brother never should have tried to run for his party's nomination in 1968. "I knew what would happen," Ted said. "I knew it in my gut, but I didn't do anything about it, did I?" In that moment, as his friend recalled it many years later, it became clear that Ted Kennedy was crumbling under the weight of not only whatever had happened at Chappaquiddick, but also what had occurred in Los Angeles back in 1968. It was as if so much tragedy had piled on in such a short time, he was having trouble separating the catastrophic events. "All of this is my fault," he concluded.

"It's okay, Ted," his friend told him, putting his hand on his shoulder. "You know what? This goddamn thing will blow over eventually and we'll sing again, I promise you that."

"'When Irish Eyes Are Smiling'?" Ted asked with tears in his eyes, referring to the family's favorite song.

"'When Irish Eyes Are Smiling,'" his friend said, "undoubtedly."

Ted could not explain his actions to his family members or even to the fifteen Kennedy aides—some of whom had worked for Jack, and Bobby's friends, and others working for Ted—who had descended upon the compound for strategy meetings, which, it was decided, would take place at

Jackie's home. Some of those present for these strategy meetings, as well as the aforementioned Burke Marshall, were: Robert McNamara, JFK's former secretary of defense; Richard Goodwin, one of the Kennedys' most fluent speechwriters and the husband of respected Kennedy historian Doris Kearns Goodwin; Dun Gifford, a trusted Kennedy confidant—he had been national campaign coordinator for Bobby's presidential campaign; David Burke, Ted's assistant; Senators John Culver and John Tunney, two of Ted's closest friends; as well as nine attorneys brought in by Stephen Smith. Moreover, Arthur Schlesinger Jr. and Ted Sorensen were brought in to fashion a public apology from Ted by way of a speech to his constituents. Schlesinger wrote a memoir/history of the administration called A *Thousand Days: John F. Kennedy in the White House,* which won him his second Pulitzer Prize in 1965. Sorensen had collaborated with the president on his *Profiles in Courage.*

"Of course, there was obviously grave concern that Ted hadn't reported the accident in a timely manner," Robert McNamara would recall many years later. "As to whether or not anyone questioned his involvement with Mary Jo Kopechne, no one in any meeting I attended would ever have broached that subject. We were just trying to sort it all out, what happened that night. And it was difficult to do because Ted was so traumatized we couldn't get a straight story."

"I know there was a public perception of a cover-up or a master plan to make the Kennedys look good, but that's not what was going on," Dun Gifford recalled in 2009. It would actually be Gifford who would be sent to identify Mary Jo Kopechne's body and would escort her body to the family's home in Pennsylvania. "Of course, yes, public relations was important; perception was always important to the Kennedys. But Ted was contrite, in my opinion, and wanting to be as forthcoming as possible. A lot was at stake, his entire political career and, it could be said, the entire future of the Kennedy dynasty. The biggest matter was that we knew he had to make a speech to the nation and we needed to be careful in how it was crafted. It was a delicate dance.

"At the house, the mood was solemn," Gifford continued. "Ethel had known Mary Jo and liked her very much. Joan knew her, too. As I recall, Joan had even once invited Mary Jo and the other Boiler Room Girls to her home for a cocktail party. So it wasn't like some stranger had been killed. For us, this tragedy had a very personal face. In a broader sense," Gifford continued, "it felt like the death of a dream. All of Ted's hopes and aspirations, all of his hard work up until that time, his dreams and those of the whole Kennedy family—those of Joseph— you could just sense them all going up in smoke. For people who had always held on to hope no matter what, it was like another death in the family. It felt like the end of Camelot, if you really want to know the truth."

"I think it's easy to retroactively overdramatize these events given their historical importance," cautioned David Burke. "I can assure you that most of us were not sitting around contemplating the notion of Camelot or the loss of any such ideal created by the media. Rather, there was very human sadness about the chain of events, and a good deal of confusion. There was a good deal of pensive thought. How did we get from Point A to Point B, and where do we go from here?"

After Jackie heard Ted's story, she stayed with the rest of the family for a couple of hours before finally going back to the home she had shared with Jack. From there, she made a telephone call to her friend Roswell Gilpatric. During their conversation, according to what he would remember years later, she told him that she "felt awful" for Joan, that her sister-in-law "looks like a ghost. It's like the walking dead here," she concluded. Jackie also said that there was no way she would be able to sleep in her home that evening, that she still had nightmares about what had happened in Dallas in 1963, which was hard for her to believe considering how much time had passed. "But when I am here with these people, it all comes back to me, I'm afraid."

As the two old friends spoke, Jackie told Gilpatric she was looking out the window of the sunroom of her home at the vista of sky and ocean, so blue and shimmering as far as her eyes could see. The green lawn in front of her house was perfectly manicured, just as it always had been when she lived there with Jack and the kids. Everywhere she looked, perennials that thrive naturally on the Cape seemed alive with color—geraniums, black-eyed Susans, Russian sage, catmint, and wild morning glories all looking hearty and alive, bursting with vivid color. There were rambling and climbing yellow and white roses covering the wall just outside the sunroom, and multicolored hybrid tea roses on long stems artfully weaving in and out of a nearby trellis. There were ground-cover roses, too, dollops of red, white, and blue. Beyond that could be seen the gentle and rolling waves of Nantucket Sound. "It's so peaceful out there," Jackie observed, "which is so ironic because in here, in this house, it's never peaceful, is it? We are always on the precipice, aren't we?"

"I think I now understand Teddy," Jackie said before ending the conversation. Gilpatric would later say that she seemed to want to choose her words carefully as she lowered her voice to barely a whisper. "I think he has an unconscious drive to self-destruct," she observed. "And I think it comes from the fact that he knows he'll never live up to what people expect of him." Roswell Gilpatric would later say he was somewhat taken aback by Jackie's observation, and by how astute it was, at least in his own estimation, having known the family for so many years. "I think, perhaps, I agree," he told Jackie. "You see, he's not Jack, is he?" Jackie continued. "And he's not Bobby. And I'm afraid that he believes deep down that what he is, is just not enough." With that comment, Jackie's voice seemed to float away. There was a long pause, so much so that Roswell Gilpatric thought for a moment that perhaps the line had become disengaged. "No, I'm here," Jackie finally murmured. "I was just thinking..."

Strategizing a Way Out

*T*he funeral for Mary Jo Kopechne on July 23, 1969, was as difficult as anyone would have imagined. A young lady's life had been tragically cut short, and the driver of the car, Ted Kennedy, was obviously responsible. Everyone knew it. Therefore, the church and cemetery were swarmed with media and curiosity-seekers. Wearing a neck brace, Ted looked as if he were in physical and emotional anguish. Ethel was quiet, doing her best not to betray her feelings about anything one way or the other. Joan looked vacant-eyed and detached. As she embraced Mary Jo Kopechne's father, it appeared that she practically collapsed in his arms. Jackie did not attend. By this time, she had left Hyannis and had gone to New York to see about her children's education.

Within five days of the accident, Kennedy's attorneys had arranged for him to plead guilty to leaving the scene of an accident involving personal injury. That would later result in a two-month suspension of his driv-er's license. After an inquest, there would be no dreaded manslaughter charge, which a lot of people found unbelievable but was true just the same.

It was hoped that Ted would now be able to save his senatorial seat. He was up for reelection in the Senate in 1970, and it was obviously feared that his present trouble would totally ruin his chances. "Prior to this time, there had been this rising, boiling feeling about this meteor getting ready to take off," Kennedy aide Robert Bates recalled in 2009. "Everyone wanted to be connected to Ted. But after Chappaquiddick, there was obviously a great deal of concern."

As Arthur Schlesinger and Ted Sorensen contemplated talking points with Ted, Joan was asked to stay upstairs in the master bedroom. They didn't want her to hear what they were saying, maybe fearing that she was already under so much stress. Earlier, Ted had asked her to call Mary Jo's mother to express her condolences, but Joan was reluctant. To her, it seemed like a big manipulation and, according to one trusted Kennedy adviser, she and Ted had a loud disagreement about it. "But Ethie called them," he told Joan, speaking of Ethel, "so why won't you?" Joan wasn't moved by that logic. "Of course, she did!" Joan exclaimed. "Everyone knows that Ethel will do anything you ask her to do," she said. "But I am not Ethel!" Eventually, she relented and made the call, but she didn't like it. "So what if he can't run for president?" she later said angrily to one of Ted's advisers. "I don't want him to run. And if you cared about him, you wouldn't want that either! Look at what happened to Jack, to Bobby? *Do you want Ted dead, too?*" Her heartfelt plea only served to make her seem emotional and unstable. She was definitely going against the tide, and thus her banishment.

Most of the Kennedy advisers present felt the odds were stacked against Ted. "There was one moment when the sisters made a fuss over the work being done by those of us trying to figure this thing out," Arthur Schlesinger once recalled. "A draft of a proposed speech by Ted said quite plainly that, because of what had transpired, he would never run for higher office. It said that he would not follow his brothers in that regard and that any aspirations he may have had to be president were now a thing of the past. 'Absolutely not,' said Eunice, with Pat and Jean joining in disapproval. 'Who knows how this thing will work itself out?' Eunice said. I remember Ted Sorensen saying to her, 'Look, Eunice, just let us figure this thing out.' Eunice looked at him with a surprised expression as if she couldn't believe he would speak to her like that. 'You are taking advantage of Ted's emotions,' she said angrily. 'He's vulnerable right now and will say just about anything you put in front of him. But he will not say that.'"

Once Rose Kennedy weighed in, there was no question about it—the line had to go. "We have to steel ourselves for a good fight now," Rose insisted. "Now is not the time to make any concessions."

There was a disagreement over another passage in Ted's speech, as well. Ted Sorensen wanted to have Ted say that he feared "some awful curse did actually hang over the Kennedys." It was a thought that Ted had said crossed his mind that night Mary Jo died, and he passed it on to Sorensen, who thought it was a powerful line. "Over my dead body" was Eunice's reaction to it when it was brought to her attention, according to someone who was present. She happened to have her rosary beads in her hand, which somehow made the moment seem even more dramatic. "We will never suggest that God has cursed this family! Mother will never approve of it."

It was Ted who brought the line to Rose for her opinion. She mulled it over. "I cannot say I disagree," she said sadly. "I don't like the line, either. But I don't like it because I fear it's the truth," she told Ted. "I won't stand in your way if you want to use it." Ted's mind was made up. "The line stays, then," he decided. It would be the first time an allusion would be made by a family member to any sort of Kennedy curse.

"All People Make Mistakes… Not Just Kennedys"

On July 25, 1969, Senator Edward Kennedy addressed the nation to explain his role in the death of Mary Jo Kopechne. Standing in the living room with him at the Big House, and out of camera range, were his male relatives and advisers. In the next room had convened all of the women, watching the broadcast on a monitor. When Joan came into the living room to stand near Ted, he asked her to leave the room and join the other women. "Why doesn't he just get a Japanese houseboy to wait quietly in the other room while he and his aides discuss his problems," Jackie would bitterly ask Joan in a letter later sent to her, "and then he can have his girls on the side and his sisters can campaign for him?"

In the end, the senator's speech was just thirteen minutes long, broadcast in color on all three networks. During it, Kennedy described the party for the Boiler Room Girls by saying it was "for a devoted group of Kennedy campaign secretaries." He strongly denied rumors that he had been intoxicated or had engaged in any "immoral conduct," claiming that "only reasons of health" had prevented Joan from being with him. He recalled the feeling of "almost drowning." He said that his failure to report the accident immediately was "indefensible" and he described the "scrambled thoughts" he had that night as being "irrational." He also stated that he "felt morally obligated to plead guilty [that morning] to the charge of leaving the scene of an accident." He didn't give much more information than that, though, other than to say he felt terrible about what happened, had no excuse for it, and that his conduct in the hours after the accident "made no sense to me at all." As expected, he said that he couldn't help but wonder "whether some awful curse did hang over all of the Kennedys," and "whether there was some justifiable reason for me to doubt what had happened to delay my report," and "whether somehow the awful weight of this incredible incident might in some way pass from my shoulders."

Ted further stated that he well understood why there might be some who would prefer that he retire from politics. But, he said, "The opportunity to work with you and serve Massachusetts has made my life worthwhile. And so I ask you tonight, the people of Massachusetts, to think this through with me. In facing this decision, I seek your advice and opinion. In making it, I seek your prayers—for this is a decision that I will have finally to make on my own."

No further charges would be brought against Ted Kennedy in the matter of Chappaquiddick even though a January 1970 inquest into the accident would result in more questions than answers. Some of the revelations from the inquest made things much worse for Ted, such as the discovery that Mary Jo hadn't really drowned. Diver John Ferrar, who was one of the first on the scene, testified, "The girl suffocated. She was totally conscious and able to hold her face deep into the foot well and availing herself of the last air in the automobile. I think she survived at least an hour, possibly as long as two. There's no question that if we had been notified of the accident, if the fire department had been notified approximately one half to one hour of the time of the accident, we would have saved her life." As such damning evidence began to emerge, and the Kopechnes didn't so much as file a civil suit against Kennedy, much of the public and media began to believe that Ted or his family or his lawyers had paid them off. However, the Kopechnes always denied any kind of payout, saying that they had received only a small amount of money from Ted and the Kennedys' insurance carrier—a total of $140,000, to be exact—for a down payment on a house.

Almost twenty years after Chappaquiddick, Leo Damore's damning book about the event, *Senatorial Privilege*, brought forth even more revelations. In it, some witnesses reported to Damore that Ted had been intoxicated before driving away from the party he and Mary Jo had attended that night and had enjoyed five rum and Coke cocktails on an empty stomach. Others, though, said he may have had as many as fifteen drinks! Had he been waiting for the effects of the alcohol to wear off before reporting the accident to the police, and is that why it took so long for him to do it? Moreover, a deputy sheriff testified that he saw Kennedy's car on a side road and that when he approached it to find out if the occupants were perhaps lost, the car sped off, heading in the direction of the bridge at a dangerous speed. Was it because Ted—who was, it was later learned, driving with a suspended license—was drunk and in a car with a woman who was not his wife that he sped off, rather than be questioned in such an inebriated state by a uniformed officer? Moreover, it turned out that there were other cottages in the area with their lights still on at that hour of the night. Why hadn't Ted knocked on someone's door and asked to use the phone to report the accident, instead of going back to the site of the party, a mile away, to summon his friends?* Of course, some of Kennedy's behavior could be explained by saying he was in total shock. However, none of this evidence was available to the grand jury, because certain witnesses were not truthful at the time and it was alleged that Ted

---

* Joe Gargan repeated these allegations in an interview with this author in March 1999.

Kennedy and some of those working for him had found ways to use their power and influence to suppress damaging evidence, thereby jeopardizing the jury's ability to gather evidence. The grand jury's foreman, Leslie Leyland, would say in 2010 that if the jury had this information in 1970, he has no doubt it would have returned with a manslaughter charge against the senator, not to mention charges having to do with witness tampering.

Luckily for Ted Kennedy, most of the revelations surrounding the events of Chappaquiddick would come too late for anyone to do anything about them—not that the information would have changed anything in 1970 anyway. At the time, the country had a warm, familial kind of feeling for Kennedy and it was difficult for many people to want to indict him, even if some didn't find his story plausible. He was the last great hope of the Kennedy dynasty, of the so-called Camelot era. If he had been anyone else, any other government official, he probably would never have been able to continue a political career. In fact, a Times-Harris poll conducted after the speech revealed that more than half of all Americans did not believe his explanation of why he was present at a party with so many single women.

There was something about what Ted Kennedy represented back then that kept most of America, for lack of a better word, hooked. It had to do with sentiment, with the loss of his brothers, with everything his family had endured—the recent images were indelible: His sister-in-law Jackie, so strong in the face of such great tragedy on the day of JFK's funeral. His other sister-in-law, Ethel, at Arlington saying goodbye to Bobby while surrounded by their many children, and pregnant with a baby he would never know. His devastated mother and father. His grief-stricken sisters. All of it was represented in snapshot images of history that could still be called instantly to mind by most Americans. The emotion engendered by his family's epic journey was what tugged at the heartstrings of most Americans, not whether or not Kennedy had made a difference in the Senate. And though much of the country would remain torn in its opinion of Senator Kennedy when it came to the Chappaquiddick incident— as it would remain for the rest of his life—he was still forgiven. Of course, some critics, some cynics, some of the less enchanted felt Kennedy had gotten away with murder—but there weren't enough of them to make a difference, and certainly not in Massachusetts. The telegrams, letters, and phone calls received by his office immediately following his speech made it clear that Massachusetts voters still overwhelmingly supported his upcoming run for the Senate.

Somehow, Ted Kennedy would manage to emerge from this imbroglio relatively unscathed. However, let there be no mistake, the man himself knew the truth: Any chance he had at ever being elected president of the United States was now laid waste, a casualty of bad luck, poor judgment, and whatever else conspired to curse him that fateful night in July 1969. He suggested as much to his friend and adviser Dun Gifford in the days immediately following his speech. "I may not be going to prison," he said at the time. "But I've been sentenced just the same. I can kiss the White House goodbye."

Ethel Kennedy, who was ever loyal to her brother-in-law, just as Bobby would have expected of her, didn't see things quite the same way. "You are a good man, Teddy," she told him in front of Rose Kennedy, Barbara Gibson, and several others. It was right after Ted had delivered his speech to the nation; he was exhausted and seemed near collapse. "This, too, shall pass," she told him as she stood before him clasping both of his hands. "You must believe me." Rose Kennedy nodded in agreement. "Don't let this stop you from doing what you have to do," Ethel continued. "Remember that *all* people make mistakes, Teddy. Not just Kennedys."

Joseph Kennedy Dies

*U*pon hearing the news of Ted's Chappaquiddick debacle in 1969, his father, Joseph Patrick Kennedy Sr., seemed ready to fold his tent and open his arms to embrace his Creator. He'd been quite sick for a good many years, ever since his stroke in 1961.

On November 17, Joseph fell into a coma.

Jackie was the first to arrive, from Greece. Then Pat from New York; Eunice and Sargent Shriver from Paris; and Jean and Stephen Smith, who had also been in Europe, showed up. Joan, Ted, and Ethel all came from Virginia.

As the family encircled Joseph's bed, Rose was barely able to stand under the emotional weight of the moment. Ted supported her with strong arms until finally she sank to her knees, her head resting on Joseph's chest. There she stayed for ten minutes, sobbing and praying. Rose rarely cried. In fact, her children could not remember the last time they actually saw her cry, despite all of the tragedies the Kennedys had experienced. She was just that stoic. But losing Joseph after fifty-five years of marriage was apparently more than she could bear. Her tears would not stop.

Finally, Rose asked that someone bring her the rosary she had cherished for years. Jackie went to fetch it from atop a dresser in the room. She gave it to Rose, who clutched it tightly and then put it to Joseph's lips. The family, still encircling their patriarch, then recited the Our Father. Emotionally drained, they spoke the verses almost as if in a trance, slowly and deliberately, while Joseph Patrick Kennedy slipped away from them forever.

Dealing with the Fallout

With the new decade of the 1970s in the offing, the Kennedy family hoped that they might enjoy a renaissance of sorts, a new beginning. So much had happened in the 1960s, much of it filled with pain and sorrow; it had left most of the family shell-shocked and in some ways fractured. Because the election for Ted Kennedy's Senate seat was to occur in November 1970, he and Joan would spend the next couple of months campaigning for votes and, as Joan put it at the time, "wondering how the fallout from what had happened would affect us both personally and professionally." Ted told the *New York Times*, "The voters need to see me, to be convinced that I'm reliable and mature. You can't counter the Chappaquiddick thing directly. The answer has to be implicit in what you are, what you stand for and how they see you." Apparently, voters in Massachusetts were still on Ted's side, though, because he did win that election and retained his seat in the Senate. But a couple of months later, on January 21, 1971, he lost to Robert Byrd of West Virginia as Democratic whip. Apparently his Senate colleagues were not quite as forgiving as his Massachusetts constituency. (The whip is elected by fellow Senate majority party members to assist the Speaker of the House and the Senate majority leader in coordinating and generating bicameral congressional support for proposed legislation that fits the majority party's agenda.)

"He had viewed his winning the majority whip position from Russell Long in January 1969 as a highlight of his career in the Senate, so losing the position was a real blow to him," recalled California senator John Tunney, who was Ted's roommate at the University of Virginia Law School in 1959 and remained a very close friend. "He wasn't surprised, though. Even though he had managed to keep his seat in the Senate, he wasn't naive. He knew that his political support had eroded a great deal as a result of what happened on Chappaquiddick Island." That said, there was still a small groundswell of support for his possible presidential nomination in 1972, the general consensus by a lot of Democrats being that the passing of time might be enough for critics to put the accident into new perspective and realize that, despite it, Ted was still a viable candidate.

Ted had made it clear when he returned to the Senate after Chappaquiddick that the presidency was not on his mind—or at least that's what he said publicly. However, it was hard for the media and the public to let it go. Even though his chances were greatly diminished and he knew it, there was still great momentum from pundits and columnists and, by extension, the public for him to at least try. It was a difficult proposition to resist—he was a Kennedy, after all. A flawed one, but a Kennedy just the same.

His friend Joe Klein, who met with Ted on Memorial Day 1970, recalled, "He seemed a ghost the day I met him…he didn't smile, seemed grim even when shaking hands with civilians; his demeanor all the more striking because we were at a classic grip-and-grin event, the annual Greek picnic in Lowell, Mass. He was scared catatonic, of course. Scared of death, obviously. There was no reason to believe, in a nation of nutballs, that he would be allowed to continue, unshot. But he was frightened of more profound things as well—overwhelmed by his own humanity in the face of his brothers' immortality, convinced that he'd never measure up, that Joe and Jack and Bobby had been the best of the Kennedys…and even after he somehow allowed a young woman to die, they still wanted him to run for president."

Though the subject of a possible future in the White House for Ted would not die in the public arena, it was rarely discussed at home. In fact, every time anyone mentioned the 1972 presidential election, Joan seemed to crumble. She couldn't even bear thinking about it, she was so worried for his safety. "I worry all the time about whether Ted will be shot like Jack and Bobby," she told *Ladies' Home Journal* in July 1970. "I try not to but I can't help myself. Ted tries to keep things from me, serious threats against his life—but I know what's going on. I know he worries about it, too. A few months ago we were in a plane and a child exploded a balloon right behind us. It sounded just like a gun shot. Ted jumped so. What a terrible thing. A balloon pops and my husband thinks he's being shot. I could read his mind, and I could have cried for him."

Ted decided to consider the disappointment of losing the whip position as an opportunity to more fully immerse himself in his senatorial duties, and in doing so he would lay what would turn out to be the groundwork for his commitment to health care reform. As the new chairman of the Senate's subcommittee on health, he lobbied hard for an increase in cancer research money. In fact, he fought for an increase to $1.3 billion over the next three years, which was four times the amount President Richard Nixon had in mind. Amazingly enough, not only was Ted's plan approved, but he secured $1.5 billion. Encouraged by that victory, and feeling once again a real sense of purpose, he devoted himself more than ever to his senatorial duties or, as he later put it, to "becoming interested in every aspect of the Senate, its arcane rules both permanent and new; its parliamentary procedure, the functions of its many committees and subcommittees, some of which were well known and others half forgotten or unsuspected of potentially great use. I doubt that anyone has ever managed to completely internalize the immense font of knowledge that these areas comprise, but I committed myself to learning it as thoroughly and in as much minute detail as I could."

As Ted worked on his political career, Joan Kennedy began to work on her life. At the end of August 1969, she lost the baby she'd been carrying—her third miscarriage. She still had three children to tend to, though, and she knew in her heart, as she would later tell it, that she needed to do something about the unhappiness that had led to her drinking. Ted was no help. In fact, he was a big part of the problem. "Why was it, she wondered, that he would go all the way to Greece to negotiate a deal for Jackie to marry Onassis, yet he couldn't find his way to the bedroom to take care of Joan as she was lying across their bed, crying?"

recalled Richard Burke, Ted's administrative assistant from 1978 to 1981. "It didn't take much to see that, for Ted, Jackie was a priority. Ethel, too, obviously. But not necessarily Joan."

During her time at the Cape in the summer of 1969 when Ted was in the midst of his Chappaquiddick ordeal, it was Jackie who suggested therapy to Joan. "I think it will help you," she told her sister-in-law. "I think you need to try." After careful consideration, Joan decided that she would do it. This was not an easy decision. For Joan, keeping Kennedy family secrets had become as much second nature as breathing; talking about such things to a complete stranger was a leap. But when she actually started therapy, it turned out to be not quite as difficult as she had expected. In fact, she had so much anxiety and confusion bottled up about the way her life had unfolded since becoming a Kennedy wife that once stories began to tumble forth, "they just came and came and came," she later said, "and I thought, my gosh, no wonder I have been so unhappy and confused! Look at how much I've been suppressing."

Joan Kennedy's involvement in therapy was in large part influenced by the growing feminist movement of the time, aspects of which today seem almost quaint, but back in 1970 were considered revolutionary. Indeed, in the 1950s and 1960s, a woman's place really was in the home and beside her man while raising her children, and this was especially true for a Kennedy woman. Anyone who thought otherwise was looked upon by much of society with curiosity. Why wouldn't a woman want to be the loving heart and soul of her home? But in the 1970s, there was a strong movement toward female empowerment, and one with which Joan fell in step a lot easier than she expected—though it would be with baby steps.*

In October 1970, Joan surprised many people when she made her concert debut in front of three thousand people at the Academy of Music in Philadelphia, playing with the sixty-member Philadelphia Orchestra in a fund-raiser for Pennsylvania governor Milton Shapp. "I guess that for much of the public, this musical appearance by Joan came out of the blue,"

---

* As was often the case, Jackie had a few words of advice for Joan, in a follow-up letter to her: "This community living has got to stop!" she wrote, referring to the Kennedy compound. "The family that really counts is his [Ted's] own. He can go to the graduations of all of Ethel's children & teach John to sail the *Victura*—but, if he botches up his own family, that will be a pretty sad record."

said her sister, Candace McMurrey. "Since when was she such an accomplished pianist? In fact, though, Joan always had a love for classical music and was actually classically trained and quite proficient at the piano, as everyone in our family well knew. Whenever there was a family gathering, it would find Joan at the piano, playing with ease and leading the rest in joyous song. She played for her brother-in-law Jack during his campaign for president—'September Song' was a favorite of theirs, with Jack singing and Joan playing—and she played for Bobby when he ran, too."

"He took me with him and encouraged me," Joan says of Bobby. "He had a theme, 'This Land Is Your Land,' the Woody Guthrie song. I'd play that on the piano and everyone would come in, feeling really great about everything. It seems like a long time ago, but it's part of my memories." Though Joan had been narrating Sergei Prokofiev's *Peter and the Wolf* every year since 1965 in special orchestral shows, the Philadelphia date was the first time she brought her musical talent to the public on the concert stage.*

On the night of her performance, the always lovely Joan Kennedy walked out onto the stage to thunderous applause wearing a striking black, formfitting Valentino gown, her dusty blonde hair pulled into an elegant French twist. She performed the second movement of Mozart's Piano Concerto No. 21 in C major, following it with Debussy's Arabesque No. 1. When she finished, she was presented with a large bouquet of cherry red roses while she bowed and accepted a rousing standing ovation from the full house. It was a decidedly big moment for her, and even though she was advertised as "Mrs. Edward (Joan) Kennedy," she still felt that the victory was hers and hers alone. Ted, who was not used to sharing acclaim with his wife, seemed at a loss as to how to respond to Joan's moment of triumph when he came backstage after the show. In truth, he was fairly dismissive of it, but at least he was there trying to be supportive. After someone poured him a shot of J&B scotch, he patted Joan on the shoulder and said, "Well done, Mommy."

---

* Joan Kennedy would later write a book in 1993, *The Joy of Classical Music: A Guide for You and Your Family* (Doubleday).

PART FIVE

Ethel

Ethel Kennedy

*W*hen the lives of Ethel Skakel and Robert Kennedy are considered, it is clear they had much more in common even than marriage to each other and being the pugnacious runts of high-profile, large, and prosperous Roman Catholic families, families fraught with both triumph and tragedy.

Ethel was born on April 11, 1928, in Chicago, to Ann Brannack and George Skakel, who made a fortune in what would later become a highly prized and successful division of SGL Carbon, a multibillion-dollar high-tech manufacturer of graphite and carbon electrodes. Ethel attended the all-girls Greenwich Academy in Connecticut as well as the Convent of the Sacred Heart before enrolling at Manhattanville College in New York, where she and Jean Kennedy became running buddies and roommates. Ethel's raucous personality and fearlessness were legendary, and some of her outrageous behavior got her and her more reserved roommate, Jean, into trouble at Manhattanville. But Ethel's practiced wiliness would more often than not save the day, helped along by her father George's deep-pocket contributions to the school's endowment. Once, when Monsignor Hartigan, a diocesan prelate, arrived at the college for a visit in a big, flashy Cadillac, Ethel was outraged at the hypocrisy and placed a placard on the car's windshield on which she had printed, "Are the collections good, Father?" The monsignor grounded the entire school until finally a chastened but unbowed Ethel came forward to admit her guilt.

Completely at odds with Ethel's peccadilloes was her deep commitment to her Catholic religious principles. In fact, she once seriously considered becoming a nun, and did attain what many Catholics might consider the next best thing: a Child of Mary.

Eventually, Jean Kennedy ended up playing Cupid to Ethel and Bobby. The problem, though, was that Bobby was interested in Pat, Ethel's older sister. When Bobby invited Pat for a holiday visit with the Kennedys in Palm Beach, Jean invited Ethel at the same time. The Bobby-Pat love boat ran aground when Pat decided Bobby was immature and too young. Fortunately, Ethel was on hand to toss Bobby a lifeline as he floundered just within reach.

Ethel and Bobby began "going steady" within a few months of the Palm Beach vacation and became engaged two years later. For many observers, the relationship seemed to lack the kind of passion usually associated with young love, more like brother and sister than two youngsters on the threshold of a lifetime commitment. (Indeed, Ethel remained a virgin until her wedding night. She once famously stated that she was so inexperienced, "Bobby was finished before I even got into the room. But," in a veiled reference to their many children, "we later got the hang of it!") The marriage took place on June 17, 1950, at St. Mary's Roman Catholic Church in Greenwich. It was a lavish affair planned and executed with great taste by "Big Ann" Skakel and witnessed by more than two thousand people, many uninvited, who jammed the flower-filled sanctuary. The couple was attended by siblings from their respective families, with JFK as his brother's best man and Pat Skakel as her sister's maid of honor.

The happy couple settled into their first home in Charlottesville, Virginia, until Bobby finished law school. Two weeks shy of their first wedding anniversary, Bobby and Ethel welcomed a baby girl, Kathleen, on Independence Day 1951. With law degree in hand, Bobby, now living in Washington, went to work briefly for the Department of Justice before resigning to manage JFK's successful Senate campaign in Massachusetts. One of Jack's key committee assignments was as a member of the Government Operations Committee, chaired by the demagogic Joseph McCarthy of Wisconsin, an avowed and outspoken anticommunist, who attained instant notoriety in his conduct of the so-called Army-McCarthy hearings, televised in real time to the nation. Bobby was hired as minority counsel to the Senate Permanent Subcommittee on Investigations, with Roy Cohn doing duty as majority counsel. With both JFK and his brother Bobby now appearing somewhat regularly on network TV, the hearing-room audience was the place for the Kennedy women, with Ethel sallying forth as pack leader, obstreperous and bossy, as she herded her sisters-in-law and others in her party to their prominent seats, usually down front.

In 1956, one hardly need recall the advice Rose Kennedy imparted to her daughter-in-law at her and Bobby's wedding reception six years earlier: "Lots of children, Ethel. Have lots and lots of children. They'll keep your marriage strong, as strong as mine." (Of course, the couple would go on to have ten children, and an eleventh would be born after Bobby's death.) While expecting their fifth child, Bobby and Ethel purchased the sprawling antebellum estate Hickory Hill from Jack and Jackie in 1957. Nine months before they moved into the property, tragedy struck when Ethel's parents, Ann and George, died in a fiery plane crash near Oklahoma City. Three days later, she joined her siblings and their families at St. Mary's in Greenwich for her parents' funeral, a solemn requiem High Mass. As was so often the case with the way her mother-in-law Rose confronted her own many tragedies, Ethel was shored up by her unwavering faith and the firm belief that God's will be done, yet there was something about the way she dealt with the death of her parents that some found disconcerting. "She didn't let it in," said a relative of hers. "The next day, it was as if it hadn't happened. She kept saying they were both in a better place, and that was the end of it. It felt as if she never really grieved, that she kept her emotions bottled and instead threw herself into her life with Bobby and the children."

Bobby soon became quite crucial to Jack's (and Joseph, the ambassador's) presidential ambitions, and over the next four years devoted himself to that successful end. When JFK and Jackie found themselves in the White House, Bobby and Ethel's stock zoomed. Now as attorney general and head of the Department of Justice, Bobby was able to claim his own place in the spotlight, Ethel dutifully at his side. She eagerly courted the press and happily fed them whenever they staked out Hickory Hill on some breaking story. The press loved her in return and rewarded her with much positive media attention when she wanted it and respected her privacy when she requested it. They were a great team, Bobby and Ethel— whom he called "Ethie" (which, of course, is where Ted got the nickname for her).

No matter how popular she was, though, everyone knew that it was her sister-in-law Jackie who was the most acclaimed of the Kennedy wives, certainly the one thought to have the most style and panache. Maybe this was unfair, because Ethel certainly had her own fashion sense and was quite the clotheshorse, too. In fact, she spent money like mad. For instance, her clothing expenses were often tripled because she liked to have not one but usually two backups for each of her designer dresses, Oscar de la Renta being her favorite designer. She also wanted de la Renta's designs in different colors. She loved imported cosmetics, as well.

"She spent so much on fancy imported cosmetics, Rose actually went over to the house one day with a clipboard to take an inventory," said Barbara Gibson, Rose's secretary, describing a day in 1970. "She sat in the bathroom...writing down the names of cosmetics and when she finished she and Ethel had a loud row about it, but Ethel didn't cut back. 'That money is mine and Bobby's as much as it's anyone else's,' Ethel said, and she was right to an extent. The money came from trusts that Joseph had set up for each family, and Ethel's, Jackie's, all of the families, in fact, got about $150,000 a year to live on—which was a lot of money in the late 1960s. [The average per capita income in 1970 was $9,350.] Rose was just afraid Ethel was going to go through it all, so she always had Stephen Smith knocking on Ethel's door to cut back; it never worked."

Still, even with her own style, Ethel apparently felt she had to defer to Jackie when it came to fashion sense. A good example: In the late 1970s, TV personality and reporter Barbara Walters happened to be in Washington for a weekend and for some reason had to go on television unexpectedly and didn't have anything appropriate to wear. Because she and Ethel wore the same size, she called Ethel to ask if she had anything in her closet she could borrow, and maybe some accompanying jewelry too. Ethel's assistant Noelle Bombardier was in the room when the call came to Hickory Hill. Ethel seemed to become very uncomfortable at the request. "Well, I'm not Jackie, you know," she said apologetically. "I mean, I do have some nice two-piece outfits that I think would look nice on television," she said. "I suppose I could send them over, as well as a couple of pieces of jewelry. But you must know, Barbara, I don't have the kinds of jewels Jackie has!' According to what Ethel later recalled, Barbara said, "But Ethel, I would never suggest that Jackie had better taste than you. Never!" Of course, Ethel knew as much, but she still felt a little embarrassed by any kind of comparison, even if self-imposed. Still, she put together a couple of outfits with matching jewelry and then had her assistant, Noelle, deliver them to Barbara at the Mayflower Hotel. It turned out that one of the outfits worked just fine.

Andy Williams, the popular entertainer, had for many years been one of Ethel's closet friends. He had also been one of Bobby Kennedy's best friends back in the 1960s. In fact, at Ethel's request, he sang at his funeral, and as a final gesture to their friendship, Bobby was buried wearing one of Andy's favorite ties. After he separated from his wife, singer Claudine Longet, in the late 1960s, Andy began to date Ethel.

"We had a lot of fun," he recalled of his many years at Ethel's side. "She was so fascinating to me, and surprising. For instance, she knew the words to pretty much every Broadway show tune, so we would sing a lot and she had a very good voice! She also knew all of my songs, 'Moon River,' 'Almost There,' all of them. We'd play golf. We'd sail. Sometimes there were so many people on the boat, along with picnic baskets and wine and sodas and all sorts of games, the boat would be practically sinking before we would even be out in deep water. She would say, 'It's okay, Andy. We'll swim back to shore.'

"I adored her but it wasn't like the fan magazines made it out to be," Andy continued. "They had us living together, married, her pregnant with my child. The truth was very different. I could never replace Bobby in her life, and I wouldn't have tried. That said, I think if she had been interested, maybe something could have come of us with the passing of time, but there was no way she could be interested in another man after Bobby. She told me once, 'My love for Bobby is eternal. Do you know how long eternity is?' she asked. I said I did. And she said, 'Well, it's a hundred times longer than what you think it is.'"

A Cross to Bear

*I*t was a sunny day in August 1969 when Rose Kennedy's secretary, Barbara Gibson, found Ethel Kennedy sitting in the kitchen of her home at the Kennedy compound, crying. "Why, what's wrong, Mrs. Kennedy?" she asked. Ethel looked up with reddened eyes and said that Bobby had been gone for a year, and as a result, chaos had broken out in her home. She said that she could not figure out how to handle her children. She had just that morning learned that Bobby Jr. was being intimate with a local girl, and of course, as a Catholic and a mother, it was against everything she believed. Ethel was clearly distressed. "He's fifteen and this is what he's doing?" Ethel asked. She then said that she didn't know how to punish her son because, as she put it, "Nothing works."

"If you want my opinion, I think you should ban him from the household altogether," Barbara Gibson suggested, according to her memory of the conversation. "Just throw him out, Mrs. Kennedy. That's what my mother would do, and that's what I would do if he were my son. That's the only thing that will teach him." Ethel looked surprised. "Can I do that?" she wondered. "Is it legal for a mother to do that?" Barbara Gibson smiled. "You're Ethel Kennedy," she said. "You're not going to get arrested for disciplining your child." The decision was made, then. Ethel said she was going to do as Barbara suggested. Now that she had a solution in place, unconventional though it may have been, Ethel seemed to feel better. That night, she gave Bobby the bad news: He was banished from the home he and the family shared at the compound. "But where am I supposed to live?" he asked. "That's your problem," Ethel told him. "If you can't live by my rules, then you can't live in this house."

That night, young Bobby Kennedy pitched a tent on the beach, where he would sleep for the next two weeks. At night, he would sneak into the homes of relatives in the compound and raid their refrigerators for food. "Sargent Shriver knew what he was up to and always made sure there was some chicken in the refrigerator for his outlawed nephew," recalled Barbara Gibson. "I don't know that the punishment did much good, though. I think Bobby just looked at it as an adventure. I felt badly for Ethel. The kids made her life very difficult when they were young. She was very complex. It took me years to understand her."

Ethel hadn't been herself since Bobby was murdered. Those who knew her well found it ironic that she'd just been on the cover of *Time* a few months before the Chappaquiddick incident in a story about her courage and bravery, in which she was portrayed as "the most remarkable member of her remarkable family." New York senator Jacob Javits described her in the article as "the greatest of the Kennedys, male or female." That was a lot to live up to, especially since privately Ethel didn't feel very courageous or brave. Rather, she was often consumed with confusion and anger about the way things had turned out for her and her family. She and Bobby had had so many plans, so much to do. He had been such a good and decent man who only cared about being of service to others. A deeply religious woman, Ethel couldn't understand why God had taken him from her and her children. Like her mother-in-law and just about all the members of the family, Ethel was a devout Catholic. "We had holy-water holders in every door of our house," her daughter Kathleen told *Newsweek*'s Lisa Miller in 2009. "We said prayers before and after every meal. We went to Roman Catholic schools. On Sundays, we put on our white gloves and shined our shoes. Women wore the mantillas. If we did something good, we got a gold star in heaven." Kerry Kennedy Cuomo said of her mother in 2010, "She still goes to Mass every day of her life. She prays on her knees before church, prays before every meal, and prays on her knees before going to bed."

Still, even Ethel's faith couldn't give her strength on what she called "the bad days." In the public eye, she knew she had no choice but to act strong. After all, as either the Kennedy patriarch, Joseph, or Bobby once put it, depending on which family member you talk to, "Kennedys don't cry." Privately, though, Ethel felt she had a right to her anger. That she had so many children to care for made things that much more difficult for her.

When Bobby was alive, Ethel's home was always filled with politicians and reporters and the most interesting mix of people. He had a knack for mixing with everyone, and enjoyed holding court as the most unlikely of viewpoints converged. He loved to debate, he enjoyed differences of opinion. Nothing pleased him more than inviting a diverse mix of people to Hickory Hill for a rousing game of touch football on the expansive lawn and then a serious debate about politics at the dinner table. It was fun and exciting, and, as Ethel put it, "it was like being at the center of the universe." But now that Bobby was gone, the house was just filled with unhappy children. It was difficult for Ethel to reconcile such a dramatic lifestyle change.

She always knew what she had to do to survive, though. The way she coped with sadness was to ignore it as best she could. It was as if she feared that to acknowledge it would have been to risk falling into a deep emotional abyss from which she could never be rescued. Therefore she never talked about the past, about Jack or Bobby, or about any of her loved ones who had died—her parents in a plane crash in 1955, her brother in another ten years later—other than to place the deceased in the context of their heavenly mission, which was to watch over the rest of the family left behind and take care of them from on high. This kind of avoidance frustrated many of her family members, especially her sons, who just wanted to have a reasonable conversation with their mother about their deceased father. For some of them, such as David and Michael, that they could never address their father's murder in some constructive way seemed to create an environment in which the only way they felt able to survive was to escape, either with alcohol or narcotics. There was also a pervasive feeling that some secret was being kept, that there was information not being revealed to them about the murders of Jack and Bobby, and as Patrick Kennedy, Ted's son, once observed, "It's your secrets that make you drink. Keeping them. Wondering about them. Fearing them."

Within just a very short time after Bobby's death in 1968, Ethel Kennedy's oldest sons, Joe, Bobby, and David, became very hard to control, especially during their annual summers in Hyannis Port. It was easy to understand that the older children were traumatized by the death of their father, and the youngest would always feel a sense of longing for the dad they barely remembered. "There was a lot of sadness," recalled one of Ethel's employees at that time. "But it was mixed with natural teenage rebellion and also a sense of entitlement. From an early age, the kids were raised to believe they were special. They got a lot of press coverage and attention and it went to their heads. And of course, there were so many of them. Ethel was at a loss. She called it 'my cross to bear.' She relied on the senator [Ted] a lot, and he did his best, but it was hard. He too was grieving."

Bobby and Ethel's oldest son, and also the oldest of the third generation of Kennedys, was Joseph Kennedy II, Joe. From the beginning, there seemed to be a lot of pressure on him. For instance, just two days after JFK's assassination, on November 24, 1963, his father wrote him a letter that suggests extremely high expectations of an eleven-year-old. "You are the oldest of the male grandchildren," Bobby wrote. "You have a special and particular responsibility now which I know you will fulfill. Remember all the things that Jack started—be kind to others that are less fortunate than we—and love our country."

Of course, Bobby Kennedy's death hit Joe, now sixteen, very hard. He not only loved his father but also admired him greatly, and therefore the despair he felt at losing him so suddenly was almost overwhelming. It had actually been his gut-wrenching duty to inform his siblings of their father's death. As it happened, Joe had been at boarding school when his dad was shot, and was flown across the country to be at his deathbed with some of his siblings who were already on that coast. When Bobby finally died, Ethel shut down completely and was unable to tell her children about it. So it was left to Joe, who was just fifteen at that time, to try to make sense of it all with his siblings. Because Bobby had been such a hero to him, Joe felt on a very deep level that there was no way he would ever be able to measure up to his father's standards of greatness, no matter how hard he tried. The fact that he sat in his father's chair at the dinner table after Bobby was gone likely didn't help matters either.

Barbara Gibson, who knew Joe very well when he was a boy, recalled, "I think he felt as if he wasn't smart enough, wasn't good-looking enough—'wasn't Kennedy enough,' is how he would put it to me—to take his father's place in the family. He was a muscular guy who started to use brawn to get his way; in other words, he became a bit of a bully. It was a defensive mechanism. We all knew it." It also didn't help that there was a sense of Joe as not being very smart. "It's a shame," Rose Kennedy told Gibson during one of their daily walks on the beach, "that Joe isn't very smart, especially with him being the oldest boy." In fact, while Joe was having a very difficult time in school, it was because he was dyslexic, not dumb—or at least that's how he sees it today. He was never tested for dyslexia, and back in 1968 no one really understood the disability. However, he was sure he had it then, and believes he still does today, and that he would have benefited greatly by some sort of treatment for it. Meanwhile, when Joe asked his mother if he could go to Spain in the summer of 1968 with a friend named Chuck McDermott, she decided to let him go. "She talked it over with Ted and they decided it would do Joe some good," said one of Ethel's relatives, "but, to be honest, I always felt that it did Ethel more good to not have to worry about the kids that summer. I think that's how Ted saw it, too."

Indeed, that same summer, 1968, Ethel sent another of her sons, David, to Mayrhofen, Austria, to attend a ski and tennis camp with his cousin Chris Lawford, Pat's son. Because both boys were just thirteen, most people on the outside of the family felt they were too young to be in Austria, even if there was adult supervision. As it happened, David lost his virginity on that trip to a seventeen-year-old girl in Austria who, while they were being intimate, told him how sorry she was that his father had been murdered. It seemed to make no sense to outsiders. However, Ethel's daughter Kathleen was seventeen in 1968 and she was sent off to teach at an Indian reservation. In fact, the family customarily sent their offspring to other countries either for vacations so they could see the world, or for work so they could be of service to others.

It doesn't seem that, today, Ethel's offspring have a very critical view of what Ethel was trying to achieve by exposing her children to the world around them at such an early age. "One of the most important things our mother did was teach us the lesson, You are what you do," says Christopher Kennedy. "She surrounded us with people who had done great things. When we went hiking it was with guys like Jim Whittaker [the first American to reach the summit of Everest]. When we played sports, it was with Rosey Grier and Rafer Johnson. What they had in common was a great sense of success and of service, and that was the example by which we were raised. We traveled a lot. We were always traveling, actually. People thought she was trying to get rid of us. That makes me laugh, really."

Still, it seems that sometimes the trips Ethel planned backfired. Chris Lawford says that the trip he took with David that summer of 1968 was a defining one in their lives, and not in a positive way. "It was a change in how we thought about being Kennedys," he recalled. "We felt differently. Or maybe a better way of putting it is that we didn't feel anything at all. Nothing mattered after JFK and Bobby died. When we left for Austria with the tennis team we were traveling with, I remember we had baggies of pot stuffed down our underwear. We were scared shitless that the Germans would figure out what was up, that we weren't the innocent thirteen-year-olds they thought we were. When we somehow got separated at customs, I was terrified that David would be scared enough to give up the drugs he had on him. I went to the camp counselor and said, 'Man, we lost David. We gotta find him!' Then, from out of nowhere, out popped a disheveled David, looking as if he'd just been in a fight. 'Thanks a lot for leaving me alone with the Nazis,' he told me. I had no idea what he was talking about, what had happened. We skied and played tennis and screwed girls the entire time we were in Austria, maybe not what our moms had in mind when they sent us there."

Also that same summer, Ethel sent Bobby Jr. off to Africa in the company of JFK's prep school roommate Lem Billings, who had become a close family friend and who would be very influential in the lives of all of the boys. Billings thought the world of Bobby and wanted to do what he could to help his friend's sons through what he knew would be a difficult adolescence. "The stories he told and the examples he set gave us all a link to our dead fathers and to the generations before us," Bobby Jr. said.

"In many ways, Lem was a father to me, and he was the best friend I will ever have."

When Bobby Jr. returned from his trip, he ended up being suspended from Millbrook School, the Dutchess County prep school he had attended for two years. Then came the episode of having sex in the compound, and his subsequent forced exile from Ethel's home. The problem was that while he was banished and sleeping in a tent, he and his brothers formed a little gang—and today, all of these years later, some people who live in Hyannis Port still talk about the Hyannis Port Terrors.

Hyannis Port Terrors

The HPTs—the Hyannis Port Terrors—was the name Joe, seventeen, Bobby Jr., fifteen, and David, fourteen, came up with for the little gang they had formed, along with several other youngsters in the Cape Cod neighborhood. The three boys would sneak out of Ethel's home in the middle of the night, race down to the Shrivers' home nearby, and meet with Eunice and Sargent's boy, Bobby, and Pat's son, Christopher, who was often visiting. They'd then don dark clothing and smear black grease on their faces to hide their identities and take off for a night of misbehavior, often high on marijuana, and on occasion even LSD. "Usually they'd meet three or four other kids in Hyannis and spend the nights causing all sorts of trouble," recalled Thomas Langford, who knew the Kennedy boys at that time. He was seventeen then and, as he put it, "a charter member of the HPTs. Sometimes I played along, when I had the nerve. We'd shoot off firecrackers, deflate people's tires, stick potatoes in the exhaust pipes of cars, turn over trash cans, mess around with girls...all sorts of mischief.

"After we did our bit, Ethel would get calls from everyone in town complaining about it. At first she used to say, 'My kids were home asleep last night, I don't know what you're talking about.' But one night she waited up, and, sure enough, she caught me, Bobby, and David jumping out one of the second-floor windows of her home. She chased us all over the compound in the middle of the night in her nightgown and bare feet, finally losing us somewhere on the stretch of beach. The next morning, the brothers told me they snuck back in the house while she was still asleep. But then she got up before they did and locked them both in their bedroom. When she finally let them out at about eight that night, they took off with one of her sheets. Apparently, during their time alone all day, they'd made a makeshift flag out of it, which had emblazoned on it the words 'HPT's Rule.' That night, they rigged it so that they could get it up on the steeple of a local church, St. Andrew's Presbyterian. I happened to be at Ethel's sitting in the living room the next day watching TV with Bobby [Shriver] when the doorbell rang."

According to Thomas Langford, Ethel went to the door to find a man standing there with a bedsheet in his hand. He turned out to be the minister of St. Andrew's Presbyterian Church. "Mrs. Kennedy, I think this belongs to you," he said. Ethel looked perplexed. "But what is it, Reverend?" He said, "It's a sheet that I think your boys hung from the steeple of St. Andrew's Presbyterian." Ethel protested. "My boys are Catholic," she said. "They would never do such a thing." The reverend then turned over a corner of the sheet and showed it to her. On it were the initials "RFK"—obviously for Robert Francis Kennedy. For a moment, Ethel had no words. "The next time your boys want to fly a flag, ask them to do so from the steeple of the Catholic church, not from mine." With that, he handed Ethel the sheet and took his leave. Ethel closed the door. Then, at the top of her lungs, she looked to the heavens and screamed out, "Give me strength!"

It was all just mischief, but troubling just the same when the stories would get back to Ethel or the other adults in the family. For instance, one prank had the boys playing in busy Hyannis Port tourist traffic, only to have one kid fall to the ground while another smacked the back of a car, making a loud noise. Then they would all gather around their fallen chum and shout hysterical sentiments at the driver, such as, "You've just killed another Kennedy!" When panicked people came to the aid of the young Kennedy sprawled in the middle of the road, the boys would milk it for all it was worth by trying to get the boy to move his legs and then saying it looked as if he'd been paralyzed. But then the fallen Kennedy would suddenly stand up and walk away. At that, the other boys would proclaim, "Look, it's a Kennedy miracle!" and then race off, leaving a crowd of very upset Hyannis Port tourists in their wake.

The stories are legendary in Cape Cod, even today. One could write an entire book on the mayhem the HPTs caused in Hyannis in the late 1960s and into the 1970s. One could also fill a tome with the many times Ted Kennedy sat down with his nephews to try to reason with them. "We're probably talking on a weekly basis," is how Thomas Langford put it. "Ethel would call in tears and Ted would come running, saying, 'Don't worry, Ethie. I'll take care of it.' That was just their dynamic. He'd put the boys in a room and give them a good talking to, telling them that their father wouldn't approve . . . that sort of thing. It didn't much matter, though. After each time, he and Ethel would reconvene and she would say, 'Well? What do you think?' and he would say, 'I did my best. Let's see if it sticks.'"

Unbeknownst to most people at the Kennedy compound during the summer week in 1969 when everyone was dealing with Ted's accident at Chappaquiddick, Ethel was handling another matter with one of her sons, minor in comparison to what was going on with Ted, but upsetting just the same. On the same night as Ted's accident, Joe got into some trouble just a few miles away. At the time, Joe was seventeen and enrolled in the private Milton Academy, living there and not at home.

On the day of Ted's accident, Joe had arrived on Martha's Vineyard to watch the Edgartown Regatta and cheer his uncle Ted, who was sailing in the race. With Martha's Vineyard being such a popular summer resort and the regatta a big event, accommodations in Edgartown were hard to come by. Eventually, Joe and a friend managed to find a double room at a quaint hotel called the Daggett House. Once checked in, they unpacked their bags and then went off to the races. They returned several hours later, but now with five friends, all of whom had been invited to stay in the room. After the owner of the establishment, Frederick Chirgwin, learned of this new arrangement, he told Kennedy he would not permit it; the five friends would have to find other accommodations. In response, Joe took off his sailing hat and furiously flung it at Chirgwin. "You can't do this to me," he shouted at him. "I'm a Kennedy. If a Kennedy rents a room, he can do what he likes with it." That outburst resulted in Joe being kicked out of the hotel altogether. He then went back to the Kennedy compound and to the small apartment Ethel had given him above one of the garages. By the time he got there, though, Chirgwin had already called Ethel. Naturally, she was quite upset.

On this particular day, the stress was already building for Ethel Kennedy. Ted's evasiveness over Mary Jo's death and the desperation it had caused in the compound—and the seeming hopelessness of it all—was more than she could handle. Enraged by the hotel owner's call, Ethel burst in on Joe and was horrified to find that he had a teenage girl in his apartment with him. "You!" Ethel said angrily, pointing at the startled young lady. "You get out of here right now, or so help me God, I'll..." Appearing frightened out of her wits, Joe's paramour gathered her delicates and made a mad dash for it. Then Ethel let her son have it. Her shrill voice could be heard all over the compound. "You think you can do anything you want just because you're a Kennedy?" she demanded to know. "Do you think your grandfather would be proud of your behavior?" She then told her son to go to his room and write a five-thousand-word essay about "Why I think Grandpa would be very disappointed in me." "I want to read it by morning."

Afterward, Rose came over to Ethel's to see what all the fuss had been about. As Ethel relayed parts of the story—carefully leaving out the details involving Joe and the girl in his apartment—she sat on the sofa with her legs crossed at the knees, her arms and hands animated as she went on about her frustration with her children and their behavior. Rose took it all in patiently. Finally, she said, "May I offer you some advice?" Ethel said she would most certainly welcome any advice from her mother-in-law, a woman who had raised so many children. "Well, dear," Rose Kennedy began, "you know, it's much more ladylike to cross one's legs at the ankle, *not* at the knee." In that particular moment, it's likely that Ethel didn't find Rose's counsel very helpful.

Pot Bust

Generally, accounts of her life over the years have had it that Ethel Kennedy raised a truly unruly bunch. It's not entirely true. The fact is, she had eleven children, and of them only three presented real problems, the eldest boys: Joe, Bobby, and David. The rest were generally well-behaved, though some of her other sons would find themselves in trouble from time to time. By the summer of 1970, Kathleen Hartington was eighteen;

Joseph Patrick II, seventeen; Robert Francis Jr., sixteen; David Anthony, fifteen; Mary Courtney, thirteen; Michael LeMoyne, eleven; Mary Kerry, ten; Christopher George, six; Matthew Maxwell, five; Douglas Harriman, three; and Rory Elizabeth, two.

Of course, each of Ethel's older boys had his own distinct personality and character, but one challenge they all faced was that they had no choice because of their lineage but to do something truly significant with their lives. "We felt a real pressure to be worthy of the name Kennedy," is how Joe once put it. "There was always so much emphasis on being of service. 'Make your life count' was something we heard a lot. Even if someone wasn't preaching it to us in the moment, all you had to do was think about the family's history and how important Jack and Bobby and even Ted had been to America to feel sort of overwhelmed by it. So, as a kid, yes, I think the best way to put it is that we were overwhelmed by it all and it could be said we acted out because of it."

A running theme throughout Joe's life and the lives of all of the third generation was the sense that they had some vitally important obligation to fulfill as members of the socially conscious Kennedy family. However, as teenagers, the youngsters couldn't wrap their minds around what it was they were supposed to do with such a unique station in life. Though their aunt Eunice would often talk to them about "being of service," they couldn't quite connect with the idea. It was so amorphous a notion that it meant little to them.

"We were often reminded that this country has been very good to the Kennedys and that we owed it some kind of reciprocal debt in return," Bobby Kennedy said. "That the money was just not all ours and the privilege and the power was not just ours to do what we wanted with, that we had to use it in some way to serve others, otherwise we would be wasting what we'd been given. I remember one time when my father returned from Appalachia where he found three families living in a one-room shack and the kids were going to bed hungry. And he came back home just in time for dinner and over the meal he said to us, 'You know, you're lucky to be eating all of this food in this wonderful house where you have your own rooms to sleep in, and I hope and pray that when you guys grow up you'll be able to do something to help people.' We clearly heard Saint Luke's admonition that from those who have been given much, much shall be expected. Was it pressure? Did we see it as pressure? Yes."

Perhaps sensing that there was no way they would ever be able to fill the shoes of their ancestors, many of the next generation of boys spent their adolescence trying to fit into a caricature-like mold of what they figured it was supposed to be like to be a Kennedy. Or as Chris Lawford explained, "From an early age, our purpose was to become more Kennedy. More brave, more reckless, more teeth, more charisma, better sailors, better football players, better with the ladies. This is what we were looking for, what we would have liked to re-create, but we never had a snowball's chance in hell of doing it. The premature deaths of Jack and Bobby Kennedy elevated them to mythic proportions. Their greatness was undiminished, their human failings forgotten. They were our benchmarks, which on a deep unspoken level we knew we would never reach."

"As adults, I think we made up for it, but as kids we were a handful," Bobby Kennedy allowed. "Our mother did the best she could, but in her defense there was pretty much no way to handle us. We were pretty bad."

On the night of July 10, 1970, Ethel and Eunice Kennedy were having dinner at Eunice's home in the Kennedy compound when a maid came into the dining room and informed them that there was a team of police officers on the property looking for them. "Now, what in Sam Hill is *this* about?" Eunice said, using a popular slang phrase of the times. Ten minutes later, the officers showed up at Eunice's front door and, much to the her and Ethel's astonishment, announced that Eunice's Bobby (Sargent III) and Ethel's Bobby Jr.—both just sixteen—were being charged for marijuana possession.

In the 1960s and 1970s, rampant drug use among American youth had increased by troubling leaps and bounds. The list of fallen adolescents included a growing number of sons and daughters of prominent families, and the Kennedys were not immune to the trend. Sargent Shriver had always recognized that recreational drugs were widely used in the Cape Cod area, and at one point he and Eunice had considered sending their sons elsewhere for the summer for that very reason. However, Eunice had said that she felt doing so would be "copping out," just to keep her children away from the temptation. "Nowhere is safe, really," she'd said, "the country is riddled with drugs from one end to the other. I think protection has to come from within the family itself." Eunice just hoped she had given her children the pride, guts, and the devotion to God and man that would keep them out of harm's way. In fact, though, the two

Bobbys—Kennedy and Shriver—had been smoking pot on and off for at least the better part of the last year. "How could I have misjudged things so badly?" Eunice now wondered.

That night, there were a lot of hysterics at the compound as Eunice and Ethel—mostly Ethel—lit into their sons. About two days later, Sargent Shriver, who had been in California, flew in to deal with the matter and to get more information as to exactly what had transpired.

"It's a setup!" Ethel exclaimed when she finally heard the details about how the arrest happened. Eunice agreed. Apparently, a policeman from Boston had gone undercover as a hippie taxi driver named Andy Moes, and over the course of a couple weeks gave the two cousins and some of their friends free rides around Hyannis Port in order to earn their trust. He even drove them to parties and observed their behavior, drinking beer and scotch. Then, during the course of one evening, he asked if they had any pot they might sell him. He offered them ten bucks a joint. Not bad, the boys decided. They each had a little stash and gave Moes a couple of joints.

Eunice felt that the operation was illegal and constituted entrapment. Ethel agreed, saying that their boys had been targeted because they were Kennedys and that the family should not stand for it. Though Sargent did his best to reason with them, it was pretty useless. According to a family member in the home at the time, Sargent maintained that the police were simply doing their job and that the Kennedy youths shouldn't be let off the hook, even if they had been tricked. Sarge also wasn't convinced that they had been targeted, since twenty-seven other youths had also been caught by the same dragnet operation involving Andy Moes. "They shouldn't be buying it, smoking it, or selling it, no matter what," Sarge maintained. "These kids are smoking pot! *That's* the issue here."

Ethel became quiet, but not Eunice. "Well, I think we should sue!" Eunice angrily told her husband, standing toe to toe with him.

"For what?" Sargent wanted to know.

"My God. I can see that you are going to be totally useless in this thing, aren't you?" a flabbergasted Eunice shot back at her husband. "This is not the time to be a nice guy, Sarge," she said, obviously alluding to his reputation as a bit of a softie. "This is the time to get mad. This is the time to fight back." Maybe that was the Kennedy way, but it wasn't always the Shriver way. Sargent was determined to keep his head, saying that he felt it would set a bad example for the boys if the adults went up against law enforcement on this matter. Perhaps it was true that the boys' names shouldn't have been revealed, he conceded, since that seemed a violation of Massachusetts law. However, he saw no recourse other than for the family to just get tougher on the boys and deal with the real issue at hand: their recreational use of marijuana.

The family managed to keep the embarrassing story under wraps until early August, when a hearing into the matter was scheduled. On August 5, Ethel, Eunice, and Sarge as well as Ted accompanied their sons to Barnstable for private juvenile proceedings. Of course, the scene was pure pandemonium during the dreaded walk from the family's car to the Barnstable district courthouse, with television cameras grinding, reporters calling out questions, strangers staring, and everyone shoving. For much of the time, Ethel seemed close to tears, while Eunice looked incredibly annoyed. Sarge and Ted seemed resigned to the moment. Both boys looked sheepish. "My uncle Teddy gets away with stuff, how come we can't?" Bobby Kennedy had asked his mother earlier in the day. He was obviously referring to Chappaquiddick. "Don't you dare bring your uncle Teddy into this," she told him angrily. "This has nothing to do with him."

Indeed, there was a consequence of Chappaquiddick that was very personal to the third generation of Kennedys. There was a pervasive feeling among many of that generation—especially some of the sons of John, Bobby, and Ted—that their uncle Ted had gotten away with a crime. Accidents happen, of course. However, there are usually consequences, especially if a death occurs. Yet in the case of the senator and Mary Jo Kopechne, it seemed to some of the younger generation that there hadn't been much of a penalty. In their minds, the way Ted had ducked justice after the accident at Chappaquiddick only served to reinforce the notion that Kennedys were born with a sense of entitlement and were not always to be held responsible for their actions. Indeed, in years to come, this kind of warped thinking would wreak havoc in the lives of some of that next generation of Kennedys.

In the end, the judge gave the boys a year of probation—standard treatment for first-time offenders—and sent them on their way.

After the hearing, both Bobbys were quite embarrassed and feeling very guilty and sorry about the whole matter. Unfortunately, Bobby Kennedy didn't have a father who might try to help him make sense of what had occurred. He just had Ethel, who was already pushed beyond her limits as a mother, and she wasn't able to be much help to him. If Bobby thought he was going to have a meaningful dialogue with her about the temptations and perils of drug use, he was wrong. Instead, Ethel just ripped into him that night, chasing him all over the compound until finally catching up to him and pushing him headfirst into shrubbery. "Give me strength," she screamed up at the sky as she headed back to her home. After that, Ethel didn't want to talk about the matter at all. In fact, the subject never came up again, except for Ethel's tearful declaration that "all these kids are bad kids and I don't think there's anything we can do about it."

Of course, Eunice Shriver was also very upset with her son Bobby—"I am quite cross with you right now," is how she put it. However, Bobby Shriver had something that Bobby Kennedy didn't have, and it made all the difference in the world. He had Sargent Shriver as a father. Sarge took his son into his study, sat down with him, and told him that while this had certainly been a bad situation, it most definitely wasn't the end of the world. "You are *not* a bad kid, and I don't care what anyone says," he told him. "In fact, you're a great kid. I know you learned your lesson, and I'm not worried about it at all," he told him, according to Bobby's later recollection. "And I don't want you to listen to a thing anyone else has to say around here, because you and your brothers and sister are *not* bad kids," he added, maybe referring to Ethel's comment. "We're going to get through this thing, son, and I know it won't happen again. I want you to know that I trust you," Sargent said. And for Bobby Shriver, it never did happen again. In fact, he considers this troubling episode a defining moment in his life. He realized how lucky he was to have a father like Sargent, and how truly sad it was that his cousin Bobby didn't have someone to guide him through this difficult terrain. True, Bobby had his uncle Ted, but apparently Ted wasn't able to make much of an impression on him. Bobby Shriver vowed to never again let his dad down.

Sargent and Eunice Shriver also made a decision to try to keep their children away from Ethel's three eldest, Joe, Bobby, and David. That wasn't going to be easy. They were all great friends. But whenever possible, the Shrivers did what they could to separate, even if gently, the Kennedy boys from the Shrivers.

PART SIX

Jackie, Ari, and the Lawfords

Jackie Talks to Rose About Her New Life

$\mathcal{B}$y 1970, Jackie had comfortably settled into her marriage with Aristotle Onassis, despite an avalanche of public opinion about it. Onassis was a squat gray-haired man almost in his seventies with a large nose and slumping figure. He wasn't exactly the kind of man most Americans, indeed most of the world, thought the queen of Camelot should end up with after having been with the dashing President John Fitzgerald Kennedy. There had been an immediate and perhaps not surprising reaction to Jackie's marriage, and it wasn't positive. In fact, it was one of outrage. Perhaps the headline from the *Stockholm Express* said it best for many people: "Jackie, How Could You?"

Though the relationship had certain limitations, there were none that couldn't be accepted by both parties. For instance, Onassis, despite being exposed to Greek art and architecture while attending private schools, took little interest in the arts, in classical music, concerts, the theater, or in any kind of culture other than Greek mythology. Jackie knew she would have to live with it, because she would never be able to change him. There were plenty of men eager to accompany her to art galleries anyway. While she thoroughly enjoyed visiting Greece, she never really made friends there and never felt at home. She was never a big fan of the yacht *Christina* either, finding its decor overdone and gauche. She also disliked most of Ari's private homes, including his prized villa at Glyfada. "It's rather like a big motel, don't you think?" she had observed. Skorpios, his private island, was, in her view, lovely but far too removed from civilization. "Of course, I cherish my privacy," she told her brother-in-law Stephen Smith, "but that's too much isolation, even for me!" When he and Jackie first married, Ari had told her he wanted to spend $4 million building an exact replica of the legendary palace of King Minos as a home for her. "Oh, please don't do that," she begged him. "I'll never want to be there, and what a waste of money that would be!" New York was home to Jackie, therefore she and Onassis would spend a great deal of time apart. In their first year of marriage, they spent a total of 140 days away from each other. However, they seemed quite content during the other 225 days. "Jackie is a little bird that needs its freedom as well as its security," Onassis famously said at the time, "and she gets both from me. She can do exactly as she pleases—visit international fashion shows, and travel and go out with friends to the theater or anyplace. And I, of course, will do exactly as I please. I never question her, and she never questions me."

Secret Service agent Jack Walsh recalled meeting Aristotle Onassis in the lobby of Jackie's Manhattan apartment building one day. "He refused to go up unless he was first announced," Walsh recalled. "He said, 'I never surprise a lady, especially a lady like Mrs. Onassis.' So I would call up and announce him and Mrs. Onassis would always say, 'Of course, send him up, Mr. Walsh. He is my husband, after all!' Later, she said to me, 'Honestly, Mr. Walsh, must you announce Mr. Onassis each and every time? I'm sure that makes him feel quite badly.' And when I told her it was always at his very specific direction, she was surprised. 'Oh, he's such a dear man for not wanting to invade my privacy,' she said.

"He would always have a gift for her, too. Once he showed up with a box and he opened it for me before he went up in the elevator. And in it was a diamond necklace that was about the biggest I had ever seen. 'Do you think she will like it?' he asked me. 'Yes, sir,' I said, 'I suspect she will.' He smiled and said, 'Do you know how much this thing cost?' Of course, I did not. He said, 'One million dollars. But worth every penny, for my queen.'"

"Every time he took her out for a meal, he would hide some little bauble in a napkin worth, likely, hundreds of thousands of dollars," reported a friend of Jackie's. "She would say, 'Ari, enough! You don't have to get me a gift with every meal.' He would laugh and say, 'Oh, yes I do, my dear. You deserve it.' He worshipped the ground she walked on, and from what I could see, she loved him too, very much." The idea of costly trinkets as bribes or to assuage one's guilt was also one that was practiced by Joseph Kennedy Sr. As JFK was fond of saying, "Every time Dad had another affair, he would pin another diamond brooch on Mother's dress."

Jackie's cousin John Davis recalls, "She was truly happy even though a lot of people did not want to believe that. She became more outgoing, more accessible. As far as I was concerned, marrying Onassis was one of the best things that could have happened to her. He was so much fun, so unpredictable, he did her a world of good. She told me, 'I never thought I would get over what happened to Jack in Dallas. Every day was joyless for me. I felt hopeless, and if not for the kids I would not have been able to go on. But Ari has made me feel that life is beautiful and should be enjoyed. He has filled my dark world with nothing but light.'"

While it wasn't always easy for some of her family members and associates to accept that Jackie had remarried, the family's matriarch, Rose, certainly had no reservations about Onassis. Jackie had invited Rose to celebrate New Year's 1969 with her, Ari and John, and Caroline, and it turned out to be a wonderful holiday for all in Greece. Rose later said she found Ari to be somewhat coarse, pretty much what she had expected. Though he was brash, she liked his directness and found it refreshing, if also a little unnerving. After all, Kennedy men never said what they meant, or at least that had been her experience with her husband. Onassis was also extravagant. He liked to spend money and had plenty of it. "Rose didn't see anything wrong with that, either—as long as it wasn't Kennedy money!" observed Sancy Newman. "Though he was about fifteen years younger than Rose, it felt as if she and Onassis were of the same generation and they really did have a lot to talk about."

For the Easter holiday in 1969, Jackie invited Rose to set sail for two weeks with her and Onassis and the children in the Caribbean. The only problem Rose had with Onassis on that particular cruise occurred when she became seasick. While she was sound asleep, Onassis slipped into her stateroom to check on her and make sure she was okay. When he later told her about it, she was taken aback. From that point on, she made sure her door was locked. That gaffe aside, she enjoyed Ari's hospitality and it also gave her an opportunity to spend quality time with her former daughter-in-law. "The problem was that every time Rose looked at Onassis, she couldn't help but remember why he was in their lives—and it was because Jack wasn't," said Sancy Newman. "Jackie couldn't help but sense Rose's sadness, which caused her to fall into despair as well."

On May 21, 1969, Jackie took Rose to see the Broadway show *40 Carats* at the Morosco Theatre, starring Julie Harris, who won a Tony for her work in the show. Accompanying them was the noted architect Edward Larrabee Barnes. They had a fun time at the show, according to what he remembered many years later. Afterward, with everyone in a jolly mood, they decided to continue the night and enjoy a dinner at Sardi's. Jackie and Rose got along as if they were the best of friends. Over the meal, Jackie talked about her new life and how lucky she was to have it. "I suppose it would surprise some people but I am very grateful for my life," Jackie told Rose, according to Barnes's memory. Jackie said that she believed she should now make the best of each day. "I've taken such a big bite out of life and I don't take any of it for granted," she said, sounding very upbeat. She added that she didn't want to one day look back on this time and feel that she had missed out on any of it, that she hadn't thoroughly enjoyed it. Rose smiled and said it was nice to hear Jackie talk like that. "After Jack died," she said, "I didn't think I would ever see you smile again."

Jackie then said that Aristotle Onassis had given her and the children an amazing lifestyle, "more than I ever could have imagined." However, she also said she wanted to make one thing clear. "Ed and I have already discussed this, so I feel free to talk in front of him," she allowed, looking at the architect. Then she told Rose, "I want you to know that I would never allow Ari to legally adopt John and Caroline." Jackie added that if anything were to ever happen to her, she wanted both children to be raised as Kennedys. "It was in my will, as you know, that Teddy and Joan should get the children if Jack and I died," she added. "But I think they have enough problems now. However, I still would want the kids to be raised Kennedys." Suddenly, the mood seemed to shift. Both Jackie and Rose became quite sad very quickly. Rose said that she had hoped Jackie felt as she did, "But I dared not ask." At that, Jackie's eyes welled with tears. "Just sitting here talking to you about this," she said to Rose, "is so hard." She then took a deep breath, got up, and, without saying a word, swept off in the direction of the ladies' room. Ed later called it a "very dramatic exit," calling to mind what William Manchester had recently written of Jackie: "My first impression of her, and it has never changed, is that I was in the presence of a very great, tragic actress."

"When Jackie excused herself, Rose and I had a few words about Aristotle Onassis," Edward Larrabee Barnes recalled. "She said that her daughter Eunice disliked Onassis but that she thought Eunice's opinion was unfair since she had never even met Onassis. Her mind was made up, though, she said. 'Personally, I like him,' she told me. 'True, he's not Jack, but really, who is?' As she sipped her mint julep, she also said that she was the one who first told Jackie to marry Onassis. She said that back when Jackie first brought Onassis to the Cape, she came to Rose as if she was her daughter and asked what she should do. Rose told her, 'Jackie, I think you should marry him. Be happy. That's what Jack would want!' Then she said to me, 'It's so sad the way the years pass us by and force us to continue to live, isn't it?' Definitely the evening's mood had changed from very gay to very downhearted, and Rose realized it. 'Funny the way a happy moment always has a sad one just under the surface, isn't it?' she observed."

Rose Kennedy then wistfully spoke to Barnes about her own life, and about aging. She would turn eighty in a year. "You know, I still feel that I am young and quite attractive," she said. "When I look in the mirror, I see a young woman looking back at me. But then someone shouts out, 'Grandma! Grandma!' and while I know I should love to hear that, I must tell you, I really don't," she confessed. "It makes me feel old. I don't want to feel that way. Can you understand that?" After Rose's comments, the two just sat staring at each other until Jackie finally returned. Jackie sat down and smiled softly. "I'm so sorry," she said, reaching out to hold Rose's hand. "I know you hate it when I get this way about Jack." Rose nodded with a sad expression, but without saying anything.

Remembering JFK

John Fitzgerald Kennedy, a third-generation Irish American, was born into a life of privilege in the Boston suburb of Brookline, Massachusetts, on May 29, 1917. Referred to as Jack by friends and family, he was the second of nine children born to Joseph Patrick Kennedy and Rose Fitzgerald Kennedy.

As president, JFK dedicated himself to his campaign pledges to improve the country's economy and saw the nation through one of its longest periods of financial stability. He was also a champion of civil rights and called for new legislation that would see fulfilled his family's longtime quest for the equality of all Americans. As earlier stated, he established the Alliance for Progress and the Peace Corps in an effort to extend America's idealism to developing nations, all of this against a backdrop of fear and paranoia as communism became a real threat. He maintained that both the United States and Russia had good reason to pull back on the development of nuclear weapons.

Putting aside Kennedy's tangible accomplishments, his fame as the young, dynamic president, and his and Jackie's and their children's image as the storybook family, there has long been a question about JFK's character in regard to his marriage to Jackie. They were wed on September 12, 1953. A great deal is now known about his philandering—especially since his Secret Service agents have spoken openly about it in the last twenty years. Obviously, he wasn't the ideal husband. Jackie did her best to cope with the unhappy situation, all the while making it clear to him that she was aware of his infidelities and that she had made the specific choice to live with them. It would seem that she loved her husband unconditionally, so much so that after his death she couldn't help but romanticize him and his thousand days in office with her myth-making allusions to the Kennedy administration as having been a sort of modern-day Camelot—romantic, victorious, and, of course, also very troubled.

Clinging to Each Other After Camelot

About a week after Jackie Kennedy Onassis, Rose Kennedy, and Edward Larrabee Barnes went to see the Broadway show *40 Carats* in May 1969, Jackie and Edward had lunch at Jackie's home. Jackie found Barnes absolutely fascinating. A Harvard graduate, he had founded Edward Larrabee Barnes Associates in Manhattan and went on to a long career designing office buildings, museums, botanical gardens, and college campuses. Among his most famous projects would be the Dallas Museum of Art and the IBM Building in Manhattan. In 1969, construction was being completed on two of his pet projects, 28 State Street in Boston and the Indianapolis Museum of Art. Like John Carl Warnecke, the architect who designed JFK's memorial for Jackie and whom she dated off and on before Onassis, Barnes was someone Jackie could talk to for hours. And she did. They had a long friendship, though it never turned romantic. He was very happily married. In fact, Jackie did have many male friends who were married and with whom she shared a great many common interests. She always thought it reductive of the human condition that there were people who believed that the opposite sexes could not have platonic relationships.

"Are you happy these days, Jackie?" Edward asked as they waited for Jackie's maid to serve lunch. The two were seated in the parlor on a couch in front of a coffee table, upon which an elegant tea setting had been prepared. Jackie smiled. "My goodness, Ed," she said, while pouring him a cup, "do you know how many people ask me that question? Almost every day someone asks me that question. Why is that, I wonder?"

Edward laughed. He told Jackie that it was likely because she was "loved by the world" and that it was widely hoped that she was finally happy and at peace, considering what she had been through in her life. "The whole world wants that for you, Jackie," he said. She nodded. "Well, that's not so bad, then, is it?" she decided. In answer to the question, she said that she now had "a new life" and that she was just trying her best to throw herself into it. "But do you know what I miss?" she asked. "I really miss politics." Edward was surprised to hear this, he said, because he never thought of Jackie as being a particularly political person. She responded by saying that when she and JFK were married, she did hate politics. But now, looking back on those days, she realized that what she really hated was "politics as a blood sport," she said. "Not the way the Kennedys played it, but the way others played it," she clarified. "Like Nixon. Oh, I am not a fan of his, I must say," she remarked with a shiver. "You know who I admire most?" she asked. "Sargent Shriver," she said, answering her own question. She then explained that Sarge and Eunice inspired her "because they believe that the way to fix our country is to fix ourselves. I think that's what politics is supposed to be about, don't you? Fixing things."

Edward nodded. "Do you miss being a Kennedy?" he asked. At that, Jackie flashed her infectious smile. "Oh, but I still am a Kennedy," she said brightly. She added that she was "absolutely surrounded by Kennedys. You saw how Rose was the other night at the show. She's like a mother to me, and I know she thinks of me as a daughter."

As Jackie's maid served the meal of lemon chicken, the two talked a bit more about Jack and Bobby and what both had meant to America. "They were men who honored their principles and values," Jackie said, adding that "you don't see that a lot these days. They were connected to the pulse of America in a way that I fear we may not see again." There was a long pause while Jackie gazed into the distance as if she'd suddenly been hit by a flood of memories. "At times it seems so sad, doesn't it?" she asked. "Here we Kennedys are, all these many years later, trying to pick up the pieces of our lives. Trying to survive after Camelot. Clinging to each other with the fear that what little that remains of our kingdom will come crashing down around us, leaving us with nothing but the memory of what was once so great. But the truth is this can never happen," she concluded, "because the family is the kingdom. And it can never fall, Ed. Not ever."

In the telling of this story, Edward Larrabee would recall years later that he didn't know how to respond to Jackie's observation, it had been so poignant. However, before he had a chance to do so, she did it herself. "Listen, if I go on like this for even one more minute, I will be depressed for the next two weeks," she said, maybe only half joking. "So, enough of this! Let's eat."

Onassis—Father Figure?

*P*rior to 1968, John Kennedy Jr.'s greatest male influence had been Secret Service agent Jack Walsh. A funny story has it that once when John was being taunted by some school chums—"John-John wears short-shorts!"—he hauled off and punched one kid right in the nose. When someone asked how he learned to fight like that, he answered, "The Secret Service!" Ham Brown, executive secretary of the Former Agents Association of the Secret Service, said, "Jack automatically became a father figure to John. It's a shame that's how things had to be, but Jack is a good man and he was happy to do it. He drove John to school and picked him up every day, just like a father would. At home, the only people around were women—Mrs. Onassis and all the maids and servants. Jack was the only man around those children until Onassis came along."

Both John and Caroline seemed to take to Aristotle Onassis when he came into their lives—John more so than Caroline. To Jackie, John had always seemed scattered and unfocused in his day-to-day activities. Though she told him not to worry about his poor spelling—his father's had been atrocious as well—she was concerned. His leg was always jiggling, he seemed nervous, hyperactive. When she looked into it, the diagnosis from doctors came back as a "learning/behavioral disability." She was very concerned about that language until it was explained to her that the phrase merely meant the boy was hyperactive and was having trouble concentrating and organizing. Some reporters over the years have said that John was diagnosed with ADD—attention deficit disorder—at the age of five, and some have even said the age of three. However, that term wasn't really used until 1980. The first edition of the *Diagnostic and Statistical Manual of Mental Disorders* (DSM) in which it appears is the third edition, published in 1980. It wouldn't be until John was twenty-three in 1983 that a doctor actually diagnosed him with ADD. It was then that he started taking Ritalin, but on an experimental basis, not consistently. Sometimes the drug made him feel nauseous, and so he often took a break from the medication, only to go back on it later to see if the effects would be the same. When John was a youngster, Onassis was very patient with him, reading him stories, forcing him to slow down, to think before he acted, or as he put it to one of his staff members, "The boy just has too much energy. He needs to stop for a minute and figure out what he wants to do, not just do everything there is to do in a day."

"I think Caroline was a little more ambivalent than John was about their stepfather," recalled Secret Service agent Clint Hill. "It was understandable. After all, she had known her real father much better than John and her memories of him were still so vivid. She missed him very much." Still, Caroline seemed to genuinely try with Onassis. He made her mother happy, and as little Caroline had said, "It's nice to see her smile so much rather than cry so much," perhaps recalling having observed her mother's abject sadness in the months after her father was buried. "All she does all day long is lie in bed and cry," Caroline said at the time. Jackie trusted her new husband implicitly with her children and was very pleased that he became a pivotal person in their lives. In fact, Ari had an easy way with children, and though he was more like a grandfather to them than a father, he would definitely be a strong presence in their lives. Onassis worked hard to win their trust. He promised the children that he was in no way trying to replace their father, and they took him at his word. He found, though, that John's biggest concern was that he was trying to take Jack Walsh's place! There was definitely an adjustment period where Onassis had to sometimes defer to Walsh when it came to spending time with the young Kennedy. "Sometimes John just wanted to be with Jack," said another agent who was a friend of Walsh's. "Onassis would say, 'Let's go and do something,' and John would say, 'No, I'm fine with Mr. Walsh.' It could get a little touchy, but they worked their way through it."

Their nanny at the time, Greta Nilsen, recalled, "Prior to Onassis coming into their lives, John and Caroline seemed to live in a golden jail, and I think they knew it. You never heard them bursting with laughter or running in the street or fighting with a friend. I had the impression they were rather melancholic. They seemed happy with Mr. Walsh when they knew they were going out with him, especially John. John did have a little sense of entitlement, though. Once when I was in the pantry preparing dinner, he suddenly came at me with a toy water gun and splashed me on my blue uniform. I ran after him and found him in the back hall and gave him a good spank. 'You are not allowed to do that,' he shouted at me. 'My mother will be very upset with you. That is not allowed in this household.' He would never treat Mr. Onassis that way, though. He had a lot of respect for him. Onassis was a big personality and he told great stories to John and explained Greek myths to him in a way I think John would never forget. I remember John doing something naughty once, and Mr. Onassis swatting him on the side of the head, and John just looked at him and said, 'I'm sorry, sir.'"

The Kennedy children—who were still being schooled in New York—thoroughly enjoyed it when they vacationed on Onassis's private isle of Skorpios, and Jackie made sure they had a busy schedule whenever they were in residence, whether it be waterskiing or other sports or even time in the local museums. "Because he knew that John and Caroline loved to fish, Onassis bought them their own twenty-eight-foot red sailboat, which Caroline christened the *Caroline*," recalled the Kennedy family photographer Jacques Lowe. (So that he would not feel left out, Onassis purchased a red speedboat for John and had his name stenciled on the stern.) "He also put at their disposal his employee Captain Anastassiadis, reputedly one of the best sailors in Greece. Since there was little chance of the children actually catching anything, Onassis ordered the sailor to keep a supply of fresh fish on board so the children could fool their mom into thinking they had caught their own dinners."

As a special surprise for Caroline and John, Onassis had a tree house built on the estate of his private villa at Glyfada. It was actually bigger than most family homes in America. When she saw it, Jackie said, "We could move in here and bring all of Ethel's kids with us, and still have plenty of room!" Onassis then had it stocked with every kind of toy imaginable, including stuffed animals. He also bought the children Shetland ponies. There seemed no end to the gifts he would lavish upon them, or the strange ways he would indulge them. When John was worried about how his pet rabbit would make the trip from America to Greece, Onassis put the animal in the care of one of his Olympic Airways pilots and instructed him to keep it on the flight deck with him, just to make sure it would reach its destination safely. John told his cousin Ted, who was Ted and Joan's son, "My mom's new husband is the king of the whole world! You oughta see the stuff he gives me! I just got my own Jeep! He's the greatest!"

One day in the spring of 1969, one Secret Service agent who asked for anonymity accompanied Aristotle Onassis, John, and Caroline on a walk through Central Park. "All of the money in the world can't buy a simple moment like this," Onassis told the agent. "I never had this with my own children," he said. "We have never had this kind of closeness. There've always been problems. So, for me, having this time with Jackie's children is vitally important." Onassis had John to his left and was holding his hand. Caroline was to his right and he was holding her hand as well. The children had never seemed more content, or so the agent would recall many years later.

"Aristotle, when I grow up, I want to be rich, like you," John said, looking up at his stepfather with great adoration. He and his sister always referred to Onassis by his first name "That's not much of a goal for you," Onassis told the boy. "You come from a family who helps people. All of your aunts and uncles help people. You should help people, too." John nodded and asked, "Like my aunt Eunice?" Onassis nodded. "But that's why I want to be rich," John said. "So I can have lots and lots of money to help people with." Aristotle Onassis patted young John Kennedy Jr. on the top of the head. "That's my boy," he concluded. "That's my boy."

Jackie and the Secret Service

She was a wonderful lady, a real inspiration to me in many ways," recalled Secret Service agent Clint Hill of Jackie Kennedy Onassis. Hill was the agent who pulled Jackie from the trunk lid of the car that awful day in Dallas after she had scrambled from her seat to retrieve part of JFK's skull that had been blown away by the assassin's bullet. For many years, he blamed himself for JFK's death, saying that if he had reacted a little more quickly he would have taken the third bullet—the most devastating of the three that hit Kennedy, "and that would have been fine with me," he said. "It's something I have had to learn to live with," he says. "I'm fine now. It took some time, though." He retired in 1975.

"We had an interesting relationship because even though it was personal, we tried to keep it professional," he said of himself and Jackie. "It was always 'Mrs. Kennedy.' It was always 'Mr. Hill.' Always.

"One memory that sticks out in my mind," he adds, "was when I drove Bobby and Mrs. Kennedy to JFK's grave three days after he was buried. Bobby had said something like, 'Let's go see our friend,' and I drove the two of them out there. I just remember standing back to give them their privacy as Mrs. Kennedy and Bobby approached the grave and then knelt before it and prayed. Then Mrs. Kennedy placed lilies of the valley on the grave. Afterward, we drove back to the White House in total silence. What could anyone say?"

Clint Hill didn't go to New York with Jackie when she moved there, his place having been taken by Jack Walsh. If it had been just Walsh guarding the children, Jackie would have been quite happy. However, the government had so many agents in the little family's midst that it became a true annoyance for her. Jackie's own protection ended shortly before her marriage to Aristotle Onassis, but as children of the president, her offspring would continue to have guards on duty around them for many more years. Therefore, there was constant communication—and miscommunication—over the years between Jackie and the government as she attempted, usually in vain, to have the protection of her children minimized.* The letters she would send outlining her concerns were usually long and very detailed, such as one she wrote on December 11, 1968, to James J. Rowley, director of the Secret Service—six typed pages,

---

* Protecting Jackie and the children wasn't cheap. According to Secret Service logs, the cost for their annual protection was about $85,000. This in contrast to the $60,000 that it cost to protect President Truman. Protecting President Eisenhower cost almost double Jackie's detail, though, at $160,000.

single-spaced! At the time, Jackie was very upset that three more agents had been added to the roster in October after new legislation was passed (a consequence of RFK's assassination). This made a total of eight agents guarding two children! It seemed preposterous to her.

"The trouble with the children's Secret Service detail now is the same as when we moved to New York in 1964," she wrote. "There are too many agents, and the new ones are not ones who are sensitive to the needs of little children."

At this point—the end of 1968—Caroline was eleven and John was eight. Jackie felt strongly that so many agents on duty were throwing their lives into "turmoil" and that they "do not care about them or understand their problems." She wanted "three young men whom they know and trust," and that was it—Jack Walsh being one of the agents she wanted on duty. She wrote that she could live with the security measures taken in New York and Hyannis Port if need be, but that what was going on in Far Hills, New Jersey, where she had a country home, was totally unacceptable.

"It's harmful rather than helpful," Jackie wrote. "Agents tramp outside the children's windows all night, talking into their walkie-talkie. Cars of each agent pile up in the driveway so that our little country house looks like a used car lot! And with all this," Jackie complained, "the agents supply the children with no protection."

Citing an example, Jackie wrote that agents on duty lost track of her children for two full hours because "they followed a wrong car out of the driveway!" She wrote that one of her neighbors, "a mother of nine," had to leave her children "and bring mine home." She detailed another example of an agent who "forcibly dragged my children home for supper" even though she "had told them they could stay at a neighbor's for the meal." She also objected to all of the security in Greece, saying that Ari had seventy-five men to enforce security "and that is quite enough." She wrote, "The children are growing up. They must see new things and travel as their father would have wished them to do. They must be as free as possible, not encumbered by a group of men who will be lost in foreign countries, so that one ends up protecting them rather than vice versa." She concluded by writing, "As the [one] person in the world who is most interested in their security, and who realizes most what threats there are in the outside world, I promise you that I have considered and tried every way, and that what I ask you for is what I know is best for the children of President Kennedy and what he would wish for them." She signed it, "Most sincerely, Jacqueline."

The response? It took almost three months, but when James Rowley finally did respond, he denied pretty much all of Jackie's requests. In explaining his reasons, he said that the government still received "communications from mentally ill persons who represent a potential threat to your children." He noted that "a curious and unwitting public" is still very interested in the activities of the Kennedy children. He also wrote of "the ever present threat of the kidnapper," and, he added, "the incidences of aircraft hijacking" were "a great concern." He did allow, though, that the agents wouldn't park on her property in New Jersey, that they would park on the road instead. He also promised to have the agents ease up on walkie-talkie communication outside the children's rooms. Small consolation for her, doubtless, considering the breadth of her complaints. Then, in what Jackie later said she considered "hard ball," Rowley pointed out that when she was in Ireland a year earlier, she had asked that Jack Walsh not accompany her to the beach. He refused. She wasn't happy about it but decided to go swimming anyway. She then went out into the churning ocean, got pulled in by an undertow, and very nearly drowned. Luckily, Walsh jumped in and was able to rescue her. Jackie lay on the beach for almost thirty minutes coughing up all the saltwater. She was very grateful, especially since earlier on that same vacation, John had been at a hot dog roast and somehow stumbled and tripped into the hot coals. Walsh pulled him out and saved him from more frightful burns than the second-degree ones he suffered on his arm. Jackie was very happy that Jack Walsh had been with her and the children on that particular trip, but not too happy about the fact that his heroic efforts were now being used as a weapon to deny her requests for less protection.

"It's a constant frustration," Jackie wrote to Lady Bird Johnson of the Secret Service detail protecting her children. "Truly, I am at my wit's end with it. They will not let the children lead normal lives, or as normal as possible considering. I guess one could say I am losing faith in this system."

Lady Bird wrote back, "I sympathize with you, my dear. We have gone through the same thing with our children. It's not the agents, I'm afraid, it's the reason for their presence. How sad that we as a nation have to go to such lengths. But after what has happened in recent years, I'm afraid we have no choice, do we?"

Considering what she herself had been through, Jackie likely agreed.

Lady Bird closed her letter with these wise words: "Put your faith in love, and it will carry you through life, no matter what happens and no matter when."

A Problem Like Maria

*T*here was one major problem in Jackie's marriage to Aristotle Onassis, and it was significant enough to cause her many years of extreme anguish. It was Maria Callas. Onassis simply would not stop seeing the famed opera star, and Callas couldn't seem to keep herself away from him either. The affair between the two had begun in 1957 when Ari was married to his first wife, Tina. Throughout the entire time he was seeing Callas, however, Onassis was also seeing other women. "He couldn't even be faithful to the woman with whom he was being unfaithful to his wife," observed Enrique Fonteyn, who worked as one of Onassis's assistants from 1966 through the end of 1969. "However, that was the Greek way back then, at least amongst powerful, rich men. I believe the affair with Maria was on hold in 1968, but not really over, when Onassis married Jackie," he said. "However, within months of the wedding—at around Christmastime, actually—Ari and Maria started seeing each other again."

Ari did try to defend his carrying on an affair even after he'd wed Jackie: His pride had been hurt in February 1970 when letters from Jackie to Roswell Gilpatric somehow fell into the hands of an autograph dealer and were made public. One was sent from the *Christina* during Jackie's honeymoon with Onassis, which was more than he could handle. "Dearest Ros," it began, "I would have told you before I left—but then everything happened so much more quickly than I'd planned. I saw somewhere what you had said and I was very touched—dear Ros. I hope you know all you were and are and will ever be to me. With my love, Jackie." The day after the letter ended up in the press, Gilpatric's wife filed for a legal separation. And Onassis cited his "hurt pride" as a reason—weak though it may have been—for his ongoing affair behind Jackie's back.

"Once Jackie knew about Onassis and Callas, she had to make a choice," said her cousin John Davis. "Do I give him up because he is doing this to me? Because he is never going to stop, and he has made that clear to me. Or do I find a way to live with it?' I think, then, the reason he had given her so many millions when they married began to make more sense. It gave him power. It gave him license to say he was taking very good care of her and that she should, in turn, just let him do what he pleases. She had gotten herself into a pickle, so to speak. She needed him more than he needed her, and he loved that, and she knew it. So, what to do... what to do? In the end, she decided to accept it. And once she had made up her mind about it, that was the end of it for her."

Indeed, for the most part, after May 1970, Jackie didn't want to know any more about Ari's relationship with Maria Callas than absolutely necessary. Rogers and Hammerstein posed the question in *The Sound of Music*: "How do you solve a problem like Maria?" Apparently, for Jackie, the solution was to ignore the problem as best she could. Though she realized that Maria was quite beautiful, she also knew that Maria was tortured by the fact that she had aged and had lost her operatic voice in the process. Her life was hell by the mid-1970s. "Jackie felt that, by comparison, she was lucky—and since she was the one who really had Onassis, she likely didn't see any reason to spend an inordinate amount of time worrying about Maria Callas" is how one of her friends at the time put it. Rather than dwell on the problem of Maria, Jackie chose to focus on the complete remodeling and renovation of a cottage on Skorpios called the Pink House—which, ironically enough, was where Callas stayed when she was on the island. Jackie also busied herself with the landscaping of certain pivotal gardens on Skorpios, trying to restore the estate to its original natural state. It bothered her, for instance, that there were snapdragons on the island. They didn't belong there—someone along the way had decided to plant them, probably Maria Callas, Jackie had decided, and she wanted them gone. Roses, too. "There shouldn't be roses on a Greek island," Jackie said. She ordered that they be replaced by wild orchids, poppies, lavender, and other Mediterranean plants. She had literally hundreds of full-grown trees brought in as well, and placed them where she thought they would look best.

"Because she had looked the other way when Jack Kennedy was unfaithful during her marriage to him, Jackie was certainly accustomed to the notion of the unfaithful husband," noted Gore Vidal. "Therefore, it could be said that her coping mechanisms were already in place for such ordeals." Her friend singer Carly Simon adds that Jackie once "told me how deeply hurt she had been" by the affairs of her husband. In a rare moment of candor about such things, Jackie told Carly, "After a while, one does turn off." ("Whenever she told you something personal, she would slip into third-person language," Carly recalled.) While in Washington with Kennedy, Jackie immersed herself in the restoration of the White House to take her mind off her troubles, and she did the same while on Skorpios with Onassis. She dealt with both husbands the same way; as long as they were there for her when she needed them to be, Jackie would be satisfied—or at least she seemed satisfied.

Enrique Fonteyn recalls witnessing a telling scene between his boss and Jackie on the *Christina* in September 1970. Jackie was at the well-stocked circular bar, sitting alone at one of the half-dozen barstools and having a drink. "I had been in the bar stocking liquor when she came in, sat down, ordered a drink, and just sat there looking quite miserable," recalls Fonteyn. "Though I wasn't the bartender, I made her a martini and left her alone." He said that Jackie—who was wearing pink capri pants, a white short-sleeved silk blouse, and her famous Jackie O sunglasses, though indoors, seemed mesmerized by the parade of magnetic miniature ships, from Phoenician to Mississippi steamboat, as they glided under the glass top of the bar. Eventually, Onassis walked into the bar. "I hate to see you drink alone, my dear," he said, sitting next to her. He asked for his own martini. Fonteyn made it for him and placed it in front of him, and then tried to look busy with his work.

"I am just so tired of fighting with you, Aristo," Jackie said. She said that the two of them had been having the same fights every day and that she found it "exhausting." "We are surrounded by beauty everywhere we go," she said. "How lucky we are, yet we don't seem to appreciate it, do we? Instead, we argue."

"I agree," Aristotle said. As he stroked Jackie's brunette hair, Onassis further added that, in his opinion, the two of them should begin to live their lives more "unapologetically." Jackie shrugged. "I suppose," she said halfheartedly. "Then it's settled," he said. "I love you, Jackie. Let's put all of this behind us now." She smiled and said she would like to do just that. He then raised his glass for a toast. "Here's to us never fighting again," Onassis said. "And to making only love," he added with a wink, clinking her glass.

Ari then asked Fonteyn to call the kitchen to have an order of marinated artichokes and petits fours sent to the bar as a snack for him and Jackie. "I have a surprise for you tonight," he then told his wife. "I think you will be very happy."

That night, Aristotle Onassis arranged a candlelit meal for himself and his wife under the stars on the deck of the *Christina*. Since he and Jackie were the only two people aboard—along with forty-five of his employees at their service, of course—it was sure to be a memorable and romantic evening. During the meal, Onassis surprised Jackie with an old friend of his named Scarola, a Neapolitan guitarist who was at the time an international jet-set personality. Jackie had so enjoyed his playing during a recent vacation in Capri that Onassis had him flown in by plane and then brought onto the *Christina* for this special evening. "We were joined on the cruise by Maestro Garibaldi, another great guitarist and friend of mine," Scarola recalled years later. "Together, we proceeded to serenade Mr. and Mrs. Onassis as they ate their meal on a large round table with white tablecloth on the deck, under a soft moonlight. Servants kept coming out with more food, more drinks, and Ari kept saying, 'More! More! More! The night must never end. More! More! More!' Mrs. Onassis was glowing with happiness and she looked more beautiful than ever behind the glow of candles on the table.

"She loved nostalgic, romantic Neapolitan songs," he continued, "and the moment I started strumming my guitar, she stopped eating and leaned forward on the table, her eyes shining. After listening to several songs, she asked me to sing her favorite, 'Sciummo' ['river' in dialect], which is a very old, sad, and romantic love song. When I sang it, she moved closer to Ari and they looked deep into each other's eyes and held hands under the table.

"The dinner lasted several hours, with many more Neapolitan songs, and was topped off by champagne and a dessert of baked Alaska—I know because Mrs. Onassis made me eat hers, saying that she was trying to keep her figure. At the end of the night, Mrs. Onassis was in tears when she came over to me and Garibaldi and thanked us for what she called 'one of the most romantic evenings of my life.'"

Pat and Peter Lawford

*P*atricia Kennedy Lawford—"Pat," who was forty-six in 1970—was an outgoing, colorful person with a great thirst for the good life who also happened to be one of Jackie's closest friends. Though the two women were different in many ways, they seemed to have a deep understanding and empathy for each other, which, according to those who knew them best, stemmed at least in part from the fact that both had dealt with infidelity in their marriages—Pat in hers with actor Peter Lawford and Jackie, of course, with President Kennedy and later with Aristotle Onassis. "Pat was a different kind of Kennedy woman," said her longtime friend Patricia Brennan, "in the sense that she didn't sit back and accept unfaithful behavior from her husband, like Jackie, Joan, Rose, and Ethel, for instance. Instead, she divorced the guy. It was really unheard of in the family, the idea of a woman divorcing her husband. In fact, it hadn't happened before. As Catholics, another level was added to the dilemma because divorce was considered such a sin. Even though the decks were definitely stacked against Pat's freedom, she went for it anyway. If you knew Pat, though, you'd know that of all the women in the family, she was most likely the one to break new ground where this kind of thing is concerned."

Given Peter Lawford's nature, most people who knew him well were not surprised that his marriage to Pat turned out to be so tumultuous. "He was well-intentioned, the nicest guy in the world, but his biggest concern during the Pat years was himself, not her," said his manager and business partner Milt Ebbins in an interview in 2000. "There was also this constant emphasis on fitting in with the Rat Pack mentality—Frank Sinatra, Dean Martin, Sammy Davis—and he never really fit in with those guys. I think the philandering was perhaps his way of fitting in. 'I've had more women than Frank,' he once told me, 'but no one will accept that.' I told him, 'Peter, you're married to a Kennedy now, at least try to be discreet.' He couldn't do it, though. He had to be a show-off. The controversy his unfaithfulness caused didn't matter to him. In fact, I think he welcomed it. On some level, he wanted to be notorious. But then there was this other side of Peter, a sensitive, warmhearted side. He could be the greatest friend in the world. He loved his kids, though he didn't really know how to express it. And, yes, he loved Pat very much, though, again, he didn't know how to express it."

In a sense, Peter Lawford's life was begun under a cloud of controversy. His mother, May Somerville Bunny, was married to another man when she became pregnant with Peter, who was born Peter Sydney Vaughn Aylen on September 7, 1923, in London. When Mary finally confessed to her husband, Captain Ernest Vaughn Aylen, that he wasn't really the child's father, Aylen immediately filed for divorce. A year later, in 1924, May Somerville Bunny married the child's true father, Sydney Turing Barlow Lawford, a captain in the British army who had served in the Boer War in South Africa. Peter began acting early in life, making his debut at the age of seven in the British comedy *Poor Old Bill*, starring Leslie Fuller and Iris Ashley. Eight years later, after the family moved to America, Peter made his Hollywood debut as a bit player in *Lord Jeff*, and then in 1942 was given a more substantial role opposite Mickey Rooney in *A Yank at Eton*. Though Peter made many successful films in the 1940s, it really wasn't until the 1960s when he linked up socially with Frank Sinatra—with whom he had made *It Happened in Brooklyn* in 1947—that Peter became truly famous. "At that time, anyone connected to Sinatra was thought of as instantly cool," Milt Ebbins said. "Peter brought the idea of *Ocean's 11* to Frank, and he was cast in it along with Dean, Sammy, and Joey [Bishop]. Pat put some of her Kennedy dollars behind the film, thinking Peter would star in it. But, much to her dismay, Frank starred in it instead. Still, when you think of all the films Peter had done by that time—thirty-one by my count—it's ironic that he's most known as one of the Rat Pack."

Peter Lawford would make another seventeen films after *Ocean's 11*—including another one with the Rat Pack called *Sergeants 3*. However, a falling-out with Frank Sinatra over the Kennedys pushed Peter out of the Rat Pack, and out of favor with Sinatra, too, for the rest of his life. Some of the Lawfords' intimates maintain it also marked the beginning of the end of their marriage.

"At the time, Bobby Kennedy was investigating the underworld with a kind of eagerness you could not believe," recalled Jeanne Martin, Dean's widow. "He was determined to not only bring down the underworld, but also J. Edgar Hoover [director of the FBI] who he believed—we all believed, actually—had it in for the Kennedys because he was constantly having the family investigated for one thing or another. Bobby felt that Hoover was a crook. During the course of his investigations into the underworld [in February 1962], Bobby stumbled onto the fact that Sinatra was tied to some very powerful gangsters such as Sam Giancana. Because of this discovery, Bobby appealed to Jack, telling him that given Sinatra's associations there was no way he could stay with Sinatra at his Palm Springs estate during an upcoming trip he was taking to California. Frank had been planning on the trip in a big way, really looking forward to it."

Frank Sinatra had very strong feelings for Jack Kennedy. He believed that the new president was a great man, someone who had not only inspired the country into service but was personally inspiring to Sinatra as well. Sinatra had been very helpful in getting JFK elected by stumping for him across the country, and had even produced his victory party after the election. The idea that JFK was coming to Sinatra's home was, as far as the entertainer was concerned, quite an honor. For Kennedy's visit, Sinatra had new phone lines installed for the Secret Service, and had even famously built a helipad for the president's helicopter. As a finishing touch, he put up a gold plaque in the bedroom in which Jack was supposed to sleep that said "John F. Kennedy Slept Here."

Though the story of what happened next has been told many times, it's still worth repeating: When John F. Kennedy decided that he wasn't going to stay at Frank Sinatra's after all, he dispatched Peter Lawford with the disappointing news rather than give it to Sinatra himself. As Peter explained to this author in a 1981 interview,* "I guess you could say that I ended up being the fall guy. One morning, Bobby called me and told me to call Frank and tell him that the president would not be staying at his home because of his [Sinatra's] ties to Giancana. Very reluctantly, I made the call, but I couldn't bring myself to tell Frank the real reason. I said it was because of security concerns. I said that the house was indefensible— that was the word I used. Still, Frank blew up and slammed the phone down. It was actually Bobby who called Frank back and, from my understanding, told him the truth. From that moment on, I was persona non

---

* Peter Lawford was dubbing lines for a rare—and unusual—guest appearance on the TV show *The Jeffersons* at CBS's studios in Hollywood when interviewed by the author.

grata where Frank was concerned. It ruined everything between us. What I felt at the time and what I still feel is that Frank had such admiration for Jack, he was disillusioned by the fact that Jack didn't come forward to talk to Frank about it man-to-man. That's not how Frank did things. If Frank had a beef with you, you knew it. He didn't send other people to do his dirty work. Frank was very disillusioned where Jack was concerned and, I guess, had to take it out on someone. And that someone was me."

It's always been reported that the primary reason Sinatra cut Lawford from his life was over the Kennedy matter, and certainly Peter suggested as much to this writer. That scenario has always made Sinatra seem a little unhinged, especially added to the oft-told story (which may or may not be true) that Sinatra then went out to the newly built helipad and, in a fit of pique, destroyed it with an ax. But Frank's very close friend and confidant Tony Oppedisano perhaps puts the event in better perspective: "From what he told me, Frank had felt for a long time that the relationship with Peter had become very one-sided," recalled Oppedisano. "He felt that Peter's loyalties didn't run as deep for him as his [Sinatra's] ran for Peter, and this event with Kennedy served to reinforce that in his mind. Loyalty mattered to Frank a great deal. If the tables had been turned, he would have fought like hell for Peter, and he didn't feel that Peter did that for him.

"Also, at this same time, Sinatra was very unhappy about the way Peter was handling Marilyn Monroe," continued Oppedisano. "Frank felt that Marilyn was very fragile and in a lot of trouble at that time with her mental state, the drugs she was taking...all of it. He cared about her a great deal. He also knew Peter was a good friend of hers, and he felt Peter should have been doing more to help her. So there were a lot of things going on at this time. It wasn't as simple as Frank just getting pissed off about the president and then cutting Peter out of his life."

"After the Kennedy snub, Frank dropped Peter from the next two Rat Pack films, *Robin and the 7 Hoods* and *4 for Texas*," recalled Jeanne Martin. "This was so devastating to Peter that it sent him into a deep and awful depression. Peter then took out his frustrations on Pat, feeling that she should have had more influence over her brothers, or at least tried to talk to them about it. But in fact, Pat really had no influence over the situation either. It was completely out of her hands."

From all accounts, Pat Kennedy was the least politically motivated of the Kennedy family, and definitely the least ambitious. In her 1987 book *The Fitzgeralds and the Kennedys*, Doris Kearns Goodwin wrote that Rose Kennedy was bothered by Pat's lack of ambition. "Although she had a good mind, a fine physique and a beautiful face which could easily have led her to excel in school, in sports or in appearance, Rose contended 'she would never make the effort to achieve distinction' in any of these areas." Actually, Pat was the Kennedy sister who, as Jeanne Martin put it, "loved a good time. She was just a regular gal and all the stars loved her—Judy Garland, Jackie Cooper, Lauren Bacall, Humphrey Bogart, Martha Raye, Jimmy Durante. She had her problems, of course. She drank too much. Of course, her marriage didn't make things any easier for her, especially the way she ended up stuck in the middle between Peter and Jack."

The sixth of Joseph and Rose Kennedy's nine children, Patricia Kennedy would grow up privileged, of course, her background including an education in the finest convent schools, with graduation from Rosemont College, a private women's liberal arts school in Pennsylvania. She traveled the world over and, like her siblings, wanted for nothing. Though she probably wouldn't have been thought of as a real beauty, she was striking just the same, with an angular face, red hair, cobalt blue eyes, a sharp nose, and of course that typically full Kennedy smile. Like everyone else in the immediate family, she was also extremely athletic.

Before having her children, Pat had been a television producer. She'd enjoyed her brief time in show business and wished it could have continued, but was instead influenced by the Kennedy women's ethos of duty to family. Any thoughts of career had to take second place to the more practical responsibilities of a mother and wife. Pat met Peter Lawford in 1949 in London and married him six years later. At the time, Pat was two weeks shy of thirty and with a personal family fortune of about $10 million. Peter, at thirty-one, was worth about a tenth of that amount. Most of the Kennedys felt he was nothing but a fortune hunter. Joseph Kennedy certainly did not approve of him; the fact that Peter was Protestant and English didn't help matters. Christopher Lawford, Pat's son, recalls his mother saying that Joe Kennedy sent her on a trip around the world in the hope that she might forget about Peter. "It didn't work," she told her son. "I got to Japan and turned right around."

It took a great deal of courage for Pat to marry Peter considering her father's disapproval of him. Eunice and Jean both married men whom

Joseph sanctioned because they were motivated, financially secure, and stable. However, Peter was much more easygoing and laid-back, not at all competitive—a lot like Pat in that respect. And while he was hopeful that his life as an actor would continue to work out, he didn't seem all that concerned about the chances that it wouldn't. An amiable fellow, Peter was well liked by the family—even if not by Joseph—and especially by President Kennedy. It's fair to say that Peter loved nothing more than being a member of America's royal family, the Kennedys. It quickly became the crux of his identity. He felt that the men in the family— Joseph, Jack, Bobby, Ted, Sargent, and Steve—were so inspiring, he was just proud to be a part of their lives. He took it all very seriously—the campaigns, the camaraderie, the closeness.

"And Pat was crazy about him," explained Jeanne Martin. "She just worshipped the guy, truly." Unfortunately, despite Pat's strong emotion, the marriage was troubled almost from the start. "I don't think Peter was faithful even from the very beginning," said Milt Ebbins. "Then, after he got involved with Sinatra and that group, forget it. His behavior really got out of control. He would be unfaithful to Pat more times than she could count. They had a lot of volatile fights about it. Pat had a temper on her, and Peter gave her plenty of reasons to express it."

"There was a point, around 1963, where she couldn't take it anymore," said one of her closest friends. "I think the difference between Pat and the other women in the family was that Pat just had a lot more anger where the infidelity was concerned. It outraged her in a way it didn't necessarily outrage Jackie or Joan, for instance. She had known that her father had been unfaithful to her mother, and it just upset her that these men got away with it. She was determined to be the one Kennedy woman to do something about it. She was determined to make a statement, so to speak. But it ate away at her, Peter's cheating. I think it's safe to say that she never really forgave him for it. She was tough, though. Pat would put up a front and act as if she was unaffected, but deep down she was very fragile. Her self-esteem was wrecked by his unfaithful behavior and I think she actually never quite recovered."

"Pat told Peter she wanted out of the marriage in 1963," confirmed Milt Ebbins. "Peter and I then went to Jack and sat down with him in the Oval Office to discuss it. The president was truly concerned. He was very sorry that the marriage was ending, but I think he felt it was Pat's fault because I distinctly remember him saying, 'It's okay, Peter, I know my sister better than you do. I understand, believe me.' He asked when it was going to happen and Peter said it was imminent. I said, 'I'm not happy about this. I'm afraid it's going to detract from the [1964] election.' And Jack agreed, saying, 'Maybe you two should wait until after the election.' Peter said he thought he could get Pat to agree to that. Before leaving, Peter said to Jack, 'I sure hope this doesn't mean the end of our friendship.' Jack patted Peter on the shoulder, shook his hand, and said, 'Don't worry, Peter. I promise, I will always be your friend.' When we left, Peter was crying, he was so moved by what Jack had said.

"Then, of course, Jack was murdered shortly after that meeting. Everyone was so devastated, it put the divorce on the back burner for almost two years. However, my memory has it that Peter and Pat weren't living together during that time."

In December 1965, Pat learned that one way to obtain a so-called "quickie divorce" from Peter Lawford was to do it in Sun Valley, Idaho, because there she would only need to establish a six-week residency before filing the necessary papers. Since it was to be the first divorce in the Kennedy family, Jackie felt that Pat would need emotional support so she showed up unannounced in Sun Valley to surprise Pat. One can only imagine Pat's amazement at opening the door to the small home she had rented in Sun Valley to see her famous sister-in-law and her two young children—Caroline and John—standing there, suitcases in hand. And one can also only imagine Jackie's surprise when she found that Ethel and Bobby and their children were already present in support of Pat. Chalking it all up to "crossed signals," Jackie, Ethel, and Pat spent three days together, during which time they solidified their bond as sisters-in-law while Bobby spent the days skiing with the many children—his, Pat's, and Jackie's.

While in Idaho, Jackie revealed that she had first noticed problems in the Lawford marriage all the way back in 1955. "I'm amazed it has lasted this long," she told Pat, who had to agree. "That's a very long time to be so unhappy."

During this time, Peter was involved with a stewardess who worked for an international airline. None of the Kennedy women could believe it. "From what I understand, Jackie kept saying, 'But Pat is so smart and funny, why would Peter end up with a stewardess? What can they possibly have to talk about?' To which Ethel said, 'They're not talking. Believe me.'"

It's interesting that Jackie—and maybe to a lesser extent, Ethel—would be so friendly with Pat. There were arguably a few reasons why the two might have had a problem with her, not the least of which was that Pat had allowed her home on the West Coast to be used by Jack for his assignations with other women. It had been Peter Lawford's idea, and he was probably pressured into it by Frank Sinatra, but still it was Pat's house too. Another reason Jackie and Ethel might have had reservations about Pat was that one of Pat's best friends had been Marilyn Monroe in the later years of the screen star's life. "You're a Kennedy now," Pat told Marilyn at one point in their friendship, which was unusual because Pat and the rest of the Kennedys were usually not very welcoming of outsiders. In fact, when Jack won the Democratic nomination, the Kennedy family was supposed to join him onstage at the convention at the Coliseum in Los Angeles. However, when Peter started to walk on with the rest of them, Pat stopped him. "You're not actually a Kennedy," she told him, "so I don't think it's right." Jack overheard her comment and said of Peter, "He's married to you, so that makes him a Kennedy, don't you think?" She just shrugged. "Besides, he's a good-looking movie star," Jack added with a wink at Peter. "So we can certainly use him up there." Peter had even taken the citizenship test just to become an American so he could cast his vote for JFK, but it didn't much matter to Pat. So for Pat to tell Marilyn Monroe that she was a Kennedy was quite unusual, and for Marilyn to then get involved with Jack (and maybe Bobby) was, as far as Pat was concerned, a bit of a betrayal.

"Pat was torn about it," said Patricia Brennan. "On some level, I think she never really believed that Marilyn, Jack, and Bobby had anything serious going on, but there was a lot of evidence to the contrary. I know that she told Marilyn [on April 8, 1962, at Pat's home in Malibu] that if it were true, she might be able to get past it to continue their friendship, but she seriously doubted that her sisters, Eunice and Jean, and sisters-in-law, Jackie and Ethel, would ever be able to reconcile it."

These kinds of friendships that sometimes crossed lines of propriety may seem odd, but really aren't strange at all if one understands the manner in which the Kennedys customarily compartmentalized their lives. In the end, according to people who knew her at the time, Pat eventually decided that whatever had transpired between her brothers and Marilyn had nothing to do with Jackie or Ethel. And apparently Jackie and Ethel didn't hold any of it against Pat. Adding to the unusual circumstances was that Jackie genuinely liked Peter Lawford too, and sought to maintain her friendship with him, despite the fact that she and Pat were so close. "The interesting thing, at least to me, was that the Kennedy women were so intricately involved with each other's spouses," said Milt Ebbins. "They were very accepting of the men's faults. It was as if none of the men could really do wrong in the eyes of the women, except if you were married to one of them and he was cheating on you. But even then, the other women were accepting. I mean, look: Jackie and Ethel were very close to Ted despite what he was doing to Joan. They were both also very close to Peter despite what was happening to Pat. I always found that so interesting."

Pat would stay behind after all of the Kennedys departed Idaho to ensure her "residency," and the divorce was then granted in January 1966.

True to her nature, Pat tried to make her break from Peter seem painless, though it was actually very difficult for her. The beach estate she and Peter owned on Sorrento Beach in California was an opulent palace that had been key to the lifestyle she had so enjoyed. The poolside parties that Peter hosted at this home at 625 Palisades Beach Road in Malibu (now Pacific Coast Highway) were the stuff of Hollywood legend. Acclaimed lensman Bernie Abramson, whom Peter and Pat considered to be the family's personal photographer, recalled, "Every celebrity in town would come to the Lawfords' for barbecues and cocktail parties—Sinatra, Marilyn, Angie Dickinson, Dean Martin, Judy [Garland]. When Pat and Peter broke up, I don't know who was more upset, the couple themselves or all of the people who loved coming to the house and enjoying themselves there. Pat was always the perfect hostess. Her brother Jack once told me, 'She gets that from Mother [Rose]. Nothing rattles her in a social situation. Whereas Jackie acts cool and collected, secretly she's a bundle of nerves. But Pat, she actually *is* cool and collected.' It was true. I still see her in my mind's eye flitting around the room in one of her colorful caftans, a cocktail in her hand, charming everyone in the room."

All of the frivolity ended, though, when the Lawfords split up. An inside joke among the family was that Pat so thoroughly cleaned out the mansion of all its valuables when she left that Peter had hundreds of five-gallon containers of water delivered to her by truck to New York, along with a note that said, "Pat, you forgot to drain the swimming pool. Peter."

In early 1966, however, Pat was determined to get on with her life, and she moved into a co-op at 990 Fifth Avenue at just about the same time Jackie moved to New York from Washington. (One block away at 950 lived Jean Kennedy Smith and her husband, Stephen, and their family.) "Jackie's children loved Pat and thought she was a hoot," said Jeanne Martin. "So they all became very close. Pat's daughter, Sydney, was Caroline's age and they would both end up going to the same Catholic girls' school together, Sacred Heart in Manhattan. They're still as close as sisters today. Meanwhile, Pat's son, Chris, became one of John's best friends."

The Lawford children always had a live-in nanny, but when the children were older Pat would give the nanny one week off a month so that she could be a full-time mom to them. (She would also turn the clocks ahead an hour so that the kids would go to sleep a little earlier and give her a much-needed break). In fact, Pat wasn't always the greatest mother. Like her sisters Eunice and Jean, she could be remote and distant—a trait all three women inherited from Rose. "After Peter and I had Christopher, Peter was very unhappy because the baby cried all the time and the house smelled like shit," Pat told Jackie at one dinner party in front of others. "So we decided it would be best if little Christopher had his own apartment down the street in Malibu. He was about two months old, actually, maybe a little young for his own place," she said with a grin. "But we rented a very nice apartment for him anyway, and he and the nanny slept there. It was just a lot easier on everyone."

The problem Pat's children faced was that, unlike their cousins, who had their fathers Sargent Shriver and Stephen Smith to turn to for parental affection and validation, Pat's children had no one after Peter Lawford was out of the picture. It would be Pat's only son, Christopher, who would suffer the most. Pat's daughters would somehow survive their troubled adolescences, but Christopher very nearly would not, as he became addicted to alcohol and drugs. Thanks to Joan Kennedy, who took her nephew to his first Alcoholics Anonymous meeting in the mid-1980s, Christopher would eventually be able to clean himself up. He remains sober to this day.

"I guess the paradox was that those kids really were Pat's life," said

Patricia Brennan. "She kept scrapbooks of everything they ever did. She kept every note, every photo. She treasured every moment with them. But there was always something that just kept her from truly connecting with them, and it had to do with Peter. She was so hurt by what she went through with Peter that something in her just clicked off. She wouldn't let anyone in, even her children. She became very protective of her emotions, very guarded, even in her friendships. She was aware of it, too. In fact, she was always a very self-aware person, even if she was emotionally damaged by her circumstances. I think the same could be said of a lot of Kennedy women who had been so very hurt by their unfaithful husbands. I remember Pat once saying, 'Something vital in you dies when you know for a fact that your husband is a cheater. And that thing, whatever it is, can never be brought back to life. I think it's your soul,' she told me. 'I think it kills your soul. At least I think it killed mine.'"

PART SEVEN

Sargent Tries Yet Again

Always in the Way

$\mathcal{D}$espite their utter disappointment about what happened in 1968, Sargent and Eunice Shriver made the very best of their lives in Paris as he began his work as ambassador there and Eunice continued her philanthropy with organizations for the mentally retarded, even starting some of her own charities in France. Of course, the Shrivers would still spend a great deal of time in America, but they worked to make Paris feel like home. As soon as they showed up in Paris, the estate where the ambassador and his family customarily lived was transformed into a mini-Timberlawn. On any given day, one might find mentally handicapped children running all over the place mingling with important diplomats, with Eunice chasing after them and trying to get them into the pool for swimming lessons. Sargent, always good-natured, could only shrug and say, "Welcome to my world." Within a very short time, Sargent and Eunice became a sort of royalty in Paris, attending all of the most important galas, rubbing elbows with the society's crème de la crème— international celebrities and governmental officials—and representing America as only they could. One year, *Paris Match* even named Sargent one of the "Five Most Popular People in France."

It wasn't to last, though. In 1970, Sargent resigned his position as ambassador, due in part to his growing dissatisfaction with President Richard Nixon's politics and his policy on Vietnam that kept the war raging on with seemingly no end in sight. Of course, as soon as Shriver announced his resignation, Democratic leaders began circling to discuss the chances of his running for president in 1972. In what by now seemed like a well-rehearsed script, the Kennedys quickly began spreading the word that if Shriver did in fact run, it would appear to them—and to their constituents—that he was taking advantage of Ted Kennedy's recent scandal at Chappaquiddick. "It never ends," a frustrated Eunice said at the time to a friend of many years. "There is always going to be some reason Sarge shouldn't run. I am just so tired of it."

"It had gotten to the point where Sargent and Eunice didn't even feel comfortable at the Kennedy compound," Senator George Smathers would recall. "Whenever they were present, there always seemed to be contention about one statement or another Sargent had made in some speech that might have telegraphed his interest in running in 1972. Ted hadn't made up his mind about whether or not he was interested in a '72 campaign. In fact, he was still sure that there was no way America would allow him to forget Chappaquiddick long enough for him to run a successful campaign. However, he wanted to keep the option open, just as he wished to keep it open for '76, too. In other words, Sargent Shriver was still in the way."

"I think Ted and some others might have liked it if Shriver just got out of politics altogether, to be candid," said Pierre Salinger. "His presence being an issue every four years had begun to cause serious problems in the family." In fact, Eunice and Ethel weren't even on speaking terms for much of 1971 because Eunice was convinced that Ethel still harbored a resentment against her husband and was working behind the scenes to help orchestrate a campaign against him within the family.

"Another issue was that Sarge had a lot of unanswered questions about Chappaquiddick," said someone who knew him very well. "He felt that Ted got away with something there and maybe he should have had just a little more humility going forward. He said to me, 'The fact that he didn't go to the very first house with lights on and say, "Jesus Christ! A girl is drowning, come and help me," is very suspicious to me. It looks like he was just trying to save his skin. I just think he could be a more gracious person considering how lucky he was to get out of that mess.'"

In the end, Sarge felt the whole Chappaquiddick matter was badly handled, anyway. He thought that the arrival of all the Kennedy acolytes, of which he wasn't one, to the compound was a terrible idea that "over-dramatized the matter," as he put it. If it were him, he said—not that he ever would have found himself in such a jam—he would have sat down in the privacy of his study, come to terms with what happened, prayed about how to proceed, and then he would have written a heartfelt speech himself. He would have then delivered it to the American public in as sincere a manner as possible. "The fact that he had to have all those people writing that speech for him, I think that was insane," he later said. "I just don't understand that." Making matters worse, as far as Sarge was concerned, was that a few weeks after the Chappaquiddick accident, Ted flew to Paris to visit with his sister Eunice at the ambassador's residence. "Was

he the least bit contrite, or humble, or sad or apologetic or *anything?*"
Sarge asked. "No. He drank the whole time, was drunk and disruptive."
As it happened, the Shrivers had another visitor at the same time, Herbert Kramer, a publicist and speechwriter with whom they were working
on a Special Olympics project. Eunice and Sarge were embarrassed by
Ted's behavior in front of Kramer. "Here we had a man Ted didn't even
know who was a guest in our home, and Ted was treating the place like
a big frat pad. I swear I wanted to punch his lights out," Sarge said to his
friend. He was definitely not a big fan of Ted Kennedy at this time.

Sargent now felt that he needed some time away from the political
arena—and away from the Kennedy family too—which is why he decided
to go into private law practice in 1971 with the large corporate firm of
Strasser, Spiegelberg, Fried, Frank & Kampelman (which, with the addition of Shriver to its ranks and the subtraction of a few others, became
Fried, Frank, Harris, Shriver & Jacobson). While he was with the firm,
Shriver's biggest client was the billionaire financier Armand Hammer.
Still, politics was in Shriver's blood and he couldn't deny it. "I felt that he
wasn't in his element," said one of the attorneys who worked with Shriver
at the firm. "I had known Sarge for a number of years. He'd always had
a glint in his eye, but I noticed it was gone when he was with the firm.
'I feel that God has a bigger mission in mind for me than what I can do
here,' he told me one day. 'I'm a public servant. That's who I am. I have to
get back to it or I'm not going to be happy.' He said that Eunice was fine
with him being out of politics, though. 'It has put her in a bad position
with her family for such a long time, I can't blame her for wanting a break
from it,' he told me. 'But she's a tough bird,' he added. 'Can you imagine her as First Lady?' he asked, laughing. 'The entire country would be
volunteering for one thing or another, or she'd be at their doors dragging
them out of bed in the morning!'"

As it would happen, Sargent Shriver would get his moment in the sun
in 1972. That was the year the Democratic presidential ticket—George
McGovern and Thomas Eagleton—would self-destruct with the revelation that Eagleton had battled manic depression for much of his life,
had been hospitalized for it, and had even undergone electroshock treatments. He had to drop out of the race. It was then that the party turned
to Sargent Shriver.

Of course some felt that Ted, as the last remaining Kennedy brother, should have been the logical choice to head the ticket. But he opted out of the primary process, saddled as he was with the negative fallout from Chappaquiddick. His absence left the field wide open for McGovern at the Democratic convention. Though he was an effective politician in the halls of Congress and on the floor of the Senate, McGovern was a dour, colorless candidate. He needed that ol' Kennedy magic, that much was certain. Therefore, he was relentless in his pursuit of Ted to join the ticket as his running mate when he had to get rid of Eagleton. In rejecting the offer, Ted insisted he still needed "breathing room" to gain more experience, and also to help raise his murdered brothers' children. He didn't publicly cite memories of Chappaquiddick as being an issue, but privately he said he believed Americans had still not gotten over any of it. George McGovern knew he needed a spark for his uphill run for the White House, but the truth was that pretty much no one of merit wanted to be on the ticket with him—five politicians had already turned him down. When Sargent Shriver's name was floated as a possibility, it certainly seemed valid, but as it happened, the main reason he ended up on the ticket was because he was one of the only people who'd been approached who would agree to do it.

From the start, it seemed like a bad idea to those who truly cared about Sargent Shriver. The ticket was such a hopeless cause, no one could understand why he would ever want to hitch himself to its wagon. Still, it was his decision to do so.

Now, as ever, the question remained: What would Senator Ted Kennedy do? And how would the Kennedy family work for—or against—Sargent Shriver?

Shriver for Vice President

*E*unice Kennedy Shriver had to admit to some ambivalence about Sargent's decision to join the McGovern ticket as vice president. Yes, it was his time; as far as she was concerned, it had been his time for many years. But was this particular race worthy of him? It was all so troubled and hopeless-seeming, she wasn't certain he should even be involved in it. In fact, she felt just barely inspired enough by it to appeal to Ted to please stay out of Sargent's way this time. In her meeting with Ted about the matter at his home in Boston, Ted nonchalantly said, "Okay, fine. I've got no problem with it, in fact. Tell Sarge he has my blessing." Though Eunice said she appreciated Ted's approval, in truth it must have felt like a bit of a hollow victory. *Of course* Ted had "no problem with it." He and just about every Kennedy loyalist was certain that George McGovern would lose the race anyway, so what did they care? In fact, if that happened, it could very well not only taint Shriver in '72 but make him "damaged goods" for '76, too—and all the better for Ted. Therefore, in a very real sense, Ted was getting exactly what he always wanted—which was, at long last, Sargent Shriver finally out of the way. "It felt unfair," said Eunice's former assistant. "Not surprisingly, considering her loyalty to the senator, we also learned that Ethel Kennedy felt the same way about Sargent's running— her feeling being, sure, why not? Suddenly, both key Kennedys were okay with Mr. Shriver in a campaign? And then we also heard that Kennedy advisers [Kenny] O'Donnell, [Ted] Sorensen, and the rest had also said, fine, no problem, lotsa luck. It was all so transparent."

While it may have seemed a bad decision to some observers, Sargent Shriver had his own reasons for wanting to join the Democratic ticket that year. First of all, he was as much a loyalist as he was an idealist. He could see very clearly the Democratic Party going down in flames, and he didn't want that to happen. He believed his party needed him, and anytime Shriver was truly needed he wanted to be of assistance. Also, he reasoned that perhaps his party would repay his loyalty in 1976 and might see fit to nominate him that year on his own merits—and that, if so, maybe the "Kennedy factor" wouldn't then matter as much. Moreover, he felt that by entering the race he could prove himself to be a strong campaigner, and that the reputation he built in 1972 might work to his political advantage in 1976. He felt he needed more visibility among his constituents, never having held elective office before, and that the campaign with McGovern might assist him in that regard. Moreover, he actually thought it possible that McGovern could win. Yes, the poll numbers were weak and the press had been terrible. Yet stranger things had happened in politics, he reasoned, and besides, there were three months left before the election. That could be time enough to galvanize the support the ticket needed. "He wasn't so naive as to think that Ted Kennedy's approval was based on anything other than Ted believing Shriver was going to go down in defeat, but it was an approval just the same," observed Senator George Smathers. "So he wanted to run with it."

And so it was that Sargent Shriver and his impeccable, blue-ribbon credentials as a social activist entered the presidential campaign in 1972 hoping that he might be elected to the second highest office in the land—the office which Adlai Stevenson first described in 1952 (referring to Richard Nixon) as "being just a heartbeat away from the presidency." After the official nomination, Shriver's acceptance speech was filled with the kind of optimism and dynamism that had characterized his personality for years, not to mention the humor. "I am not embarrassed to be George McGovern's seventh choice for vice president," he said. "We Democrats might be short on money, but we're not short on talent. Ted Kennedy, Ed Muskie, Hubert Humphrey, Abe Ribicoff, Tom Eagleton— what a galaxy of stars. Pity Mr. Nixon—his first and only choice was Spiro Agnew." Sargent also couldn't resist cracking a joke about Ted Kennedy, who was sitting nearby. "Look at him with that pensive look," Shriver cracked. "The great Ted Kennedy. I wonder what he's thinking about." A lot of other people wondered, too, especially when promises of campaign funding from the Kennedys did not come through as expected. The ticket was in serious financial straits from the very beginning, and it was clear that the Kennedys were not going to help at all.

In retrospect, it would seem that George McGovern's campaign was pretty much doomed the moment he flip-flopped on Eagleton. "One day he was for him '1,000 percent'—even in light of the revelations about him—and five days later, Eagleton was out," Hugh Sidey recalled. "It made McGovern look as if he didn't know what he was doing—and why hadn't he more thoroughly checked out Eagleton's past history, anyway? It was a sore subject that colored the entire campaign."

Of course, there were other significant problems too, not the least of which was just a general sense of disorganization in the ticket. Sargent Shriver was a multitasker—long before that term became part of the pop culture vernacular—who never knew how to prioritize his schedule, and no one who worked for him was able to assist him in that regard. "He was hard to manage," said Donald Dell, who worked for the campaign in its earlier days, maintaining the schedule of events. "He was a wonderful man who wanted to do good things and be all things to all people, and that kind of politician is difficult to control. I could never get him where he needed to be because he was always off doing something else he felt important. I used to say, if we had ten Sargents, that would work. But one is not enough. There was constant disarray.

"Besides a matter of finances and scheduling, there was a huge controversy over whether or not Nixon had blown the Paris peace talks," continued Dell, "which pitted Sarge against Nixon in a very acrimonious way. Sarge said a lot of unkind things about Nixon, suggesting in speeches that he was a crook, a liar, and worse. Nixon retaliated by trying to undermine Sarge's reputation and his knowledge of the peace talks. It seems hard to believe now, but at the time Nixon was popular. People tended to believe him.

"Then there was the matter of Eagleton, which never went away and which was always at issue and in need of a response from Sarge. It was very distracting and kept pointing to McGovern's lack of common sense and lack of judgment. In short, it did not go well for Sarge out there on the campaign trail, though he did get the public recognition that I think he wanted."

Still, though most polls predicted that the Democrats would go down in the worst defeat in modern American politics, there was Sargent Shriver on the front lines, always believing there to be an upswing in support of the McGovern-Shriver ticket. "You just can't predict these things," he said at the time. "You have to roll with the punches." With his patrician mien, outfitted in banker's tailoring, Sarge was a tireless spokesman for a renewed liberalism, his charisma and Kennedy-like demeanor hard to resist. Newspaper columnist Mary McGrory assessed it this way: "To rouse his audience, he does everything but administer open-heart massage." Meanwhile McGovern, downbeat and dispirited, failed to galvanize much support during the three-month campaign. Stanley Karnow of the *Washington Post* noted, "Although there is nothing less prestigious than running for the vice presidency on a weak team, Sargent Shriver is probably the most sparkling of the four candidates on the electoral race. In contrast to George McGovern, whose nasal piety borders on the self-righteous, Shriver exudes a natural sense of humor that seems to suggest that he considers the election is a game even if he is playing to win."

Also playing to win was Eunice. She had finally decided that she would give her all to the campaign, and once she made that decision there was no stopping her. Not only did she make campaign forays on her own, but she and Sarge as a team spent fifteen-hour days crisscrossing the campaign trail in search of voters for the McGovern-Shriver ticket. "She was a force of nature out there," said Doris Kearns Goodwin, the Pulitzer Prize–winning writer and presidential historian who worked in a public relations capacity for the Shriver team. "There was nothing she would not do, knocking on doors, handing out flyers, speaking to a small group of women, shaking hands with factory workers...she would do it all with that characteristic Kennedy flair and so much energy you wondered where it all came from."

Frustrating for Eunice, though, was the ever-lackadaisical support from the rest of the Kennedy family. Of course, they made some obligatory appearances—Ted and Joan, Rose and even Ethel—but they seemed halfhearted. There wasn't much sparkle from any of them, especially not from Ethel, and Eunice felt the strong sting of their rejection. She didn't focus on it, though. There was a lot to do and she wanted to do it all, as always. But she was very unhappy with the family, especially given all that Sarge had done for them in the past. It was disappointing,

The strongest family support the Shrivers received was from Jackie and Aristotle Onassis, who donated a large sum of money to the campaign. This was a surprise, because Eunice and Sarge hadn't had much patience for Jackie's relationship with Ari. However, in recent months, Eunice and Jackie had begun speaking about it and Eunice had apologized for having been so chilly. It was as if she now more fully understood what it was like to be on the outside looking in, and she wanted to make amends to Jackie and Ari. In return, Jackie made a number of appearances for Shriver and spoke well of him every chance she got. Characteristically, Shriver sent her and Ari a note a week after the election in 1972 to show his appreciation: "Both Eunice and I are grateful for all your encouragement and support during these past months and it gives us comfort to know you're thinking of us now." As a postscript, Shriver added, "Jackie, you were so solicitous and sensitive to my situation that I must add a note of special thanks."

The loss was a big one, in fact, maybe even bigger than expected. Friends, business associates, and dozens of others came together at Timberlawn to watch the poll results, which from the beginning Eunice knew would be shattering. "This will be a hell of a night," she said. "The first time a Kennedy loses an election." In the end, Richard Nixon and Spiro Agnew would go on to win the election by an overwhelming majority. Nixon won 60 percent of the popular vote and 520 electoral votes to McGovern's 17. Unbelievably, Nixon carried forty-nine of the fifty states, with only Massachusetts coming through for McGovern-Shriver. It was difficult to imagine a bigger defeat in any major election. "Well, we did our best," Sargent Shriver said that night. "We didn't have the support I had hoped for, I must admit. But you can't take these things personally. You give it your best shot. That's all you can do. That's what Eunice and I did."

"Same Ol' Sarge"

*T*hough he put on a brave face in public, privately Sargent Shriver was crushed by his recent loss. It would take him years to get over it, if he ever actually did. It wasn't so much the election. That was politics and he understood it was all a game anyway—a high-stakes one, true, but a game just the same. What really bothered him was the way the Kennedys, and especially his brother-in-law Ted, had let him down. A friend of some years' standing tells the story of a meeting he had with Sargent about a month after the election. The two were at the Kennedy compound, in the living room of the Big House. "I don't feel very much at home here these days," Sargent said, according to his friend's account of the conversation. "I try to be above it, but I admit, I'm pretty pissed off."

"Hey! You have a right to be pissed off," his friend told him. "Look, they screwed you over, Sarge. That's clear."

Shriver nodded. "But I'm trying to rise above it," he said. "It's my wife's family. What the hell can I do?"

"You can be pissed, that's what you can do," his friend said. "Why take the high road all the time, Sarge? It's never done you any good in this goddamn society of Kennedys."

"I know," Sargent agreed. "But I have a responsibility to my kids to handle this thing the right way."

The two men smiled at one another. "Same ol' Sarge," his friend said.

A rare photo of the Kennedys celebrating family patriarch Joseph's birthday, at his and Rose's home in the Kennedy compound. Left to right: Sargent Shriver, Steven Smith, Ethel Kennedy, John Fitzgerald Kennedy, Jean Kennedy Smith, Rose Kennedy, Robert Kennedy, Eunice Kennedy Shriver, Pat Kennedy Lawford, Ted Kennedy, and Joan Kennedy. Jackie Kennedy kneels next to Joseph Kennedy, who is showing the effects of a recent stroke. He turned seventy-four on September 6, 1962. (*Courtesy John Fitzgerald Kennedy Library, Boston*)

A family party at Rose's and Joseph's. Left to right: Joan Kennedy, Eunice Kennedy Shriver, Jackie Kennedy, Ethel Kennedy, Jean Kennedy, Ted Kennedy, Robert Kennedy, John Kennedy, and Steven Smith. (*Courtesy John Fitzgerald Kennedy Library, Boston*)

President John F. Kennedy drives some of his nieces and nephews in a golf cart through the Kennedy compound in September of 1962. Ted Kennedy once observed of this younger generation, "Even before they had a chance to make important achievements and accomplishments in their lives, they have been public figures." (*Robert Knudson, White House/John F. Kennedy Presidential Library and Museum, Boston*)

President Kennedy and Jackie with John Jr., Caroline, and the family pets in Hyannis Port, August 1963, just three months before the President's death. "I should have known that it was asking too much to dream that I might have grown old with him and see our children grow up together," Jackie would observe. (*Cecil Stoughton, White House/John Fitzgerald Kennedy Library, Boston*)

Ethel and Bobby Kennedy with six of their children. Left to right: Joseph, Courtney, Kathleen, Robert Jr., Michael (on Bobby's lap), and David. "Oh, how he would have loved seeing what his kids would become," Ethel would say of Bobby. *(Ed Clark/Time Life Pictures/Getty Images)*

Ted and Joan Kennedy with two of their children, Kara (left) and Ted Jr., at home in November 1962. *(John Loengard/Time Life Pictures/Getty Images)*

Peter and Pat Kennedy Lawford with their children, Christopher, three, and Sydney, eight months. "I remember smiling for cameras long before I could talk," Christopher once recalled. (*J.R. Eyerman/Time Life Pictures/Getty Images*)

Jean and Stephen Smith with their sons, William (in her lap) and Stephen Jr., in January 1961. (*Walter Bennett/Time & Life Pictures/Getty Images*)

Eunice and Sargent Shriver with their children, Robert, Maria, and Timothy, kneeling in prayer at President Kennedy's grave site on the first anniversary of his death, November 1964. *(Lee Lockwood/Time Life Pictures/Getty Images)*

For many years, Sargent Shriver would have a complex and often baffling relationship with his brother-in-law Ted Kennedy (both seen here on June 2, 1966). Kennedy and his advisers continually stymied Shriver's political aspirations and perhaps even prevented him from one day becoming president. *(John Fitzgerald Kennedy Library, Boston)*

Eunice Kennedy Shriver, playing ball in 1969 with a mentally handicapped child in Paris, where her husband, Sargent, served as ambassador to France. As founder of the Special Olympics, Eunice made her life's work the understanding and treatment of those with mental retardation. *(Liaison)*

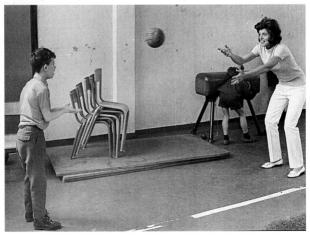

Though Jackie outraged much of the world when she married Aristotle Onassis, the Kennedy family generally approved of her second husband. He was actually quite hard to resist. The two are seen celebrating Jackie's fortieth birthday in July 1969 in Athens, Greece. *(SCU Archives/Everett Collection/Rex Features)*

Jackie, the architect Edward Larrabee Barnes, and Rose attend a performance of *Forty Carats* on Broadway, May 21, 1969. That night, Jackie told Rose that should anything happen to her, she wanted her children, John Jr. and Caroline, to be raised as Kennedys. She did not want them to be adopted by Onassis. *(Pictorial Parade/Getty Images)*

After Bobby's death, Ethel turned for comfort and companionship to singer Andy Williams, seen here at the Kennedy Center for the Performing Arts Gala Preview on May 22, 1971. Because of her loyalty to Bobby's memory, Ethel would never allow herself to become romantically involved with any other man. "My love for Bobby is eternal," she told Andy. *(Ron Galella, Ltd./Wire Image)*

No one could ever question Ted Kennedy's loyalty and devotion to his children. When Teddy Jr. was diagnosed with cancer and had to have his leg amputated, his father was his greatest support. Father and son are seen together at the Joseph Kennedy Foundation's International Symposium at the Kennedy Center, October 16, 1971. (*Ron Galella/Wire Image*)

Jackie at Bobby Kennedy's grave at Arlington National Cemetery on June 6, 1972, the fourth anniversary of his murder. Despite the passing of years and her marriage to Aristotle Onassis, she remained shattered by the assassinations of her husband and brother-in-law. (*Retro Photo*)

Newly widowed after Onassis's death in March of 1975, Jackie made it a point to remain an active part of the Kennedy family. She, Ted, and Ethel attended the Robert F. Kennedy Pro-Celebrity Tennis Tournament at New York's Forest Hills Stadium on August 23, 1975. *(Ron Galella/Wire Image)*

On June 12, 1977, the family came together at the groundbreaking ceremony for the John F. Kennedy Presidential Library and Museum in Boston. From left to right: Rose Kennedy, Jean Kennedy Smith, John Kennedy Jr., Caroline Kennedy, Jackie Kennedy, and Pat Kennedy Lawford. *(Allan Goodrich, John F. Kennedy Library, Boston)*

"Yeah," Sargent said with a resigned smile. "Same ol' Sarge." A few moments later, he smiled sadly and concluded, "Funny thing is, I like Teddy. I respect him. I always have. Which just makes the whole goddamn thing worse."

His friend had to agree. "Think you might try again one day?" he asked

Shriver laughed heartily. "Hell no," he said. But then, after a beat, he added with a chuckle, "Well...maybe."

Though Sargent Shriver tried to protect his children from the disappointment, there was no way around their feelings about what had happened. "My experience with politics was one of loss," Maria Shriver would say many years later. "My father lost his vice presidential bid on the McGovern-Shriver ticket in 1972. The rejection of my father was so painful, so personal; I remember the sting of that defeat....People who said they would support him didn't. I'd learned early on that political life was about constant travel and being surrounded by fifty people in the house, and either you lose or you get assassinated. So I wanted nothing to do with that."

Of course, Maria would have to have a change of heart about her interest in politics when her husband, Arnold Schwarzenegger, told her he wanted to run for governor of California in 2003. Before she knew it, he won and she was the Democratic First Lady of a Republican administration.

Or, as her father used to say, "You just can't predict these things. You have to roll with the punches."

PART EIGHT

The Third Generation in Trouble

An Accident Results in Paralysis

It was August 13, 1973. Ethel and Jean Kennedy along with three Kennedy employees—including Rose Kennedy's secretary, Barbara Gibson—were standing in the lobby of Cape Cod Hospital. Pacing nervously, Ethel seemed out of breath and in great distress, as if she were having a panic attack. "I demand to see my sons," she said to a nurse who happened to be walking by her. She grabbed the nurse by her elbow and held on tightly. Startled, the nurse looked to Jean Kennedy for assistance. "Why are you standing there looking at me?" Jean demanded to know, also seeming very anxious. "We've been standing out here for an hour and no one has said a single word to us about anything." When the nurse told the Kennedy women that a doctor would be seeing them soon, Ethel sighed heavily and collapsed into a nearby chair. "As you can see, Mrs. Kennedy is very upset," Jean said, motioning to Ethel. Then, to Barbara Gibson, she said, "Call my husband [Stephen Smith] and ask him to meet us here as soon as he can get here. Tell him that David and Joe have been in a car accident and we need him here." As Gibson walked to a pay phone, she heard Ethel say, "I don't know what these kids have done now, Jean. And I'm afraid to find out."

Another hour passed. Finally, Stephen Smith arrived. "I'll take care of it," he told Eunice and Ethel. "You two wait here. I'm going back there." When a nurse looked as if she might try to block Smith from going beyond a door that was marked "Staff Only," he said, "I am staff. I'm Kennedy staff. And I'm going back there, so it's probably best that you don't try to stop me." The nurse let him pass. Within fifteen minutes, Stephen Smith brought a doctor out to meet with Ethel and Jean, and he had Joe with him. Ethel jumped out of her chair and wrapped her arms around her son. "Thank God," she exclaimed. After a beat, she backed away from him and closely studied his face. Then she hauled off and smacked him on the shoulder with her open hand. "Where's David?" she demanded. "And what happened? You tell me this instant what happened," she said.

Joe seemed pale and shaken. It had been just a day since he and Ethel and Ted had sat down and had a heart-to-heart about his responsibility as a Kennedy. He was the heir apparent to the Kennedy dynasty and Ethel and Ted wanted to remind him to be careful, to "make the right decisions," as Ted had said. "The other boys are looking up at you for example," Ted reminded him, "especially David. And we just want you to be aware." And now, only twenty-four hours later, he found himself in a hospital at a loss as to how to explain to his mother how he and David had ended up there. "It's my fault," he said. "David's here because of me, Mom. It's because of me."

Here's the story Joe Kennedy told his mother:

On Sunday, August 12, Joe—who was now twenty-one—invited David, eighteen, and his girlfriend at the time, Pam Kelley, nineteen, to a barbecue with some other friends at Nantucket. The brothers and their friends spent the day sailing, and then that night enjoyed a barbecue on the beach. The next morning, Monday, everyone went swimming before their intended trip back to Hyannis Port. Joe borrowed a friend's Jeep to drive David and Pam back to the jetty. "I guess I was driving too fast," Joe told his mom and his aunt and uncle, his voice quivering. "And on the way back in the Jeep, it somehow turned over and everyone sort of spilled out of it."

"What do you mean, you *guess* you were driving too fast?" Ethel demanded to know.

"Okay," Joe conceded, "I was driving too fast, Mom."

Ethel just shook her head angrily. She was holding her rosary beads and gripping them so tightly that her knuckles had become white.

"And now everyone's hurt except me," Joe said. "I don't know what else to say."

Ethel looked at her son with cold eyes. The suspicion on her face indicated that she knew there was more to the story. However, she decided to let it go. Now she just wanted to see David. When a doctor finally took her, Jean and Stephen Smith, and the others to David's room, it was very difficult for her. Lying in bed in a traction device, David appeared to be paralyzed. Barely able to move his head, he just stared straight up at the ceiling when the small contingent came into his room. Ethel went to his bedside and held his arm, Jean standing behind her with her hand on her sister-in-law's shoulder. Barbara Gibson was also present. "Whatever happened," Ethel finally told David, according to Gibson's memory of these events, "it doesn't matter. As long as you're okay." As David looked up at his mother, a single tear fell onto his pillow. "I'm sorry, Mom," he said. Ethel nodded. "I know you are." At that moment, according to Gibson, Stephen Smith said, "I should call Ted." Joe smiled. "Yeah! Uncle Teddy can get us out of this mess," he said happily. Ethel just glared at him. Meanwhile, Smith left the room and went to a pay phone in the hallway. As she later walked by him, Barbara Gibson heard Steve speaking on the telephone to someone she believed to be Ted Kennedy: "It's not good," Smith said. "I think we have a real problem on our hands here, Ted. These kids are out of control. We have a lot to consider in terms of how this thing is going to play out in the court of public opinion." In that moment, Smith saw Gibson standing in the hallway. He glared at her and said, "Whatever it is that's your job for my mother-in-law, I suggest you do it. Now!"

Of course, there was much more to the story than what Joe had told, as his mother had suspected. As it happened, there were five girls in the car with Joe and David, including David's girlfriend, Pam. "It was Kennedy horseplay, of course," Pam Kelley would say many decades later. "We were all laughing and screaming and having a good time as Joe spun the Jeep 'round and 'round and 'round. And at one point, someone said something about going to a rest area across the street. Joe turned the car around and headed over to that spot at a fast speed. He didn't notice a station wagon coming down the street. When he finally did, he steered hard to avoid it. He swerved. We hit a ditch. That's when the Jeep started flipping over and over. I remember David and I holding on to the roll bar to keep from flying out of the vehicle, and I can still in my mind's eye see David's face as we were forced to let go of the Jeep and start tumbling out of it. That's the last thing I remember, David's face. I hit the ground real hard. Then I tried to get up. But I couldn't. I couldn't move."

Pam and another of the girls were hospitalized in serious condition, while the other three young women were all treated and released. David's injuries included a severely sprained back, but Pam's spinal injuries were much more serious. After a three-hour operation, it was clear that she would be paralyzed. Tragically, she would spend the rest of her life in a wheelchair. To think that a girl had been paralyzed for life as a result of her son's reckless driving was very difficult for Ethel to accept. "My own boys are responsible for this," she said at the time, "which makes me responsible."

Joe was inconsolable that the accident had resulted in permanent paralysis for a girl he barely knew. It caused a rift between him and David that would take years to heal—and in truth, things were never quite the same between them again. "He would visit me every day," Pam Kelley recalled of David. "Ethel would come too, almost every day. She would try to cheer me up, bringing presents, and act optimistic. My impression of her at that time was that she couldn't deal with any more upsetting news, so she was just cheery, cheery, *cheery*. David hated that about her. 'She just can't be real,' he told me, 'or she'll fall apart. And she can't fall apart because she's Ethel Kennedy and Ethel Kennedy can never fall apart. It's a vicious cycle.'"

One day, Ethel and Ted brought Rose Kennedy to the hospital to see Pam. On this day, Ethel couldn't seem to force herself to be jovial. She stood against a wall in the room and looked somewhat stricken as Rose and Ted spoke to Pam. Eventually, Ted pulled up a chair to the bed so that his mother could sit down next to the patient. Ted stood behind Rose, his hands resting on her slim shoulders. "You know, sometimes things happen in life that we can't predict or understand," Rose said. "In my own life, I have seen so much tragedy. But take it from me," she said, smiling gently at Pam. "God does not make mistakes," she added, looking upward. "We have to accept that He knows what He is doing, and we have to go on. In my heart," she concluded, "I don't believe He will give us more than we can take."

After they chatted for about thirty more minutes, Ted helped his mother out of the chair and said it was time for them to take their leave. Rose kissed Pam on the forehead. She then pulled a rosary out of her purse and placed it on the girl's chest. "This is for you," she said. "This will give you strength." Rose was then helped from the room by Ted.

After the two left, Ethel approached Pam and put her hand on her shoulder. "I just want you to know that I am praying for you," she said. The girl looked up at her and nodded. Ethel then reached out and touched the rosary. After holding the crucifix in her fingers for a few moments, she nodded and smiled sadly at Pam. "God bless you," she said. She then turned around and walked out of the room, seeming very much older than her forty-four years. Obviously, all of this misfortune was hard on Ethel. Years later, one of her personal assistants, Noelle Bombardier, would recall, "She could be very guarded and you wouldn't see a lot of emotion.

Sometimes, though, I'd find her alone by the pool, crying. She'd stop as soon as she realized someone else was there."

"Uncle Teddy didn't go to jail after Chappaquiddick, and that was a lot worse than this. So I don't think you have to worry too much," David Kennedy told his brother Joe on the day Joe had to face a judge. "I sure hope you're right," was Joe's response. In fact, the Nantucket Police Department would only charge Joe Kennedy with negligent driving. He could—and some observers felt should—have gotten two years in jail, especially considering what had happened to Pam Kelley. Instead, he was just given probation and a $100 fine.

"You had a great father and you have a great mother," the judge told him. "Use your illustrious name as an asset instead of coming into court like this." There was a strong sense that the Kennedy name had leveraged Joe out of a tight scrape, a theory strengthened when it was learned that the judge had been a friend of his grandfather Joseph's.

By autumn, David Kennedy and Pam Kelley had ended their relationship.

Today, Pam Kelley is a divorced mother who works as executive director of the Cape Organization for Rights of the Disabled (CORD) earning $57,000 a year. Though there would always be stories of a huge settlement with her from the Kennedys, in fact not a lot of money was offered, or taken. When she received $688,000 from Joe Kennedy's insurance policy back in the 1970s, she was satisfied with the sum and told a reporter, "There's no way I'd be able to spend that money if I lived to be 102." But of course, that wasn't the case. Years later, her brother, Jim, explained, "Since she was a minor, her father became trustee of the small fortune. Within about four years he had managed to turn it to zero dollars. She was broke.

"During the first couple years following her accident, Pam fought with depression, drugs, and alcohol," Jim Kelley, said. "Through her own tenacity and force of will she overcame those demons and worked her way to become director of CORD. She was married for a while and out of that she has a daughter. She has had to work hard for everything she had accomplished and then work even harder to retain it. If I had to pick a person I most admire for their courage in the face of adversity, I would certainly pick Pam."

Over the years, Pam Kelley would continue a friendly relationship

with Joe Kennedy, who would sometimes call to see if she needed anything; if so, he would do what he could to provide it to her. She's said that
he's given her about $50,000 over a thirty-year period.* Sometimes the
two would be on good terms, other times not as much. "I feel like he
thinks I'm a piece of trash sitting in a wheelchair," Kelley told the *Boston
Herald* in 2005, obviously during a period when she was not happy with
him. In response, Joe said, "I have a very strong sense of responsibility for
Pam and her circumstances. I have helped Pam many, many times over
the years, and Pam knows I will continue to do so in the future."

David Kennedy was in the hospital for just eight days, but those would
be days that would change him forever. During that time, he was treated
with morphine, which, as it would turn out, was the worst possible drug
for him. David's hospitalization after the accident would mark the beginning of a slow and terrible decline for him into serious drug abuse. "Taking morphine, that's when I really felt for the first time that things were
okay in my life," he would recall years later. "The morphine, man, it was
the thing that made me forget how miserable I had been since Dad died.
It was the thing that made me forget my pain." In the weeks to come,
when David would visit Pam in the hospital, he would fake back seizures
just so that he could get another dose of morphine.

"This was the beginning of the end for David Kennedy," Christopher Lawford would say many years later. "I don't think he was ever the
same after the accident. Things would go from bad to very bad to worse
in a very short time. The years after the accident were the worst years,
by far."

---

* Today, Pam Kelley receives $2,004 a month from Joseph Kennedy in a settlement that
will last until the year 2016 and that includes a confidentiality clause. After many pre-
liminary discussions with her, it was decided not to interview her for this book in order
to honor her settlement agreement. Her quotes in these chapters were taken from previous interviews she has given about what happened to her in 1973.

November 1973: Ten Years

*I*t's all just so unfair," Ethel Kennedy said to Jackie Kennedy Onassis while holding both of her hands.

It was November 1973, ten years since the assassination of President Kennedy. Tributes and other memorials to the president had come in across all the media, forcing the Kennedys to once again relive one of the family's most catastrophic days. To commemorate the sad anniversary, Ethel hosted a memorial Mass in the large Pool House at Hickory Hill, attended by most of the Kennedys, including, of course, Jackie.

Ethel and Jackie usually didn't spend a lot of time commiserating about their sadness. They had both tried to move on with their lives, Jackie being more successful at it than Ethel. However, gatherings for the anniversaries of Jack's and Bobby's deaths couldn't help but bring to the fore the widows' mutual anguish.

"Just look at us," Ethel said, weeping. "We're all wrecks, Jackie, and we'll never get over it." She and the former First Lady were in the company of Ethel's personal assistant, Noelle Bombardier, who'd just recently been hired, and a host of Kennedy relatives.

"Oh God," Jackie exclaimed, now swept away by emotion and also crying. "Nothing could be worse than this, could it? Could it get any worse?"

"It's all so senseless," Ethel agreed. "It didn't have to happen, Jackie. It just didn't have to happen."

As the two women embraced, everyone around them stared, moved and speechless.

What could anyone say?

Ted Jr.'s Cancer

*A*t the time of the ten-year anniversary of President Kennedy's death, the country was being shaken to its core by Watergate, which would result in the resignation of President Richard M. Nixon. Soon, Nixon would refuse to hand over tape recordings and documents subpoenaed by the Senate Watergate Committee. Then an Advisory Panel on White House Tapes would determine that an eighteen-minute gap in Watergate tape was due to erasure and of no consequence. Later, in March 1974, a grand jury in Washington, D.C., would conclude that Nixon had indeed been involved in the Watergate cover-up. Seven people, including former Nixon White House aides H. R. Haldeman and John D. Ehrlichman, former attorney general John Mitchell, and former assistant attorney general Robert Mardian would be indicted on charges of conspiring to obstruct justice in connection with the Watergate break-in. They would be convicted the following January, although Mardian's conviction would later be reversed. (In 2005, *Vanity Fair* revealed that W. Mark Felt, ninety-one, a former FBI official, was the Watergate whistle-blower Deep Throat who helped bring down President Nixon.)

In Ted and Joan Kennedy's home in McLean, Virginia, a more personal emotional drama was unfolding. On November 6, Ted noticed a reddened and painful-looking lump on his son's knee. Though Ted Jr. had complained about it in the past, saying it had prevented him from playing football, his dad wasn't immediately concerned. After all, if Kennedy men worried every time they had a sports-related injury, there wouldn't have been time for much else in their lives—they were often hobbling around with one injury or another. Therefore, Ted let it go for a few days. However, when it seemed to be getting worse, he summoned a physician to his home. It was quickly decided that a battery of tests should be conducted at Georgetown University Hospital.

On November 9, Dr. S. Phillip Caper met Ted at the Boston airport upon his arrival from a business trip to Washington. "I'm afraid your boy has a tumor in his leg," he told him as a stunned Ted stood in the airport. "It doesn't look good, my friend," said the doctor. His ominous words hit Ted like a freight train. "Are you saying he has cancer?" Ted wanted to know. The doctor nodded. "But he's just twelve!" Ted said in disbelief.

That weekend, Ted played a game of father-son touch football with his boy, fearing that it could be the last time he would ever see him run freely. There would be some sort of surgery, he knew, and it would probably involve the amputation of his son's leg. This emotional upheaval took Ted right out of his usual self-absorption, which wasn't surprising to those who knew him well. "When his children [Kara, thirteen at the time,

Patrick, six, and Ted Jr.] faced a real crisis, he would always be there for them, there was no doubt about it," recalled his friend Senator John Tunney, Ted Jr.'s godfather. "Obviously, the same was true of Ethel's kids, and of Jackie's. He loved them all and only wanted the best for them, felt a responsibility to them. He was never too busy for them. If they were sick, he would do the most amazing things to cheer them up. For instance, I recall once that when Douglas [Ethel's son] was sick, he invited the entire Washington Redskins team to Hickory Hill to cheer him up. That was certainly going the extra mile! When it came to that third generation, they could always count on Ted."

While Tunney makes a good point about Ted as a father, it should also be noted that he was at the same time very tough on his boys, usually not willing to allow them any moment of apparent weakness. He and Joan fought a great deal, for instance, about how to treat Patrick's asthma. Though it was a serious medical concern, Ted saw it as something that needed to be overcome, not treated. Nothing annoyed him more than seeing the boy with an inhaler, for instance, or seeing Joan trying to soothe him after an attack. "You have to stop coddling the boy," Ted would tell her. As far as Ted was concerned, Joan overreacted when it came to problems with their children. She happened to be vacationing in Switzerland at the time of Ted Jr.'s diagnosis, and the last thing Ted wanted to do was call her and give her the news. He would later say he just didn't have the energy to deal with her. He waited as long as he could until finally, at the end of the weekend, he felt he had no choice but to telephone Joan. Of course, she was frantic with worry about Ted Jr. when her husband told her the news.

At this time, Ted Jr. was in the seventh grade at the St. Albans School in Washington. Like all of the Kennedys, he was athletic and, though slight in build, a proud player on his school's football team. He was also a good student. His parents expected a lot of him scholastically, and he generally delivered. He was also a little defiant—which Ted Sr. actually admired about him. For instance, when he was eight years old and tired of his dad's hammering away at him over his homework, Ted Jr. angrily penned a note to his dad: "You are not ascing [asking] me questions about the five papers. You are not creting [correcting] my homework. It is a free world." Ted thought the letter was so spirited, he called it "The Ted Rebellion," framed it, and hung it in his office.

After a biopsy was taken on November 13 and examined, it became evident that the initial prognosis had been accurate. Moreover, Ted Jr.'s leg would have to be amputated above the knee, and immediately, before the cancer could spread. There seemed to be some good news, though. Apparently, he had chondrosarcoma, a cancer of the ligaments, as opposed to the more deadly osteosarcoma, bone cancer. Still, the survival rate was just 25 percent and death could come within eighteen months. The operation was scheduled for Friday, November 16.

How do you tell your twelve-year-old son that he has cancer and will have to lose one of his legs? Ted was at a loss. Not knowing how to proceed, he needed time to think. In private, with his friend Senator John Tunney, he had to wonder, once again, about the so-called Kennedy curse. "'Maybe my generation, my brothers, we aimed too high," he told Tunney. "And we achieved it, we got what we set out to get. And you know, I have to wonder, if maybe there's a price to pay for wanting too much."

The evening before Ted Jr.'s scheduled surgery, Joan returned to the States. Later that same night, Ted and the doctor sat down with Ted Jr.—without Joan—to give him the devastating news. "I'd heard and delivered more than my share of bad news in my life, but this was the worst of the worst," Ted would later recall. He further remembered that Ted Jr. "started crying and I was fighting back emotion with every ounce of my being. I held Ted in my arms and told him that I'd be there with him, that we'd face this problem together. It was the battle for his life, and I wanted to be on the front line."

It was during the time of his son's medical crisis that Senator Ted Kennedy began to more fully understand the serious problems most Americans faced when it came to health care. "I guess you could call it the silver lining of what was going on at the time," Ted would later say, "that I developed a deeper understanding of something that would become one of the biggest interests of my life and career." Most of the parents Ted met at the hospital in the months and years after his son's surgery (as his treatment continued) were simply unable to afford the kind of continuous treatment of their children that had been afforded Ted Jr. Their insurance coverage wouldn't allow for the treatment for one reason or another, and some cases the parents didn't even have coverage and would soon have to take their children elsewhere for treatment. "Ted was astonished and saddened to find that some of the people he met at the hospital had no choice but to negotiate their way out of their financial predicament by trying to figure how much treatment they actually could afford—and how much their child's life would then be compromised as a result," recalled Tunney. "He began to recognize how fortunate the Kennedys were and began to fully grasp the fact that had it not been for the family's wealth, power, and prestige, they very well could have lost Ted Jr." It was true. After all, Ted, Sr. had the resources to fly doctors into Boston from all over the country to discuss various treatments and then to settle on one. He was able to see to it that the best doctors treated his son at the best hospitals. Certainly money would never be an issue for the Kennedy family when it came to treating Ted Jr. Ted had all the money, all the insurance advantages, and all of the other resources necessary—including the kinds of connections most people would never dream of—to take care of his son.

In speaking to other concerned families at the hospital, the senator heard the stories of those who had borrowed as much as banks would allow in order to pay for treatment, of those who had refinanced their homes in order to borrow against them, and others who had no choice but to declare bankruptcy. In most cases, there wasn't even a guarantee that the treatment—whichever one they had settled on—would work, as there rarely is in cases of cancer. "He realized that there needed to be more much more funding for cancer research so that perhaps a cure could actually one day be found," added Tunney. "Indeed, during the time that his son was sick, Ted came face-to-face with real Americans in crisis—both insured and uninsured, as well as the underinsured—and he would never forget the stories he heard and the friends he made during this time. He knew now more than ever that he had to devote himself fully to health care reform in America and also to better funding for not only cancer research but the research of all illnesses. From this time onward, Ted Kennedy would steer his Senate health committee's work in that direction."

Because Ted Jr. had a cold on the day scheduled for his surgery, the operation had to be delayed until November 18. This caused a bit of a scheduling conflict because Ted's niece, twenty-two-year-old Kathleen—Ethel and Bobby's eldest daughter—happened to be getting married on that day to twenty-six-year-old David Townsend. As father figure for the Kennedy clan, Ted had already agreed to give her away. He certainly didn't want to let her down, but he had to wonder if he was emotionally equipped to juggle such a joyous moment with the devastating one that was also scheduled to occur on that same day. He knew it would take everything he had to get through it, and he did.

Very early on the morning of the eighteenth, Ted Sr. spent time with Ted Jr. at the hospital as he was awaiting surgery. He then left his son with Joan for several hours to perform his role at the wedding. He knew that he would return to the hospital as quickly as possible after the ceremony. He drove a few blocks down the street to Holy Trinity and gave Kathleen away, as promised. Singer Andy Williams was at the ceremony, and as he recalled, "I sang 'Ave Maria,' just as I had at Bobby's funeral five years earlier. Of course, it was a beautiful, traditional wedding. Rory—who I think was about four—and Douglas—about six—were ring bearers. The church was full of Kennedy friends and relatives—Sargent and Eunice, Jackie, Pat, Jean and Stephen, and the whole gang. Kathleen was in a classic long and flowing wedding gown picked out for her by her mother. Teddy was there, very distracted but with his game face on. I recall that Joan stayed at the hospital with little Ted. Everyone was aware of the ordeal going on." Before Ted Sr. went back to the hospital, he made sure everyone would remember to sing the family's favorite song, "When Irish Eyes Are Smiling."

By the time his father returned to the hospital, Ted Jr.'s surgery had been completed and he seemed to have come through it well.

Just when Ted Jr.'s family had begun to relax a bit after his ordeal, doctors conducted more tests and concluded that he did have bone cancer after all, and that it had spread to the remainder of his leg. Now it was time to fight, and fight harder than ever before, his father decided. As part of his quest to help his son, Ted summoned doctors from all over the country to meetings at his home to discuss new and maybe even experimental treatments to deal with cancer before finally settling on Dr. Edward Frei III of Boston Children's Hospital. It was decided to treat Ted Jr. with an experimental drug called methotrexate, which was quickly becoming known for effectively destroying cancer cells. This chemotherapy treatment would begin on February 1, 1974, and would continue for the next two years. It was especially grueling, lasting for three days every three weeks and involving hospital stays, intravenous drips, and the emotional tumult one might expect of such an ordeal. "Helping Ted recover took precedence over every other activity in my life," Ted Sr. would recall, "including my duties in the Senate. I slept beside him in his hospital room. I would hold his head against my chest when the nausea overcame him. In time, I learned the technique of injecting him myself."

In the years to come, to his great credit, Ted Jr. would use his frightening teenage ordeal as the catalyst for his life's work as a health care attorney. As an adult, he would dedicate himself to advocating for cancer patients, first with the Wellness Community, as well as with his own health care advisory and financial services firm, the Marwood Group. "I remember the emotional isolation I experienced, losing my hair, and dealing with that as a seventh grader," Ted Kennedy Jr. would recall. "No one ever asked me how I was doing, or thought that my mental attitude would have an impact on how I approached the challenges I faced. Even though my parents found the best, most brilliant doctors that existed at the time to treat the cancer in my body, no one really ever addressed how I was doing emotionally.

"Cancer had an enormous impact on how I approach my everyday life," says Kennedy. "It sensitized me to a lot of issues for people facing cancer, and not just the psychosocial issues but the legal issues as well. That is why I'm a health advocate. I also learned to pay attention to my body, not in a hypochondriac way, but to listen to what my body tells me. I think anyone who has faced a life-threatening disease really has a chance to reflect on his or her life. For me, I am incredibly grateful for everything today."

In closing, he says, "I have to credit my parents with my recovery. They really came together when it mattered most. They had their problems, as everyone knows. But when it came to their kids, they would come together and make it work . . . and make us a real family."

Hickory Hell?

I don't care. That woman is fired!" Ethel Kennedy exclaimed. "She's out of here! I want you to get rid of her, now!"

It was a stressful March day in 1974 at Hickory Hill, with various adolescent Kennedys running wild all over the property, as usual, while Ethel attempted to pack suitcases in her third-floor bedroom. She had just gotten back from an Aspen vacation with her children and was now preparing to take another trip, this time with Eunice and Sargent Shriver to New York City, to attend a benefit gala for the Peace Corps. As she and her assistant, Noelle Bombardier, raced about the huge, cluttered bedroom in search of a specific pair of designer shoes, Ethel asked a maid named Connie to fetch a jar of face cream she wanted to remember to pack for the trip. Apparently the maid had difficulty understanding English and, minutes later, presented Ethel with a box of tampons. Though it was a simple—and maybe even comical—misunderstanding, Ethel became instantly enraged. "What is *wrong* with you?" she demanded to know of the maid as she stood up and faced her. One thing led to another, angry words were exchanged, and suddenly Ethel hauled off and slapped the employee right across the face. For a second, the three women—Ethel, her assistant, Noelle, and the maid, Connie—stood staring at one another with wide-eyed astonishment, as if in complete shock. But then the maid broke the silence by bursting into tears and fleeing from the room, with Noelle Bombardier following her. Meanwhile, Ethel sank into a nearby chair and began to cry. It was quite a scene.

By the beginning of 1974, Ethel Kennedy's fragile emotional state seemed to be getting no better, and in fact, it could be said that it had only gotten worse. Maybe because she'd never really dealt with her feelings of anger and loss where Bobby was concerned, the dark rage that had been bubbling under the surface since 1968 with only occasional eruptions had now become a dominant part of her personality. The only person who could really reach her was Ted. However, it had gotten to the point where Ethel refused to allow anyone to call him on her behalf. "He has enough to deal with," she would say. "I'm a grown woman. I can take care of myself." Maybe so, but this occasion hadn't been the first time she had slapped a person—in the same week!

Just a few days earlier, Ethel's assistant, Noelle, heard a ruckus in front of Hickory Hill while she was taking a landscaper around the property to freshen it up for spring. She walked down to the front entrance and saw a taxicab parked there, with Ethel and the cabbie standing outside of it arguing, Ethel gesturing wildly. As the assistant approached, she heard Ethel scream, "I don't care what the meter says. I know you have overcharged me and you're not going to get away with it." To which the driver responded, "Look, just don't tip me then, lady. But you have to pay what the meter says." Ethel glared at the cabbie, asked, 'Did you just call me *lady*?" and—crack!—slapped him. Alarmed, Noelle ran to Ethel's side to calm her down and convince her to go with her back up to the main house. After getting Ethel settled, she then ran back down to pay the cabbie. "That woman is crazy," he told her. "She's lucky I don't have her arrested!"

Now, just days later, Noelle was trying to solve yet another problem as she stood before the sobbing maid. "I have never been struck before," Connie said through her tears, "and I don't like it one bit. I quit!" Noelle asked her to just stay put for the time being, "and let me talk to Mrs. Kennedy."

"Mrs. Kennedy, she really is the best maid we have here," Noelle, minutes later, said to Ethel, who was now sitting on the bed, staring straight ahead and showing no emotion. "She's here when she's supposed to be and she does her job well. I really don't think we can afford to lose her."

"Too bad," Ethel said. "I don't like her. She's finished."

The heated debate went on for fifteen more minutes, until finally Ethel relented. "Fine," she said. "I don't care if she stays or goes. If you want her to stay, fine. Just keep her away from me."

"Perhaps you might consider apologizing to her, Mrs. Kennedy?" Noelle suggested. The way Ethel's face darkened again, it was clear that no such apology would be forthcoming.

"I know she felt badly about the incident, though," Noelle Bombardier would recall many years later, "because about a week or so later, Connie injured herself in the kitchen right in the middle of a dinner party that Mrs. Kennedy was hosting. I slipped into the dining room to whisper into Mrs. Kennedy's ear what had happened and to tell her that I needed to take Connie to the emergency room. I truly didn't know what her reaction would be, given what had happened earlier with this same maid. But Mrs. Kennedy said, 'No, let me. I want to do it myself.' She then stood up and said to her guests, 'One of my maids has just hurt herself badly. I have so many valuable people working for me, but she's one of the best. So I hope you don't mind, but I really must take her to the hospital.' Everyone agreed. Mrs. Kennedy then left her party to tend to the maid. After the night was over, I said to her, 'Mrs. Kennedy, that was a very nice thing you did for Connie.' She just smiled and nodded. We always had an understanding, she and I. There was just something between us from the very first moment we met."

Ethel Kennedy and Noelle Bombardier (then Noelle Fell) met in late 1973 when Noelle—thirty-three at the time—applied for the job of Ethel's personal assistant. After she heard about the opening from Ethel's interior decorator, Bombardier called Hickory Hill to make an appointment. Days later, she found herself at 1147 Chain Bridge Road in McLean, Virginia, walking the ten steps up to the enormous red door that gave entry to the main four-story house of Hickory Hill. After she was let into the house by a uniformed maid, she walked through the high-ceilinged entryway past a massive library on her right and then, to her left, the spacious Victorian-influenced living room, decorated in colors of burgundy and gold—always referred to by Ethel, she would later learn, as "the drawing room." There, in the middle of the room, on a silver pedestal and enclosed in a glass box, was perhaps the strangest souvenir Noelle had ever seen displayed in any person's home: a pope's mitre, gleaming and gold, an enormous version of the chess piece it inspired. Noelle stood in front of it, transfixed. She'd never seen anything quite like it up close, and she couldn't help but wonder which pope it had belonged to and how in the world it ended up at Hickory Hill. Her eyes then searched the room for a couch to sit on, but there wasn't one. Instead there were several round red oak tables and enormous matching chairs with red velvet cushioning situated here and there as individual separate conversational areas. Perhaps the best way to describe the room would be to say that it looked royal, not necessarily comfortable. As she sat down near a grand piano, she heard a voice say, "Hello!" It was Ethel, coming down an elaborate staircase wearing blue flared knit leisure pants and a pink top with a small red heart at its center. A gold chain with a cross on it hung at her neck. She also had on her wedding ring. With her short blonde hair and lively bright eyes, she at first seemed quite outgoing, but the downward-sloping way she extended her hand in Noelle's direction definitely suggested a certain formality. Noelle bolted up from her chair. "Very happy to meet you," Ethel said as the two women shook hands. She then turned to a maid who had followed her into the room. "Do get us a pot of tea, won't you?" Ethel said to her. "And some of those lovely butter cookies, too. That would be nice."

"My first impression of her was, 'My God! What royal presence she has!'" Bombardier recalled. "When she came down those stairs, honest to God, I felt like saluting. I also think that she carried so much baggage in terms of American imagery, it was impossible to not be impressed."

"Noelle is such a pretty name," Ethel said. "Andy's daughter is named Noelle," she added, referring to Andy Williams. As the two women chatted away, Ethel learned that as a youth Noelle had attended a boarding school and nunnery for eight years. "That's very interesting," Ethel said. "You know, I am very religious. I go to church every day. In fact, I start each day at seven in the morning at church." After they talked for about an hour, Ethel said, "Okay, you're hired."

"But don't you want to see my résumé?" Noelle asked.

"Nope," Ethel said, "I have a good feeling about you."

The two women did seem to have an instant affinity for one another. Ethel would later say that she sensed it would be easy to open up to Noelle, and as it turned out, she would do so often in the seven years that they would work together.

"Let me take you on a tour of this place," Ethel said. "It's called Hickory Hill," she said as the two women walked through the dining room with its large mahogany table that could seat at least thirty people, and then out the sliding glass doors that faced one of the swimming pools. "But you may end up thinking of it as Hickory Hell," Ethel continued with a chuckle, "because trust me when I say that this place can be a real madhouse. But I don't like that word, hell," Ethel cautioned, "so let's not use it."

Ethel Kennedy's Hickory Hill estate sat majestically atop a grassy knoll on six sprawling and green acres. The house itself was exquisite, a grand Georgian edifice with high ceilings, gleaming chandeliers, thirteen bedrooms, and an equal number of bathrooms. It became immediately clear to Noelle that despite the formality of the surroundings, the environment was also perfect for children, with two swimming pools for water sports, tennis and basketball courts, and all sorts of athletic equipment everywhere for football, baseball, and soccer. As the two women walked along a manicured pathway and chatted, Noelle noticed a sign that said "Trespassers Will Be Eaten." "My boy, David, put that there," Ethel said, laughing. "It's pretty funny, don't you think?"

Jacques Lowe, the esteemed photographer who documented much

Kennedy history over a forty-year period, once recalled of Hickory Hill, "It was a place that had to be seen to be believed. It wasn't just the Kennedy kids overrunning the place, it was all of their friends and all of their cousins, too. And there was Ethel running around chasing after them while hollering at them and nursing their bruises. In the midst of all of this were so many servants working there, I couldn't keep track. It was beautifully landscaped and the interior was quite austere. On one hand, you felt you were standing in a royal palace, but paradoxically there was all of this craziness going on there at the same time, lots of kids, lots of chaos, people getting thrown into the pool fully dressed. One's senses were definitely on high alert the entire time."

"My impression was that Mrs. Kennedy had created a hectic environment around her as, perhaps, somewhat of a distraction," said Noelle Bombardier. "Of course, there were a lot of children and their friends and cousins, but it really didn't *always* have to be what she called 'a madhouse.' It seemed to me that she wanted this kind of chaos around her at all times. She did not want any alone time. She did not want to eat lunch by herself, or dinner, or any meal, in fact. There were times when I felt she could use some private time, but no, that wasn't her. 'Where are the kids? Where is everyone?' she would ask. I would tell her that I'd just got them all settled somewhere else so that she could have a few moments of downtime to relax, and she would say, 'I don't relax, Noelle. When have you ever seen me relax? Bring me my kids. I want my kids.'"

Bombardier would have many unusual and memorable experiences as Ethel Kennedy's personal assistant, but what stands out in her mind all these years later is her former employer's ongoing—and at times even somewhat troubling—devotion to the memory of her late husband, Bobby.

"In many ways, the house was a shrine to RFK," Bombardier recalled, "in the sense that there were photos and posters of him everywhere. Truly, you could not walk into a room, even the bathrooms, without seeing his smiling and handsome face. The walls of Mrs. Kennedy's bedroom and the tops of bureaus and chests there were fairly covered with photographs of her and her husband, all in elaborate frames, all in specific places, which Mrs. Kennedy did not want moved. It was vitally important to her that every picture be in its rightful place. In time I began to feel that she, in so many ways, felt a certain powerlessness about the way her life had turned out, so she would try to organize her life in a way that made her feel in control of what was at her immediate disposal, namely her private environment.

"Every summer when we were getting ready to relocate to Hyannis Port, it became my job to gather up all of the photographs in Mrs. Kennedy's bedroom and take them to her home at the compound. I would then place the pictures in the exact spots in that bedroom as they had been in her Hickory Hill bedroom. She wanted both rooms to look as much the same as possible. It made her comfortable and feel in control. However, not that it mattered, but it made me feel very, very sad. It was just so... *upsetting.* Many a time, I would find myself sitting on the bed, trying to compose myself, trying not to cry. The more I got to know and care about Mrs. Kennedy, the harder it was to accept that she was always in such sorrow, that she had not reconciled her husband's murder."

One day, as Ethel and Noelle sat in the kitchen at Hickory Hill going over the scheduling of the children's events that day, they began to talk about Bobby Kennedy. "Oh, he so loved it here," Ethel said wistfully. "You know, we bought this place from Jack and Jackie fully with the intention of living here until we were both very old. That was the dream, anyway. It didn't turn out quite the way I expected..." Her voice trailed off. "Do you want to know something?" Ethel then asked. "For a moment, I actually thought he would live after he was shot. Why, he opened his eyes, Noelle, and he looked right up at me. And I thought, 'My God! He is going to live! *He is going to live!*' But then he closed his eyes. And that was it. He never opened them again."

"Maybe you should have a little distance from it," Noelle told her boss, taking a leap and hoping to not offend. "I know how much you miss him. I worry about you, that's all."

Ethel nodded with a sad smile. "I know what you mean, Noelle," she said. "But I have found a way that works for me. I just have to do it my way. I have all of these kids. I'm sure you understand."

"I do, Mrs. Kennedy," said Noelle as she reached for Ethel's hand.

PART NINE

Poor Ari

Onassis's Many Problems

*B*ut this isn't what I want, Aristo," Jackie Kennedy Onassis told her husband, Aristotle Onassis, in front of his lawyer, Stelios Papadimitriou. It was spring 1974 and the three were at the Onassis home on Skorpios, in the library.

"But it's what I want," Onassis told her.

"But it doesn't *look* like you want to divorce me," Jackie said, approaching him. She took both his hands in her own and looked at him intently. "Why are you doing this?" she asked. "Don't you love me anymore?"

Onassis looked downward as if he couldn't bear to meet her gaze. Then he just shook his head and pulled away from her.

"If there is nothing I can do to prevent this," Jackie said sadly, "then I guess I'll just have to accept it. But I'll never forget the wonderful times we had," she said. "Please tell me you won't either."

Onassis had no response.

Jackie kissed two of her tapering fingers and then gently touched Onassis's lips with them. With that, she turned and walked away from him.

Actually, it had been coming for some time. Onassis hadn't been himself for more than a year since the death of his twenty-four-year-old son, Alexander, back in January 1973. Alexander had been in a terrible plane crash in Greece while piloting a small aircraft. As soon as they heard about it, Ari and Jackie left New York to be at his side. Though Onassis and his son had a stormy relationship, the two still had a deep and abiding love for one another. "In my life, there is no one like my son," he often said. "A Greek father and his son have a bond that can never be explained, nor can it ever be broken." Alexander was bright, charming, and smart, though much more withdrawn and moody than his father. Jackie liked him very much. "Jackie, I want you to pray to Saint Rita of Cascia," Eunice Shriver told her when she called the hospital to see how Alexander was faring. "She is the patron saint of all that is impossible. Sarge and I are praying to her and we invite you to do the same, Jackie.

Please promise me that you will." Jackie said she would. Unfortunately, Alexander died the same day, on January 23.*

Of course, no one knew Onassis's heartbreak more intimately than Jackie. In the last year, she had done everything she could think of to help him recover from the loss of his son, but to no avail. The couple had gone on many cruises, had taken many vacations, and had spent a fortune trying to escape his sadness, but it was impossible. Even his business dealings had suffered, and in fact he had lost a great deal of money in the last year because he had become a less astute and intuitive businessman than he had been for all of his adult life. With his airline, Olympic Airways, facing bankruptcy and his wealth now cut in half from a billion to a still staggering five hundred million dollars, Onassis began to feel like a failure. Worse, he had somehow decided that his turn of bad luck was not only his own fault as a result of his own poor decisions in life, but Jackie's too. His vengeful daughter, Christina, had planted that seed in his head years earlier—that along with Jackie Kennedy would come great misfortune. Cruelly, she had cited the murders of Jack and Bobby as evidence. Now inconsolable in his grief, Ari decided that Christina had been right. "I was a happy man before I married her," he would often say. "Then I married Jackie and my life was ruined."

By the beginning of 1974, Aristotle Onassis seemed to be fading faster with each passing day. Much to everyone's dismay, he was diagnosed with the very serious and also rare autoimmune neuromuscular disease myasthenia gravis, a debilitating condition affecting first the muscles that control eye and eyelid movement and facial expressions, and then finally the muscles that control breathing and neck and limb movements. The onset of the disorder can be quite sudden, as it was in Onassis's case. To fight it, doctors prescribed extremely high dosages of cortisone, a drug with which Jackie was all too familiar since it was the same medication JFK had used to treat his Addison's disease. However, in Onassis's case, the

---

* A day earlier, on January 22, Jackie got the news that President Lyndon Johnson had died. She felt terrible about it; he had always been kind to her. His wife, Lady Bird, was still a dear friend, and Jackie called her immediately from Greece to extend her sympathies. On February 14, 1973, Lady Bird wrote to thank Jackie for the call: "You were so kind to telephone me at a time when I know your own heart was so full," Lady Bird wrote. "These have been emotion packed days, but there is still a certain feeling of insulation from the deep sadness I am sure must come."

medication only made matters worse in that it precipitated the onset of Cushing's syndrome, which hit Ari hard with its symptoms that include weight gain, back pain, skin problems, and a litany of other issues that just a year earlier would never have been believed possible in Onassis.

The sicker he got, the meaner he was to Jackie. "Onassis treated her so badly," said the celebrated photographer Peter Beard, who was a friend of Jackie's. "I can't tell you how many meals I sat through on Skorpios when he would scream at her, and she would just continue eating. She took a lot of shit from him. Constantly, he would make insulting comparisons between Jackie and Maria Callas, suggesting that Jackie was just interested in superficial gossip whereas Maria was a real artist and substantive person. It was all very hurtful."

In the spring of 1974, Aristotle told Jackie that he wanted a divorce. He had actually been preparing for it for some time, because six months earlier he had instructed his lawyer, Stelios Papadimitriou, to draw up divorce papers. Moreover, he wrote out his last will and testament and handed it to the lawyer for safekeeping. In it, he stated that Jackie had "given up her hereditary rights on my inheritance" and thus he intended to "limit the share for her and her children." (He was no doubt referring to the agreement Jackie had signed when she married him.) Now, upon his death, in accordance with his wishes, Jackie would receive just $200,000 a year for life, and $25,000 a year for John and Caroline, but only until they reached the age of twenty-one. Jackie would also receive a 25 percent share in Skorpios and the *Christina*. Moreover, if she decided to dispute the will, she would immediately forfeit any money she would have received. He also specifically stated his desire that his attorneys fight her in that regard "through all possible legal means." Papadimitriou later recalled, "It was as if he wanted her to hate him—as if, even in death, he wanted her to be sorry she had married him. But when I told him that in order to file for divorce in Greece he would have to outline his criticism of her, what she had done wrong, why he was divorcing her, he blew up at me and said, 'I will never do that. I will never say anything bad about Jackie. Forget it.'"

Jackie and Sinatra

*I*t wasn't that he didn't love her, Aristotle Onassis had told Jackie, he just no longer wanted her in his life. It didn't make any sense to her when he finally explained it in the spring of 1974, but so much of what had happened in recent years had defied explanation. This was just something else Jackie would have to accept. She was even free to date, Onassis had told her, though most people in her life thought that an unlikely scenario. However, in the early fall of 1974, Jackie did enjoy a night out on the town with someone who might have been considered an improbable suitor: Frank Sinatra. In fact, Jackie liked Frank a great deal, found him interesting and charming and—true to the way the Kennedys compartmentalized their feelings—didn't hold against him any of the longstanding rumors that he had been one of JFK's "wingmen" when it came to introducing the president to other women. "Her feeling was that whatever had happened fifteen years ago happened fifteen years ago," said one of Jackie's closest friends. "If she didn't hold it against Jack, she surely wasn't going to hold it against his friends. For instance, she didn't hold it against Peter Lawford either, and he was a part of that contingent as well. Jackie didn't live in the past, anyway. When she looked back on the Camelot years it was usually in a romantic, not critical, way. Therefore, she was always interested in socializing with people who had been connected to that time and place in her life. It made her feel good, it made her feel connected to a period that still meant the world to her."

"Though they spoke often over the years, Frank and Jackie hadn't seen much of each other after that incident when the president refused to stay at Frank's home in 1962," recalled Frank's close friend Tony Oppedisano. "But there was always a strong connection there because of Jack. Frank loved Jack, no matter what had happened. When he was with Jackie, it brought back a lot of those old feelings for that time and place, as I think it did for her too. But the relationship with Jackie was one of his relationships that, when it came to explaining the depth of it, Frank was very tight-lipped about, even with me. He just made it clear that there were feelings there."

At the end of their evening together, Frank—who was single at the time—and Jackie ended up at Jilly's, a popular nightspot on 52nd Street owned by Frank Sinatra's longtime friend Jilly Rizzo. Tony Oppedisano was at the time a jazz guitarist and vocalist who happened to be working at Jilly's the night Sinatra and Onassis showed up there. "I was on a break and Jilly had me come to his table and we were sitting and talking when there was a loud buzz in the room. We turned around and in walked Frank with Jackie. They sat down and seemed very happy, holding hands—not to say that it was a romantic gesture because they also could have been holding hands as old friends, but they *were* holding hands. Maybe an hour or so later just as the food was being served, in walked Aristotle Onassis. There was no big deal made about it; it wasn't as if Frank looked up and said, 'Oh shit! What's *he* doing here?' Jackie seemed very happy to see Onassis. So he joined them and there was then a lot of conversation and a lot of laughs. It was all very friendly."

At about three in the morning, according to Oppedisano, Jackie and Ari left the popular nightspot, followed by Tony and Jilly. Before taking his leave, Onassis shook hands with Sinatra, with Rizzo, and then with Oppedisano. He looked at Jackie and said, "Okay, I'll be in the car. Take your time." He then walked across the street by himself and halfway down the block where his limousine awaited him. "It surprised me," recalled Oppedisano, "that he left Jackie there with Frank, but in my opinion, Onassis respected that Frank and Jackie had a relationship that predated him. I think he sensed that there was a strong connection. I remember thinking at the time, well, he's not well, he's been diagnosed with myasthenia gravis, maybe he thinks, 'I'm not going to be around much longer and Jackie could do a lot worse than end up with Sinatra.'"

About a year later, on September 17, 1975, Jackie Kennedy Onassis would spend another evening with Frank Sinatra, this time when she accompanied him to his concert at the Uris Theater in New York and then, afterward, for drinks at the "21" Club. When pictures of the couple appeared in the press the next day, Ethel Kennedy was concerned enough to telephone Jackie to remind her that Sinatra had been involved in the more infamous White House shenanigans. Some in Jackie's circle claimed she was upset that Ethel had brought the matter to her attention, while others have said she wasn't really moved one way or the other about it. What is known, though, is that it never got serious between Frank and Jackie.

An interesting postscript to the story of Jackie Onassis and Frank Sinatra: It would be almost twenty years later, in May 1994, when Frank got word of Jackie's death. It hit him hard. In fact, he was so distraught he couldn't perform opening night at the Foxwoods Casino in Ledyard, Connecticut. "He just wasn't able to work," recalled Tony Oppedisano. "Frank Jr. [who was conducting the orchestra for his father at this time] did the show that night. In fact, the audience was told that they could get refunds for their tickets *and* see Frank Jr. I was up with Frank [Sr.] the whole night, until the sun came up the following morning. In the past, I'd spent hundreds of hours with Frank until three or four in the morning, sometimes with all laughs, sometimes much more serious. But that weekend there was just silence. He didn't want to talk about it. He just wanted me around as a friend.

"The next day, he slept the entire day," continued Oppedisano. "That second night, again, he was too distraught to go on. He just couldn't pull it together. There was nothing physically wrong with him; he had made himself ill because he was so upset. Frank Jr. performed again that night. Finally, on the third day, we realized Frank [Sr.] wasn't going to be able to continue at all. We canceled the rest of the engagement and rescheduled it for November. In my mind," Oppedisano concluded, "Frank's reaction to Jackie's death spoke volumes for the way he felt about her."

Ari Dies

On February 2, 1975, while terribly ill with the flu in Glyfada, Aristotle Onassis called his wife Jackie in New York to tell her that he missed her and wanted to see her. By this time, he wasn't even able to keep his eyes open because of the myasthenia gravis. He had lost forty pounds in two months, was slurring his speech, and seemed as if he were wasting away. Christina summoned cardiologist Dr. Isadore Rosenfeld in New York and asked him to fly to Greece to see her father. "Jackie accompanied me on that trip," recalled Rosenfeld. "After I examined Onassis, I determined that he was suffering from gallbladder disease and I felt strongly that he should go to New York for intensive treatment. However, Onassis's gastroenterologist, Professor Jean Caroli, felt he should be sent to Paris for treatment. Jackie let the decision rest with Christina, who agreed with Caroli. Thus Onassis was moved to the American Hospital in Paris.

"Jackie was very upset," continued Dr. Rosenfeld. "She did her best to get along with the daughter. They tried to put aside their differences so that decisions could be made. They both loved Onassis, even if they didn't get along with each other.

"A few days later, Onassis was operated on in Paris. I was concerned. I did not believe he would survive an operation at that time; he was that weak. The operation did not go well; Onassis seemed ready to give up. This was not the kind of life for a man who had lived so fully."

Jackie was told that her husband could hang on for days, maybe weeks. Therefore she decided to return to New York to be with her children. Some questioned her decision to leave her dying husband's side and wondered how she could do it. Surely, said the skeptics, if she really cared about him she would never have left him in Paris at such a crucial time.

Once she was back in Manhattan, Jackie Kennedy Onassis telephoned a number of old friends, including the architect Edward Larrabee Barnes. A few years earlier, Barnes had solidified his reputation as a world-class architect with his highly acclaimed Walker Art Center in Minneapolis. Though he and Jackie had continued occasional correspondence, they had not actually seen each other since June 1969 when they went to the theater to see 40 Carats with Rose Kennedy. When he arrived at her home at about noon on March 12, 1975, Jackie greeted him at her elevator in the foyer. She did not look well. "She had on a cream-colored silk robe, her hair pulled into a little ponytail, no makeup on," he recalled many years later. "I had never seen her like that. Jackie ordinarily didn't accept visitors that way. She looked older than she had when I last saw her. As soon as she saw me, she gave me a warm embrace. I noticed that she had rosary beads in her hand."

"I'm so sorry we haven't seen each other," Jackie said, according to his memory. "But it was impossible, Ed. I had to cut out of my life every male friend I ever knew before Ari. He was that jealous. It wasn't worth the fights with him. I hope you understand." Jackie said that she had also called a couple of other men she'd known before Ari to apologize, and mentioned one by name—the noted writer George Plimpton, whom she had also dated prior to marrying Ari.

"Of course, I understand, Jackie," he said. "These things happen."

The two then went into the living room. With shaky hands, Jackie lit a cigarette and curled up on a couch across from the architect. A maid brought in a tray of teas with a pot of hot water. The two then spent about thirty minutes catching up on each other's news. Jackie was particularly interested in Barnes's latest projects. "There's no one like you out there," she said to him. "Do you realize that? You are so unique in your field!" (It's possible that Jackie was stroking his ego, because it is clear that she had the same high regard for I. M. Pei, to whom she had awarded the job of designing the Kennedy Library and Museum.)

Finally, Edward asked, "So, how's Ari?"

"He's not doing well, Ed," Jackie said softly. "I should have stayed there, I know that now. But I am so disliked over there by everyone—his daughter, Christina, his family, his friends. And for what? What did I ever do?" She shook her head. "He loved me. I loved him back. Was that so wrong?" Jackie continued, saying that she intended to go back to Paris in a week. "To tell you the truth, I need time to steel myself for what I know is coming," she said. She also said that she was in touch with Onassis's oldest sister, Artemis, who had promised to let her know if Ari's condition changed. "But I pray to God nothing happens before I get back," she said.

Edward studied her for a moment. "I'm worried about you, Jackie," he told her.

"I'm not well, Ed," Jackie said, her voice a soft whisper. It was not a characteristic remark. No matter how difficult things had ever been in her life, she had always attempted to put forth an image of strength and resolve, even if secretly she was crumbling. However, it was as if she now had no energy left for image-making, especially for the benefit of a close friend.

"Have you talked to any of the Kennedys?" Edward asked.

"Oh yes," she said, brightening a bit. "They have all been so wonderful to me." But she said that Rose had told her that she should return to Paris as soon as possible to be at Ari's side. Rose felt that if something happened to Ari while Jackie was in New York, she would never be able to forgive herself. "And she's right," Jackie said. "I never would."

After about an hour, Jackie rose from the couch and, now seeming completely spent, asked Edward to leave. She felt she had to take a nap. "Will you please call me tomorrow," he asked, "and let me know how you are?" She said that she would do so. However, she did not. In fact, this occasion would mark the last time Edward Larrabee Barnes would ever lay eyes on Jackie Kennedy Onassis. For years, he would wonder why she would seek him out after so many years, only to then decide not to stay in touch. He would never have an answer.

A couple days later, on March 14, 1975, Onassis's sister, Artemis, called. Ari had taken a turn for the worse. "I'll be there tomorrow," Jackie said.

The next morning, Artemis called again just as Jackie was packing to return to Paris. Ari had died.

Who Should Represent the Kennedys at the Funeral?

*O*h my God," Ethel Kennedy exclaimed. "Onassis is dead? What a terrible shame."

At the time, Ethel was standing in the cockpit of a United Airlines jet en route to Los Angeles. One of the more unusual perks of being a Kennedy was that if something newsworthy involving one of them occurred while they were on a flight somewhere, the airline generally allowed them to be contacted via the pilot's communications system with ground control. The purpose of this admittedly unusual practice was to alert the family member of whatever had occurred so that waiting press at the gate upon landing would not come as a total surprise. A statement could be at the ready, if necessary. It didn't happen often, but it did happen. On this particular day in March 1975, Ethel was sitting in first class winging her way to the coast when a stewardess came up to her to inform her that the pilot needed to see her. She must have known there was a problem as she walked up the aisle and into the cockpit. She was handed a telephone, and her assistant Noelle Bombardier was on the other end, informing her of Ari's death.

"How shall I prepare for this?" Noelle asked her, according to her memory. "Will you want to go to Greece for the funeral?"

"Oh my God," Ethel repeated. "I don't know. I don't think I can do it, Noelle. Another funeral? And Jackie? It's all just too much. Call Teddy and ask if he will go and represent the family."

When Ethel landed in Los Angeles, she immediately called Noelle from a pay phone at the airport to see if she had talked to Ted. Noelle told her that the senator said he had a prior engagement and couldn't possibly go to Greece on such short notice. Many other Kennedys could have gone, true. But Ted felt that it should be Ethel. She and Jackie had the most public recognition, and to Ted's mind, it seemed only right. However, this was the last thing Ethel wanted to do. At the risk of seeming selfish, she said that she simply couldn't handle another funeral that involved Jackie. "Even all of these years later, just seeing her like that again will bring it all back to me," she said, "and I can't do it. But, okay, if I must, I must. Will you go with me?" she asked Noelle. "Because I can't go alone."

Noelle Bombardier agreed that she would accompany Ethel to Greece. However, later that day Ted Kennedy changed his plans and said he would attend the funeral to represent the family. "Oh, thank God for Teddy," Ethel told Noelle, "because, truly, I did not want to go."

"Let's Try to Move On with Our Lives"

*A*ristotle Onassis rescued me at a moment when my life was engulfed in shadows," Jackie said as she stood at a podium in front of the media gathered for a press conference in Paris. As flashbulbs popped all around her, the former First Lady—now twice a widow—was dressed all in black and seemed somewhat dazed in her grief. "He meant a lot to me," she continued, a bit stiffly. "He brought me into a world where one could find both happiness and love. We lived through many beautiful experiences together which cannot be forgotten, and for which I will be eternally grateful."

The condolences for Jackie on Ari's death had came pouring in by the time she returned from the funeral. "The sad news, which reached me this weekend, sent my heart winging your way," Lady Bird Johnson wrote to Jackie on March 17, 1975. "I know that you are heavily involved with painful arrangements now.... The shadow of grief which has pulled at your life seems an unbearable one. I wish there were words to tell you of my sympathy. It is equaled only by my admiration for your strength and composure and courage. I know they have been put to the severest of tests, always in the public eye." (Jackie immediately wrote back to Lady Bird, thanking her for her "beautiful letter" and adding, "You are a person who is incredibly kind.")

Now that Onassis was dead at the age of sixty-nine, there was bound to be much haggling between Jackie and his daughter, Christina, over the terms of his will, and likely—as Lady Bird had put it—"always in the public eye." Jackie had signed all sorts of other paperwork over the years—including the couple's original marital agreement and several revisions to it—limiting the amount of money she could receive at Onassis's death. Now it was felt that she had made a number of mistakes along the way. Even with his recent business reversals, Onassis's estate was still worth half a billion dollars and his wife of seven years was entitled only to $200,000 a year. In fact, Ted Kennedy met with Jackie at her country home in New Jersey to tell her that he felt she should contest the will. Though Onassis had stipulated that if Jackie did so she would be cut from it entirely, Ted felt sure that none of it would hold up in court. He promised Jackie that the Kennedy family would access the best attorneys available and that they would mount a major and lengthy court battle for her. The thought of such public contention made Jackie cringe. Still, if she did contest the will and she won, under Greek law she would be entitled to 12.5 percent of Onassis's estate, or more than $60 million. That had to make Jackie wonder.

That Christina Onassis showed up in New York one day, cornered Jackie, and demanded to know, "How much do you want to just go away?" did not help matters. What had Jackie done to incur the wrath not only of Aristotle's daughter but also of so many people connected to Onassis? If she had spent even $10 million of his half billion over the last seven years of marriage, that probably would have been an inflated estimate. Plus, she had tolerated his relationship with Maria Callas the entire time she was married to him, and had never been unfaithful to him. To add insult to injury, she learned that Ari had even called Maria during the last days of his life when Jackie was in New York, and that Callas had visited him at the hospital. It was obviously to be expected given their tempestuous but long-term relationship, and Jackie likely understood as much after she had time to think about it. Still, one would imagine that it hurt her.

In time, the many attorneys representing Jackie and Aristotle worked out a financial settlement for Jackie rather than risk a lengthy and embarrassing court case. In the end, she agreed to a sum of "just" $25.5 million, $6 million of which would go to estate taxes and $500,000 for her attorneys, leaving her with $19 million. She would also receive $150,000 a year for the rest of her life. John and Caroline would each also receive $50,000 a year until they turned twenty-one. At that time, $100,000 a year would be added to Jackie's annuity. In return, Jackie gave up her interest in Skorpios and the *Christina*, as well as all of Onassis's homes.

Most people believe that Jackie was left a huge amount of money when Onassis died. However, when one considers that he was worth at least $500 million at the time of his demise, it's surprising to learn that she ended up with just $19 million and an eventual maximum of $250,000 a year for life. In fact, Ted Kennedy was bowled over when he heard the final figures from André Meyer. Meyer said that he had suggested to Jackie that she not agree to the terms. He felt strongly, as he usually did when it came to such matters, that she was being shortchanged. "But I will not fight Christina any more than I already have," Jackie said, exhausted by the whole matter. "So let's just let it go now, and try to move on with our lives."

A few weeks after Aristotle Onassis's death, Jackie had a conversation with a very close mutual friend of theirs about him. "He was also so fascinating and so, I don't know, so *funny*, I guess," Jackie told this friend. "Once, he said to me, 'You know, Jackie, a woman is like the world.' I had no idea what he meant and asked him to explain. 'At twenty years of age, she is like Africa. She is semi-explored,' he said. 'At thirty, she is India. She is warm and mature. She is mysterious. At forty, she is America. She is technically perfect, but it is all superficial. Deep down, she remains troubled. At fifty, she is Europe. Completely in ruins. And at sixty, she is Siberia. Everyone knows where she is, but no one wants to go to her.'

We laughed at that because that was so...*him*," Jackie said. "You would think there would be something insulting about those observations, but if you knew him, you knew that this was his humor. After we had a good laugh, I made him promise to tell me that story every ten years, and then we kissed," Jackie concluded, "and I knew in that moment that he loved me. And I knew in that moment that, at sixty, he would still come to me. And I also knew that I would still be waiting for him."

PART TEN

Rosemary and Rose

"We Must Never Give Up"

*I*n the winter of 1975, Eunice arranged for her sister Rosemary to leave St. Coletta's in Jefferson, Wisconsin, for a visit with her family in Palm Beach, Florida. Rosemary, who was now fifty-seven years old, had been at St. Coletta's for more than thirty years. From 1969, with Joseph's passing, she was a permanent fixture in the minds and hearts of the Kennedys, mostly because Eunice made sure of it. Eunice desperately wanted her sister to be an active part of the family, and even though Rosemary's visits to Hyannis Port and Palm Beach were usually fraught with problems, Eunice believed them to be of great importance to everyone, especially Rose.

Rosemary still had her own small three-bedroom, one-bathroom house—the Kennedy Cottage—on the well-manicured grounds of the Alverno Nursing Home operated by St. Coletta's. There she lived with two nuns—not always the same two but rather a number of sisters over the years. "I think it could be said that she had a good life," said Sister Joseph Marie, who is now retired, but worked primarily at the Alverno Nursing Home from 1973 through 1999. "She was like a little child, and she had a child's innocence in many ways," she recalled of Rosemary. "At times, I would think she had the mental capacity of someone who was perhaps five or six years of age, and other times she struck me as a teenager. She was a very large woman with expressive eyes and dark hair, so she could be a bit intimidating. Her hair never really turned gray, no matter her age. It was always very black, and toward the end of her life just streaked with gray.* She could be very temperamental and cause quite a scene when she wanted to.

"The house in which she lived was a lovely little cottage. A small kitchen, very charming. I didn't live there, but I did visit quite often and would talk to Rosemary. We would have tea, and I would read to her from

---

* When one considers the photos of Rosemary as a teenager, one is struck by how attractive she was. She was considered the best-looking of all the Kennedy girls, as pointed out in the recent History Channel documentary *The Kennedys' Home Movies*.

magazines like *Life* or *Look*, and she would sit and listen. Sometimes, I was sure she knew what I was relaying, and other times I wasn't so certain. She loved game shows—*Let's Make a Deal*, those kinds of programs. She also knew all of her siblings, but we never spoke about them in terms of their celebrity. She would sometimes say, 'My brother Jack is coming,' or 'Bob is coming,' and I would correct her, saying they are gone, but it never really sank in.

"Rose, Eunice, and many of the Kennedys often came to St. Coletta's to visit Rosemary," Sister Joseph Marie continued. "I would often see Ted, Jean, or Pat. Mostly, though, Eunice was present, sometimes every month. Often she would bring Rose, but by the mid-1970s it was just easier for Rosemary to go to one of the family homes for a visit. As for those visits outside of St. Coletta's, she never really wanted to go. It was not easy to convince her to leave, and I have to say that after every visit she would be agitated and it would sometimes take weeks to get her back on track."

"Rosemary's occasional visits to Palm Beach and Hyannis Port, though well intended, were usually a source of great frustration for her," says Kennedy neighbor Larry Newman, who met Rosemary many times. "She knew she didn't fit in, and there was no way for her to feel comfortable no matter how much the family tried to accommodate her. This is why two sisters always accompanied her. It was a steadfast rule." Indeed, Sister Joseph Marie along with another nun, Sister Juliane, accompanied Rosemary to Palm Beach in 1975 to the estate there, La Guerida. It was not easy."

On the first two days of that particular visit in 1975, Rose did what she ordinarily did when she was with her daughter—she tried to act as if everything were fine and nothing was out of the ordinary. She did her best to make her daughter feel at home. "However, Rosemary felt more comfortable with the chaperoning nuns than she did with her mother," said Sancy Newman, Larry's wife, who also knew Rosemary quite well. "At times, she would burst into tears for no apparent reason, causing Rose to run from the room, upset. It was heartbreaking. 'I have never known how to deal with her,' Rose told me. 'After all of these years, one would think I would be able to be a better mother to her, but it's never happened.'"

Rose was always distressed about her daughter's diet at St. Coletta's, which was high in fatty foods, and she knew that chocolate was often used to reward Rosemary for good behavior. "She's fat because you keep giving her French fries," Rose chastised Sister Joseph Marie in front of Barbara Gibson. "And every time she asks for one, you give her a candy bar. I am opposed to this. I don't like the way her teeth look!" When her children were young, Rose rarely allowed them to have sweets. Or as Eunice once put it, "That so-called 'flashing Kennedy smile,' that got to be a part of the trademark after we grew up and some of us entered public life. Well, you don't flash unless your teeth are good. Mother monitored our intake of sweets. And the tooth brushing... oh, the tooth brushing!" she quipped.

"The nuns had a system in place for Rosemary, and one that had been in place for many years," said Gibson. "They were not going to change it."

"I admit, there was too much chocolate being given Rosemary," said Sister Joseph Marie many years later. "But she had so few pleasures in life and she so loved chocolate. I'm afraid we overdid it, though."

The situation changed dramatically on the second day when Eunice arrived with her daughter, Maria, and her sister Jean. As soon as Rosemary saw her two sisters, she lit up. She was seated in a cushioned chair when Eunice and Jean walked into the room. "Don't get up," Jean told her sister, "I'm coming over there to give you a big hug."

For the rest of the week, Eunice doted on Rosemary, telling her stories, reminding her of certain moments in family history, and doing whatever she could think of to make the visit enjoyable. Always present in Eunice's hand or in her purse was a notepad that she would constantly take out and jot down a note about one thing or another. At the end of the day, after Rosemary was asleep, she would review these notations with both nuns. On one afternoon, her notations included such observations as: "Rosie needs new shoes"; "Too much time in the sun, not good"; "Which books are being read to Rosie?"; and "Find out how Rosie is sleeping. Naps?"

"One day, Eunice insisted on bringing Rosemary out on one of the family's boats," recalled Barbara Gibson, "which turned into quite a scene. Apparently Eunice kept pushing Rosemary into the water to try to get her to swim. She was roughhousing with her pretty much the way Kennedys always did with each other, but not taking into consideration Rosemary's limitations. Sister Juliane was very angry about it. She and

Sister Joseph Marie both went to Rose and complained. Rose was in the middle of getting a massage and listening to her French-language tapes when they barged into the room and told her the story. Rose looked at them and said, 'I find it hard to believe that two grown nuns such as yourselves are tattling on a grown woman. I trust that Eunice knows what she's doing; have you not heard of the Special Olympics? So I'll thank you to mind your own business.' Duly chastised, the two nuns just stood there with their mouths open."

Barbara Gibson has another memory of that week. "Rosemary was prone to sudden fits of anger," she recalled, "and we never knew when one would occur. One day I was in the kitchen with Rose having lunch with Rosemary and it was all very pleasant until suddenly Rosemary stood up from the table and started screaming at Rose, *'I hate you! I hate you!'* There was no provocation for it whatsoever. I bolted out of my chair in fear. 'Now, now, dear,' Rose kept saying, looking up at her from her seat, but there was no stopping Rosemary. 'I hate you!' she kept repeating. Then she started screaming, *'Damn that baby! Damn that baby!'* I wondered, where in the world had she heard that? Was she parroting something she had heard in her childhood? I was at a loss, stunned and afraid. In that moment it seemed to me that she really did hate her mother and maybe even blamed her in some way for what had happened so long ago. I thought, what a true family tragedy this is, and there are two victims— Rosemary and Rose. Finally, Sister Juliane got Rosemary out of the kitchen. Afterward, Rose looked up at me with a dazed and very startled expression. Then she stood up and walked over to me at the sink. She opened her mouth and I thought she was about to ask for a glass of water, but instead she just collapsed into my arms. I don't think I had ever seen her cry before, and of course the family would always say that she never showed emotion. But on that day, she certainly did cry, and the tears kept flowing."

In the middle of a week that certainly had its troubling moments, Jackie Kennedy Onassis showed up with her daughter, Caroline. (John Jr.'s whereabouts at the time remain unknown all these years later.) "Jackie seemed to have no problem communicating with Rosemary," said Larry Newman. "In fact, I recall seeing the two of them easily conversing on the beach, Jackie often with a patient smile on her face. Caroline and Maria also got along well with their aunt and spent a lot of time swimming in the ocean with her or on the beach lying in the sun and just talking."

At one point that week, Ted flew down to see his sister Rosemary and spend the night. Rosemary would have all of her meals with the family, and during the evening when Ted was present he sat next to his sister at the dinner table and tried to interact with her as much as possible, but she seemed uninterested. Trying to be helpful, Rose repeatedly prompted her son, making suggestions such as, "Tell her the story about when…" or "Maybe Rosie would like to hear what happened when…" Always a great storyteller, Ted would do his best to entertain Rosemary, but there seemed no reaching her. "Oh, she's just tired," one of the nuns explained. Jackie didn't say a word during the meal, just smiled nervously, whereas Caroline and Maria tried to lighten the mood by telling stories about their friends at school.

Finally, after an uncomfortable hour, Rosemary suddenly announced, "I want to go to bed now." With that, the nun helped her from her chair and took her to her bedroom. As soon as she left the dining room, a heavy silence fell over the room as the Kennedys spent the next moments just staring down at their plates. Finally, Jean said, "Well, she seems healthy, doesn't she?" Rose didn't respond. "Yes, I suppose one could say that," Ted remarked, still looking at his plate. Eunice smiled knowingly at her family members. "It's difficult, I know," she told them with characteristic assurance. "But we must keep trying. We must never give up on her."

The next morning, Rose Kennedy and Barbara Gibson were swimming together in the sparkling Olympic-sized pool, which had been enclosed for year-round use. As the two women swam and talked about the day's schedule, one of the nuns rolled in Rosemary in a wheelchair. (Though Rosemary was fully ambulatory, she often used a wheelchair to navigate the Kennedy compound.) Without saying a word, the nun stopped the chair right in front of Rose at the lip of the pool. Then she turned the chair so that Rosemary was not looking at her mother but instead was in profile. It was a very odd thing to do. The nun then locked the brake so that the chair wouldn't move, and she left the area. There Rosemary sat in her chair, her outline an imposing presence as she stared blankly into the distance while her mother and her mother's secretary floated in the water. Barbara Gibson recalled that it was as surreal a scene as she ever witnessed in all of her years working for Rose Kennedy. As Rose paddled in the water she looked at her daughter with great sadness, shook her head, and then murmured, "Oh, my sweet Rosie. What did we do to you? *What did we do?*"

Rose's Precious Yesterdays and Priceless Tomorrows

*I*n September 1975, the Kennedy family congregated at their compound for a weekend-long celebration of Rose Kennedy's eighty-fifth birthday. All of her surviving children (with the exception of Rosemary), sons-in-laws, daughters-in-law, and twenty-nine grandchildren came together to pay homage to the family's enduring matriarch.

When one considers the life of Rose Kennedy—and at 104 years, it would be a long one—one is struck by the immensity and consistency of its tragedies. She was preceded in death by her husband of almost fifty-five years, Joseph P. Kennedy, after he suffered a debilitating stroke. There were the losses of four of her nine children within a twenty-four-year span, the near death of her youngest in two separate accidents, and in years to come she would suffer the death of a beloved daughter-in-law and the demise of two grandchildren. She also spent decades coping with the mental incapacity of her daughter and namesake, Rosemary, to whom she dedicated her 1974 autobiography *Times to Remember*. In the book, Rose acknowledges that it was her faith and commitment to God that got her through the unimaginable horrors she endured, events that she shared with reporter Robert MacNeill in 1974 in a lengthy interview conducted in Palm Beach for A&E's *Biography*: "God will never give me a cross heavier than I can bear," adding that her strength also came from "the thought of Mary standing at the foot of the cross as She watched Her Son being crucified." In the same interview, Rose remembered thinking after the murder of her third son, Bobby, "It seems impossible that the same kind of disaster would befall our family twice in five years. In fiction, I would have just put it aside as incredible."

As a mother, Rose was a tough disciplinarian and openly admitted to striking her children with wire hangers when the occasion called for it. She was usually not a soft, sentimental woman, and her daughters—Eunice, Pat, and Jean—would take after her in the way they raised their children. All three could be very tough, though there are certainly no stories of wire hangers where their second generation is concerned. (However, Rose and her wire hangers did become the stuff of family legend, so much so that once when Rose came to visit her daughter Eunice, the Shriver children went all over the house in search of hangers to either hide or throw away lest Rose got hold of them.) It would not be accurate to leave the impression that Rose's children have bad memories of growing up with her, because from all accounts they have given over the years, they don't. "Baby carriages are my earliest memory of Mother," Eunice would say. "It seems there was always a big navy blue baby carriage out on the lawn, and there was always somebody in it. Mother would wheel the carriage, and we kids would hold on to the sides. When I was about four, I can remember Mother saying, 'Hold on! Don't run ahead! Just hold on.' It seems like I never really let go."

"I don't think you really appreciate your mother until you have kids of your own," Pat Kennedy said in 1990. "With us, Mother was always very understanding, and that isn't easy when you have a lot of children. After [Rose's sister] Aunt Agnes's death, there were twelve [with the addition of the three Gargan cousins], and they fit right in. Mother said, if you can have nine you can always raise twelve. We were a very close unit, all of us together, and there was a lot of love.... Mother had a tremendous curiosity and we grew up with maps all around, in the dining room, in the kitchen, and if someone talked about an event in a foreign country or another state, we knew where it was on the map."

Rose's eighty-fifth birthday actually fell on July 22, 1975, but her party was postponed so that everyone could be assembled. Even at her present age, Rose was a formidable woman. She remained sharp, funny, and vigorous. If there is a distaff version of the Renaissance man, it would be Rose, with a vast knowledge and interest in art and literature, in gardening, music, the public libraries, the theater, ballet, languages, and politics, for which she had acquired an especial taste and which had proven so beneficial in the careers of her sons.

"She still played golf, her score in the 80s," recalled Barbara Gibson, Rose's secretary. "What's also interesting about Rose is that as she got older, she became sweeter to her family—but not to her servants, I might add, with whom she was still very demanding. To her family, though, no longer was she the chilly, remote family matriarch she'd been as mother to her children. As a grandmother, she was much more emotionally available. She loved taking long walks on the beach with her grandchildren." Also, while she had always played a significant part in the political successes of her boys and they were quick to acknowledge her role—giving speeches, hosting teas, organizing tours, and working the telephones—now she was more a sounding board to Ted, interested in his well-being, not really in his politics. Still, she remained politically savvy and always ready with an anecdote. Years later, her granddaughter Kathleen Kennedy Townsend would say that Rose used to pin quotations to her blouse as a precaution. "She'd say, 'You never know when someone's going to ask you to give a speech and you have to say something appropriate,'" Kennedy Townsend said.

"She changed our lives," recalled Kerry Kennedy, Bobby's daughter. "She was always the focal point; she was the one we all looked up to. Not just the grandchildren, but the whole family. She always pushed us as grandchildren to think, to dig a little deeper, to question everything, to ask why. We'd go to Mass, and afterward she'd ask, 'What was the Gospel about? How did it relate specifically to your life?' And this was to a seven-year-old."

Indeed, her religion practically consumed her. She still attended Mass every single day in Hyannis or at her home in Palm Beach, usually wearing a knee-length white dress, white gloves, matching shoes, and a lace mantilla over jet-black hair. "She sat in the front and usually alone," Barbara Gibson recalled, "and daily put one dollar—neither more nor less—into the collection plate." She apparently had an ironic sense of humor about her religious image too. "One day she dipped her fingers in some holy water and sprayed it at my face," added Gibson. "'People say I'm a saint,' she told me, then wryly added, 'so this is my blessing.'"

"You just keep busy," Rose told *Life* in the summer of 1975 while trying to explain her longevity. "Some people get bored and are boring. You keep interested in other people and in different activities. I've always had a mind that was probing and curious, and I've had the opportunity to use it." She may have been eighty-five, but her son-in-law Sargent probably said it best when he said, "Mother can still whip all our butts whether in a good debate or on the golf course, so make no mistake about that!"

At the last minute on the Friday night before Rose's birthday party, there was confusion as to whether or not Jackie would be able to attend the festivities, since she was just getting over a bad flu. With most of the family together in the living room on Friday night, talking and laughing, it was assumed that she would not be showing up. However, at one point after supper, Jean excused herself, saying that she had to run next door to Ethel's to retrieve something she had forgotten there. Ten minutes later, she walked into the living room with none other than Jackie. "Surprise, everyone!" she exclaimed. "Look who I found wandering around out there!" Of course, everyone jumped to their feet and surrounded Jackie with hugs and kisses. Finally, Jackie walked over to Rose, who was sitting on one of the floral print chairs in the living room, knelt at her side, and whispered in her ear. When Jackie kissed her on the cheek, Rose lit up with joy.

"In preparation for this weekend, all of Rose's grandchildren had participated in compiling a leather-bound volume of memories, anecdotes, poems, and drawings relating to their experiences with her, seven months in the making," recalled Hugh Sidey from *Time* magazine. "As part of the big Saturday night celebration, they read passages of it to everyone in the parlor."

Standing in the center of the room and holding the thick book, David—Ethel's son—began, "This is dedicated to our grammar instructor and favorite linguist, the great golfer and consummate swimmer, our movie operator and manners authority, Florida propertier [sic] and midnight dancer, Parisian swinger and general leader." Then Ted Jr.—Ted and Joan's boy—took over from his cousin and read some of the riddles found in the book. "She always corrects your...?" he asked the group. Everyone in the room shouted out, "Grammar!" as Rose laughed. "Tardiness at her meals leaves you...?" he asked. Immediately, everyone chimed in, "Hungry!" as Rose nodded in agreement. Maria, Eunice and Sargent's daughter, took over from Ted, reading, "She is slight and beautiful, yet her granddaughters have thunder thighs and boulder bottoms! Thanks a lot, Grandma." Anyone present would have felt the love in the room and the sense of community as, later, the children and their parents danced to rock and roll music played by a band Eunice had hired for the evening. Caroline, seventeen, showed her cousin Doug, eight (Ethel's son), and her mom, Jackie, how to do the Bump. Meanwhile, Bobby Shriver and his date, the flaxen-haired Judy Arbuckle, kicked off their shoes and did a barefoot dance for the guests.

Eventually, everyone gathered for a family portrait, all of the Kennedys together—except for Ted and Joan, who had to tend to Patrick, who had suddenly come down with a stomachache after having eaten too many clams at dinner. Later, Ethel's daughter Rory, six, and Patrick, eight—now recovered—presented her with a large round cake that had been baked by Ethel and decorated by Jean. As well as an assortment of candles, it was festooned with an American flag and, around its perimeter, the names of each of her grandchildren in frosting. As everyone sang "Happy Birthday" to her, Rose beamed. Then she blew out the candles to raucous applause.

"*Speech! Speech!*" the family members shouted out. Rose was never one to shy away from a good spotlight, but on this evening she was almost too choked up for words. "I am so happy this weekend," she finally said, standing in the middle of the room and completely surrounded by loved ones, some on their feet, some sitting on the floor, others on chairs and sofas. "Having you all here means the world to me. We certainly have had our trials and tribulations, haven't we?" she asked. Everyone nodded knowingly. "But we are here, still a family, still madly in love with one another," she observed. "I want you to be well aware of who else is here," she said. "Grandpa is here watching over all of us," she announced to a big round of applause. Then, looking directly at Jackie, she added, "And, dear Jackie, Jack is here too." There was more applause as Jackie wiped tears from her cheeks. Then, looking at Ethel, Rose said, "And Bobby too, my dear Ethel. Bobby is here too," as the room burst with more cheers. "And Kick and Joe, and each and every one of our loved ones who have passed on are here with us, right now," she continued as the applause continued to ring out. Rose let the noise die down. Then, after a moment of reflection, she said, "My wish for us all is a simple one. Let us never forget our precious yesterdays," Rose Kennedy concluded, looking at one and all, "and let us always thank the dear Lord for our priceless tomorrows."

PART ELEVEN

Shriver for President

Sarge Takes a "Leap of Faith"

*A*n old saw alleges that once you dip your toe into the roiling waters of politics, the longing for a full-on dive into the swirling eddy is too difficult to resist. It turned out to be all too true with Sargent Shriver, as he announced his decision to seek his party's nomination for president in 1976. However, as had always been the case, his affiliation with the Kennedy family did him no favors. Of course, Sarge first had to make sure the coast was clear where Ted Kennedy was concerned. As he did every four years, Ted vacillated between running and waiting, and, as also seemed to be the case every four years, expected Shriver just to wait for his decision. But eventually, Ted made a firm choice to not run in 1976, clearing the way for Sargent. When Shriver and Kennedy met to discuss Shriver's entering the race, Sarge put it to Ted straight: "If you're not going to run, what about me?" In a response that was one step removed from being grudgingly, Ted said, "I wish you well," hardly a ringing endorsement. Ted said he wouldn't oppose Shriver's running for president, but that Sargent shouldn't expect a lot of help from him either.

Shriver had never before sought political office on his own, and he called his decision a "leap of faith." However, he couldn't seem to make up his mind about whether he wanted to play off the obvious Kennedy connection. "On one hand, I think Sarge hoped to establish his identity independent of his famous family's," recalled Hugh Sidey. "But on the other, he felt that the Kennedy name might go a long way toward helping reinforce his own credibility. In the end, he decided to go with the Kennedy connection." Thus when Sarge made his announcement, the Kennedys showed up in full force to at least appear to be supportive— Rose, Ethel, Pat, Joan, and Jean were present and all had signed on as members of the "Shriver for President Committee," with Jackie joining as well. "I'm fortified by my family—by my mother who has seen twenty-three presidential campaigns, by my wife, Eunice, and our sons and daughter, by my brother Herbert, by Rose Kennedy and Ethel Kennedy and Jackie, by Jean, and Pat, and Joan, and my most admirable sister-in-law, Willa Shriver of Baltimore," Shriver said in his announcement speech, notably leaving out Ted's name. "In peace and war, in public and private life, they know the demands and duties, the joys and sorrows of the kind of course I'm taking, and have encouraged me to take it."

During his speech, Shriver also invoked the name of JFK and tried to establish a clear connection between himself and the late president's ideals. "Let us remember there is no conservative or liberal remedy for the sickness of the national spirit," he intoned. "The cure will come from honest, truthful leadership that summons the best in us—as we remember John Kennedy once did. His legacy awaits the leader who can claim it. I intend to claim it, not for myself alone, but for the family that first brought it into being, for the millions who joyfully and hopefully entered public service in those days in order to produce a better life for all, and to those billions of unknown, uncounted human beings who I've seen all over the world—in Asia, South America, Western Europe, and the Soviet Union—for whom the memory of those days and of John Kennedy is still an inspiration to their minds and a lift to their hearts. That's what we must all be proud of once again."

It was pretty stunning rhetoric but, as it would happen, perhaps a mistake for Shriver to connect himself so closely to JFK. The presence of the Kennedy women onstage as well as the reference to JFK suggested that Shriver didn't have his own platform on which to stand but was instead trying to create some sort of allusion to Camelot. "It wasn't like he had much choice, though, because when he tried to distance himself from the family, a reporter would inevitably corner Ted Kennedy to get a comment from him, and that comment would usually end up working against Shriver," recalled Arthur Schlesinger Jr. "Though Ted watched the proceedings from a safe distance, I think maybe the idea that Sargent might become president was a little more than he could handle." In fact, Ted couldn't contain his professional jealousy. He still believed that if there were going to be a president or vice president in the family, it should be he, and if not he then no one else. At one point, Ted even told a reporter, "I can't help it if Sargent wants to run." When asked if he supported him, he said, "Sure I'll support him." The reporter wasn't convinced. "If Mussolini was running, would you support him, too?" Ted laughed. "Yes, if he was married to my sister," he answered. Indeed, the Massachusetts senator was always at the ready with a lacerating quip when the subject of a rivalry between Sargent Shriver and himself was broached.

Unfortunately, after Sarge made his announcement that he would be campaigning for a place on the Democratic ticket, the Kennedys made a hasty exit from his campaign and were rarely seen again. "I'm waiting for Ted to run," Jean's husband, Stephen Smith, told one politico when asked why he wasn't more involved in the Shriver endeavor. When told that Ted wasn't planning to run in '76, Smith said, "I'm still waiting for him to run."

"I think it's just awful," Jackie Kennedy Onassis told Stephen Smith in the presence of two mutual friends and two business associates during a meeting in New York. The small group was in Smith's New York office discussing certain stocks her children had in common with the Kennedy family when the subject of the Shriver campaign was raised. Jackie was unafraid to speak her mind on such matters, especially when they involved Sargent. About a year earlier, in April 1975, Eunice thought it would be fun if Jackie allowed John and Caroline to go to Russia with the Shrivers for a vacation. Jackie agreed, but because Caroline had other summer plans, John went alone. While John was with the Shrivers, Sargent spent many hours telling him long and detailed stories about his father, the president, so much so that by the time John got back to the States he had a whole new respect and admiration for his dad.* That Sarge had taken so much time with her son made Jackie love him all the more. "This family is acting like some kind of cult and I'm very disappointed," Jackie told Stephen Smith. "Sarge is such a good man," she said. "It's a real shame."

Smith disagreed. "Obviously, Teddy does not want him to run," he said, "so I don't understand why Sarge keeps injecting himself every four years. He's so stubborn. He wants what he wants," Smith said, getting heated. "Well, it doesn't matter," he concluded, "because it's Teddy who will always have the last word."

Now Jackie was upset too. "It's Teddy who wants what he wants, and at

---

* John also became very close friends with his cousin Timothy Shriver on that trip to Russia. A year later, during the summer of 1976, Sargent asked Jackie if—in the true Kennedy tradition of service—she would allow fifteen-year-old John to accompany sixteen-year-old Timothy to Central America to help the Peace Corps after a massive earthquake there. John would be accompanied by his Secret Service agent, of course. (Interestingly, in November 1976, he would turn sixteen, which marked the end of his Secret Service protection.) Jackie said, "Absolutely." Even though the two boys would be sick the entire time they were there—living in a tent, no less!—it was a worthwhile experience they'd never forget.

the expense of everyone else," she exclaimed. Jackie added that it was well known within the family that, deep down, Ted did not want to be president, nor did he want to be vice president. But Sarge wanted it, badly, she said, and he was qualified to do it and deserved to do it, at least in her opinion. "And not only that," she concluded, "this country needs him."

Stephen Smith just shrugged and said that the two would have to agree to disagree. "I can tell you this much: The family will never support Sarge running for president or vice president." he added. "Even if Teddy runs, wins, and serves two terms and Sarge *then* wants to run, the family will *still* not support it."

Jackie's eyes widened. According to the witnesses, she stood up and demanded to know of Smith, "Since when do you speak for the whole family? I happen to be a part of this family, and you do not speak for me." She then turned and walked out of the room without so much as a goodbye.

Stephen and Jean Kennedy Smith

Jean Ann Kennedy was the eighth of nine children of Rose and Joseph Kennedy, born in Boston on February 20, 1928, coincidentally the eighth birthday of her older sister Kick. Along with Joe Jr., Kick was like a surrogate parent and role model for her sisters Eunice, Pat, and Jean, much as Joe was to his brothers Jack, Bobby, and Ted. Jean was a quiet, sensitive child and seemed at sea among the frolicsome folderol of her older siblings and nearly forgotten by her mother. It remained for her Irish nursemaid Kico to give Jean the maternal nurturing that Rose seemed unable or unwilling to provide.

Jean lived largely out of the Kennedy limelight—whether of her own choosing or happenstance—and would do so throughout her developing years and even into adulthood. This seems at odds with her physical appearance in that when Jean—handsome and statuesque, as tall as most of the men—would enter a room, she exuded a certain presence that everyone recognized, a kind of physical charisma she shared with many of her siblings. Even her marriage to Stephen Edward Smith on May 19,

1956, at the Lady Chapel, a small, exquisite chapel behind the main altar in New York City's St. Patrick's Cathedral, seemed her way to remain outside the Kennedy spotlight. While her brothers and sisters pulled out all stops when it came to their weddings, with big, expensive, formal affairs, Jean said that when she was given two options by her father—a big wedding with a small gift or a small wedding with a big gift—she chose the latter, the big gift being an expensive diamond pin. As if to assure her father that she was serious about cutting corners, Jean wore the Hattie Carnegie gown that her sister Pat had worn for her marriage to Peter Lawford two years earlier. Even her maid of honor, sister Eunice, wore one of the bridesmaid's frocks from her own ceremony three years prior. One can only imagine Jacqueline Bouvier making such a frugal acquiescence when she married JFK.

However, as much as Jean avoided taking a key role in the family's high-profile and very public activities, her husband Stephen did not shy away from the Kennedy spotlight. He was especially unhappy with the attention being heaped on one person whom he seemed intent on casting as a rival, Eunice's husband, Sargent Shriver. If Sarge ever considered Stephen at all, it would certainly not be as a potential rival for the public's and family's approval. When Sarge left his position as managing director of the Merchandise Mart to join JFK's administration, Smith was chosen to replace him at the Mart. In addition, Stephen handled the Kennedy family's extensive real estate and financial holdings, and from all accounts did a superior job. Sarge was always complimentary of Stephen's work, but it has to be said that seldom was the reverse true. The brothers-in-law just didn't get along, mostly because Stephen had such a dim view of Sarge's desire to be a politician and was doubtless jealous of the obvious high regard in which some of the family held Shriver.

Jean's marriage to Stephen was troubled. Whether the problem was sexual in nature or not, by many accounts she engaged in some sort of long-term relationship with the ten-years-older Alan Jay Lerner, the dapper, urbane lyricist and librettist of such Broadway musical hits as *Brigadoon*, *My Fair Lady*, and *Camelot*, in collaboration with composer Frederick Loewe. Ironically, Lerner had been a classmate of JFK's, and of course the lyrics he wrote for the title song in *Camelot* came to define the idealism and tragedy of the Kennedy administration. In truth, Jean's connection with him may have had a lot to do with the hurt of "a woman scorned." After all, Stephen was widely known as an inveterate woman-izer, often leaving Jean alone for entire weekends as he sought validation of his sexual prowess with a series of beautiful young matrons.

Jean always seemed to sense that her life should be easier, that she should be happier. In fact, there was a period in the late 1970s, after she followed Joan's lead and went into therapy, when she began to lay the blame for her unhappiness at her mother's feet.

"You shipped me off to boarding school when I was young, and you never really cared for me," she told Rose one day in 1978 in front of Rose's secretary, Barbara Gibson, as the three women were swimming in the pool.

"My memory of it is very different," Rose said. "I wanted all of my chil-dren to have a wide range of experiences, and that's why we sent you to boarding school."

"But that's the reason I'm so screwed up," Jean charged, "and I also think it's the reason I have made such bad choices."

"Well, I don't know what you've expected of me, dear," Rose said, try-ing to stay calm, "but your father and I did the best we could. I find it quite alarming that you don't see it that way."

For Jean to have spoken to Rose in that manner was a little surprising. Rose's children seldom stood up to her or criticized her. Afterward, Rose was very upset by the scene. "Exactly what was I to do?" she asked Gib-son. "I was left alone with all of those children while Joseph did whatever he was doing. I did the best I could. I would like to see Jean do better, I really would." Later, after she had calmed herself, she told Gibson, "It's interesting isn't it, this 1970s thinking that the problems of today's youth are directly linked to their parents? If you ask me, by the time you turn fifty [Jean's age at this time], you should be able to pull yourself up by your bootstraps and take responsibility for your own life."

By the late 1970s, Jean and Stephen Smith had sold their home in the Kennedy compound and bought a new summer house on Long Island. They seemed eager to put some distance between themselves and the rest of the family. This isn't to say that the summers at the Kennedy com-pound would end entirely, because they didn't. The Smiths would often lease a house near the other Kennedy homes and spend time there. But they made their point—they wanted their distance.

Ten years after JFK's death, Jean founded the Very Special Arts, now known as VSA, a nonprofit that seeks to promote the artistic talents of the mentally and physically challenged, much as older sister Eunice's Special Olympics addresses the physical limitations of retarded youngsters. VSA is now an affiliate of the Kennedy Center. It would be impolitic to suggest that Jean was thinking of the Smith legacy in her creation of VSA or to impugn her motives in founding a program that seems to be inspired by Eunice's work with retarded children. While the parallel will undoubtedly be criticized, to ignore it altogether would also be wrong. Jean was trying to make her own mark, but in some ways it also seemed that maybe she was trying to compete with Eunice.

Some would argue that Jean and Stephen Smith—for whatever part they played in the Kennedy family's accomplishments in the betterment of the lives of Americans—will always remain second-stringers in the drama played out by the powerful political family. Others might say that in a family of so many who were committed to social change, not everyone had the temperament to play that sort of role. For instance, it could be said that Ethel, Joan, Jackie, and even Pat did little for social change. Indeed, the standards set by Jack, Bobby, Ted, Eunice, and Sargent were so high, not everyone would be able to reach them.

Yet Another Disappointment for Sarge

Although Sargent and Eunice Shriver hit the campaign trail vigorously on Sarge's behalf, they simply couldn't get any traction there. "It was very difficult for Eunice," said Senator George Smathers. "Weekends at the Kennedy compound had never been more tense, I can tell you that much. To be honest, I think Eunice didn't even have her heart in it, though. I think she almost feared what fresh hell her life would be if Sarge actually won the nomination—and who knows what her family would have done if he had won the election! I think she could look into the future and see nothing but heartaches and she made a decision— even if she never gave voice to it—that she would just as soon Sarge not get the nomination."

"I'm sure there were times Eunice wished Sarge was tougher, meaner, more of a bulldog," said Pierre Salinger. "But that wasn't his way. He was a gentleman, a diplomat. Shriver could look at a problem from every angle and consider it to the conclusion—that there were no good guys and bad guys taking part in it. Situations were not as black and white for him as they were for the other Kennedy men. Whereas JFK and RFK had staunch allies and enemies, Shriver had staunch enemies who were often also allies. In many ways, I think the Kennedys actually appreciated Shriver's sense of diplomacy and his even-tempered approach, and with the passing of years, they had repeatedly used it to their advantage. But that didn't mean they respected it. He was a nice guy, and you know what they say about nice guys?" Salinger concluded. "It's reductive and not even true to say that Shriver finished last. But he didn't always finish first, that's for sure."

As it turned out, Sargent Shriver did not secure his party's nomination in 1976. Instead, the Democrats went for the virtually unknown Jimmy Carter to head the party's ticket. In the post-Watergate era, with Nixon leaving office in disgrace, it was as if the country simply wasn't interested in high-profile, controversial figures, especially those who couldn't seem to get along without their high-profile, controversial family members. To a large extent, the public and the media had grown weary of the persistent Kennedy question as it applied to Sargent Shriver—whether the family was in or out, whether Ted cared or didn't . . . and on and on. Such an ongoing narrative just made Sargent Shriver look as if he wasn't his own man. "A lot of people thought I was just an in-law trying to capitalize on my relationship with the Kennedys," Sargent told the *Chicago Tribune* in 1987. "And who in the hell wants to have an in-law of the Kennedys? If you want to have someone who stands for what the Kennedys stand for, have a Kennedy. They thought I was running for president on the basis of the fact that I was related and [the public thought] what a cheap, low level kind of thing that was. Even after Jack was killed, I was the brother-in-law of the former president of the United States or the brother-in-law of the Attorney General or the brother-in-law of the Senator. You're always devalued. There were times I'd say to myself, 'wouldn't it be great if I could just get out from under and be myself?'"

Yes, there were other problems with Sarge's 1976 campaign, related to philosophical issues such as his apparent waffling on the subject of abortion (he and Eunice were definitely pro-life, though at times his speeches seemed to indicate otherwise). However, by far the biggest obstacle Sargent Shriver faced in his 1976 bid for the presidential nomination was the same one that had dogged him in 1964, in 1968, and in 1972, and it wasn't just the public's perception of his relationship to the Kennedys, as Sarge so very diplomatically outlined to the *Chicago Tribune*—it was that the Kennedys and their acolytes really and truly did not want him to succeed where Ted hadn't yet. It was as simple as that.

Certainly, one would think there should have been a place in American politics for a noble man like Sargent Shriver, a visionary and idealistic thinker whose own brand of philanthropy had nothing to do with money or worldly possessions, but everything to do with his wealth of ideas in contributing to the public good. It wasn't meant to be, though; 1976 would bring the election of Jimmy Carter over Gerald Ford. Meanwhile, Ted Kennedy was that same year reelected to the Senate. And so it remains for Sarge's firstborn and namesake, Bobby Shriver, to sum up during an interview what happened to his dad in that bicentennial year: "Ted didn't do shit for my father in 1976."

PART TWELVE

Ted's 1980 Campaign

Ted's Presidential Decision

*H*e had put it off year after year, campaign after campaign. He had also made it clear that he didn't want his brother-in-law Sargent Shriver to participate in any of those races either. However, despite his reluctance, it was always presumed by many Americans, Republicans as well as Democrats, that Senator Edward Kennedy would one day run for president of the United States. For his part, Ted was always more realistic than idealistic when it came to running for the presidency. He understood America very well and he knew that even though he had been forgiven enough after Chappaquiddick to continue in the Senate, the chances of his being elected to the highest office in the land were slim to none. Though eleven years had passed, Ted understood that there were still people in the country who would not forget what happened to Mary Jo Kopechne and his part in it. In truth, he couldn't forget, either. "I am haunted by it," he once told his friend Dun Gifford. "I keep thinking about her gasping for breath in that car under water, and it kills me inside. If I spend too much time on it," he said, "I wouldn't be able to get on with my day. It's that paralyzing." Despite such upsetting memories of the past, Ted had never lost his drive to serve his country, to honor his brothers' memory, and he wanted to go forth on a bigger platform than just the Senate—if America would allow it.

There was also a question of national expectations. In his memoir *True Compass*, Kennedy articulated how his party's goals in 1976 were not in alignment with his own. "Whether consciously or not, they seemed enthralled by the dream that the dash and vaulting aspirations of the early 1960s would return again. My actual vision of the presidency . . . was a good deal more complex and less romantic. My concept of myself as president had little or nothing to do with Camelot. It wasn't about Jack, or Bobby, or my father. The eras that shaped them had passed. The present era was quite different in mood, in collective experience, and in the challenges the nation faced. Jack's and Bobby's great legacies inspired me, but cold reason told me that I could not run as their surrogate, nor could I govern according to their templates. My goals, my style would derive from my own judgments as to what I wanted to accomplish."

Besides concerns about ghosts of the past and expectations of the future, Ted Kennedy's family was also a concern. His running for president was a concept with which most Kennedys had a love-hate relationship. "They wanted to see Ted fulfill what, in some ways, seemed to be his destiny, yet they were also afraid of what might happen to him should he ever be elected," said Senator John Tunney. "Ted was also fearful. Though he had long ago made peace with the possibility that he could one day be the target of another assassination—'I decided I would not live my life in fear of the shadows,' he said—he was never able to reconcile what such a tragedy would do to his mother and the rest of his family. Could he in good conscience allow them to possibly suffer a third time what they had endured in 1963 and 1968?" When Ted chose not to run in 1976, his mother confirmed that his safety was an issue for her when she said he had "promised me faithfully that he would not run. I told him I did not want to see him die too, that I could never stand another tragedy." It was a chance that, by 1980, Ted was ready to take, albeit reluctantly, primarily because he so strongly disagreed with so many of incumbent president Jimmy Carter's philosophies as well as his general attitude about the country and its future.

Though both were of the same Democratic Party, President Carter and Senator Kennedy were never friendly. Carter had serious reservations about Ted, though he never articulated them publicly. However, privately he said he believed the Kennedys to be spoiled personalities who felt above the law and often acted with a sense of entitlement. If it had been up to him, he would just as soon never even appear in the same photograph with Ted, which is probably why he never accepted Ted's offer of assistance in his campaign. Indeed, at the 1976 Democratic convention, Carter decided not to give Ted a speaking role at all. Throughout Carter's four years in office, he and Kennedy continued to butt heads.

By late 1979, the climate in the country had changed to a point that gave Ted Kennedy grave concern. Not only was the economy suffering, but the energy crisis seemed to be worsening by the month. Carter had said during his campaign that he believed health care coverage should be mandatory and universal, making it seem as if he and Kennedy agreed at least on that important issue. Carter went so far as to promise that health care reform would be a priority of his administration. However, when he got into office, his goals changed. As many political pundits at the time considered understandable; Carter decided that his first priority would have to be an energy bill. Health care would have to wait. Over the course of his four years in office, though, he seemed to continually stymie Ted's efforts in the Senate to get any legislation passed relating to health insurance concerns. Ted also suspected that Carter felt threatened by Kennedy's power in the Senate.

Simply put, Kennedy believed that Carter was not a man of action. In his view, Carter loved taking meeting after meeting and pontificating about what might be best for the country—indeed, the world. But at the end of the day, he would inevitably stop short of taking true, decisive action. "He loved to give the appearance of listening," Ted once said. Of course, Carter enthusiasts would disagree with such a harsh assessment of his presidency, but it was Ted's firmly held opinion. Ted's animus for Carter seemed to have no bounds. For instance, he was also derisive about Carter's mandate that no liquor be served in the White House, writing in his memoir that it was the first thing one was reminded of when entering the presidential home, "in case you needed reminding." Carter, according to Kennedy, "wanted no luxuries, nor any sign of worldly living," which is also why, Ted felt, he had sold the presidential yacht, Sequoia, at auction. The sale of that yacht really seemed to stick in Ted's craw. He had a strong emotional connection to the yacht because JFK had held strategy meetings on it during the Cuban Missile Crisis, and had even celebrated his last birthday on it. Ted couldn't believe that Carter viewed the vessel as nothing more than a status symbol that needed to be eradicated from the presidential landscape. "When he got rid of the boat, that's when Ted was sure Carter was full of it," said Senator George Smathers.

By the fall of 1978, President Carter definitely had put health care reform on the back burner, to the point that it seemed not even to be an issue for him. Instead he focused on inflation, and to that end he proposed a number of budget cuts that would, in Ted's view, adversely affect the elderly, the poor, and blacks as well as the unemployed. By the end of that year, Ted had started speaking out openly against some of Carter's policies. In response, Carter asked Ted to issue a blanket statement that he would never consider a draft from his party to run for president. When Ted said he wouldn't do it, it became clear to President Carter that he might truly have an adversary in Ted Kennedy, one who might affect his political future.

It wasn't until July 15, 1979, though, that Ted was sure that President Carter's presidency should be challenged. That was the evening Jimmy Carter—with his approval ratings way down because of the country's fatigue over the energy crisis, long gas lines, and other problems, including the intensifying concerns over the Iran hostage crisis—gave his so-called "malaise" speech. Though he never actually used the word "malaise" in the speech, it is thusly known because of the suggestion Carter made that Americans were the cause at the heart of their own problems because they'd lost confidence in themselves and their country. The speech was viewed by many as a moral indictment, and it outraged many Democrats because of its perceived pessimistic bent and critique of consumerism. Or, as Ted put it, "It was a message contrary to—and in conflict with—all the ideals of the Democratic Party I cherished. I tried to imagine President Kennedy or Bobby Kennedy ever abandoning their optimism in the face of adversity and giving vent to sentiments remotely this melancholy."

By August, Governor Ronald Reagan of California had begun to edge out Jimmy Carter in important popularity polls. It seemed to Ted as if his Democratic Party was in serious trouble. Those same polls suggested that Ted might actually have a chance against Reagan, should they both run. "I began to think I had no choice," Ted would later recall. "I began to think that I had a responsibility to run. It started to make sense to me, again."

"S.O.S.! The Elephant Is Chasing Amy Carter!"

On May 19, 1979, Ethel Kennedy hosted her twenty-first annual Hickory Hill Pet Show to benefit one of her favorite charities, Runaway House. The annual event, held on the grounds of the estate, was always well attended by celebrities and the public. Hundreds of people would park as far away as downtown McLean, about three miles from the estate, and be bused onto the property. There would always be horses and other large animals, as well as a petting zoo with goats and chickens. Many people would bring their dogs to the fair as well, to show them off and enter them in different competitions. It was a gala affair, a circuslike atmosphere that even had a ringmaster, usually the columnist Art Buchwald, resplendent in red jacket and black bowler hat, walking around with a microphone and interviewing the people who had brought their pets to enter them in events. That year, some of the Washington Redskins were in attendance to play ball with the fans. Meanwhile, representatives from different foreign embassies were recruited to prepare foods from their respective countries. It was an event the Kennedys looked forward to every year, and one that Ethel took great pride in presenting. The young actor Gary Coleman was one of the celebrity guests that year. Jackie Kennedy Onassis was also present, with her children, all surrounded by Secret Service agents, as were Ted and his family and most of the other Kennedys. Ethel had even invited President Jimmy Carter and First Lady Rosalynn, as well as their eleven-year-old daughter, Amy. However, the Carters planned to be at Camp David that weekend, but said Amy would love to attend the Pet Show. So they sent her to Hickory Hill, along with a team of Secret Service agents. There were likely three thousand people on the premises.

The highlight of the extravaganza was to be the appearance of a six-thousand-pound elephant named Suzy. "I think it's the biggest elephant in the world," Ethel enthused after she managed to secure the animal for the show. She was very excited.

All was going well with the day, until suddenly...not so well. As Noelle Bombardier roamed the property making sure everything was in order, someone summoned her on her walkie-talkie—"*S.O.S. S.O.S. The elephant is chasing Amy Carter! S.O.S. S.O.S. The elephant is chasing Amy Carter!*" Bombardier happened to be in the area where the incident was occurring and turned around to see the enormous mammal pursuing poor little red-haired Amy while everyone around her cleared away. Before Bombardier had a chance to react, one of the Secret Service agents scooped up the frightened girl just as the charging elephant came within twenty feet of her. He then tossed her right over a fence, where another agent was waiting. Though it was all over quickly, it was quite frightening just the same. Because she had some minor scrapes and abrasions, Amy had to be taken to the hospital.

Afterward, Noelle Bombardier ran over to Ethel Kennedy, who was clearly mortified. "We have to get back to the house and call the First Lady before she hears about this from someone else," Noelle told Ethel, who wholeheartedly agreed. However, when they got back to the house, Ethel didn't want to talk to Rosalynn Carter. "What do I say to her?" she asked her assistant. "You tell her. I can't! It's too embarrassing!"

Bombardier got on the phone with the First Lady as Ethel stood next to her. "Well, Mrs. Carter," she began, "you see, we have an elephant here who, I guess, must have loved little Amy because she...well...she got a little too close to her."

Rosalynn Carter was instantly upset and wanted to speak to Ethel. However, Ethel stood next to Noelle shaking her head to indicate that she definitely didn't want to talk to her. "But you really don't have time to talk to Mrs. Kennedy," said Noelle to the First Lady. "You should call the Secret Service at the hospital right away to make sure your daughter is okay." She then hung up. Fifteen minutes later, Mrs. Carter called back and this time demanded to speak to Ethel. Ethel had no choice but to come to the phone. "I am just so sorry," she told the First Lady. "I don't know what to say! Nothing like this has ever happened before!" Rosalynn apparently told Ethel that Amy was fine, but was still crying because she'd been so scared. It was an embarrassing phone call for Ethel, to say the least. She hung up with the First Lady, turned to Noelle, and said, "I want you to get that damn elephant off my property, like *yesterday!*"— which is what Noelle did.

That evening, Ted Kennedy and Jackie Kennedy Onassis were in the main house with Ethel and several friends and relatives, talking about the day's unbelievable event. "I just don't understand," Jackie said, "why, with so many *thousands* of people here, why in the world that elephant went after Amy Carter?"

"Me neither," Ethel said, mystified. "I can't figure it out."

"Well, isn't it obvious?" Ted said, a mischievous glint in his eye. Everyone turned to him for an explanation. "Obviously," he concluded, "the elephant must have smelled *peanuts* on the kid."

"Oh, Teddy!" Jackie exclaimed. Obviously, Ted was alluding to Jimmy Carter's famous reputation as a former peanut farmer. "That's not funny!"

Everyone laughed, though, because it *was* pretty funny.

The Joan Factor

*P*erhaps it was easy to understand Ted Kennedy's concern, and that of most of his family, when it came to what some advisers began referring to as "the Joan Factor." The situation with Joan Kennedy could pose some potentially lethal problems to Ted's campaign, should he decide to run. Still, wasn't this a matter for Ted to take up with Joan privately, since it had to do with their marriage? Some may have thought so, but that wasn't the way it unfolded. In the summer of 1979, Ted called a meeting of psychiatrists and doctors—some of whom had treated Joan in the past and some who had not—to confer with him, Joan, Jean, Ethel, Eunice, and his aide Richard Burke, to decide how to handle the problem at hand—namely Joan. It was decided to have the conference in a hotel in Crystal City, Virginia, territory deemed "neutral" and thus a safe zone to pose some difficult questions, such as: Was Joan up to the challenge and rigors of a political campaign? If so, how would the Kennedy spin doctors be able to explain some of the particulars relating to her private life?

By this time, Joan's face was appearing constantly on the covers of women's magazines such as *Good Housekeeping, Ladies' Home Journal, Redbook,* and *McCall's,* all with very personal interviews discussing her battle with alcoholism. Indeed, by the end of the decade, Joan's drinking problem was well known to anyone who cared to read about it. The avalanche of press had begun to roll back in February 1976, when Joan checked into the Smithers Rehabilitation Center in New York City for alcohol abuse. Coincidentally, a freelance writer had been in treatment at the same time as Joan. He sidled up to her one day, gained her trust, and from that moment on took copious notes about her confessions during group therapy. He then sold Joan's warts-and-all story to the *National Enquirer.* More damage was done when other newspapers, including the *Washington Evening Star,* published reports based on the *Enquirer's* exposé, infuriating the Kennedy family, particularly Eunice, who wrote an angry letter to the newspaper for having "violated every canon of honorable journalism." It was quite a missive. "You who sit in splendid judgment of us all, whose lives can be saved or broken at your whim," she wrote, "have turned thumbs down on a gallant and admirable woman. There's no triumph here for you. Only deep shame."

About a year earlier, Joan moved out of the home she shared with Ted and the children and took an apartment in Boston. Most of the Kennedys were baffled by her decision. How could she leave her husband and children to fend for themselves? That was certainly not the Kennedy way. Rose told Joan that she'd wanted to take off many a time when she was married to Joseph, "but if we all did exactly as we pleased, what kind of world would this be?" With the new living arrangement, Joan Kennedy would see her children on weekends and on special occasions, while "the help" took care of them and Ted in her absence. All of it promised to be difficult to explain to Ted's constituents—thus the meeting.

Joan wasn't told of the confab until the last possible moment for fear that she would become so nervous about it she wouldn't show up. In a sense, it was handled as if it were an intervention. After Joan appeared at the hotel with her children—nineteen-year-old Kara, eighteen-year-old Ted Jr., and twelve-year-old Patrick—she was quickly whisked away to a conference room. Once there, she was taken aback to see the other Kennedys present, along with the team of doctors.

During the meeting, Ethel made it clear that she felt Joan had "licked" her alcoholism. She didn't really understand it as a disease but rather thought of it as an emotional problem that could be taken care of with therapy. Eunice had a better understanding of the situation and felt strongly that Joan had a long way to go. The two women butted heads about it for a while, until Ethel finally suggested that Joan stay with her at Hickory Hill and that between the two of them they'd figure out a solution to the problem. Joan was against that idea, though. "I'm not a child," she protested.

"Well, I want to be president," Ted finally said, cutting to the chase. "I think the timing is right. I can do this. I believe I can win. People are sick of Carter. The energy crisis, the economy. People need a change, and that's me." However, he also said that if his aspirations would in any way hurt Joan, then "forget it. It's not worth it. I won't do it. I will only proceed if I have the full support of everyone in this room," he said, "including my wife."

Joan's children also spoke up, all agreeing that the only way they would go along with their father's ambition to be president would be if their mother was for it as well.

Joan then looked at Ted and said that she too wanted the presidency for him and that she would do whatever she had to do to help him reach that goal. "I think you'd make a great president," Joan told Ted in front of the observers. "But I need more time to work on myself, I really do."

After some discussion, the decision was made that if Ted should in fact run, they would keep Joan's involvement in the campaign to a bare minimum. She would hold a single press conference at her home—which they would schedule for December 1979. It would be an event that Joan and her therapists could prepare for in earnest. Then, if that went well, she might make appearances with Ted on the campaign trail.

"Okay, kiddo, then it's settled," Ethel said. "I, for one, am looking forward to us being in the White House. And I think Ted can do this country a lot of good. Oh, I'm so proud of you, Teddy," she exclaimed, jumping up to embrace him. "Isn't this just great?"

"It sure is, Ethie," Ted said, embracing Ethel. "It sure is."

Eunice wasn't so sure. Not only was she worried about Joan, but she was also savvy enough to know that America was going to have a lot of questions about what was going on with her marriage to Ted. "Sarge and I see a lot of roadblocks down the line," she warned everyone. "The way the climate is now after Watergate and"—she paused—"Chappaquiddick," she said, after a beat, "people are really looking at the character of their candidates and their wives. I think this is going to be a big problem."

Jean had to agree with Eunice. "We're going to have our work cut out for us to try to explain away all of . . . this."

Ted nodded. "It's not going to be easy," he said. Then, looking at Joan, he asked, "Are you up for it, Joansie?"

Joan answered Ted with total silence. She must have known in that moment, though, that her options were limited. "She already felt such tremendous guilt for having presented so many problems to the family as a result of her personal problems," noted her former assistant, Marcia Chellis. "How could she now deny them their last chance at the presidency? Besides that—as she would later tell it—she so believed that Ted Kennedy could make a difference in this country, she didn't want to be the reason he could not run for office."

"Yes, of course I want to try," Joan Kennedy said at the meeting. "More than that, I will do it. You'll see," she told Ted. "You'll be proud of me." He smiled at her. "That's my Joansie," he said, patting her on the shoulder. Everyone left feeling somewhat encouraged.

The Roger Mudd Interview

*B*efore Senator Ted Kennedy even had an opportunity to officially announce his campaign, there was a serious public relations imbroglio concerning a televised interview he would do with CBS's Roger Mudd. Ted gave the interview to Mudd from his summer home on Squaw Island for a CBS special broadcast. However, after it was over, the CBS crew was concerned that they'd gotten nothing of substance from the senator. He had been evasive and even seemed somewhat unprepared. When Mudd asked for another interview, Ted reluctantly agreed to it. It was during that second interview, then, that Mudd asked the big, headline-making questions relating to Chappaquiddick. Ted felt cornered, as he later recalled it, because he never expected those, claiming his agreement with Mudd had specified no questions about Chappaquiddick.

After the two interviews were completed, Ted was unhappy enough about the results that he telephoned Roger Mudd to request a third interview. In that third interview, which took place at Ted's office in Boston, Mudd pointedly asked Ted about the state of his marriage to Joan. "Well, I think it's a—we've had some difficult times," Ted said, seeming unable to find the right words. "But I think we'll have...we've—I think, been able to make some very good progress and it's—I would say it's—it's—it's—I'm delighted that we're able to share the time and relationship that we—that we do share." He could not have answered the question more disastrously. When asked if he and Joan were separated, his response was, "Well, I don't know whether there's a single word that should—have a description for it." Eventually, Mudd asked Ted the most obvious of questions: Why did he want to be president? Again, Ted faltered; his halting answer was almost unintelligible. First, he rambled on about the country's "natural resources" and "greatest political system in the world" and then mentioned something about inflation. He also touched on unemployment and education and, in the process of trying to hit every talking point, basically gave an answer that—at least in a single viewing—didn't make much sense. Today, many historians point to that single televised moment as the one that would end up costing Ted Kennedy the presidency—and he hadn't even announced his candidacy yet.

As might be expected, Ted was quite angry about the entire Roger Mudd affair and felt that the interview, when finally broadcast on November 4, 1979, had been edited to make him look much worse than actually had been the case. In fact, though, Ted had ample time to prepare, at the very least, for the third interview, which he himself had requested. It still seems inconceivable all these years later that he would not have had an answer at the ready for the obvious question about the reasons behind his presidential ambitions. Ted insisted that he had good reason to be thrown by the question since he had not yet announced his candidacy. To follow that logic, though, is to also believe that a candidate doesn't think about his reasons for running for the presidency until the day he makes the official announcement—which was obviously (one hoped) not the case in this instance. The Kennedy family was for the most part mystified as to why Ted had fumbled the answer. Of course, he was well prepared—Kennedys were always well prepared when it came to big PR moments. He most certainly had compelling answers to the questions. He just didn't give them. It was as if he had purposely sabotaged his chances to occupy the White House before he'd even made his campaign official. In the end, though, the family was certainly not going to support Roger Mudd in the controversy. They would be there for Teddy. That's just the way it had to be. It could be said that Ethel Kennedy spoke for the whole family when she told one reporter—off the record, of course—"That Roger Mudd is a dirty, rotten so-and-so. If he, in *any* way, has hurt Teddy, I'll go after him myself!"

Ted: *"The Dream Never Dies"*

On Wednesday, November 7, 1979, at Faneuil Hall in Boston, Ted Kennedy officially announced his intention to challenge and overthrow the incumbent president, Jimmy Carter. Yes, he would seek his party's nomination, and his chances seemed quite good: In fact, every poll showed him with a two-to-one lead over Carter among Democrats and independents. Ted recalled, "As I stood quietly behind the lectern in Faneuil Hall, I was enveloped in the moment. My personal past, my family's past, the Boston past, the American past—it had all coalesced in this room, where patriots had once gathered before the Revolutionary War to shape the American future. Jack had made his final 1960 campaign speech here. I was forty-seven years old, one year older than Jack when he died. Jackie smiled at me from the audience of 350 friends and relatives—and half again as many reporters."

Next to Jackie sat Eunice and Sargent Shriver. If anyone thought the two of them held any kind of grudge against Ted for his woeful and continual lack of support where Sargent's political ambitions were concerned, he would be wrong. "They could compartmentalize it all in a way that I found fascinating," said Hugh Sidey. "At the end of the day, Eunice was still a Kennedy and she would be there for Ted, no matter how slighted she may have felt by the way he had handled Sarge over the years," he added. "That always astonished me and I think said a lot about her as a woman, and about Sarge, too, who was also present for Ted." Eunice also made sure her children would be available to Ted. She sent her son Bobby a telegram at this time, which author Edward Shorter quoted in his definitive volume *The Kennedy Family and the Story of Mental Retardation*:

"Ted's career as politician at absolutely crucial stage next two weeks. Friends prove their friendship by helping out now. Everybody making sacrifices. Some of time, others money, jobs, careers, even family, Ted's record of helping Dad [Sargent] politically is inadequate but in other ways very good.... Consider all this in planning your vacation. One year from now I don't want you to look back and say, I wish I had done something at the crucial period. Churchill said, 'These are the years—nineteen to twenty-six.' You can change things! Love, Mother."

Jean and Stephen Smith, Pat and Ethel Kennedy, and even Rose were also present when Ted formally announced his candidacy. Kennedy's announcement speech took just fifteen minutes to deliver, and during it he made it clear that America was no place for President Carter's sad-sack brand of pessimism. Kennedy said that he stood for a hopeful and ambitious future and he asked people not to buy into Carter's "myth that we cannot move." After exuberant applause, Ted then took questions, as expected. However, one of the first questions was directed at Joan and concerned her feelings about Ted's presidential ambitions. She answered by saying she was enthusiastic about the prospects and eager to one day soon meet with the press to answer in greater detail any other questions they might have of her. She seemed at ease. In about a month's time, she would host the promised press conference at her home in Boston, and during it she answered as many questions as she could about Chappaquiddick, her alcoholism, and her marriage. It was definitely true that most of the media felt Joan had no choice but to be as open as possible about the most personal matters, and she played along gamely.

In many respects, Joan Kennedy felt a new life in the offing for her as First Lady. She thought the important national position might give her structure and purpose, and the more she thought about it the more appealing the idea became to her. She also still loved her husband very much. No matter what he had done, she couldn't help herself—as she so aptly put it at the time, "I guess it's true that the heart wants what it wants." They had a history together, he was the father of her children and still very much a part her life. If she could acquit herself in his eyes, she would definitely not turn down the opportunity. If in the process he should decide he wanted to give their marriage another chance, she would not turn him away.

For Ted, the bar was raised to perhaps unreachable heights by a constituency intent on having another Jack or Bobby leading the party. True, when Ted announced his intention to run, he was ahead in the polls. But with the passing of time he began to lag behind Carter—and he never regained his footing, even though his message certainly had value. After Carter's "malaise" speech, Ted stayed on point against it. "At other times in our history when we were facing problems, we didn't throw up our hands in despair," he said in Philadelphia. "We didn't talk about malaise in the American spirit. We rolled up our sleeves and set out on the job to be done. And we can do it again." He voiced his disdain for Carter's leadership. He charged that Carter should have expected the hostage situation presently unfolding in Iran and accused the president of not paying attention to warning signs indicating that trouble was imminent. He felt strongly that a good solid debate with Carter about important and obvious issues such as foreign policy, health care, and the economy would win him solid approval by Americans, but Carter was against it.

Ted Kennedy even broke new ground by openly campaigning for gay rights at a time when the idea was, to say the least, novel. However, a big problem for him was that he often seemed long on rhetoric and short on specificity. Yes, he gave rip-roaring speeches in the great Ted Kennedy tradition, but it was as if he hoped his power as an orator might mask the fact that he didn't have much of a plan. Moreover, he was a liberal, and as such was viewed by some critics as an impractical spendthrift, someone out of place during economically depressed times. He never quite found his stride. He seemed ill-prepared, troubled, and distracted, causing some people to wonder why he was even in the game. "Why is Kennedy even running?" California governor Jerry Brown asked. "What is his debate with Carter? The only issue is career advancement."

There were other reasons Senator Kennedy's campaign for his party's nomination was troubled, starting with the huge hit his campaign funding took by his loss of the all-important Iowa caucuses in January. Further complicating things, Stephen Smith, who was orchestrating the campaign, felt constricted by safety concerns. Because of fear that Ted was a marked man, there were Secret Service everywhere, which many people found off-putting. Even trotting out the Camelot mythology didn't help relax people. After some of his speeches, a six-piece band would play the music from *Camelot* while Kennedy took his bows. However, by the end of 1980, it seemed, at least according to most tallies, that most Democrats would not vote for Ted under any circumstance, Camelot or no Camelot.

Looking back on it now so many years later, it's clear that the biggest stumbling block Ted Kennedy faced during this campaign had to do with the all-important question of character. Ted believed that his personal life shouldn't have been an issue for the public when evaluating him for high office, that his record in the Senate—and it was a very good one—should have been enough for voters to understand that he deserved to be president. Perhaps with some politicians that would have been the case, and it may even be the case with some today. However, in 1980, Senator Edward Kennedy came with too much baggage to ignore. After what he'd done at Chappaquiddick and after what Nixon had done with Watergate, the media was looking for any flaws it could find, and Ted didn't work very hard to camouflage his.

For instance, Ted seemed not to want to make an effort with Joan on the campaign trail, so much so that he sometimes acted as if he were annoyed by her presence. "Her success in front of a critical audience seemed to vex him, not fill him with pride," is how Marcia Chellis put it. Did he feel that her alcoholism was a factor in keeping him from the White House? If so, perhaps he got the idea from *Time*, which had recently published a very unflattering piece on Joan. "Public life has not been kind to Joan Kennedy," reported the magazine. "Its wounds can be seen in the puffy eyes, the exaggerated makeup, the tales of alcoholism. Today she is a sadly vulnerable soul and an unknown factor in her husband's electoral campaign." The writer—no byline was given—further stated, "She sometimes seems unnerved by her infrequent reunions with Ted. One woman friend recalls a scene a few months ago when the Senator's car pulled up in front of Joan's apartment as she stood nearby. 'Oh Christ,' said Joan. 'Here he comes. I'm getting out of here,' and she strode rapidly away."

One wonders how Ted and Joan Kennedy hoped to deal in the future with their fractured marriage if in fact they actually ended up president and First Lady. "They intended to just move into the White House together," Richard Burke later said, "and have separate rooms like Jack and Jackie did, and that would be the end of it. He would do his thing and she would do hers. But what they didn't get is that Joan was never able to operate like that, which is one of the reasons she became an alcoholic. She had never been happy as the wife of a senator who had girlfriends, so what made them think she could be happy as the wife of an unfaithful president? There were a lot of unrealistic propositions on the table at the time, not the least of which was the question of how the public would accept this kind of marriage between the president and First Lady. The girlfriends were bound to come out. In JFK's day, no. The media was different and not as likely to turn on the president, thus no one knew about him and Marilyn Monroe, for instance. But in 1980? Forget it. You couldn't have those kinds of secrets after Nixon."

Ted's troubled marriage aside, the events of Chappaquiddick were constantly being brought into question by the press, and often by the public—which Ted had certainly expected but was upsetting just the same. While he was campaigning in Louisville, detractors showed up with placards bearing Mary Jo's name as well as a dummy of a female corpse and a sign that said "Killer." In Alabama, Ted was confronted by someone holding a placard that posed the question, "How Can You Rescue the Country

When You Couldn't Even Rescue Mary Jo?" At another stop, a group of detractors played the song "Bridge over Troubled Water" over a sound system just as Ted's caravan pulled into town. After Jackie appeared at a fund-raiser at Regis College in Weston, Massachusetts, she told Joan Braden, "I could see the whole Chappaquiddick question on their faces. It's on people's minds." Ted certainly didn't help matters when *Time* quoted him as having said, "The essence of the event for me is that the girl is dead. There is nothing else for me to say." Did he really feel that way? No, of course not. In truth, he was racked with guilt about what happened to Mary Jo Kopechne, at least according to those who knew him best. But he wasn't going to go that far with the media about it. He wanted to appear done with the matter so that the rest of the country would join him there. However, he wasn't going about it very well in terms of his public statements regarding Mary Jo, which just made him sound callous and uncaring.

A press conference at the airport in Sioux City, Iowa, stands out in the minds of those involved in the Kennedy campaign, mostly because of its brevity. Ted stood at the mic ready to answer questions with Joan standing behind him. But the first question was to Joan. "Mrs. Kennedy, do you believe your husband's version of what happened at Chappaquiddick?" For a moment, Joan looked stricken. She seemed blindsided by the question. Two articles about Chappaquiddick had just been published the week of the press conference and she had been quite upset by them. It was doubtless the last thing she wanted to talk about, but she knew she had no choice. As she approached the microphone Ted moved aside. She stood at the podium for a long moment. "Yes," she finally said. "I believe my husband's story, which he told me right after the incident. And I don't believe that these stories in the last few days are going to come up with anything new." In a small, shaky voice, she continued, "It's just such a shame…" With tears in her eyes, she concluded, "I mean, it's such a shame that all of this has to come out again. I don't know what else to say…I just don't."

"It wasn't what Joan had said that day as much as it was how she said it," recalled Richard Burke. "She looked so sad and unhappy—and so immensely vulnerable—the hardened press corps was actually stunned by her appearance. There was a long pause in the proceedings as Joan went back to her position behind Ted. And then, surprisingly enough, there were no more questions. The reporters just quietly dispersed without words of explanation." Indeed, it had been a one-question press conference, the first of its kind in the campaign and—who knows?—maybe the first of its kind ever in any campaign. According to Burke, Ted turned to Joan, his voice still audible on the live mic feed, and said, "Good. That was good, Joan." But he didn't reach for her, try to embrace her or show her any warmth at all. Even the most hardened reporter might have, in that moment, wanted to give Joan Kennedy a hug, but her husband seemed indifferent, even cold to her. It was hard to overlook, and even more so when Ted repeatedly spoke of Joan's personal issues as "her" problems rather than "our" problems. "He was such a lousy husband," Marcia Chellis observed, "you had to wonder what kind of president he'd be. Of course, one has nothing to do with the other, but still, at least if you were a woman, you had to wonder."

In the end, Ted's inadequacies, not only in regard to the relationship with his wife but also as they related to the pertinent campaign issues, were too much to overcome. Thus the decision was made by the end of the summer of 1980 that he would withdraw his challenge to Carter's presidency. The presidency was not to be for him and—at least judging by the way he had stumbled through much of the campaign—perhaps he knew it all along. "He had to know it," observed Richard Burke, "because I had never known a workhorse like Ted Kennedy. No matter how much you threw at him, he would tackle it and know what he was talking about. But throughout this time, he was just not on his game. It wasn't like him at all. His heart wasn't in it."

At the Democratic convention in August 1980, Ted Kennedy officially withdrew his intention to seek his party's nomination, and ironically enough, the sad occasion would afford him one of his most shining moments. Truly, the Senator Kennedy who walked onto the stage that night was finally the man his supporters had always believed him to be—eloquent, thoughtful, and powerful in every way. "May it be said of our party in 1980 that we found our faith again," Ted said from the stage. "And may it be said of us both in dark passages and bright days, in the words of Tennyson that my brothers quoted and loved, and that have special meaning for me now: 'I am a part of all that I have met, too much is taken, much abides, that which we are, we are. One equal temper of heroic hearts, strong will, to strive, to seek, to find, and not to yield.'"

With Joan and his children—Kara, Ted Jr., and Patrick—surrounding him, Ted concluded, "For me, a few hours ago, this campaign came to an end. For all those whose cares have been our concern, the work goes on, the cause endures, the hope still lives, and the dream never dies."

Much was made of the fact that Ted seemed to refuse to join and then elevate the hand of the incumbent Carter. It was viewed as a sign that Kennedy didn't really support Carter. In his memoir, *True Compass*, though, Ted made it clear that Carter didn't seem to want to elevate his hand either—that there was no effort on the part of either of them. (Of course, it would be argued that Carter had no reason to do so.)

President Jimmy Carter still believes today—and many historians agree—that a consequence of Ted Kennedy's efforts to assume the presidency was a divisiveness in the Democratic Party that would ultimately lead to the election of Republican Ronald Reagan. "However, Ted never subscribed to such thinking," said Senator John Tunney. "He always maintained that Carter's popularity had already been on the wane. Had that not been the case, he said, he would not have sought his party's nomination in the first place."

The question remains, though: If Ted had won the nomination of his party and had run against Reagan, would he have won? Reagan was incredibly popular partly because of his unflagging optimism during a time many Americans felt especially disenfranchised, so it's difficult to imagine that he could have been defeated. Perhaps a more interesting question has to do with what sort of damage it would have done to Kennedy's political career had he actually lost a presidential election. There was already great concern that he was risking much of his Massachusetts constituency by attempting to overthrow Carter, and that if he didn't bow out when he did he might also risk an erosion of his influence in the Senate. If he were to ever have lost a presidential election, it's likely that Ted Kennedy would not have become the great power in the Senate that he did, which would arguably have been a real loss to this country. Or as Rose Kennedy so aptly put it at the time, "We Kennedys believe that things work out the way they're supposed to work out. God sees to it."

"It was okay, the way it turned out. In fact, I think it was better than okay for Ted because, at long last, he was finished with the notion of being president of the United States," observed Richard Burke. "The responsibility to at least try for highest office had been weighing on him for so long, he now felt a great sense of relief that it was 'over and done with,' as he put it." Had he ever really wanted it? Or was it just something he felt he had to do for his family, for his country—for his brothers? Only he would know for sure, but most people who knew him well felt he was quite satisfied with and proud of his work in the Senate—as well he should have been—and that he would be very happy to continue to serve in that way. Indeed, now that the presidential weight had finally been lifted from Ted Kennedy, the senator from Massachusetts could begin to enjoy the second act of his life of service, and never look back.

End of a Marriage

*T*he statement of January 21, 1981, was short and concise:

"With regret, yet respect and consideration for each other, we have agreed to terminate our marriage." It was decided that Patrick, who was thirteen, would live with his father at the Kennedys' home in McLean Virginia. Kara, twenty, and Edward Jr., nineteen, were in college. Joan would continue to live alone in Boston. It would be two years before the divorce would be final. Alexander Forger would negotiate a lump sum for Joan of about $5 million from Ted, as well as monthly alimony; she would also receive the condominium in which she had lived since 1977, and the house she and Ted had shared on Squaw Island, near the Kennedy compound.

Barbara Gibson was with Rose Kennedy when Ted called to give her the news of the divorce. "Yes, dear," Rose said, according to Barbara's recollection of her side of the conversation. She was very calm. "I see, dear," she said. "So, is there somebody else?" she asked.

"I'm so sorry," Jackie told Joan when she called to see how Joan was faring, according to what Joan would later recall, "because now I feel that I should have told you to do this fifteen years ago. I just didn't know back then what we know today." The two were talking on the telephone shortly after the divorce announcement was made. Jackie went on to say that she felt "terrible" because, she reasoned, if she had encouraged Joan out of the marriage sooner, "maybe you wouldn't have gotten so sick," she said, referring to Joan's alcoholism. "But I couldn't have done it anyway," Joan responded. "Times were so different. We did the best we could back then, though, didn't we?" Jackie had to agree. "We sure did," she concurred, "with what we had to work with, anyway."

The conversation brings to mind a letter Jackie wrote Joan in the summer of 1979. Reading it, one has to wonder if Jackie's views hadn't sprung from personal experience. She wrote that she suspected Ted had arranged to have his long-distance phone calls billed to their mutual friend the architect John Carl Warnecke, so that Joan would be unable to monitor them. (This had to have hurt Jackie. She liked Warnecke a great deal and had even dated him several times after JFK was killed and before she married Aristotle.) Thus, Jackie wrote, "he is able to talk to Mootsie or Pootsie every night—right in the house with his wife & children—and then bring them there when you're away. What kind of woman, but a sap or a slave, can stand that & still be a loving wife—& care about him & work like a dog for him campaigning?" She continued, "This is the 20th Century—not the 19th—where the little woman stayed home on a pedestal with the kids and her rosary. Your life matters—as much as his—you love him but you can't destroy yourself. You are the mother of three children and they're your children and you want to be around to bring them up as you feel they should be brought up. A mother is more important to children than a father," Jackie posited. "That is the parent it hurts children most to lose, and you are not going to let that happen."

Joan later said that Jackie's letter so touched her, she cried upon receiving it.

Despite everything she had been through with Ted, though, Joan Kennedy was still unsure if she'd made the right decision to let him go. Perhaps that's why, on the very afternoon that the Kennedys made public that they were ending their marriage, Ted received a huge basket of colorful tulips and poppies delivered to his office. They were from Joan.

PART THIRTEEN

David's Story

"The Kennedys' Biggest Shame"

She had a new pair of white shoes on," twenty-seven-year-old David Anthony Kennedy told authors Peter Collier and David Horowitz for their book about the Kennedys in 1983. He was talking about a photo he had seen of his aunt Rosemary, the Kennedy sister who had been lobotomized at Joseph Kennedy's behest. "The thought crossed my mind that if my grandfather was alive the same thing could have happened to me that happened to her," he said. "She was an embarrassment; I am an embarrassment. She was a hindrance; I am a hindrance. As I looked at this picture, I began to hate my grandfather and all of them for having done the thing they had done to her and for doing the thing they were doing to me."

Unfortunately, David Kennedy's downward slide had continued with the passing of the years. In the ten-year period between 1974 and 1984, things had gone progressively from bad to much worse, and there seemed no reaching him.

"Oh, my David. My sweet little David," Ethel's personal assistant, Noelle Bombardier, said when asked to remember the young Kennedy who had often been put in her charge. "He really liked me and I liked him so much," she recalled. "Though he was so charming, he often acted strangely. For instance, he would use the bathroom without closing the door and I would walk by and holler at him and say, 'David! Please!' But nothing bothered him. Yet at the same time, everything bothered him. At first, I didn't know what was wrong with him. I thought, well, maybe he's just depressed. But it all came out from Mrs. Kennedy one day."

On the day in question, Ethel asked Noelle to pick up a skirt especially made for her by Oscar de la Renta, her designer at the time. "Okay, Mrs. Kennedy," Noelle said, "but I'll have to wait until a little later because I don't have my car."

"Oh, is something wrong with your car?" Ethel asked.

"Well, actually, I let David use it to run an errand."

"What!" Ethel exclaimed, suddenly very alarmed.

"Don't worry, Mrs. Kennedy," Noelle said. "He told me he would be back within a half hour."

"You should never have done that!" Ethel exclaimed. "Don't you know that the boy is on *drugs?*"

Noelle was completely shocked. She said she had no idea. She had figured that something was wrong with him, she said, but she certainly didn't know it was a drug addiction. Ethel then explained that when David was twelve, he had seen his father murdered while watching television. "We were in Los Angeles, as you know," Ethel said, "and Bobby had just won the primary in California and had just given a speech to thank his supporters. I had some of the kids in Los Angeles with me— Courtney, Michael, Kerry, Chris, Max, and David. I remember, I said, 'This is family history. The kids should see this.' And David was at the hotel staying up late, watching the TV, while I was with Bobby at the Ambassador Hotel. Then, as we were going through the kitchen, Bobby was shot. I was standing right there, Noelle," Ethel said, "and this... this...*person*...killed my husband," she concluded, her voice cracking with emotion. "And my son saw the whole thing on TV."

Noelle was so horrified by Ethel's story, she had to sit down.

"David and Bobby were so close," Ethel continued, now taking a place next to Noelle. "They were inseparable. David was small, a runt like Bobby had been. And Bobby just took to him, you know?" Ethel then explained to Noelle that David had always been a very sensitive youngster, very introverted, "not like the other boys. He and I would go and pick flowers while his brothers were killing each other with their crazy games," Ethel recalled with a smile. "If he ever got in trouble, he didn't really care what I thought about it. He cared what *Bobby* thought. If Bobby was unhappy with him, it was the end of his world." On the very morning of Bobby's death, David had gone into the ocean in Santa Monica with some of his siblings to play and was pulled under by a dangerous undertow. "Bobby just jumped right in and saved him," Ethel said. "He saved David's life the very same day he lost his own, and David never really could understand any of it. It was as if he thought God had traded his life in for his dad's," she concluded sadly.

Young David Kennedy was never quite the same after that awful day in June 1968, according to his mother. He became sullen, depressed, his behavior so erratic that "we took him to a doctor and the doctor put him on some medication. One thing led to another," Ethel continued, "and I think that's how he got addicted. But we were so worried about him, we just did what the doctors said. I think that's how it happened," Ethel reasoned, according to Noelle's memory of the conversation. "Or maybe it was the treatment he had after the Jeep accident he and his brother were in...I just don't know..." Ethel stopped talking and just stared off into the distance. "I know there were sleeping pills," she said, seeming now to rack her memory, "because he couldn't sleep...I know that much."

Almost at a loss for words, Noelle apologized profusely for allowing David to use her car.

"Well, you didn't know," Ethel said, taking her off the hook. "It's not like we tell everyone! But now that you know, never let him drive, Noelle. You must promise me!"

Noelle promised.

Just as the two women were finishing their discussion, they heard the loud screeching of brakes outside. David had returned. Moments later, he ran into the house, out of breath and sweating profusely. Immediately, Ethel jumped up from her chair to confront him. "David Kennedy, don't you dare ever ask Noelle for the keys to her car again," she scolded him. "She didn't know that I don't want you driving, but you know it and you took advantage of her!" David seemed unfazed. "Oh, okay, cool, Mom," he said. Then he glanced at Noelle, said, "Sorry," flashed her a big smile, and ran up to his room. "Oh my God," Ethel said, sitting down again. "Well, at least he didn't hurt himself, or anyone else."

In the spring of 1978, David suffered an overdose; Stephen Smith told the press that he had pneumonia. When he got out of the hospital, Ted and Ethel sat down with him to try to reason with him once again. "What do we have to do, David?" Ted asked him, as Ethel looked on, according to what Ethel later recalled to a friend of some years. "What is it that you need from us? Because we don't know what to do. You tell me. And I'll do it, David. Just tell me." David thought it over. "I want you to bring back my dad, how about that?" he said, suddenly very angry. "How about *that*, Uncle Teddy. Can you do *that*?" It was such an upsetting moment, Ted didn't know how to respond to it. He just hung his head and shook it sadly. Ethel, as she would recall it, stared at her son and wondered how things had gotten so ugly. "Didn't think so," David said as he jumped up from his chair and bolted from the room.

Several months later, in 1979, the family got word that David had been beaten and robbed in Harlem while trying to score drugs in the same location where, four years later, his brother Bobby would also be known to buy drugs. Then, a week later, he was hospitalized with an overdose and suffering from endocarditis, an inflammation of the heart often associated with intravenous drug use. He nearly died. Apparently scrambling to cover up his illness lest it affect Ted's presidential bid at that time, Stephen Smith issued a statement saying that David was "suffering from an ailment similar to drug addiction." The word was out about him, though, and no one was fooled by Smith's unusual way with words.

"I toss and turn all night thinking, what would Bobby do?" Ted Kennedy said one day to an administrative assistant. The two were in the study at Hickory Hill, virtually surrounded by framed pictures of Bobby on all of the walls. "I rack my brain thinking, what would he do?" he said while motioning to one of the last photographs of Bobby ever taken, at the Ambassador Hotel right before he was shot. "What would Bobby do?" Ted asked. "And, I swear to Christ, I don't have a *clue* what Bobby would do. And I think, Jesus Christ, if Bobby were alive, none of this would be happening."

"Look, you can't beat yourself up over this thing," the assistant told Ted. "You're doing what you can."

"But I promised I would be there for these kids," Ted said, now looking down at the floor. "I promised Ethie. I feel like I'm letting her down."

The assistant would later recall that he had rarely seen Ted so upset. Apparently Ethel had been listening to the conversation from another room, because she suddenly walked into the study and stood right before Ted. Looking down at him with her hands on her hips, she said, "I never want to hear you say that, Ted Kennedy. I never want to hear you say you are letting me or Bobby down. Because it's not the truth. It's not the truth, Teddy. *It's not the truth.*"

Ted looked up at Ethel and nodded. The moment hung. "You're all I have," Ethel said, now almost in tears. "I don't have anyone else, Teddy. Just you. Please, just never say that again!" Ted looked stunned. It now felt as if the two should embrace or offer some other demonstration of affection. But then, as was often typical of the Kennedys at the unfolding of an emotionally powerful moment, one of them quickly short-circuited it; Ethel suddenly turned around and walked out of the room. After she was gone, Ted and his assistant just sat looking at one another, not knowing what to say.

"Of course, Mrs. Kennedy was very, very worried about him," recalled Noelle Bombardier, "but she was also embarrassed. I recall one afternoon when Princess Grace Kelly was coming to visit Hickory Hill with her brother Jack and sister Lizanne. Mrs. Kennedy had planned a wonderful luncheon for them. Meanwhile, David was walking around high or drunk or . . . really, I didn't know what was going on with him, but he definitely wasn't right, stumbling about and bumping into the furniture. Mrs. Kennedy was frantic about it and finally said, 'Okay, look, Noelle, first things first. We have to get him out of here. We don't have time to do anything else!' I called the senator and he said, 'Okay, bring him over here to my house.' He lived just down the street on Cambridge Road. So I got David into the car, drove over there, and dropped him off. 'Tell Ethie I'll take it from here,' the senator told me as he took David. Then I raced back to Hickory Hill just as Princess Grace and her siblings were arriving. We had our lovely afternoon, though it was quite disconcerting knowing what was secretly going on behind the scenes. Mrs. Kennedy was practically jumping out of her skin the entire time. Finally, Princess Grace and her family members left. Within seconds of their walking out the door, Mrs. Kennedy said, 'Okay, go get David and bring him back.' So I raced back to the senator's house, he handed David back to me, and I brought him home.'"

Soon after David's treatment for endocarditis, another very troubling incident at Hickory Hill occurred. Noelle Bombardier arrived for work one morning to find Supreme Court Justice William O. Douglas pacing the floor in the drawing room with a woman named Gertrude Ball who handled business affairs for the Kennedys. Ethel was at the Kennedy compound at the time.

"What's going on here?" Noelle asked.

"Oh, my, it's just *terrible!*" Gertrude Ball exclaimed. She then explained that earlier that morning David had called her to say that a burglar had broken into his bedroom, that there had been a bloody fight, and that the room had in the process been completely ransacked. She didn't explain why Douglas was present, and Bombardier didn't ask.

"Well, has anyone been up there to see if David's okay?" Noelle asked. The answer was, "No. We're both too afraid to go up there." Noelle then asked if they had called the police. They were just about to do so, Ball said. "No, wait, let me go check it out," Noelle decided.

Noelle would later recall thinking that the story seemed suspect, primarily because David's room was on the third floor and she couldn't imagine how an intruder would be able to get a ladder to that level of the house. After running upstairs, she gently knocked on David's bedroom door. No answer. She then slowly opened the door while bracing herself for fear of what she might find. She peeked in and saw David passed out on the bed with a young woman at his side. Taking a quick look around, she noticed that a window had indeed been broken. There was also furniture scattered about, as if a fight had occurred. Worse, there was blood on the floor. She went over to David and shook him by the shoulder. He looked up at her with a groggy expression, said he was fine, and then passed out again. Noelle decided that whatever had occurred in that room had involved drugs, and that it would be best to not call the police. She raced back down and told Douglas and Ball of her theory. "Whatever shall we do?" Ball asked. "Well, I think you should call Mrs. Kennedy," Noelle said. "Heck, no, I'm not calling her. You call her," was Ball's response. "Oh, good Lord," Noelle said. She ran into the kitchen and got on the phone with Ethel at the Kennedy compound to tell her what was going on. "I don't think it was break-in, though," she reported to Ethel. "I think David was on drugs and just trashed the room himself. Or maybe he had some friends over and they had a party that got out of hand, I don't know..."

"But David is supposed to be at Teddy's house!" Ethel exclaimed.

Before she left for the Cape, Ethel had asked Ted if he wouldn't mind watching over David for a couple of weeks while he finished school and before he joined his mother at the Cape. Ted had said he would do it. However, David only stayed with his uncle for two days before he announced that he was returning to Hickory Hill. He promised that he would not misbehave, and that was the end of it, as far as he was concerned. Ted did what he could to make David stay at his house, but what could he do, really? David was a grown man, not a child. He returned to Hickory Hill, saying, "My uncle is no better than I am. He needs a babysitter more than I do!" When Noelle explained all of this to Ethel Kennedy, suffice it to say, she was not pleased. "Well, then, fine," she said. "You march right back up there and you tell David to clean up his room." It was an odd response, to say the least, considering the circumstances.

"Mrs. Kennedy, I can't do that, Noelle protested. "That doesn't seem reasonable. This is more than just an untidy bedroom..."

"*I don't care,*" Ethel said, according to Noelle's recollection of the conversation. "You tell David to clean up that mess!"

"But Justice Douglas is here with Mrs. Ball and they want to call the police."

"What in the world are *they* doing there?" Ethel wanted to know. "*What the heck is going on there?* Don't you dare call the police," she warned. "You just do what I am telling you to do. You go up to David's room and you tell him that his mother said to straighten out that mess. Now!" With that, she hung up the phone. Obviously, Ethel hadn't fully connected with the gravity of what was going on, or she just didn't want to do so.

Noelle agreed with Ethel that the police should not be called. She got the two visitors out of the house and off the property as quickly as she could, telling them that she would handle the matter. After they left, she called Ted Kennedy and told him what had happened. "Holy Christ!" was Ted's response. "You know, I tried to get him to stay here," he added, his tone a little defensive. "But he wouldn't do it. But I told Ethie he needs to be in a hospital, not here at my house. What do you think we should we do?" Ted Kennedy asked. "*What should we do now?*" That this is what it had come to—Senator Ted Kennedy asking Ethel Kennedy's personal assistant for advice—suggests a hard truth: No one knew what to do about David Kennedy.

Intervention for David

*P*erhaps no one in the Kennedy family understood that better than his long-suffering aunt, Joan Kennedy. Because she had been battling an addiction to alcohol and prescription pills for so many years, she could obviously relate to David's complex emotional issues, and she also understood what it was like to feel like a complete outcast in the close-knit family. She certainly never felt that she belonged either. When she saw David at a family function, the two had a chance to really talk, and David confided in her. He said that he felt everyone in the family was staring at him during the ceremony "because they know I'm a junkie. I'm sorry I'm so weak," he told Joan. "I just don't want you or anyone else I love to lose faith in me." He also told his aunt that he felt he "wasn't good enough to be a Kennedy," and that all he had done in recent years was "bring shame upon my family." Joan somehow got David to admit to her that he was using everything from pot to coke to heroin to Demerol to methadone, and that he was also drinking heavily. He also claimed that his uncle Ted had been so tremendously upset with him recently that "he threatened to lock me away like his sister Rosemary, for the rest of my life in some psychiatric facility." Joan was understandably upset by everything her nephew had revealed to her. Had Ted actually said that to David? "Of course not, Joansie," he said when she confronted him. "I would never say such a thing to him. Why would he tell you that?"

"I think we should have an intervention," Joan suggested to Ted in a meeting with him, Richard Burke, Stephen Smith, Eunice and Sarge Shriver, and several other people, including key Kennedy family PR people and attorneys. A strong proponent of therapy for some time now, Joan firmly believed in the value of carefully executed interventions—a therapeutic process during which the addict's friends and family members confront him to remind him of the consequences of his actions and also to tell him how those actions have affected them and, most important, to make it clear that if he doesn't get help they will cut him out of their lives. "I have done a lot of research into this," Joan said, extracting a stack of brochures from her large purse. "I've talked to a number of doctors and psychiatrists and here's what they have told me." She spent about thirty minutes detailing the possible benefits of an intervention. Everyone was quite impressed.

"Well, I think that's just a *marvelous* idea," Eunice decided. She said that she too had talked to several psychiatrists about the very subject, and as she put it, "I am totally convinced of its viability as a solution."

Sargent Shriver wasn't so sure. He was concerned that it would appear to David as if everyone was piling on him. "That will just piss him off," Sarge offered. "Then what?"

"It has to be Ethie's decision, then," Ted said, according to a recollection of the meeting. "Let's run it by her and see what she thinks. I agree with Joansie, though, we have to do something. And I like this idea. Good one, Joansie," he said, smiling at her. She beamed back at him. It must have been a good feeling for her to know that she had contributed something important.

When the drastic idea of an intervention was later presented to Ethel Kennedy at a follow-up meeting, she, like Sarge, expressed some ambivalence. She agreed that David might feel that everyone was ganging up on him, and she wasn't sure what good that would do him. In the end, though, she had to admit that she was at the end of her rope, so she agreed to it. She decided, though, not to be a part of it. "God knows, he knows how I feel," she explained, "and we're at such odds right now, he'll just start lashing out at me and, to tell you the truth, I can't take it." Everyone understood.

"So David's brother Joe and I planned the intervention at a nearby hotel," Richard Burke later recalled. "To my memory, all of his brothers and sisters were present. We had a psychiatrist there who acted as a mediator. We had a facility lined up and the plan was to take David right over there from the hotel. They all told David how much they loved him and how disappointed in him they all were, and that if he didn't straighten up his act they were going to stop communicating with him. It was standard intervention material. Very tough. Very upsetting. Lots of tears. I recall that when someone brought up that his uncle Teddy was disappointed in him, David really lashed out. 'The way he drinks,' David said, 'and the way he has lived his life and treated Aunt Joan? How does he get off being disappointed in me?'

"To be honest, I don't think it did any good," Richard Burke continued. "I'm not sure we understood the depth of his shame, that the guilt he felt about the relapses was partly responsible for his wanting to continue to medicate himself, if you will. He was so ashamed, and he kept saying as much. Even with the shrink there, I just had a feeling we were in over our heads with this thing. He absolutely refused to go to the facility, and short of dragging him over there, what could we do? The next day, I reported back to the senator that I didn't think the intervention had been successful. He was crestfallen. 'Goddamn!' he told me. 'I don't know why, but I just thought it would work. I really did.'"

The next couple of years would amount only to more of the same for David Kennedy—unsuccessful treatments at rehabilitation centers followed by relapses, unhappiness, shame, and despair. He would lose track of the many meetings he would take with his uncle Ted about possible strategies to help him with his addictions. "I am always being chewed out by my uncle," he would say at the time, "and I feel really bad about it. The whole thing is messed up."

In the spring of 1983, events took an even more dramatic turn when author David Horowitz contacted David Kennedy, now twenty-seven, to interview him for a book he was writing about the Kennedys. Horowitz had been around the family for a couple of years, brought into the fold by Bobby when he asked Bobby to help him network into the third generation. The relationship with Bobby started off peacefully enough, with Horowitz promising not to write about the young Kennedys' drug issues unless any of them became news and thus public information. Still, the more Horowitz hung around Bobby Kennedy and Chris Lawford, the more exposed he was to their private worlds and became privy to some of their more private moments with women and, yes, drugs—much of which would end up being detailed in his book, cowritten with Peter Collier.

Horowitz said that he believed David Kennedy had been the scapegoat for many of the family's problems, and that he wanted to give the young and troubled Kennedy a voice. Perhaps at the risk of exploiting David's vulnerability and certainly appealing to his sense of having been so misunderstood, the writer guaranteed that if David agreed to further interviews for the book, it would set the record straight once and for all. David, who wasn't very untrusting of the media as a rule, thought it over and ultimately agreed to be interviewed. He then spent four days being questioned by Horowitz—four days that he would soon regret. "I feel they should have done something earlier," David told the author in speaking about how the family had handled his addictions. "My mother, although in a sense she wasn't really competent. But even more, Ted, Steve Smith and the rest of the group who were always figuring out ways to keep Joe, Bobby and Chris from having to pay the piper, just let me go. When they finally did do something, it seemed like it was more to keep me from OD'ing in the street and causing a problem for Ted's campaigning, than anything else."

On September 10, 1983, David entered yet another rehabilitation program in Spofford, New Hampshire. His ex-girlfriend Pam Kelley—who had been paralyzed in the auto accident years earlier—spoke to David after he finished the program at Spofford, which was just six days. "He seemed somewhat better," she would recall. "He said he was hopeful. He was tired of being looked at as the Kennedy screwup. He wanted more for himself and his family. 'I get it now that I'm totally responsible for my own problems,' he told me. 'I want to be better. I don't want to be this guy who is always so ashamed of himself and of what he is doing to his family. I will be better. I have to get better.'"

Bobby Jr.'s Surprising Drug Bust

*J*ust one day after David Kennedy checked into the program in Spofford, Ethel Kennedy got a troubling telephone call from a family friend in Rapid City, South Dakota, an attorney named John Fitzgerald. He had bad news—as if she needed more bad news! Her son Bobby was being questioned by police there after apparently overdosing on a Republic Airlines jet from Watertown to Rapid City. He had also been found in possession of heroin, a small amount in his carry-on bag. (The authorities would decide to keep the luggage for further inspection, and two days later they would find even more evidence of the drug.) After about three hours of questioning, Bobby was released.

Many years later, in 2000, John Fitzgerald recalled, "Unfortunately, yes, I was the one who had to call Ethel Kennedy and give her this news. As it happened, Bobby called Ted to tell him what had happened, and Ted called me and asked me to handle it. He suggested I call Ethel, telling me that he couldn't bear to do it himself.

"It was not an easy call to make. I thought for some reason she would be more stoic, but that was not the case. She was upset. 'I already have my hands full with David,' she told me. 'I can't go through this with Bobby, too.'"

A series of intense telephone calls between the Kennedys took place over the course of the next two days while Bobby was holed up in a hotel in South Dakota. He was in trouble and needed help, that much was clear. But the idea of sending another young Kennedy to rehab wasn't easy to accept. "David was the Kennedy screwup, not Bobby," said Christopher Lawford. "So this was a real wake-up call."

Even though he had obviously been in some trouble in the past—such as when he and his cousin Bobby Shriver were arrested for pot possession back in 1970—Bobby, the third of the eleven RFK children, was thought of as the one most likely to follow in his father's footsteps. He had cut a striking figure as a teenager—back in the days when Ethel would ban him from the house and he would sleep in a tent on the beach—very tall and lanky with shoulder-length black hair and always with his pet falcon on his shoulder. A Harvard and University of Virginia Law School graduate who now worked as an assistant district attorney in Manhattan, he was viewed as sensible and focused. Though he failed his bar exam on the first try, he did pass it on the second try. "I don't want the pressure of doing great Kennedy-like things in my life," he had said, "but I see that there's no escaping it." One classmate at Harvard recalled a speech Bobby delivered in jurisprudence class. "He talked about the eighties and how self-indulgent they were and how, in the sixties, people cared. He made this incredible comment about the loss of ideals since the sixties. At that point, I think we realized—hey, this kid really is Bobby Kennedy's son."

Bobby married Emily Ruth Black (a classmate from the University of Virginia Law School), in March 1982, but the union was troubled from the start; she complained that he had "a lot of suppressed and not-so-suppressed anger." After the two moved into an apartment that had been bequeathed him by close family friend Lem Billings, Bobby used drugs to cope with his troubles. At first, it had been alcohol and marijuana as a teenager with his cousins, and then cocaine and, eventually, heroin, which, like his younger brother David, he would score in the streets of Harlem. Everyone knew it. It wasn't a secret. After all, he'd been using for fourteen years. It was just that so much focus had been on David's troubles, Bobby's weren't viewed as being that serious.

"I was part of a generational revolution that looked at drugs almost as a political statement—a rebellion against the preceding generation which had opposed the civil rights movement and promoted Vietnam," Kennedy would observe many years later. "At the time, I don't think any of us were aware of how damaging drugs could be. I'd always had iron willpower and the ability to control my appetites. At nine I gave up candy for Lent and didn't eat it again until I was in college. After I started taking drugs, I earnestly tried to stop. I couldn't. That's the most demoralizing part of addiction. I couldn't keep contracts with myself."

It was eventually decided to send Bobby to Fair Oaks Hospital, a treatment center in Summit, New Jersey. Once there, he issued a statement through Ted Kennedy's office saying, "I am determined to beat this thing." Later he would plead guilty to drug possession and would be sentenced to community service.

Ironically, this unfortunate incident would turn out to be the best thing ever to happen to young Bobby Kennedy, because afterward he would never again use drugs. To his credit, this former member of the HPTs—the Hyannis Port Terrors—really turned his life around. He has been sober for twenty-eight years. "I'm one of the lucky ones: I've never had a single urge since," he says. "Once I completed a twelve-step program, the obsession I lived with for fourteen years just lifted. I would describe it as miraculous."

Like his mother and many of his family members, Bobby Kennedy is today extremely religious. He carries a rosary in his pocket wherever he goes, and he says the prayers of the rosary every day of his life.

"I Love You, Mom. That's All I Got."

It was January 1984, the beginning of a new year. "I keep praying that each year will be a better one for us," Sargent Shriver said in his New Year's toast while surrounded by many of the Kennedys' third generation of sons and daughters. Much of the family had convened at Sargent and Eunice Shriver's home for a New Year's get-together, and even David was present. "I hope this will be that year," Sarge said.

As it happened, David Kennedy had spent much of the last two years in Sacramento, isolated from the family as he attempted to build a new life there, all the while continuing to do drugs and remaining as unhappy and disillusioned as ever. Ted and Ethel didn't want him to go, but his mind was made up. He wanted to be away from Hickory Hill. In some ways, Bobby's drug bust had just made things worse for him. It had been Bobby's first bust and first time at rehab, and the family was solidly behind him in a way that David envied. Bobby had been using drugs as long as David and, in David's eyes, had only been better at hiding it. So why should he now have so much familial support? David really was blind to any support the family had given him—it was as if he was just too far gone to recognize it.

After Bobby's return from rehab, Ethel seemed even closer to him than before—and this probably made no sense to David either. Why was she always so angry at him, yet not mad at Bobby? Also, Bobby's recovery somehow seemed easy for him—which made David feel all the more inadequate. All of it seemed unfair, and in David's eyes the family's typical dynamic was always to see the odds stacked against him.

"I'm just trying to hold this family together," Ethel had earlier told Jackie during the reception after the September wedding of Sydney, Pat's daughter, at the Kennedy compound. In truth, Ethel wasn't really doing such a bad job. If anything, David's ongoing turmoil stood in stark contrast to what was going on in the lives of his siblings by 1984.

For instance, by this time, David's oldest sister, Kathleen, thirty-four—the first of Rose and Joseph's grandchildren—had spent almost the last ten years raising two children by attorney David Townsend. She'd gotten her law degree in 1978 and was working as a property program analyst at the Massachusetts State House in Governor Mike Dukakis's Office of Human Resources. David was a stay-at-home dad, writing a novel. "He represents the new kind of father," Eunice said at the time. "He really enjoys taking care of the kids." The couple soon moved to Santa Fe, New Mexico, which is where two of their children, Meaghan and Maeve, were born—at home, via Lamaze. "There is a tradition in New Mexico that after a home birth you bury the placenta and plant a tree over it," Kathleen explained years later. "My mother arrived the day after and looked in the icebox. 'What is this?' she asked. I said, 'A placenta.' She said, 'What's it doing there behind the milk?' I said, 'Well, there's this tradition...' She went out and bought a piñon tree and buried the placenta herself. She's open to all new experiences." David, with nothing but the knowledge of a police manual, delivered Maeve himself, since no local doctor could be found who would attend a home birth. "She was born in the amniotic sac, as Meaghan had been—a sign of great grace, according to an old midwife legend," he said. "I had to chew through the sac or she would have drowned." They were then—and are still—an unconventional couple, and very happy together.

David's older brother, Joe, thirty-two, had married Sheila Rauch in 1979 and had twin boys in early 1983. To his credit, after the accident that had paralyzed Pam Kelley, Joe really did turn his life around and stayed out of trouble. He was presently running the Citizens Energy Corporation, a nonprofit energy company started by Richard Goodwin, who had been a speechwriter for JFK and had also worked as an adviser to Bobby. Joe was toying with the idea of running for office. In two years, he would be elected to the U.S. House of Representatives from the Massachusetts 8th Congressional District, and it would certainly seem as if he would have perhaps the brightest political career of any of the Kennedys' third generation.

As earlier stated, Bobby, twenty-nine, had done very well in his drug rehabilitation in New Jersey after his recent surprising drug bust. He and his wife, Emily, would go on to have a boy together in 1984 and in another four years a girl. The following year, Bobby would join the Riverkeeper organization to satisfy his fifteen hundred hours of community service. He worked with the group to sue alleged polluters of the Hudson River, and after his community service was completed he would end up taking a job with the organization as its chief attorney. Bobby would also found (and is the current chairman of) the umbrella organization Waterkeeper Alliance. In 1994, Bobby and Emily would divorce and he would marry an architect named Mary Richardson, with whom he would have four children. In 2010, he would file for divorce from Mary after sixteen years of marriage, just three days before she would be charged with drunken driving.

Mary Courtney Kennedy, better known as Courtney, twenty-eight, had gotten a job as a producer at the Children's Television Network and was now married to ABC sports producer Jeffrey Robert Ruhe. The marriage would be over by the late 1980s, making Courtney the first in the third generation of Kennedys to divorce. She would get remarried in 1993 to Paul Michael Hill, an Irishman who was wrongly imprisoned for fifteen years over IRA activity. He was one of the Guildford Four convicted of bombing two pubs outside of London. (The 1993 film In the Name of the Father was based on this case.) They would have one child together and be legally separated in 2006.

Meanwhile, Michael Kennedy, twenty-six, had married Victoria Gifford, daughter of legendary New York Giants halfback, Hall of Famer, and sportscaster Frank Gifford, in 1981. By the beginning of 1984 they had one son, and would have two more children in the coming years. In 1984, he would graduate from the University of Virginia Law School.

Mary Kerry Kennedy, better known as Kerry, twenty-five, was now working as a human rights activist, and in four years she would establish the Robert Kennedy Center for Human Rights.

Christopher George Kennedy, twenty-one, was attending Boston College in Chestnut Hill and would graduate in two years with a BA degree. He would marry Sheila Sinclair Berner in 1986 and they would have four children. Earlier, in 1979 and 1980, he worked for his uncle Ted's campaign for the Democratic presidential nomination, and in 1988 he would become treasurer of the campaign committee for his brother Joe's reelection to the U.S. House of Representatives.

Matthew Maxwell Taylor Kennedy, better known as Max, nineteen, was about to enter Harvard, where he would graduate with honors. He would later attend the University of Virginia Law School and then go on to become an assistant district attorney in the juvenile crime unit of the Philadelphia prosecutor's office. He and his wife, Vicki, also an alumna of UVLS, would go on to have three children.

Meanwhile, Douglas Kennedy was seventeen and Rory Kennedy sixteen, and both were in private schools.

Now, if only the family could get twenty-eight-year-old David on the right track.

"What's troubling you, David?" Noelle Bombardier asked him one night in early 1984 when he had arrived from the West Coast for a visit. Everyone was gone from Hickory Hill, and David, not wanting to be alone, had asked Ethel's assistant if she wouldn't mind staying at the house for a few extra hours before returning to her own home. He might have been almost thirty, but he was still such a little boy at heart. She agreed to stay and have dinner with him, as she often did. "Why are you so very sad?" she asked him. "Tell me the truth." David then sat down and told Noelle the exact same chilling story of witnessing his father's death that Ethel had earlier relayed to her. "I was in my room all by myself," he said, his voice devoid of all emotion. "All the politicians and grown-ups were downstairs, and I didn't want to go down there, so I stayed in my room. I was watching television and then all of a sudden I saw my dad get shot, and I saw my mother kneeling over him, and I thought, that's it. He's dead. It just plays over and over in my head," he concluded. "Over and over and over..."

"I understand," Noelle said, taking him into her arms. "I understand."

The two then had dinner, but there wasn't much either of them could say after David's heartbreaking story. It had been just that distressing.

About a week later, David and his mother, Ethel, had another confrontation that spoke volumes about the hopelessness and exasperation everyone was feeling at this time. Actually it was a showdown that had been building all day. That morning, Ethel walked into the drawing room to find a picture of her and Bobby from their wedding day placed on the coffee table instead of hanging in its place on the wall. When she picked it up and examined it, she found powdery traces on it. Clearly, someone had been using the glass as a base from which to sniff cocaine. In her mind, this was one of the most sacrilegious things she'd ever heard of; it was more than she could handle. She broke down into racking sobs in the living room, clutching the wedding picture to her bosom. Noelle recalled her being "absolutely inconsolable for hours."

That night, Eunice and Sargent were scheduled to have dinner at Hickory Hill and then meet with the third generation of Kennedys to discuss certain philanthropic endeavors in which they hoped to involve them. David didn't show up for the meal, much to Ethel's embarrassment. Afterward, he finally made his appearance, looking tired and disheveled. Throughout the time Sargent spoke to the young Kennedys about the importance of being of service, mother and son exchanged angry stares.

Finally, after Sargent finished his talk and was surrounded by eager Kennedys asking him questions, Ethel pulled David into the kitchen by his arm. Concerned about what might happen in there between them, a couple of his siblings followed them, as did two of his friends. "How dare you show up looking like this?" Ethel demanded to know of David. *"What is wrong with you?"*

David didn't answer. He just stood in front of his mother looking defeated.

"And was it *you* who used the wedding picture of me and your father to do drugs?" she demanded. "It *was* you, wasn't it? Who else?" she asked. *"Who else?"*

Still no answer.

"Answer me," Ethel demanded, looking at her son with angry eyes.

But now she was crying. "You answer me this very instant, David Kennedy!" David took a deep breath and let it out slowly. Then, seeming very ashamed of himself and with tears in his eyes, he very quietly said, "I love you, Mom. That's all I got."

Ethel seemed taken aback. The two just stared at each other for a few moments. What else was there to say? "Oh my God, David," Ethel said, sounding as if someone had just knocked the wind out of her. Then, with tears streaming down her face, she did what any mother would probably have done in a similar circumstance: She took her son into her arms and held him as tightly as she could.

A Kidnapping Attempt at the Compound

Look, I have *tried* to talk to her about it," Senator Ted Kennedy said to Ethel's assistant, Noelle Bombardier, "but it's like talking to a brick."

"But, Senator, it's ridiculous," Noelle told Ted. "All the windows are always open, as are the doors. Anyone can get in here. I don't feel that any of us are safe."

"I know," said Ted, who was certainly no stranger to such fears. "You just learn to live with it, you know?"

Bombardier was referring to the fact that neither of Ethel Kennedy's homes—at Hickory Hill nor at the Kennedy compound—were equipped with security systems. It made no sense to anyone, especially given what had happened to Jack and Bobby. However, Ethel was adamant. She didn't view the extra security as a precautionary measure but rather as something that would be foisted upon her because of what had happened to Bobby. "I don't want to live in fear," she said. "I won't do it." Everyone knew this was how she felt, and everyone just had to deal with it.

What spurred Bombardier's conversation with Kennedy was this: The night before, there had been a frightening break-in at Hickory Hill. An apparent vagrant broke into the main house and actually entered fifteen-year-old Rory's bedroom on the third floor. "Where's your mom's room?" he demanded to know. Scared out of her wits, the girl said, "Down the hall." At the same time, Ethel apparently heard something in the hallway, turned on the light in her room, and then opened the door to find a strange man standing on the other side of it. She screamed out at the top of her lungs. In moments, the entire household was awake, including all of her sons, who quickly tackled the intruder to the ground. It turned out that the intruder was what Ethel later called "a harmless wacko." Still, one might think this event would have been enough to frighten her into changing her mind about a security system. It didn't, though. After that event, Ted did everything he could to convince Ethel that the situation was dire, but she wouldn't accept it. "There are too many activities going on here," she told him, "and I don't want bells going off all the time. It would drive me crazy. So the answer is no!"

About a year later, in the spring of 1984, something even more frightening occurred.

Noelle Bombardier was at the Hyannis Port home getting it ready for Ethel and the family's summer stay. She was in the process of having it painted by four male students she'd recruited from Harvard to do the job. As the work was being done, a woman with a small child knocked on the door and asked to use the phone. She said that Ted often allowed her to come onto the property. Noelle instantly knew that the woman was lying. However, as it happened, anyone could actually walk up to the house. From the street side, a guard station was in place, ostensibly to prevent tourists from getting to the compound's homes. But from the beach, all one had to do was walk right up to any of them. Bombardier told the woman to leave the premises immediately or she would call the police. She left, but a little while later she returned, this time alone. Then, while Noelle was in another room of the house, the intruder approached Noelle's daughter, Danielle, who was about ten. "Would you like to meet my little girl?" she asked. Before long, Danielle was walking off hand in hand with the intruder—the painters all believing the intruder to be one of the household's maids.

When Noelle realized her daughter was gone, she understandably became frantic. Hysterical, she called the police. She then got into her automobile and began driving down the beach, looking for her daughter. She soon found her, still walking with the intruder. "I drove along keeping my eye on them, thinking, how do I kill this woman and not hurt my child in the process?" Noelle recalled. "I was twenty feet away and ready to push on the gas when, from out of nowhere, I was suddenly surrounded by police. As the cops drew their guns on the woman, I got out of my car and ran to my child and pulled her away from the intruder. She was then handcuffed. 'What were you trying to do?' the police asked her. 'I was trying to kidnap Rory Kennedy,' she admitted. 'She thought my daughter was Rory Kennedy!'"

After the abductor was carted away by the police, Bombardier drove her daughter back to Ethel's house, from where she immediately telephoned her boss at Hickory Hill.

"Oh my God, that is *terrible*," Ethel said, seeming genuinely shocked.

"And now I have to go down to the police station and file criminal charges against the woman," Noelle said.

There was a long pause on the line. Then Ethel finally said, "Absolutely not. You'll do no such thing!"

"But Mrs. Kennedy, she thought it was *Rory* she was taking," Noelle said, according to her memory of the conversation. "Of course we must press charges."

"I said, *no!*" Ethel repeated. She explained that if criminal charges were filed, the media would find out about the incident, which meant it would generate press. She didn't want that kind of attention. Moreover, she said she was afraid such publicity would spur copycat attempts. "So let's just forget it ever happened," she told Noelle. That might have been something Ethel Kennedy could have done, but arguably not most people. Noelle was very upset. "Okay, fine," she said. "Then I quit."

"Now, you are really overreacting, Noelle," Ethel said, trying to stay calm. "Just go get a good night's sleep and we'll discuss this tomorrow. But do *not* file charges." Very early the next morning she telephoned Noelle as she was packing her things to leave the compound. "But if you leave now, who is going to let the maids in later this morning?" Ethel wanted to know.

"Do you think I'm worried about your damn maids?" Noelle shouted into the phone, raising her voice to her employer for the first time in seven years. "Why, three cops had to spend the night here with me and my child because we were so afraid. Don't you get it?"

"But the woman is in custody," Ethel exclaimed. "I don't understand what you are so afraid of!"

The two argued for a while longer before hanging up. Noelle then left the compound to drive herself and her child back to Virginia. The next day, she showed up for work at Hickory Hill. "I certainly hope you have changed your mind about quitting," Ethel said to her. "I really don't want to lose you, Noelle." She was clearly making an attempt at smoothing things over.

"Then let me press charges," Noelle insisted.

"Absolutely not," Ethel said. "I explained to you my reasons and you'll just have to accept them. Now that's the end of it!"

"Well, I'm sorry, Mrs. Kennedy," Noelle said, "but I can't act like this is okay. This was my child. And it could have been Rory. I'm afraid I have to leave."

"But it's just such a shame," Ethel said, seeming to really mean it.

"Yes, it is," Noelle agreed. "It's such a shame."

The two then parted company. "It wasn't necessarily on bad terms," Noelle Bombardier said many years later. "I just couldn't stay on after what had happened, and after the way Mrs. Kennedy had reacted to it. I was heartbroken by it and, I have to say, very concerned about Mrs. Kennedy's safety under the circumstances, and that of her family."

Always Tomorrow?

$\mathcal{M}$ost people who knew David Kennedy point to the then-imminent publication of *The Kennedys: An American Drama* by David Horowitz and Peter Collier as being the catalyst to David's final meltdown. In his interviews with Horowitz, David had been very candid about not only his drug use but also that of other family members. In fact, he had been critical of just about everyone, especially his own mother. The authors quoted him liberally. Worse yet, pretty much all of Bobby's and Chris's drug exploits were in the book as well. Perhaps venting about his family's dysfunction had made him feel better in the moment, but afterward David was racked with guilt about it, and very sorry he had ever participated. Paula Sculley was with David when he reviewed excerpts of the book for the first time, which were published in *Playboy* along with a photo of David shooting up. "He bent his head over and said, 'My God, this is awful. It's trash,'" she remembered. "He felt betrayed and used."

On March 19, 1984, David entered the drug program at St. Mary's Rehabilitation Center in St. Paul, Minnesota, his fifth stint in a rehabilitation center. "This is it, David," his uncle Ted had told him. "I'm very serious. We're running out of solutions here." Now he was as frustrated as he was sad. "It's time for you to be a real Kennedy," he told him, falling back on elements of the family's standard credo as a last resort. "Kennedys don't quit," Ted said. "Kennedys don't fail. Kennedys don't let each other down." It was all well-meaning, of course, but the senator was basically verbalizing David's worst fears about himself: David *did* feel like a quitter, he *did* feel like a failure, and he *did* feel as if he was letting everyone down.

Unfortunately, the program at St. Mary's was just a twenty-eight-day program—certainly not enough time to make much of an impact, especially given that the first excerpt of the dreaded Kennedy book hit the streets in *Playboy* pretty much as soon as David got into St. Mary's.

After David finished his stay at St. Mary's, he was scheduled to join much of the family in Palm Beach to spend Easter with his grandmother Rose. Since she was not well, the Kennedys wanted to be sure to celebrate this particular holiday. In fact, they were sure it would be her last. (Actually, the ever-tenacious Rose would live another ten years!) Because there were so many relatives present when David arrived on April 19, there was no room at Rose's mansion, so David stayed at the nearby Brazilian Court Hotel and Beach Club—a luxury destination for affluent tourists—as did several of his siblings.

While in Palm Beach for the next six days, David would visit daily with his grandmother. He hadn't seen her in some time and was deeply saddened by how much she had deteriorated. He loved her, as did everyone, and hated seeing her so small and fragile and sick.

Meanwhile, back in Virginia, Ethel Kennedy was still frantic as to what to do about her son. On Monday morning, April 23, she called her nephew Michael Skakel. "She told me that David was back on drugs," Michael recalled. "I wasn't surprised. I didn't think twenty-eight days at St. Mary's was going to do anything for him. She begged me to find another place for him, so I started checking around. The problem was that she didn't want me to use the Kennedy name. She was afraid that if I was canvassing rehab centers and using the Kennedy name it would get out, and she didn't want any more bad press about her son. She was adamant about that. 'You must be discreet,' she told me. In the end, though, without being able to say he was a Kennedy I couldn't get the kind of special treatment Ethel wanted for David. I might have been able to get him into a good rehab in a few weeks, but not instantly—and she wanted instantly."

On Tuesday afternoon, April 24, Ethel placed four telephone calls to Palm Beach lawyer Howell Van Gerbig Jr., a friend of the Kennedy family's. She was extremely agitated, the attorney would later recall, and wanted to know if there was anything he could think of to help David. "She was at a loss," Van Gerbig said. "She said that David had been abusive to some of the staff working at his grandmother's estate, and even to some of his relatives there. When I asked her what drugs he was on, she seemed confused. As far as she knew, she said, all he was taking was the sedative Mellaril. When I observed that he must certainly be on other drugs, she said, 'He promised me he stopped doing heroin, but I'm afraid he's lying to me.' I recommended a doctor in Florida who might be able to be of assistance. I also offered to meet with David myself at dinner. Ethel begged him to call me to set it up, and he did. But then David didn't show for the dinner. She called me first thing in the morning [Wednesday] and when I told her that he didn't show, she was upset. I was almost as worried about her as I was about her son."

"David would start with the drinking and drugs early in the afternoon, usually vodka," said Terrence Murphy, a friend of David's who was summoned by the young Kennedy and asked to join him in Palm Beach. "I flew down and met him at a bar called Doherty's, just around the corner from the hotel. It was about one in the afternoon. I walked in looking for David and saw what looked like an old guy nursing a drink, sitting at the bar with his back to me. When I approached him and he turned around, I couldn't believe it was David."

After the two greeted one another, Terrence took a seat next to David and asked him how he had fared at rehab. "Oh yeah, it was well worth the money my uncle Teddy spent on it," he said. Then, raising his double vodka on the rocks, he added, "Cheers, buddy!" Terrence observed that David's drinking at such an early hour wasn't a good idea, saying that it was making him look like an old man, at least according to his recollection of the conversation. "I *am* an old man," David remarked as he lit a Marlboro. "How's your mom?" Terrence asked. "Same as always," David said. "Have you heard about this book I'm in?" David then asked, changing the subject. He added that he had "spilled my guts to some punk writer," and he was afraid of how his family would react when the book was finally published. "I really did it this time," he said.

Terrence smiled and put his hand on David's shoulder. "Well, there's always tomorrow," he offered.

David stared ahead blankly. "Not always," he said.

Room 107

*I*t was Thursday, April 26, 1984, and Ethel Kennedy was pacing nervously back and forth between her kitchen and the study at her home in Hickory Hill. "Has he called yet?" she asked her new assistant, Leah Mason, who had that very week replaced Noelle Bombardier. "No, Mrs. Kennedy," came her response. "Well, where is he?" Ethel asked urgently, not really expecting an answer. She had been upset all morning, saying she had a feeling, a premonition, that something was wrong with David. "A mother just knows," she told Mason. "I have a terrible feeling."

Two days earlier, on Tuesday night, David was supposed to attend a dinner at Rose Kennedy's. He didn't show up. The next day—Wednesday— he was supposed to take a flight from Palm Beach back to Boston where he shared an apartment with Paula Sculley. The last Paula had heard from him was earlier that day when he called to tell her he was on his way. The two had planned a vacation to the Bahamas, and they chatted about it for a few moments. David also mentioned looking forward to an AA meeting he planned to attend once he got back to Boston. That was the last anyone had heard from him.

On Wednesday night, when Paula called Ethel to ask if David had shown up there, Ethel immediately knew that something was wrong. She called the hotel in Palm Beach and asked for David's room, 107. He had not checked out, yet there was no answer.

She called again, and again, and again. No answer.

"Room 107," she requested at midnight. Still no answer.

Finally, Ethel went to bed, though she would not sleep a wink. A curious unease had taken hold of her.

At three in the morning, Ethel called again. "Room 107." No answer.

By the next morning, she was completely frantic. She called again. "Room 107, please." Still no answer.

And again an hour later. "Room 107." The phone just rang.

Ethel then called all of David's siblings. No one had heard from him.

Her son Douglas, seventeen, was still at the same hotel. So Ethel called his room. No answer.

She then called her sister-in-law Jean Smith, who she knew was still in Palm Beach. No answer there either. It was maddening.

Finally, at 9:45, Ethel called Caroline Kennedy—who was still in Palm Beach at Rose's house—and asked that she go to the hotel and check on David. Fifteen minutes later, Caroline and her cousin Sydney Lawford went to the hotel and called from the lobby, but got no answer. They went to David's door and knocked repeatedly. Again, no answer. Finally, they left, went back to Rose's, and called Ethel to tell her that they thought David was simply not in the room. "Well, then where in the world is he?" Ethel asked Leah Mason in exasperation.

At 10:30, Ethel called David's room again, then again at 11:00. Still no answer.

At 11:15, Ethel's phone rang. She jumped to answer it, thinking it was David. It was Jackie. Caroline had called her mother to tell her that David was missing. The two cousins had grown very close in recent years and Caroline was frightened. It's not known what Jackie said to Ethel, but from Ethel's side of the conversation it seemed that Jackie was offering to send a private investigator down to Florida to find out what was going on there. Ethel thanked Jackie and said she would get back to her soon if David didn't show up.

After Ethel hung up with Jackie, Ted Kennedy called. Again, Ted's side of the conversation is unknown. However, Ethel was heard telling him, "I'm just not as strong as you are, Teddy. I'm falling apart here. I don't know what to do!" Apparently he asked if he should come to her side. He must have been out of town, though, because Ethel's response was, "No, I can't have you come all that way just for me. I have my boys. I'm okay." She thanked Ted for his call and promised to get back to him as soon as David was located.

After hanging up with Ted, Ethel crumpled into the leather chair behind her mahogany desk in the study and stared into a cup of cold black coffee as she said the rosary. When she finished, she began waxing nostalgic about her son to Leah Mason. "I remember when David got the idea to collect sand in little plastic baggies and sell them to tourists as 'Kennedy Sand' for a dollar a bag," she said with a smile. "Oh, I was so mad at him for that," Ethel said. Then, after a beat, she added, "I wish now I had not been so mad." She sighed deeply. "Why was I always so... *mad?*" Taking a deep breath, she then reached for the phone on the desk and dialed the number to the hotel once again. In Palm Beach, Josephine Dampier—secretary to the hotel's manager—picked up the phone.

"This is Mrs. Kennedy again," Ethel said. "I'm sorry to keep bothering you, but no one has heard from my son David. I've called his room repeatedly! My niece was just at your hotel and said there was no answer at his door. So I need someone to get into room 107 and make sure my boy is not in there."

"Of course, Mrs. Kennedy," Dampier said. "Would you like me to call you back?"

"No," Ethel said. "I'll stay on the line. Could you do it now?" she asked.

"Of course."

"I put her on hold and took a deep breath," Josephine Dampier would recall many years later. "Call it a mother's instinct, because I have my own kids, but I knew. For some reason, I just knew.

"I sent a desk clerk and a porter up to the room. Five minutes later, the desk clerk called me from the room, nearly hysterical. She had found him lying on the floor between twin beds that appeared to not have been slept in. He was wearing cutoff denim shorts and a pink long-sleeved preppy-looking shirt and white sneakers. His packed green duffel bag was nearby on the floor. A red light on his telephone was flashing—he had messages. From his body position on the floor, David looked as if he had been trying to get to the phone. The desk clerk knelt next to him and touched his face. It was cold. She felt for his pulse in his neck, and then at his wrist. There was none. 'He's gone, he's gone,' she told me, very upset. 'He's dead!' 'Oh my God,' I thought. 'How am I ever going to tell this to Mrs. Kennedy?' I said a quick prayer and got back on the line."

"Mrs. Kennedy," Josephine Dampier said into the receiver, "we have to call you right back because we have to call the paramedics now."

"Oh no," Ethel exclaimed. "Oh my God, no! *What happened?* Is he okay?"

"I promise you we will call you back." With that Josephine quickly hung up the phone before she could be asked any more questions. Meanwhile, at Hickory Hill, Ethel Kennedy and Leah Mason sat in the study staring at each other with fear in their eyes.

Ten minutes later, the phone rang. Ethel grabbed for it. It was Gerald Beebe, an executive from the hotel.

"Mrs. Kennedy," he began, according to his memory. "We found your son. The paramedics have arrived and—"

Ethel interrupted him. "He's dead, isn't he?" she asked. Her voice wasn't small and fearful, rather it was demanding and forceful. She wanted to know the truth, and she wanted to know it now.

"Yes, Mrs. Kennedy," came back the answer. "I'm afraid so, ma'am. Your son is dead."

At that, Ethel Kennedy let out a sickening wail. "Oh dear Jesus," she exclaimed. "No! No! No!"

"Without Faith and Family, We Have Nothing"

$\mathcal{A}$ couple of days after his death, about forty of David Kennedy's family members and friends gathered at Hickory Hill to view his emaciated-looking body in one of the mansion's many elaborately appointed drawing rooms. Almost everyone seemed to be present—Ted and Joan; Jackie; Pat; Eunice and Jean and their husbands, Sargent and Stephen; as well as all of David's siblings and many people closely connected to the Kennedy family. His brothers and sisters looked stricken. "If only David had known how much we loved him," a saddened Joe later said. "But I don't understand how he didn't know it. That's just who we are, especially the brothers. I mean, who is closer than the Kennedy brothers? The thing we have, only we brothers understand it, and we just always know it's there. I just don't understand how he didn't know it. I just don't..."

Because she was so ill, Rose Kennedy stayed behind in Florida. David, who would have been twenty-nine in less than a month, would soon be buried next to his grandfather Joseph in the family plot at Holyhood Cemetery in Brookline, Massachusetts.

In two days, there would be a funeral Mass for David. Arthur Schlesinger Jr. would later recall of it, "It was held on the terrace at Hickory Hill—a lovely day, fragrant with spring, the deep green grass rolling away toward the swimming pool and tennis court. I thought of all the happy times I have had through the years at Hickory Hill and the sad times, too. The younger brothers read prayers, Kathleen spoke charmingly about David, as did Ted Kennedy, choking back tears. I looked at Ted and Sargent Shriver, once so young and slim, now both gray and portly. Ethel was composed, pale, rather beautiful. It was a profoundly sad occasion. The cover of the program was a letter that David—then twelve years old—had sent his mother after Bobby's death—the John Donne quotation: 'Death be not proud...' carefully written and decorated—heartbreaking."

Before the funeral Mass, though, there was a wake at the house. "David is with his father and uncles now," Sargent Shriver was heard to have said as he approached Ethel at the wake. "We have to believe that God had a plan for David and that he is happy and at peace now. It's all we have, isn't it? Our faith and our family," Sargent observed, his rosary beads in his hand.

Ethel nodded. "Without that, what do we have?" she asked her brother-in-law. "Without faith and family, we have nothing." The two then embraced and held each other close, speaking softly to one another. Ethel tried to be her uplifting self, but on this day she seemed as if maybe she was on some sort of medication. She looked vacant-eyed and extremely distant. "He never got over his father's death, did he?" another mourner, not a family member, later asked her. Ethel shook her head vehemently. "His father didn't just die," she said, her tone crisp. "His father was *murdered*," she added bitterly. "And, no, to answer your question, none of us have ever gotten over his father's *murder*."

During the wake, the Kennedys did what they usually did in such circumstances—they tried to be strong for each other. However, it was obviously difficult. Many of them felt they had let David down.

In most accounts of David Kennedy's life and death over the years, the suggestion has been that the Kennedy family abandoned him, making him feel alone and isolated and thus contributing to his death. However, anyone who has ever dealt with a family member in the throes of addic-tion understands that the story is rarely so black-and-white. In fact, David did what many addicts often do; he pushed away those in his family who didn't support his addiction. Could Ethel have done more for him? Could his siblings, or other relatives? Ted? Of course, that is a question only they would be equipped to answer, but what is certain is that David Ken-nedy would also have needed to take care of himself—and he didn't. Or maybe he couldn't. After all, addiction is a disease. Oftentimes people who are addicted have a difficult time being decisive on their own. An addiction affects the brain in many ways, and one of those ways has to do with the decision-making process. Addicts usually don't make the most reasonable or responsible or accountable decisions for themselves. The most important thing a recovering addict can do is surround himself with responsible people who can help him make better decisions, and from all appearances, it does seem that David at least did that much for himself. Still, the fact remains that in the years between 1976 and his death in 1984, he had four overdoses, was arrested four times, had six stints in rehab and five hospitalizations. Every time David's loved ones sent him into rehab, it was to help him in the only way they could think of, and each time they hoped and prayed he would recover. Sadly, he never did.

"I wish now we had handled all of it differently," one of his brothers would say, "but I don't know what else we could have done."

Needless to say, there were a lot of mixed emotions at the wake. Some relatives were quite angry at David because they felt he had let them down, and himself too. Others were angry at themselves, feeling they could have done more for him. Ted seemed to understand these sorts of conflicting emotions, going to many of his relatives and patting them on the shoulder while telling them, "You did what you could." However, for the senator to hold up the rest of the family on this day was not an easy task. He too felt tremendous guilt and sadness about his nephew. He and Ethel were seen commiserating quite often, embracing one another. At one point, Ethel was seen wiping a tear from Ted's cheek. Trying to shake it off, Ted eventually did what he often did at weddings and funerals: He led the crowd in a rendition of the family's favorite, "When Irish Eyes Are Smiling." It was halfhearted at best.

At the end of the family wake, Ethel asked that she be allowed to spend a few final moments alone with the dead son she often seemed unable to reach in life. There were some who felt she could take no more grief that day, because she looked as if she had never been more overwrought or inconsolable. "Let Ethie do what she wants to do," Ted Kennedy said when asked by Bobby if he thought it was wise. "That's her boy in there. Let her do what she wants."

As Ethel Kennedy walked very slowly toward the open casket with her head bowed, all that she would have been able to see, at least at first, would have been the top of David's wavy blond hair. It must have been a shock, because she stopped for a moment to steel herself. She took a deep breath and let it out slowly. Then, as she continued toward the coffin, her son Joe quietly closed the door to the drawing room.

PART FOURTEEN

Kennedy Upheaval

Disagreements About the Kennedy Foundation

By the spring of 1984, the four surviving children of Joseph and Rose Kennedy—Eunice, Pat, Jean, and Ted—were concerned, and some might say with very good reason, that the next generation of Kennedys—their children, the third generation—would never be able to live up to the standards set not only by the adults but also by history. Most of the members of that third generation simply weren't interested in any of the Kennedy charities, most notably the Kennedy Foundation, which under Eunice's leadership had taken on the cause of mental retardation. Eunice and Sargent's four children were heavily invested—but it's not as if they had much choice. "These are important times," Eunice wrote in one of her many missives to her son Bobby in 1984. "We cannot, must not, squander these opportunities for growth and for a fuller and deeper understanding of MR and all that it involves. I implore you as I do your brothers and sister to be involved. It is part of our mandate as Kennedys and Shrivers that we do all we can, give all of our time. Please plan your vacation this summer with my wishes in mind, and those of your father. Love, Mother."

One would have been hard pressed to find other Kennedys as involved with the Kennedy Foundation as Eunice and Sargent's offspring were. Certainly Jackie's children, John Jr. and Caroline, had little to do with the foundation, just like most, if not all, of Ethel's children. Even Ted's children seemed uninterested.

"I have recently decided that this must change," Eunice said at a meeting at Ted's home on April 9, 1984, according to the minutes of that meeting. Besides her and Sarge, attending were her son Bobby; Pat Kennedy; Jean and Stephen Smith; Ted Kennedy; Ted's son Ted Jr.; Ethel; Ethel's sons Joe and Bobby; and a half-dozen Kennedy Foundation employees and financial advisers such as Bob Cooke and Joe Hakim. "I think we have to recognize that it can't just be me and Sarge forever running this foundation," Eunice told the others. "The next generation must come forth. This is a family matter. And I am now of the opinion that they must come forth now."

"Well, I don't see how," Ethel said, "when, let's be honest, Eunice, you won't let anyone near the foundation—and certainly not the kids."

"That is not true," Eunice shot back quickly. "And in fact, that is a complete mischaracterization of my role here and you know it, Ethel!"

Others at the meeting recall the two women staring at each other for a tense moment. Then Eunice started angrily riffling through a gigantic leather portfolio of memos and correspondence and other material relating to the foundation. "I have right here..." she began, referring to one document in particular that she may have thought would prove something important. Ted cut his sister off in order to restore peace. "It is true," he said, according to the minutes, "that the next generation has not stepped forward in a timely fashion. I am not convinced, though, that the reasons for their lack of interest are as Ethie here has suggested. However, it would help, I think, if there was perhaps more transparency as to how the foundation is run."

Eunice and Sargent stared at Ted. Was he also suggesting that the Shrivers—and Eunice in particular—had commandeered the foundation?

In truth, the Kennedy Foundation had always been Eunice's venture. Long before she started Camp Shriver, Eunice had wanted to transform the public's point view of mental retardation, and in the process also be of assistance to the mentally handicapped. It may seem reductive to put it in these terms, but the truth is that, more than anything, she just wanted to make a difference. Because of her family's many connections, she had the power and influence to do so. Joseph sensed that of all his daughters, Eunice was the one who was the most astute, the most focused, and, it's safe to say, the most like him. Therefore, her opinion mattered to him a great deal, and from 1947 on she was very instrumental in advising him about the kinds of charities she felt were most deserving of the Kennedys' interest and financial support. Of course, she wanted to prove to her father that she could do it—that she could, in fact, do anything he wanted her to do, and do it as well as any of his sons. But she also truly believed in the cause, and much of her emotional attachment to it had to do with the plight of her sister Rosemary. In the end, it's safe to say that if not for Eunice, the Kennedy Foundation never would have thrived. After all, it was her drive and passion that fueled its many projects, and it was because of her resolve and persistence that she was able to get legislation passed that would make significant changes in the way the government thought of and handled the plight of the mentally retarded. Ted said it best in a letter to Jean Kennedy Smith dated March 1, 1981: "The Kennedys owe her a debt of gratitude that we as a family have been so associated with a cause as worthwhile."

By the mid-1970s, though, Ted, Jean, and Pat—who were also trustees of the foundation—were pushing hard for it to begin to support causes other than MR. At the time, the foundation's annual income was a little over $2 million, and Eunice wanted to spend all of it on causes related to mental retardation. But her siblings had other ideas. For instance, the John F. Kennedy Library needed help in organizing the hundreds of thousands of documents that were being stored there; the facility was greatly understaffed. Jean felt strongly that some portion of the foundation's money should go to the library, and she even managed to get Jackie's support in that regard, which under most circumstances would have all but guaranteed success for any family venture. But not for this one. Eunice wasn't impressed with the idea, and Jackie's support of it meant little to her. "The library is its own entity," she wrote in a letter to Jean. "Perhaps money can be siphoned from the Foundation's endowment for this purpose, but most certainly not from its annual income." Moreover, the properties on the Kennedy compound needed structural work, and it was Pat who felt that some of the foundation's money should go to that purpose. Ethel—not a trustee of the foundation but obviously a powerful family member—agreed with her. That proposition was unreasonable to Eunice, though. Home renovations did not fall under the purview of responsibilities of the Kennedy Foundation, at least in her opinion.

In the spring of 1977, Eunice met with Ted, Pat, and Jean at Jean and Stephen Smith's home in the compound to discuss the siblings' ideas for spending the foundation's money. In the minutes from that meeting, it is clear that Eunice would not be swayed from her point of view. She really could wear down her siblings if she chose to—and she chose to.

At the meeting, no matter what the others came up with as a valid reason to spend money on something other than MR, Eunice countered with an equally valid reason as to why the expenditure shouldn't occur. "Then it is decided," she said—even though it really wasn't—"that $2.3 million will continue to be spent from the annual income for the mentally retarded." The others didn't say anything, but it's doubtful that they were completely happy. Eunice then ran from the Smiths' home to Rose Kennedy's house—and that was quite a distance!—to discuss the matter with her mother. She had such extraordinary energy and stamina that no one could keep up with her as she darted from one person's home in the compound to another's, taking care of important business as only she could. According to Eunice's notes, she spent "considerable time" with Rose, discussing with her what her siblings wished to do with the foundation's money and how she so vehemently disagreed with them. According to what Eunice later wrote, Rose confirmed for her that the foundation had been started specifically to help the retarded and that its money should be spent only for that purpose and nothing else. With her mother's approval, Eunice then ran back to the Smiths' and told them that the family matriarch agreed with her—and that was the end of it. For the time being, anyway.

By the fall of 1983, the Kennedy siblings again had other ideas for the Kennedy Foundation's money, and again the JFK Library and the Kennedy compound had come to their minds as projects to be taken seriously; now they were also concerned about some structural repairs necessary to the Kennedy Center for the Performing Arts. One meeting at Ted's home in Virginia between himself, Pat, Jean, Stephen, and Eunice and Sargent became particularly contentious, according to its minutes.

"I'm sick and tired of the same old arguments," Eunice told her siblings. "Father's intention for the Kennedy Foundation was clear from the outset and it was that mental retardation be at its forefront, not the restoration of any of the homes we own."

Ted wasn't so sure. "I do not recall Father being quite so adamant," he said.

"Well, I *do*," Eunice insisted.

Actually, Eunice was stretching the truth. In fact, Joseph had started the Kennedy Foundation mostly as a tax shelter for the Merchandise Mart in Chicago, and it was Eunice who ended up using it as a way of furthering her own cause of mental retardation when she took it over in 1960. Joseph was only mildly interested in the cause of MR; it was Eunice who really propelled it forward, turning it into her life's work. That was the way it happened, but not the way Eunice chose to remember it. In fact, it was stipulated in Joseph's will that the Kennedy Foundation's money be used "to fulfill its dedicated purpose." Joseph's will said nothing about mental retardation. As the meeting ended, the siblings were not happy with Eunice at all, yet they were wondering if maybe she was right and they were wrong; that's how compelling Eunice was when it came to debating.

A couple of weeks later, it was Bobby Shriver—instead of his parents, Eunice and Sargent—who met with Ted Kennedy, which suggests that animosity was definitely building between Eunice and Ted. Ted and Bobby agreed that yet another meeting should be held to discuss the Kennedy Foundation, and at this next meeting, Ted said that he wanted to see some proof that his father's intention behind the foundation was that it be solely directed to the cause of mental retardation. According to a later recollection, when Bobby told his uncle that he was not comfortable going back to his parents with such a request, Ted had to laugh. He probably knew what his nephew would be up against, and he felt badly for him. But it had to be done.

Sarge on the Kennedy Curse: "So Be It"

At the same time that Eunice Kennedy Shriver was in discussions with her siblings over the business of the Joseph P. Kennedy Foundation, her husband, Sargent Shriver, was dealing with a predicament of, arguably, much greater importance—a crisis that would provide him with an opportunity to once again consider his faith.

When Sargent used to say that he had never been sick a day in his life, it wasn't just hyperbole. No one who knew him well recalled the man ever even having so much as a cold. That's why it was such a surprise in the fall of 1983 when he woke up in the middle of the night with a wrenching, searing pain in his abdomen. He was sixty-eight at the time. Eunice was on a business trip and the only other person in the house was his son Anthony. The pain was so severe, Sargent was not even able to get out of bed. Anthony had to pick him up and carry him downstairs, then put him in the car and drive him to Georgetown Hospital.

After two weeks of tests, no one seemed to have a clue as to what the problem might be with Shriver, and it was decided that he "probably" had stomach cancer. More tests would have to be conducted, though, to be sure. "So they decided I should go and see this top-notch cancer guy," Sargent recalled to this author many years later in 2002. "Can you imagine that there is such a thing? A cancer guy?" he asked, laughing.

Of course, the Shriver family was greatly concerned about Sargent's health. However, to hear him tell it, he wasn't all that worried. "Something just made me feel that I didn't have to be concerned," he said. "So I went to see the cancer guy. And he did all of his tests and, sure enough, even he didn't know what was wrong except that I *probably* had cancer. I asked him what he knew for sure, and he said, 'Nothing, really. I think we need to do more tests.' But the timing was a little off," Sarge recalled with a laugh. "You see, the cancer guy had to go to Hawaii for a medical convention. So he gave me a bag full of awful medications and said for me to take them and then come back to see him in a couple weeks. I left there thinking, 'Okay, so let me get this straight. The cancer guy is going on vacation—I mean on a medical convention—and meanwhile I have to sit home and have cancer? No,' I decided. 'I'm not going to accept it.'"

Sarge discussed the matter with Eunice, who simply could not reconcile the possibility that her husband had cancer. "There's only one solution," she said. "We have to pray. And we have to pray like we never prayed before," she said according to his memory, "because there is no way I will accept this." Of course, Sargent agreed.

That day, Sarge, who had gone to church nearly every day of his adult life, went to his place of worship, Holy Trinity, in Georgetown—the same church in which JFK had attended his last Mass before he was assassinated. Founded by the Jesuits in 1794 and administered by them ever since, it's the oldest Catholic church in the nation's capital. There, sitting in a wooden pew in an empty church, Sargent Shriver contemplated Jesus Christ's agony in the Garden of Gethsemane after the Last Supper. As described in the Gospels of Matthew, Mark, and Luke, during the agony in the Garden, Christ's human will had to decide whether or not to submit to the divine will expressed by the Father's command that Jesus offer redemption to all of humanity through His painful and public death by crucifixion. Presumably since Christ's human will was free, in His human nature He did have a choice in this matter. His agony was that, as a human being, He did not want to suffer, just as no human being does. This point is important in the teaching of Christianity in that it suggests that Christ is not merely a distant deity but also someone who deeply identifies with man's sufferings while remaining perfectly divine. In the end, despite His understanding of the suffering He would have to endure, Christ willingly submitted His human will to the command of His Father. "Though there was no justification for the pain Jesus was to suffer," Sarge would observe, "He accepted it anyway. He didn't cry about it. He didn't whine about it. He didn't try to figure out a way around it. He just accepted it as God's will. And that day in church, I thought, hell, if He could accept death like that, then who am I not to accept whatever it is that is causing me this present problem? I sure as hell can do it if He did it. And as I was thinking this thing over, really mulling it over, something washed over me. It was a peace and calm such that I had never before experienced. I knew in that very moment that it didn't matter if I had cancer and it didn't even matter if I didn't. I was fine. I knew I was perfect and whole no matter the outcome, that it didn't make any difference what was going on in my body, my soul was okay. And from that moment on," Sarge recalled, "I am not kidding you, from that moment on, I began to feel a hell of a lot better."

In fact, two weeks later, Sargent Shriver had never felt in better shape. The pain he'd had in his stomach was gone. He went back to the doctor, who conducted all of the tests Sarge had intended to take upon his return. The results all came back negative. "And I was sitting there in the doctor's office," Sargent recalled, "and the doctor looked at me and said, 'Sarge, I don't know what you did, but you sure did it. There's nothing wrong with you.' I just looked at him and said, 'I know, doc. You're not telling me anything I don't know.' And that was the end of it."

Sargent Shriver said he felt uncomfortable relaying this particular story, "Because the suggestion is that it's a big deal and the first time anything like that ever happened to me. In fact," he said, "I have had many times in my life when I was saved—especially when I was in the service, times when everyone was killed but me, or times when I had escaped death just at the last minute. People ask me why I am so religious," he said. "It's because I have just always known that my faith protects not only me, but my family. All of us have felt the same way.

"And some might say, well, what about the Kennedy curse?" Shriver asked. "To that I say, we as a family have always believed that there's more to consider than just our human experience, something better, something richer and more important. And if we Kennedys and we Shrivers and we Smiths are in some way cursed to experience the hereafter just a little sooner than the rest of humanity, well then, so be it. That's how I look at the Kennedy curse, anyway. So be it."

Eunice Faces a Family Revolt

Soon after Sargent Shriver's health scare, the disagreements over the Kennedy Foundation continued. Bobby Shriver went back to his mother, Eunice Shriver, with Ted Kennedy's request of some proof that their father intended the foundation to focus its attention solely on the cause of mental retardation. Eunice was, not surprisingly, quite angry. "This again!" she exclaimed, probably referring to the fact that the issue had been raised at the last meeting. "Does he think we are lying?" she asked her son. Bobby said his uncle "just wants proof." As expected, this didn't sit well with Eunice at all. She got on the telephone with her brother and told him that the "proof" he wanted was not written, it was in fact verbal. In many conversations that Joseph had with her and with Sargent, she said, the family patriarch made it quite clear that all of the money from the foundation should be used for the purpose of researching mental retardation. "It's what Father wanted and it's what Mother wants," Eunice said, according to one recollection of the conversation. "And I am not going to stand by and allow the trustees [meaning her siblings] to continue to question my own ethics or that of the foundation." In other words, she was sick of the debate and not going to engage in it any longer.

There were several more meetings in late 1983, but Eunice would not be swayed by her siblings. It was finally becoming clear to them that even as trustees they had no power to make decisions where the Kennedy Foundation was concerned, or as Ted put it in a letter to Sargent Shriver at this time, "I am sure my father intended for all of his children to take part in the decision-making process, and I am not sure that this is what has been occurring."

Finally, in January 1984, Ted, Pat, and Jean shot off an angry letter to Eunice telling her that, as far as they were concerned, the foundation was a family business and, as such, it should support all of the areas of philanthropy viewed worthwhile by the different members of the family. In other words, the foundation didn't belong to Eunice—it belonged to all of them. They still had the same goals in mind for the way the money should be spent, according to what they wrote to Eunice, namely: the Kennedy Center, the Kennedy Library, work on the Kennedy compound, as well as several charities that interested Jean and Stephen, such as Jean's own venture, the Very Special Arts.

The siblings maintained that they were also unhappy about the way the Kennedy Library was being run as it related to researchers. Several Kennedy biographers had gotten hold of documents through the library that they were able to utilize in their work, books of which the family did not approve—such as the aforementioned *Kennedys: An American Drama* by Horowitz and Collier, which they felt had just added to the myriad problems young David Kennedy was experiencing. The Kennedy siblings wanted more restrictions placed on documents made available to researchers, which also meant a complete review of the library's holdings—and that was going to cost money. In Eunice's view, that concern was chiefly to do with the family's image. It might have surprised outsiders to know that she couldn't have cared less about how the family was portrayed in books about them. "Do you think it matters in the least?" she would later say. "People will always write what they will write. We should be used to that by now." Her interest was in mental retardation, not family public relations. (Of course, Eunice was also the first one to shoot off an angry letter to a newspaper if they published a falsehood about a family member, but as she would explain it, "I believe there's a different standard for newspapers to be reliable. Books, you either believe the author or you don't. But a newspaper, a daily newspaper, you want to know that what they are putting out there is the news, and it's the truth.") The Kennedy siblings also mentioned in their missive that "the next generation" of Kennedys needed to be brought into the business of the foundation as soon as possible and that if it were to survive it could only do so if the grandchildren began to take an interest in it.

Now this matter, which had been brewing for years, had turned into a bit of a war. As far as Eunice Kennedy Shriver was concerned, the siblings (or trustees, as they were referred to) were engaged in a mutinous battle against her. The only thing she agreed with them on was that the next generation should be brought into the decision-making process of the foundation. That was it, though. Everything else she disagreed with. Moreover, in her view, getting the next generation involved in the foundation's business wasn't going to happen overnight; it would likely take five to ten years, she said. Eunice was now quite disenchanted with her siblings and wasn't very friendly to any of them from January to April of 1984—which brings us back to the meeting at Ted's home on April 9, 1984.

"I have changed my mind," Eunice announced at that meeting, "and I now think we should not wait five to ten years to bring in the next generation. I think we should do it now."

"Exactly," Ethel said. "This is what I have been saying all along."

"I know that, Ethel," Eunice said. Then, as she scooped up a pile of papers and started busily inserting them into file folders in a large notebook, she added crisply, "And I am agreeing with you, all right? I will concede that point, but will not make any concessions as to how the foundation's money is spent." In other words, she was trying to strike a compromise by giving them something—not much, though, since the real issue on the table wasn't really when the third generation would come into power as much as it was the question of how the foundation's money was to be spent—just on mental retardation causes or on other charitable ventures as well?

Since Ethel really had no knowledge of the back-and-forth about the foundation's expenditures, because she was not a trustee and this was one of the very rare meetings she attended related to this matter, she didn't have much else to say.

In the end—not surprisingly—Eunice prevailed. The trustees finally agreed with her that the Kennedy Foundation would continue to be devoted solely to the cause of mental retardation as long as the next generation would now be allowed to play a bigger role in its decision-making processes. That was fine with Eunice. It was substantially what she'd been fighting for anyway. It gave her more time to do what she wanted with the foundation's money without having to answer to her siblings about it. The war was over.

So what about that next generation—the third generation—as it would relate to the Joseph P. Kennedy Jr. Foundation? The problem the family faced in regard to that generation's participation in the foundation was that the only people truly invested in the cause of mental retardation were her and Sarge's children. After all, it had been their mother's life's work for as long as they could remember, and it was also a cause that their father had helped her implement over the years. Of course, the other young Kennedys saw the cause as valid and important—but it was "Aunt Eunice's mission," not necessarily theirs. Eunice realized that one day the situation would probably arise where the foundation would be run by a generation perhaps not so interested in mental retardation, and maybe that would be a battle her children would have to fight. It was eventually decided to establish the Associate Trustees Committee for the Joseph P. Kennedy Jr. Foundation and automatically enroll the entire third generation in the hope that somehow they would organize themselves into a governing unit. "It was their first foray into letting go and sharing power," says Christopher Lawford, Pat's son. "It was not easy for them. I remember my aunt Eunice coming to me before the first meeting and nervously asking if I was going to lead a revolt and try to move the foundation away from mental retardation to something that had more relevance to me and my generation. I assured her I wasn't, but that tension was always present."

Following the death of Eunice Kennedy Shriver, her children and many of her nieces and nephews have made it their mission to make certain that the cause of mental retardation remains at the forefront not only of the Kennedy Foundation's interests but also of their own. She would no doubt be very happy about that. In fact, Timothy P. Shriver, the third of Eunice and Sarge's five children, is currently serving as chairman of the board of directors and chief executive officer of the International Special Olympics.

Looking back so many years later on this Kennedy uprising, the question remains, how had Eunice Kennedy Shriver handled it? It could be argued that she could—or maybe should—have been a little more understanding of her siblings. It could be argued that she could—or maybe should—have given them more latitude. In fact, a great many arguments could probably be made against the way she behaved during this bit of a family rebellion. However, her daughter, Maria, has a favorite saying on a T-shirt that probably sums it up best when it comes to women like Eunice Kennedy Shriver. It says: *Well Behaved Women Seldom Make History*.

Peter Lawford Dies

*F*lash back to June 1966.

"What the hell do my kids need *me* for?" Peter Lawford said to Jackie Kennedy in the presence of his friend and partner Milt Ebbins. Jackie and her children had accompanied Peter on a vacation to Oahu, Hawaii. "They're Kennedys," Peter said of his children. "They have all that power. All that money. They don't need me. I'm nothing."

According to Ebbins's memory, Jackie leaned over and put her hand on Peter's. "Why, that's just not true," she told her former brother-in-law. "You are a wonderful man. In fact, I still feel that you and Pat should be able to make it work. I'll talk to Pat when I get back. I'll see what I can do."

"It was an unusual vacation, to say the least," Milt Ebbins recalled many years later. "Peter had planned to go with his children Christopher and Sydney and soon found out that Jackie was going to be on the same island at the same time. He said to me, 'I don't think I can go now.' He was heartbroken because it had been everything he could do to convince Pat to let him take two of the kids on this vacation. I said, 'Look, call Jackie and see if she will mind.' So he did. She said she didn't mind at all. In fact, she said, 'Why don't we all fly over together?' Jackie was just that kind of woman—nothing really bothered her when it came to familial relations. So she and her kids flew to San Francisco and met up with me, Peter, his kids, and a few other friends and we all flew to Hawaii together. The trouble began when we got there and were photographed together. Pat called me in a complete rage. 'Why didn't you or Peter tell me that Jackie was going to be there?' she demanded to know. I know why I didn't; it was because I thought Peter had done it. But when I later asked Peter, he said he was afraid to tell her because he was afraid she would say no and that the trip would then be canceled. Then, when I asked Jackie about it, she looked at me as if I was out of my mind and said, 'Why, Milt, why would I?' 'Maybe because you and Pat are best friends?' I wanted to answer. However, I didn't. That's just the way it was with the Kennedys."

While in Hawaii with Jackie, Peter took it upon himself to make certain that she and her children had a wonderful holiday. At one point, he arranged an elaborate cocktail party at the Kahala Hilton for her and about a hundred friends of his—or perhaps friends of friends. "It was the hotel on the island at the time," Ebbins recalled. "It had just opened about a year earlier, very exclusive, a real celebrity hangout at the time. [Peter and Jackie were staying in separate rented beachfront properties near this hotel.] On the day of the party, everyone was in suits and ties, gowns and high heels, on the beach, waiting and waiting for Jackie, who had gone off sightseeing for the day with John and Caroline. I remember Peter pacing back and forth, very nervous because he thought she wasn't going to show. 'I'm going to look like the biggest fool if she doesn't show,' he told me. All of a sudden, a helicopter appears and lands right there on the middle of the beach, sand blowing all over the place causing what looked like a huge dust storm. The door opens and out of the chopper descends Jackie, wearing some kind of little beach frock, a sort of caftan that was billowing in the wind, with sandals. It was quite the entrance. Peter, in his three-piece suit, ran over to Jackie and escorted her to the party. Standing there watching her approach, we guests all looked at each other in complete dismay as it become clear that *we* were overdressed."

It was at this party that Jackie and Peter had their conversation about Peter's feelings of great inadequacy. "You know how much Jack loved you, don't you?" Jackie told him. "You are a wonderful man. I wish you knew that, Peter." Peter then informed Jackie that Bobby had recently telephoned him to tell him that he didn't want him to have anything further to do with Pat or with any of the Kennedys. "You're out," Bobby told Peter, according to what Peter said. "We don't want to see you around here ever again, do you understand that? You are *out*." This was the cruelest blow of all. After all, Peter had been forced to sacrifice his close friendship with Frank Sinatra because of his allegiance to the Kennedys, and now he was being expelled from the Kennedys' lives too. "Don't you dare let Bobby get away with that awful threat," Jackie said, clearly upset. "Do you think Ethel would stand for it for one second?" she asked Peter. "Ethel loves you," she said. "Call Ethel. Talk to her about this! Promise me you will." Then, according to Milt Ebbins's recollection of the conversation, Jackie added with a soft smile, "The Kennedys can be overbearing, Peter. I know this better than most. Remember, I never really fit in, either," she added. "So don't worry about it."

For the next twenty-three years, Peter Lawford would continue to spiral into a deep abyss of alcohol and drug abuse, never really regaining his footing after the divorce from Pat. "He had so loved the Kennedys, I don't think he ever got over Jack's death, first of all, nor could he ever reconcile being ousted from the family," said photographer Bernie Abramson. Bobby's admonition aside, Peter did try to have a relationship with Pat and the other Kennedys, but to no avail. Even Ethel seemed to fall by the wayside after Bobby's death, but in her defense, she had her own problems by that time with some of her sons. Only Jackie continued a friendship with Peter, and, try as she might, she was never able to convince Pat to find any forgiveness for what Peter had done to her during their marriage.

"In years to come, Peter would be, for the most part, an absentee father," added Bernie Abramson. "He loved his children dearly and they felt the same about him, though I think there was a lot of strain between them all. Peter blamed the Kennedys for many of his life's problems, even though, in all fairness to the Kennedys, he certainly had enough time to straighten them out on his own, and in fact married three more times after the divorce from Pat [to Mary Rowan in 1971, Deborah Gould in 1976, and Patricia Seaton in 1984]. With the passing of the years, though, Lawford's career fell into a complete shambles. It was a shame."

In 1981, Peter recalled to this author, "When you're going up against the Kennedys, you're going to lose, and that's what I have had to accept. They don't want me around. I admit I am not the best father in the world, but in all fairness to me, the Kennedys have made it exceedingly difficult to have any sort of meaningful relationship with my children. Pat has thwarted me every step along the way, as have other members of her family. My conversations with Pat led me to believe that I was useless as a father. As if she was the perfect mother?" Peter asked. "I will always love Pat and I'm sure I hurt her repeatedly," he admitted, "but she hurt me too. The Kennedys can be quite cruel and that is a fact I have learned to live with. When you are out of their inner circle, you're out. And I am out."

On September 17, 1983, Lawford found himself among the Kennedys again when his daughter Sydney married James Peter McKelvy. The ceremony took place at Our Lady of Victory Church in Centerville, Massachusetts, and then there was a reception on the lawn of Rose Kennedy's home in the compound. (This was actually the last family wedding Rose was well enough to attend.) It was a difficult day for Peter, though. Giving away his daughter in marriage was very important to him, yet he would later say he couldn't help but feel uncomfortable given the tense relationship between him and Pat. The two kept their distance, though they were cordial when absolutely necessary. Ted seemed quite happy to see Peter, though. Ted later said that it was as if Peter's presence in the compound had transported him back to a glorious time in his life, back when Jack was alive and so many things were so very different. However, it was Jackie who took Peter under her wing that day. Guests couldn't help but notice how protective she was of him. "Coming back here to this place after all of this time can't be easy for him," she was overheard telling Ted. "He doesn't look well. It's as if the circumstances of his life have taken a terrible toll on him. I'm worried about him." In fact, when Peter's son, Christopher, married nearly a year later in November 1984 in the West Indies, Peter was not well enough to be present.

Sadly, on December 24, 1984, the Kennedy family got the news that Peter Lawford had died of cardiac arrest at the age of sixty-one in Los Angeles. He would be cremated the next day, on Christmas Day. "The death of Peter Lawford is a special loss to all of us in the Kennedy family, and my heart goes out to his children, Christopher, Sydney, Victoria, and Robin," said Ted Kennedy in a statement to the media. "We take comfort from the fact that we know he will also be missed by all the people who enjoyed his many roles in films and on television. He was a dedicated and creative actor as well as a loving father and loyal friend to all of us, especially in the challenging days of the New Frontier. The legacies of his love and his fine performances will be a cherished treasure for his family, his friends, and his many admirers."

Pat Kennedy Lawford was with her now grown children at her New York home in the midst of a big holiday celebration when she got the call that her troubled ex-husband had died. In the moment, she seemed numb, unable to connect to any true feeling about the loss. She had never remarried, saying that she simply did not know one single person she believed was truly happy in a relationship. She maintained that anyone who professed to be content in a romantic relationship, be it just dating or marriage, was probably lying about it and she wasn't going to count herself among them. The truth is that after Peter, she was never able to bring herself to trust again. She had also never gotten past her anger at him. Still, he did represent a very important, pivotal time in her life, and of course he was the father of her children.

She was therefore filled with conflicted emotions about his demise. She chose not to attend the small funeral in Los Angeles, and neither did Jackie, though Jackie had arranged with the hospital to be contacted the moment Peter passed away, and she did immediately telephone his widow, Patricia Seaton Lawford, to offer her condolences. As well as by his own children, the Kennedys were represented at Peter Lawford's funeral by Jackie's daughter, Caroline; Ethel's children Bobby Jr. and Courtney; and Sargent and Eunice's children Maria and Timothy.

Intervention for Pat

*A*fter the death of Peter Lawford, Pat Kennedy Lawford arranged for her four children and their spouses to go to Jamaica for a brief vacation in order that they might come to terms with their grief as a family. However, rather than go along, she stayed behind in New York and, says Christopher Lawford, promptly "fell apart. My father's death may have left me cold, but I think it did a number on her. She had been battling with her own drinking demons for years. In the winter following my dad's demise, her condition turned critical."

In January 1985, it was decided that Pat's alcoholism was so out of control that an intervention had become necessary. "I don't know what else we can do," Eunice said, according to one of the family's attorneys. However, Ted wasn't so sure of the wisdom of such a move. "These things never work," he said at the time. "We did this for David, and you see how that turned out." Eunice was adamant, though, that something needed to be done, and Jean agreed with her, as did Pat's children. "Her four kids were afraid Pat would face the same fate as their father if they didn't do something and do it right away," recalled Milt Ebbins. When Eunice contacted Jackie to ask her to attend, according to another reliable source, Jackie was against the idea. "Pat will not have a good reaction to it," Jackie said, according to the source. "I know her very well and I'm not in favor of this at all. I think we should come up with another idea." Jackie was overruled, however.

"Eunice, Jean, Ted, and Pat's four kids—Christopher, Sydney, Victoria, and Robin—showed up at Pat's New York City home to confront her about her drinking," recalled Patricia Brennan. "When Pat walked into the living room and took one look at them all sitting there, she instantly knew what was going on. One of them started reading from prepared notes she had made telling Pat how concerned she was about her and how much she had hurt them all. After a few minutes, Pat turned right around and went back into her bedroom, and would not come back out. She was angry, mostly at her children. She was beyond angry, actually. 'How dare they?' she told me later, in quite the rage. 'I am their mother. They should have more respect for me than that.' As she went on and on, it was clear to me that she didn't want to be helped. Not at that time, anyway. I always knew, though, that there was a small part of her that wanted help. I always knew it."

A few weeks later, Pat sent her son, Christopher, a note saying that she felt it would be wiser in the future if the Lawfords worked on their problems internally as a family "without importing Eunice, Jean and Ted." She said that she found the idea of her siblings present for an intervention "repugnant" and added that she would not be discussing the matter any further.

She signed the note, "Love, Mommie."

PART FIFTEEN

Caroline, John, and Maurice

Caroline Kennedy

$\mathcal{E}$thel Kennedy would be the first to say that she never really understood the reasons for the troubles of some of her children, primarily the older boys. Ted felt the same way about his offspring, and so did Pat and Jean. In their eyes, the third generation of Kennedys truly had it made. After all, they were young; their inheritances and trust funds had made them wealthy; they had a strong, practically royal lineage; there seemed no reason why they should ever have dabbled in drugs or done anything at all to shame the family. Ted, in particular, said he wished he could reclaim his own youth. "Those kids don't know how lucky they are," he once said. Maybe it was because Jackie always viewed her offspring, Caroline and John, as being in a very unique situation—children of a United States president—that she worked so hard to be sensitive to their needs and vitally aware of the challenges they would face as they grew up. It's certainly true that both children never had the sorts of problems Bobby's had—or even Ted's for that matter.

Over the years, one reason proffered for why Caroline and John turned out so well was because Jackie purposely kept them away from Ethel's more unruly bunch, fearing a bad influence. However, this is simply not true. Both women commiserated about the raising of their children and lent helping hands many times along the way, just as they were involved in the raising of all of the other young Kennedys. In this large family, no child was isolated from the others. Caroline and John spent plenty of time with Ethel and Bobby's offspring, just as they did with Joan and Ted's, and with all of their other cousins.

The real reason Caroline and John turned out so well has to be traced back to Jackie's basic parenting skills and some of the choices she made along the way. She was strict. She was tough on them, and so in a sense she had that in common with Ethel. The difference was that her kids listened whereas many of Ethel's didn't. Jackie believed in communication. If the children had questions about their father's murder, for instance, she tried to answer them. She didn't avoid such questioning or try to change the subject. Both of her children were raised to come to her first if they had a problem, and to no one else. They were also raised to depend on one another because Jackie feared that one day she might be gone and they would have no one but each other. Moreover, they were raised by a courageous mother. Though she had her vulnerable moments, Jackie was a powerfully strong woman who had endured more than her share of heartache. Yet she somehow went on and continued to live a very good, very rich life. Her children would later say that they couldn't help but be influenced by her strength.

"Caroline's only scrape that I can recall was when Jackie found out that she was growing pot in the backyard of their home on the compound," recalled Rose Kennedy's secretary, Barbara Gibson. "Caroline said that she was doing it for her cousins, that she didn't smoke it herself. Jackie was suspicious of that, of course. There was a lot of discussion with both John and Caroline, but Jackie handled it internally, making sure not to involve any other family member. It was just very expeditiously taken care of, not made a big federal case. In fact, I don't even know how or even if Jackie punished Caroline, that's how discreet she was about it."

It should go without saying that the lives of Caroline and John were unusual in almost every way. For instance, on the night their father died, Lyndon Johnson wrote them both letters to express his sympathy. "He was a wise and devoted man," he wrote to Caroline. "You can always be proud of what he did for his country." And to John, "It will be many years before you understand fully what a great man your father was." (That he sat down and took the time to write these letters considering all that was going on that night certainly speaks well of President Johnson. "What those letters will mean to them later—you can imagine," Jackie later wrote to LBJ. "The touching thing is, they have always loved you so much, they were most moved to have a letter from you now.") Moreover, LBJ always sent Caroline and John letters and telegrams on their birthdays, such as the one he sent Caroline on her ninth in 1966: "I remember when my own girls were nine. It is such a pleasant memory that I just wanted to add my happiness to yours on this special day." Or the one to John when he turned six that same year: "When I was six, I wanted to be sixteen. At sixteen, I couldn't wait to be twenty-one. But today, I wish I were six again, like you! You have my affection and deep interest—Lyndon Johnson." (Jackie responded, writing to LBJ, telling him that he was quite a "psychologist" in that "you always know just what to say to a boy and just what to say to a girl." She said that John was fascinated to know that the president of the United States wished that he was six again, "but he's also not sure whether or not to believe it.")*

Because she was older and had so many more memories of him, Caroline had a more difficult time than John in accepting the death of her father. The two had been very close. For the first couple of years after Jack's death, Jackie was constantly on the telephone with child psychologist Erik Erikson trying to find ways to help her daughter best express in a constructive way the anger she felt at losing her dad so suddenly. Whereas Caroline had once been such an outgoing and polite little girl, after November 1963 she was withdrawn and combative, often seen walking around with her hands clenched. Sargent Shriver once recalled visiting Jackie in New York in 1970 and being taken by Jackie to Caroline's bedroom to see what Jackie called "her little project." Peeking in through the half-opened doorway, he saw the tot sitting in a room with bright pink walls. Strewn about were stuffed animals, lions, giraffes, and teddy bears. On the floor was Caroline, her legs crossed over each other, a magazine in one hand, a pair of scissors in the other. She proceeded to cut out a photo of her father, Jack. Then another of her uncle Bobby. As her mother and uncle watched, she stood up and walked to a small desk in a corner of the room and took a tape dispenser from one of its drawers. Then she taped the two pictures onto a wall where they joined dozens of others in the same space. It was heartbreaking.

Jackie would never forget another devastating scene that took place shortly after she and the children moved to their first home after leaving the White House, in Georgetown. Secretary of Defense Robert McNamara had come to visit and brought with him a lovely oil painting of Jack as a gift. After Jackie propped it against the fireplace to admire it, the two old friends parted company. Later that night, she telephoned McNamara in tears. "I'm sorry, but you'll have to come back and get the painting," she told him. "I can't keep it." When he asked why, she

---

* Jackie joined many people of her generation who felt that receiving a telegram was very special. Nothing pleased her more on her own birthday than sitting at the dinner table after a meal and opening congratulatory telegrams. A telegram itself was thought of as a gift. In fact, countless handwritten letters from Jackie exist thanking friends and colleagues for birthday telegrams.

explained that Caroline had come downstairs, saw the painting, and then rushed over to it and began kissing it repeatedly. Seeing this, John soon joined in. Before Jackie knew it, both were sobbing, as was she. "It's more than I can take, Bob," she concluded. "Please come and get it. Everything, right now, is more than I can take."

For Caroline in particular, the emotional scars of losing her father in such a painful manner would never really disappear. Yet with the passing of years she would somehow adjust to life without a father who, while very much a historical and well-known icon to millions of Americans, was someone she simply wished she could have known much better. She would remember the fantastic stories he had told her at bedtime, the games of hide-and-seek he would play with her in the White House, the way he looked when the family went sailing in Hyannis Port, always dashing with his shock of wavy brown hair blowing in the sea breeze, his cobalt eyes gleaming. She would always remember his brilliant smile. Indeed, his presence would feel very real to her—long, long after he was gone.

As a child, Caroline attended the Brearley School and Convent of the Sacred Heart, both in New York City and within walking distance of Jackie's apartment. She graduated from Concord Academy in Massachusetts in 1975. She received her bachelor of arts degree from Radcliffe College at Harvard University in 1979, and by 1985 she was attending Columbia University Law School. Caroline toyed with becoming a photojournalist, just as her mother had once been, and even interned at the *New York Daily News* in 1977 for $156 a week. "She was a loner but not necessarily by her own choosing," said Laura Burke, who also interned at the same time. "People were afraid to approach her. She carries with her so much history, there's an intimidation factor. I have to say that she was very nice once you got to know her. I had lunch with her almost every day. I made the mistake once of asking about her mother. It was a simple question like 'How's your mom?' But she just closed down. I'm not sure she even answered."

In 1980, after graduating from college, she got a job as a research assistant at the Metropolitan Museum of Art, also near her home. Soon she began to act as a liaison between the museum and production companies interested in filming there. "She was personable and smart," said Lisa McClintock, who also worked at the museum. "People just wanted to do business with her because of who she was, though. It was always in the air, the celebrity factor. Anyway, I went to the lunchroom one day to have my meal and Caroline was in there and invited me to join her. While we were eating, her mom showed up and sat down at our table. Well, what could Caroline do at that point, disinvite me? I could tell she wasn't comfortable, but there we were, the three of us having lunch. At one point, Caroline went to the ladies' room. I found myself alone with Jackie Kennedy Onassis."

"So, tell me," Jackie said after a few minutes of idle chatter, according to McClintock's memory. "Does Caroline have a lot of friends here?"

"Well, she's a bit of a loner," came back the careful answer from Lisa.

"That's always been a problem," Jackie said with a frown. "She's not like her brother. John, you can't shut up. But Caroline . . . she's very much like me, I guess. Would you do me a huge favor?" Jackie asked. "Would you encourage her to be more outgoing? I would love for her to be more social."

At that point, Caroline rejoined them. "What are you two talking about?" she asked with just a bit of suspicion.

"Oh, I was just telling your friend that I simply adore her scarf," Jackie said, flashing a conspiratorial smile to Lisa.

"From that time on, I would often dine with her and Jackie," said McClintock. "I think Jackie liked me. However, I have to say that Jackie could be critical of Caroline from time to time. For instance, Caroline liked her desserts. Jackie never touched them. One afternoon, Caroline ordered a slice of pie. As she sat eating it, Jackie just stared at her. Then, when she finished, Jackie said, 'Well, dear, I hope you're satisfied. That was at least three pounds right there.' Caroline rolled her eyes and said, 'Mother, there's more to life than being thin.' Jackie shot back with, 'Really? And how would you know that, dear?' It was a catty little exchange.

"Later, Caroline told me, 'Sometimes I order desserts just to get her goat. She so hates it when I eat sweets.'" Once, according to what Caroline told Lisa McClintock, Jackie asked her, "Have you ever seen a fat Kennedy? No, you have not. And I'll be darned if you're going to be the first one." Apparently, Jackie felt Caroline would never find a husband if she were overweight. "I think it's a generational thing," Caroline told me. "I don't know how else to explain it, it's so ridiculous."

Actually, it was while working at the museum that Caroline met the man who would soon become her husband—exhibit designer Edwin Schlossberg. By 1985, the two were dating seriously and contemplating marriage. "I had dinner with Caroline, Ed, Jackie, and John Jr. very early in the courtship," recalled Lisa. "I remember Jackie being a little distant, not eager to let this new person into the circle, or at least that's how it appeared to me. She spent a lot of time studying poor Ed as if he was on display. At one point, Ed went to the restroom and Caroline said, 'So, Mother, what do you think of him?' Jackie very carefully said, 'Well, dear, he's not exactly…*interesting*, now is he?' To which John responded, 'Heck, Mom. Let's face it. That guy's the biggest bore who ever lived!' We all laughed. Then poor Ed came back to the table having no idea that such a harsh judgment had been passed on him. The next day, Caroline said to me, 'Mother, John, and I are so close, it's difficult for us to imagine anyone else in the picture.'"

John Kennedy Jr.

$\mathcal{B}$y 1985, John Kennedy Jr., despite almost flunking out, had graduated from Brown University with a bachelor's degree in history. Jackie knew his difficulty in school was due in large part to his ADD, and it didn't help that he had other obligations. During his second year, when she received a letter from Brown telling her that he was in danger of being expelled because of his poor grades, she responded by writing, "I have never asked for special consideration for my children because I feel it is harmful to them, but there was an extra burden John carried this year that other students did not…he was asked to campaign almost every weekend for his uncle. His other cousins took their freshman year off from college to do this, but he just was as anxious to go to Brown as I was to have him go." She wrote that "the problem is getting himself organized," and added, "this scare should teach him the vital lesson to allot every second of his time. I am sure it will as he frantically tries to make up his work." She closed by saying, "I look forward to hearing that he is off probation and to never get another notice that he is on it." He graduated but with just mediocre grades. Now he was working for the New York City Office of Business Development and was contemplating going to law school, which was a pursuit his mother encouraged rather than the one he seemed most interested in at this time—acting. Steven Styles, a good friend of John's, recalled, "He was so funny, so charismatic, such a great character. I think of all the third-generation Kennedys, people in the family would have to agree that John was the golden child, partly due to his parentage and partly due to the fact that, in truth, you really couldn't help but gravitate to him. He was good-looking as hell, not necessarily book smart but very intuitive. He also had great empathy. He felt terrible about what had happened to his cousin David, for instance. Many times, I heard him say, 'That could have been me.' He felt fortunate to have been raised as he'd been. He adored his mother and had a lot of respect for her."

John's memories of his dad were fewer than Caroline's, and he would later admit that he wasn't sure which were actual reminiscences and which were just the result of photographs he had seen over the years or stories he had been told by others. He spent quiet moments in his college room at Brown sitting in a special chair—the very same one his father used in the Oval Office. "He'd sit in his chair and he had this book of speeches his father had made in the first one hundred days," says Chris Oberbeck, who was at Brown at the same time. "He goes, 'Can you believe all these speeches that he made? In those first hundred days?' He was just amazed. He had a great sense of himself as a representation of his dad and believed that as JFK's son he had a certain standard to uphold. 'I'm not just any guy,' he once told me. 'I'm the son of one of the greatest presidents of our time. And my mom is so revered, I can't get into trouble. It's not even a possibility.'"

As teenagers, Caroline and John were certainly not exempt from the kind of experimentation with drugs done by their more unruly cousins. Both smoked pot from time to time, and John tried cocaine a couple of times. "He and I did coke together," Stephen Styles confirmed. "It wasn't a big deal, just something to do, but John was always too afraid of getting busted to really enjoy himself. He was always looking over his shoulder, as if some invisible authority figure was lurking about ready to reprimand him. 'If I am ever arrested on a drug charge,' he once told me, 'my mother would kill me.' I laughed. And he looked at me very seriously and said,

'No, you don't understand. *My mother would kill me.*' Once we had a few drinks and he was feeling a little drunk and he said, 'You know what I think is unfair? My cousins get loaded all the time and it's cool and everyone accepts it. But me, I have to feel guilty every time I have a drink.'"

Still, John apparently did have his fun. Jackie's housekeeper Marian Ronan, who was responsible for taking care of Jackie's Red Gate Farm on Martha's Vineyard, recalled, "After partying over Memorial Day weekend [1993], John and his friends left the house a pigsty. When I walked in, I couldn't believe my eyes. The house was strewn all over with wet towels and empty champagne bottles. The carpets were stained. There were half-eaten plates of food discarded in every room, and food had even been splashed onto the walls. I also found marijuana buds in one bathroom and bedroom and leftover marijuana joints lying on a bathroom sink counter. It took me two days to clean up that mess." She said that when Jackie found out about it, "she banished John from the main house."

Though Caroline didn't have many boyfriends in her teen years and into adult life, John had more than his share of romantic escapades. He never had a shortage of amorous partners in his life. Some observers couldn't help but draw comparisons between him and his father, President Kennedy. They would say that John took after his father in the sense that he had a very active sex life and was thought of as quite the ladies' man. In 1985, he was dating Christina Haag, a Brown alumna and actress, in a relationship that would be on and off for about six years. "There was another girl named Sally Munro that John dated," said Stephen Styles. "She went to Brown, too. Very nice girl. 'My mom is lukewarm on her,' John told me. 'I get it. There's probably no one she will ever approve of.' I asked why and he was very matter-of-fact about it. 'She's extremely overprotective,' he said. 'But you have to take the bitter with the sweet in this life. She kept me out of trouble by raising me as she did. The flip side is that she can be overbearing. I just learn to live with it. Yin and yang, you know?' He was pretty philosophical about it."

John and Madonna

In 1988, when John was twenty-eight, he spent six months trying to navigate the erratic terrain of a relationship with Madonna. At the time, Madonna was a thirty-year-old, widely successful pop star who had carved a niche for herself in the entertainment world with a string of hit records and medium-defining music videos. Though both were public figures, John and Madonna certainly had very different perspectives about fame. He'd been famous since the day he was born, and there were days when he wished he could live his life anonymously. But she'd been famous for only about five years, and so far she seemed to savor every second of it. She would do anything she could to generate publicity for herself, in fact, and was already considered a master media manipulator. The old saw "opposites attract" comes to mind when one tries to understand why John even wanted to date her. He said he thought she was complex and, as he put it to friends, "endlessly fascinating."

During their brief relationship, Madonna stunned John one day with her admission that she would sometimes call photographers to tell them where she and her husband, Sean Penn, would be so that the media could photograph them there, thereby generating publicity for herself. (And, yes, she was married to Penn while dating Kennedy.) She said that when Penn found out about it, he was upset with her. "Why in the world would you do such a thing?" John wanted to know, according to two of John's friends who had witnessed the conversation, which took place in his apartment. "Why else? To get my picture in the papers," Madonna answered matter-of-factly. This was certainly a surprise to a person like John who had spent pretty much his entire life dodging photographers. "But Madonna," he said, "you're so much better than that." He reminded her that she had talent, she was intelligent, focused, driven, a real artist. "Don't you see that by inviting photographers into your life that way, you're setting yourself up for future misery?" he asked her. According to the witnesses, Madonna just looked at him blankly. "In other words," he continued, "you may think it's cool to put yourself out there like that, but I guarantee you there'll be consequences to it one day." In John's view—and he had made it clear many times to friends and associates—

when a celebrity invites photographers to take pictures of what might be considered a private moment in public, such as an intimate dinner in a cozy restaurant with a loved one, it suggests that the celebrity doesn't value his privacy. The implication is that there are no boundaries, that every moment in that celebrity's life is open to public scrutiny. "Your whole life becomes public property," he once explained, "and you can't reverse that perception once you've established it." In trying to explain his theory to Madonna, though, he might as well have been speaking in a foreign tongue. "But I want *fame*, John," Madonna insisted. "Fame means power. And I want *power*." John said that perhaps this was a valid thought, especially coming from a woman in a male-dominated show business world. "But if you were really famous, why would you have to call photographers to come and take your picture?" he reasoned. At that, Madonna just glared at him. "Exactly what is it you are trying to say, John?" she asked. He shook his head as if to indicate that he was done with the subject. "You know what they say," he concluded. "What price fame, Madonna? What price fame?" She mulled it over, but it didn't take her long to come up with an answer. "Any price," she said.

In the end, John Kennedy Jr. decided that because he and Madonna had such different sets of values, there was no way it could ever work out for them. She was invested in building a certain iconography, not in trying to find ways to control it. She was more than happy to cast herself as a public person. Luckily, Madonna had great talent and ambition to go along with her hunger for attention, and her star would continue to ascend. His time with her wasn't a lost cause, though, as far as John was concerned. "John always thought it valuable to see a different perspective of any issue he found important, especially as it related to media," said one of his friends. "He stayed friendly with Madonna. 'Her life works for her,' he told me. 'Who am I to judge her?'"

One more telling story about John and Madonna:

In the summer of 1988, Madonna was jogging with John and one of John's closest friends in Central Park when, again, the subject of fame and celebrity came up between them. As they kept a rapid pace together, Madonna turned to John and asked, "Do you know how big a star you could be if you only acted like a real Kennedy instead of just some ordinary guy? I mean, my God! You could be huge." John seemed bemused. "But I haven't done anything to merit that kind of acclamation," he said.

"I'm just a guy." According to the witness, Madonna stopped running to look at John. "I don't get you," she said. "You're not 'just a guy,' you're a *Kennedy*. That sets you apart, John. You are a historical person. Don't you see that?" John paused and then, while running in place, said, "You can be the star in this family. How's that?" Then, flashing his winning smile at her, he sprinted off. As he ran off, Madonna stared at John's friend for a moment and shook her head in dismay. "He is just so odd, isn't he?" she asked before running after him.

Career Girl

*B*y the middle of 1985, Jackie Kennedy Onassis was, much to the surprise of a lot of people, working at Doubleday and Company. She had taken the job a few years earlier, in 1981. She would come into the office three days a week—Tuesdays, Wednesdays, and Thursdays—and work as an editor, not only assisting authors in the development of their books but also shepherding their beloved projects through the complicated maze of publishing, from book proposal to actual publication.

Jackie had worked in the early fifties for the *Washington Times-Herald* as a reporter—the "Inquiring Photographer"—interviewing random people on the issues of the day as she roved the streets, snapping their pictures and folding their answers into a daily column. It became so popular that she would go on to interview Richard Nixon for the column and was assigned to interview Dwight D. Eisenhower and covered the coronation of Queen Elizabeth II. Decades later, after meeting several writers in New York with whom she became friendly, she decided she wanted nothing more than to work as a book editor. She started at Viking Press in 1975. But in 1978, the company published Jeffrey Archer's novel *Shall We Tell the President?* Set in a future fictional presidency, it was presumably modeled after Ted Kennedy and described an assassination plot against him. When the *New York Times* gave it a scathing review and suggested that she was irresponsible for allowing its publication, Jackie resigned from Viking the next day. Eventually she found herself working at Doubleday.

To some, it certainly seemed strange: Jackie Kennedy Onassis—

former First Lady and internationally known socialite and fashion icon—working in New York as a book editor. She obviously didn't need the money; her affluence was well known. But it didn't seem strange to her at all. She loved the job, got along famously with her colleagues, and felt she was doing something with her life that truly mattered, something she knew she was good at, and, most importantly, something that made her abundantly happy.

As mentioned earlier, this author first met Jackie in 1983 at Double-day, where we had a lively discussion about celebrity culture in her small, cluttered office that featured just one window. Her desk looked like organized chaos: heaps of magazines in neat piles, large manila envelopes in stacks, other kinds of mail sorted in a specific way perhaps known only to her. There were two empty foam coffee cups in one corner, and two unfinished pastries as well. A square glass container held a jumble of pencils, all different colors, each one with a sharpened point. There was an ashtray filled with cigarette butts. No pictures of any Kennedys anywhere—just a poster of a ballerina on the wall. "Oh my, I do adore Diana Ross," she said, mentioning the subject of my first book for Double-day. "She is so...I don't know...what's the word I'm looking for?" We stared at each other for a moment before it came to her: "...*enigmatic.* That's it." She nodded her head. "Say, can I ask you a question?" "Of course," I replied. "Speaking of enigmas, do you know Michael Jackson? Because I also find him absolutely *fascinating.*" I did, in fact, know Michael Jackson. "Really!" she exclaimed. "Well, we should talk about *him* one day. I love people in the public eye who I sense have an inner life that is somewhat..." She paused. Then, with a mischievous twinkle in her eye, she finished the sentence: "...*secretive.* I guess you could say I love people who have secrets," she added, laughing. "Isn't that just *awful?* But, really, what would be the point of writing about a celebrity if you weren't going to reveal his or her secrets?" she asked. "I mean, that's what makes a book a juicy and fun read, isn't it?"*

---

* As it happened, Jackie would acquire and in 1988 edit and publish a book from Michael Jackson called *Moonwalk,* and would write a three-paragraph introduction to the book.

Maurice Tempelsman

*E*ver since Maurice moved in, I feel out of sorts."

It was the spring of 1985 and Jackie Kennedy Onassis was dining with her old friend Roswell Gilpatric at an upscale restaurant in New York City. The two were speaking about her present companion, Maurice Tempelsman. "Well, you two get along, don't you?" Roswell asked. "Oh, of course we do," Jackie said. "But I'm just so set in my ways. I had such a routine," she said with a soft, barely concealed chuckle. She added that her days used to unfold like clockwork. She always knew what she was going to do and when, in a very structured manner. "But now I can't make heads or tails of anything," she said, seeming exasperated. "The phone is always ringing for Maurice. There are visitors all day, people coming and going. Why, it's like Grand Central Station at my apartment!" Roswell, according to his memory of the conversation, couldn't help but laugh. He told her that this kind of change was probably good for her. "It's nice to shake things up a bit," he said. Jackie had to agree.

Jackie told Roswell that after Aristotle Onassis died, she never imagined being in another relationship. "And I certainly never thought I would live with another man," she said. "Why, I'm fifty-five," she exclaimed. "I'm old, Ros," she added. The two friends laughed again. "And I'm so stubborn. I like things done my way. You know me. I'm quite fussy, aren't I?" Rather than answer the question and state the obvious, Roswell just smiled at her and told her that these were her best years, that it's fun to throw caution to the wind at her age. "But must I do it for another man who smokes cigars?" Jackie asked, laughing.

By 1985, Jackie had become fully committed to her latest romantic relationship, one quite different from those she'd enjoyed in the past. His name was Maurice Tempelsman, someone very familiar to those in Jackie's circle but not necessarily to the public that remained fascinated by the former First Lady or, at least, to the media that kept constant tabs on her every move. Tempelsman was born on August 26, 1929, the same year as Jackie, to the Yiddish-speaking Orthodox Jewish Leon and Helene Tempelsman in Antwerp, Belgium. When he was about eleven, he and his parents and only sister moved to the United States to escape the Nazis' invasion of their homeland during World War II. They settled on Manhattan's Upper West Side in a refugee community. At sixteen, he began working for his father, who was a diamond merchant, while also attending New York University, where he took night classes. Though Tempelsman never graduated from college, Rachel Gotlieb, a childhood friend, remembers a teenage Maurice as being scholarly and "on the timid side." It wasn't long before he joined his father in the diamond merchant business—Leon Tempelsman and Son, Inc. "I had an inner conflict abut whether I really liked the business," he would say in 1982, "and part of me still wonders." Soon, though, he began making his own fortune.

Late in 1949, Maurice, then twenty, married Lilly Bucholz, two years his senior, who had also fled Antwerp with her family. Her father was also in the diamond mining business, though not as successful at it as Maurice's father. They would have three children—Rena, Leon, and Marcy—but by the 1970s their marriage was on the rocks and the couple was just staying together for the sake of their children.

"In 1979, Jackie's financial adviser André Meyer died," Roswell Gilpatric recalled. "I attended the funeral with her and walked home with her afterward. She was very upset about it. She knew he cared about her very much, and even though it wasn't romantic for her, she felt protected.

"She'd already been seeing Maurice, but after André died her relationship with Maurice really took hold. She would tell me in that lovely, breathy voice of hers, 'He's a smart man, and tough, too.' In the 1950s, she told me, he went into business with the U.S. government stockpiling African diamonds for industrial and military purposes. He had a lot of ties in Africa, and became a major power there in his field. Because he also had strong ties to the Democratic Party, he was well known to the Kennedy family. Jackie first met Maurice when JFK was a senator. I believe it was Ted Sorensen who introduced them. The senator wanted to meet Sir Ernest Oppenheimer, the diamond and gold mining entrepreneur who was a friend of Maurice's, so Maurice arranged the meeting and Jackie went along. She told me she very vaguely remembered meeting Maurice at that time. However, the two continued seeing each other on a social basis whenever Jackie was in New York, all the way through her marriage to Onassis. Then, when Onassis died, Maurice made it his intention to win Jackie over, which is what he ultimately did."

Maurice Tempelsman had some commonalities with Aristotle Onassis.

First, they shared some physical traits: He was short in stature—barely five feet eight inches—a little overweight, and balding. He had a long and swooping nose and wasn't the most attractive man in the world. When it came to choosing men, though, Jackie had always looked beyond the exterior attributes of the opposite sex and was intensely attracted by a man's wit, his curiosity, his intelligence, his sense of humor, and, it would be safe to say, his financial resources. "He enjoyed the arts, was a collector of Roman and Greek antiques, was well-read and -traveled, fluent in French, like Jackie, and had a wonderful sense of humor," said Tempelsman's cousin Rose Schreiber. He was also affluent—owned his own yacht, which couldn't compare to Onassis's but was impressive just the same—and was socially well-connected. He was distinguished in many ways, not the least of which was the fact that he was—is—one of just a handful of site holders permitted to make, ten times a year, direct purchases of diamonds from the De Beers diamond cartel, the internationally based diamond mining and trading company that has controlled the flow of diamonds in the U.S. marketplace for decades.

Tempelsman was also an astute businessman and financier, like Onassis. He was running a multimillion-dollar diamond trading business, and doing so very successfully. Over a period of years, Tempelsman would take complete control of Jackie's finances and build her $25.5 million settlement from Onassis into a fortune that would be estimated at between $100 and $200 million.

It could be said that the biggest difference between Tempelsman and Onassis was his temperament. Tempelsman was easygoing and affable, never volatile. He would gladly acquiesce to Jackie's desires just to see her smile, and he wouldn't have dreamt of being combative with her. "Why should I try to fight her on anything?" he once asked, privately. "She's smart. She knows what she likes, who she is, what she wants. Who am I to come into the picture and try to dictate to her?" Attorney Samuel Pisar, a friend of Maurice and Jackie's, put it best: "With Maurice, everything slowed down. She was at peace with him."

Also like Onassis—and to a certain extent like JFK—Tempelsman was somewhat paternal where Jackie was concerned. She was a woman who liked being taken care of—and he did his part of the bargain well for her. It could be said that the only problem Jackie had with Maurice Tempelsman wasn't his fault: His wife, Lilly, refused to give him a divorce.

An Orthodox Jew who was apparently more devoted to her faith than Maurice was, she simply refused to do so, even after he left her in 1982. Her refusal kept him tied to her pretty much for the rest of their lives, but once he was with Jackie—he moved into her home in 1984—it was Jackie who had his heart, not Lilly.

Early in their relationship, Jackie considered ending it rather than continuing with a man who was married. But she had to wonder if that was a reductive way of looking at the relationship with Maurice. After all, divorce was not an option due only to the religious convictions of his wife, not because the marriage was still viable. He was a good and decent man, Jackie knew, and she didn't want to let him go. Plus, she sensed that he would be faithful to her, and considering what she'd experienced in her lifetime, this was a refreshing turn of events. Still, why was he living with his wife? Just as Jackie was trying to figure out what to do, Maurice's wife made the decision for her. By this time, ironically, Lilly had become a marriage counselor at the Jewish Board of Guardians. She was tired, she said at the time, of seeing photos of her husband and Jackie all over New York and on Martha's Vineyard—where Jackie had an estate—and she wanted him to move out. Therefore, in November 1982 he left their home and moved into a hotel. Then in 1984 he moved in with Jackie, taking the bedroom (next to hers) that had once belonged to Aristotle— the one in which she kept her exercise equipment when Onassis wasn't in residence.

"He was quiet. He was discreet. He kept her secrets," says R. Couri Hay, a publicist who is also a friend of the Kennedy family's. "Jackie liked having strong men around like him. If you look at JFK, Onassis, and Tempelsman, they seem very different, but really they're not. They were all strong father figures, in a sense. She felt very safe with each of them. She felt protected."

Former congressman Tony Coelho, a Tempelsman friend, says, "The more you talk to him, the more you like him. He is a person who can be a natural confidant. They were natural together. Most people put her up on a pedestal, but with Maurice it was different. He didn't regard her as a trophy."

"He was a man of honor," adds Stanley Gottwig, also a Manhattan investor at the time who worked closely with Tempelsman. "Once committed to someone, he was totally committed. I had many meetings with

Jackie and Maurice and I saw the mutual admiration they had for one another, and also the respect they shared. After one such meeting, she pulled me aside and said, 'Have you ever known anyone sharper than Maurice?' She was quite charmed by him."

Stanley Gottwig recalls a particular meeting with Maurice and Jackie in March 1986 during which they discussed the structuring of her complex finances and the building of certain annuities for her children. Jackie was about to announce the engagement of her daughter, Caroline, to her beau, Ed Schlossberg. Certain financial matters needed to be addressed in light of the upcoming nuptials. The three were in Tempelsman's New York office, which was filled with antiques and hundreds of books. They were seated at a long mahogany conference room table sipping hot coffee. "I can't believe my little girl is getting married," Jackie said. "It seems like just yesterday when I held her in my arms." Then, with a laugh, she added, "Oh my, that is so trite, isn't it? But it's true!"

Toward the end of the meeting, Maurice told Jackie, "Now, not only will Caroline be taken care of, but her children will be taken care of as well. And their children's children, too."

Jackie looked up from a stack of papers in front of her. "You really do care about Caroline and John, don't you?" she asked Maurice earnestly.

He seemed surprised by the question, at least according to Stanley Gottwig's memory. "Of course I do, my dear."

She smiled at him. "You are such a dear, dear man," she said, reaching out for his hand. "I don't know that I deserve you, Maurice."

"Oh, but I know that you do," he said, taking her hand into his own and returning her smile. "I know that you do."

Caroline Kennedy and Maria Shriver Both Marry

There were three Kennedy weddings of note in the spring and summer of 1986, two of them full-blown American royalty affairs that gave the family a great opportunity to reconvene: Eunice and Sargent's daughter, Maria, to actor Arnold Schwarzenegger, and Jackie's daughter, Caroline, to Ed Schlossberg. The third wedding was a very low-key event—Timothy, the son of Eunice and Sarge, to Linda Sturges Potter.

"Don't look at him as a Republican," Maria Shriver told her uncle Teddy when talking about her fiancé, Arnold Schwarzenegger. "Look at him as the man I love. And if that doesn't work, look at him as someone who can squash you." Ted had to laugh. Actually, he took no issue with his niece's choice for a husband and liked him very much. Eunice and Sargent felt the same way. Thus the wedding between Maria and Arnold, on April 26, 1986, was a joyous affair. It was interesting that Maria and Arnold had known each other a full seven years before marrying, nearly mirroring her parents' long courtship of nine years.

At the time, Maria was just beginning her career in television with a job in Philadelphia. She first became interested in broadcasting in 1972 during her father's vice presidential race when she was sent to the back of the campaign plane during travel time—where the media was seated. She now calls those orders "the best thing that ever happened to me." As a seventeen-year-old, she kept her ambition to be a reporter a secret because she feared her family would be against the idea. After all, the Kennedys often had a contentious relationship with the media, and, mirroring the concerns of her cousin John Jr. in years to come, she was afraid some of her relatives might feel she'd joined the enemy's ranks.

Maria's career would be a fast-moving one. After college and a degree in American studies, she ended up working in a training program at KYW-TV in Philadelphia at the age of twenty-one, doing any job she was asked to do, from getting coffee for the news director to scouring the wire services for possible leads. She started at the bottom and worked her way up, given no preferential treatment because of her family and, if anything, maybe having it a little tougher, courtesy of people who viewed her as spoiled and privileged before even knowing her. Not only was she tenacious and determined, but she also had a real passion for news, which would carry her far. Eventually she found herself working as a field producer at WJZ in Baltimore and then, finally, on the air as a correspondent for the syndicated evening program *PM Magazine*. From there she would work for CBS News as a field reporter, and in years to come she would coanchor the *CBS Morning News* with Forrest Sawyer from 1985 to 1987, and then move to NBC from 1987 to 2004.

Her mother, who always had been very strict with her, seemed quite proud that Maria was making her own way with her own career. "I know I have been hard on her," she told friends at the wedding rehearsal dinner the night before the ceremony. "I imagine it is quite the challenge being the daughter of Eunice Shriver," she said with a smile. "But, like all mothers, I have only wanted the best for her."

On her special day, Maria wore a lovely silk mousseline gown, very traditional with long white veil and train, while Arnold was dapper in a perfectly tailored black morning suit with a frock coat. As stunning as the couple of the day looked, though, it was difficult to take one's eyes off Eunice and Sargent Shriver. They made another stunning couple, full of good cheer, Sargent in a gray top hat offsetting his tailored formal black cutaway outfit; Eunice was also wearing a large chapeau. "I can only hope for a marriage like my parents'," Maria said at the time. "When I think of the ideal marriage, theirs comes to mind. That's what I want for myself, my husband, the children we will have."

Equally special, though much more intimate, was the wedding on May 31, 1986, of Sargent's and Eunice's son Timothy to Linda Sturges Potter, a young woman he had known for a number of years. Because the rehearsal dinner and reception were not held at the Kennedy compound, it was guaranteed to be less of a media event. The couple was wed in an ecumenical ceremony, conducted by a New York Episcopal bishop and a Catholic priest, at Georgetown University's Dahlgren Chapel of the Sacred Heart.

The third of the Kennedy weddings that summer was that of Jackie's daughter, Caroline, to Ed Schlossberg on July 19, 1986, which happened to be the groom's forty-first birthday. It also happened to be the seventeenth anniversary of Ted's devastating accident on Chappaquiddick Island.

Edwin Alfred Schlossberg is the son of Mr. and Mrs. Alfred and Mae Schlossberg of New York and Palm Beach, Florida, his father a successful textile designer and manufacturer. Born on July 19, 1945, Ed grew up on the Upper West Side surrounded by a very large family of Russian Jewish immigrants. All four of his grandparents had landed on Ellis Island from Poltava, Ukraine, and, like Maurice Tempelsman, Ed's family was deeply steeped in Jewish orthodoxy. He graduated from the Birch Wathen School and Columbia College and then received his PhD in science and literature from Columbia University in 1969. Ed was described by a family spokesman as "a specialist in interactive media," though most people were at a loss as to exactly what that meant. Even Jackie, when asked by a Doubleday colleague what Ed's profession was, said, "I have no idea. He could work for the CIA, as far as I know." In fact, Schlossberg was—is—an incredibly creative person, an artist who worked with unusual materials such as aluminum, Plexiglas, or even rice paper and bamboo rods. He didn't just paint pictures; he also designed and created artistic display pieces on a large scale. In addition to being the author of nine books, mostly instructional manuals, he was the president of Edwin Schlossberg, Inc., a New York company specializing in the design of museum interiors and exhibits.

Ed is twelve years older than Caroline—interesting only in that her parents were also twelve years apart in age; JFK was thirty-six, Jackie twenty-four when they married. Because Schlossberg is Jewish, there were rumors at the time that the family—Rose, in particular—was unhappy about the union. The rumors weren't true. The entire family supported Caroline's decision to marry Ed. The fact that he agreed to raise any children the couple had as Catholics probably helped, though.

"All our lives, it's just been the three of us," John said while delivering the toast at the rehearsal dinner the night before the ceremony. "My mother, Caroline, and me. Now," he said, turning to Ed, "there are four." John's emotional and always appropriate turn of phrase was very much in the Kennedy tradition, reminiscent of his father's and his uncles' way with words.

On the day of the wedding, Caroline walked down the aisle resplendent in a white silk organza gown with a tulle petticoat, shamrock appliqués, lace veil, and a twenty-foot train. It was designed for her by Carolina Herrera, with no input from Jackie. The Church of Our Lady of Victory in Hyannis was filled with many of JFK's loyalists, including Arthur Schlesinger Jr., Ted Sorensen, and Pierre Salinger.

For her part, Jackie played the role of mother of the bride beautifully, trying her best not to steal focus from her daughter—no small feat when one is Jackie Kennedy Onassis. The pushing crowd of onlookers outside the church could barely contain themselves when she arrived for the ceremony, alone. She was wearing a Herrera-designed pistachio-colored crepe suit and gloves, holding a clutch bag with one hand and waving to the crowd with the other. "It was a hot, muggy day," recalled Steve

Heaslip, who was a photographer at the *Cape Cod Times* assigned to the wedding, "with 50 or 60 media people waiting at the entrance of the church. Jackie sent over a big cooler of soft drinks and water for the press. I thought that was a classy thing to do."

John Jr. was Ed's best man on this special day, and according to all onlookers, provided one of the most memorable moments of the night when he took his mother into his arms and danced with her during the reception.

Ted, who gave the bride away, offered an emotional toast at the reception, which was held under a large tent set up on the grounds of the Kennedy compound. "I'm filling in for my brother Jack," he told the guests. He first paid tribute to Rose, who would soon turn ninety-six. She was elderly and feeble but still seemed determined to live a good life and be a part of the family's many activities. "To the mother of us all," Ted said, raising his glass to Rose. Turning to Caroline and Ed, he then said, "We've all thought of Jack today, and how much he loved Caroline and how much he loved Jackie...Caroline, he loved you so much." With tears flowing all around him, Ted continued by toasting Jackie, "that extraordinary woman, Jack's only love. He would have been so proud of you today."

PART SIXTEEN

William Kennedy Smith and the Palm Beach Scandal

Eunice's Dire Prediction to Ted

The 1980s had all but confirmed Ted Kennedy's status as the consummate legislator, one of his greatest gifts being that he made few enemies while staying true to his personal convictions. He was known to forge friendly relationships with many Republicans, such as Senator Orrin Hatch, with whom he worked on a number of health-related issues. Throughout the decade, he worked hard during a period in which the Republicans had captured not only the presidency with Ronald Reagan, but control of the Senate as well. Though Ted found himself part of the minority party for the first time in his political career, this did not stop him from devoting himself to liberal causes such as women's issues and gay rights. He was also at the forefront of funding for AIDS education, concerns, and treatment during a time when most people simply didn't understand the disease and wanted nothing to do with learning more about it. Ted had a good heart. He genuinely cared about people from all walks of life and was always intensely interested in how the so-called "other half" lived. He wanted nothing more than to make a difference as a civil servant, which had always been his intention.

Despite his great success in government, though, Ted was floundering in his personal life by the end of the 1980s. It could be said that the decade had been one of debauchery for him, with his drinking habit spinning completely out of control. As a single, wealthy, and very prominent man, there was no limit to the number of women he could score—not that it could be argued that there had been any limit when he was a married man—and he was often caught in embarrassingly compromising positions, such as when European paparazzi photographed him having sex with a young lady on a motorboat. Those kinds of sensational moments became commonplace for Kennedy in the 1980s and did nothing but distract from the good work he was doing in the Senate. Many people perceived him as being a disgrace to the Kennedy name, which had to have been frustrating to a man who so loved his family and wanted nothing more than to represent them in the best way possible. Still, his demons were what they were—and there seemed no getting around them. In his personal life, he always seemed to make the worst decisions, and they were definitely coloring the public's perception of him. JFK and Bobby could get away with it. But after Watergate, all eyes were on politicians, and the tabloid media had created an environment that was now unforgiving in its exposure of the personal lives of political figures. Though not referring specifically to his uncle, maybe Ted's nephew John Kennedy Jr. would put it best in a March 1998 editorial in his *George* magazine when he wrote, "Hellish torment awaits those who mix an undisciplined libido with a political career."

In January 1991, Ted Kennedy was sitting at a poolside table on a patio of the Kennedys' sumptuous Palm Beach estate with two of the family's attorneys. He looked dreadful. He was overweight by at least thirty pounds, his eyes were bloodshot, and his face was unshaven and blotchy. His drinking problem was so serious that he was said to suffer blackouts after a night on the town. On this morning, he was obviously hungover. "I had sex with a couple of knockout hookers last night," he told the lawyers awkwardly. "I'm not as young as I used to be, though," he said with a chuckle, "because I think I fell asleep before I finished." The attorneys laughed tensely. Just then, Eunice Kennedy came sweeping into the room.

At almost seventy, Eunice was now, maybe more than ever, quite the vibrant presence. As she got older, her personality was just as dominant as ever, even if she was physically much more frail, no doubt the result of her years-long battle with Addison's disease (the same ailment from which her brother Jack suffered). As honorary chairman of Special Olympics International, Eunice was still a very busy woman. This coming summer of 1991, she was looking forward to the International Special Olympics in Minneapolis. At seventy-five, Sarge was getting older too, but was still involved in many charities despite a bout with prostate cancer.

Eunice was actively involved in her children's lives as well. All her children were, not surprisingly, of great service to others. Her eldest, Bobby, had turned into a fine young man and was now living in Los Angeles and working for the Special Olympics. Anthony was head of a charity called Best Buddies, whose goal was to forge friendships between the handicapped and college students. Timothy was deeply involved in educational charities concerning AIDS prevention and drug addiction. Mark was invested in a social program in Maryland called Choice. Meanwhile, Maria was doing very well in her television broadcasting career. As

Eunice's only daughter, she spoke to her mother almost every day from her home in Los Angeles. The older Maria got, the more she looked like Eunice. Eunice would make an excellent, if also sometimes quite strict, grandmother to Maria and Arnold's children as they came along—four in all.

Eunice sat down and took her brother in with slanted eyes behind thick-framed glasses. There she sat, staring at him, not greeting him or anyone else, just staring at him with a stern expression. She had her rosary clutched tightly in one hand and was fingering the beads. When a Kennedy functionary came to the table to ask if she would like some breakfast, Eunice dismissed the servant with a quick wave, not even glancing in her direction lest she take her eyes off her brother for even a moment.

"Good morning, Eunice," Ted said with a smile, perhaps trying to break the uncomfortable silence of her sitting there staring at him. "And how is my lovely sister faring on this glorious day?"

"Just look at you," Eunice said, ignoring her brother's attempt at levity. "Why, Ted Kennedy, you look a fright." She said she was worried about him and that she knew fully well why he had been drinking. "You want to escape," she told him. "Yes, we have a lot of sad memories. But we can't escape them, Ted. We have to face them."

"I know that," Ted said sadly.

"As your sister who loves you, I am asking you to please take a good long look at yourself," Eunice said, never softening her steely gaze. "You must change the way you want to be perceived by others, and govern yourself accordingly." She then ticked off a list of the public relations disasters that had occurred in the recent past, behind which she suspected was his drinking. She knew of every incident, too, and had a memory for the specifics of each episode that most people would have found amazing. "Jack and Bobby are depending on you, now as always," she said, invoking the names of their dead brothers—which no one ever did in the family unless they meant business. According to the two lawyers present, she also said that there was "a whole generation of Kennedys coming up now," many of whom have their own personal dysfunction, "and they need you to set an example for them. In fact, this family needs you now more than ever."

Ted nodded in agreement. Eunice's commentary had to have made an impact on him. After all, Ted had done his best to be a strong male influence on twenty-four Kennedy children—two of Jack's, eleven of Bobby's, four of Peter Lawford's, and now four of Stephen Smith's, not to mention his own three children. It had never been easy, but he had done his best and he had done so despite his tendency to be self-absorbed—which made it all the more a challenge.

"My fear is this," Eunice continued. "If you don't straighten up, something terrible is going to happen. All hell is going to break loose again, and by that time we'll all be too damn old to deal with it." Then, rather than soften the blow by saying anything else, Eunice glanced at her watch and exclaimed, *"Oh my God! I'm going to be late!"* And with that, she pushed herself away from the table, rose, and walked away quickly, leaving Ted sitting with the two attorneys, perhaps embarrassed and maybe even saddened. But that was Eunice. She wasn't the kind of woman who would coddle a person after she let him have it. She wanted the moment to stick, not be defused by some meaningless pleasantry. Ted had to know that Eunice was right, though. In fact, it would take less than a month for her dire prediction to come true.

Ted's and Jean's Sad Memories

*I*t was to be just another Easter weekend for the Kennedys at La Guerida in Palm Beach, or at least that's how it was anticipated. "I suppose we'll do what we usually do," Jean Kennedy Smith, who was then sixty-three, said when asked how she planned to spend the first Easter without her husband. "My children and I will go down to Palm Beach. Probably Ted will be there, too. And anyone else who wants to join us. We would love to see Jackie and Maurice," she said. "We're hoping..."

As it happened, the holy holiday brought out something melancholy in Ted and Jean, who were both deeply grieving the recent death, in August 1990, of Stephen Smith, Jean's husband. Smith had always been a tough, uncompromising person, but had been integral to nearly all of the campaigns of the brothers over the years, and as such commanded a great deal of respect among the Kennedys. He also ran the family's finances as chairman of the family's business office in New York after Joseph passed away. Ted had become extremely close to Stephen over the years, and as it became clearer that Stephen would probably not live much longer, Ted took it harder than most people, with the exception being, of course, Jean. Stephen was barely sixty when he died of cancer. "He was the last one left," Ted said of Smith, "the last great man in this family." (Sargent Shriver might have taken offense to that statement, but then again, it was never very surprising when Ted discounted Sarge.)

Though their marriage was troubled almost from the start, at the end it was appropriate that Jean would be the ever-present and dutiful wife to the ailing Stephen. She'd never stopped loving him, after all. He had just been very difficult to love, given his unfaithful behavior over the years. However, they had adopted two children together and had two of their own, so, in the Kennedy tradition, Jean felt a real responsibility to them and to the rest of the family to at least try to have a good marriage. She had history with Stephen. That counted for a lot. There was comfort, there was familiarity. He was a good man in many ways, smart, funny. It certainly wasn't the worst thing in the world to stay married to him. Now that he was gone, she missed him terribly.

Jean's life changed a great deal in the 1980s and into the 1990s. She began to take responsibility for some of her own decisions and stopped blaming her mother for her unhappiness. Her work with her charity, Very Special Arts, had forced her to focus on the problems of others, and it was to her own advantage. She began to express a much more clear-eyed assessment of her childhood and life as the fourth—and not as well known— daughter of Joseph and Rose Kennedy. She had also become a force to be reckoned with when it came to raising her own children. Not surprisingly, she was a lot like the mother she had often criticized. She was forceful and strong in the way she raised her children and, also like her own mother, Rose, she didn't much like it when they stood up to her or defied her.

On the night of Good Friday, March 29, 1991, Ted, Jean, and some friends—including retired FBI agent and RFK's personal bodyguard William G. Barry (who had leapt from the crowd and wrestled Sirhan Sirhan to the ground after he shot Bobby), along with his wife, son, and daughter-in-law—began reminiscing about Stephen and other loved ones from the past as they sat by the pool listening to Frank Sinatra records on the sound system. The Kennedys were customarily stoic about their lives and times, rarely discussing among themselves the many tragedies that had befallen them, so this was an unusual night for Ted and Jean.

The conversation went from one topic to the next:

Joseph's debilitating stroke, on a golf course in Palm Beach, and how different things might have been had it never occurred.

The shootings in Dallas and in Los Angeles, and how such cruel twists of fate had taken Jack and Bobby from Jackie and Ethel, from their children, and from all of their loved ones.

Joan's alcoholism.

The tragic accident at Chappaquiddick and how very different things might have been for Ted if only it had never happened.

Ted Jr.'s cancer.

David's death—also in Palm Beach.

Their recounting of so much painful history evoked such strong and unexpected feelings of bittersweet nostalgia that it's no wonder the experience took a toll on both Ted and Jean. By the time they were ready to retire for the evening, both were emotionally spent. "I found at the end of that conversation that I was not able to think about sleeping," Ted would later recall. "It was a very draining conversation."

Jean went right to bed, but not Ted. Unable to sleep, his face flushed from the night of drinking, he wandered aimlessly through the expansive mansion in his grief and sadness, looking for someone else to talk to, someone to perhaps take his mind off his troubles. By this time, Jean's grown children Kym and Steve had left the family home, leaving behind her daughter Amanda and son Willie—whose full name was William Kennedy Smith. Ted soon found his son Patrick and nephew Willie standing by the glass windows adjacent to the patio. He opened the door. "Say, do you guys want to go out for a drink?" he asked them. "Sure, why not?" they answered.

An Alleged Rape at the Kennedy Estate

The week preceding Easter 1991, Ted Kennedy and his son Patrick and his nephew Willie made many visits to a place called Au Bar, a disco and nightclub on Royal Poinciana Way in Palm Beach. There, they would pick up women and bring them back to the Palm Beach estate where they would, according to most accounts, have sex with them—something else that never would have been allowed to occur had Rose still been in residence.

At this time, Patrick was a recovering addict after having spent time in a rehab about five years earlier dealing with a coke problem. He was much better now, but determined not even to drink lest he relapse. He was turning out to be a fine young man despite his troubles in the past. Ted and Joan were both proud of him. He had been the youngest member of the Kennedy family to hold elective office when, in 1988, he won a seat in the Rhode Island legislature at just twenty-one. He would also suffer from bipolar disorder and depression for most of his life. In 1991, he was young—twenty-four—and single, and some thought that there was certainly no reason he shouldn't be allowed to have sex with consenting women if he wanted to. It was just that he would sometimes be with his father when the two men met available women, which rubbed people in the media, and also in the family, the wrong way. "If my dad was alive, I could never do it, that's all I can say," John Kennedy Jr. had said. "But, you know...to each his own, I guess."

Willie, who was thirty years old, had a full, thick Kennedy-like mop of black hair and thick dark eyebrows. The youngest son of Stephen and Jean, he was completing his final year at Georgetown Medical School to attain his doctorate after graduating from Duke University with a degree in premed. Previously, he had attended boarding school at Salisbury School in Salisbury, Connecticut. He was generally thought of as a decent young man, one of the less spoiled of the third generation, and though he got into trouble from time to time with his cousins, Jean Kennedy Smith always felt that he, as she put it, "has his head on straight." He had given a moving eulogy at his father's funeral; *Time* reported that "he outshone Arthur Schlesinger." The children of Jean and Stephen Smith kept a low profile, much like their parents. They were seldom featured in stories about the Kennedy family. "Don't put them on a pedestal," Stephen Smith had said of his children to one reporter. "They are children just like any other." Many years later, Willie recalled, "I think the first time people from my high school were aware that I had a connection to the Kennedy family was when my uncle Teddy spoke at my graduation."

At the club, Ted, Patrick, and Willie met Anne Mercer and Patricia Bowman. Though the two Kennedys and Smith were trying to have a good time, it wasn't working out for them. Ted's dark mood was apparently contagious. "You look like you're having a great time," Anne said to Patrick, being playfully sarcastic. "Who are you to say anything?" Ted shot back angrily, as he threw back another Chivas scotch. Later, Anne called Patrick a "bore," adding, "with genes like this, there'll be no more Kennedy dynasty." To which Ted indignantly responded, "How dare you speak in this manner? This young man is a member of the legislature of Rhode Island!"

By about 3:30 in the morning, Ted's back was bothering him, he was drunk, tired, feeling his age, and ready to go home. Therefore, he and Patrick—along with a twenty-seven-year-old waitress Patrick had met named Michelle Cassone—headed back to La Guerida, leaving Willie behind with Patricia Bowman, who was a twenty-nine-year-old single mother.

Once the three got back to the estate, they talked for a while—"mostly the senator held court," Cassone would recall. At a little before four, the two young people excused themselves and went into one of the downstairs rooms, leaving Ted alone. They were cuddling in that room when suddenly Ted appeared in the doorway without his trousers and wearing what appeared to be nothing but a long nightshirt. He cleared his throat, as if to announce his presence. "Then he just stood there with this very strange look on his face," Cassone would recall. Was he just wandering the house and had stumbled upon them? What in the world was going on? "To tell you the truth, I was completely freaked out," Cassone recalled. She jumped to her feet. "Okay, I'm out of here," she said. She and Patrick went outside, where she asked him, "Does your father embarrass you?" The two then engaged in a conversation about Patrick's relationship with his dad.

Meanwhile, Willie had apparently returned to the mansion with Patricia Bowman. By all accounts, the two began to have sex by the pool. Willie would later say he "pulled out" and was glad he had because, as he would tell it, he had a "bad feeling" about Bowman. She seemed like one of those women the young Kennedy cousins often talked about, the kind who were only interested in them because "we are Kennedys"—as if they didn't use their family name and heritage to interest women in the first place. That said, Willie would later tell Patrick he was glad Patricia left, driven away, apparently, by Dennis Spear, the estate's caretaker. But then she showed up again for no reason he could think of, and, as he would recall it, "my heart skipped a few beats, I was so freaked out when she just popped up again. And I thought, man, this girl is whacked."

All of this was going on while Jean Kennedy Smith was sound asleep upstairs in the ocean-view room that had for decades been used by her mother. Of course, Jean would never have condoned any of what was going on that night, but Kennedy women had long ago abandoned any hope that they might influence the men in the family when it came to their personal behavior.

On Saturday morning, Jean rose early as she always did and took a long, five-mile walk along the beach. When she returned, she went for a swim in the estate's pool. After lunch, she went shopping. When she returned, she found Ted playing tennis and watched the game. The family seemed fine, Willie and Patrick giving no signs that anything strange had happened the previous night, and certainly no sign of it from Ted either. What no one knew was that Patricia Bowman had gone to the police that afternoon to file rape charges against Willie.

Tough Love

*T*hings quickly went from bad to worse.

When William Kennedy Smith was finally officially charged with sexual battery, the floodgates of controversy opened and the nation became quickly spellbound by the unfolding melodrama, the latest Kennedy scandal. With his mother at his side, Willie surrendered to the Palm Beach police to be booked. While he looked concerned and almost stricken, Jean looked strong and defiant. "We will get to the truth, I can assure you," she told reporters. "I am very distressed that someone is trying to hurt my son. He says he has done nothing wrong and I believe him. We all believe him."

The Kennedys did what they always did in times of trouble—they closed ranks. An attack on one of their own was an attack on all of them. Bobby Kennedy Jr. called a meeting of his brothers and sisters to tell them that they had to stick together, "now more than ever," as he put it. Outraged by the charges brought against one of their own, the Kennedys fought back with a vengeance. Who was this accuser, anyway? As well as calling her sex life into question, the Kennedy investigators assigned to look into her background told the family that she supposedly had been a user of cocaine, had had three abortions, had a child born out of wedlock, and even had received seventeen traffic tickets—though actually it was impossible to know what was true and what was not true about her. On April 16, she was even named in the *New York Times*. Up until that time, releasing the name of an alleged rape victim was unheard of in the reporting of such an incident. The *Times* was widely criticized for its decision and later explained its reasoning to name her by saying that it "did so only after her identity became known throughout her community and received detailed nationwide publicity." None of this mattered to the Kennedys, though. What was important was that they present a united front. Did they consider that Willie could be guilty? No. Or as one friend of the family put it, "I believe the sense in the family was that even if he did it, there was nothing anyone could do about it at that moment except just be supportive. There wasn't, I think, a lot of concern about the victim. Only about Willie, which I guess is, as a family, understandable."

To help prove their case, the prosecutors eventually found three women—a doctor, a medical student, and a law student—who claimed that Willie had had rough sex with them between 1983 and 1988, forcing himself on them just as, allegedly, he had done to Patricia Bowman. Even though their testimony would ultimately be judged inadmissible in court—a devastating blow to the prosecution—it received national attention and helped paint Smith as a man out of control and possibly a sexual predator. Still, Jean remained unfazed.

"I don't care what anyone says. I support my son no matter what," she told one attorney during a meeting in his office to discuss the case. Present were Jean, two attorneys, Willie, and a legal secretary. Jean reiterated her belief that her son was innocent and said that she would "not allow him to be victimized like this. Family means everything to the Kennedys," she said, "and if someone is attacking our family, I believe we have no choice but to fight. Family matters, that's what my father always said," Jean continued, "and it is the credo by which we have lived our lives from the very beginning. We will remain strong and defiant through this," she concluded. "That's exactly how my father would handle it."

When Willie said he was afraid that the public would believe the charges, Jean shot him an annoyed look. She was in his corner, but clearly she was also quite angry with him. "I'm just saying..." he continued, according to witnesses. Jean cut him off. "Quiet," she commanded in a very sharp tone. Smith just nodded and looked down.

One of the attorneys present then said that the family would be able to fight the charges but that doing so would take time and money. "Oh, that's easy," Willie said with a slight smile. "We have plenty of both." Everyone looked at each other in silence. It seemed like the most inappropriate thing William could have said in that moment. In response, Jean very slowly rose from her chair, walked over to her son, and stood directly in front of him. "I'd like to talk to you in the hall," she said looking down at him. With a sheepish expression, he looked up at her and said, "Yes, Mother." The two left the room. Jean returned fifteen minutes later, but without her son. "Now," she said, sitting back down and addressing the attorneys. "Where were we?"

Jean's antagonism toward her son did seem somewhat odd to the observers, as if something else was going on that only the two of them knew about. "Though Jean was obviously annoyed at her boy, she was still involved in every strategy meeting," recalled Dominick Dunne, who was in the courtroom for the proceedings and wrote about them for *Vanity Fair*. "The lawyers didn't know much about her. They all knew about Eunice, Jackie, Rose, Ethel, Joan, and even Pat because of the Peter Lawford marriage. But Jean? In terms of the women in the family, most people knew virtually nothing about her, but they came to find out that she was quite formidable. They learned that she was determined, focused, and driven—decidedly a force to be reckoned with.

"There were strategy meetings every night at the Kennedy mansion— often over dinner—where all of the lawyers were staying," continued Dunne. "You might say it was a command center. In those meetings, Jean displayed a fiery temper, especially with her son. The sense was that she loved him very much but was also quite unhappy with him. She would freely chastise him, often in the company of others, and had a tough-love approach to dealing with him. Most found their relationship to be quite tense. When he wasn't around, she spoke lovingly of him. But when he was present, it was a different story."

One attorney very close to the case but not authorized to speak about it recalled, "William owned a cell phone, which was about the size of a small brick, typical of the times. During one particular meeting around a conference table, it rang and he pulled it from his jacket to answer it. 'No, Willie,' his mother said, glaring at him. 'But it might be urgent,' he said. 'Nothing is more urgent than what is going on here,' she said. 'I am quite sure you will agree.' He nodded his head and then put the phone back in his pocket.

"There was another instance when William seemed to not be paying attention to a point Mrs. Kennedy Smith was trying to make regarding the case. In his defense, he was obviously under a great deal of pressure. After all, he was facing fifteen years in prison, and also pretty much the end of his medical career. On this day, he seemed distracted. At one point, he seemed to be drifting off, staring into space. While his mother was speaking, she very casually stood up, went to a bookshelf, and pulled a book from it. We all thought she was going to look something up. Instead, she stepped behind her son, raised the book over his head and dropped it with a loud thud on the table right in front of him. He was obviously startled, as were the rest of us. Then she just went back to what she was saying, all without missing a beat."

Another moment stands out in the minds of many who were intimately involved in the case. While the defendant's attorneys were going over his testimony with him and his mother, Willie explained that at one point during his time with Patricia Bowman, his accuser had, as he put it, "masturbated me to ejaculation." It was an uncomfortable moment, especially given that his mother was sitting right there next to him.

"Well, I certainly don't like the way *that* sounds," Jean noted of the word "masturbated." According to witnesses, William was visibly embarrassed. Noting as much, Jean glanced at her son, shook her head, and put her hand on his shoulder as if to put him at ease. "I am just saying that there must be a better word," she continued. A few alternate phrases were put forth by those in the meeting, each one sounding worse than the other. Finally, Jean decided, 'We shall use the word 'massage.' I think that sounds better.'"

It was as if Jean Kennedy Smith had resolved to not be the least bit flustered by the testimony, no matter how embarrassing. And, by God, she wasn't.

Victoria Reggie

*I*n the fall of 1991, Ted Kennedy was a year from turning sixty. It was as dark a time for him as he'd ever known, and that was saying a lot. A recent *Boston Herald*–WCVB survey showed that 62 percent of those who had responded felt that he should not run for reelection in 1994, that's how much damage had been done in Palm Beach. At about this time it was announced that Richard Burke, a former aide to Kennedy, was planning a tell-all book about Ted that would include stories of the senator allegedly doing drugs with his children and having sex with young interns. The allegations made headline news, even though they had not been proven, and later even Burke's own credibility would come into question.

Meanwhile, Joan Kennedy—who was now fifty-five—found herself in trouble once again. On May 14, 1991, she was arrested for driving under the influence. Two weeks later she would plead guilty, receive a suspended ninety-day sentence, and be ordered to spend two weeks in an alcohol treatment center. This was not the first time she'd been arrested for drunken driving, but because of what was going on with Ted and Patrick in Palm Beach, it generated a great deal of media coverage. Poor Joan was so humiliated, she didn't even want any family members with her when she appeared before the judge. It was just her and her lawyer. When her son Ted Jr.—who had just graduated from Yale—also checked into a drug and alcohol program in Hartford, it seemed like the entire family was in turmoil. He had been arrested in 1980 for pot possession, and over the years unfortunately became an alcoholic. (To his credit, though, this stint in rehab for Ted Jr. would be his one and only; he remains sober to this day.) Luckily, Ted's daughter, Kara, was spared any headlines. It was as if Eunice's prediction had manifested itself not only in another jam for Ted, but also one for William, Jean, Joan, and Ted Jr.

That Ted had been present in the club on the fateful night in question, that he had taken his son and nephew there for drinks and had later showed up in just a nightshirt when his son was alone with Cassone, did not bode well. He might as well have been charged with a crime, that's how bad the press was for him. "The living symbol of family flaws," *Newsweek* dubbed him.

Ted maintained he was simply in the wrong place at the wrong time, and expressed as much in his memoir, *True Compass*, by writing, "I could have avoided any involvement in the trial if I'd simply taken a walk on the beach by myself that night instead of asking my son and nephew to accompany me to the bar." That doesn't take into account, though, the fact that he had been courting this kind of disaster with his bad behavior for many years. It also bears mentioning that he allotted no more than five brief paragraphs in his book to the entire William Kennedy Smith ordeal.

If ever it could be said that a turning point needed to happen in the life of Ted Kennedy—a time when he would finally take stock and decide to change it—it would have to be now. At the same time, he began dating a woman who would help to trigger just such a change—in fact, in *True Compass*, Ted titled the chapter about this person "The Woman Who Changed My Life."

She was Victoria Anne Reggie, known as Vicki, a dark-haired, hazel-eyed thirty-eight-year-old beauty with the most dazzling of smiles. She'd long been a friend of the family's, her father, retired judge Edmund Reggie, also having known the Kennedys for many years. He'd run the Louisiana campaign for JFK in 1960 and had also organized Bobby's and Ted's primary campaigns in that state. A recently divorced mother of two small children—a boy, Curran, who was eight and a girl, Caroline, six—Vicki worked as a partner in a Washington corporate law firm. She'd been raised in Crowley, Louisiana, and was of Lebanese Catholic descent. She had attended New Orleans's Tulane University and Tulane Law School. She was a strong, determined woman—a tough and aggressive lawyer—nothing like some of the women Ted had been seeing since his divorce from Joan. She was also very funny, with a ribald sense of humor.

Ted had known Vicki casually for many years. She'd even interned for him in 1975, though he would have to admit to having no memory of her whatsoever. However, when he saw her at a party he attended celebrating her parents' fortieth anniversary on June 17, 1991, he realized that he had a connection to her that was strong and powerful. "What's the matter?" she said when he showed up at the party alone. "Couldn't get a date?" He laughed. "Well, I was thinking you would be my date," he said. Feigning disbelief, she shot back, "Dream on, Kennedy!" From that moment on, their rapport was immediate—playful and even flirty. "I hadn't felt that relaxed or lighthearted in a long time," Ted would recall. Before the night was over, he asked if he could call her again for a date. When she said yes, that was just the beginning for them. Within months, they were very much in love.

"I was this little shy five-year-old, and I didn't quite know what to make of this man who, as Mom said, came to dinner every night and was this amazing presence," Vicki's daughter, Caroline, recalled in 2009. Curran added, "He just really made an effort to connect individually with me. In addition to being this father figure that was always there and always so supportive, he was just such a great friend. He and I shared a love of sports, which he kind of spent a lot of time to get to know well, to have that bond with me."

Vicki recalled, "It was such a surprise to me. When we were still dating he said, 'Well, it's Halloween. I'll be there to take the children trick-or-treating.'" She added, "My neighbors were in shock. It was the talk of my street. He loved those kid things so much. I think his life was defined by family."

From the outset, Ted seemed to understand that Vicki would not tolerate bad behavior from him, and that included any unreasonable outbursts. She wasn't fragile or starstruck as had been some of his earlier conquests; rather she had high expectations of him and made as much clear. "I believe you can be a better man than what most people expect you to be," she had told him. She wasn't referring to his work in the Senate, either. For years he had been acquitting himself nicely in that venue. She was talking about his personal life.

After a few dates with Ted, Vicki sensed not only his kindness and need to be of service, but also his abject loneliness. Following his divorce from Joan, he had moved into the Big House at the Kennedy compound in Hyannis Port, which had been his mother and father's home and where Rose still lived. He would spend his weekends there, flying from his home in Virginia to Connecticut with a posse of single male friends, such as Senator Chris Dodd, with whom Ted often got into high-profile trouble regarding their relationships with women ranging from very famous and wealthy socialites to unknown exotic dancers and waitresses. Once at the compound, Ted and his buddies would behave as if they were overgrown frat boys, sailing on his boat, the *Mya*, drinking lots of Irish whiskey, eating copious amounts of seafood, and carousing with women, all while Rose Kennedy was upstairs in her bedroom suite being tended to by nurses and aides.

It's interesting to note that throughout his life, no matter how bad his behavior, Ted was always devoutly religious, his Catholic faith of the utmost importance to him. Critical observers have often wondered how someone who cheated on his wife and drank to excess could also be a man of such great faith. "What's to rationalize?" his nephew Timothy Shriver asked Lisa Miller of *Newsweek* in an article she wrote about Ted's faith in 1999 titled "The Believer." "You mean you shouldn't pray if you haven't got your s—t together? This is another fairly common misconception of faith, which is that people who go to church, or people who pray, or people who talk about their faith or religion must be, somehow, more pious or ethically rigorous or have more morally cleansed lifestyles. The high correlation is supposed to be between faith and your search, the depth of your search, your willingness to try, your willingness to admit error, your hope and belief in the ultimate meaning and value of that search."

"Ted Kennedy never held himself up as a paragon of good behavior," added Rose Kennedy's former secretary, Barbara Gibson. "I think, deep down, he was always very self-critical. 'I keep trying,' he once told me. 'I go to church in the hope that it will sustain me. But I don't pretend to think that I am not a flawed man.'"

Even so, Ted's freewheeling lifestyle made no sense to Victoria. As she would later tell it, she believed that one of the reasons he had been behaving so badly in recent years was that, despite all of his female company, he was very much alone. The reason he was so self-involved, she believed, was because he was a man who had no romance in his life, no one to really care about other than his brothers' children and his mom. He had his religion, true. But there was no intimacy for him, no real sharing. She hoped to change that.

Maybe Ted said it best when, in speaking of Vicki to his old friend Senator George Smathers, he said, "She did something no one else ever did. She read my heart."

"Mad as Hell"

One story about Ted Kennedy and Victoria Reggie and the way they trafficked in the early days of their relationship is very telling. The couple was at Baxter's Fish 'n' Chips and Boathouse, one of the oldest of Cape Cod restaurants, on Pleasant Street on Hyannis Port, sharing a seafood platter of whole clams, scallops, gulf shrimp, and haddock. It was a warm afternoon in August 1991 and Ted, according to witnesses, seemed quite angry. Perhaps it was because the couple was so accustomed to being in the restaurant that they didn't seem to care who could overhear their conversation. They made no effort to be discreet. There were at least a dozen witnesses to their heated exchange that day.

"That girl is lying," Ted said, perhaps referring to Patricia Bowman, though it's not known for certain. "I know she's lying. She knows she's lying. And Willie knows it, too. Everybody involved knows it, so I don't understand how this thing has gone this far." His face was getting red, a sure sign that he was becoming infuriated.

"Calm down," Vicki said. "I'm sure she is lying, too. But you can't blow up like this, Ted. Not in public."

"Why not?" Ted asked. "I am entitled to be angry," he added, now raising his voice to a rolling thunder. "I'm mad as hell," he roared. "That's just who I am. And you just have to put up with it."

"And why is that?" Vicki asked, her voice now also rising, ignoring the startled stares of other diners in the establishment. Incidentally, in years to come, Vicki would become much more discreet and even protective of Ted. For instance, if he was drinking in a restaurant and she saw a photographer lurking nearby, she would make an effort to cover the drink with a napkin, or even move it so that it would appear to be hers. But in the early days of their relationship, things were different.

"Because this is what you've signed up for," Ted said, answering Vicki's question, "if you want to be with Edward Kennedy. That's why."

"Is that so?" Victoria said as she gathered her things. "I remember negotiating no such agreement. But I'll try to refresh my memory. Elsewhere!" With that, she got up and left the restaurant in what can only be described as a huff. Ted's lack of self-control and sense of entitlement would usually be in evidence when he was drinking heavily, and it soon became clear that Vicki would be having none of his bombastic outbursts.

Ted then ordered his meal—lobster salad with a side of clam chowder—and sat alone eating it for about a half hour, looking sad and dejected with a wool cap pulled over his head. Finally, Victoria returned. As soon as he saw her, his spirits seemed to lift. With a boyish grin, he rose, kissed her tenderly on the cheek, and whispered what appeared to be an apology in her ear. Looking at him warily, she sat back down. The two then spoke quietly, holding hands across the table for another hour before finally leaving together, arm in arm.

Ted Recognizes His Shortcomings

*I*n the fall of 1991, Ted Kennedy decided it was time to come clean about some of his behavior and also to make amends for it. With his career in the Senate hanging in the balance, he really had no choice. He received a pitiful 22 percent approval rating in a national Gallup poll after the recent Clarence Thomas hearings adjourned—the lowest rating of any senator on the committee. Things had never been so bad. The only strategy that made sense at this juncture was for Ted finally to take full responsibility for his actions. He had done as much after Chappaquiddick in his televised address to the nation, and even though a lot of people in the country didn't buy his explanation of events, his coming forward did ingratiate him with his constituency and went a long way toward ensuring his enviable place in the Senate. And now—a week before jury selection was to begin in the trial—it was time to take similar action. "He knew people had concerns and he felt it was important to address these concerns," said Paul Donovan, a Kennedy spokesman. "He felt he owed it to the people of Massachusetts."

Did he also owe it to his family? Perhaps. He definitely felt that he had let them down. There was a telling moment at his home on the Cape in the summer of 1991 when the Kennedys convened for a holiday. When some members of the third generation—two of Ethel's children and one of the Shrivers—commented that they viewed Ted as a huge disappointment, Ethel, who had overheard the conversation, lit into them. "How dare you say that about your uncle Teddy!" she demanded to know. He had always been present and available to them throughout their lives, Ethel reminded them, and, as she put it, "It's your duty now to be there for him. So don't you ever say one bad word against him," she warned them, "or so help me God, I'll kick you all right out of here," adding, "and you *know* I will." Most certainly, Ted would have been proud of his "Ethie" that day.

The venue chosen for Ted's speech was Harvard's John F. Kennedy School of Government in front of an audience of eight hundred, and many millions more by virtue of its televised broadcast. The date was October 25, 1991. In what would amount to an extraordinary thirty-minute speech by the senator, who was dressed in a conservative navy blue suit, he said, "I am painfully aware that the criticism directed at me in recent months involves far more than honest disagreements with my positions, or the usual criticism from the far right." Looking up from his prepared text, he continued, "It also involves the disappointment of friends and many others who rely on me to fight the good fight. To them I say: I recognize my own shortcomings—the faults in the conduct of my private life. I realize that I alone am responsible for them, and I am the one who must confront them." He added, "I believe that each of us as individuals must not only struggle to make a better world, but to make ourselves better, too, and in this life those endeavors are never finished."

Ted also referred to the Clarence Thomas hearings, but in a way that some thought might suggest a personal awakening and maybe an end to his high-profile womanizing ways, especially considering his new relationship with Victoria Reggie. It was speculated, incidentally, that she helped him write the speech, but Ted later said this was not the case. She didn't know what he was going to say, he would recall, until he was onstage saying it. "Some of the anger of recent days," he said, "reflects the pain of a new idea still being born—the idea of a society where sex discrimination is ended and sexual harassment is unacceptable—the idea of an America where the majority who are women are truly and finally equal citizens."

"Unlike my brothers," Ted Kennedy intoned, "I have been given length of years and time, and as I approach my sixtieth birthday, I am determined to give all that I have to advance the causes for which I have stood for almost a quarter of a century."

The William Kennedy Smith Trial

The William Kennedy Smith trial, which began on December 2, 1991, was as sensational as one might have expected given the high-profile nature of the case and the appearance of various Kennedys coming and going from the courthouse, all under the microscope of intense curiosity. In fact, it's safe to say that this was one of the most heavily scrutinized and widely publicized rape trials in history, right alongside those of Fatty Arbuckle, Charlie Chaplin, and Errol Flynn in Hollywood's halcyon days of the 1930s. Along with the Supreme Court confirmation hearings of Clarence Thomas, the Persian Gulf War, and the resignation of Mikhail Gorbachev as Russia's premier, it was the biggest story of the year. Part of the reason for the huge exposure of the case was the growing tabloid influence on news reporting. Suddenly, sleazy stories about the Kennedys were being picked up from gossip newspapers and disseminated all over the world by mainstream media; in the process, the *National Enquirer* had somehow become the go-to place for up-to-date Kennedy news.

William Kennedy Smith was represented by Roy E. Black—viewed by many as one of the finest legal minds in the country—Mark Schnapp, and Mark Seiden. The prosecutors were Moira K. Lasch and Ellen Roberts.

Jean and her other son, Steve, and her daughters, Kym and Amanda, were present on the first day of testimony. Wearing a lime green linen dress, white heels, and pearl earrings, Jean looked elegant but somehow very tiny, as if dwarfed by the chaos around her. Never before had Jean Kennedy Smith been thrust under such a hot spotlight. If anything, she had done all she could to stay out of the public eye, and even her participation in the Very Special Arts was pushing it as far as her comfort level could go when it came to being the focus of attention. "To go through this so soon after Steve was taken from her was very difficult," one friend of hers recalled. "She was used to turning to him in times of crisis. Without him, she felt lost." In the end, the judge ruled that because Jean was a potential witness at the trial, she would not be permitted to sit in the courtroom during testimony.

At the end of that first day, the members of the family who had flown down for the proceedings gathered at the estate on North Ocean Boulevard to discuss how it had gone and what was in store. In all, nineteen members of the Kennedy family would attend the trial, many of them present at that gathering after the first day of testimony.

Perhaps emblematic of the star power of such a large congregation of Kennedy family members, and of how no one is immune to being dazzled by their presence, Mary Lupo, the Florida circuit judge presiding over the Smith sexual assault case, asked Roy Black to take her picture with Sarge on his first day in her courtroom. Of course Eunice was also present, as was her son Bobby. Jackie had also wanted to appear and had actually made plans to do so, but at the last minute Jean called her to say she feared that her presence would cause a media circus that would be impossible to contain. Jackie had to agree. For her part, Joan was just too upset about the matter to be present for it, and Rose, of course, was much too aged at 101. John Kennedy Jr. would show up before the end of the trial, though Caroline would not. Ted wasn't allowed to be present for the proceedings since he, like Jean, would likely be a witness.

The mood at the manse was serious, but not necessarily depressed. Ethel and Pat added a certain levity to the atmosphere, as they usually did to any family gathering. "Did you see the way we looked on the news?" Ethel asked Pat. "You and I look like dowagers, Pat! When did we get so old?" Pat laughed. "One thing is for sure," she said, "we could both use new wardrobes and maybe even a fashion consultant." At that, Eunice piped in, "Where is that Jackie Kennedy when you need her?"

In discussions to determine how the family members should be transported to and from the courthouse in the days to come, the idea of having them show up in limousines was floated by one of the third generation. "Absolutely not," Jean said. "We will continue to show up in the Mercury station wagon. And it will be driven by Bridey [Sullivan, Jean's longtime housekeeper]." Jean understood that public relations was as important as any legal strategy at this time when the eyes of the world were once again on the Kennedys, and she didn't want the family to appear privileged or entitled. That said, it was a curious sight to see the famous Kennedys tumbling out of a beat-up 1989 station wagon driven by their housekeeper. Also, there would be no parties during the time this crisis was going on, no public outings, and, most definitely, no photos taken of anyone coming and going from expensive "in" restaurants.

"We will behave in a respectful way," Jean told all of the nieces and nephews. "I don't want to hear a single peep out of anyone," she said. Ted Kennedy, also present at that dinner meeting, addressed the third generation as well. "This is the time during which we all have the opportunity to show the world what we are made of," he told them. "We have to stay strong, be composed, and behave in a dignified manner. Is that understood?" Everyone agreed. "We'll attend Mass at St. Edward's every Sunday, as always, and we'll receive Communion, as always," Ted continued. "Understood?" Again, everyone nodded in agreement. Though they were all adults at this point, there was still a sense—especially given the circumstances—that the next generation had to be told how to behave.

One of the more unusual days of the trial—the third day, during which Patricia Bowman was scheduled to testify—found Eunice Kennedy Shriver being introduced by her nephew William to the press corps outside the courtroom, literally hundreds of reporters. With William at one side of her, Jean at her other side, and Ethel standing behind her, it looked as if the lionesses in the family had come to protect their cub. Standing before a bank of microphones in a soft drizzle, and holding an armful of sweaters and shawls she had brought with her to protect her and the other Kennedy women from the air-conditioning inside the courtroom, Eunice held court. "I'm very happy to be here with my sister Jean," she told the press in a voice that had almost the exact same cadence as her brother the late president's. "She is a very courageous woman," she continued, of Jean. "She has raised four very wonderful children and enjoyed a long and marvelous marriage with a wonderful man, Stephen Smith, who recently left us. She has also started Very Special Arts, which is an international program that gives arts to all disabled people. So I am very happy to be here for her. As for William, he has the same kind of loyalty from his cousins, who he grew up with and who love him very much. Most of them are coming down here to stay with him, thirty of them in fact. That loyalty was taught by our parents," she continued. If the Kennedys were American royalty, Eunice was most certainly the dowager queen, or at least she comported herself as if she were, especially as she ended her speech in a very royal way with, "So to all of those who are going to watch this trial over the next—this rather sad trial, over the next two weeks, I wish you a happy Christmas and the gift of loyal family relationships. Thank you very much." In her view, the family was on trial as much as was Willie. She felt a need to remind people of Kennedy family values. Later, she admitted, "There was a lot more I wanted to say, as one can well imagine. However, one has to know when to stop, doesn't one?"

When Patricia Bowman showed up, the press corps didn't even recognize her. The single mother of a two-year-old, Bowman had never made any public appearances, so few people even knew what she looked like. Imagine the mad scurry to photograph her when the identity of the attractive yet also ordinary-looking five-foot-six-inch woman in a pageboy haircut finally became clear. Dressed very conservatively in a gray suit, accessorized by a single strand of pearls and a gold pin, she struggled through graphic testimony that was clearly very difficult for her.

Bowman said that she had met William at the bar, thought he was a kind, charming man, and happily gave him a ride back to the Kennedy manse. "I was taking him to the Kennedy home, which I assumed would have security," she said. "There was a senator there. I didn't feel I was in any danger whatsoever." But once at the estate, he allegedly disrobed to take a naked swim, and that's when things went sour. He later tackled her, she claimed, pinned her to the ground, "and I was telling him 'no' and 'stop' and I tried to arch my back to get him off of me, but he slammed me back on the ground and then he pushed my dress up and he raped me. I thought he was going to kill me." During one dramatic moment, she pointed at Willie Smith and said to his lawyer, "Your client raped me!"

Ethel and Eunice sat in the spectators' section of the courtroom and seemed not to blink the entire time Bowman told her tearful story. Occasionally, Ethel could be seen whispering angrily in Eunice's ear and shaking her head in the negative. Eunice—her face usually devoid of any expression—would inevitably raise both her palms to Ethel as if signaling her to calm down. When the testimony became particularly graphic, both women looked extremely embarrassed and appeared to wish for a hole to crawl into. At one point, Eunice reached into her purse, pulled her rosary from it, and began praying.

The problem with Patricia Bowman's testimony was that there were numerous inconsistencies and gaps in her account, which the defense was able to use to its great advantage. Perhaps what many people will remember from the gavel-to-gavel televised trial coverage—besides the graphic testimony—is the gray electronic circle superimposed over Bowman's face, lest her identity be revealed on television.

The day Ted Kennedy testified was of course one of the high points of the proceedings. He looked surprisingly fit, and it was clear that he had been taking care of himself. Bolstered by his new relationship with Victoria Reggie, who was in the courtroom and with whom he would share an occasional look, he was in much better shape than he'd been in prior public appearances. In fact, he'd lost twenty-five pounds and his skin even had a glow to it. Vicki had also helped coach him on his testimony. His sister Pat was also present in the courtroom. Testifying as to the events that led up to the alleged attack, the club he and his family members attended, what they did there and who they met, Ted seemed in complete control, totally commanding the room during his forty-five-minute testimony. He was emotional when he explained why he had been in Palm Beach that fateful weekend—this being because he wanted to spend more time with his sister Jean following the death of her husband, Stephen.

"[He] was very special to me," Ted said of Stephen Smith as Willie brushed away tears. "He was next to a brother, really. We lost a brother in the war. When Jean married Steve, we had another brother. And when Steve was gone, something left all of us when we buried him."

The jury was completely transfixed as Ted talked about the night on the patio of the Palm Beach estate during which he and Jean became lost in melancholy memories, and how difficult it was for him, preventing him from being able to sleep, and thus his night on the town with his son and nephew. It was as if the jurors were getting an inside peek into the lives of the enigmatic Kennedys; based on the rapt expressions on their faces, they were swept away by the experience.

"Could you tell us who Bill Barry is, what his relationship to the family is?" Roy Black asked.

"Well, Bill Barry was a former FBI agent who now specializes in security matters," Ted answered. "He was probably Jean and Steve's—one of their two or three best friends. He was one of my brother Bob's very best friends. And he provided security for my brother Bob in the 1968 campaign. And he was with my brother when he was killed." Black added, "In fact, is he not the man who knocked the gun out of Sirhan Sirhan's hand?" Ted answered, "Yes." Of course, none of this had anything to do with the trial, but it was all inside information about the Kennedys that seemed to personalize them for the jury and, in a way, help the jury to feel more sympathetic not only to the family but also, by extension, to the defendant.

Black asked if the family had tried to spend more time with Jean after Stephen's death. "I have tried," Ted said. "We spend a lot of time together. I think my sister Pat, who is here, and Eunice have spent a lot of time with her too. I have tried to. The other members of the family... Ethel has. Jackie has. We are a very close family."

Jean's testimony was brief. Wearing a light blue linen jacket and large glasses, she looked like a college professor—an angry one at that. She seemed confident, poised—and annoyed by the questioning. The only reason her son had been in Palm Beach, she explained, was because it was the first Easter without her husband and she wanted her children to be with her. She didn't know anything about the events of that Good Friday, she said, and heard no screams or anything else that would have given her some hint as to what was going on below her bedroom window as she slept.

After her testimony, Jean would return to the family estate, where she would watch Willie's testimony on television while repeatedly saying the rosary.

There was a tense moment in the courtroom prior to Willie's testimony when Bobby Kennedy Jr. was unhappy with his seat. The Kennedys were allotted three seats in the courtroom, as was the family of the accuser. Kennedy wanted to sit on the aisle for his cousin's testimony in order to have a better view. However, that seat was taken. "I'd appreciate it if you'd move," he told the occupant, who refused to do so. Kennedy then went to a bailiff and asked that the person be moved. When he refused to accommodate him, Kennedy went back and persisted. "You don't understand," he said, "we're family." The person sitting in the seat said, "You don't understand, we're family, too!" It turned out that the person sitting in the seat was one of Patricia Bowman's stepbrothers. Kennedy finally relented and went to another seat. Just as he sat down, he looked over and saw his mother, Ethel, regarding him carefully, a look of extreme disapproval washing over her face.

In his own testimony, which took just twenty-nine minutes, William Kennedy Smith—called "Will" by his attorney in court—admitted to having sex with Patricia Bowman, but claimed it was consensual and that she had even guided his hand along the way. He said that the consensual sex with Bowman turned ugly when he called her the wrong name—"Kathy." He said, "She sort of snapped... got very upset." But he also said she apologized before leaving the estate, saying, "I am sorry I got upset. I had a wonderful night. You're a terrific guy." But then she showed up at the estate just minutes later claiming that he had raped her, and repeatedly calling him "Michael." It certainly sounded like both had had plenty of alcohol that night. At one point during his testimony, Willie Smith testified that he had ejaculated twice, once on himself and then soon after while having intercourse with his accuser. "What are you, some kind of sex machine?" prosecutor Moira Lasch asked, her voice dripping with disdain. In the spectator seats, Ethel was noticed shaking her head and scowling.

The difference between Smith's testimony and his accuser's was glaring. Whereas she sometimes seemed confused and unclear as to the chain of events, he was precise and specific. Some argued that the victim's memory would have been understandably foggy due to the traumatic experience she'd been through, and Smith's would have been sharper since he was a public person, accustomed to being in the spotlight, and also well rehearsed by his battery of Kennedy attorneys. Others just felt that she was lying and he was not.

The trial lasted from December 2 through December 11, 1991. The outcome was swift. The jury of six (four of them women) deliberated just over an hour—including the time it took to pick a foreman—before returning with a verdict of "not guilty." Only reasonable doubt had to be shown, and in their estimation, it had been. Jean was in the courtroom for the verdict and seemed close to tears when it was read. Willie looked over at her and smiled broadly. As she left the courtroom, she seemed to be on shaky legs, as if the ordeal had finally gotten to her. She had been a rock throughout the entire trying experience, but now that the matter was finally concluded, it was as if she had nothing left. "Yes, I am relieved," she told one reporter. "I am also exhausted, as you can imagine. But above all, I am thankful. I never doubted my son, not for a second."

Forty-five minutes later, Willie stood before a bank of microphones in front of the Palm Beach County Courthouse. "They say that gratitude is the memory of the heart," Willie told the crowd of reporters and other onlookers after his acquittal, referring to a quote from Jean-Baptiste

Massieu, the eighteenth-century French priest and scholar. "And I have enough memories in my heart to last a lifetime. I want to say thank you, most of all to my mother. I don't think it's possible for a child ever to repay the debt they owe their parents. I only hope I can be as good a parent to my children as my mother has been to me." Jean looked on, seeming exhausted and, finally, almost at the verge of collapsing. "My life was in their [the jurors'] hands and I'm so grateful for the job they did and the seriousness with which they took it," he said. "I have an enormous debt to the system and to God and I have a terrific faith in both of them. And I'm just really, really happy. So we'll see you guys later."

"It's the [best] acquittal that money can buy," Patricia Bowman told Dominick Dunne when he interviewed her after the verdict. "They had nine months to come up with their story. I had to give five statements. My deposition took three days—720-some pages—and there were three defense attorneys and two prosecutors and one of my attorneys. And this is over a period of eight months that I had to give these statements. When did Willie ever give a statement? He had nine months. He had five of my statements and everybody else's statements. He had the forensic evidence. He had all kinds of resources, which they've already testified that they used. He had all this material with which to concoct a story. And that's what he did. He concocted a story. He fit every nook and cranny. Everything I couldn't remember, because of rape-trauma syndrome, he could come up with something for. Everything that fit in with the forensic evidence, he found an answer for it."

She continued, "I'm now standing up and saying, 'No, I am not crazy. I am not a drug addict. I've never been treated for any drug problems. I've never been treated for any alcohol problem, because I've never had one. I'm not nuts. I'm not a prostitute. I'm not promiscuous. I have a small child. I have a life, a beautiful, full life that was tampered with, that a man tried to destroy on March 30, and that a group of men tried to destroy after that through the criminal process. But they haven't destroyed me. I'm a survivor. And I will stand up each and every time and say, 'What you did to me was wrong.'"

In 2004, a former employee of the Center for International Rehabilitation alleged that William Kennedy Smith had sexually assaulted her five years earlier when he was her superior, and she brought a civil action against him. Smith denied the charges, calling them "outrageous" and saying that "family and personal history have made me unusually vulnerable to these kinds of charges." Her attorney, moreover, had to acknowledge that the employee continued to work for Smith for the next six months, and during that time had consensual sex with him on a number of occasions. It didn't make sense to a lot of observers that she would continue to be intimate with him if he had raped her. On January 5, 2005, the court dismissed the lawsuit.

Today, William Kennedy Smith leads a quiet life of service, practicing medicine and heading an organization he started, Physicians Against Land Mines, a laudable venture that calls to mind Princess Diana's commitment to land mine eradication.

Jean Kennedy Smith—Ambassador

*J*ean Kennedy Smith had always striven to create a life of fulfillment for herself outside of her marriage, and as part of that effort, she was deeply and heavily invested in her Very Special Arts charity. In a sense, she had used Eunice's Special Olympics as a template for how such a venture might be organized and run. At first it was a daunting task. There was a sense among the sisters—Jean and Pat—that no one could ever compete with Eunice's philanthropy. Since the Kennedys had always been so extremely competitive, if one couldn't do something better than another there seemed little reason even to try. But in the 1970s, when Jean first founded Very Special Arts, she became heartened by its tremendous success. It gave her a real sense of purpose and made her feel that perhaps she wasn't so much in Eunice's shadow after all. In June 1989, Jean hosted the first International Very Special Arts Festival, and more than a thousand handicapped people came from all over the world to converge upon the White House. President George H. W. Bush hosted this contingent, and the closing festivities were taped by NBC for a splashy television special. Jean felt that she was contributing on Eunice's level, which was saying a lot.

Still, the last couple of years had been very difficult for Jean. She now felt a need to do something new and exciting with the years she had left—she was only sixty-four—and if she could be of service, she would feel as if she were doing something worthwhile. During the summer of 1992, she visited Ireland, and while there also visited the American ambassador's residence in Dublin. As Irish Americans, the Kennedy family—especially the first and second generations—had a strong affinity for Ireland. In talking to friends in Dublin about it, she began to wonder what it might be like to serve in Ireland as American ambassador. When she returned to the States, she mentioned the idea to Ted. "It just came to me in a flash," she once recalled. "I think my husband gave me the idea. It's from heaven. I mean I think he [Stephen] must have in some kind of way because it just hit me that it would be a really good idea at this point in my life. And I think it sort of fit, you know? I knew how crazy they [the Irish] are about Jack and I thought, 'Why not try?' You know, I wasn't very optimistic I'd get it. There would have to be a lot of [other] people wanting it."

It was at around the time Bill Clinton was elected to office in 1992 that Jean decided to throw her hat into the ring and let it be known that she would be interested in an ambassadorship. Of course, there was some opposition from critics who didn't know much about her. In fact, prior to the William Kennedy Smith trial, most people didn't know her at all, and those who thought they did perceived her as one of the less ambitious or powerful of the Kennedy women, especially as compared to Eunice. For her part, Jean had had been very involved in the political career of her brother Jack, going all the way back to his 1947 congressional campaign, his 1952 Senate campaign, and of course his presidential campaign in 1960. Moreover, her husband had been intimately involved in all of her brothers' campaigns; anyone who felt she'd not been privy to the working mechanics of all of those races didn't know how much Stephen Smith confided in his wife about such matters. Besides that, Jean had been a member of the board of trustees of the Joseph P. Kennedy Jr. Foundation since 1964. She had also been a member of the board of trustees of the John F. Kennedy Center for Performing Arts since that same time. More importantly, though, she had been running her own Very Special Arts charity for almost twenty years. Those who had worked with her over the years could attest to her focus and tenacity; those who dealt with her during her son's trial could certainly attest to her strength and determination. Also, having been born into a family that courted tradition and ceremony and had always observed the proper protocol in all manners, Jean Kennedy Smith was well suited to carry out the duties expected of an ambassador, of which so many were purely ceremonial and usually in the public eye.

However, it was true that Jean had not been involved in any sort of diplomacy, and thus for some it was quite a stretch to imagine her representing the United States' interests in any foreign country. As far as Ted was concerned, though, her lack of experience in that regard didn't matter. He loved his sister and wanted her to have exactly what she wanted at this time in her life. He felt that he had let her down in recent years, and in a sense he wanted to make it up to her if he could. He had such admiration for the way she handled herself throughout the trial of her son, and knew that his friend and brother-in-law Stephen was smiling down on her. He wanted to help her. So even though there were others in the running who were perhaps more qualified, Ted was willing to risk any opposition he might face and any criticism that might be leveled at him, and use whatever influence he might have to appeal to President Clinton on his sister's behalf.

As it happened, Clinton liked the idea immediately. Of course, he realized that Jean Kennedy Smith had no history of diplomacy, yet he couldn't help but see the sentimental value to appointing her as ambassador to Ireland. An admirer of the Kennedy family, he felt that this family had long ago established the paradigm for the ideal representation of Irish Americans. Certainly their sensational personal histories didn't reflect who they were in total. It was their devotion to being of service that framed them historically, their long history of duty to America that went all the way back to JFK in 1960, and even before that with the Kennedy brothers' years in the Senate and even their father's ambassadorship to the United Kingdom in the 1930s. No matter what had happened over the years, or what personal difficulties the family had faced, what was inescapable about them was that they not only, as they say, talked the talk but walked the walk. The next generation, the third, was busy making its own impact by this time as well, many of them in government positions themselves. Jean wished to now take her own place as a representative of the previous generation.

President Clinton nominated Jean Kennedy Smith to serve as ambassador to Ireland on March 17, 1993, fittingly on the day we honor the patron saint of Ireland, Saint Patrick. She was confirmed by the Senate on June 16, 1993. A short time later, in 1994, Jean would make headlines by championing the granting of a U.S. visa to the leader of the Sinn Féin political party in Ireland, Gerry Adams. Sinn Féin—which translated from Irish means "ourselves" or "we ourselves"—is a left-leaning wing of the Irish Republican Army. In his memoir, *True Compass*, Ted Kennedy recalled, "Jean was convinced that Adams no longer believed that continuing the armed struggle was the way to achieve the IRA's objective of a united Ireland," and that "it took only a couple of hours' conversation with Jean after we landed to discover what was the most important thing on her mind—the opportunity for a breakthrough in the Northern Ireland stalemate."

"I was privileged to serve as America's ambassador to Ireland during the critical time that gave birth to the peace process," Jean would recall in 2008, "and I saw up close the immense struggle in the North to overcome bitter partisan divisions and finally achieve peace. One man more than any other embodied the persevering spirit and inspiring vision that led Northern Ireland out of its darkest night of the soul—Nobel Peace Prize winner John Hume. At many difficult moments, the tactics of wily opponents of any peace agreement appealed successfully to divisive interests and supporters of violence, but John helped us all cling to the vision of a better future." Jean further recalled that after a bombing at London's Canary Wharf in 1996, which seemed to indicate that the cease-fire had come to an abrupt end, Hume did not give up. Jean had a gathering at the ambassador's residence that night and "John stepped to the center of the room and led us all in a song of hope." She added, "What John Hume taught me was similar to what my brothers President Kennedy and Robert Kennedy taught me earlier—that we need leaders who speak to our sense of hope, to the easily forgotten sense of fellowship that we all have with one another, and to our aspiration to live our lives in service to a worthy cause."

Siobhan Walsh, who was a member of Jean's staff in Dublin, recalled of her, "I found her to be a fascinating woman, very smart, very dedicated to the notion of peace in Ireland. 'All people should have the freedom and ability to assemble, to speak, to choose their leaders,' she said. She's a refined person who had her boundaries with people and made them known right away. There has been a lot of sadness in her life, we all knew that. But she was loath to discuss it. In fact, she practically never mentioned her family. If you thought you were going to get anecdotes out of her about JFK or Bobby or Ted, you were very wrong. Their names rarely, if ever, came up.

"I can recall many times when Ted or Pat or Eunice had visited, and I have to say, there was something rather stiff about the way they comported themselves. They were very formal with one another, or at least that's how it appeared to me. Perhaps they were more familiar with each other when in private, but when in public they seemed quite stiff. For instance, I recall the ambassador taking her sister Eunice on a tour of the house one day. Eunice—who was wearing a gray cashmere sweater, a pair of charcoal capri pants, and sensible shoes—had a very thick notepad and was taking copious notes as Jean spoke about possible renovations. She was just writing feverishly, page after page after page. When they were finished, I recall Eunice telling her sister, 'I shall have these notes typed up by my secretary and will have them delivered to your office posthaste.' That's how they talked! The language they used with one another was very formal, which I found curious. 'Shall you be joining us for dinner?' Jean would ask her sister. 'Why, yes, I would be most delighted to join you,' would be Eunice's response."

Jean's term as ambassador, which would end in September 1998, would not be without its controversy, though. For instance, in late 1996 she was accused of pressuring embassy staff members to spend taxpayer money to refurbish the ambassador's residence in Dublin. The residence, a sprawling white Georgian-style mansion built in 1776, is quite spectacular. Over the years, the guests staying there have included President Kennedy and George H. W. Bush, as well as celebrities like Bing Crosby and Princess Grace of Monaco. Jean didn't see why taxpayers' money shouldn't be used to maintain the mansion, but found that there was, not surprisingly, a great deal of bureaucratic red tape attached to those kinds of decisions. There was also some controversy concerning an allegation of violations of U.S. conflict-of-interest laws. In 2000, the United States Department of Justice announced that she had paid $5,000 in a civil suit to resolve the matter.

"Jean's work as ambassador gave her a sense of purpose like nothing else could have during one of the darker times in her life," said one of the Kennedy family lawyers. "Her husband, Stephen, would have been proud of her, as would have her brothers Jack and Bobby."

PART SEVENTEEN

Kennedy Wives— Old and New

Ted and Vicki Marry

*I*t had become clear to most observers by the end of 1991 that Ted Kennedy was quite serious about Victoria Reggie and that he intended to marry her, if she would have him. Ted made it official on January 14, 1992, when he proposed to Vicki during a performance of *La Bohème* at the Metropolitan Opera House in New York. The couple kept it a secret for a couple of months before telling all of their children in March. They asked their offspring not to say a word to anyone for a while, and everybody promised. However, Vicki's six-year-old daughter, Caroline, mentioned the happy news to a friend in her kindergarten class, who then told his parents—one of whom apparently worked for the *Washington Post*! So that was pretty much the end of that secret. At that point, Ted felt that the proper thing to do would be to ask Vicki's father for her hand in marriage. "We knew they were dating so we weren't surprised when the senator called," recalled Vicki's father, Edmund M. Reggie. "Vicki was on the line, too. Ted said, 'As you must know by now, I love Vicki very much. I would love to make her my wife and I've asked her to marry me. So now I want to ask you and Doris for her hand in marriage.' It was very nice. Of course, Doris and I were thrilled." The official announcement was made on March 16.

The press immediately contacted Joan Kennedy for a comment. Unfortunately, she didn't know anything about any of it and was taken completely by surprise. She seemed rattled by the call from a reporter from the *Boston Herald*. "Oh? Is that true?" she asked when told of the announcement. "I can't talk now," she said before abruptly hanging up. She was very upset. She spent a couple weeks in seclusion, not speaking to anyone but her closest friends. "It wasn't that she had any hope of reconciling with Ted," said one, "but, you know, there was always that little part of her that wondered if, maybe...And this announcement ended that for her and made her come to terms with the fact that he was gone from her for good. It wasn't easy. I'm not sure she ever fell out of love with him, even after all that had happened. So, yes, it was hard. I know she spoke to Jackie about it, and also to Ethel and Eunice, though I don't know exactly what their conversations entailed. Joan simply would not discuss it."

Most of the other Kennedys were happy not only that Ted had finally found someone to love, but also that she was a strong-minded, independent woman who would see to it that he would live a more dignified lifestyle than he had in the past. "If you don't," she had told him jokingly, "I'll cut your throat with a rusty razor!" In truth, Vicki wasn't opposed to Ted's drinking—just his overdoing it. She enjoyed a cocktail at the end of the day too, and she had a sense of humor very much like Ethel's or Pat's. That said, Vicki's assimilation into the family was not easy.

No member of the second generation or their spouses (with the exception of Jackie) had ever remarried. Other than Jackie bringing Aristotle Onassis to the compound back in 1968, it just hadn't happened that outsiders were brought into the original second-generation royal family of Camelot. Certainly, their accepting or not accepting Onassis into the fold wouldn't have had major repercussions, since he and Jackie lived an independent and affluent lifestyle all their own. But it was harder to imagine what might have happened had Ethel remarried. Her new husband would have had to get along with not only all of his new relatives, but her many children as well. Ethel already had her hands full with her brood; bringing a mate into the mix would not have been easy. This was precisely the problem Ted Kennedy faced in trying to blend Victoria Reggie—who had two young children of her own, Curran and Caroline—into his family. There was immediate suspicion where Vicki was concerned, and many of the family members didn't take to her easily.

The first big controversy had to do with Ted's three children—Patrick, Ted Jr., and Kara—and their feelings about their father's new relationship. How would it affect their inheritance, which was at the time estimated at roughly $30 million? The only way to control what might happen to their inheritance—and how it might end up being split with Vicki and her children—was for their father to insist on a prenuptial agreement. Ted considered as much, but ultimately decided against it. It was that decision that set the stage for many years of future suspicion where Victoria was concerned. Had she influenced him in regard to the prenup? If so, what was she after? Ted insisted that Vicki had nothing to do with his choice, that he felt that insisting on such an agreement was tantamount to saying that he didn't trust her or their marriage. It wasn't a matter of trust, as far as his children were concerned, it was a matter of practicality, and maybe even loyalty. Still, it was Ted's money, not his children's, and he said he could handle it as he wished. He had set up very substantial trusts for them, and that would have to be enough.

The other Kennedys of the second generation stayed out of the fracas, but that's not to say they didn't have strong opinions. "I don't know for sure that I trust her yet," Ethel told Eunice of Victoria in front of relatives. She had always been so protective of Ted, it was difficult for her just to blindly go along with the new program. "But I don't know that I don't trust her," she added. "However, if this is what Teddy wants, we have no choice but to support him and then just wait and see what happens next." Eunice agreed; she was also not inclined to be critical of Vicki. "I'd be more unhappy if he broke up with her," she said. "I think she's the only reason he's so happy now and we should be grateful to her for that." That Vicki had somehow convinced Ted he was only allowed three drinks a day—two cocktails and a glass of wine—seemed like a small miracle to Eunice. She had long been trying to restrict his drinking and hadn't been successful at it, so she had to hand it to Vicki, she said. Then, proving that Pat wasn't the only Kennedy sister with a wicked sense of humor, Eunice concluded, "Sarge and I are too old to worry about Ted and Vicki now. We're too busy taking all our medications."

Ted and Vicki were married in a civil ceremony on July 3, 1992, at Ted's home in McLean, Virginia. "I can't remember the last time I saw my dad so happy," Ted Jr., who was now thirty-one, said in his toast later at the wedding reception, "and it is all due to Vicki."

Two Very Different Kinds of Kennedy Wives

In 1993, Ted Kennedy and his nephew Joseph—Bobby's son—found themselves embroiled in controversies involving their marriages and the Catholic Church.

It started with Joseph Kennedy II—Joe. Back in February 1979, he married Sheila Brewster Rauch in Gladwyne, Pennsylvania. She was a bubbly, enthusiastic person, full of life and someone the Kennedy family seemed to like a great deal. The couple went on to have twins in 1980—Matthew Rauch Kennedy and Joseph Patrick Kennedy. However, when the marriage hit a rough spot in 1990, it never recovered and ultimately ended when Sheila filed for divorce. It was granted in 1991.

Two years later, Joseph became involved with a former staff member named Anne Elizabeth Kelly, known as Beth. Earlier, in 1986, when Joe won his first election to Congress, succeeding former House Speaker Tip O'Neill in Massachusetts's 8th Congressional District, Beth had gone to Washington with him to work for him there. They soon fell in love, and now he wished to marry her in the Roman Catholic Church. However, he couldn't, because the church doesn't recognize divorce. Like his uncle Ted and his aunt Pat before him—both of whom were divorced—he was also unable to partake in the sacraments of the church, such as Holy Communion or Confession. For Ted, this had been an issue ever since his divorce from Joan. He was deeply religious, his faith handed down to him by his parents. "The most important element in human life is faith," Rose Kennedy has said. "If God were to take away all His blessings, health, physical fitness, wealth, intelligence, and leave me with but one gift, I would ask for faith, for with faith in Him and His goodness, mercy, and love for me, and belief in everlasting life, I believe I could suffer the loss of my other gifts and be happy."

"I am an American and a Catholic," Ted said in 1983 in a speech he gave at Jerry Falwell's Liberty University. "I love my country and treasure my faith." As much as he loved his religion, Ted defied the church on issues such as abortion and later gay marriage, believing that the Catholic faith was too restrictive and exclusive. Privately, he thought some of the church's laws were unfair, but it was the Catholic Church's rules that governed him. Other than making his opinions known and continuing his work in the Senate for change in certain laws, there seemed nothing more he could do. Or was there? After all, Kennedy was a lawmaker himself, and in a sense he was used to making changes to rules and regulations. Why should this matter be any different?

In discussing the situation with lawyers and family priests, Ted wondered what the chances might be of having his marriage to Joan annulled. An annulment would signify that the marriage was not really recognized in the Catholic Church, and it was usually granted very soon after a marriage had taken place (because a marriage was materially flawed in some way, by fraud, for instance, or lack of judgment, or some other misunderstanding, such as claim from one of the spouses that he or she had been mentally incapable of entering into the union). But there were cases, the Kennedys learned as they looked into it, of annulments being granted years after the fact. Indeed, they were stunned to learn just how many annulments were granted every year—as many as sixty thousand. Most of them were to eradicate short-term mistakes, but quite a lot were to rid people of marriages that had lasted for decades.

Once he realized that an annulment might be an option, Ted Kennedy decided he wanted to pursue it, and in fact he couldn't believe that it had never before occurred to him. One thing he knew for certain was that he could usually convince Joan to acquiesce to his wishes, and it would be fair to say that he'd taken advantage of that from time to time. But this was really pushing it, and he knew it. "Do you think we can get Joan to agree to such a thing?" he asked one of his attorneys in a meeting.

"Gosh, Ted, I don't see how," the attorney answered, according to his memory of the conversation.

"I know," Ted allowed. "I've been such a prick to her over the years. Why the hell would she?"

The two men stared at each other for a moment.

"I have to try, though," Ted decided. "Joansie knows how much my faith means to me. Maybe she'll cut me some slack."

"Maybe," said the attorney.

At just about the same time that Ted Kennedy was trying to figure out how to proceed with Joan, Joe Kennedy decided to move ahead with an annulment from his own ex-wife, Sheila. He asked for the annulment and filed the appropriate papers with the Boston Archdiocese in 1993. Sheila immediately opposed the idea. Then, when the Boston Archdiocese seemed to drag its feet on the issue, Joseph went ahead and married Anne in a civil ceremony at his home in Brighton, Massachusetts.

Meanwhile, Ted also went forth with his own annulment from Joan. When he asked Joan for it, she agreed to it, much to everyone's surprise. Perhaps it was because of the way Ted had appealed to her, sitting down with her and apologizing for the many years of torment he had caused her. This was certainly a new Ted, the Ted that seemed to have manifested itself from his new relationship with Vicki. The old Ted would have just stated his case and walked out the door. But the new Ted atoned for his sins and tried to make things right with Joan. He said he was sorry for everything that had ever happened between them, that he loved her and wished her well, that he wanted nothing more than to commit himself to his spirituality, and that he couldn't do so without an annulment. It had nothing to do with his feelings for her, he told her, or his memories of their marriage, but only to do with the Catholic Church's laws, which, he had to admit, he viewed as archaic. Touched by him—as she always had been—and even more so by his honesty and kindness toward her, Joan simply could not turn him down. Thus she agreed to the annulment on the admittedly unusual grounds that Ted's marriage vows to be faithful to her had not been honestly made. In time, the Catholic Church granted the annulment. It was all done quickly and also, maybe more importantly, quietly. There was no mention of it in the media.

One of the reasons Joan agreed, say those who knew her well, was because she was worried about the divisiveness Ted's marriage had caused within the family. She wished to set an example to her children that if she could put her personal feelings aside for the sake of Ted's happiness, perhaps they could as well. "It was a difficult decision for her to make,' said Joan's former personal assistant, Marcia Chellis. "After all she had been through with him and their marriage, to then say, okay, the union was never legitimate was, well...it was gut-wrenching. But it was Joan's decision, just the same."

Unfortunately for Joe Kennedy II, Sheila Rauch was no Joan Kennedy. In 1996, a couple years after he married his new wife, the Catholic Church surprised him and Sheila with the news that it had granted him his annulment—this despite the fact that Sheila had opposed it. Sheila Rauch, an Episcopalian, decided *not* to just go quietly into the night. She had always been a very determined person. When she had gotten married to Joe, she'd had her own minister standing right next to the Catholic priest as she and Joe took their vows—and she did not promise to obey. She was a smart woman with a degree from the Harvard School of Design, who had worked as a city planner until the birth of her children, at which time she gave up her career for her family.

The result of her unhappiness can be found in a book she wrote called *Shattered Faith: A Woman's Struggle to Stop the Catholic Church from Annulling Her Marriage*. In it, she explained that she opposed annulment because it would have meant that her twelve-year marriage following a nine-year courtship had never actually occurred. She suggested that the Kennedys were using their power and influence to eradicate, effectively, twelve years of her life. In a sense, that was true. Generally, the Kennedys, when faced with an obstacle preventing them from doing what they wanted, would find a way around it. But Joseph and his lawyers weren't really trying to deny Sheila her marriage memories or her principles. In fact, Joe looked at the whole thing as "Catholic gobbledygook," or at least that's what he told Sheila. He and his team simply had their eye on the prize—an annulment so that he could marry in the Catholic Church. In their view, it had nothing to do with Sheila. Why, they asked themselves, was she being so incredibly vindictive? Of course, a better question might have been, why was he being so incredibly narcissistic? When it came to Kennedy men, though, it wasn't news that they could be maddeningly self-serving in their relationships with women.

In the end, Sheila's book wasn't as much about herself and Joe as it was about the subject of annulments in the Catholic Church, and how they ran counter to the church's own teachings. "When you go to get forgiveness for murder, the priest doesn't try to convince you that you didn't kill someone. If you had an abortion and try to get forgiveness, you're not told you were never pregnant," she wrote. Still, the book generated a great deal of international attention and did Joseph a lot of political damage. Thus the family was furious with her. It seemed that every time Ethel Kennedy turned around, she would later confide to a friend, she would see her former daughter-in-law on television lambasting Joseph and, it seemed, the entire Kennedy ethos. (Joe was the second of her children to have a failed marriage, Mary Courtney being the first.) She found it all very upsetting and couldn't understand why Sheila felt the need to expose the private details of her life. Joe seemed set to become the next governor of Massachusetts, but after his ex-wife's story became public knowledge—and at the same time as the story of his brother Michael's relationship with a sixteen-year-old babysitter—he was forced to withdraw from the race. It was a shame, said his supporters, because he had been such a devoted public servant and exceptional congressman. He was invested in many human rights causes, such as the development of low-income housing, and of programs to encourage banks to subsidize the renovation of poor neighborhoods. But the American press, in particular, came down hard on Joe, helping to shape (and even reflect) opinion against him. It was as if the public had finally had enough of the Kennedy men's apparent mistreatment of women, and people weren't going to tolerate it anymore. Within the family, though, Ethel—and many other Kennedys joined her in this feeling—just felt that Sheila was being selfish, that she was putting her own concerns before the greater good. For goodness' sake, why couldn't she be more like Joan?

"Ted was particularly unhappy about it," said one Kennedy family adviser. "I was in his office when Joe came in for a meeting of strategists to figure out how to handle the Sheila matter."

"It's way out of control," Ted told his nephew Joe, according to the source. "You gotta shut her up, Joe. *Shut her up!*"

"I can't shut her up," Joe told his uncle. "What the hell am I supposed to do, Uncle Teddy?"

"You just call her and tell her to shut up," Ted said, raising his voice. "I don't see what the problem is." He may have been the new and improved Ted in a lot of ways, but there was still a male chauvinist in him who from time to time would make an appearance.

"You don't understand women," Joe said. "They don't just do what you tell them to do anymore. This isn't the 1950s." The last thing Ted needed to do was try to incite Joe, though. Joe's anger issues were always a matter of concern, and had certainly contributed to the end of his marriage to Sheila.

"Well, your wife has done a shitload of damage," Ted said. "This is a disaster."

Joe had to agree.

In truth, Sheila Rauch was just telling her story, which it could be argued she had every right to do and there was nothing the Kennedys could do about it. She and Joan were very different kinds of women from two very different generations. Joan was used to being discreet, to keeping the family's secrets. She was from the golden age of Camelot, when every time she opened her mouth and revealed something she shouldn't have—such as when she mentioned to reporters that Jackie wore wigs or that JFK's back was so bad he couldn't even pick up his children—she felt terrible about it. She loved the Kennedys and would always put their needs above her own. That was just her personality, her character. Even when she gave interviews to women's magazine's about her sobriety, she never trashed Ted. However, Sheila was a modern-day woman with strong convictions that had very little to do with what might have been in the Kennedys' best interests, and everything to do with what she felt was right and fair to her and to her children. Whereas Joan could be counted on to be a model of Camelot discretion, Sheila could not.

"There was a whole conspiracy of silence," Sheila Rauch recalled. "I was being told, 'Kennedy wives don't talk,' but they were having it both ways. First Joe's saying we were never married, and then he's saying I'm supposed to be quiet because I was once a Kennedy wife! So I had to speak. I wasn't going to tell all, but I was going to speak in an appropriate and responsible way." Two different women, two different approaches to the same problem—one whom the family had a great deal of respect for, and the other about whom the family couldn't have been more unhappy. The one thing they had in common, though, was that their marriages to Kennedy men were anything but easy. Joan's problems were well known by all. And Sheila had her own set of private issues with Joe (many of them very familiar to Joan), most of which remain unknown to the world because Sheila chose not to reveal them in her book.

In the end, Sheila Rauch proved herself to be every bit as formidable as the Kennedys and their team of lawyers and priests, because she managed to get the annulment overturned by the highest appellate tribunal of the Roman Catholic Church, the Roma Rota, in 2005. Joseph could appeal the decision, but the story had already done so much damage to him personally and politically that he decided to just leave well enough alone.

The New Wife

*T*he new wife likes things done a certain way," Joan Kennedy told one of her sons in the summer of 1992, "and I guess that's her prerogative. Still, it can be hard."

The new wife—that would be Vicki—certainly did make a big impression as soon as she and Ted Kennedy married, and it wasn't always a good one. The first thing she did was have "No Trespassing" signs posted on the beach in front of the Big House in Hyannis Port. For decades, the

Kennedys had allowed their neighbors to cross the beach in front of their home as a shortcut, or even just to take a nice walk. No one ever bothered the family. It just had always been that way—that is, until Vicki moved into the Big House. Suddenly signs went up to prevent access, and most people didn't take it well. It was as if she were sending a bigger message— no interference in her marriage—no trespassing there, as well as on the beach.

Vicki also did a massive remodeling of the Big House. Barnstable County official James Cummings, who attended many Thanksgiving parties hosted by Ted and Vicki at the compound (and was often one, if not the only, Republican present), recalled, "[When they moved in] the house was kind of like a museum, photographs all over the place. You would look at the photos and the one thing you noticed was that everyone in them was dead! So that was a little tough to take, you know? I mean, in terms of having a good time there. It was a little...depressing. But when he married Vicki, she got rid of most of the pictures, just keeping the ones up that she thought mattered. Ted would take you around and stand in front of each picture and have a little story to tell about it. The house didn't look like it had been modernized in quite a long time. It was almost looking dilapidated before Ted married Vicki. But she took care of that as well, just really giving it an overhaul. To a certain extent, I just think she made it a happier place, not so much a place that just housed old history, but a real home."

When Ted's three children and their own families showed up at the house unannounced, it bothered Vicki. She therefore asked that they call first as a courtesy. She also had locks installed in the pantry to keep them and others from raiding the refrigerator. Vicki also fired the longtime cook at the house and hired someone new who specialized in healthier gourmet cooking. Needless to say, it became quite contentious between Ted's children and his new wife. Ted tried to stay out of it by saying that he trusted his new wife's judgment, which didn't make matters any easier for his children.

"My impression of it," said a longtime friend of Victoria's, "was that Vicki had heard all of the stories of the way the family ran roughshod over Joan, and she wasn't going to let it happen to her. Maybe she went a little overboard, but she was trying to make a point early on, which was that she had her boundaries and she wasn't about to let anyone cross them. To say that some of her decisions created uneasy situations would be putting it mildly."

Vicki had even managed to cow some of the Kennedys of the second generation. Ethel, for instance, just wanted to keep the peace and didn't want to cross Vicki if she could help it. She wasn't happy about some of the new regulations, but because she wanted to respect Ted's wife, she tried to be agreeable.

For instance, the pool at Rose and Joseph's home had always been open to all of the Kennedys. It only made sense. It was the *Kennedy* compound, after all. However, when Victoria moved in, she quickly became tired of having her pool filled with noisy Kennedys and their children and grandchildren. "Enough is enough," she decided. "There's a whole ocean out there, why is everyone in our pool?" She had little signs put up around the pool indicating quite clearly that the pool area was reserved for Ted Kennedy's immediate family. One can only imagine the reaction these signs generated from the other Kennedys. One day, Ethel walked out of her home and over to the Big House and, much to her astonishment, found Joan in the pool with her daughter, Kara (now Kennedy Allen), and her children. This was a direct violation of the new rules! After all, Joan was no longer "immediate family." Such family drama had put Ethel in a bad position in any case. Her first loyalty was always to Ted, everyone knew that. But still, she loved Joan too. In the end, she just didn't want any trouble. As she comically put it at the time, "I am way too old for trouble."

"Joansie," Ethel called out to her former sister-in-law. "What are you doing in the pool?"

Joan didn't hesitate. "I'm babysitting Ted's grandchildren," she said.

Ethel laughed. "Good answer, Joansie," she said. "Good answer!"

In all fairness to Vicki, there was no way she would have evicted Joan from the pool anyway. To hear Joan tell it, the two women actually met on an airplane flying over Nantucket shortly after Vicki started dating Ted. "I didn't know her at the time but she came over, introduced herself, and said she'd had the occasion to meet all three of my children," Joan recalled. "She said they were wonderful people, so unspoiled. I was very flattered. It was like mother-to-mother." Vicki then reached out to Joan shortly after marrying Ted to see if there was some way the two could work together to achieve harmony. They liked each other; there was no bitterness between them. In fact, one story has it that Vicki was sitting out on the veranda of the Big House one day when she saw a lone figure walking on the beach, all bundled up in a coat and scarf. "Who is that?" she asked the maid. "I don't know," the maid replied, then asked, "Shall I tell her she is trespassing?" No, Vicki decided, she wanted to check it out for herself. When she got out onto the beach, she realized it was Joan. The two women greeted each other and spoke for a few moments—it's not known what they said. Then they continued walking down the beach, talking to each other as they made their way.

Any rapport Vicki and Joan shared was not accidental. According to all accounts, they had to work at it and talk through problems whenever they arose. Understandably, situations arose that couldn't be avoided.

For instance, every year even after the divorce, Joan had still spent Christmases with Ted and her children at Ted's home in Virginia. After he married Vicki, though, that no longer seemed appropriate. Also, Joan had customarily spent every Thanksgiving at the compound with Ted and their children. Again, right after he married Vicki, this too seemed no longer possible. Thus the first few Thanksgivings were hard on Joan. There would end up being two turkeys—one for Ted and family, and then one the children would bring to Joan and share with her. In the coming years, though, Vicki felt comfortable inviting Joan to her Thanksgiving table—and Joan appreciated the invitation and accepted. She then joined her ex-husband, his new wife, and all of their children (and grandchildren) for Thanksgiving at the Big House, and did so for many years afterward. "Vicki is very cognizant of treating my mother with due respect," said Ted Jr. at the time. "She realizes that my mother deserves something."

Pat's Regrets

*I*t was the winter of 1993 and Pat Kennedy Lawford was lunching with her friend Patricia Brennan in Beverly Hills at the Polo Lounge of the Beverly Hills Hotel. It was a bimonthly affair. Brennan recalled, "Every other month, she would call and say, 'I'm coming to Los Angeles, so we're due,' and I knew what that meant. And even though we hadn't seen each other in two months and would probably not see each other for two more months because she lived in New York, for those three hours, we were as close as two old friends could be."

At this winter 1993 lunch, Pat Kennedy said, "Jackie's so lucky. She had a couple of fabulous marriages and never really had to worry about her kids. They just turned out so well. I don't know how she did it."

"You've been a good mother too," Patricia offered.

"Oh, please!" Pat Kennedy said. "I was a *terrible* mother." After adding that she felt she was a much better grandmother, she explained, "Don't forget, I'm the one who rented a house across the street for Chris and the nanny when he was an infant so Peter and I wouldn't be disturbed by the crying." At that, the two friends burst into almost uncontrollable laughter.

As the two women talked, Pat said that she still believed her children never forgave her for leaving their father. "They loved Peter so much," she said, "and they felt that I ripped them away from him and forced them to live three thousand miles away in New York. I think they never got over it," she concluded sadly. "But I could never explain to them that their daddy had been such a bastard to me. You just can't do that to a child. No matter how old they are, you still can't do that to a child."

"On some level, I think they knew," Patricia observed.

Pat just nodded. "I sometimes think I drove Peter to it," she said again, according to her friend's memory of the conversation. It seemed like an odd statement. Patricia asked what Pat meant by it. "Oh, you know how we Kennedys were back then," Pat said with a soft smile. "We were so full of ourselves, weren't we? All of that power and money. Why, we were at the center of everything. I think maybe I looked at Peter as not really belonging." She said that she hated to admit as much, but she feared it was the truth. She had to wonder, she said, if "perhaps I drove him into the arms of other women. I just don't know anymore..." As her voice drifted off, the two women just stared at one another.

At seventy, Pat Kennedy Lawford was still a striking woman, with bright red hair and a full Kennedyesque smile. She'd had a tough life, though, battling alcoholism for a long time. After the family's unsuccessful intervention, Pat's drinking continued unabated. Finally, in June 1988, a car she was driving careened into a tree and she was arrested for driving under the influence. Always stubborn when it came to her drinking, she wouldn't listen to anything anyone had to say about it, even when Joan tried to talk to her about her own personal experiences. Finally, after the arrest, it was Jackie who appealed to her old friend Pat, telling her she was, as Jackie put it, "too good a person to have to be thought of in that way." She asked Pat to spend time with her at her summer home on Martha's Vineyard—a lavish estate, isolated in the middle of 375 acres. During that time, the two women connected once again as "sisters," enjoying together the limitless peace of the Vineyard. Afterward, Pat significantly cut back on her drinking. Most people credited Jackie's influence for that small but important victory. By 1993, Pat was no longer drinking at all and, in fact, never had another relapse. "The hardest thing I ever had to do was get sober," she told one relative. "I think I didn't know how strong I really was until I realized that, yes, I had actually done it. It's truly my biggest personal victory. For the first time in years, I feel good about *me*."

Like Eunice and Jean, as the years went on, Pat would become invested in several organizations that served the mentally retarded, but in a way that was not high profile. It was interesting to those who knew her well that when she had been younger and married to Peter Lawford, she'd had such a penchant for Hollywood and a celebrity lifestyle, yet as an older woman she retreated into a much more private life in Los Angeles and New York.

By this time—the winter of 1993—Pat's children were all grown, most with children of their own. Chris was thirty-nine, married with three children. He'd had terrible bouts with alcohol and drug dependency but had been sober for about eight years. In years to come, he would write a couple of books about his struggle for sobriety, thereby making it a public and very inspiring story. An actor, writer, attorney, Chris would go on to become an activist and public speaker. He definitely had his father's charisma and sense of panache. Pat's daughters Sydney, thirty-eight, and Victoria, thirty-five, were also now married with four children and three, respectively. Robin, thirty-two, was unmarried at the time. "They've been better to me than I've been to them, I fear," Pat told Patricia Brennan.

"I don't necessarily believe that," Patricia said.

"Well, I do have some regrets," Pat concluded. "But it's been a wonderful life just the same. Who was it that said something like, 'Maybe the best one can hope for is to at least end up with the right regrets'?"

"That was Arthur Miller," Patricia answered.

"Oh yes, Marilyn's husband," Pat said, maybe flashing back to all of the history she'd shared with Marilyn.

"Do you ever see Jackie?" Patricia asked.

"Of course," Pat said. "All the time." She said that Jackie had never changed, she was "still pretty terrific" and always knew "just what to say and do in every situation. Oh, she's so perfect, I hate that woman," Pat added with a wicked laugh. "I just hate her!"

At that, the two friends again dissolved into laughter.

PART EIGHTEEN

Jackie: Her Final Years

"Life Goes On"

I guess life goes on for us," Jackie Kennedy Onassis said during the 1993 holidays, according to her longtime cook Marta Sgubin. "I am beginning to finally feel that we're just like any family," she added of herself and her children. "Nothing major has happened in years. Thank God for that!" Indeed, by this time it seemed that life was, at long last, serene for Jackie and her two children.

Jackie's daughter, Caroline, now thirty-six, had three children—Rose, Tatiana, and Jack, who was just a baby. The children called her "Grand Jackie," and Jackie doted on them. Caroline's marriage to Ed Schlossberg was rewarding, and very private. She never wanted to be a public person, and for the most part managed to avoid the spotlight, with the exception of an occasional speech given at a benefit or a Kennedy-related tribute. When she turned down an offer to be chairwoman of the 1992 Democratic National Convention, many people were surprised, but not her own family. "We know who Caroline is," her uncle Ted said at the time. "She's like her mother. Could you see Jackie doing it? No. So we shouldn't expect it of Caroline."

Caroline's friend Alexandra Styron, the daughter of writers William and Rose Styron, observed of her at this time: "She seemed to have come into her own. I'd never seen her happier. She looked beautiful, though she was stick thin. Her skin glowed. She and Ed were as much in love as any married people I had ever seen. They had a very quiet social life. They went out to occasional dinner parties given by friends, but they stuck pretty close to home. Caroline was extremely unassuming, down-to-earth."

John, now thirty-three, had turned out to be devastatingly handsome, with his wavy dark hair, penetrating eyes, and athletic body. One of his great appeals, though, was that he was viewed as an "everyman" by most Americans in the sense that, despite his famous pedigree, he still seemed somewhat fallible. For instance, he'd had a great deal of trouble in school—failing math a couple of times and later failing the New York State bar exam twice. Flunking the bar was embarrassing but, typical of John, it was also something he played off of with characteristic self-effacing humor, at least in the public arena. Privately, though, he was worried—mostly because Jackie was unhappy about it and felt he had simply not applied himself.

"I remember him saying, 'My mother is all over me about this thing,'" his friend Stephen Styles recalled of John's trouble with the bar exam. He added that John then said, "For a Kennedy to flunk even once is not acceptable. Twice? They throw you off the compound for that. Three times? It's out of the family for good then." Styles added, "He was joking, but he was also concerned. 'I have to pass the third time, or I'm in deep shit with my mom,' he said."

Jackie tolerated John's private life as well as could be expected, even though she'd not been very happy about some of the women who came his way. One in particular who seemed to be a thorn in Jackie's side at this time was actress Darryl Hannah.

John first met Darryl in 1978 when both happened to be vacationing in Saint Martin with their families, then again at the 1988 wedding of Jackie's sister Lee Radziwill to director Herb Ross. At the time that he began dating Darryl, he was dating a string of other women, including actresses Christina Haag and Sarah Jessica Parker and model Julie Baker. As the story goes, in September 1992, Darryl was apparently the victim of domestic violence at the hands of rock star Jackson Browne, with whom she had been involved for about a decade. According to several friends and many news accounts, she ended up with a black eye, a broken finger, and numerous bruises. When Darryl called John to tell him what had happened, he flew to Los Angeles and brought her back to New York with him. Their monogamous romance started at that time.

Also at about this time in 1992, John had quit his job as a Manhattan assistant district attorney—after arguing six trials and winning convictions in all six—and had moved into Darryl's Upper West Side apartment. "Jackie was not happy about any of it," recalled Stephen Styles. "I was at Darryl's with John when I overheard a telephone conversation between him and his mom. 'Look, I'm just living my life, Mom,' he said. 'What do you want from me?' I don't know what she said to him, but his response was, 'Well, I'm sorry, but that's just not going to happen. I will see you tomorrow night at dinner and we can talk it over. I'm fine, Mom. I really am.'

"Later, when I asked John about the conversation, he said, 'She's not thrilled about this thing with Darryl. She's afraid we're going to get married. But she doesn't even know her.' What was her biggest beef about Darryl? I asked. 'The fact that she's an actress,' he said. 'She doesn't want me involved with a public person because that throws me even more in the spotlight, and that's not what she wants for me.' He also said no woman was ever going to be good enough for him in his mom's eyes. He added, 'But, that's mothers for you, right? Why should mine be any different?'"

John was also thinking about possibly running for office one day, though nothing was concrete in his mind about it. In 1993, he said, "If your father was a doctor, and your uncles are doctors, and all your cousins are doctors, and all the family ever talks about is medicine, there's a good chance maybe you're going to be a doctor too. But maybe you want to be a baker." Jackie was also against his entering politics, though. Again, too high profile for her taste.

Jackie, who had turned sixty-four in July 1993, was for the most part living at her estate on Martha's Vineyard, though she maintained her residence in New York City. She had curtailed her activities at Doubleday somewhat, but was still going into the office three times a week. Meanwhile, she and Maurice Tempelsman were very happy together. "They bickered like an old married couple," said a friend of theirs. "You would be out with them and Jackie would say, 'Maurice, stop putting so much salt on your food.' And he would roll his eyes and put the salt shaker down. Then, when she would turn her back, he would very quickly salt his food. They laughed a lot. He was good to her. He was exactly what she deserved."

In August 1993, Maurice went to Russia on business, and while he was gone, Jackie missed him tremendously, recalled Marian Ronan, who worked for Jackie at her Red Gate Farm on Martha's Vineyard. "On the day he was due to return, Jackie was like an excited kid on Christmas Eve. She brushed her hair until it shimmered like silk, put on white jeans and a T-shirt, and paced up and down until she heard his car coming. Then she ran to the front door with a huge smile on her face. When Maurice came in she slipped her arm through his and kissed him tenderly on the cheek, led him into the living room, and closed the door. It was a very touching scene."

Ronan also recalled Jackie going into a "blind panic" when she thought she'd lost a ring Maurice had given her. "She phoned the house and, her voice shaking with anxiety, told me, 'Marian, I don't have my ring. I'll die if I've lost it!' The gold eternity ring was encrusted with priceless emeralds and sapphires and she often described it as 'my most treasured possession.' I quickly searched the house and found the ring right where she'd left it—on an antique china plate she kept in her bedroom. When I phoned Jackie back and told her I'd found it, she was incredibly relieved and told me, 'Oh, thank you! Thank you so much!'

"She insisted that we call her madam, but she always treated us more like family members than servants," said Marian Ronan. "For all her social position, wealth, and fame, Jackie looked happiest while sipping coffee with her hired help in the home's small kitchen, which was off the big main kitchen. She'd be sitting there in a swimsuit and bare feet with curlers in her hair, chatting away like a housewife."

For a woman like Jackie Kennedy Onassis who had lived such a high-profile, even historic life, it was refreshing to her friends and family members that her concerns these days were anything but extraordinary. As she enjoyed her sixties, her biggest interests had to do with her job, her children's welfare, and staying fit—she was a resolute dieter, a yoga enthusiast, and a proponent of anything else she felt would help her stay in shape and remain healthy.

Of course, Jackie was still in touch with the Kennedy family, though she didn't see all of them as often as she might have liked. She and Ted remained very close, though she didn't know Vicki well. She also remained in close touch with Joan, Ethel, and Pat. And she made it a point to speak to Eunice and Sarge as often as possible. However, there was still a sense that everyone wasn't as close as they had once been. "But that's what happens when you get older," Jackie reasoned in 1993, "you start devoting your life to your grandchildren, I guess."

"She never spoke about her late husbands, JFK or Onassis," recalled Marian Ronan, "and she never discussed any of the Kennedy family. But in the kitchen there was a wall clipboard covered with a montage of photos showing Jackie, JFK and their kids, and Onassis."

"She never looked back, except to do so in order to remember the good times," said her longtime cook and good friend Marta Sgubin, who worked for Jackie for twenty-five years. "In my eyes, Madam was not a person who would ever grow old. She had a childlike persona, an innocence, this despite her obvious sophistication. She was so thoughtful, I would always find little Post-its on the refrigerator complimenting me on the meal I had made the night before. 'In all of your life, you will never make such an incredible dessert as you did last night with the mango ice cream,' she once wrote. Another time, she wrote, 'Bravo et Merci. Everyone said it was the best dinner in New York.' She liked things just so, and she appreciated it when things were done that way. Madam felt it was important that people in her life knew that she appreciated them...that was vitally important to her."

Not surprisingly, Jackie always remembered birthdays. In April 1993, when Ethel Kennedy turned sixty-five, many of her family members were gathered at her home for a celebration when the phone rang. "I'll bet I know who that is," Ethel said. When one of her sons handed her the phone, she smiled broadly as soon as she heard the whispery voice on the other end of the line. "Jackie," she exclaimed, "in all of these years, you have never once forgotten my birthday. How in the world do you do that?"

In fact, Jackie's secretary, Nancy Tuckerman, once revealed that Jackie made it a point to transfer all of the birthday dates of the many different Kennedys from one calendar to the next every year so that she would remember either to send a card or make a call—especially to the women in the family. Perhaps that was because Jackie was usually estranged from her own sister, Lee Radziwill. The two saw each other only occasionally. Therefore it may have been all the more important to Jackie that she maintain her ties to her Kennedy "sisters."*

It's not known what Jackie said to Ethel on the occasion of her sixty-fifth birthday, but Ethel's response was simple and to the point: "Thank you for calling me, kiddo. God bless you, Jackie."

Marian Ronan will never forget the last time she saw her employer. It was at the end of the summer 1993 at the Red Gate Farm on the Vineyard. "As we stood saying goodbye in the kitchen, she shook my hand and looked at me with those wonderful eyes. She said softly, 'Thank you so

---

* Jackie's relationship with her younger sister, Lee, had always been fraught with problems, some of which could be traced all the way back to 1963 when the two went sailing with Aristotle Onassis. From most accounts, Lee had a romantic interest in Onassis, who was more taken with Jackie. Of course, Jackie was married to Jack at the time and certainly would never have thought twice about Onassis. However, when she later ended up marrying him in 1968, Lee was quite upset about it; it was just one of the many slights she felt as the less famous, less popular sister. Over the years, there would be many such feuds between the two women, with sisterly jealousy being the most dominant theme of their disagreements. To say that they disliked each other, though, would be untrue. In fact, they had a deep and abiding love for one another. They simply could not get along.

much, Marian, for all you've done this summer. Have a good winter. Take good care of yourself and I will see you next year.' Little did we know that we were saying goodbye for the last time."

Jackie's "Bad News"

*I*n November 1993, the nation commemorated the thirtieth anniversary of the assassination of President John Fitzgerald Kennedy. For Jackie, November 22 was still a day shrouded in a lot of pain and trauma. Of course, she had gone on with her life, but she had never really gotten over the ordeal of witnessing the brutal killing of her husband, the father of her two children. "I think about that day every November and it takes me right back to Dallas," she once told Joan Braden. "But I also think, in a sense, that it's a good thing, as painful as it is. I think we should never forget. We should forge ahead. But we should never forget."

This particular year, Jackie, still an enthusiastic equestrian, decided to retreat to Middleburg, Virginia, to observe the anniversary and to enjoy some horseback riding. However, a terrible accident occurred one day when she somehow took a tumble off her favorite horse, Clown. Though she had taken many such falls over the years, this one was particularly nasty. She was knocked out cold for almost half an hour. "Everyone was quite concerned," said Margorie Maitland, who witnessed the event. "It was terrifying. The ambulance came and they worked on her for about thirty frightful minutes. Then she got up as if nothing had happened. I remember her just rising like a phoenix, standing straight up and looking quite fit despite what had just happened. 'I'm totally fine,' she kept saying. 'Please don't fuss over me.'"

Despite Jackie's nonchalance, the unfortunate accident was the first in a chain of calamitous events that would forever change the course of her life. First, when Jackie was taken to Loudon Hospital Center for treatment immediately after the fall, the examining doctor noticed what he thought was a swollen lymph node on her right groin. Believing it to be nothing more than an infection, he gave her an antibiotic and sent her home. A few weeks later, as Jackie spent Christmas with Maurice and her family at her New Jersey country retreat, she seemed fine. But then, during a Caribbean vacation with Maurice a short time later, she began to experience painful swelling of the lymph nodes in her neck, as well as a persistent cough and terrible stomach pain. Now she was concerned. Cutting the vacation short, she went back to New York to consult with a head and neck surgeon at the New York Hospital–Cornell Medical Center. The news was anything but good. A CAT scan detected swollen lymph nodes in Jackie's chest and stomach, a biopsy of which then revealed that she was suffering from non-Hodgkin's lymphoma. Stunned, Jackie didn't know how she would ever be able to break the news to John and Caroline, but with Maurice at her side, she was somehow able to get through her talk with them. Of course, they were both distraught and in shock, as was Maurice.

The first person in the Kennedy family that Jackie told the stunning news to was Eunice Kennedy Shriver. "I have what I'm afraid may be bad news," she reportedly told her. "But I don't want to worry you. I just want to inform you."

It was interesting that Jackie decided Eunice should be the first of the Kennedys other than her own children to know the news. It was as if she felt that of all the women in the family, Eunice was the most resourceful, the most formidable, and perhaps Jackie felt a need for Eunice's special brand of strength and resolve at such a worrisome time. The specifics of what the two women discussed remained known only to themselves. However, it is known that Eunice was so upset that she was barely able to get through the conversation without betraying her true feelings of great worry and concern. She wanted to be strong for Jackie, but as she would later tell it, it was very difficult. For Eunice Kennedy Shriver to not be able to rally when necessary suggests that she really was shaken right to the core by Jackie's news. As soon as she ended the conversation with Jackie, Eunice called Ted, who within fifteen minutes telephoned Jackie to remind her that she was well loved and to assure her that he had no doubt she would be just fine. Fifty percent of such cases are curable, he reminded her, and he said he was certain that she would beat the odds. "We Kennedys always beat the odds," he told her. It was an optimistic way of looking at things and very much like Ted and the rest of the Kennedys. Sadly, in this case, it wouldn't prove to be true.

No Words

$\mathcal{J}$ackie, how are you feeling?" Ted wanted to know. It was January 1994. Ted, Vicki, and two of his grown children were standing in the living room of the Big House—where Ted and Vicki now spent much of their time—greeting Jackie, who had flown in from New York City. "Oh, I'm just fine, Teddy," Jackie said as she walked in looking thin and elegant. She embraced him. She then greeted everyone else in the room with warm hugs.

"I felt I needed to see Grandma," Jackie said finally. "I don't know why. I just thought it was important."

"Well, she's on the porch," Ted said.

"And how's she doing?" Jackie asked.

"She has her good days and her bad days," he answered. "Today is a bad day."

By this time, Rose Kennedy was 103. Confined to a wheelchair, she was now blind and deaf, the ravages of old age having taken their terrible toll on her. "They would wheel her out every now and then," *Cape Cod Times* photographer Steve Heaslip would later recall, "and she was so wasted away behind blankets and so many different layers of clothing, it felt like an invasion of privacy to even photograph her. So we [media photographers] started backing off."

Almost every year, the Kennedys used to host a big birthday party for Rose and invite the media to the gathering. But by the end of the 1980s, Rose was no longer well enough to even go outside to meet the press who had shown up for the festivities. Therefore, Ted would invite them into the Big House. Karen Jeffrey, a reporter for the *Cape Cod Times*, remembered one of those occasions:

"The room Rose was sitting in was a den, maybe a TV room," she recalled. "The walls were covered with pictures of her boys and herself with international leaders, the Pope, etc....I noticed that there were no pictures of her daughters on the walls! The rugs were very worn and the furniture old—not antique, just very old. The television had to be at least thirty years old, one of those giant wood consoles. Ted stood on one side of Rose, who was seated, and Eunice was on the other. Jean was nearby and Pat was, as well. Ted's twinkle and the way he interacted with Rose was very genuine. It certainly didn't feel put on for the press. He would say, 'Mother, look here,' or 'Look there,' or 'Smile for the camera,' and she would do as she was told as everyone shot pictures and took frantic notes. It was a little sad, I suppose. But endlessly fascinating."

Jackie walked through the living room and out to the porch where Rose Kennedy sat, all bundled up in a wheelchair. The Kennedy matriarch had a colorful scarf on her head and was wearing a down vest over a sweater with a wool blanket draped around her legs. She was also wearing large sunglasses. She looked very tiny, unbelievably frail at about eighty pounds. Only she knew what she was thinking these days; since she seldom said a word, one couldn't help but wonder if she thought of the past or, indeed, if she now lived in the past. "It has been said that time heals all wounds," she had written in her memoir. "I don't agree. The wounds remain. Time—the mind, protecting its sanity—covers them with some scar tissue and the pain lessens, but it is never gone."

Sitting at Rose's side in an Adirondack chair was a nurse in a crisp white uniform saying the prayers of the rosary. When she noticed Jackie approaching, she rose. The two women nodded at each other, and Jackie took the nurse's place in the chair. As the nurse walked away, Jackie held Rose's hand. The two then sat in silence as the waves from Nantucket Sound crashed upon the deserted beach before them.

There were just no words.

One Regret

I have a terrible feeling I brought this onto myself," Jackie said. It was April 13, 1994, and she was lunching with fashion designer Oleg Cassini, an old friend who had designed many of her spectacular gowns during her White House years, and with whom she was now interested in doing a book. Cassini would recall that on this afternoon, she was wearing an obvious wig and had a Band-Aid on her cheek. Other than that, he would recall, she seemed fine. She had no appetite, though, as evidenced by the way she just picked at her Chinese chicken salad.

"What do you mean, Jackie?" he asked her.

"The smoking," she said.

"Oh no, Jackie," he exclaimed. "Please tell me you don't still smoke."

Jackie shook her head sadly. "Oleg, my one regret is that I do—at least up until a couple months ago when they made me stop. In fact, I'd been smoking three packs a day for more than forty years."

Oleg would recall being stunned by her admission. "Why, I don't think I have ever even seen a picture of you smoking," he said.

"I guess you could say it's my dirty little secret," she said. "I never wanted to encourage anyone else to start by being seen doing it myself. So I have been exceedingly careful in public." Jackie said that she had tried to quit "at least ten times" over the years, but to no avail. "And now here I am, stuck with this damned cancer. I can't help but wonder."

"You have taken such good care of yourself otherwise," Oleg said. "Yoga, your diet...I just don't think..."

"I know...and all of that deprivation of sweets I would have so loved over the years," Jackie added with a wry smile, "and for what?"

The two just looked at each other.

"I suppose when faced with one's own mortality," Jackie finally said, "the first thing one does is wonder what she did to hasten things. I would just feel so stupid if I did this to myself," she remarked sadly.

Again, Oleg didn't know what to say.

"Oh my," Jackie finally said with a smile obviously intended to lighten the mood, "let's just have dessert. Something chocolatey and decadent. Shall we share one?"

"But Jackie, you never eat dessert," he said.

"Oh yes I do, Oleg," she responded with a wicked smile. "Believe me, these days I most certainly *do* eat dessert."

Too Young to Die

*B*y the winter of 1994, Jackie had been undergoing chemotherapy for a couple of months, and as is often the case, the treatment seemed much worse than the disease itself. Immediately her hair began to thin, she lost weight, and in just a short time she seemed to age at least ten years. Lady Bird Johnson sent Jackie a letter at this time expressing her concern for her health and wishing her all the best. The two women had been corresponding for the better part of forty years, good friends since before their White House days. Jackie's letter of reply is interesting in that one can detect a change in her handwriting. Whereas it had always been quite legible, her penmanship neat, in this letter to Mrs. Johnson, which is undated but appears to have been written in the winter of 1994, her handwriting seems shaky. "Everything is going wonderfully," Jackie wrote, being as optimistic as possible, "and I hope to see you on the Vineyard again next summer. Much love, Jackie." This would be the last letter she would ever write to Lady Bird Johnson.*

Jackie had also actively begun getting in touch with old friends, which suggested that perhaps she sensed she was now facing her own mortality. One of those people was the architect John Carl Warnecke—the designer of JFK's gravesite at Arlington National Cemetery—whom she hadn't seen or talked to in some time. By 1994, Warnecke was retired and living in the San Francisco area. There had been some disenchantment on Jackie's part when she learned that Ted had apparently been using Warnecke's telephone to call his mistresses in order that Joan not see the numbers. However, because Jackie was never sure about what was going on, she decided to ignore the evidence and just chalk it up to more examples of Ted's bad behavior.

"She called in March to tell me that she had a special project at Doubleday that I might be interested in," Warnecke recalled in an interview many years later. "She said it was a book of architecture. We made an appointment to talk more in-depth on the phone in a week's time. But on the appointed day, her secretary called to tell me that Jackie wouldn't be in the office, would I mind calling her at her home instead? Of course, I agreed."

---

* The next letter in the voluminous files of correspondence between Jackie Kennedy Onassis and Lady Bird Johnson is one from Caroline Kennedy, dated May 28, 1994. Caroline wrote, "I wanted to let you know how much we appreciated the effort you made to come to New York last week to wish my mother farewell. I'm sorry I didn't get a chance to see you. Love, Caroline."

"Why, John, how are you?" came the familiar voice on the other end of the phone when John called Jackie's apartment.

As the two began to talk, it wasn't long before the conversation turned to Jackie's illness. "They thought it was in remission," Jackie said of the cancer. "But then they found out that apparently it has spread to my brain. So they have this marvelous therapy," she continued, "where they actually put a stent into your head and pour the chemotherapy into your brain. Doesn't that sound just ghastly?"

John was too stunned to comment. That Jackie could so easily describe such a treatment was a little more than he could bear. "I don't know what to say," he told her.

"Oh, John, I know it's hard," Jackie told him, her voice well modulated and controlled. She said that perhaps she should be more careful about the way she doled out such startling information to her friends. "It's a bit of a shock, I know," she added. "But you mustn't worry. I am too young to die. Why, I'm only sixty-four, and I refuse to go," she concluded. "Believe me, they will have to drag me kicking and screaming from this earth, because I will not go of my own accord."

The two old friends laughed.

"Do you know that my son John plays the guitar?" Jackie asked at another point in the conversation. She said that John had recently visited her and, while sitting in her living room, "played the guitar and sang the most lovely Spanish songs to me. It was marvelous," she said. "I didn't know he had such a wonderful singing voice. Funny what you don't know about your kids, isn't it?"

The two spoke for about half an hour more. Though John Carl Warnecke wished to keep private the details of what they discussed, he did share one moving memory. "How are you dealing with it all?" he asked Jackie.

"I'm fine," she said, predictably enough. "One must remain strong," she said. But then, after a pause, she added in a low voice, "However, I do cry from time to time. In the shower. Where no one can hear me. I think that's best."

John hung up the phone after wishing Jackie "all the luck in the world" with her continued treatment. Ten minutes later, he realized that they had never discussed the architecture project she had in mind. He thought about calling her back. But he decided against it. Perhaps there had never been a project anyway, he thought. Maybe she just wished to reconnect with him. Instead of calling her back, he sat at his desk and remembered a note he had written to her many years earlier. In it, he had explained his concept for JFK's gravesite at Arlington on a grassy slope overlooking the Potomac, and the incorporation into it of the Eternal Flame, which Jackie had lit at JFK's funeral. Somehow, on this day, John Carl Warnecke's words in that note reminded him more of her than they did of the memorial he had created for her late husband. "The total design and composition must be simple," he had written, "and out of its simplicity and dignity... will come its beauty."

Vigil

*I*t was Thursday, May 19, 1994. About a month earlier, Jackie Kennedy Onassis's health had taken a dramatic turn for the worse when she collapsed with perforated ulcers in her stomach. Terrified, she was convinced that this was to be the end for her. "I'm dying," she whispered to Maurice as she lay on the floor, according to someone close to him. The ulcers were caused by a reaction to prednisone, the steroid she was taking as part of her treatment. Indeed, she could have bled to death if the condition had not been taken care of immediately. Doctors removed a portion of her stomach that had been bleeding. Upon her release from the hospital a couple of days later, her attitude changed. Whereas she had once been unfailingly optimistic, now she was just exceedingly quiet. The chemotherapy had taken its toll on her, not only physically but emotionally. She stopped taking calls from friends and loved ones, staying close to Maurice and her children. It was as if she sensed that the end was near and she simply didn't have the energy to console all of those who would be devastated by her death. Always with an eye toward how she wanted to be remembered—and with consideration to the privacy of some of her friends—she went through the many years of correspondence she had saved. With her friend and longtime assistant, Nancy Tuckerman, at her side, she read each letter aloud. Some, she saved. Others, she tossed into a roaring fireplace.

Days later, Jackie came down with pneumonia and ended up back in the hospital. There, she was told that the cancer had spread to her liver. Though no one said as much, Jackie seemed to know that all hope was lost. When offered additional chemotherapy treatments, she declined them. In fact, she said she didn't even want to be treated for the pneumonia. "Just take me home," she told John and Caroline. "I want to go home. It's okay," she told her distraught children. "In my heart, I know it's okay."

With the passing of a few more days, Jackie slowly began to slip away. It was as if she had let go, as if she had reconciled herself to her fate and was fine with it. If anything, she seemed peaceful. Finally, Caroline began making the dreaded phone calls to friends and loved ones to inform them that there wasn't much time left.

On Thursday morning, May 19, at about 11:30, Jackie was given the last rites of the Roman Catholic Church by Monsignor George Bardes of St. Thomas More Church. As he finished, Jackie looked up at him and smiled. "She was physically weak," he said later, "but spiritually strong." He also said he later found Caroline in her old bedroom, weeping. John met him in the hallway and walked him to the front door. "Thank you for coming," John said, looking exhausted. "My mother really wanted to get that over with. You know how she is. Always with a checklist." The two men smiled sadly and shook hands.

Later that same day, many of Jackie's friends and family members came to her home on Fifth Avenue to say goodbye to her. She had decided weeks earlier that, with the exception of her son and Maurice, only women should be permitted to sit by her bedside in her final hours. Her friend Bunny Mellon was present, as was singer Carly Simon, another close friend. There were many others coming and going—colleagues from Doubleday; longtime Kennedy acolytes; friends of Aristotle Onassis; people she had met from so many different walks of life over the years, some appearing to be almost in a daze as they talked among themselves, sharing their memories. Jean Kennedy Smith was present, as was her son William Kennedy Smith. Ethel's sons Joseph, Bobby Jr., Michael, and Douglas were present, as well as Pat's son, Christopher. Jackie's sister, Lee Radziwill, was there, with her son Anthony and his wife, Carole. Sargent Shriver—looking particularly shaken—was present, as was his daughter, Maria Shriver. Of course, Ted Kennedy and his wife, Vicki, were there. Caroline had Ed Schlossberg at her side. However, John and Darryl Hannah were having trouble in their relationship at the time, and she was in

Los Angeles. Obviously too ill to make the journey was Rose Kennedy. Also, Joan couldn't make it; she was just too upset.

Down below on Fifth Avenue outside Jackie's building were scores of news crews reporting the story around the world that the Queen of Camelot might be near death. Jackie's spokeswoman issued a statement saying that Jackie "is fighting another phase of her illness with great fortitude." As a result, traffic was all but stopped in front of 1040 Fifth Avenue, the building Jackie had moved into so many years earlier when, still shocked and confused by the tragic turn her life had taken in Dallas, she decided to start anew.

Soft Gregorian chants filled Jackie's home and lights were dimmed as the procession of friends, family, and loved ones continued throughout the afternoon and into the evening. Slowly, people came and went from the apartment in solemn tribute to a woman who meant so much to so many, some of the female guests being permitted a few moments with Jackie in her bedroom. Candles were lit all about the apartment, lending an almost religious atmosphere to the proceedings. As people milled about, occasionally someone would tell a humorous story about Jackie or about one of the other Kennedys that would elicit soft laughter.

Eunice and Pat were already present when Ethel came rushing in at about 3 p.m., but it was when the three Kennedy women exchanged greetings in the foyer that an almost palpable shift in energy seemed to occur. "It was as if a blanket of overwhelming sadness had descended upon us," recalled one visitor. "Whereas all day long it felt as if everyone was trying to be strong, no tears but the kind of stoic strength they knew Jackie would have approved of, when the three elder Kennedy women converged, everyone sort of lost it. It was as if that's when reality hit, when we all knew that this was true, that it wasn't just some awful nightmare, that Jackie was, indeed, dying. I just remember the three of them—Ethel, Pat, and Eunice—walking into the living room with such devastated expressions on their faces. I'll simply never forget it."

Just five weeks earlier, Jackie had called Ethel with her annual birthday greeting, this time for Ethel's sixty-sixth. According to what Ethel recalled, the two shared a laugh when Ethel complained, "I feel more like ninety-six!" To which Jackie responded by saying, "Well, if you ask me, you don't look a day over fifty-six!" And now it had come to this—Ethel about to walk into the bedroom in which Jackie lay dying, with her sisters-in-law Pat and Eunice at her side.

Always Jackie

*A*s Maurice Tempelsman opened the door to Jackie's coral-and-peach-colored bedroom, the Kennedy women—Pat, Ethel, and Eunice—walked in, took one look around, and then stood in place for a moment as if in a state of shock. Pat, her eyes wide with disbelief, seemed to crumble a bit; Eunice put her arm around her shoulders and held her tightly. There in front of them was Jackie, lying peacefully in her large, canopied bed. Wearing a print scarf, she was on her back, her eyes closed, her mouth slightly open, and her hands folded peacefully over her chest. She was partially under a blanket with an intravenous tube connected to one arm through which morphine was being administered. Though unconscious, she looked quite beautiful and even regal as she lay bathed in the soft and gentle glow of three antique lamps.

Ethel walked into the room first. "Oh my God," she said, seeming overwhelmed. "It can't be true," she said as she sat in a chair to Jackie's left and took her hand. "It just can't be true," she repeated. Eunice and Pat then walked to the other side of the bed. As Eunice took Jackie's other hand into her own, Pat, standing behind her sister, began to murmur, "No, no, no." It was then that Maurice closed the door to the bedroom.

The three Kennedy women never spoke of their last, private moments with Jackie. However, one of Ethel's sons—who wished not to be identified—said in a 1999 interview, "My mother told her how much she loved her and how much she had always meant to her, no matter their petty differences. However, she said that she wasn't sure that Aunt Jackie understood what she was saying or if she was even awake. She said that the room was beautiful, that there were flowers everywhere, soft music playing, Jackie's books all around her. There were manuscripts and bound volumes. Books by Isak Dinesen, Jean Rhys, and Colette. Record albums. The music she loved. But in the middle of it all was this vision, Aunt Jackie. She said she had never seen Jackie look more lovely, more peaceful. The word she used was 'serene.' I remember it because that's a word I don't think I had ever heard my mother use. She said, 'Jackie was just so serene. I had never seen anyone look that way before.' I don't think she ever thought it possible that Aunt Jackie would not be here."

The Kennedy women were with Jackie for about thirty minutes. By the time they emerged, they seemed to have a newfound strength. Now there were no tears. It was as if their time with Jackie had somehow bolstered them, enabling them to accept the inevitable.

"She's going to be fine," Eunice told Caroline, according to several witnesses. "God is with her now, as always. He's with all of us. Do you believe that?" she asked her niece.

"I do, Aunt Eunice," Caroline said, seeming determined to be strong. The two embraced. Eunice reached into her pocket and pulled out a chain of rosary beads and gave them to her niece. Caroline's husband, Ed Schlossberg, then hugged Eunice, followed by Ethel and, finally, Pat. "Thank you for being here for my wife," he told them.

Before taking her leave, Ethel asked to see John. He came from the kitchen, his dark eyes red-rimmed and bloodshot. Now thirty-three, he was wearing a beautifully tailored dark blue suit with a crisp white shirt and aqua-colored tie. With all of that wavy thick hair and his jaw so strong, he was a strikingly handsome man. But on this night, he somehow looked just like the lost little boy who had saluted his slain father's casket so many years earlier.

"Kiddo, I have always loved you like one of my own," Ethel said, reaching up to brush the tears from John's eyes. "Your mother doesn't want you to cry now, John," she said. "You have to be strong. Your mother was always so strong. She wants you to smile now."

John tried his best to force a smile, but it simply wouldn't come. Ethel placed one hand on each side of his face and pulled him close. Then, looking at him with great warmth, she said, "Your parents will be together in heaven very soon. And they will look down on you and Caroline. And oh, how they will love you, John. Oh, how they will love you!"

At that, John's face broke into a small, sad smile as he wrapped his long arms around his beloved aunt and held her close.

At quarter after ten that evening, May 19, after everyone had departed, leaving only Caroline, John, and Maurice to spend their final hours with her, Jacqueline Kennedy Onassis departed from this world—always a legend, always an icon, always a mother...a woman greatly admired. Fittingly, she would be buried at Arlington National Cemetery next to her beloved first husband, the president.

PART NINETEEN

John and Carolyn

John Kennedy Jr. at a Crossroads

*F*lash back to June 9, 1990. Ethel Kennedy's daughter, Kerry, had just married Andrew Cuomo* at St. Michael's Church in Washington, D.C. After the nuptials, Ethel Kennedy hosted a lavish reception for the two political families—the Cuomos and the Kennedys—at her Hickory Hill estate. Recently, Ethel's sons had set up a flying fox on the property— an aerial cable usually used for military maneuvers. Jackie took one look at it and, turning to Sargent Shriver, said, "How long do you think it'll be before John is up there on that thing?" Sarge just smiled. No sooner had Jackie spoken than she noticed a commotion behind her. "Come on, John, get up there," Ethel's sons Joe and Bobby were saying to John Kennedy Jr. "Just try to stop me," John said as he took off his suit jacket and loosened his tie.

"Oh, no. Really John, must you?" Jackie said.

"Yes, Mother, I must," he said with a laugh.

John jumped up onto the flying fox's small seat, grabbed the pulley, and pushed off from a platform. Soon he was sailing in the air about twenty feet off the ground, right across Ethel's property and into a smooth-as-silk landing just a couple of feet away from his aunt Ethel. "My God! You almost hit me," Ethel shouted at John. "Almost doesn't count, Aunt Ethel," he said with a big grin as he jumped off the apparatus and ran from her. At that, Ethel grabbed a chocolate cupcake off a platter and hurled it at her nephew. He yelped as it hit him right in the back of the head. "You're right," Ethel said, laughing, "almost doesn't count." Jackie just laughed at the sight and shook her head in dismay. Turning to Maurice Tempelsman, she remarked, "I don't know what I'm going to do with that boy."

He had always been impulsive and unpredictable, but after the death

---

* The son of former New York governor Mario Cuomo, Andrew is currently the governor of New York, having assumed office in 2011. He and Kerry had three daughters, Cara Ethel, Mariah Matilda, and Michaela Andrea, before divorcing in 2005.

of his mother in 1994, there seemed to be a great deal of pressure on John Kennedy Jr. to do something important with his life. Jackie's passing caused some political pundits and Kennedy watchers to look to John as perhaps the next great Kennedy. It was as if Jackie's death signified an end of the Camelot era, that is unless someone stepped in to continue the epic tradition. Adding to the pressure was that Jackie had also sometimes been critical of John's lack of focus. Though she would not have wanted to see him in public office, she definitely felt he was too old not to have some direction in his life, a real career. A lot of others felt the same way, both in his private life as well as in the media. After all, he was JFK's one and only son. Surely he should be the Kennedy to do something truly noteworthy.

Few people knew that John gave generously to several charities and spent a great deal of time working with inner-city children in Harlem and in Bedford-Stuyvesant in Brooklyn. Moreover, he helped start Exodus House, a school for Harlem children. He also helped tutor students there. In 1995, he established Reaching Up, Inc., a nonprofit organization that trained caregivers for the mentally disabled, and a very personal undertaking for him in that it mirrored his aunt Eunice's work. He also worked with the Robin Hood Foundation to help poor children in New York. These endeavors did not generate a lot of press for John—which was by design. He didn't want the attention, he just wanted to make a difference. Thus most people weren't aware of John's personal philanthropy—even many of his cousins didn't know about Exodus House, for example— and felt he should be doing something in the political arena. After all, there were Kennedys in office making significant contributions as public servants—why not John?

For instance, Ted's son Patrick had become the youngest member of the Kennedy family to hold elected office when he won election to the Rhode Island House of Representatives at age twenty-one. He would serve two terms in the Rhode Island legislature and go on to become the chairman of the Democratic Congressional Campaign Committee from 1999 to 2001. He served from 2001 until his retirement in 2011 as a member of the Rhode Island delegation to the U.S. House of Representatives, with membership on a number of its standing subcommittees. In true Kennedy tradition, he was the sponsor of the Mental Health Parity

Act in 2008. In November 1986, Bobby's son Joseph Patrick Kennedy was elected to the U.S. House of Representatives from the Massachusetts 8th Congressional District. He served there until 1999. Bobby's daughter Kathleen Kennedy Townsend would become the sixth and first female lieutenant governor of Maryland when she was elected in January 1995. She would serve until 2003.

By 1995, John was definitely at a crossroads. When he was with his cousins at the compound, it had gotten to the point where nobody even mentioned his career—or lack of it. In a way, that just made things worse. It was as if people had begun to accept that he had no real career and it was okay with them. He seemed to be getting a free pass just because he was JFK's son.

One of the greatest misconceptions about John Kennedy Jr. was that while he was a sincerely nice man, he wasn't very bright, sort of like a golden retriever—sweet but dumb. Doubtless, this was the result of the problems he had passing the bar and of all the publicity he had received the two times he failed it. True, maybe law wasn't his calling, but he had brains, drive, energy, and ambition. He was vastly intelligent in other areas, especially in the area of politics. In fact, he lived and breathed politics. Being of service to others was a code he had lived with all of his life. It was something in which he truly believed.

Here's a telling story about John:

Back in 1988, when he met Al Gore for the first time at the Democratic convention at the Omni in Atlanta (at which John was one of the speakers), Gore was annoyed by the demands of the pressing crowd and said to John, "Can you believe these people? What a pain in the ass this is! They are always wanting something from us." John was stunned. He didn't say anything at the time, but from that moment on Al Gore was not a person for whom John had much respect. In fact, Gore's sentiments were completely antithetical to everything John thought a public servant should aspire to be. "I was deeply offended by it," he told Richard Bradley at *George* magazine when recounting the memory. "I thought, man, are you crazy? These people are why we're in politics! They're looking up at us. They believe in us. And your attitude is that they're a pain in the ass?"

In truth, the reality of John Kennedy Jr. was much more interesting than his public persona because—unlike what some thought of him— the real JFK Jr. was thoughtful and introspective. "But one also has to

Somehow, growing up in the public eye was easier for Caroline Kennedy and John Jr. than it was for pop star Michael Jackson. The three are seen in 1978, when Jackson was in New York filming *The Wiz*. (Jackie Kennedy Onassis would later edit Michael's autobiography, *Moonwalk*, for Doubleday.) (*J. Randy Taraborrelli Collection*)

David Kennedy's death of a drug overdose at the age of twenty-eight on April 25, 1984, was something his mother, Ethel, and his many siblings could never quite reconcile. David, pictured here at the Kennedy compound, was a kind, gentle young man whose problems could be traced back to his having witnessed his dad's murder on television in June 1968. (*Michael Grecco/Getty Images*)

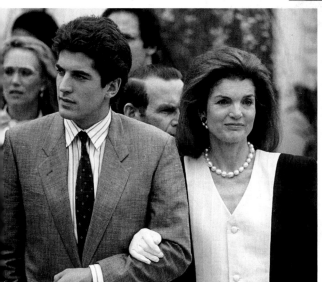

As far as Jackie was concerned, no woman would be good enough for her son, John. "But that's mothers for you, right?" John once observed. "Why should mine be any different?" The loving mother and son are seen here at the wedding of Maria Shriver to Arnold Schwarzenegger on April 26, 1986. (*Steve Heaslip/Cape Cod Times*)

Despite Ted Kennedy's many flaws, Jackie remained utterly devoted to him. He was always there for her after JFK was killed, and he even negotiated her marital contract with Aristotle Onassis. The two are seen at the wedding of Jackie's daughter, Caroline, to Ed Schlossberg on July 19, 1986. (*Cape Cod Times/Steve Heaslip*)

Jean Kennedy Smith never wavered in her belief that her son, William Kennedy Smith, was innocent during his rape trial in December 1991. During the ordeal she proved herself to be a tough, formidable woman, qualities she would later display as U.S. ambassador to Ireland (1993–1998.) Mother and son (with Robert Kennedy Jr. visible behind them) are seen arriving at court days before "Willie" was acquitted. (*Acey Harper/ Time Life Pictures/Getty Images*)

The Kennedys have always loved sailing. Here, Jackie and her companion Maurice Templesman (far right) go for an outing off of Martha's Vineyard in August 1993 with, left to right, President Bill Clinton, Ted Kennedy Jr., Victoria Reggie Kennedy, Ted Kennedy, Caroline Kennedy, Washington lawyer and activist Vernon Jordan, Ed Schlossberg, Hillary Clinton, and Chelsea Clinton. (*Kevin Wisniewski/Rex Features*)

Caroline Kennedy and Edwin Schlossberg, seen here in November 1993, have been married for more than twenty-five happy years. *(Rex Features)*

After Aristotle Onassis, Jackie found love again with diamond merchant Maurice Tempelsman. Though the two were a perfect match, it wasn't to last: Less than six months after this picture was taken, Jackie would be gone, the victim of lymphoma, on May 19, 1994. *(Brian Quigley/Time Life Pictures/Getty Images)*

Eunice Kennedy Shriver (left) and Sargent Shriver (far right) with their daughter, Maria, and her husband, Arnold Schwarzenegger, at the premiere of his movie *True Lies* in Westwood on July 12, 1994. *(Ron Galella)*

Ethel's sons Michael and Joe Kennedy, with John Kennedy Jr., campaigning for their Uncle Ted in 1994. (*Kevin Wisniewski/Rex Features*)

A deeply grieving Pat Kennedy Lawford embraces her nephew Christopher at his brother Michael's funeral in January 1998. Michael had died in a skiing accident in Aspen. (*Kevin Wisniewski/Rex Features*)

John F. Kennedy Jr. gives his wife, Carolyn Bessette Kennedy, a kiss on the cheek during the annual White House Correspondents dinner on May 1, 1999, in Washington. The two had a somewhat challenging relationship marked by difficult arguments and passionate reconciliations. (*Tyler Mallory/Getty Images*)

Ethel Kennedy and her daughter Rory await news of John Kennedy Jr.'s missing plane on July 17, 1999, the day Rory was to be married. Tragically, they would soon receive word that John, his wife, Carolyn, and her sister, Lauren, had all perished in a crash. (*Kevin Wisniewski/ Rex Features*)

Senator Edward Kennedy speaks to his sister Eunice outside his Senate office on February 12, 2002. "I am asking you to please take a good, long look at yourself," Eunice once told her brother. "You must change the way you want to be perceived by others, and govern yourself accordingly." (*Vince Dewitt/ Cape Cod Times*)

At the 29th Kennedy Center Honors dinner at the Department of State in Washington, D.C., in December 2006. Left to right: Congressman Patrick Kennedy, Sargent Shriver, Jean Kennedy Smith, Eunice Kennedy Shriver, Victoria Reggie Kennedy, Senator Ted Kennedy, and an unidentified guest. (*Greg Mathieson/Rex Features*)

Ted and Vicki Kennedy, seen here on September 16, 2008, always had a lot of fun together. Many people credit Vicki with having changed the senator for the better. She certainly helped him recognize his shortcomings and live a much better and happier life. *(Cape Cod Times/ Steve Heaslip)*

Ted Kennedy's recent diagnosis of brain cancer did not stop him from stumping for Barack Obama during the latter's presidential bid in 2008. The two men appeared together a year later at the signing of the Edward M. Kennedy Serve America Act at the SEED Public Charter School in Washington, D.C. *(Ron Sachs/Rex Features)*

Ted Kennedy's two wives, Joan and Vicki, walk to St. Francis Xavier Church in Hyannis during the funeral procession for Eunice Kennedy Shriver on August 14, 2009. The two women had definitely managed to forge what many considered an unlikely friendship. *(Darren McCollester/Getty Images)*

Of course, Joan was very distraught over the death of her former husband, Ted Kennedy. Despite their difficult relationship, she always had a great deal of forgiveness for him. Toward the end of his life, he tried to make amends to her for the problems he had caused her in their marriage. Joan is seen here with her son Patrick Kennedy as they arrive for the funeral at Our Lady of Perpetual Help Basilica in the Mission Hill neighborhood of Boston. (*Washington Post/Getty Images*)

Ted's children, Patrick, Kara, and Ted Jr., and his widow, Vicki (along with President Barack Obama), at the funeral mass for Senator Kennedy on August 29, 2009. "He always believed that our best days were still ahead," the family said in a statement, "but it's hard to imagine any of them without him." (*Rex Features*)

The picture of grief. Ted Kennedy's wife, Vicki, on the day of the senator's funeral, responding to friends and former staff members who'd gathered on the steps of the Senate to pay a final tribute to the Massachusetts Democrat. Kennedy's hearse paused at the Capitol before moving on to Arlington National Cemetery, where he was buried near his brothers, John F. Kennedy and Robert Kennedy. (*Rex Features*)

As the only surviving child of President Kennedy and Jackie, Caroline Kennedy remains, for many, the living embodiment of Camelot. Here she is at the signing of the Health Care Bill in Washington, D.C., on March 23, 2010. (*Rex Features*)

In many ways, Ethel Kennedy is today the family's matriarch. Few have had as much courage as Ethel, who raised eleven children on her own after the murder of her husband, Bobby Kennedy. She is seen here on January 21, 2011, at a Justice Department ceremony commemorating the fiftieth anniversary of Bobby's swearing-in as U.S. attorney general. (*Mark Wilson/Getty Images*)

On February 14, 2011, President Barack Obama presented Jean Kennedy Smith—the youngest daughter of Rose and Joseph and the sole remaining member of the Kennedy family's golden generation—the 2010 Medal of Freedom. Jean, who would turn eighty-three six days later, is currently the secretary of the Board of Trustees of the Kennedy Center. "In some ways it seems like a lifetime ago," Jean said of the family's storied history, "and in other ways...just yesterday." (*Ron Sachs/Rex Features*)

beware of anyone who says that John was a certain way and always acted a certain way," said Richard Bradley. "In fact, he was never consistent, always fluid in his thinking and in his reactions. His thinking was never monolithic. He was also smart enough to know how simplistic his public persona was. He understood that JFK Jr., as a cultural figure, was completely disconnected from the reality of his true character and personality. In fact, he understood the culture and the mechanisms of culture better than most people because he had lived it all his life. He was attached to people's memories, and that was okay with him, if a little frustrating. He understood that there were special demands on him, though. Just because of who he was."

Certainly, it was relatively easy for some of the other Kennedys to go into politics and start with a clean slate. After all, who really knew anything about Ted's son Patrick? And who even knew who Bobby's son Joe was? And could anyone pick out Kathleen Kennedy Townsend from a crowd, other than in her own state? Not really. Those politicians were distinguished by their fathers and their family lineage—and then later by their politics—but John came with all sorts of baggage having nothing to do with his parents but rather with what people thought of him specifically. What they wanted him to be. What they expected him to be. Therefore, he was reluctant to just jump into politics and do battle with all of those preconceived notions. He wanted to take his time. He wanted to think about the best way to proceed. Yes, he was interested in public service—but at his own speed, in his own time.

It would be at this juncture of his life—the time following his mother's death—that John Kennedy Jr. became seriously involved with a woman he had dated only casually a few years earlier. With the passing of time, she would confound and confuse as much as she would bewitch and beguile. She would also turn out to be his greatest encourager. If John had been granted the gift of old age, it's likely that this particular woman might have been someone he, in his senior years, would have looked back on as one of his most seminal relationships even though it's doubtful that they would have ended up together for the rest of their lives. She was likely destined to just be an important chapter in the great book of his life and times. However, as it would happen, she would be John Kennedy Jr.'s last love. She would be his wife. And not until death would they part.

Carolyn Bessette

*C*arolyn Bessette was born in White Plains, New York, on January 7, 1966, the youngest child of William and Ann Marie Bessette. The couple also had twin daughters, Lauren and Lisa. Her father was an architectural engineer, her mother a schoolteacher and school administrator. When Carolyn was four, her parents separated and soon after divorced, her mother later marrying an orthopedic surgeon with three daughters of his own. The blended family then moved to Greenwich, Connecticut, where Carolyn went to elementary and high school. In 1983, she enrolled at her mother's alma mater, Boston University, from which she graduated in January 1988 with a BA in elementary education.

"She was a popular, very interesting girl," said Mary Cullen, who knew Carolyn very well at this time, having been raised in the same neighborhood. "She was one of those girls who seemed to have it all, good looks, a great personality, smarts. She could be self-involved, though. I remember spending many nights with her over coffees where all we would do would be to talk about her and her life and her boyfriends. As we would be walking out the door at the end of the night, she would turn to me and say, 'And what about *you*? We never talked about *you*!' But she was so entertaining, you didn't mind the moments of self-absorption. She would say, 'I'm not self-absorbed, am I? Tell me the truth.' Then we would spend a half hour talking about whether or not she was self-absorbed."

From all accounts, Carolyn was not only model beautiful with her long brown—and later blonde—tresses and deep, penetrating eyes, but she was also funny and warm, the kind of young woman most men found irresistible. "Guys loved her," said Stewart Price, who knew her after she graduated from college. "She was tall—five feet ten and, I guess, a size six—flirty, fun, stunning. We'd laugh because I knew her motto with men was something like, 'Get them. Train then. Drop them.' The other thing about her is that she was a hugger," he continued. "She was constantly hugging everyone as they came and went from her day, and not just a polite hug but a real bear hug. She would also touch you a lot when talking to you, always making contact with you."

Richard Bradley, who would be the executive editor of John's *George* magazine in a couple of years, said of Carolyn, "She had so much physical charisma. John had a charisma to him too, obviously, but he had charisma that was borne of a cultural obsession with him. Carolyn didn't have any of that but she could walk into a room and command the room by sheer physical presence, not because of what people knew of her family or what they thought of her, but merely because of her physical intensity."

In 1988, Carolyn appeared on the cover of a cheesecake calendar called *The Girls of Boston.* Afterward, she posed for fashion photographer Bobby DiMarzo, flirting with the idea of maybe becoming a fashion model. She certainly had what it took in terms of physical appeal, though, as described by Oleg Cassini, who met her in Boston at a fashion show, "It was almost extreme—the sharp features, the alabaster skin, bright fire engine red lipstick, long blonde hair pulled tightly back, simple jewelry, little makeup other than lipstick. It was very spare, the look of the future, a kind of WASP-patrician appearance, the sort of thing that appealed to Calvin Klein. She had expressive eyes and a fetching way of moving her head and smiling. Her appearance made a statement—the vibrant big-city female professional."

Eventually, Carolyn ended up working in retail at a Calvin Klein boutique in Chestnut Hill, outside of Boston. That job eventually led to another in the corporate headquarters of Calvin Klein in New York. Calvin Klein was a big fan of hers and felt she was a terrific representative of his company, eventually moving her into the public relations department.

John actually first met Carolyn a year before he began to get serious about her. At the time, he was still with Darryl Hannah. His friend John Perry Barlow—the American poet, essayist, and political activist—recalled, "It was a difficult time in his life. John wanted to do the right thing. We were at Tramps, a nightclub [in the fall of 1993]. He was in a sad mood. He told me, 'I have met a woman and I can't stop thinking about her. I don't want to act on this now because I want to be true to Darryl.' He said, 'Darryl and I are having some difficulties, but I truly want for this thing to work out between us.' I asked, 'Who is she?' He said, 'She's an employee of Calvin Klein. Somebody ordinary.' I responded by saying, 'John, if you can't stop thinking about her, she must not be that ordinary.'"

One thing led to another and Darryl decided that she wanted to "take a break" in her relationship with John. It seemed to not be going anywhere. She wanted marriage, but for years he had been resistant. Therefore, she was now thinking about going back to Jackson Browne— or maybe it was just a ploy to make John jealous. At any rate, John wasn't sure how he felt about it. However, he did know that if Darryl was to be out of the picture, he wanted to get to know Carolyn Bessette. So he took Carolyn away for the weekend, to the sleepy beach town of Emerald Isle on the southern Outer Banks of North Carolina, where they stayed at a rental resort called Sea Song. They were accompanied on the trip by John's cousin Anthony Radziwill and his wife, Carole, both of whom liked Carolyn a lot and in fact decided that she was much better for John than Darryl. However, as often happens in long, complicated relationships, John and Darryl reunited when Darryl said she wanted to give it one more try, and John felt he owed it to her. Within days of his weekend getaway with Carolyn, John came clean with her, telling her that he was in an on-again/off-again relationship with someone else, that it was troubled, that they had been "on a break" but that now he was going to try again with her. Though Carolyn would say that she admired John's honesty, he would one day live to regret ever having opened up to her about Darryl.

A year later, John and Darryl were close to ending it—again. Meanwhile, Calvin Klein's wife at the time, Kelly Rector Klein, invited John to a charity function and then to the showroom for the fitting of some custom-made suits. It was she who reintroduced him to Carolyn. Upon meeting her again, John was, this time, bowled over by her. He immediately ended whatever was left of his relationship with Darryl Hannah.

"It was like one day we turned around and Carolyn Bessette was in the picture, and she stayed," recalled Gayle Fee, who works for the *Boston Herald*. "The first time he was spotted with Carolyn was in Martha's Vineyard. It was my scoop. They were out boating. A paparazzi got a photo of them and JFK Jr. was sort of helping her either out of or into a sort of diaphanous black skirt, and she was quickly known as this mystery girl in the white thong. Since everyone thought he was still with Darryl, this was quite a big deal. If I recall, her hair was more brown at the time than it was blonde. Everyone wanted to know who this new girl was. . . . it was a real sensation for a while."

John Perry Barlow remembers one of his first meetings with Carolyn: "We were at a café near Lincoln Center in New York City. Then we left to see the Financial Center in southern Manhattan. There, we passed many hours talking, till two or three a.m. We didn't talk about people, but of our views of life. Carolyn had the air of a chic hippie. If she was allowed to be totally free, I think she would have worn faded and psychedelic clothes. She was a little odd, believed in astrology, very carefully studied the stars. She was also interested in the tarot. At the end of the evening I said to her, 'Do me a favor. Fix me up with someone like you, will you?'"

"I remember the day John called me and said, 'Dude, I've met the one,'" Stephen Styles recalled. "I said, 'John, where have I heard that before?' And he said, 'No, this time it's for real, my friend. Wait until you meet her.'

"About a week later, he invited me to meet Carolyn at Bubby's, a restaurant in Tribeca just up the street from John's place. When I walked in, there was this girl sitting at a table talking to some people in a real animated fashion with this super personality just sort of filling the room, saying something about how much she loved the place's pecan pie. She was lean and angular, tall, with her hair sort of pulled back from her face, light makeup on. As I walked over to her table, here comes John from the men's room, with a big smile and wearing the black knit cap that I happened to know was the last gift his mother had ever given him. He said to me, 'Buddy, this is the girl I was telling you about.' She flashed me pretty much the greatest smile ever and—bingo! We spent the whole afternoon laughing and talking.

"I remember that we talked about John's flying. He had started taking lessons after his mom died. He said, 'Mom wouldn't have allowed my flying even for a second.' To which Carolyn said, 'Smart lady, your mom.' I asked her, 'You're not so thrilled with the fact that John's taking flying lessons either, are you?' She replied, 'Between you and me, I think he's got a screw loose.' We laughed. 'No way will he ever get me up there, I can tell you that much.'"

In the summer of 1994—just months after Jackie died—John decided he was serious enough about Carolyn to bring her to the Kennedy compound to meet the family. It was while at the compound with John's family that Carolyn got her first taste of the way John was perceived by his family. Everyone seemed to be involved in some sort of political or philanthropic endeavor—everyone, that is, but John. No one pressured him about it—they just didn't bring it up at all. It somehow seemed wrong or, at the very least, inadvertently hurtful that everyone talked about their many ventures, leaving John out. He was taking flying lessons. That was his project at the time. Fun, but not exactly significant—which, if anything, mirrored the way he was viewed by the family.

"What do you want to do with your life?" Carolyn asked John, according to what she later recalled to her friend Mary Cullen.

On its face, Carolyn's was a simple question, but was it ever loaded! Though embarrassed to admit it, John said he wasn't sure how to answer the question, that he had been thinking about it for some time and was hoping to soon find something that would distinguish him—but he didn't know what that was, not yet, anyway. This probably wasn't easy for him to admit. However, his admission seemed to bring them instantly closer, as Carolyn would later remember it. Prior to this time, John had seemed distant and removed. However, here in Hyannis, at the compound in which he had spent so much time with family and loved ones, he was different. He was reaching out to her, being honest, and she found it compelling.

In the months to come, whenever John had an idea as to how he might proceed, Carolyn took great interest in it and enthusiastically spoke with him about it. It doubtless made John feel that the relationship had great potential because it mirrored some of the great marriages he had seen in his own family. After all, behind many of the great Kennedy men had often been a strong, powerful woman—such as had been the case with his own parents, Jackie standing behind Jack, loyal to him, no matter what. Even before them, of course, his grandmother had stuck with his grandfather even in the darkest of times.

"The greatest power couple in our family has to be my aunt Eunice and uncle Sarge," John told Jacques Lowe, the Kennedy family photographer. The two had met to go over photographs Lowe had taken in the 1960s, which he now wanted to donate to the JFK Library. "That's what I'm looking for in my own life," he said, holding a picture of Eunice and Sarge taken by Lowe. "A woman who will support me the way my aunt supports my uncle. That's golden, what they have," he said. "If I could find that kind of woman, I'd be a happy man."

Rose Kennedy Dies

On January 22, 1995, Rose Kennedy passed away at the Kennedy family compound in Hyannis Port from complications of pneumonia, just a few months short of her 105th birthday. At her bedside were Ted, Vicki, Pat, Jean, Eunice, Ethel, and many of her grandchildren. As well as her five surviving children, she had thirty grandchildren and forty-one great-grandchildren.

In his memoir, *True Compass*, Ted Kennedy wrote that Rose's death "came as an even more heartbreaking blow than I could have anticipated. It was not as though I hadn't understood for some time that this was going to happen. Mother had grown enfeebled (in body, but not in spirit) from a series of strokes even before she turned one hundred." Ted gave a stirring eulogy for his mother during her funeral Mass at St. Stephen's Roman Catholic Church in Boston, where Rose had been baptized. "Mother knew this day was coming, but she did not dread it," he said. "She accepted it and even welcomed it, not as a leaving but as a returning. She has gone to God. And at this moment, she is happily presiding at a heavenly table with both of her Joes, with Jack and Kathleen, with Bobby and David."

"At Rose Kennedy's service, there was bedlam outside the church," recalled *Cape Cod Times* photographer Steve Heaslip. "There was a huge crowd outside the church, and when Arnold Schwarzenegger came out of the church with Maria Shriver the crowd started chanting, 'Ah-nold! Ah-nold! Ah-nold!' He was visibly upset and looked angrily at the crowd. You could tell that he thought that was inappropriate. There were carloads of Kennedys at that funeral. I don't think I have ever seen that many Kennedys all in the same place, and all with that exact same smile. It was a little overwhelming."*

---

* Rose's daughter Rose Marie—Rosemary—did not attend the services for her mother. However, in July 1995, she would visit the Kennedy compound at Eunice's and Ted's behest. Now seventy-seven years old, she was a rather large woman with thick glasses and short, jet-black hair. Rose spent a weekend in the Big House with Ted and Vicki and was often seen sailing with Sargent and Eunice. She had two nuns from the home with her the entire time, neither of whom were dressed in habits but instead wore blue jeans and colorful T-shirts with whimsical Cape Cod graphics on them.

After the service, the family went to Hickory Hill, where Ethel had arranged for a catered meal in Rose's honor. Everyone was present except Ethel's son Michael. It was later learned that he had checked himself into an alcohol rehabilitation program.

"It's just so hard to believe," Ethel was overheard saying to her sister-in-law Pat. "First Jackie. Now Grandma."

For Ethel, Rose's death was another big blow, because the two women had been neighbors at Cape Cod for so long. Contrary to what a lot of people may have thought—and what had been reported about them in the press—she was truly attached to her and thought of her as a great friend as well as a mother-in-law. The two had spent countless hours together planting flowers on the expansive property and talking about family matters, trying to make decisions about myriad problems, always coming together as the backbone of the family. Ethel treasured those moments. Even in Rose's declining years, Ethel took comfort in knowing that she was right next door at the compound, and that she was okay. It had been incredibly difficult for Ethel to watch as Rose's condition deteriorated over time, and she dreaded the day Rose would be gone for good. Now that day had come.

"But you still have me, Ethie," Ted Kennedy told her as he held her tightly in his strong arms.

"I do, don't I?" Ethel said, looking up at him with a sad smile.

"Mother loved you so much," he told her in front of the others. "And you remember what she would always say, don't you? She would always say, 'No matter what happens, God wants us to be happy. After all, birds sing after a storm...'"

Ethel finished Rose's quote: "...so why shouldn't we?"

Pat, too, had a very difficult time with Rose's passing. She still hadn't gotten over Jackie's death, which had hit her hard. In fact, it was safe to say that Pat still hadn't reconciled Jack's or Bobby's deaths either, even though those tragedies had occurred so many years earlier. The same could be said of most of the Kennedys, though, and whenever there was a family funeral—such as Rose's—it all came back to them, the overwhelming sadness, the emotional devastation, the terrible grief they felt, first, when Jack was murdered, then when Bobby was taken from them. All of it was always present, just under the surface. Somehow, they managed to prosper and even grow as a family despite it, but it was always there.

Pretty much all of the Kennedys were present at the compound after Rose's service, including John, of course, who had brought Carolyn. It was the first time she was present for an important family occasion, and as always, she made a favorable impression on everyone. After meeting her for the first time, Jean pulled John aside and, in front of a gaggle of his cousins, told him, "Now, don't you dare mess this up, John. She seems like a good girl." She then slapped him lightly—playfully—across the face. "I'm watching you," she warned him, "but more importantly, so is Grandma." She pointed to the heavens above. John had to laugh. "Then I know I'd better toe the line," he said, smiling at his aunt.

Paparazzi War Zone

*A*s often happens when people sense they are perfect for one another, things moved very quickly between John Kennedy Jr. and Carolyn Bessette. By late summer 1995, the two were living together in John's loft at 20 North Moore Street. They soon became a Manhattan staple in that they were quite social, always attending parties, dinners, galas, and charity events, constantly being photographed coming and going. Yet Carolyn never seemed very happy. Though she loved John deeply and was privately very content with him, the intrusion of paparazzi everywhere she went—even when she was not with John—had quickly become more than she could handle. She'd never wanted to be famous, she just wanted to date John Kennedy Jr., and even though she fully understood that the two notions—fame and John—went hand in hand, that didn't make it any easier for her whenever she saw those long black lenses poking out from behind a parked car or some bushes.

Publicist R. Couri Hay, a friend of the Kennedys, recalled, "Over time, a strange phenomenon began to occur where Carolyn's image was concerned. Simply put, people began to hate her. All you ever saw were pictures of her looking really pissed off and stories about how mad she was, and people began to think, hey, what right does she have to be so unhappy? I soon began to see her not as an asset to John, but as a liability. He had big plans, or so he told me once. He had his eye on the Senate one day, and, who knows? Maybe even the presidency. But she couldn't even handle Tribeca; how was she going to handle Washington?"

Stephen Styles recalled, "Friends would come to me all the time and ask, 'Why is she so pissy? What does she have to be so unhappy about? She's got JFK Jr. What's wrong with her?' And I would defend her, saying, 'But you don't know her, she's nothing at all like those pictures you've seen, like those stories you've read.' It didn't matter. The perception was being engraved in stone that she was ungrateful and difficult, and it quickly got to the point where there was nothing anyone could do about it."

In truth, some collective jealousy of Carolyn Bessette was inevitable, especially from the women of America. In particular, women of all generations felt a real connection to John Kennedy Jr., whether it was motherly, sisterly, or sexual. If America had a prince he was it, and she was the woman who had landed him, and no one had ever heard of her. Who was she? There was a real cultural fascination about her, and a sense that if she was going to be the woman who landed the prince, the least she could do was share him with people, be open about her life. Be outgoing. Be what people expect from someone in that role. This was expecting an enormous amount from her, because Carolyn Bessette was, at the end of the day, a very private person.

This cultural cattiness about Carolyn created an ongoing dynamic because the tabloid press coverage of her put her in direct opposition to John. No one was going to write anything negative about John. Even the editor of the *National Enquirer* had told John that the publication's audience didn't want negative stories about him. And since all stories about celebrity couples hinge on conflict, because happy couples don't sell, if they weren't going to write negatively about John, then who would be their target? It was preordained to be Carolyn. Or as Richard Bradley so aptly put it, "She could have been as beautiful as she was and with the personality of Mother Teresa and it still probably wouldn't have made any difference."

That the tabloid media generate millions of dollars in revenue by publishing stories based on nothing but the unfettered imaginations of their writers is something Carolyn Bessette never really considered—that is, until such stories began to be fabricated about her and her life. "She would be standing in a checkout line and there on a rack would be a magazine whose cover would be some ghastly, awful picture of her glaring at someone, and the headline was about how she and John were fighting. She just couldn't ignore it," said Mary Cullen. "First of all, it infuriated her. Then it hurt. 'I don't know what to do about it,' she told me one day, 'because John doesn't want to hear about it. He keeps saying he has had to live with it all his life, as if that means I should be okay with it, too. But I'm not.'

"It was a huge frustration for her because she saw the obvious link between the fabricated stories and the unflattering pictures, and it became an issue between her and John. It soon mushroomed into what she saw as a communication problem. After all, she worked in PR. She felt that maybe there was something that could be done to mitigate the damage that was being done. 'Maybe we could figure something out, if he would just talk about it,' she told me. 'Maybe we could strategize things better instead of just walking out into the middle of a freaking war zone every single night of the week. There has to be a better way.' In the end, she just wanted to be heard, but it was a subject John didn't want to discuss. It turned into, 'The fact that it bothers me should be enough for you to care, but it's not. Why is that?' You know how every couple has that one fight they keep having over and over again without any hope of resolution? This was theirs."

The irony is that John never had a problem with the tabloids, prior to this time, anyway. In fact, he subscribed to them and, in a strange way, had an appreciation for them. He enjoyed the narrative some of the reporters would spin to tell a good—even if untrue—story, mostly because John also loved to tell a good story. And besides, what was being written about him was far enough from the truth that it didn't matter to him.

Adding another layer to an already unhappy situation, some of the New York paparazzi began to dislike Caroline because they felt she had poisoned John against them. He had always been very nice, but now, almost overnight, he was combative. Suddenly he was confronting the photographers, screaming at them to "get the hell out of the way," and becoming confrontational.

At one point, John even called Jacques Lowe, an award-winning photojournalist who once served as the official campaign photographer for JFK, just to discuss with him photographers and how they might be better handled. "It's completely out of control," John said, "and I don't know what to do about it."

"My best advice is for you to tell Carolyn to just accept it and roll with it," Lowe told John, according to his memory of the conversation. "Since her public image is obviously being shaped by tabloid photography, the least she can do is smile, for God's sake. Even if she doesn't mean it, she has to smile, John. No more frowning or scowling or putting a hood over her head. That's just the way it has to be. Otherwise, she's going to be perceived as a new kind of Kennedy woman, all right. The pissed-off kind!"

"Of course I have tried to tell her that," John said, "but she won't listen. The other thing is that her mother is encouraging her that she shouldn't have to put up with it. And I wish she'd stay out of it."

"Oh, no. Once the mother gets involved, forget it," Jacques said. He told John that his mandate would have to be to make both Carolyn and her mother understand that "if Carolyn is going belong to you, she's also going to belong to the world," Lowe concluded. He reminded John that likely no woman in history abhorred paparazzi as much as John's own mother had, "but you never saw pictures of her glaring at them. Even when she was angry at them, she somehow looked beautiful. Rage can actually be attractive," he told John, "that is, if you know how to pull it off."

"Yes, but I'm afraid there will only ever be one Jacqueline Kennedy Onassis," John said.

Jacques Lowe had to agree.

John's Risky Proposition

John Kennedy Jr. was always interested in the media. In fact, one of the reasons he usually tolerated photographers was because he knew they had a job to do, that they served a purpose, whether it was to provide mindless entertainment to the masses as a diversion from people's troubles, or to document some important touchstone moment in history. John not only was fascinated by celebrity and the way people handled it, as we have seen from his relationship with Madonna, but also was intrigued by the way the rich, famous, and influential molded and shaped their images for public consumption. John had seen the way the public was now reacting to Carolyn Bessette as a result of the way she was captured by paparazzi, and though it bothered him a great deal and he thought it grossly unfair, it intrigued him just the same and in many ways reinforced for him the wisdom of the way he had always dealt with the media. "He assumed the best about people and never became cynical about their motives," his close friend Dave Eikenberry said, "and that's amazing, given the sycophants and leg humpers he had to deal with every day. It took enormous fortitude for him to stay well grounded in the face of his bizarre celebrity, but he did it."

"As I see it, even the trashiest tabloid writer has a responsibility that he clearly does not take seriously—shaping the way people think of others, and by extension, the way they perceive themselves," John told this author in 1994. (Interestingly, he introduced himself to me simply as "John Kennedy," leaving out the "F." and the "Jr.") "It's all tied together. When it's about politics, the way the media reports and distorts or otherwise makes decisions about the way to ultimately present information to the masses can, obviously, have huge ramifications. This is a subject that has long interested me."

Before his mother died, John often talked about publishing a political magazine. Jackie was ambivalent. On one hand, she was happy to see that he had passion for something, and publishing was certainly an interesting proposition. Of course, she and her family had always been on the other side of the equation, often trying to control the way they were perceived by the media and, by extension, the public. However, she had started a career as a photojournalist many years earlier, and Jack had also worked as a reporter. So maybe John's idea wasn't that much of a stretch. But Jackie wasn't sure. "John, you're not going to do the *Mad* magazine of politics, are you?" she asked, which couldn't have made John feel very supported. He said no, "But I thought it was good advice to keep in the back of my mind [in terms of] what direction we wanted to go," he later told Larry King. Then Jackie got sick and John's idea was derailed for a bit. When he eventually mentioned it to Carolyn Bessette, she thought it was terrific. The more the two of them discussed it, the more persuasive Carolyn was—and the more John began to believe that the venture had potential.

Things moved quickly. Soon, John had partnered with an old friend, Michael Berman—who had a background in public relations and marketing, but none in publishing—in the idea of a political magazine that would emphasize not only politics but also pop culture, along with how society views politics. It would be a political lifestyle magazine—that was the best way to describe it—and they would call it *George*, as in George Washington. The two then went about the business of raising the money for the venture—in the area, they learned, of about $30 million.

It obviously wasn't difficult for John Kennedy Jr. to network in the publishing business. Magazine and newspaper publishers eagerly accepted his calls and took meetings with him. Most of the executives who met with John saw something in him that they didn't know existed because he didn't give a lot of interviews to the press and, other than the tabloid fictions, not a lot was known about him. They found that he actually had keen insight into the cultural habits of others. He understood, or at least tried to understand, what made people tick. This was partly because he always made calculated choices to remain tethered to "normal" people in his life. He socialized with celebrities at fund-raisers, but that was about it. His friends were not all in show business and they weren't all in politics. He had friends in all walks of life. Therefore, he understood people, which would serve him well as a publisher. Also, he had known and was still friendly with many politicians, and had a strong foothold in that world just by virtue of his famous lineage. Of course, all of the Kennedys were just as immersed in that world, but none were JFK's only son. As John Kennedy Jr., he was a guy who had special access. In other words, he could call the president of the United States and it was likely he'd get through—and likely on the first try.

As it happened, it would be Pierre Salinger, who had been the White House press secretary to President Kennedy, who set John on the right path with *George*. Salinger, who was living in Paris at the time, was visiting Georgetown when John asked to take a meeting with him. "This guy is historical," he told Carolyn in front of friends over drinks. "He's an old friend of my dad's, and he knows media like no one's business."

"Yes, John and Carolyn Bessette met with me," Pierre Salinger recalled many years later. "I had known John all of his life, so I was proud to see how he turned out. He was well-spoken, intelligent, ambitious. I was also impressed with Carolyn. She shared John's vision for a political magazine. She didn't say a lot; she felt to me like a quiet power. Of course, my job, as I saw it, was to talk him out of such a risky idea."

John and Carolyn met Pierre at a restaurant in Georgetown, John wearing a black jacket and red tie, Carolyn a brown Prada suit. "It's far too risky a proposition," Pierre Salinger told him, according to his memory of the meeting. He warned the young Kennedy that he would "lose your shirt in this venture," reminding him that most magazines fail in their early stages of development.

"We're aware of that," John said, referring not only to himself but also to Carolyn at his side. "But there's nothing like it on the market. It would do for politics what *Rolling Stone* did for rock music," John said. "Politics is, today, driven much more by personality than ideology. That's what this magazine is about."

"But why not just write a column for *Vanity Fair*, or something like that?" Pierre asked.

John laughed and glanced at Carolyn, who did not betray the way she may have felt about the idea. She just sat quietly, sipping her vodka and grapefruit juice. John said he could sit down and write a column for *Vanity Fair*, which would take about an hour out of his day. Or he could devote "my life to a project that actually matters to me," he said, "like this one."

"Again, it's too risky, John," Salinger persisted. "Why not just work for your uncle Teddy in the Senate?"

At that, even Carolyn had to chuckle. "You may as well forget trying to talk him out of this thing, Mr. Salinger," she finally said. "He's going to do it. He really believes in it."

"And what do you think, my dear?" Pierre Salinger asked her.

"I think it's great," she said. "Only someone like John could make it work, though," she added. Then—even though there was probably a lot more she could say—she looked at John to fill in the blanks, as if recognizing that it was his place, not hers, to continue. Before he had a chance to speak, Pierre asked John another question: "Is this your way of entering politics?"

"Not right now," John said after pondering the question for a moment. "But in the future, who knows?" He noted that he could most definitely see himself running for office one day, but that at this time in his life he liked "the proximity to it that a magazine like this could afford me."

Pierre Salinger had to smile to himself. He would later admit that the idea of John Kennedy Jr. in politics appealed to him greatly, mostly because he knew how incredibly proud his father would have been to witness such a development in his son's life. "And you know, your concept is not really such a stretch," he told John. Salinger then cited JFK's fabled debate with Nixon as a perfect example of personality over ideology. "Even though your dad had it all over Nixon, it was his image that helped him win the debate as much as it was his politics," said Salinger, according to his memory of the conversation with John. "So, in a sense, what you're proposing isn't new. Yet it feels new just the same, doesn't it?"

Of course, John's father, JFK, did grasp the vital importance of image-making in American politics. He was in office at a time when television was becoming the primary medium for news-gathering and he, more than any president before him, knew how to use this new medium to its—and his—best advantage. After JFK, Ronald Reagan and Bill Clinton successfully used the medium, while others, such as LBJ and Richard Nixon, never really understood it, as future historians would point out.

"Well then, okay, let me see what I can come up with for you," Pierre Salinger told John Kennedy Jr.

George

*T*rue to his word, a couple of days after their meeting with him, Pierre Salinger called John Kennedy Jr. with the idea of having him contact Hachette Filipacchi Media, the world's largest magazine publisher. Headquartered in France, its interests would later include book publishing. "I knew that the French loved the Kennedys," Salinger would recall, "mostly because of Jackie's celebrity there. And I had a strong sense that David Pecker [who at the time was in charge of the magazines' operations in the United States] might be interested in what John had to offer."

John met David Pecker over lunch at an Italian restaurant on East 60th Street. "He arrived on his bike with his briefcase slung over his shoulder," recalled Pecker, who also remembered being "skeptical" once John explained his idea. "I told him that magazines about politics and religion don't sell," said Pecker. "Why should I invest Hachette's money in this? He said he'd put celebrities on the cover—commercialize the covers. He handed me the results of a direct mail campaign which he had paid for himself. It cost him hundreds of thousands of dollars. That's how confident he was, and it was reassuring to me that he was willing to put his own money at risk. When we finalized the deal [in February 1995] we had dinner at Rao's at 114th Street and Pleasant Avenue in Harlem. After dinner, he just walked over to his bicycle and put his cap on. As he was going down 114th Street in the middle of the night, photographers were all chasing him."

Once word got out that JFK Jr. was publishing his own magazine, the novel idea caught on like wildfire, and enough advertising space was purchased to fill eight issues before the first one was even published! The magazine's headquarters would be centralized in an office building at 1633 Broadway, and as far as Kennedy and his partner, Michael Berman, were concerned, everything was off to a good start. The partners spent the next few months staffing the publication with people such as Matt Berman (no relation to Michael), who became its creative director, and Richard Blow (now Richard Bradley, after he changed his last name to his mother's maiden name) as senior editor and, eventually, managing editor. The first five issues would publish bimonthly, after which the intention was for the magazine to hit the stands every month.

The plan was for each issue to feature an interview that John would personally conduct with a notable person. For its first issue, John and Gary Ginsberg, senior editor and head of legal affairs for the magazine, flew to Montgomery, Alabama, to interview former Alabama governor George Wallace, the infamous white supremacist and JFK's fabled nemesis. They spent three days interviewing the politician, who by this time was elderly and nearly deaf. It went fairly well; Ginsberg and Richard Bradley returned to finish the job. Later, Kennedy flew to Los Angeles with Michael Berman to interview the movie producer Oliver Stone, which did not go quite as well. Stone, who had made the controversial film *JFK*, could not resist peppering John with questions about his father and about his opinion of the Warren Commission's report on President Kennedy's assassination. John didn't mind talking about his father, but the assassination was definitely off-limits. "Why would any person think it's okay to talk to a stranger about the way his father was murdered?" John would later ask one of his staffers. Perhaps Stone couldn't be blamed, though. After all, the subject of Kennedy was one of his great passions. He was sitting with the president's only son—what else could he do but ask questions? Still, John excused himself from the interview, which was ultimately canceled. The story was replaced by one about Warren Beatty.

Many of the interviews John did for his magazine would turn out to be more revealing of him than they were of the subject. From the kinds of questions John asked, one could sense that he was thinking about going into public service and was realizing that once in that arena, he wouldn't be able to leave it easily, if at all. It was as if he wanted as much data as he could amass before taking the leap. He was on a quest and was smart enough to use the venue he had created to gather for himself as much information as possible, not just about politics but also about a whole spectrum of experiences from a wide range of subjects, such as Muhammad Ali, Colin Powell, Madeleine Albright, Louis Farrakhan, Don Imus, Bill Gates, and Northern Irish politician Gerry Adams.

In September 1995, John Kennedy Jr. officially announced the publication of *George* at a much-touted press conference in the rotunda of Manhattan's Federal Hall National Memorial on Wall Street, which stands on the site of Federal Hall, where George Washington was inaugurated as the first president of the United States. There were more than 150 reporters and photographers present, including this author. John joked that he hadn't seen that many newsmen in one place since the results of his first bar exam created a media firestorm. He was funny, interesting, candid, and, more than anything, struck people as a humble guy just wanting to make a valid contribution, much like so many other members of his family. "My uncle Teddy said that if he was still speaking to me by Thanksgiving, I'm not doing my job," he said with a grin. He then displayed the cover of the first issue of *George*, featuring Cindy Crawford dressed as George Washington (it would be the October-November issue of 1995). Of course, her clothing was scant, the point being, as John explained, that "politics doesn't have to be dull. It can be interesting, even tantalizing."

For the rest of the year, John would work hard to promote his magazine, doing television and radio interviews with the likes of Howard Stern, Larry King, Barbara Walters, and Oprah Winfrey. He even had a cameo on the sitcom *Murphy Brown*, starring Candice Bergen. It was the first time most Americans got to know John as an adult—witty, candid, funny, but also, in his own way, quite guarded. Like his mother, he presented himself in such a way that an interrogator sensed it would be inappropriate to ask him personal questions. It felt somehow wrong to bombard him with questions about Jackie, for instance.

One of the biggest splashes the magazine made was when John put Drew Barrymore on the cover dressed as Marilyn Monroe for the September 1996 issue. The caption read, "Happy Birthday, Mr. President." A great many people were confused by that particular cover, but if you knew John, it made a lot of sense. Of this cover, John told Oprah Winfrey, on the first show of her eleventh season, "My family is used to all manner of controversy. In the grand scheme of things, this probably didn't register too high on the Richter scale."

"John was very aware of the cultural semiotics of the Kennedy iconography," said Richard Bradley. "He was actually trying to do a couple things with that cover. One was to push back the boundaries of the box in which he found himself. The Kennedy iconography had become like a straitjacket for John, and playing with it that way was his Houdini-like way of moving his muscles and bones to get out of the straitjacket. He was saying, 'Back off. Give me some room. I'm a living breathing person, I'm not a statue.' At the same time, he was also saying that it was dangerous to set such iconography in stone. He was saying, 'My father was human and, yes, he had a full life and it's not all untouchable. He is not a deity.'

"That said, John was also very protective of his parents' memories," continued Bradley. "For instance, he was unhappy about the Seymour Hersh book *The Dark Side of Camelot* for the simple reason that he thought it was reductive of his father's place in history. He felt that his father was a great man and that this kind of book was destructive of his memory. John was very conscious of the power exerted by the memory of his father. He could very easily step outside his own personal memories or the personal impact his father had on him and see what his father meant to the masses, how his father had inspired people. So to have writings that sort of splattered mud on that shining inspiration seemed to him to be shameful.

"Beyond that, he believed very strongly that public service was worthwhile, that we should encourage people to go into it and that if we violate the personal lives of politicians, we not only discourage people from going into the field but we distract the public's attention away from serious issues."

Though off to a good start, within a year the magazine would begin to founder. "Yes, the magazine had its problems," said Richard Bradley, "and we did our best to address them, but it wasn't easy. Was it a political magazine or was it about celebrities? The audience didn't understand it. John wasn't willing to compromise or pander, either. Maybe if he had been, it would have been more successful, I don't know.

"John went to Cuba to interview Fidel Castro. Imagine the history of that! It was amazing to even think about, let alone for it to happen. But it didn't seem to make much of a difference. What should have mattered to people didn't matter as much as one might have thought.*

"That said, John was true to his convictions; he wanted the magazine to be taken seriously, so he rejected interviews with pop culture people that might have given the magazine a broader appeal. Therefore, we ended up with Billy Graham, Dan Quayle, Gary Hart, and Cokie Roberts...and maybe a younger demographic didn't really get that or want that from us."

"Sometimes, it felt like a college newspaper," said a former staffer. "John was always a presence, but he had a casual way of commanding and the staff liked him a lot, even if sometimes they were confused by him. For instance, we were once on deadline, feverishly trying to get the magazine out, and he walked in and said, 'Let's go to the park and play touch football.' People were appalled, but they appreciated a gesture he made in the fall of 1996, when the staff was again putting an issue to bed. John decided they needed to unwind: He called the Yankees front office and procured forty-one skybox passes to a World Series game. No one complained that time."

---

* It should be noted here that John's cousin Maria Shriver beat him to the punch where Castro was concerned, having conducted her own interview with the Cuban dictator for NBC News in 1988.

John Proposes to Carolyn

$\mathcal{A}$t John Kennedy Jr.'s side throughout the development of *George* had been his greatest encourager, Carolyn Bessette. In fact, three weeks before the press conference to unveil the first issue, John had asked Carolyn to marry him, giving her a ring of diamonds and sapphires, a duplicate of a ring Jackie once wore and loved. Much to John's surprise and dismay, though, Carolyn didn't exactly jump at the chance to be his wife. In fact, she said she wanted to think it over.

"She called me and said, 'John popped the question last night,'" recalled her friend Stewart Price. "I said, 'Wow, congratulations, sweetheart! When's the wedding?' And she said, 'Well, I didn't say yes. I told him I had to think about it.' 'What's the problem?' I asked her. She paused for a long moment. 'Of course I love him,' she said. 'But I really have to think about it. Do I want to live my life under a microscope? Running from photographers every day? For the rest of my life?'"

Another problem Carolyn identified as she got to know John was that she saw so many people around him who, either consciously or not, preferred to identify themselves as people who knew him rather than as individuals with their own independent lives. "He saw that all around him and was very conscious of it," observed Richard Bradley. "I think he was torn between the fact that sometimes it was useful to have people like that around and the fact that, on a deeper level, he knew he was better served by having people who could tell him when they thought he was wrong or making a mistake, people who could retain some distance from him."

"Carolyn didn't want to get sucked into John's world and lose her own identity," said Stewart Price. "Or, as she told me, 'I don't want to be a Kennedy. I am who I am and I'm okay with that. I don't want to just be JFK Jr.'s wife, and let that be what defines me for the rest of my life. That's not what I want.' Knowing her, I understood that. 'What are you going to do?' I asked her. 'I'm not sure,' she said."

Indeed, it would be months before Carolyn would officially accept John's proposal.

Relationship Woes

*T*hough obviously in love, John Kennedy Jr. and Carolyn Bessette were also two very passionate and expressive people who sometimes allowed their heated emotions to get the best of them. When they argued, it was as if they completely lost their minds, at least according to those who knew them best. "They definitely knew which buttons to push in each other," said one close friend. "They knew how to inflict the most damage."

There had always been the problem of stalking paparazzi, and discussion of that particular subject seemed always to end in a fight. However, in the last six months or so, a new and arguably more serious difficulty had begun to emerge: Carolyn's insecurity, which, as it often did, manifested itself in her extreme jealousy of other women. She was beautiful, charming, smart—the total package, if ever there was one. Yet the manic way people usually reacted to being in John's presence—especially the way some women behaved—caused Carolyn to second-guess his loyalty and fidelity to her. As far as John was concerned, he never gave her reason to be suspicious because he had never cheated on her. He simply wouldn't have done it. It wasn't in his makeup. Or was it?

In fact, John had taken Carolyn away for a weekend while he was still technically in a relationship with Darryl Hannah—and Carolyn would never let John forget it. "John was sorry he had ever told her about Darryl," said Stephen Styles. "Carolyn had that on him and she was relentless with it. 'If you cheated on Darryl with me, how do I know you're not cheating on me with someone else?' Of course, he and Darryl had been on a so-called break at the time, and it had been Darryl's decision to call for the hiatus, but that didn't matter. It became a part of the running narrative of their relationship that John had 'cheated' on Darryl with Carolyn, and now Carolyn couldn't trust him. John could simply glance at a woman in an admiring way and he would later be accused of having been interested in her. From waitresses to celebrities, it didn't matter—if she was an attractive female and Carolyn sensed that a moment had occurred between them, it all but guaranteed a good fight."

As an example, John and Carolyn were having breakfast with two mutual friends at Socrates restaurant in Tribeca on a Sunday morning.

Throughout the meal, an attractive woman across the room kept trying to get John's attention. She seemed to be winking at him, flirting with him. He couldn't help but notice, as did, of course, Carolyn. Finally the woman came over to John's table and asked if she could have her picture taken with him. He declined. However, she was persistent. She went on and on until finally John relented. She handed someone a camera and the picture was taken. "You know, this isn't the first time we met," she then said to him. He looked confused. "Do I know you?" he asked. "You don't remember?" she responded, somewhat mysteriously. "A couple of years ago? On the Cape?" John looked at her closely, scrutinizing her face as if trying to place her. "Nope, I don't remember," he said finally. "Sorry." After an uncomfortable moment, the woman said, "Well, it doesn't matter. Thanks, John. Bye." And with that, she was on her way.

"What was that about?" Carolyn instantly wanted to know.

"Beats me," John said. After sizing him up, Carolyn then asked why John appeared to be so nervous. "Is it because you thought she was hot?" she asked, throwing down the gauntlet. Now his temper was rising. He repeated that the lady in question was just a fan. Carolyn still wasn't satisfied, though, and continued to push. "Jesus Christ, Carolyn," John said, now raising his voice. "You're so much smarter than this. Come on!"

"And what's *that* supposed to mean?" she demanded to know.

Before he knew it, he was having a full-on argument with his fiancée in front of his friends about something that, in his view at least, couldn't have been more ridiculous. Finally, Carolyn excused herself and left the table in tears. John was visibly shaken. "I don't know what to do now," he said to his friends. "Should I go after her, or what?" he asked. His friends said yes, he must. He then got up, threw some money on the table, and said, "What a great way to start the day, huh?" before running after her.

By the winter months of 1996, John and Carolyn were, according to what he was telling his friends, "averaging about one good knock-down, drag-out a week," and usually over the same two themes: her unhappiness with paparazzi and her insecurity about other women. Because the two were so constantly monitored by the very photographers who had become an issue in their relationship, it seemed only a matter of time before one of their dustups would be caught by a video camera.

It happened one Sunday morning in February 1996. After having breakfast, John and Carolyn were seen arguing in Central Park, with her laying into him, screaming at him and gesturing wildly. He retaliated by shouting back at her, his face twisted with rage, his leashed Canaan dog, Friday, looking up at him. At one point, she hauled off and hit John hard on the shoulder with a closed fist. John seemed to be unglued as he grabbed Carolyn by the shoulders and shook her. As she pulled away, he snatched her hand and yanked the engagement ring from her finger. The struggle continued as he pushed her and she pushed back, all the while hollering within inches of each other's face. At one point, the two appeared exhausted and dazed, with John sitting down on the curb and crying in front of stunned passersby. Carolyn bent over him. "Give it to me," she said to him. He reached into his pocket, pulled out the ring, and handed it to her. With ring in hand, Carolyn knelt down next to John and touched her head to his. Then she began to cry as well. However, he pushed her away. The fight began again, with Carolyn trying to wrestle the leashed dog from John. "You got your ring," John told her. "You're not getting my dog!" After a tug-of-war, John finally said, "Fine!" and gave Carolyn the leash. Finally, the two of them began walking down the street together, talking to each other quietly and appearing to be making amends.

"She accused me of having an affair with [fashion model] Claudia Schiffer," John later explained to another one of his cousins when talking about the fracas. "And I lost it. I don't even know Claudia Schiffer," he added. "The jealousy gets to you. I lost it. She kept pushing and pushing and pushing until, finally, I just lost it."

John and Carolyn Marry

John Kennedy Jr.—arguably one of the most famous men on the planet in 1996—managed to do the seemingly impossible when he married Carolyn Bessette. He did it in secret, far from the prying eyes of stalking paparazzi and the rest of the news media. On September 21, 1996, the glamorous couple exchanged vows on remote and inaccessible Cumberland Island, the largest and southernmost of Georgia's barrier islands. Only eighteen miles long and three miles wide, the island has no grocery stores, no gas stations, and very few commercial establishments. In fact, only about a hundred people live there, and most of them work for the National Park Service.

At the time, the handsome Kennedy scion was thirty-five, his new wife thirty. The ceremony, which was romantically illuminated by the glow of candles and kerosene lamps, took place in a white clapboard chapel, the First African Baptist Church, a quaint one-room church on the north end of Cumberland Island, which had been built by former slaves back in 1893 and then rebuilt in the 1930s. No longer an active church, it serves as a local historical monument. Constructed with whitewashed logs, it has only eleven handmade pews that seat no more than forty people, providing the setting for certainly one of the most intimate of Kennedy weddings.

John looked, as expected, quite dashing on his wedding day in a midnight blue wool suit and white vest, one of his father's shirts, JFK's watch, and, along with his groomsmen, a blue cornflower as a boutonniere. It had been JFK's favorite flower. Carolyn was elegant in a pearl-colored silk crepe bias-cut gown with a veil of silk tulle, along with long gloves. Her bouquet was fashioned from lilies of the valley, Jackie's favorite flower. Holding her hair in place was a comb that had belonged to Jackie, a gift from Caroline. Father Charles J. O'Byrne, a Jesuit priest who had known John ten years earlier when John was a student at New York University, performed the ceremony by reading from the Bible with a small flashlight.

Most certainly, when that single dreamy color photograph of John and Carolyn made the magazines and newspapers, he kissing the hand of his beaming bride, most Americans were taken completely by surprise. If anything, it proved that even the most high profile of celebrities can have private moments if there are people around them who adhere to one simple practical principle: Don't talk about it.

It's true that everyone involved in the planning of the wedding—from the caterer and the florist to the designers and family members—wanted the best for John and Carolyn. But to say they kept a big secret for him would be inaccurate. Actually, they didn't know he was even getting married. The weekend before the service, John called the people on the guest list and told them he was having a party on Cumberland Island and that they should make plane reservations right away and be sure to attend. He was adamant that it was a party they would not want to miss. Everyone took the bait. Of course, to everyone's credit, no one blabbed about the "party" either.

But of necessity, the occasion had to be kept small and intimate. Thus many of John and Carolyn's personal friends could not attend; there simply wasn't enough room to accommodate them. Those family members present who managed to keep the couple's secret were: Anthony Radziwill, who was ill at the time with cancer and who served as John's best man; Caroline Kennedy, who was matron of honor, and whose daughters, Rose and Tatiana, were flower girls, and whose son, three-year-old Jack, was the ring bearer; Caroline's husband, Ed Schlossberg; Ted and Vicki Kennedy; Jackie's sister, Lee Radziwill; Ethel's son Bobby Kennedy Jr.; Jean's son William Kennedy Smith; Maurice Tempelsman; and members of Carolyn's family, including her mother, Ann Freeman, and one of her sisters, Lisa Bessette.

The greatest loss, without a doubt, was that Jackie wasn't present to see her son wed. "Carolyn resembled Jackie strongly," John Perry Barlow said, "in the sense that her nature was complex, subtle. Jackie was the most exceptional woman I ever knew, and Carolyn reminded me of her. Carolyn, too, was unconventional, charismatic, and, like Jackie, she had so much compassion for others. But I think what they had in common overall was their absolute femininity. Carolyn's femininity was almost mystical. She was something like the Delphic oracle. I never knew a woman who knew how to handle men so well. As for John, her love for him was at once absolute and tinged with ferocity."

The reception for the newlyweds was held at the Greyfield Inn, a luxury hotel on Cumberland Island that was built in 1900 and was once the home of Margaret Ricketson, daughter of Thomas and Lucy Carnegie. It's so secluded that guests can only arrive by ferryboat or helicopter. The Kennedys rented the entire thirteen-room inn for the occasion, buying out anyone with prior reservations. During the festivities, the couple cut a three-tiered butter-cream wedding cake. Then a very happy Ted Kennedy toasted the happy bride and groom as his own wife, Vicki, beamed at him. "Jack and Jackie would have been very proud of you and full of love for you as you begin your future together," he said while raising a flute of champagne to the newlyweds.

PART TWENTY

Michael's Story

Michael Kennedy's Troubles

On New Year's Eve 1997, many members of Ethel Kennedy's family—some of the third generation of Kennedys and their children who were the fourth—were at the scenic Sundeck restaurant atop Aspen Mountain, surrounded by spectacular views of snow-covered mountains, enormous aspen trees, and a cobalt blue sky as far as the eye could see. Eating duck quesadillas and sipping hot chocolate in the wood-and-glass-structured restaurant designed as a very large chalet, they excitedly talked among themselves while waiting for the mountain to clear of skiers so that they could play a very dangerous game, which they unofficially called ski football. The Kennedys had been playing it all week, dividing themselves into teams and then careening down the slopes on skis at high speeds, usually without the protection of helmets, and without poles and dangerously close to one another. They would jettison a football toward each other, making improvised goals. It was a fast and furious kind of game, the kind of sport most people wouldn't have dreamed of playing, and which the ski patrol definitely did not endorse. More than once that week, the Kennedys were told that the sport was too deadly to be played on the icy slopes and that it was feared the family was encouraging such activity among the other vacationers. Someone was going to get hurt, the patrol warned—or worse. By late afternoon, the sun was going down, the temperature was dropping, and the hills were becoming icy. Though most skiers were finished for the day, the Kennedys—there were thirty-six in their party—were waiting for everyone to get off the slopes so that they could begin their game.

* * *

Michael LeMoyne Kennedy, thirty-nine, was an expert skier and quarterback who loved the risky sport so much he enjoyed taking video footage of his siblings as they raced about the mountain, throwing a small plastic football among themselves. "Michael really had a tremendous drive for living on the edge. Whether it was kayaking or skiing, he just did it," says James Hilliard, a longtime friend and former business associate of Michael's. "It wasn't arrogance in his personality, it was just his strength."

The year 1997 had been a terrible one for Michael. Previously he had been running his brother Joe's Citizens Energy Corporation as chairman, and helping his uncle Ted win his 1994 Senate reelection campaign. He was thought of as a giving, openhearted person, a philanthropist and expert political strategist who, it was believed, could very well forge his own political career. Like many of his relatives, he cared deeply about a wide range of causes, some of which most people would never even consider. For instance, he was a founding board member of the Angola Education Assistance Fund and had traveled often to Angola, where he helped open a Roman Catholic university. He also helped to fund loans to female-owned businesses in Ecuador and even operated a company that provided heat to 150 homeless shelters in Boston. He was also scheduled to begin work on Joe's campaign for governor of Massachusetts, a campaign that would have to be abandoned because of the public spectacle of Joe having asked his ex-wife, Sheila Rauch, for an annulment. Coinciding with Joe's high-profile scandal, unfortunately, would be his own.

In April 1997, Michael was accused of having had a sexual affair with the family's former babysitter, allegedly beginning when the Massachusetts girl was just fourteen. It was an awful and, for some, unbelievable accusation. Yet from all available evidence it seemed to be true, and it was made even more disturbing by the fact that his wife, Victoria, reportedly found him with the girl in one of the bedrooms of their enormous harborside home back in 1995. Michael and Victoria were so close to the parents of the girl in question, they had attended the inauguration of Bill Clinton together. Understandably, everyone was quite shocked, hurt, and angry. As a result, Kennedy's entire life seemed to implode. The incident would eventually mark the end of his sixteen-year marriage to Victoria, which had resulted in three children—Michael, Kyle, and Rory. She actually stayed with him after finding him with the girl, hoping that the marriage could be repaired. Michael explained that he had been under the influence of liquor when he bedded the babysitter, and promised to get help. He then sought professional treatment for his alcoholism in 1995 and, a year later, for sex addiction. But then he continued seeing the girl—who was very mature for her age and, from most accounts, also in hot pursuit of Michael—and being intimate with her. When Victoria found out about that, she finally had had enough and left him.

What was so strange about the situation to many people inside the family's circle was that Michael Kennedy had always been such a level-headed and reasonable person, not given to the errors of some of his siblings and cousins. However, something seemed to have snapped in him in 1994—it's not known what—and he began drinking heavily and becoming extremely depressed. Eventually, Michael admitted that he had been intimate with the girl, but said that she was sixteen, not fourteen, when he first started having sex with her. She was nineteen when the story broke. Apparently the two had been involved for several years, to the complete astonishment of Michael's family. He passed three polygraph tests with his version of events, which didn't make the relationship any more acceptable, but at least it didn't rise to the level of statutory rape, according to the laws of Massachusetts. Even so, Michael Kennedy still appeared to a lot of people to be nothing more than a megalomaniac with no moral code whatsoever—an image that the Kennedys had long fought against as a family, but that persevered just the same, precisely because of these kinds of sordid events. To people who thought that the Kennedys played by a different set of rules and didn't care what others thought, this episode was all they needed to prove their belief. As the *New York Post* put it in its April 26, 1997, headline, "They're At It Again!" What made Michael Kennedy want to do such a thing? And what made him think he could get away with it? These were the questions with which his stunned and disappointed family members grappled, and to which they never really got good answers.

Because the babysitter's parents declined to press charges, the whole ugly mess eventually blew over, but not without a great deal of heartache suffered by all concerned. "Ethel was so humiliated by it," recalled a close friend of hers. "Frank Gifford [the Hall of Fame football player, TV announcer, and Victoria's father] had been a very close friend of hers for many years, as was his present wife, Kathie Lee. It was just very sad."

"I can tell you that Michael also felt horrible about what he had done," says close friend John Rosenthal, a real estate developer. "His biggest concern was the impact it had on his children."

Kennedy tried to move past it, though. In October 1997 he appeared at an AIDS conference at the John F. Kennedy Library in Boston. At the time, there were also reports that he and Victoria might reconcile after they missed at least one divorce hearing and were then seen dining together in various Boston restaurants. "Probably the central thing in Michael's life was his wife and his children," said Larry Spagnola, a documentary filmmaker and Michael's former Harvard roommate. "It was definitely his intention to reconcile."

It was around this same time, the autumn of 1997, that Michael and his brother Joe were mentioned in one of John's controversial editorials in *George*. In an effort, it has to be assumed, to be provocative, John Kennedy Jr. posed apparently nude for the photograph that accompanied the essay, showing only limbs, chest, and face as he pondered a dangling apple. The headline was, "Don't Sit Under the Apple Tree."

"I've learned a lot about temptation recently, but that doesn't make me desire any less," John wrote somewhat cryptically. About Michael, John speculated that his cousin "was looking for a hedge against mortality." He "fell in love with youth and surrendered his judgment in the process." He also suggested that Joe and Sheila Rauch "chased an idealized alternative to their life" and that Joe had "left behind an embittered life." Speaking about the public condemnation of both, he wrote, "Perhaps they deserved it. Perhaps they should have known better. To whom much is given, much is expected, right?"

To this day, it's often reported that John in the autumn 1997 article labeled his cousins the "poster boys for bad behavior." That's not true. The quote was out of context. The point Kennedy was making was that the public—not he himself—had decided that his cousins fit that description. He was actually defending his family members, not indicting them. "The interesting thing was the ferocious condemnation of their excursions beyond the bounds of acceptable behavior," he wrote. "Since when does someone need to apologize on television for getting divorced?" At the time, some people in the family apparently reacted to the press reports about the column, and didn't actually read it themselves. As a result, this became one of the rare times—and maybe the only time—that JFK Jr. at least temporarily fell out of favor with some members of the family. Of the editorial, Joe said, "I guess my first reaction was, 'Ask not what you can do for your cousin, but what you can do for his magazine.'"

Of course, such flare-ups were common among the third-generation cousins and often didn't represent anything more than just momentary venting. After all, they'd known each other since they were kids. They often argued. Joe had the kind of temper John didn't condone. And Joe always thought John was kowtowed to, made to seem more important than the other Kennedy sons because of his parentage. Still, though they didn't always get along, the cousins had a deep and abiding love for one another. Joe knew who John was at his core, and John knew the same of his cousin. Bobby better understood the context of what John was trying to say. "You have to read the actual editorial John wrote, not just the press about the editorial," he told this writer in November 1997. "Is my brother [Joe] upset about it? I guess. Maybe. But most of my family read the text and we knew what John was trying to convey. And even if some of us were mad, we're Kennedys. We don't stay angry for long. We can't," he said, laughing. "We're thrown together too much to stay mad at each other."

To celebrate the holidays, Michael Kennedy just wanted to be with his family in Aspen, nursing his wounds, relaxing and have a few laughs, not worrying about the media, its coverage either of John's editorial or of his own unfortunate exploits. With his mother, Ethel, back at the restaurant sipping cocoa and nursing a hurt shoulder from a tumble she had taken earlier, he and his family members went noisily up to the slope and then divided themselves into two teams—Michael the captain of one and his sister Rory leading the other.

Apparently the stakes were high. On the previous day, the score had been tied between the two teams. "We'll play tomorrow," one of the Kennedys had proclaimed, "and death to the loser."

"Oh My God, Not Again!"

*I*t was on this December 31, 1997, at about four in the afternoon, that a dangerous game of ski football was under way. At lightning speed, Michael Kennedy, who was once described by former U.S. Olympic ski coach Bob Beattie as the best natural skier he'd ever seen, set off down the mountain with his camera in one hand and a football in the other. "Photo op! Photo op!" he yelled out as he took photos of the others while skiing backward. Wearing a bright copper ski suit and no helmet or any other kind of protection, he was followed by his son, Michael Jr., fifteen, and daughters Kyle, thirteen, and Rory Jr., ten.

R. Couri Hay, a publicist, reporter, and friend of the Kennedys who had often skied these slopes with them, was present that December day and recalled the events. "I didn't play," he remembered. "Though I am a good skier, the idea of whooshing down Aspen Mountain playing football was beyond my athletic capabilities and, to tell you the truth, beyond my imagination, too. But they were such daredevils, the Kennedys, and I wanted to be part of the fun because I was a friend of Michael's. So I said, 'I'll carry the poles.' And that's what I did. I carried Michael's poles.

"After the first goal, which was made by Rory, Michael got serious about the game and gave the camera to a friend so he could concentrate on it. 'Michael! Michael!' someone called as the football sailed his way. Michael turned around to get the pass and he caught it. But in doing so, a terrible thing happened. He veered off the trail in his determination to get the pass and slammed into a massive spruce tree. It was awful. His skis hit the tree first, then his head hit and he just crumpled like a rag doll and fell backward onto his back. The crash was as loud as a head-on collision of cars. It was traumatic to witness. I was about twenty feet away and got to him as fast as I could, but I knew the truth immediately. I knew he was dead. Blood was pouring from his nose. His face had gone completely white."

There was chaos as frantic Kennedys descended upon Michael from every direction. Rory Sr. kicked off her skis and ran over to her brother. Trying her best to stay calm, she went to work on him. "There's no pulse," she screamed out. "There's no pulse! Somebody call the ski patrol!" She then laid Michael on his back, pried his bloody mouth open with her fingers, and began giving him mouth-to-mouth. Counting off, "One. Two. Three. Four," she breathed into his mouth and pounded on his chest, trying to get his heart moving again. "I've got a pulse!" Rory exclaimed. She then turned Michael on his side as he began to once again breathe, in order that he not choke. There was a fleeting moment of disbelief and exhilaration when it seemed as if Michael was going to be okay. Exhausted, Rory dug her hand into the snow and wiped her face with it before spitting Michael's blood from her mouth. She leaned in close to him. "Michael," she said to her brother through her tears, "now is the time to fight. Don't leave us," she begged him. "Do not leave us, Michael! Please! Please!" Meanwhile, each of Michael's three crying children made the sign of the cross and fell to their knees. No one told them to do so, it somehow just came naturally to them, as if by instinct. "As they kneeled in the snow and prayed," R. Couri Hay recalled, "their prayers were interrupted with their cries of, 'Please, God, not my daddy! Not my daddy!'"

"Our Father who art in heaven..." they began to pray, and they continued to pray and weep—along with all of the others present—until the paramedics arrived and began working on Michael. Finally, Rory gathered up the children and told them to "think good thoughts" as the paramedics fit Michael with a cervical collar and put him on a toboggan, covering him with a yellow blanket. "Let's go pray for Daddy," she told them through her tears.

"When I came upon him, it didn't look like he was aware of anything," says Davis Factor, an L.A. photographer who was skiing that day and stopped to help. "I don't think this guy knew what hit him."

"At this point, I started to back away from the scene because I realized that this was an intensely personal and tragic family moment," recalled R. Couri Hay. "As the toboggan took Michael down the slope, I took the poles and slowly skied behind the toboggan... it was eerie, unbelievably sad."

Michael Kennedy was dead by the time they got him to the hospital, the official cause listed as "massive head and neck trauma." In an instant, another Kennedy life was over. It was impossible to reconcile. "Oh my God, not again," Ethel Kennedy cried in the hall outside of the emergency room as she fell into her daughter Rory's arms.

Reckless or Accidental?

*O*f course, there was a great deal of media coverage about this latest Kennedy tragedy, much of it focusing on what was perceived by many critical observers as Michael Kennedy's reckless behavior, suggesting a kind of hubris that makes the family feel somehow invincible. It's actually a reductive and simplified way of looking at them. Yes, they're a big family that enjoys adventure, which obviously puts them in danger from time to time. It could be said that their passion for sports runs a close second to their passion for politics. However, much of the press about Michael's death suggested that he was just the latest Kennedy killed while engaging in some sort of sporting activity, as opposed to the truth, which is that he was actually the first. As for real "risk-taking," of course, most of the family will admit to a certain amount of it, but not so much in terms of their participation in sports as in what they have done as public servants. "My family has often been called 'risk-takers,' a phrase said with an undercurrent of opprobrium, an explicit or implied understanding that a life lived with such risk is inexcusable and unjustified," noted Max Kennedy. "It is true that my father took risks. But it is also true that nothing can ever be achieved without risk. In a book on the literature of ancient Greece, he underlined a sentence that read, 'Life for him was an adventure, perilous indeed, but men are not made for safe havens.'" When Max Kennedy and most of his other family members think of "risk-taking," they think of his father exploring the bottom of a communist-controlled mining operation in Santiago, Chile, in order to get a better understanding of the dangers faced by people working there. Or traveling to South Africa during a time in the 1960s when apartheid was simply unheard of by most Americans. Or going to the Mississippi Delta to assist in aiding starving children. Or meeting with gang members after the Watts riots. Or prosecuting some of the world's most notorious mobsters. But sports activities? While risky, they don't necessarily rise to the standard any Kennedys would consider particularly perilous. Maybe a more accurate explanation, although it too is weak, can be found in the notion of the so-called Kennedy curse, which encompasses all of the tragedies the family has suffered, something Sargent Shriver once dismissed by saying, "So be it." "The Kennedy Curse" is what screamed out of *Newsweek*'s cover, with a photo of Michael and a headline that read "Another Reckless Life—and Tragic Death."

As to whether or not Michael's death was the result of carelessness, maybe that was a different story. But even there, one would find some debate. One witness to the accident, experienced skier Ted Widen, recalled, "I felt they were asking for trouble. I like having a distance of about twenty-five to fifty feet around me when I ski," he said, "and these people, some of them were skiing at an arm's distance from each other. It was way too close. They were cutting each other off and barely missing each other on their way down. I remember thinking they were playing a very dangerous game. I didn't know they were Kennedys, by the way. I just knew they were a rowdy group of people playing a crazy game—and by the way, never in my life had I ever heard of playing football on skis. I told the friends I was with, 'Look, let's stay as far away from those people as possible.' Just as my group was getting ready to move to the side, down the hill comes one of the guys from that group, full steam ahead and just barely missing one of my friends. And he sailed right by us without a care in the world. I waved my fist at him and screamed out, 'Hey! Come on! Slow down!'"

Some of Michael's friends rose to his defense when magazines quoted witnesses as saying they thought the Kennedys had been out of control. One friend, Blake Fleetwood, wrote a letter to *Time* in response to its reporting of the accident, saying, in part, "Michael was the best all-terrain skier I have ever seen. He was skiing at a moderate speed on a well-lit and well-groomed intermediate slope, playing a game with his children, something many of us have done without incident for nearly 20 years. Like all sports, including ski racing and ski jumping, ski football has an inherent risk, but Michael's death was far from reckless; it was a tragic accident."

Michael's older brother Bobby Kennedy Jr. was particularly upset with R. Couri Hay, who contacted the *New York Daily News* and the *National Enquirer* immediately after the accident—before Michael even had arrived at the hospital—to file a firsthand witness report.

"Look, I want you to stop giving interviews about what happened to my brother," Bobby Kennedy told Hay in a very heated telephone call about a week after the accident. "You're betraying your friendship with Michael, with me, with all of us," he said. "What the hell is wrong with you, Couri?"

"I'm just telling the truth, Bobby," Hay explained.

"But you quote Michael as having said, 'We'll play tomorrow. Death to the loser.'"

"Well, he *did* say that."

"I don't give a shit," Bobby countered, according to Hay's recollection of the conversation. "Michael said a lot of things. No one would even know about it if you hadn't blabbed it."

"I'm a reporter," Hay said in his defense. "This is my job. You guys can't control the news."

"Jesus Christ, don't give me that bullshit!" Bobby said, exasperated. "You contacted the press before Michael was even at the hospital! That's terrible, man. Bottom line," Bobby concluded, "is that my mother wants you to knock it off."

"But your mother is quoted in *Time* as having had a conversation with an official at Aspen Ski Corporation asking her to stop the game."

"What!" Bobby exclaimed. "That's a lie! My mother never talked to anybody," Bobby said. "All of these stories are ridiculous. Stop talking to the press, dude. I'm serious."

"I can't promise that," R. Couri Hay said, holding his ground. "If I can save one life, one limb, one child from being hurt by calling attention to ski safety, I think it's my responsibility to do that."

"Fine, then," Bobby Kennedy said, sounding defeated as he ended the phone call.

Grace Under Pressure

*I*t was Friday morning, January 3, 1998.

"Bagels! We need bagels," Ethel Kennedy exclaimed. "And coffee. There will be a lot of people here. Do we have enough coffee?" As she ran about the house giving orders to servants like a general on campaign, it was obvious that Ethel was quite upset and just trying her best to hold it together. After all, friends and family would be arriving at the Kennedy compound in a couple of hours to pay their final respects to Michael, whose closed coffin sat in the parlor of her home facing a window overlooking the Atlantic Ocean. It was here that Michael had spent so much of his life with his loved ones, and it was here that they had all come back the previous night to say goodbye to him.

"The wake continued until almost midnight," recalled Brian O'Conner, a press aide to Joe Kennedy, "and Mrs. Kennedy was there the whole time, consoling, trying to make everyone else feel better."

Another close friend of the Kennedys, Philip Johnson, added, "It was very much an Irish affair. Being Irish Catholic myself, I had seen it before. Yes, laughter and the funny anecdotes of Michael's life, laughter about moments on the campaign trail and, yes, tears. A lot of tears. At times there were occasions when Mrs. Kennedy prayed and led some of us in prayer. Would that we all had her strength."

At Ethel's request, the Reverend Michael Kennedy, who is a distant cousin of the family, flew to Massachusetts from Ireland, where he is a parish priest, to assist with the wake. "She is a woman who relies on her faith to get her through these times," he said. "She believes in God's promise of a hereafter, and it sustains her."

"I'm so sorry this has happened, my love," Andy Williams told Ethel after the service, according to his memory. "I don't know what to say." He recalled that the evening had been so emotional, he was "near tears the whole time, just trying to hold them back because, you know . . . that's what we'd been doing for decades, ever since I sang at Bobby's funeral. Grace under pressure. I guess that's the best way to describe how we've handled these things."

"Now, now. You mustn't be sad," Ethel told him as she took her old friend's hand. "Michael is with David now. And with Bobby. They'll take care of him, Andy. He'll be just fine."

"But what about you, Ethel?" Andy asked. "How are *you* doing?"

Ethel gazed at Andy and, for just a moment, her eyes seemed to mist over and it appeared that she might begin to crumble. However, she quickly shook it off. "Andy, why don't you go find Bobby Jr. and tell him you're here," she said, changing the subject. "He would love to see you. Now, go. We'll talk later."

Of course, Ethel Kennedy was obviously a very strong, resilient woman, but one had to wonder just how much more she could take. Given a life checkered with so much tragedy, it seemed a wonder that she could muster the strength to be available to others during yet another crisis. It was clear to most observers, though, that an integral facet of Ethel's coping mechanism at this time involved helping others deal with what had happened to Michael, almost as if to distract and protect herself from the full impact of the tragedy. However, she appeared exhausted, as if she might buckle at any moment.

"Ethie, come and take a little walk with me," Teddy finally said as he took her by the arm.

"No, Teddy," Ethel protested. "No!"

"Just a little walk, Ethie," he insisted, his tone gentle but firm. "We'll be right back, don't worry."

She exhaled deeply. "Okay," she said, giving in to him. "Just a little walk."

Ethel and Teddy walked through the parlor, past Michael's casket, and out the door into the cool ocean air. Hand in hand, they slowly continued across the expansive green yard and then down to the beach, the same stretch of sand and sea upon which Ethel had spent many a day and night with her beloved Bobby and their children so many years earlier. A few moments later, Ted Kennedy could be seen holding his "Ethie" in his arms under a gray New England sky.

"Okay, Lord. The Kennedys Have Had Enough."

*T*he funeral Mass for Michael Kennedy was held at Our Lady of Victory Church in Centerville, a Cape Cod community near Hyannis Port. It was the same church in which Caroline Kennedy, Sydney Lawford, and Kara Kennedy had married. Referring indirectly to the way Michael died, Joe Kennedy, in his moving eulogy, framed his brother's athletic prowess as "one of the glories of his life and it should not be diminished by his loss." Always so eloquent, he added, "He was not made for comfort or ease. He was the athlete dying young of A. E. Housman's verse: 'Like the wind through the woods, through him the gale of life blew high.'" The service also included the reading of letters from President Clinton, Coretta Scott King (the widow of the Reverend Dr. Martin Luther King Jr.), and Nelson Mandela, the president of South Africa.

Andy Williams, who began the funeral by singing "Ave Maria," recalled, "I don't know what it was about this Mass, but this one was so hard. Maybe it was because some of us old-timers were just getting older and this kind of thing involving the younger generation was just so hard. In fact, I think that was it. You get to a point where it just becomes too much, and I think that's how we were all feeling that day. I barely got through the song, I have to say. I was standing up there looking at Ethel, and it was ... it was incredibly difficult."

Certainly no sight could have been more heartbreaking than that of fourteen-year-old Michael Kennedy Jr. struggling to hold up the front of his father's coffin after the Mass, and then breaking down into racking sobs after the casket was loaded back onto the hearse. "I just remember John Kennedy Jr. holding Michael Jr. in his arms with all of his might," said Gary Andover, another family friend who was also at the funeral. "I saw Sargent Shriver break down and his daughter, Maria, go over to him to hold him and support him because, for a moment, it looked like he might collapse. Michael's estranged wife, Victoria, also looked devastated. She was with her dad Frank Gifford and his wife Kathie Lee Gifford, who were holding the hands of Michael's little girls, Rory and Kyle. And of course, there was Ethel, her face so sorrowful. She seemed older, more fragile, and just so very sad. Eunice was at her side, holding her hand."

Michael's siblings, especially the brothers who were all so close, did what they could to hold it together during the Mass, but afterward they began to take comfort in what Michael had been to them, and how important he'd been in their lives. "On the hour-and-a-half drive carrying Michael's body from the funeral home in Hyannis Port to the cemetery in Brookline, we were told there was room for only one of us in the hearse," recalled Joe Kennedy. "But all of us [brothers] ended up going. Bobby and I squeezed into the front seat with the driver; in the back, Max, Douglas, and Chris scrunched in next to Michael's coffin. The Mass had been tearful. Bobby and I had both eulogized Michael. But now, in the car, the conversation was full of the great fun Michael was to us. We all laughed heartily, unfettered. A windowed partition between the front and the back muffled some of the conversation, and each of us kept pushing it back and forth in order to hear the stories better."

Though Michael's brothers were feeling somewhat better by the time everyone got to Holyhood Cemetery in Brookline, there was no avoiding the overwhelming sadness of seeing the mahogany coffin that held Michael's body ready to be lowered into the cold ground. Michael was to be buried with his favorite football and a medallion that marked three years of sobriety for him. "Everyone was in such absolute shock and feeling such tremendous grief, you couldn't even speak," said football star

Brian Holloway, a friend of the family's who attended the services, of the cemetery service. With him was his daughter Kerry, named after Kerry Kennedy, who is also her godmother. "We just put our arms around each other because there weren't any words," he said. "I was standing right next to John Jr. at the family plot where David Kennedy was also buried. John and I looked at each other and nodded sadly, and then I put my arm around his shoulder. He did the same, put his arm around mine, and we just stood there in disbelief that this terrible thing had happened to someone so young and so athletic and as full of life as Michael."

"I went over to John, who was standing with Carolyn," Gary Andover recalled. "Carolyn had her hair pulled severely back from her face into a little bun with just light makeup on. Her eyes were very, very red. She looked bereft and incredibly thin, though my memory of her was also that she moved with such facile grace she somehow reminded me of Jackie. Both she and John were dressed in black. They seemed so devastated. Two weeks later, I saw photographs of them from this awful day in some ridiculous tabloid being used to illustrate how unhappy they were in their marriage, which was most certainly not what was going on that day.

"I'm so very sorry your family has to go through this again," Andover told John as the three of them walked away from the cemetery, Carolyn at John's side.

"I know," John said. "It sure seems unfair, doesn't it? I'm really worried about my aunt Ethel, I gotta tell you. She doesn't look good to me right now."

Gary agreed and put his arm around John's shoulder as they continued walking.

"You know," John said, his voice sounding very weary, "they say the Lord doesn't give you any more than what you can handle."

"Yeah, that's what they say, all right," Gary agreed.

John stopped walking. Then, with a small, weak smile, he gazed up at a gray winter's Cape Cod sky and said, "Okay, Lord. The Kennedys have had enough now, thank you."

PART TWENTY-ONE

A Peaceful Time

Ethel's Change for the Better

On April 11, 1998, Ethel Kennedy turned seventy years old. In the months before her birthday, she had been understandably overwhelmed with grief at Michael's sudden death. In fact, for days afterward she simply couldn't stop crying. She was grief-stricken and inconsolable for so long, her children stayed close by her side. But then something seemed to change in her. With the passing of just a few months, she went through what appeared to be some sort of emotional transformation, the result of which was that she seemed to become more accepting of Michael's death and less angry about it than she had been about other deaths in the family.

As everyone who knew her well realized, there'd always been an undercurrent of suppressed rage in Ethel's personality, and it could be argued that it was with good reason. Ever since Bobby was murdered thirty years earlier, she'd suffered one heartache after another with her children. But maybe because of wisdom that comes with age, she had begun to realize that there was nothing she could have done about the unpredictable and often tragic ways life had unfolded for her and her family, so why bother wasting time being so incredibly angry about it? Or maybe she had begun to rely more on her Catholic faith than ever before, and she was finally finding a comfort in it that perhaps had previously eluded her. "She goes to Mass every day of her life," her daughter Kerry said at this time. "She prays on her knees before church, prays before every meal, and prays on her knees before going to bed."

With Ethel, it was always her actions that spoke volumes, not necessarily her words. She had always proclaimed in press interviews and at public events that she was just fine, even when she wasn't. However, by the time she turned seventy, she somehow did seem better. From all accounts, there was a certain tranquility and ease about her. She was more nurturing as well. "She's become the greatest source of strength to all of us," her oldest child, Kathleen, said right after Michael died. "She's filled with love. She makes people feel special. She listens. She validates us. She acknowledges us. She has created a safe harbor for all of us and, yes, we go there often." These days Ethel was more—to use a word she had chosen in trying to describe Jackie at the end of her life—"serene." Except that Ethel Kennedy was nowhere near the end of her life. She still had many years to live, so much more to give her family, and now, as she embarked on her eighth decade, she was truly living once again and not just going through the motions.

"What I think is that after the kids were grown and on their own, Ethel started to mellow," said one of her longtime friends. "So in a sense it started before her seventieth birthday. Gradually, she just became more relaxed. Let's face it, the biggest problem she faced was that the older boys were always in trouble. As adults, that trend seemed to continue, but she was much less invested in the outcome."*

"I remember that after Jackie died in 1994, that's when Ethel seemed to start down a better road," said her former assistant, Leah Mason. "'Jackie was so young and taken like that,' she [Ethel] said. 'How dare we not enjoy this life God has given us, while we still can?' She also said, 'I'm just going to try to be happier, you know?' She'd had a lot of misfortune in her life and I think she began to recognize that she'd let it get to her, though she never said as much. Playing tennis, going golfing, sailing…all the things that she had always done she was now really and truly enjoying, instead of just acting like it. 'Maybe the point of death is to teach us about life,' she told me."

Only Ethel's close family members knew of her sometimes overwhelming sadness and anger. Others simply enjoyed being in her company.

"I always knew that Ethel was a complex person," says her longtime friend the singer Andy Williams. "You knew that there was this sadness

---

* Ethel Kennedy's worries were not only about her own boys, but also relatives on the Skakel side of the family. The Martha Moxley murder, for instance, weighed heavily on her. As the story goes, the family of fifteen-year-old Martha Moxley were friends and neighbors of Ethel Skakel Kennedy's brother Rushton, in an upscale section of Greenwich, Connecticut. On October 30, 1975, the teenager and some of her friends walked one block to the Rushton Skakel mansion to attend a Halloween party. Before the evening was over, Martha would be dead, her partially nude body discovered the next day beneath a tree in the backyard of the Skakel home. A broken golf club, the apparent murder weapon, was found nearby. The investigation into the murder would last twenty-three long years, with Thomas and Michael Skakel, Ethel's nephews, under scrutiny. (The case would remain cold until Michael's indictment and conviction for the murder on June 7, 2002. He received a twenty-year sentence). It was just one more tragedy in a long list of them in Ethel's life.

about her and maybe a certain amount of anger, but if you weren't close to her, you'd never know it. She didn't want people to feel sorry about her. Plus, she had an image of being strong and stoic, and to a certain extent, that's the way the family promoted her. Therefore, I think she felt an obligation to be that sort of woman, at least for the world.

"Of course, having known her for more than forty years, she and I talked a lot about her sadness, but I would never divulge what she'd said to me," continued Williams. "But, always, there was that other fun-loving Ethel at the ready.

"I remember one of my birthdays, for instance, when she took me to a high-class restaurant [the Jockey Club of the Ritz-Carlton Hotel in Washington, D.C.] to celebrate. I had on a beautiful and expensive suit. She brought out a big cake and sang 'Happy Birthday' to me. As I was getting ready to blow out the candles, I leaned in and, sure enough, she palmed the back of my head and pushed my face right into the cake. 'Happy birthday, kiddo!' she said, laughing. But that was Ethel. I still get a Valentine's Day card from her every single year. On it she always writes, 'Will you be my Valentine, Andy? Love, Ethel.'"

Brian Holloway, the former NFL offensive tackle for the New England Patriots and Los Angeles Raiders, and his wife, Tammy, are good friends of Ethel's and of many of the other Kennedys. "What do you think the Celtics are going to do this year?" Ethel asked him one day when they were sitting out on the porch enjoying a beautiful, sun-drenched Cape Cod afternoon. She was always full of sports questions whenever she was in Brian's company. "Who's going to win the playoffs?" she would want to know. "Do you think the Rams should have left Los Angeles?" she asked. As they were talking, Ethel suddenly got an idea. "Come on, let's go see Dionne Warwick." It was so random a suggestion, but very much like Ethel these days. "I don't have anything to wear," Brian protested. "Oh, just wear what you have on now," she said. "You're a football star, you can get away with it." Within thirty minutes, the two were in Brian's car, racing to see Dionne Warwick at the Cape Cod Melody Tent in Hyannis. "And there we are in the front row enjoying the show," he recalled. "Afterward, we went backstage and, much to my amazement, Ethel and Dionne seemed like best friends! Who knew? Then Ethel and I went back to the Cape and we had a fabulous dinner. It was all so spontaneous and fun, I thought to myself, 'Wow, Ethel Kennedy sure knows how to live!'"

"Ethel is definitely the matriarch," Brian's wife, Tammy, recalled. "Everyone will be seated for dinner—her children and their friends—and then Ethel will walk into the room and everyone stands, led by her children. She sits, and everyone else follows suit and sits down, so there is definitely that kind of formality. Everyone in the family is very respectful of her.

"One thing I noticed over time is that she has French fries at every dinner. Whatever was being served, be it lobster, chicken, steak, or whatever, there would always be a bowl of French fries on the table. So I asked Ethel about it. And she said, 'Oh, that's what Bobby and I had on our honeymoon. French fries. So we have fries with just about every meal.'

"You definitely still feel Bobby's presence all over," Tammy Holloway continues. "For instance, Mrs. Kennedy still wears her wedding bands. I once asked her about it and she said, 'It would be like cheating on Bobby if I ever took them off, so I never have.'"

Every Sunday at 3 p.m. while the family is in residence, a priest says Mass in Ethel Kennedy's living room. If you happen to be at the compound at that time, you are expected to attend. "You honor that request, whatever your beliefs," said Tammy Holloway. "It's lovely, beautiful, everyone sitting around in couches and chairs in the living room while the priest says Mass. Sometimes the little kids get up and read scripture."

The main bathroom downstairs is the biggest attraction of Ethel Kennedy's house at the Kennedy compound, said Tammy Holloway. "Whenever someone new comes by, it's always, 'Have you been to the bathroom yet?'" she recalled, laughing. "Everyone who doesn't know better wonders why it takes so long for people to come out of the bathroom. It's because there are black-and-white pictures of Ethel and Bobby's entire life, everywhere—on the burgundy-and-white-papered walls and under Plexiglas on all of the counters. It's such a tribute to her life and times, all of the Kennedys represented with all of their children at different ages, different times of their lives. You'll see JFK here and Jackie there, Eunice, Sargent, Ted and Joan, all of the kids of the third generation, John Jr., Caroline—all of it displayed so lovingly. When you're in this bathroom, you feel that you have to stop and take in every single photograph because it really hits you that, truly, this is your American history just as much as it is the Kennedys.'"

In 2009, Ethel was in attendance at a Daughters of the American

Revolution benefit performance in Washington, D.C., with Ted Kennedy and her friends Andy Williams and John Glenn when she found herself greeted by a face from the past—her former personal assistant, Noelle Bombardier. "I actually didn't even know Mrs. Kennedy was there," Bombardier recalled. "I first saw Andy's manager and went up to him to say that I knew Andy from my days with Ethel Kennedy, and that I wanted to say hello to him. And the manager said, 'Why, Mrs. Kennedy is here too! Why don't you come backstage after the show and say hello?' The curtain then went up, I enjoyed the show, and afterward I made my way backstage."

As Noelle was walking down a hallway to the backstage area, she saw her former employer standing in a corner talking in an animated fashion to Andy Williams. She stood and smiled at her for a moment, remembering all of the rich history the two shared, much of it involving Ethel's lost son David. Ethel stopped talking to Andy and stared at Noelle with a look of astonishment as if she couldn't believe her eyes. It had been thirty years since the botched kidnapping attempt on Noelle's daughter that caused her to quit Ethel's employ. "Is that you, Noelle?" Ethel asked. "Is that really you?" The two women then embraced and had a warm reunion. "The years have passed, but we still look pretty good, don't you think, Mrs. Kennedy?" Noelle asked as she smiled at Ethel. "Heck, yeah, we do, kid," Ethel said, laughing. "You betcha we do!"

Flynn

On July 4, 1998, John and Carolyn joined the Kennedys for a major family celebration of the Independence Day holiday at the Kennedy compound. The festivities started with a special Mass under a tent in Sargent and Eunice Shriver's yard during which the sacrament of Communion was offered. Then there was a family cruise in Hyannis Harbor with at least thirty Kennedy relatives on board, including Rosemary Kennedy, who was visiting from St. Coletta's.

Carolyn Bessette Kennedy could roughhouse with them as if she'd been born into the family, chasing John's cousins around the property, playing football with them, jumping into the ocean and dunking them. On this day, she spent an hour on the sand with the youngest Kennedys of the third generation, trying to teach them how to do cartwheels and somersaults. Meanwhile, Ethel stood on the beach and admonished her, saying, "Carolyn, don't do that. You're going to hurt yourself!" John chuckled. "Don't worry, Aunt Ethel," he said, "she's made of rubber. I think it's all that yoga." Ethel had to laugh. "She's me at that age, you know?" she told John. "I used to be able to do somersaults too, way back in the Stone Age." The two smiled at each other and embraced.

An hour later, John and Carolyn took a walk out onto the pier. A photographer appeared from nowhere. John walked over to a bucket, filled it with ocean water, walked over to the photographer—who was snapping pictures the whole time—and threw the bucket of water at him. "Just thought I'd cool you down," John said, laughing. "It's really hot out here!" It didn't seem malicious, though. Rather, it was a light moment, so much so that the photographer started laughing, as did John.

Later, at the buffet table, John and Carolyn joked about how John had only complex carbohydrates on his plate—macaroni and cheese, potatoes, and corn. "Now that's what I call a meal, Kitty Cat," he said, using his nickname for her. Carolyn picked up a grilled steak and put it on his plate along with some avocado, fresh green beans, and some sliced tomatoes. "I don't know what I'm going to do with you," she said, kissing him on the cheek. Ted, witnessing the scene from his table, remarked to Pat, "God, those kids are so in love, aren't they? It's like watching Jack and Jackie again, all these years later."

Pat, eccentric as ever, was wearing an Independence Day–inspired leotard: one leg designed with white stars against a blue background and the other all red and white stripes. She also had on a colorful red baseball cap and a red, white, and blue ribbon around her neck. Pat seemed to be in a better mood on this day than she'd been in quite some time. She and Ted couldn't help but sit and watch John eat, laughing all the while. Since he was a kid, John had had a habit of eating his food very quickly while hunched over his plate with one arm around it, as if he were trying to protect it from being stolen. "No one's going to take your food away from you," Pat told him with a smile. As John and Carolyn sat talking to Sargent, Eunice, their daughter, Maria, and her husband, Arnold, a bunch of Kennedy nieces and nephews scurried about the yard chasing eastern cottontail bunnies. "You'll never catch them," John told the kids with a big grin. "Those things run faster than Kennedys, and that's really saying something." Then, gazing at Carolyn lovingly, he added, "Sometimes, though, it's nice to get caught."

Most of John's family adored Carolyn. They knew that she fully supported John in everything he wanted to do, and she represented, in their view, a real anchor for him. She had quit her job at Calvin Klein and was now taking trips to Europe for John on *George* business. At this time, John was upset that circulation had begun to drop off and was even worried that Hachette might close it down. He was courting other possible investors and Carolyn was behind him all the way. Though at first apprehensive about it, she was also now very supportive of his flying, and went up with him quite often. It was while soaring through the clouds with John, she said, that she felt closest to him. "We can talk up there with no interruptions," she told her friend Mary Cullen, "and if that's what it takes to finally be alone with my husband, then I'm all for it." It was funny, she said, but she just didn't feel any fear when she was with John. Other people in his life had said the same thing about him over the years. He was so secure and confident and capable no matter how risky the sport in which he was engaged—skiing, sailing, kayaking, flying—that he just seemed invincible. "I mean, what are the chances of JFK Jr. dying?" is how Carolyn put it, "and of little ol' me just happening to be there at the exact same time? That just would never happen." In fact, Carolyn said she was planning on taking flying lessons herself very soon so that the hobby would be something the two of them could truly share.

"I think they were coming to grips with a lot of their problems by the summer of 1999," said R. Couri Hay, "and were on their way to a serious rebuilding of their relationship. The fact that they were going to Rory's wedding was, I felt, a symbolic decision for them. I think they wanted to present themselves at the wedding as a united couple for the benefit of anyone who had lately heard otherwise of them. In the next year, I think they would have had a child."

"I know that they had been talking about having children," confirmed John and Carolyn's friend John Perry Barlow. Barlow says that John told him that he and Carolyn were trying to decide how to bring a child into the world knowing that the baby would be the subject of such intense scrutiny. "They were already in this unremitting klieg glare," he said, "and they couldn't imagine what it would be like with a child. Would it be fair to the baby? How would they, as parents, handle it?" These were their concerns, says Barlow.

What John really wanted was a son. He may not have been sure when it would happen, but he knew it would one day. And he wanted to name him Flynn.

John Kennedy Jr.—Running on Water

*I*t was July 1998 and Tammy Holloway and John Kennedy Jr. were sitting on colorful cotton towels on the cool sand of a stretch of beach at the Kennedy compound. John was wearing nothing but a blue swimsuit, and according to Tammy's memory, "he was so beautiful, just this amazingly chiseled body, the chest hair, the tousled black mop, the gleaming white teeth. He had a five o'clock shadow, too, very casual, very sexy. It was a beautiful, sunny morning on the Cape, and I was just so happy to be spending it with him."

"It's so good to see Brian again," John said, speaking of Tammy's husband. "He's so cool."

"He feels the same about you, John," Tammy said, according to her memory. "Thank you for having us here, really. We love coming here every July."

"Tell me, Tammy," John said, looking out at the sea with a pensive expression. "How many kids do you guys have now? What is it, like, a hundred?" he asked. He turned to her and smiled.

"Actually, Wendell makes seven," she said, returning his smile.

"Well, you must have a lot of help, nannies and that sort of thing," John said.

"No, actually we don't," she said. "I just want to raise my own kids, you know?"

"That's so awesome," John said. He told her that he and Carolyn definitely wanted children and that when they had them, he wanted to be a real part of their lives, too, just as his mom had been for him and Caroline. "She was there for us all the time, no exceptions," he said. "And she had a real code of behavior for us. I can still hear her voice," John continued. "'Just because you are a Kennedy doesn't give you license to be unkind to others. I don't care whether he is rich or poor, black, white, whatever...every single person deserves your respect.' That's what she used to tell us, and I daydream about telling my kids that." He lay back and closed his eyes, letting the sun wash over his already tanned face. "So, how did you and Brian meet?" John asked, his eyes still closed.

"It was a blind date," she answered.

"Wow," John said, sitting up again and now looking at Tammy with fascination. "So, okay. He's this big, famous football star, right? And you're a person in the so-called regular world. And the next thing you know you're married to this sort of celebrity, right? And you have this new life, photographers pestering you and all of that." He seemed to be turning the thoughts in his mind as he was speaking them. "So, how did you deal with it?"

"It's not easy," Tammy said. "I mean, you have to have a real strong sense of self. At first I wanted my old life back. I once had privacy and my own friends and all of a sudden I was thrust into this new world," she continued, "and I didn't like it. I didn't like that people were in my face all the time!" At this point, as Tammy recalls it, she began to wonder if perhaps John was thinking of his wife, Carolyn Bessette, as he asked her these questions. Carolyn wasn't with him at the Cape, and the reason for her absence was never explained. "I wanted to be a doctor," Tammy continued, "and I gave all of that up to be a part of Brian's world. But then I started having some second thoughts about it."

"So what did you do?" John asked.

"I talked to Brian about it, and I told him how I felt," she recalled. "And he understood. But it wasn't about him at all. It was about me. I had to find the strength in myself to deal with it. And I had to do whatever it took to not lose my identity."

"That's so interesting," John said, nodding. His eyes were narrowed and it looked as if he was taking in the information. "I think that's true," he agreed. "You have to be a strong person, or the whole thing can just eat you up. It's really something else, a real sort of freak show," he concluded.

At that point, John pulled a ratty old pair of sneakers from a cloth gym bag. He then put them on his bare feet and tied their laces. "I think I'll go for a run," he said.

"My God, John, you need some new sneakers!"

He grinned. "Yeah, I know. But these are so comfortable, I can't seem to give them up," he said, shrugging. Then, looking out at the wide vista of cobalt blue sea and sky, he added, "Man, I sure do love it out here. I love the water, you know?"

"What is it about the Kennedys and water?" Tammy wondered. "Throughout history, we have seen Kennedys here on this very spot, sailing and enjoying the water, year after year for, what? Forty years? What is that about, John?"

John smiled to himself and nodded. "It's because when we're out there in the sea, we are by ourselves, finally, and we are at peace. It's a beautiful thing, really, that kind of isolation. It's completely still, quiet. Out there," he said, gazing out at the sea with great admiration, "it's like," he paused, struggling for words, "it's like heaven."

She nodded. "I have seen pictures of you running on the beach, and I swear, it looks like you are actually running on the surface of the water. Do you know what I mean?"

He laughed. "That's a little trick of mine," he said. "Promise not to tell?" he asked, winking.

She did.

"There's this little ridge and it's right at the point where the water meets the sand," he said, pointing out at the sea. "It's my secret spot. And if you hit it just right, from back here on the beach, it actually looks like you're running on the top of the water." He stood up and stretched. "Wait and see," he said. "I'm going for a run now, and when I come back this way, take a look. And you'll see for yourself, okay?"

"I'll be watching," Tammy said.

With that, John Kennedy Jr. shot Tammy Holloway a big grin and was off with a flash, running across the long stretch of sand- and pebble-covered beach. She followed him with her eyes until he was just a small dot on the far-off horizon. Then he turned around and headed back her way, this time a little farther out into the ocean so that he was running in perhaps just a few inches of water. And as he got closer to her, he found his secret spot and, sure enough, it looked to Tammy as if John Kennedy Jr. was running on the surface of the sea. Knowing how it must have appeared to her, he gave her a broad smile and a thumbs-up as he passed her by . . . and then he just kept on running.

PART TWENTY-TWO

Camelot Loses Its Prince

Mike Tyson's Advice

*I*t was March 1, 1999. The black Mercedes pulled up to the runway of a small airport in Montgomery, Maryland. The driver, Virgil McLyn, was employed by boxer Mike Tyson as his bodyguard. He'd been asked to pick up a friend of Tyson's who was flying down to visit the fighter in jail. At the time, Tyson was serving a one-year sentence at the Rockville Detention Center for assaulting two motorists after a traffic accident. As McLyn pulled up, he noticed that the small private plane had already landed. In a few moments, the cockpit door opened and down the metal ladder walked a smiling John Kennedy Jr. wearing dark suit pants and an open white shirt and carrying a garment bag. "How you doin'?" he said to McLyn as he extended his hand. The two men spoke for a moment before McLyn opened the rear passenger door of the Mercedes for Kennedy. "No, that's all right," he said. "I can sit up front with you." As the two drove along the highway, McLyn had soft jazz playing in the vehicle. "Do you have anything else?" John asked. "Maybe some hip-hop or something?" Sure. Seconds later, the two men were bopping their heads to Wu-Tang.

"John, I'm going to take you to Mike's house first to see his wife, Monica, and the kids," McLyn explained. "And if you don't mind, maybe take some pictures with them? Is that cool?"

"Sure," John said. "Sounds good."

"And you know what?" McLyn said. "My mom, man, she loves the Kennedys. I hate to ask, but if I could get a picture with you too, that would mean the world to her."

John had to laugh. "Sure. I think we can arrange that," he said.

The two men then drove to Mike Tyson's mansion, where they were met by Tyson's second wife, Monica Turner, a physician; the couple's two small children, Rayna and Amir; and Monica's child from a previous marriage. John excused himself and went to wash up. He emerged a few minutes later wearing a gold tie and a suit jacket. After he took pictures with everyone, it was off to Rockville.

Once at the detention center, John and Virgil were escorted to the visitors' ward, a small concrete room with a glass window on one of the walls, on the other side of which would sit the prisoner. As they walked in, the four guards present looked as if they couldn't believe their eyes. As soon as Kennedy sat down on one side of the partition, Tyson showed up on the other side. McLyn stood directly behind John.

"So, what's up, Mike?" John asked.

"Nothin', John. Just trying to get through this thing, you know?" Tyson answered.

"Obviously the two of them were friends," recalled Virgil McLyn. Indeed, these seemingly unlikely pals had known each other since June 1997 when John attended Tyson's Las Vegas fight, the legendary bout during which the boxer bit off part of Evander Holyfield's right ear. Madonna was at that fight, too. The two spoke afterward, Madonna asking John, "Do you think he swallowed it?" referring to Holyfield's ear. "No," John said, chuckling, "I'm pretty sure I saw him spit it out." John felt Tyson's sentence was ridiculous, that he was being targeted for who he was. "It's like [Bob] Dylan's *Hurricane* song," John said. "It's racism that has Mike back in jail, pure and simple."

"At the jail, John was just trying to lift Mike's spirits," recalled Virgil McLyn. "They talked about how it was going. Just pleasant chitchat. A little bit about boxing, too. And they talked about Mike's public image and how the media seemed to always be on his case. John offered some advice, just told him to try not to let it get to him, that this jail sentence was just a misstep but that he'd be back strong soon, that kind of thing. After about an hour, we were getting ready to leave. It must have been about three in the morning."

"So, what did you do, fly down here?" Mike asked John.

"Yeah, sure."

"I can't believe that," Mike said. He added that John took the plane from one location to the next "as if it was some kind of flying taxicab."

John smiled. "I do love it."

"Virgil's not a fan of small planes," Mike said, looking at his bodyguard and laughing.

"Yeah, I had to take a little plane up to Indiana," Virgil said, according to his memory. "It was me, Mike's wife, and his lawyer. And that was some scary shit," he said. He added that the plane "was dropping and bouncing" so much, he never prayed so hard in his entire life.

"Yeah, well, it can get a little turbulent up there sometimes," John said, laughing.

"You're not flying back tonight, are you?" Mike asked.

"Sure I am," John said.

"Dude, really," Mike said. "You oughta spend the night and fly back tomorrow."

"No, I'm cool," John said.

"I don't know," Mike said. "I think flying that little plane is nuts, John." John smiled. "Look, you love your bike, right?" he asked Mike. "And you were in a wreck a couple years ago. Yet you wouldn't give up your Harley, now would you?"

Mike laughed. "Yeah, but that's different," he said. "At least I'm on good ol' terra firma."

"But you can't imagine how beautiful it is up there, Mike," John said.

"Do me a favor, John," Mike said. "Promise me something."

"What's that?"

"Promise me you won't bring anyone you love up there with you," Mike said. "You want to fly? Cool. But fly alone, John. Not with anyone you love. Promise me."

John just smiled again. After a few more minutes of conversation, he and Virgil McLyn left. The reason for the late-night visit had been so that John could slip in and out unnoticed. Of course, it didn't work out that way. As soon as they got outside, John was surrounded by reporters. He said a few kind words about Mike Tyson, let the press take some pictures, and then got back into the Mercedes with McLyn.

On the way back to the airport—Wu-Tang still playing—John said he wanted to stop at a 7-Eleven and get a cup of coffee. "Dude, to stay awake?" Virgil asked, alarmed. "I mean, if that's the case, let me take you back to the house and you can fly tomorrow." However, John insisted he was fine. After they stopped, Virgil offered to go into the convenience store with John. "No, I'm fine," John said, getting out of the car. As Virgil watched from the car, John went inside, poured a cup of coffee, and took it to the counter to pay for it. Every person inside—maybe five or six— stopped what they were doing and stared. Then, as John left, everyone ran to the glass door and peered outside, disbelief registering on all of their faces.

Soon after, Virgil pulled up to the airport and then onto the runway.

The two men got out of the car and Virgil walked over to John. "I liked him so much," Virgil said, years later. "I mean, he was such a regular guy. And I don't know why I said it, but I did." Indeed, as he shook John Kennedy Jr.'s hand, Virgil McLyn said, "You know what, man? For a white boy, you sure are cool."

John laughed. "Thanks, my friend. So are you," he said.

John Kennedy then walked over to his plane, jumped into the cockpit, and, ten minutes later, pulled onto the runway. Then, as Virgil stood watching, the plane began to speed down the asphalt and smoothly lift off the ground. Soon it was soaring. Within a minute, it was just a dot. Then it was gone.

"The Worst That Could Happen"

On Saturday, July 10, 1999, Ethel and Rory Kennedy were sitting in Ethel's living room at the Kennedy compound with thick notepads in their laps, talking to Holly Safford, the caterer for Rory's upcoming wedding. Ethel has a longtime cook at the compound, who also travels with her. For special events, though, she uses Safford and her company, The Catered Affair, which is located outside of Boston. Safford had been catering Kennedy events for many years, starting with Rose Kennedy's hundredth birthday in the summer of 1990. "You have voluminous notes when you leave a meeting with Mrs. Kennedy," Holly Safford recalled. "She has a vision, which is the whole look of the space, the tablecloths and the china and everything that is going to be used, and then you move to the menu very quickly, which is paramount to her because she's extremely food-oriented. 'There is a lot of mediocrity in food,' she's told me, 'but I'll have none of that.' She's very specific about every detail. So specific that, once, she drew a picture of the exact size of the crouton that she wanted for a Caesar salad, put it in an envelope, addressed it by hand, and sent it to me in the mail. And it was positively miniscule!"

On this day, bright sunlight streamed through every window, making Ethel's decor—yellows, pinks, and pale blues—seem all the more vibrant. It was cheery, bright, and inviting. It was also the first time Holly Safford would meet the bride-to-be, since all of the decisions relating to food preparations had been made by Ethel.

"So we have a final menu now, is that right?" Ethel asked.

"We do," Holly said, according to her memory of the conversation. "Let's see," she began enthusiastically, now referring to her own notes. "For the main course, the guests will choose between grilled-to-order six-ounce sirloin steaks, grilled portobello mushroom caps, or orange-cured salmon filets. We'll have a salad of Maine organic potatoes with summer truffles and leek, towers of grilled summer vegetables, and orzo salad with shrimp, pink grapefruit, and mint. There'll be orecchiette with white beans, grape tomatoes, Asiago, and fresh basil. And we'll also have a Caesar salad."

"Wow, that sounds great, Mom," Rory said, excited. This was to be a special time for Rory, who was now a filmmaker. The last of Bobby's and Ethel's children to be born—Ethel was pregnant with her when Bobby was murdered—she was set to marry Mark Bailey in just one week, on July 17, 1999. Rory was—is—a remarkable documentary filmmaker and producer, with dozens of films to her credit, her subjects illuminating the human condition and revealing her own social consciousness. For instance, she has made movies about women imprisoned for using drugs while pregnant and disabled mothers fighting to raise their children.* Just eighteen months earlier, she had tried to breathe life into her brother, Michael, after he careened into a tree in Aspen. Getting over the trauma of that ordeal was hard, and in fact she never really did—she just got past it, somehow. Now she was about to start anew.

"You know us Kennedys," Ethel said. "We like our good food. But what about dessert?" she asked. "We have the wedding cake, but what else?"

"Well, we'll have ice cream," Holly offered. "Double vanilla and chocolate."

---

* In 2007, Rory would direct *Ghosts of Abu Ghraib*, an examination of the events of the 2004 Abu Ghraib torture and prisoner-abuse scandal. After it aired on HBO, it would be nominated for four Emmys, winning the award for Outstanding Nonfiction Special. A year later, she would direct *Thank You, Mr. President: Helen Thomas at the White House*, which was, of course, about the veteran White House reporter, and also aired on HBO. She most recently directed *The Fence (La Barda)*, which premiered on opening night of the Sundance Film Festival 2010. The film made its debut on HBO on September 16, 2010.

"That's it?" Ethel asked, her eyebrows raised.

Holly nodded.

"Oh, well, I'll want coffee ice cream too, and peach as well," Ethel said. "And Chunky Monkey, too. That's Teddy's favorite, so we must have Chunky Monkey, all right? And let's do something fun," she continued. "Let's not serve it in bowls but, instead, let's have ice cream cones passed to everyone and they can then scoop out what they like. Doesn't that sound like fun?" Ethel asked.

Rory and Holly nodded with big smiles. "Oh, and don't forget the jimmies and color sprinkles," Ethel said.

Holly made a note.

"Oh, I wanted to ask you something," Rory said, turning to Holly. "What is the very worst thing that you've ever seen happen on a person's wedding day?"

It was an odd question, so much so that Holly was taken aback. She immediately recalled quite a few scenarios, but none that she felt comfortable sharing for fear that they would put a damper on an otherwise very happy day. For instance, what came to mind was the time one of her clients learned that her father was terminally ill. The bride-to-be moved the wedding up three months just so that he would be able to attend. But then he died the very morning of the wedding. Though devastated, his daughter went ahead with the wedding because she knew that's what her dad would have wanted. Years later, Holly recalled, "I was sitting there looking at Rory and trying to decide how to answer her question when it occurred to me, 'Is she having some sort of premonition about her own wedding day?' If so, I didn't want to say anything that would set any fears in motion."

"Well, actually, we haven't had anything significantly bad ever occur with any of our brides," Holly answered, fibbing. "I do remember that story about the gal in New York who was getting married at the Essex Hotel, and not only did the bridegroom not show up, he and his best friend used the honeymoon airline tickets and went off to Hawaii together for a good time, leaving his fiancée at the altar. He didn't show up, call, or anything."

"Oh my gosh, that poor girl," Rory said, her eyes wide with astonishment.

"Heavens to Betsy!" exclaimed Ethel. "How sad!"

"That's like the worst that could happen at a wedding, isn't it?" Rory asked. "My gosh!"

"I know!" Holly said. "It doesn't get worse than that, does it? But nothing like that has ever happened to any of my brides."

"And nothing bad will happen to this bride, either," Ethel said. "What a great day this will be for you and Mark, kiddo," she added as she reached out to touch her daughter's hand. "I'm just so happy for you."

"Please Tell Me John's Not Dead"

On Friday night, July 16, 1999, the rehearsal dinner was held for Rory Kennedy, Mark Bailey, and their wedding party at Ethel Kennedy's home on the compound. All of the guests had participated in the making of a large quilt for Rory, with each person contributing a specially selected colorful square. Afterward, the women in the bridal party had their hair styled by Christina Rivers of Hyannis. All in all, it had been a very successful event, the happy prelude to what was sure to be a memorable wedding the next day. Of course, many of the Kennedys would be present for the occasion—all of Rory's siblings and their spouses and all of their children were expected, as well as a wide assortment of aunts, uncles, and cousins, including, of course, John Kennedy Jr. and his wife, Carolyn. John's sister, Caroline, would not be present as she was planning to be rafting with her husband, Ed, and their children. They were celebrating their thirteenth wedding anniversary, and also Ed's fifty-fourth birthday.

On the night of July 16, John and Carolyn were scheduled to fly in John's single-engine Piper Saratoga from Essex County Airport at Fairfield, New Jersey, to Hyannis Airport on Cape Cod for the wedding. John had recently been wearing a cast after having broken his ankle in a paraglider crash just three weeks earlier. Now that the cast was off, he was able to fly solo again and he couldn't wait to get up in the air. This would mark his first flight without a copilot since the accident, though he was still limping badly. He had actually told Caroline that—just to be on the safe side—he would have a copilot on this particular trip too. But apparently he changed his mind.

On the way to Hyannis, John and Carolyn were going to stop in Martha's Vineyard to drop off one of Carolyn's two sisters, thirty-four-year-old

Lauren. At around 8:30 p.m., the three of them took off from the airport in Fairfield, New Jersey—John, of course, in the pilot's seat, and Carolyn back-to-back behind him in a passenger seat facing Lauren. Kennedy was flying under visual flight rules, or VFR in aviation terms, meaning he was not required to file a flight plan with the FAA and was navigating on his own rather than relying on instruments. However, when Lauren wasn't at the airport on time at a little after 9:30, the friends who were to meet her there became concerned. By ten o'clock, John's plane was half an hour late. Something was wrong.

Ted Kennedy had arrived in Hyannis Port with Vicki earlier on the sixteenth for Rory's rehearsal dinner. At around midnight, he got a call telling him that John's plane had not arrived in Martha's Vineyard on time. There was mounting concern. Ted got out of bed, Vicki made a strong pot of coffee, and the telephone calls began. Ted called John and Carolyn's apartment, and when someone answered the phone, he must have had a second of relief. But it was just a person staying at the apartment for the weekend since the air-conditioning wasn't working at his home. Yes, John and Carolyn had left on time, as far as he knew. Now Ted was getting worried. He called Joe Kennedy, Ethel's son, who was staying at her home, and told him not to wake his mother yet, but there was a problem. Joe got on the phone and started making his own calls. The FAA and the First Coast Guard District Command in Boston were contacted—but no sign of John's plane. By 3 a.m. the FAA had alerted the Air Force Rescue Coordination Center at Langley Air Force Base in Virginia. Radar had tracked the plane at 2,500 feet as it left the Rhode Island area at 9:26 p.m. At 9:40 p.m. and 20 seconds, it was tracked at 2,200 feet, having dropped 300 feet in fourteen minutes. It dropped 300 more feet in only four seconds, 300 more in the next five, and 500 more in the five seconds after that. Then it was...lost.

Ted waited until around 5 a.m. to call Ethel to tell her that there was trouble. He woke her from a sound sleep. From that time on, frantic telephone calls were made by many of John's close friends and relatives. "But there was this sense, you know, that John would show up," said Brian Holloway. "People were saying, 'You know John, he's just going to walk right through that door at any second with a big grin plastered on his face.' 'Man, you will not believe what just happened,' he would say. And he would then tell this phenomenal story, and at the end of it we would be looking at each other and say, 'Only to John would this kind of thing happen.' That was the dream, anyway..."

By 6 a.m. White House chief of staff John Podesta contacted President Clinton at Camp David to tell him that JFK Jr.'s plane was missing. Clinton said that he would authorize whatever was needed to find the missing plane, and by 7:45 a fleet of aircraft including fifteen Civil Air Patrol planes had taken off in search of any debris in the ocean or along the hazy and foggy coast. By about 1 p.m., debris began washing onto the shore of Martha's Vineyard, very close to the home that Jackie had owned that now belonged to John and Caroline.

Stephen Styles recalls, "I was home on Saturday morning and a friend of mine called and said, 'Tell me that John's not dead. Please tell me that John's not dead.' And I said, 'What in the world are you taking about?' He said, 'Turn on the TV right now.' I hung up the phone, ran to the television and turned it on, and all I saw was a screen full of blue ocean and blue sky with the words 'JFK Jr.'s plane missing' scrolling across the bottom of it. I immediately got sick to my stomach. I ran to the bathroom and threw up. And then I just started crying, kneeling in front of the toilet, bawling like a baby because I just knew. I just knew."

The phone at Ethel Kennedy's home didn't stop ringing all morning, of course, and Ethel would jump every time it did, hoping it would be good news. "Holly, they are going to find him," she told her caterer Holly Safford when she called at nine in the morning to express her concern. She told her that as far as she was concerned, the wedding was not canceled. She reassured her that John would be found.

"I told Mrs. Kennedy that I would stand by," Safford recalled. "I hung up and called Rory. I told her how sorry I was that this thing had happened. 'What a horribly unbelievable turn of events,' I said. 'I'm so terribly sad for you and your family.' She carried herself with tremendous dignity. She was very, very concerned about her cousin... 'It takes just one second for a moment to change the entire lives of a whole family,' she said. It was a very sad conversation.

"Then, it was the wedding is on. The wedding is off. The wedding is on. The wedding's off—seesawing like that all day," she recalled. "There was a glimmer of hope still late Saturday morning, even though it was waning. People were holding on to whatever they could hold on to that John had somehow gone off course and there had been weather or fog or the plane was disabled, or he was somehow, somewhere injured, but alive. When you don't know, you hold on to the slightest thread of hope."

At Ethel Kennedy's urging, deliveries for the wedding continued throughout the day on Saturday—the flowers, the food, the tables, the tents, and all of the other makings of another Kennedy wedding. The ceremony—with 380 guests, many from out of town—was to be at six, and it was as if Ethel felt that to cancel it would have been to give in to the tragedy at hand, and she wasn't going to do it. Not yet, anyway.

"We Need a Miracle Now More Than Ever"

I still believe in miracles," Ethel told her longtime secretary, Leah Mason, who was no longer working for her but was at the compound as a friend. "I believe God knows what He's doing and that John, Carolyn, and Lauren will be found. I have to hold on to that belief, and I will."

"I believe that, too," Mason said. She would recall years later that though determined to remain strong, Ethel seemed much older on that day than she'd ever before noticed, as if years of tragedy had finally taken their toll.

Ethel told Leah that the Kennedy family had been dealing with the heartbreak of airplane crashes for years. It had first brought them sorrow in the 1940s with the deaths of the family's first- and fourth-born children—Joseph Patrick Kennedy Jr., twenty-nine, on August 12, 1944; and Kathleen, known as Kick, twenty-eight, on May 13, 1948. Years later, of course, Ted almost died in a plane crash. Prior to that, Ethel's parents and her brother George were also killed in separate airplane accidents. It was impossible to imagine that yet another might now claim John Jr. "My poor Johnny," Ethel said, her eyes filling with tears. "We need a miracle now more than ever before."

Finally, by noon on Saturday, it looked as if there would be no miracle. John was gone, along with his wife and her sister. In a blink of an eye, all of the problems with which he had been grappling in recent months— the many questions about his marriage; his cousin's cancer (Anthony Radziwill would also die within just three weeks' time, at the age of forty);

the flagging sales of *George*—all of it was suddenly rendered moot. The many threads that had constituted the fabric of his life were unraveled and swept away in just a matter of minutes.

At about one o'clock, Lynn DeLaney from the RFK Memorial Foundation called Holly Safford to tell her that the wedding was definitely off. She said that Ethel and Rory decided to invite all guests who were not in the immediate Kennedy family to the Sheraton Hyannis Resort and serve in the ballroom the food that had been intended for the wedding. It was an opportunity for those not in the Kennedys' inner circle to come together and share their horrendous feelings of grief and loss. At the same time, a small gathering was planned on Ethel's deck for family members and closest friends, and they would be served there by the remaining catering staff.

Later that day, thirty-year-old Rory walked on the beach of the six-acre Kennedy compound, with the protective arm of her fiancé, Mark Bailey, also thirty and a book and film editor, draped over her shoulder. After a while, Ethel joined the couple on the long stretch of beach. Holding Rory's hand, she spoke in her ear while intrusive helicopters swirled above, causing the kind of cacophony to which she and the rest of the family had long ago grown accustomed. The two were seen embracing, with Ethel stroking her girl's blonde hair and, it appeared, consoling her.*

At about five o'clock, the family gathered for a Mass performed by three fully robed priests on the porch of Ethel's home, attended by about fifty family members. Ethel stood behind Ted and his wife, Vicki, during the service. Behind her was her sister-in-law Jean Kennedy Smith. Next to her, Eunice and Sargent Shriver. Following the Mass would be the family gathering on Ethel's porch.

"That family gathering had a very quiet, subdued, solemn tone, as you can imagine," said Holly Safford. "There was a short cocktail hour and then dinner. They were devastated and stunned and in a state of disbelief, but also very dignified and very unified. It was not something they were unfamiliar with, that kind of shocking turn of events. It was heartwarm-

---

* Rory Kennedy and Mark Bailey would eventually be married in Greece on August 2, 1999, at the home of shipping mogul Vardis Vardinoyiannis. As of this writing, the couple lives in Brooklyn, New York, and they have three children, Georgia Elizabeth (born 2002), Bridget Katherine (born 2004), and Zachary Corkland (born 2007).

ing to see the way they clung to each other. You don't want to intrude on their grief, and with each passing hour it was more and more clear that the news would not be good."

"It was very, very hard," said one of Ethel's sons. "I just remember my aunt Eunice and uncle Sargent, and Aunt Jean and my mom, all so heartbroken. Everyone was just devastated. Uncle Teddy was grief-stricken. John had been such a light in our lives, we couldn't imagine how we would ever be able to go on without him."

By this time, Sargent was eighty-three and Eunice seventy-three. Both seemed physically unwell and emotionally unable to handle the unfolding turn of tragic events. Pat, who was seventy-five, had not yet arrived, but was on her way. One of the guests watched as Jean, who was seventy-one, was seen trying to console her sister Eunice. Eunice seemed to be crying—a rare display of emotion from a woman who had lived much of her life being stoic and strong. Eunice just nodded her head sadly in response to whatever Jean was whispering to her.

Ethel, who as earlier stated was now seventy, joined Eunice and Jean and held both their hands. The three then talked quietly among themselves, Eunice repeatedly shaking her head as if in disbelief. Soon the little group was joined by Vicki Kennedy, Ted's wife, who was only forty-five. She looked as if she were very concerned about the older women. For Vicki, who well knew all that they had been through in their troubled lifetimes, it must have been difficult to watch them experience such overwhelming grief at their advanced ages. "Please, ladies, let's all go someplace else and take a little break from this, okay?" she said. Everyone agreed. The women then followed Vicki to another part of the house, all of them walking very slowly as if emotionally and physically exhausted, all except for Ethel. "I have something I must do," she said, leaving the others.

Ethel walked into the kitchen. There, she sat at the table and stared at the phone for a few minutes, as if trying to pull herself together. She went to a drawer and pulled rosary beads from it, and began fingering the beads. She then dialed the number of Clint Flagg, owner of Vintage Flowers in Osterville, Massachusetts, who had handled the floral arrangements for the wedding. In planning the wedding, Ethel had said that, more than anything, she wanted her daughter to have peonies for the ceremony. However, as it happened, that particular flower was out of season. Undaunted, Flagg had searched the world over and was able to locate peonies in England and have them flown to Hyannis Port. "Rory and I want to thank you so much for what you did for us," Ethel told Flagg. "May I ask you for one more favor?" Ethel then requested that the petals from all of those peonies be placed in plastic bags. "I'm not sure, but I suspect John, Carolyn, and Lauren will be cremated and their ashes scattered at sea," Ethel said sadly. "If so, I would like those petals to be scattered as well. I think Carolyn would like that very much, don't you?"

A Sister's Grief

*A*s Ted Kennedy pulled up to Caroline Kennedy's two-story wood-shingled weekend house in Sagaponack, Long Island, on Sunday morning, July 18, he saw hundreds of people congregating outside a long driveway barricaded by yellow police tape, more than a dozen state troopers, and a slew of squad cars. There were also at least a hundred reporters on the street, many of them positioned in front of TV cameras delivering what appeared to be live broadcasts, likely around the world. It looked like a crime scene. Inside, behind tall hedges and iron fences, Caroline sat in her living room, answering the telephone, talking to relatives, and trying, all the while, to be supportive of her three children, Rose, eleven, Tatiana, ten, and John, seven. With her were her cousins Maria Shriver and William Kennedy Smith, as well as, of course, her husband, Ed Schlossberg. President Clinton had called earlier to assure her that everything possible was being done to find John. The two spoke of the last time Clinton had seen John, in February 1998 when John attended a dinner honoring British prime minister Tony Blair. At that time, Clinton took John and Carolyn on a personal tour of the White House. John had said that some of it "looks vaguely familiar." Of course, John had been there a few times in recent years, and the tour was mostly for Carolyn's benefit. Clinton would recall her walking around with eyes as big as saucers trying to take it all in. It had been a very exciting day.

As soon as Ted's driver announced to the police that the senator was in the car, they released the tape and allowed the car to slowly roll through the entranceway and down the long driveway. Meanwhile, as the crush of people realized who was in the car, they pushed forward, almost causing a mob scene as they were shoved back into place by the officers.

It had been earlier, on Saturday, July 17, when Caroline first learned that her brother's plane was missing. She and her family had been in Idaho only a day, having arrived there to celebrate Ed's birthday on July 19. The Schlossbergs' plans for this trip were made before they knew the exact date of Rory's wedding, and after Caroline and her cousin had discussed the matter, it was agreed that they were not to cancel their trip. Instead, Caroline and Ed would visit Rory and Mark as soon as they returned from their honeymoon. It had been John's cousin and very close friend Anthony Radziwill who informed Caroline of her brother's missing plane. He hadn't been able to contact her because the telephone switchboard at the Mountain Village Resort, where the Schlossbergs were staying, in the sleepy resort town of Stanley, was turned off for the night. Desperate to reach his cousin, Anthony contacted the authorities at the Sun Valley Police Department and asked them to track Caroline down at the resort and have her call him. He said it was an emergency. It was about 4:30 a.m.

Responding to Radziwill's call, a police officer drove to the hotel and called Caroline to tell her that an emergency situation had developed and that she should call Anthony. When she did, Anthony told her the devastating news, though he could barely get the words out. He would later say it was the single worst telephone call he had ever made. Of course, Caroline was worried, but not as much as one might have thought. After all, she'd talked to John the previous Thursday and had made him promise that if he was going to fly to the Cape for the wedding, he would take along a flight instructor. Also, he would be sure to fly during the day. Since he hadn't flown alone in some time due to his broken ankle, she had been concerned. Maybe just wanting to placate her, John agreed.

In fact, John's interest in flying had always been a point of serious contention between sister and brother. John had actually quit taking flying lessons ten years earlier, in 1988, when Caroline and Jackie sat down with him and begged him to stop. Jackie told him that if anything ever happened to him, she simply would not live through it. Caroline agreed with her mom that if John was killed in a plane crash, she would never recover from it. Moved by their emotional appeal, John stopped. But then, about two years after Jackie's death, he decided he wanted to resume his flying lessons. He and Caroline actually had a falling-out about it because, as she told him, "Nothing's changed except that Mother isn't here. But I still am, and I'm afraid, John!" Caroline even appealed to her sister-in-law, Carolyn, to try to get John to stop, but Carolyn was unsuccessful. John kept insisting that he would be fine, that he knew what he was doing, and, moreover, he had even convinced Carolyn that the danger was minimal. So he started flying again.

After Michael Kennedy's death in 1997, Caroline appealed to John again. Her cousin's sudden death reminded Caroline of the fragility of life and she begged John to please reconsider his flying lessons. He agreed, again, to stop. Three months passed. Finally, John called his sister to tell her that he really missed flying and would appreciate it if she would just support his decision and not give him any more grief about it. He said that Carolyn was "on board"—his words—and that she had even given him a Saint Christopher medal for protection. All of this was little comfort for Caroline, but she knew her brother and knew that his wife would have little influence over him once he'd made up his mind. Caroline therefore decided there was nothing she could do but accept John's decision, even though she didn't like it. She usually didn't even want to know when he was going to be in the air because of the anxiety it would cause her.

When Caroline called Ted after having spoken to Anthony, she told him that she felt that there must be some mistake and that she had spoken to John on Thursday and he had indicated that he would be flying during the day, not at night. But there was no mistake, Ted told her, John's plane had indeed left New Jersey at night. He must have had a change of plans, Ted said. One can only imagine the feeling of dread that must have washed over Caroline at that moment. But Ted said to his niece that perhaps John did have a copilot and perhaps they were all safe somewhere. He told her to just stay put and not come to Hyannis. "When news of this gets out, it's bound to be a zoo here," he told her. "I promise to keep you posted." Of course, there was no way Caroline and her family could stay in Idaho now. She just wanted to get home as quickly as possible. The Schlossbergs chartered a plane and returned to New York.

Ted decided to leave Hyannis Port and fly to New York on Sunday morning to check in on Caroline. He was glad he did. She was of course very upset. Once Ted settled in, he and Caroline and Ed went into the yard and dropped the American flag on a tall flagpole to half-mast. They returned to the confines of the house and Ted then played basketball with the kids for a while so that Caroline and Ed could have some time with her cousins. Caroline had been insistent that she wasn't going to cry in front of her children—which was very much the way her own mother had handled matters when her father was killed. Ted realized, though, that Caroline needed to break down, that what she was going through was overwhelming, which is why he took the kids. After about an hour, Caroline and Ed went for a bike ride to relieve some of the anxiety.

That evening, after Caroline went to bed, Ed and Ted spent a few hours talking, trying to come to terms with what had happened. Before leaving, Ted said he wanted to check on his niece. He went up to her room expecting to find her fast asleep. Instead, she was sitting cross-legged on her bed, looking at a scrapbook of photographs of her brother and her mother and weeping. He sat down next to her, took her into his arms, and rocked her, just the way he had done so long ago when Jack was killed.

"Our Prince Is Gone"

*T*he next few days would be an awful blur.

On Tuesday night, the wreckage of John's plane was found at the bottom of the ocean. While it appeared that John's body was still strapped in the plane, the bodies of Carolyn and Lauren seemed to be missing.

A Navy ship, the *Grasp*, went out on Wednesday to collect what was left of the Piper Saratoga and also to recover the bodies. Sure enough, when divers went below, they found John in his pilot's seat. Nearby on the ocean floor, they found Carolyn and Lauren, also still strapped to their seats. As Ted Kennedy and his sons, Ted Jr. and Patrick, watched in utter disbelief from the deck of the ship, the three bodies were brought to the surface and then placed on gurneys and taken away. There were very few dry eyes on the vessel as the emotion of the moment seemed to catch up with even the military personnel. It was decided that an autopsy would be performed on John, but not on his passengers. A decision had to be made about whether or not autopsy photos would be taken, as required by law.

Ted was against it for fear that they would end up in the wrong hands and be published in some tabloid. It was agreed that photos would be taken but the film not developed unless there were some question raised about the investigation into the deaths.

No one wanted answers, though, not really. The answers to most of the questions being asked were unbearable.

For instance, it was speculated by the FAA that it probably took just three minutes for John's plane to complete what was called "a graveyard spiral" into the ocean at nearly 5,000 feet per minute. Hitting the water at such a tremendous speed, they said, was comparable to the plane slamming into solid concrete. The National Transportation Safety Board later ruled that the crash had most likely been caused by "the pilot's failure to maintain control of the airplane during a descent over water at night, which was a result of spatial disorientation." Weather conditions in the area at the time were clear below 12,000 feet, with visibility at ten miles. With just a little over a year of flying experience, John was not licensed for instrument landings and likely not equipped to handle the kind of extremely overcast, foggy conditions that presented themselves that night.

Interestingly, John's good friend John Perry Barlow later recalled, "I had a phone conversation with him a couple of weeks before the accident and I said, 'You know, it occurs to me—because I'm a private pilot—that you know just enough now to be dangerous, you know what I mean? You have confidence in the air, which could harm you. You're going to find yourself flying in instrument conditions because you think you can.' I said, 'You're in that narrow window between three hundred and five hundred hours where a lot of pilots get killed,' which is a generally true statement. It didn't have anything to do specifically with him, it was just an observation. He listened intently. 'Interesting,' he said. 'I just have to be careful.'"

Within eight hours after being located, the three bodies of the deceased would be cremated. John's cousins Doug and Max were at the crematorium as the bodies were being destroyed, knowing in their hearts that some members of John's family should be present.

For the Kennedys, all of it was simply unbearable. But those who worked with John at *George* were also overcome. Said the magazine's former editor in chief, Richard Bradley, "Within the office, there was a professional relationship, of course, but underlying it there were profoundly personal feelings of warmth and loyalty for John, and I would even say love. I don't think it's wrong to say that people who worked for John just loved the guy. For the people who worked there, he was much more than a boss. He was someone we cared very deeply and personally about, and that's why when John died, the office was much more affected than anyone on the outside realized, and part of that is because I don't think people realized how much contact we had with John. I think the most common question I heard about John at that time, and even now, is, did he ever come to the office? He was a presence in our lives every day. Losing him was more than most of us could ever reconcile."

Within days of the cremations, seventeen members of the Kennedy and Bessette families, including Ted Kennedy and his sons, Patrick and Ted Jr.; Caroline Kennedy; Maria Shriver; William Kennedy Smith; Richard and Ann Freeman, Carolyn's stepfather and mother; and Lisa Bessette, Carolyn's sister, found themselves sitting in wooden folding chairs aboard the destroyer USS *Briscoe* as it steamed out to sea. The two families had asked that the *Briscoe* sail as close as possible to the exact patch of ocean that had claimed John's plane. In front of the mourners on a card table were three very small pale blue boxes inside of which were the ashes of John, Carolyn, and Lauren. "We commit their elements to the deep, for we are dust and unto dust we shall return," prayed the Navy's deputy chief of chaplains, Rear Admiral Barry Black, "but the Lord Jesus Christ will change our mortal bodies to be like His in glory, for He is risen the firstborn from the dead. So let us commend our brother and sisters to the Lord, that the Lord may embrace them in peace and raise them up on the last day."

Also on the boat that day was John's cousin and best friend Anthony Radziwill, who was battling cancer. During the summer of 1999, John was agonizing over Anthony's slow decline. In fact, over a five-year period, Anthony's illness took a great toll on John, and eventually on Carolyn too, who had grown to love Anthony and his wife, Carole. "Once it was the four of us with all our dreams and plans and then suddenly there was nothing," recalled Carole Radziwill, who wrote a moving account of this time in her life called *What Remains: A Memoir of Fate, Friendship, and Love.*

In trying to understand the relationship between John and Carolyn, it has to be understood that Anthony's cancer was a constant, often mind-numbing issue in their lives, providing day after day of dread and concern. It was unrelenting. No matter what was going on in their lives, in the background, Anthony was dying. By the summer of 1999, John had reconciled himself to the inevitable. However, he felt that Anthony had not done so, and it worried him. Therefore, he began talking to Anthony's wife, Carole, about what he felt needed to be done to prepare Anthony for his own death. To that end, he was reading *On Death and Dying* by Elisabeth Kübler-Ross, he told Carole, and he had started really thinking about the "Five Stages of Death"—anger, denial, fear, acceptance, and peace. Carole didn't want to discuss it with John, though— not yet, anyway. As Anthony's wife, she'd been through so much turmoil in the last five years, she was emotionally and physically exhausted. She promised that one day soon, she and John would discuss whatever they needed to in order to help Anthony with his transition. Meanwhile, John began writing Anthony's eulogy, which he knew he would be delivering at the funeral. "A true gentleman," John wrote in a first draft of the eulogy, which was later found in his office desk, "he was humble, decent, charming and down to earth. He had humor, intelligence and a heart as big as the ocean. You couldn't help but love him."

John ended his eulogy with: "Good night, sweet prince."*

Now, by an awful twist of fate, it was John who was gone, not Anthony. Sadly, Anthony would follow him in just three weeks.

Not long after John and Carolyn died, it was as if someone opened a floodgate to sensationalism and all sorts of stories began to be published alleging, among other things, that at the time of their death John had been cheating on Carolyn or she had been cheating on him, or that one or both of them were addicted to drugs. The list of unsavory allegations seemed endless. Who knows if any of these stories is true? As Jackie Kennedy once put it, "No one knows what goes on in a marriage except the two people in it." That said, there's no solid evidence to support any of those allegations. No credible sources have any real proof of any of these stories. "It was a difficult summer," Carole Radziwill allows. "And I'm not going to say that it wasn't. It was. John's magazine, *George*, was struggling and Anthony was dying, and we were—we were not, any of us, really, in

---

* The ending, in addition to being a quotation from *Hamlet*, may have alluded to the fact that Anthony was the son and scion of Polish royalty, Prince Stanislaw Radziwill.

a good place. And there were reports that they were in marriage counseling, and that's true. But I think what distorts everything in life is not understanding the difference between fact and truth. The fact was they were in marriage counseling. The truth is they loved each other. And I have no doubt that they would have been okay."

After the priest finished the service, an officer in dress whites carried the first box down a ladder to the choppy waterline, where he opened the box and scattered the ashes. As he did so, a brass quintet from the Newport Naval Base played Christian hymns, in place of the military taps. The officer returned for the other two boxes. All of the ashes were scattered into the same sea to which the Kennedys had been so devoted for so many years—the same sea John F. Kennedy Jr. had often said assured him a sense of peace and solitude, the sea he had said represented heaven. John was just thirty-eight. Carolyn was thirty-three, Lauren thirty-four.

"It is an interesting biological fact that all of us have in our veins the exact same percentage of salt in our blood that exists in the ocean," John's father, President Kennedy, had said many years earlier on September 14, 1962, during a toast to the America's Cup racing crew, "and therefore, we have salt in our blood, in our sweat, in our tears. We are tied to the ocean. And when we go back to the sea—whether it is to sail or to watch it—we are going back from whence we came."

What Families Do

There would be a funeral Mass in New York for John and Carolyn at St. Thomas More Roman Catholic Church on Friday, July 23, 1999, and then another the next evening for Lauren at Greenwich's Episcopal Christ Church. Somehow, the families would get through it all, but for the Kennedys, there was an almost palpable sense that nothing would ever again be the same. With John gone, the brightest light in their lives had been extinguished. That he was also a direct link to President Kennedy, the man about whom the family had always been the proudest, made the others feel as if he deserved a special kind of respect. After all, he was his father's son, and as long as John Kennedy Jr. walked among them, it felt as if President Kennedy was still somehow present, too. Now father and son were both gone, leaving in their wake a kind of emptiness that was impossible to quantify. "Our prince is gone," is how Maria Shriver put it, and that was most unusual phraseology for her. The family never used royal titles when speaking about themselves. But in this case, it just seemed appropriate. Because it was true.

"Once, when they asked John what he would do if he went into politics and was elected president," Ted said in his moving eulogy during the service for John and Carolyn, "he said, 'I guess the first thing is call up Uncle Teddy and gloat.' I loved that. It was so like his father.

"How often our family will think of the two of them," he said of John and Carolyn, "cuddling affectionately on a boat, surrounded by family— aunts, uncles, Caroline and Ed and their children, Rose, Tatiana, and Jack, Kennedy cousins, Radziwill cousins, Shriver cousins, Smith cousins, Lawford cousins—as we sailed Nantucket Sound. Then we would come home, and before dinner, on the lawn where his father had played, John would lead a spirited game of touch football. And his beautiful young wife, the new pride of the Kennedys, would cheer for John's team and delight her nieces and nephews with her somersaults.

"We thank the millions who have rained blossoms down on John's memory," he intoned to the mourners, including President Clinton and Hillary Clinton. "He and his bride have gone to be with his mother and father, where there will never be an end to love. He was lost on that troubled night, but we will always wake for him, so that his time, which was not doubled, but cut in half, will live forever in our memory, and in our beguiled and broken hearts. We dared to think, in that Irish phrase, that this John Kennedy would live to comb gray hair, with his beloved Carolyn by his side. But like his father, he had every gift but length of years.

"We, who have loved him from the day he was born, and watched the remarkable man he became, now bid him farewell.

"God bless you, John and Carolyn. We love you and we always will."

After the funeral Mass, many of the Kennedys congregated for a few moments in the vestibule of the old Gothic-style church. The Kennedys were on their way outside to greet the mourners, many of them longtime friends, who had come to say goodbye and to also pay tribute to John and Carolyn and were now spilling out onto East 89th Street. Alone for a few minutes with each other and a few close friends, the family members spoke briefly about how Jackie used to take John and Caroline to this same church every Sunday for Mass. It was also here that she and her children commemorated the anniversary of Jack's death each November. As Ted Kennedy stood in the vestibule with Vicki, Caroline—who had also given a reading at her brother's service of Shakespeare's *The Tempest*—approached him and embraced him warmly. Ethel peeked outside at the pressing crowd, shading her eyes from the sun and waving. She then stepped back inside. Soon, Eunice and Sargent were present in the vestibule, as were Pat, Joan, Jean, and some of their grown children, including Bobby and Timothy Shriver; Christopher Lawford and his sister, Sydney McKelvy; Ted Kennedy Jr.; William Kennedy Smith; and Bobby Kennedy Jr.

"You know, I've been thinking about Grandpa all day," Sargent Shriver said to the small group, according to the recollection of one of the relatives who was present. "And Jack and Bobby too. It's all gone by so fast," he said sadly.

At that, Caroline seemed to crumble. She had managed to maintain her composure all day, but now she appeared to be completely worn down by sheer emotion. Her husband, Ed, grabbed her from behind and seemed to hold her up by her elbows, while her oldest daughter, Rose, who was just eleven, stuck close to her side. Eunice's daughter, Maria, walked up behind her mother and wrapped her long arms around her, putting her head on her shoulder. Maria hadn't been able to stop crying all day, her eyes hidden by large sunglasses. "Granny would say, wipe that tear away," a comforting Eunice had told her earlier, referring to Rose Kennedy.

"Never would I have ever believed this day would come," Ethel said sadly. Her sons Bobby and Joe each took one of their mother's hands and held tightly. "But we will pull together, though, and we will go on," she told the small, tearful group, "because we are family. And that's what families do," she concluded. "They go on."

The small group of Kennedy family members finally composed themselves enough to walk outside the small church and then to their cars, all the while forcing smiles and waving to a world that had long wondered about them, long speculated about them, long loved them, and, yes, even at times hated them too. They would do what they'd been doing for more years than many of them cared to remember—they would choke back their tears.

PART TWENTY-THREE

Transitions

Rosemary Kennedy—Free at Last

*F*lash back to Labor Day weekend in September 1994. Four generations of Kennedys gathered at the Cape to celebrate the nation's one hundredth Labor Day holiday, and as was very often the case, Eunice, Pat, Jean, and Ted arranged for their sister, Rosemary Kennedy, to visit the family for the holiday. She had lived more than fifty years in Wisconsin at St. Coletta's, although after Joseph's death in 1969 she did enjoy many one-week visits with her family during summers in Palm Beach and in Hyannis Port. Still, Rosemary, who was now seventy-six, obviously had led a very sad life. As much as the Kennedys loved their father, Joseph, they never really reconciled his actions toward his daughter, basically deciding as a family that they had no choice but to move forward and not dwell on the past.

Rosemary arrived with two nuns from the Wisconsin facility on August 24. When Rosemary showed up, she was greeted by many members of the family who had congregated at the Big House to greet her warmly, including her sisters and brother as well as Sargent Shriver, Stephen Smith, and Ethel Kennedy. Rose—who at 104 was in a wheelchair and could barely speak or hear—seemed happy to see her daughter once again. That evening, the family had a quiet meal, and then Rosemary retired early, saying that she was exhausted from the trip.

The next morning, Eunice and Pat planned to take Rosemary on a drive into town to buy some T-shirts, flip-flops, and other items Rosemary said she wanted for her stay at the compound. The three sisters and one of the two nuns who'd come with Rosemary piled into Eunice's SUV, drove through the exit of the compound past the guards usually stationed there, and into one of the small Cape Cod towns. They found a small gift shop that the Kennedy women loved. It looked like a little home, a wooden structure with a flag in front of it and a couple of Adirondack chairs on a small porch, one yellow and one blue. As they shopped, Rosemary seemed to become impatient and said she wanted to go outside and sit down. One of the nuns accompanied her, and the two left the store to sit on the porch. After about ten minutes out there, according to what the nun would remember years later, someone pulled into the small parking lot in front of the store, got out of his car, and walked up to her and Rosemary. He asked for directions. Since she'd been to the Cape many times with Rosemary, she thought she might be able to help and the two began discussing the driver's route. Confused about something, he walked back to the car to get a map, and the nun followed. They spoke at the car for about five minutes, the entire time looking down at a map. It had been just five minutes, but when the sister glanced up at the porch she realized that Rosemary was gone. Since it had been such a short time, she assumed that Rosemary had gone back inside to join her siblings. She continued talking to the motorist for about another five minutes before he left and she went back inside the store. Inside, she saw Eunice and Pat debating over bath salts. She looked around the store—no Rosemary. "Is Rosie in here?" she asked the Kennedys. "What!? She's not with you?" was the response. It didn't take long to realize that Rosemary had disappeared.

Panicked, the three women ran out of the store and started calling Rosemary's name. But she was gone. "How could you allow this to happen?" Eunice demanded of the nun. According to the sister's later recollection, Eunice was understandably upset. The nun's explanation of what had happened didn't make matters much better. "That was very irresponsible of you," Eunice scolded her. "I can't believe this has happened." Eunice was so hard on her, the nun actually burst into tears. "There's no time for that now," Eunice said. "We have to find my sister."

Pat went one way, Eunice another, and the nun yet another, all in search of Rosemary. "She couldn't have gone far," Eunice said. Thirty frantic minutes later there was still no sign of her. It was then decided that Eunice and the nun would take the car and go looking for Rosemary while Pat stayed behind at the store in case she returned. So the two women got into Eunice's car and drove very slowly down a street that ran parallel to the beach. It wasn't long before they saw a large woman in a red tracksuit, red, white, and blue baseball cap, and large spectacles walking slowly on the beach, just seeming to enjoy the day. She seemed not to have a care in the world as she walked along, taking in the view. When she stopped to look at the ocean, the nun exclaimed, "Let's go get her, quick." Eunice pulled over to the side of the road, about twenty feet behind Rosemary. "No, let's wait," she said as she studied her sister.

"What in the world is she doing?" the nun asked. Eunice smiled. "I guess she's doing what we Kennedys have been doing for generations," Eunice said. "She's enjoying the beach. Let's leave her be."

As Rosemary walked along, Eunice drove very slowly behind her, the two women keeping a close eye on her the whole time. "I'm sorry I was so angry at you," Eunice told the nun as the two sat in the car watching Rosemary. "I had no right," she said.

"No, Mrs. Shriver, of course you had a right," the nun said.

"Oh no, my dear," Eunice said. "You see, I lost Rosie too, once. It was twenty years ago," Eunice said, smiling at the memory.

"We were in Chicago," Eunice remembered. "Sarge was running for vice president at the time. Rosie and I went to church in the morning, and after the service we were in the vestibule and I was looking at some rosaries and candles and, I don't know... I became distracted. I turned around and she was gone. And it didn't end as quickly as this, either," she said.

As they drove slowly along and continued to watch Rosemary, Eunice explained that back in Chicago, Rosemary had no identification on her and no money either, yet had wandered out into the street and then become absorbed by the bustling city of Chicago. It had been the first time in twenty-four years that she was free. Eunice said that she was "absolutely terrified," so much so that she had no choice but to call the police. She and an officer then drove all over the vicinity looking for Rosemary, trying to pick her out of crowds of swarming people. But they couldn't find her. Finally, as Eunice recalled it, they had no choice but to issue an all-points bulletin with a description of Rosemary. "A reporter who had heard the bulletin about a missing person saw someone fitting the description," Eunice told the nun. "She was walking down the street, looking at all of the shopping store display windows and having what seemed to be a very nice time," Eunice said. "So the reporter approached her, asked if she was looking for me, and she said she was. The next thing I knew, we were reunited. I had never been so happy to see her. I knew then that she was a very independent woman, and I had to acknowledge that about her," Eunice said. "Anyway... I'm very sorry I lashed out at you."

Of course, the nun accepted Eunice's apology. Then the two women continued to drive at a very slow pace along the side of the road, watching

Rosemary Kennedy enjoy her freedom for, likely, the first time in twenty years. "I have never seen her so relaxed," Eunice said with a soft smile. "You know, I think I shall never forget this moment," she said as she watched her sister. After about an hour, they got out of the car, walked down to the beach, and greeted Rosemary as if nothing were wrong, rather than scold her and ruin her lovely day.

It's likely that Rosemary Kennedy never forgot that day in Cape Cod either, a morning when she was able to walk on the beach alone, unsupervised. It probably had been an even richer experience for her than her Chicago getaway, simply because there were no pressing crowds to make her nervous and fearful. It had just been Rosemary and nature on the Cape, a moment for her to collect her thoughts in exactly the same manner as her many relatives by now took for granted since it had been their way for so long. In many ways, she was a good deal stronger than most people knew. After all, she'd survived a very challenging life, living it her own way and, eventually, on her own terms, which was not so surprising considering the Kennedy blood that ran through her veins.

On January 7, 2005, Rose Marie Kennedy—Rosemary—died at the age of eighty-six of natural causes. Eunice, Pat, and Jean were at her side at Fort Atkinson Memorial Health Hospital in Fort Atkinson, Wisconsin, as was Ted. She had lived a long and very sad life, but one hopes she knew how much her family loved her. It was difficult for all of her siblings to say goodbye to her, but a little tougher for Eunice. After all, Rosie had inspired Eunice's life's work. Indeed, so much of who Eunice was as an activist and humanitarian was intrinsically tied to who her sister had been in her life and in the lives of her mother and siblings. In years to come, Eunice would often say she would never forget the sight of her older sister alone on the beach, enjoying the day with nary a concern or restriction. It would carry her through.

Rosemary would be buried next to her parents, Rose and Joseph, at Holyhood Cemetery in Brookline.

An Ongoing Struggle

*I*n March 2005, life took yet another sad turn for Joan Kennedy, who was now sixty-eight. Still battling alcoholism, Joan relapsed yet again, and this time in a very public way. She took what ABC News later described as "a drunken fall" in Boston and was found lying bleeding and alone on a Beacon Hill sidewalk. "She said she was okay, but she did not look okay," recalled Constance Bacon, who shielded the helpless Joan from the rain as they waited for an ambulance. "She was conscious. She had just hit her head pretty hard. She knew that she had fallen and she tried to get up and she couldn't. So I just waited until the ambulance came. I had no idea who she was."

Unfortunately, Joan's fall resulted in a concussion and a broken shoulder. When the accident made the national news, it was difficult for those who loved and cared for Joan to realize that she was still waging what, at least from all outward appearances, seemed to be an unsuccessful battle against alcoholism. She had always been such a generous and caring person; it was difficult to reconcile that she was still in great turmoil and pain. From the hospital, Joan called her son Ted Jr., who then called Patrick and Kara with the upsetting news. When Patrick arrived at the hospital, he looked exhausted and extremely upset. "You want to make sure there's someone there for her all the time," he said, "but at the same time you don't want to encroach on her privacy too much. When things like this happen, it makes you feel as though maybe you should have done more to make sure there's someone with her 24/7, and perhaps that might become necessary." Soon after, Patrick announced that he was dropping plans to run for the Senate in 2006, a move he had been contemplating for some time that would have seen him challenge Republican senator Lincoln Chaffee. "My family means too much to me," he said, obviously referring to his mother since he was not married and had no children.

After that very troubling incident, Joan's children intervened in her affairs, obtaining a court-ordered guardianship that put Ted Jr. in charge of his mother's care and her $9 million estate. The details found in papers filed in Barnstable Probate and Family Court on Cape Cod were disturbing. It was alleged by her children that Joan had stopped attending Alcoholics Anonymous meetings and had been surreptitiously drinking vanilla extract and mouthwash in an attempt to become inebriated, so much in fact that she had done damage to her kidneys. If she continued at the rate she'd been going, doctors feared she could end up on dialysis within a year. They also stated that Joan had been suffering from bipolar disease and depression as well as alcoholism. In the end, Barnstable judge Robert Terry ruled that Joan was "incapable of taking care of herself by reason of mental illness."

It was at this same time that Joan's children found out that she had transferred title of the Squaw Island home—the house she and Ted had owned for many years, and which she got as part of her divorce settlement from him—to a trust that was to be controlled by Webster Janssen, a man Ted Jr., Patrick, and Kara claimed to not even know! Understandably, they became suspicious and feared that someone was taking advantage of their mother in her emotionally weakened state. The result was an awful family feud that left Joan feeling bullied by her children and as if she had no power over her own life and affairs. She retaliated by putting the Squaw Island house on the market. As far as her children were concerned, this was the proverbial last straw. They loved that house, had grown up there, felt it was theirs as well as their mother's, and weren't going to allow it to be sold. "Basically, my mother is taking it out on us by trying to sell the house," Ted Jr. stated at the time.

So how did all of this happen?

It started a couple years earlier, in the spring of 2003, when Joan's second cousin Webster Janssen picked her up from her home in Boston to drive her to Maine to visit relatives there. On the trip, Joan seemed particularly anxious. She had just been released from a treatment facility in Blairstown, New Jersey, after a seven-month stay and, as she explained to Janssen, "It cost me a fortune. I'm very worried about my future," Joan said. "I'm getting older. I feel I need to be saving money, not spending it."

"What about Ted and the kids?" Janssen asked. "Surely they can help you out?"

Joan shook her head and didn't respond. Her relationship with Ted was fine, mostly because she kept him out of her business and he didn't ask questions about it. They had been divorced for more than twenty years and, of course, he was now married to Vicki. He'd just barely been available to Joan during their marriage, so she certainly didn't expect much from him now, other than simple kindness—which he did offer. However, Joan's now grown children were a different story. Joan was adamant that she didn't want them telling her what to do, yet she was always in such emotional distress that it was difficult for them to stay out of her affairs. The more they pushed to help her, the more she felt her freedom being chipped away. As much as they all loved one another, there was a great deal of anger and disappointment bubbling just under the surface. It was a family dynamic that had been many years in the making, going all the way back to when Joan left home to move into her own apartment in the early 1980s. By 2005, she had been in and out of rehabilitation centers for the better part of thirty years. It had not been easy on anybody.

"Maybe I can help you," Webster Janssen offered as he drove Joan to Maine. As it happened, Janssen had grown up with Joan in Bronxville. His mother, Belle Bennett, and Joan's, Ginny Bennett, were cousins. He had been a frequent date at school functions, an usher at her wedding to Ted (and, he recalls, danced with Jackie at the reception), and had maintained a relationship with her over the years. He was one of the first to call her after the Chappaquiddick incident in 1969. Because he'd worked on Wall Street as a trust investment officer at Citibank and Morgan Guaranty Trust, he felt qualified to help Joan. "I'll take a look at your portfolio and we'll see what we can do."

"When I looked at her portfolio and saw how her investments had been managed, I realized she really could benefit from my experience," Janssen recalled. "I thought I could help her. That I would give her the best advice."

Joan and Webster came to an arrangement whereby she would pay him by the hour to advise her on her assets, which he found in looking at the books came to about $9 million. However, since her money was hopelessly entangled in mortgages and other long-term investments, Joan had good reason to be worried. She was cash poor.

For the next eighteen months or so, Joan and Jannsen continued to work on her finances and straighten out myriad problems. "I would come to Boston once a month and we would sit down and try to figure it all out," he recalled. "Without getting into detail, a lot of people had taken advantage of her. She is a very nice person, and somewhat naive. I found that she wasn't knowledgeable about her investments or finances, and she was really in over her head."

"What about the house on Squaw Island?" Webster asked Joan during one of their meetings. "How often do you actually go there?" Joan said she stayed at the home about two months of the year every summer. "It's not worth it, then," Webster advised her. "I think you should sell it. You could probably get about $7 million for it. That would put money in your pocket and you wouldn't have to worry for the rest of your life."

Joan seemed relieved. It sounded like a very good idea. Therefore, she and Janssen established a trust, transferred title of the Squaw Island house to it, and prepared to sell it.

When Joan told Ted that she was working with Webster Janssen, he said he was happy about it. He said he was relieved that she had found someone she could trust and he was happy not to have to worry about her. Apparently, Joan decided not to tell her children she was working with Janssen, and Ted didn't give them that information either. In fact, the children didn't know a thing about Janssen until Joan had her street accident in Boston and they began delving into her affairs. "Who the hell is this guy?" Ted Jr. asked his mother. "It's none of your business," Joan told him. "These are my affairs, not yours."

It was when Joan Kennedy put the Squaw Island house on the market that her children—Ted Jr., Patrick, and Kara—decided to take her to court over the sale of the property, with a trial being set for June 2005. They also wanted the interloper Janssen out of the picture. It was all very unfortunate—"extremely disrespectful to Joan," is how Janssen put it— and couldn't have done much to ease Joan's unhappiness at this time. However, in their defense, Joan's children were genuinely worried. They didn't understand why she felt it necessary to keep her relationship with Webster Janssen a secret, and they were very concerned. It got ugly.

In the end, Joan didn't have the strength or energy to fight her children. A court case was avoided when she settled the matter by dissolving the trust established by Janssen and taking the Squaw Island house off the market. She also reluctantly agreed to strict court-ordered supervision with a guardian to make sure she did not drink. Meanwhile, her finances were to be handled by two court-appointed trustees. Tired and feeling overwhelmed, Joan then went into rehab again. This time, she was *required* to stay sober, otherwise her children would be granted permanent custody of her.

Webster Janssen says, "My reputation took a beating. Let's just say the Kennedys were not kind to me in the press. It never even occurred to me when I started helping her there would be any opposition since I was a family member and had the qualifications. There were things that showed up in local newspapers impugning my professionalism and integrity, statements I could have sued them for, but I didn't want to go up against the Kennedy machine. It would have cost an arm and a leg and taken years in litigation, and quite frankly, I didn't want to drag Joan through it. It cost me more than you will ever know in time and personal anguish."

Within six months of the settlement, Joan was much stronger emotionally and decided to put her foot down. She was selling the house, and that was the end of it. So she put the property back on the market for $6.5 million, just as she and Webster Janssen had intended. Ted had the right of first refusal, but apparently he didn't have the cash or the credit since he was heavily leveraged on other properties, including the Big House on the compound. Joan's children said they didn't have the money either. In the end, the house was sold to a stranger. "If it had been sold under the trust that Joan and I had established, there would have been a provision that the new owner would have to allow Joan to lease it every summer for two months, as she had for years," said Webster Janssen. "But under the new arrangement, that was not possible. So it was all very sad."

As of this writing, Joan Kennedy is committed to her sobriety and attends Alcoholics Anonymous meetings seven days a week in Boston, where she lives. She remains sober. Her relationship with her children is still somewhat strained, but they continue to try to make it work. "At the end of the day, we're family," Patrick Kennedy said, "and, as we've well learned over the years, it's family that matters most."

Pat Kennedy Lawford Dies

On September 17, 2006, Pat Kennedy Lawford passed away at the age of eighty-two from cancer and complications of pneumonia.

In the later years of her life, Pat had devoted her time to organizations that served the mentally disabled and those helping people with substance abuse problems. She may not have had the kind of high-profile life of her sister Eunice, the activist, or Jean, the ambassador, but as she got older she was very happy with the life she had made for herself. "She distinguished herself in one important way," Ted Kennedy once said of her. "She was a very good friend. In fact, you could never have a more loyal, kinder friend than my sister Pat."

When Pat learned that she had throat cancer in 2003, she made a decision not to fight it. She was against the idea of chemotherapy and felt strongly that it never worked and that anyone who believed it did was fooling himself. "That was always Pat's way," said her friend Patricia Brennan. "She was very definitive and pragmatic. It was the way she felt about marriages never working out. Anyone who said she was in a happy marriage was lying about it, at least as far as Pat was concerned. The family was very worried about her and sort of ganged up on her and made her go on chemotherapy. In the end, though, Pat was right—it didn't work and it made her life a living hell. If it had been up to her, she would have died in 2003, not 2006. The last three years were brutal. It was a shame. 'If everyone had just let me do it my way, this would be all over by now,' she told me in 2004. She wasn't afraid of death, not at all. She was more afraid of living a life of great pain than she was of dying. When it was her time to go, she was happy to do it, I must say.

"The last time I talked to her was in 2005. She could no longer make the trips to the West Coast, so our lunches were a thing of the past. On the phone with me, I could barely hear her because her voice was just a whisper now. She said, 'No tears for me, Patty. I have had a very good and very rich life. So, not one tear should be shed for Pat Kennedy Lawford,' she concluded, 'and if you cry for me, I swear to God I will come back and haunt you.' And then we laughed. My goodness, how we laughed!"

Patricia Kennedy Lawford was survived by her son, Chris, three daughters, Sydney, Robin, and Victoria Frances, and ten grandchildren.

Ted Kennedy and the Obama Endorsement

I'm proud to stand here with him today and offer my help, offer my voice, offer my energy, my commitment to make Barack Obama the next president of the United States."

It was January 2008 and a now older Ted Kennedy—in his fifth decade as a senator—stood next to his niece Caroline Kennedy onstage at a morning campaign rally in Bender Arena on the campus of American University in Washington, D.C., delivering a ringing endorsement of Barack Obama's campaign for the nomination of his party for president.

Almost ten years had passed since the death of John Kennedy Jr.—ten years of family life, of children, grandchildren, and the passing of glorious summers in Hyannis Port. Back in 2002, "No Child Left Behind," which Ted had cosponsored, was signed into law, giving states and school districts more freedom over how they spent federal dollars, but also requiring them to raise student achievement. He was very proud of that legislation. Then, in 2006, Ted easily won an eighth term that was to extend his Senate career to an even fifty years in 2012. A year later, Congress approved an increase in the federal minimum wage, something else Ted had been fighting for in the Senate for quite some time. Indeed, though many things had changed over the years for the Kennedys, some things remained the same—such as Ted Kennedy's commitment to public service, his need to be of assistance, and, most of all, his ability to get things done.

Throughout 2007, Ted had remained neutral in the race even though his support had been avidly sought by all three presidential contenders—Obama, Senator Hillary Clinton, and Senator John Edwards—proving pretty much the obvious: that a political endorsement by Ted Kennedy was still significant almost fifty years after his brother Jack took office. It was Caroline Kennedy who first spoke to Ted about endorsing Obama. She believed in him and had decided to lend her support. It wasn't an easy decision. She would not be able to forget Chelsea Clinton's emotional support six weeks after John died when Chelsea joined Caroline and her family on a sailing and waterskiing trip off Martha's Vineyard. Chelsea had been a good friend, and Caroline also counted Hillary and Bill Clinton as close friends. She called all three and spoke to them personally to tell them that she had decided to support Obama. Those were difficult calls, say sources close to the Clintons. "Bill understood and seemed to roll with it, but Hillary and Chelsea were very hurt and they let Caroline know it," said the source. "But Caroline has been around politics long enough to know that you can't take it personally, and she was surprised that Hillary and Chelsea didn't see it that way."

The Kennedys' support of Obama was a crushing blow to New York senator Hillary Clinton, who had been a colleague and a friend of the Kennedy family for years. In fact, the Clintons had long been friends with Ted and Vicki. On a personal level, they had entertained the couple at Martha's Vineyard—along with Jackie when she was alive—and, professionally, Bill Clinton had sought Kennedy's counsel when he was threatened with impeachment over the Monica Lewinsky scandal. Also, of course, when John Jr.'s plane went down, President Clinton mobilized the full resources of the federal government in searching for the plane and the victims of the crash. Moreover, Ted had worked closely with Hillary Clinton on health care reform and other legislation. Ted liked Mrs. Clinton and advised her not to make the same mistake he made in 1980 when it came to the Secret Service. He said that he felt that the Service had made it impossible to connect with voters during his campaign that year and warned her to try to keep them at bay, even though, of course, they needed to do their job in protecting her and her husband. However, Hillary didn't seem to be Ted's cup of tea as a politician. She was too brash and, he felt, divisive. He was also quite disenchanted when Bill Clinton made some statements suggesting that the primary reason Obama had so much momentum was because of the support of African Americans, thus injecting race into the campaign, at least in Ted's view. He had appealed to Bill to stop making such statements in a couple of very heated telephone calls, but to no avail. Later, many people in the Clinton camp would say that she lost Kennedy's support because of her husband, and in fact Bill did play a lesser role in her campaign after the Kennedys endorsed Obama.

In the end, though, Ted just didn't think Hillary could win, even though some of his own family strongly disagreed, such as Ethel's children, former Maryland lieutenant governor Kathleen Kennedy Townsend, Bobby Jr., who was now a global environmentalist, and Kerry, a human rights activist. Ethel was also behind Barack Obama. In 2005, she had invited him to speak at a ceremony commemorating what would have been Bobby's eightieth birthday and she said at the time that she felt he would be "our next president." "I think he feels it. He feels it just like Bobby did," Mrs. Kennedy said in an interview that day, comparing her late husband's quest for social justice to Mr. Obama's. "He has the passion in his heart. He's not selling you. It's just him." Jean was also behind

Obama, which was difficult for her because, after all, Bill Clinton had named her ambassador to Ireland. "But as I think back on my brothers' lives and John Hume's words and example, I know that my experience, my conscience, and my heart all point to Barack Obama, the messenger of hope, who speaks to the same principle of unity and the common good that John Hume and my brothers believed in," Jean said at the time. "He offers the right moral vision for America in our dangerously divided but increasingly interconnected world." Rarely had the family ever been so split on their support of a political candidate, and Arnold Schwarzenegger went on record saying that in thirty years he had never seen such a thing happen. His wife, Maria Shriver, sided with Ted Kennedy in his support of Obama, while Republican Schwarzenegger eventually backed his party's candidate for office, John McCain.

"There was another time, when another young candidate was running for president and challenging America to cross a new frontier," Ted said in his endorsement of Obama. "He faced criticism from the preceding Democratic president, who was widely respected in the party," Kennedy said, referring to Harry S. Truman. "And John Kennedy replied, 'The world is changing. The old ways will not do.... It is time for a new generation of leadership.' So it is with Barack Obama," he added. "Now, with Barack Obama, there is a new national leader who has given America a different kind of campaign—a campaign not just about himself, but about all of us. A campaign about the country we will become, if we can rise above the old politics that parses us into separate groups and puts us at odds with one another. With Barack Obama, we will turn the page on the old politics of misrepresentation and distortion. With Barack Obama, we will close the book on the old politics of race against race, gender against gender, ethnic group against ethnic group, and straight against gay."

Ted, who had been introduced by Caroline that morning, said that Obama "offers that same sense of hope and inspiration" as did her father. "Your mother and father would be so proud of you today," he told Caroline.

Ted's son, Representative Patrick Kennedy, also endorsed Obama from the stage that day, saying that "we now find ourselves standing on a precipice of crisis.... We need a leader who can galvanize a new generation of citizens."

"Today isn't just about politics for me. It's personal," Obama, who was forty-six at the time, said when it came time for him to speak. "I was too young to remember John Kennedy and I was just a child when Robert Kennedy ran for president. But in the stories I heard growing up, I saw how my grandparents and mother spoke about them, and about that period in our nation's life—as a time of great hope and achievement." He added, "I know what your support means. I know the cherished place the Kennedy family holds in the hearts of the American people. And that is as it should be, because the Kennedy family, more than any other, has always stood for what is best about the Democratic Party and what is best about America."

Meanwhile, the Clinton campaign issued a statement from Kathleen Kennedy Townsend. "I respect Caroline and Ted's decision, but I have made a different choice," Ms. Townsend said in her statement, adding, "At this moment when so much is at stake at home and overseas, I urge our fellow Americans to support Hillary Clinton. That is why my brother Bobby, my sister Kerry, and I are supporting Hillary Clinton."

Within days of his endorsement speech, Ted Kennedy hit the road in support of his candidate. New Mexico, California, New Jersey, Connecticut, Massachusetts, Maine, Pennsylvania, Washington, Maryland, Virginia, Ohio—the schedule was grueling but Ted loved it, as did Vicki. "I felt joyous and exuberant through the inevitable exhaustion of the Democratic primary campaign," he wrote in his memoir, *True Compass*, "as I had felt in Wyoming and West Virginia in 1960 for Jack, and in Indiana and California in 1968 for Bobby."

Doubtless, the persuasive power of Ted Kennedy helped Barack Obama secure the nomination of his party. In effect, Kennedy had set aside any fears that Obama didn't have the experience to be president just by virtue of being willing to go out on a limb and lend him his support. After all, one of the greatest criticisms Hillary Clinton had of Obama was his lack of experience. Once that became a nonissue, Obama's candidacy seemed all but guaranteed. It was an important time not only for the country, but for Ted Kennedy as well. He felt invigorated by the possibility of what was to come. It was just the beginning. And maybe nothing said it better for him than when, in Maine on February 8, 2008, he led the crowd of Obama supporters in song, as he often did from the podium after a rousing speech. On this day it was a familiar old chestnut about his heritage of which he was so proud, one he had sung at rallies more times over the years than he could possibly remember. It was "When Irish Eyes Are Smiling." Indeed, in the midst of making a big difference by supporting the candidacy of a man who could be America's first African American president, it was a time in Ted Kennedy's life when all the world seemed bright and filled with hope.

Ted's Diagnosis

As the primary season came to a close, Ted Kennedy, who was now seventy-six, was at his home preparing for the start of the sailing season in Hyannis when he suffered a seizure on Saturday, May 17, 2008. "We woke up as usual, went downstairs to have coffee," Vicki—who by this time had been married to Ted for sixteen years—would later recall. "He took the dogs [Sunny and Splash, both Portuguese water dogs] out for their first walk, as usual, and read the newspapers. Then he was taking the dogs out again, and suddenly I heard Judy, a wonderful friend of ours who's been with us at the Cape for a long time. [Judy Campbell was the Kennedys' household assistant.] She said, 'Vicki! *Vicki!*' And I ran into the dining room, and Ted was sitting in a chair there. I knew something very grave was happening." Ted later recalled, "I felt disoriented. I moved toward the door leading to the porch, where several spacious chairs face the lovely prospect that I've known since childhood: a view to Nantucket Sound and the several masted boats at anchor in the nearby harbor. 'Well,' I told myself, 'I'll just go outside and get some air.' I didn't make it outside....I lowered myself into a chair. That's the last thing I remember until I awoke in the hospital."

Ted was rushed to the Cape Cod Hospital and then flown by medevac helicopter to Massachusetts General Hospital. His children hurried to his side, as did Caroline. Tests were conducted, the results of which were swift and shocking. By Tuesday, doctors were certain Ted had a malignant brain tumor. One doctor opined he had two to four months to live. "It just didn't compute with him," Vicki said. In truth, Ted would never accept such a diagnosis. He'd seen cancer in his own family—Ted Jr. when he was a boy and, more recently, his daughter, Kara. Seven years earlier,

Kara was told that she had "inoperable" lung cancer and that there was little if any hope for her survival. She was only forty-two and the mother of two children, Grace and Max. It was devastating news, but Ted refused to give in to it. He called in the best doctors from all over the country to confer about possible treatments before settling on one that was risky but held the best hope, basically the removal of part of Kara's lung. It was everything he could do to keep his daughter's spirits up as she underwent aggressive chemotherapy and radiation. Where Joan was concerned, Ted also did what he could to help her through the ordeal, too. This time, unlike when Ted Jr. was sick, Ted was really there for Joan. In fact, today Joan credits Ted with "saving my daughter's life," because, somehow, Kennedys being who they are, Kara beat the odds. Now, seven years later, she was still alive and doing very well, as was of course Ted Jr. Ted Kennedy had not given up on his kids, and he certainly wasn't going to give up on himself either.*

The news hit hard across party lines. Ted had so much respect from both Democrats and Republicans, it was difficult to imagine a time when he would not be in the Senate fighting tooth and nail for his beliefs. "I think you can argue that I would not be sitting here as a presidential candidate had it not been for some of the battles Ted Kennedy has fought," said Barack Obama. "He is someone who battled for voting rights and civil rights when I was a child. I stand on his shoulders."

The family was distraught at this sudden turn of events. It seemed impossible to imagine that a time might be imminent when Ted would no longer be with them. Ethel, for one, simply refused to believe that Ted was dying—which is perhaps not so surprising. "I will not accept this," she told Ted's son Patrick, according to his later recollection. "Teddy can beat this," she said. "He has to. He just has to…"

"The fact that he had always been there to take care of everything was an incredible relief to us," Ted Jr. said in 2009. "He instantly took on the situation, whatever it was. Whether it was John's death or whatever

---

* Sadly, Kara Kennedy died very suddenly of an apparent heart attack on September 16, 2011, after exercising at a health club in Washington, D.C. Her brother Patrick speculated that her cancer treatment had left her physically weakened. Her mother, Joan, added, "She was very healthy. That's why this is such a shock."

situation was facing our family, he was in the director's chair and he really helped all of us emotionally and logistically."

Though the next few months would be difficult, rarely did Ted allow his illness to get the best of him. He continued on the good path his wife Vicki had set for him years earlier. "He was incredibly generous to anyone who approached him on the Cape," says Karen Jeffrey, a reporter for the *Cape Cod Times*. "He made an effort to stay in touch with people, to reach out to people, especially on the Cape. If he heard someone in a family he knew even vaguely was sick, he would send a card or make a phone call. He wrote his own thank-you notes, and I am in receipt of some of them. For instance, when he was sick on the Cape, I happened to say to a press person who knew him, 'Tell the senator he should spend as much time on that porch getting sun as possible. And tell him I hope he's feeling a lot better.' Two days later a handwritten note came in the mail, thanking me! He had very nice handwriting and the first thing you thought of when receiving one of his notes was, 'Rose trained him well.' It was definitely a throwback to another era, the handwritten note. Jackie was known for it as well. There are probably thousands of notes from Jackie circulating about from people who received them in her lifetime, and the same is true of Ted."

Ted's greatest comfort at this time was, as it always had been, sailing on his boat, the *Mya*, and enjoying the Nantucket Sound on a blustery day just the way Kennedys had been doing for so many decades. "When you're out on the ocean, do you ever see your brothers?" the former award-winning *Boston Globe* columnist Mike Barnicle, a friend of Kennedys', once asked Ted. "Sure," Ted answered. "All the time...all the time. There's not a day I don't think of them. This is where we all grew up. There have been some joyous times here. Difficult times, too. We all learned to swim here. Learned to sail. I still remember my brother Joe, swimming with him here before he went off to war. My brother Jack, out on the water with him...I remember it all so well. He lived on the water, fought on the water. The sea," Ted concluded, "there are eternal aspects to the sea and the ocean. It anchors you."

Mike Barnicle has many telling stories about Ted, including this one:

In August 2009, Barnicle would resign from the *Boston Globe* after a stellar twenty-five-year career, over charges of plagiarism concerning two of the approximately four thousand columns he had written for the paper.

It was a dark time for Barnicle. One night at about 11:30, there was a knock on the screen door at his home on Cape Cod, not far from the Kennedy compound. He opened the door to find Ted. "You have to hang in there," Ted told Mike, handing him a pair of rosary beads. "Everything passes, even the darkest of nights." That's the kind of man Ted Kennedy had become by this time in his life.

Another close friend of his recalls a conversation he had while sailing with Ted on the *Mya* under a low gray sky. Ted was wearing his favorite straw hat and windbreaker. "You know, I think sometimes, why me? But then I think, hell, why *not* me?" he observed. "Maybe it's my turn, you know? I think about Joe and Kick. Jack and Bobby. And Mother and Father. And Jackie. And David and Michael. And John Jr. and Carolyn. I think, none of them wanted to go either, did they? So, maybe I'm going now. Maybe it's my time to go." His friend refused to accept such reasoning from Ted. "It's not your time," he insisted. "Don't give in to it, Ted." Ted smiled. "It's okay," he said. "This is a slow thing. It gives me a chance to say goodbye. It gives everyone that chance. We didn't have it with my brothers Jack and Bobby. So I'm glad to have it," he concluded.

The Troops Rally

*T*ed Kennedy's goal was to be well enough to speak at the Democratic convention in August. It was a long shot, but he knew he could do it if he just kept a positive attitude and also, of course, prayed. Meanwhile, despite many health setbacks in the next few months, he was eager to continue to work—he was in the process of drafting legislation for universal health care that he hoped to give Obama should he win the election—and, maybe more important, to enjoy the good life on the Cape.

In June 2008, Ted Kennedy underwent delicate brain surgery to extract as much of the growing malignancy as possible, though it was always clear that there was no way to eradicate the cancer but just to, one hoped, extend Ted's life a little longer. The family troops rallied in a big way that summer. Ted Jr.—who never forgot how his dad had helped him deal with his own cancer so many years earlier—moved into his uncle Jack and aunt Jackie's house next door so that he could be available to his father. He brought along his wife, Kiki, and their children, Kiley and Ted III. Jean and Joan both rented houses nearby so they could be present as well. In fact, Joan's son Ted Jr. was often seen tooling about town on his moped with Joan on the back—hanging on for dear life, a scarf over her head, looking fit and every bit "the Dish" of old. Eunice was not well at all, but still found a way to spend much of that summer in Hyannis with the family. Of course, Ethel was in her home, as always, welcoming many of the third and fourth generation of Kennedys as guests.

Within a month, Ted was back at the Senate to give Democrats a much-needed vote to pass Medicare pricing legislation. Upon entering the chamber, Ted received a standing ovation. Recognizing that the legislation was on the verge of being approved, nine Republicans switched their votes to side with him.

The Fourth of July 2008 was tough for everyone. Just as they had done for years, the Kennedys gathered at the Cape for their big annual family barbecue. This time it seemed that even more of the third generation showed up than usual and with their children, too—the fourth generation of Kennedys, many of them throwing Frisbees and footballs across the yard and out onto the sandy beach with typical Kennedy flair. Though Ted was quite weak, his hair thinned and his face drawn, he was also in great spirits as he joked with all of the youngsters present, including his four grandchildren. He and Joan also spent a great deal of time talking to one another, often isolating themselves from the others. At one point, they walked out to a long sandbar and stood in their bare feet for an hour, talking and laughing. How wonderful it must have been for their children to witness parents who had once been so at odds reconcile any animosity that had resulted from their tumultuous union. Still, it was difficult to escape the sense that the gathering was as much a farewell to Ted as it was a celebration of Independence Day. "I see the kids hanging on his every word," Joan later said, "and it kills me because I know what they are thinking."

"When I'm not around, I want you all to remember this day," Ted said at one point as he offered up a toast. "And I want you to remember how happy we are and what kind of a family the Kennedys are. And I want you to take solace that we *are* Kennedys, each and every one of us. And that we are family. And there is nothing more important than family."

At that, everyone cheered. Everyone, that is, except Ethel. Instead, she became visibly upset, and as the applause rang out all around her, she put down her glass and fled from the room.

"Wise Men Never Try"

I am here to pay tribute to two men who have changed my life and the life of this country—Barack Obama and Edward M. Kennedy," said Caroline Kennedy on August 25, 2008, in front of an enthusiastic audience at the Pepsi Center in Denver. It was the first night of the Democratic convention.

Though he was not well and seemed to be getting weaker by the day, his chemotherapy and radiation treatments taking their awful toll, somehow Ted was able to rally enough to make it to the convention. Just hours before he was scheduled to speak, however, most people in his contingent thought it unlikely that he would be able to take the stage. To make matters worse, as he was rehearsing his speech he felt a sharp pain in his side and lower back. Kidney stones. He'd never had them before, so the timing was incredibly poor. As it happened, the drugs the doctors wanted to give him to deal with the pain threatened to impair his performance onstage. He had worked so hard to get to the point where he'd be able to speak at the convention, the idea that he wouldn't be able to do so was more than Vicki could take. Usually unflappable, she actually burst into tears in front of the doctors, telling them that if they gave her husband the drugs they prescribed, they were taking away Ted's right to make a decision about speaking. He would be so out of it, there was no way he would even be awake! The doctors agreed, and calibrated how much painkiller to give the senator so that it would be out of his system in time for his moment onstage. But then an uninformed nurse made a mistake and gave Ted another dose of the drug. When Vicki found out about it, she let the nurse have it! But it was too late. The damage was done. The drug was coursing through Ted's bloodstream, and all he and Vicki could do was cross their fingers and hope that the effects would wear off before Ted was scheduled to speak. Vicki was uncertain of the wisdom of even allowing him to go onstage, but she also knew that once he got out there he would somehow be reinvigorated and would likely acquit himself well. She didn't want to deny him his moment. She didn't want to deny the audience either.

When Caroline Kennedy introduced her uncle Ted, he walked out onto the stage greeted by thousands of placard-waving people—the signs boasting the name "Kennedy" in bold white letters against a blue back-ground. It was a dramatic appearance, as expected, perhaps one of Ted's most memorable in front of an American audience, given the attention his illness had generated in recent months. Somehow...he had made it.

"It is so wonderful to be here," he said, with a big smile, "and nothing, nothing, is going to keep me away from this special gathering tonight." In a blue suit, pale blue shirt, and blue print tie, he looked strong and vital as he again lent his support to Obama. "We are all Americans," he intoned in his moving speech. "We reach the moon. We scale the heights. I know it. I've seen it. I've lived it. And we can do it again." Many delegates wiped away tears as Ted spoke. "I pledge to you that I will be there next January on the floor of the United States Senate," Kennedy said, drawing loud cheers and applause. "The hope rises again, and the dream lives on," he said in conclusion of his seven minutes at the microphone, as delegates waved hundreds of Kennedy signs.

"There he was," said one witness, "the shock of white hair, older, stately, dignified, the Lion of the Senate, still representing Camelot, rep-resenting our American history. Unbelievable. To be there, well, it was a moment I'll never forget."

Of course, Barack Hussein Obama II would be elected the forty-fourth president of the United States, the first African American to hold the office. He would be inaugurated on January 20, 2009. Ted was pres-ent, just as he had promised. However, at the inaugural luncheon later that day after Obama's swearing-in ceremony, he suffered a seizure and had to be taken to the hospital. The seizure was witnessed by fellow con-gressmen, many of whom seemed visibly shaken. Representative Pete Sessions (R-TX) said Kennedy's hand began shaking and he appeared to have "a seizure" or "a stroke" and was almost immediately helped by emergency personnel. Ted's longtime friend Senator Chris Dodd (D-CT) quoted Ted as saying, "I'll be okay, I'll see you later," as he was put into an ambulance. "He gave me that Irish smile, so I think he's going to be all right," said Orrin G. Hatch (R-UT). In fact, Ted was awake and answering questions when he arrived at the hospital and was able to receive a phone call from President Obama. Vicki and Patrick Kennedy were at his side.

In November 2008, the day after Thanksgiving, Ted and Vicki had hosted a party at their home in the Kennedy compound, the Big House—the same house in which the Kennedys had rejoiced when Jack was elected and grieved when he was assassinated, the same house in which Joseph had died, in which they mourned Bobby, the house in which everyone convened when Ted faced the nightmare of Chappaquiddick—indeed, a house filled with so many poignant memories, both good and bad. This was another opportunity for friends and family to come together, this time to give thanks for the year that had just passed and the one now on the horizon. "We have so much to be grateful for," Ted said in addressing the guests, about a hundred in all, including people who went all the way back to Ted's days in grammar school. "Let's remember what's important. Friends, family, loved ones, and our faith. Thank you for coming, and God bless you all."

Joan was present, as were Ted's three children and his grandchildren, not to mention a wide array of nieces and nephews. Though chemotherapy had definitely taken a toll on Ted and he seemed somewhat weaker, there was still that great smile and twinkle in his blue eyes. At one point, he went to get up, faltered, and sank back into his chair. Ethel looked alarmed. She went over to him and helped him stand. Then she helped him walk to the bathroom and waited outside until he was finished. Afterward, she helped him back to his chair. "Guess she's my nursemaid now," Ted said, slightly embarrassed. Ethel patted him on the shoulder and smiled down at him. "I love you, Ethie," he said to her as everyone around them became quite choked up. Ethel seemed unable to speak; instead, she just continued to pat him on the shoulder, her head nodding up and down.

"Let's have a musical number," Jean shouted out at one point when everyone was seated in the parlor. It certainly never took much to convince Ted to break out in song. He sat down in a straight-backed chair next to the piano. When someone began to play, he began to sing one of his favorites. He may have remembered singing it forty years earlier on the *Christina* in Greece when Jackie was being romanced by Aristotle Onassis. Or maybe not. But he had certainly sung it many times since then, and on many occasions. *"Some enchanted evening,"* he began, *"you may see a stranger . . ."* Soon Vicki began to sing along with her husband, and then, one by one, everyone in the living room joined in.

PART TWENTY-FOUR

Looking Ahead

Kathleen Kennedy Townsend

*I*t's certainly not been easy for the third generation of Kennedys to have to constantly compete in the public's minds with the historic legacies of JFK, RFK, and EMK. "We had always evaluated ourselves, and others evaluated ourselves, on how Jack and Bobby and my father were and what was going on with the Kennedys in the 1960s," Patrick Kennedy has recalled. "Here we were, growing up and growing up fast, but our mindset was always turned backward." It's no wonder. After all, they are the last generation with direct memories of Joseph P. Kennedy, and the last with memories of JFK and Bobby, too. And as the women marry, change their last names, and have children of their own, they are, arguably, also the last generation that will accurately be described as "Kennedys." The public has expected the family to continue the Camelot tradition, but it has not been that simple. Times are different. Just having the last name Kennedy holds no guarantees in the political arena. Still, the Kennedys all grew up with the mandate that they must be of service. It's what Kennedys do, after all. Therefore, even though the names of most of the third generation might not be widely known, many of them have made significant contributions not only in public but also as advocates of many important causes. Of the bunch, though, it's Ethel's kids who have really distinguished themselves, so much so that even Pam Kelley, who was paralyzed so long ago in the Jeep accident while Joe Kennedy Jr. was driving, has to admit, "You can only surmise she did well by them. Despite their screwups, they're all committed to public service and they're all sincere about it."

Without a doubt, Ethel's daughter Kathleen Hartington Kennedy is the most politically accomplished of the third generation of Kennedy women. In fact, she had always had a keen sense of social responsibility. When she was twelve, her father, Bobby, wrote her, "You seemed to understand that Jack died and was buried today. As the oldest of the Kennedy grandchildren, you have particular responsibility now, a special responsibility to John and Joe [Jr., killed in World War II]. Be kind and work for your country. Love, Daddy." She was the oldest of Bobby's and Ethel's children, and Ethel put her in charge of the rest of the brood when

Bobby was killed, mirroring Rose's decision that the oldest of the second generation care for the youngest. As it happened, Kathleen was a very nurturing presence in the lives of her siblings and, some might argue, at a level that exceeded even her own mother's during the most difficult of familial times in the 1970s. By David's own admission, Kathleen had taken him under her wing, for instance, when much of the rest of the family didn't know what to do about him.

Kathleen attended Radcliffe College, as would her cousin Caroline. Fully dedicated to the antiwar movement in the 1970s, she found herself working for the George McGovern presidential campaign in 1972. It was then that she met her husband, David Townsend, who was finishing his doctorate at the time. They married in November 1973, the date—as previously mentioned in this book—falling at the same time that Ted Jr. was hospitalized, causing a conflict for Ted Sr., who was to give his niece away. The couple then moved to New Mexico, where she found work with a human rights organization. After having three children in six years, they moved back east to earn their law degrees at Yale. The couple is still happily married, perhaps heeding Grandma Rose's advice to Kathleen: "Make sure you never, never argue at night. You just lose a good night's sleep, and you can't settle anything until morning anyway."

After working for her uncle Ted's 1980 presidential and 1982 senatorial campaigns, Kathleen became intensely interested in politics. She said she was influenced by her father and her uncles to want nothing more than to be of service when she ran for the House of Representatives in Maryland's 2nd Congressional District in 1986. She lost that election, however, becoming the first Kennedy to lose a general election, but certainly she did not lose any of her desire to serve. (It was interesting that she ran using her married name, Townsend, not wanting her maiden name to give her any kind of advantage.) Dedicated to the notion that nowhere do children learn to be of service more than when they are in school, she soon became the president of the Student Service Alliance of the Maryland Department of Education. She also worked as the assistant attorney general of Maryland and in the U.S. Department of Justice as a deputy assistant attorney general for two years during the Clinton administration. In 1994, Parris Glendening chose her as his running mate when he ran for governor of Maryland, winning that election (and using the Kennedy name this time) and also the next one four years later.

When this author first met her in October 1996 at a seminar on the history of the Kennedy women at the John F. Kennedy Library in Boston, I was struck by the force of her personality, the intensity of her presence. People seemed to naturally gravitate to her as she stood in a corner of a large theater room and held court. "In talking to you," I told her, "I can't help but think of your father, your entire family. Do you realize how much baggage comes with just being...*you?*" She laughed. "Good and bad baggage, I suppose," she said, "but mostly good, I hope. The family's legacy carries with it a big responsibility and my brothers and sisters have always recognized it," she continued. "But you can't let it overwhelm you. You could easily be paralyzed by it, it's just that daunting. So I try to stay focused on the here and now and just do my job. But, yes," she concluded, "my father, my uncles, my relatives are never far from my mind just as I know they're not far from the minds of most people who look into my eyes for the first time."

In 2002, Kathleen ran for governor of Maryland, but lost that election. Since leaving office she has continued working for nonprofit groups benefiting Democratic causes and candidates and serves on the boards of many organizations, including the John F. Kennedy Library. She has also written a book, *Failing America's Faithful,* about the value of organized religion as a motivating force to encourage people to be of service and how in her view churches have lost their way in that regard in recent years.

Many people—her constituents as well as Kennedy followers and even her own family members—strongly maintained that Kathleen Kennedy Townsend could, indeed *should,* have gone even further in politics than she did. However, time, place, and circumstance seemed not to be on her side. Plus, she seems not to have had the desire to continue after 2002, though she hasn't ruled it out as a possibility one day.

The Third Generation

Kathleen Kennedy Townsend wasn't the only one of Ethel and Bobby's children with the potential to achieve high political office. Joseph Kennedy, Ethel's second child, served as a member of the U.S. House of Representatives from the 8th Congressional District of Massachusetts from 1987 to 1999. As earlier stated in this book, he also founded and still leads the Citizens Energy Corporation. With the death of his uncle Ted, Joe's name was mentioned as a possible candidate for his Senate seat. In an Associated Press article, Democratic strategist Dan Payne said, "He wouldn't be human and he wouldn't be a Kennedy if he didn't give serious consideration to running for what is known as the 'Kennedy seat' in Massachusetts." (The six-year term of the seat ends in January 2013.) However, Joe wasn't interested. (The seat eventually went by appointment to Paul G. Kirk, and later by election to Republican Scott Brown.) There's little doubt that if not for the massive onslaught of negative publicity he received in 1996 and 1997 with the attempted annulment of his marriage to Sheila Rauch as well as the allegations regarding his brother Michael and the babysitter, Joe Kennedy would have enjoyed greater success in politics.

Two other children of Ethel's also could have been serious political contenders: Christopher and Maxwell.

Christopher Kennedy, Ethel and Bobby's eighth child, has worked for Merchandise Mart Properties in Chicago since 1988, his grandfather's flagship company and the greatest source of income for the entire family. Some consider him the only true businessman of the Kennedy family, with the kind of acumen not seen since the days of Joseph P. Kennedy and his son-in-law Stephen Smith. Involved in a number of family campaigns—including his uncle Ted's 1980 presidential campaign—Christopher actually considered running for the Senate in 2009, but decided against it. In August of that year, he was appointed to the University of Illinois board of trustees by Governor Pat Quinn the day after his uncle Ted's death. Like his sister Kathleen, Christopher has had a long happy marriage. He and his wife, Sheila, married in 1987 and have four children. In January 1998, Merchandise Mart and several other commercial properties owned by the Kennedys were sold to Vornado Realty, a real estate investment trust, for $625 million. It was a deal Christopher helped to broker, and one that guaranteed much of the third generation of Kennedys (Smiths and Shrivers included) millions of dollars in yearly annuities—as per the provisions in their grandfather's will should the company be sold—instead of hundreds of thousands, and for the rest of their lives. The sale of Merchandise Mart was the end of an era in the sense that the venture was the family's last operating business, now leaving the Kennedys' holding company with securities only. Christopher continued working for Merchandise Mart Properties after its sale and is presently the company's president. Today, more than three million people annually come through the Mart—which spans two city blocks and rises twenty-five stories—to attend the many trade, consumer, and community events hosted there, as well as to visit its many showrooms and retail shops.

Matthew Maxwell Kennedy, Ethel's ninth child, better known as Max and named after General Maxwell Taylor, chairman of the Joint Chiefs under JFK, has always been very interested in politics, having worked as a field organizer for family campaigns, including his brother Joe's 1986 congressional campaign and his uncle Ted's 2000 senatorial race. In 2001, much of the East Coast media touted Max as a possible candidate for Massachusetts's 9th Congressional District, filling Democrat Joe Moakley's seat. However, Max never declared his candidacy. Behind the scenes, his uncle Ted was concerned about his nephew's chances. Max had recently given a speech honoring his father and had mumbled his way through the whole thing, looking very uncomfortable and not at all ready for a wide audience. Then word got out that, years earlier, he and his first cousin Michael Skakel (now in jail for the murder of Martha Moxley) had been arrested back in 1983 for assaulting a Harvard campus cop. It was a minor incident that hadn't even made the news when it happened, but now it was suddenly a big story. Max began to experience firsthand what he had always known to be true, which is that as a politician his entire life would be up for scrutiny. He had given up alcohol at the age of twenty, attended regular AA meetings—still does—and had worked hard to have a good life. He didn't want to see it judged so publicly, so he decided politics wasn't for him—at least not at that time. After talking to his uncle Teddy about it, he dropped out of the running.

Years later, Max campaigned tirelessly for Barack Obama early in the primary season at about two hundred events in swing states. He is also the author of the bestselling book *Make Gentle the Life of This World: The Vision of Robert F. Kennedy and the Words that Inspired Him*. The title is from the Greek poet Aeschylus. RFK had recited it on April 4, 1968, in giving the news of Martin Luther King's assassination to an audience in an Indianapolis ghetto. "The 1960s saw such terrible turmoil in this country," Max says, "and I think that the phrase 'make gentle the life of this world' could, in many ways, have been the theme of the last few years of my father's life."

Max has been married to the same woman, Victoria Anne, since 1990. They have four children.

Max's younger brother, Douglas Kennedy, who is sometimes a Fox News Channel reporter, is also a recovering alcoholic and has been married to his wife, Molly, since 1998. The couple has three daughters. "Most of the time, people don't know who I am," he has said, "and I don't tell them. I value being part of my family, but I have a clear sense of who I am and what my job is." It's sometimes been easy for the media to paint all of Ethel and Bobby's offspring with a wide brushstroke and suggest that they all have criminal records, but that's just not true. In fact, though most of the brothers have had minor scrapes with the law, only Joe, Bobby, and David had truly problematic adolescences—the infamous Hyannis Port Terrors—and, later as an adult, Michael obviously had gotten himself into serious trouble as well.

Except for Ethel's children Kathleen and Joe, perhaps no one in the family has had a more distinguished career in politics than Ted's son Patrick Kennedy. He served as the U.S representative for Rhode Island's 1st Congressional District from 1995 until 2011. He joined his father in sponsoring many pieces of legislation benefiting health care reform, such as the Mental Health Parity Act in 2008 that required group health plans to cover mental health issues in a way comparable to that provided for the physically challenged. Patrick has done so much for the advancement of health care reform in this country, many of his supporters felt it was a shame that his personal problems—such as his bipolar disorder, alcoholism, and an addiction to prescription medications such as OxyContin—have sometimes stood in the way of his political career. He has had numerous stays in rehabilitation centers over the years and said his recovery is "a lifelong process." Patrick Kennedy married Amy Petitgout, a sixth-grade public school teacher from New Jersey, at the Kennedy compound in July 2011.

One fundamental difference between the second and third generations that most certainly came to bear as they were being raised was that Jack, Bobby, and Ted had one interest and one interest alone: politics. Whereas the third generation has a wide array of philanthropic concerns, the three sons of Ambassador Joseph focused only on holding public office, and they never wavered from that goal. They also never allowed their personal lives to interfere with their political ambitions—their father, Joseph, simply wouldn't have allowed it. Another advantage the brothers had was that they weren't necessarily famous as youngsters (though they were certainly known), and thus didn't have to live their lives, and make their mistakes, under as much public and media scrutiny. "Our lives were relatively free of the spotlight," Ted Kennedy once recalled. "That is totally different for my children's generation. Even before they've had a chance to make important achievements and accomplishments in their lives, they have been public figures."

Politics aside, many members of the Kennedy family's third generation have made and are still making a big difference in the world. Obviously, one doesn't have to be a politician to be the catalyst for great change, and it's sometimes easier if politics can be taken out of the equation altogether. "My mom changed the world without being elected to office," Bobby Shriver said of Eunice Kennedy Shriver. "Period. End of story."

In fact, Ethel's daughters Mary Kerry, Mary Courtney, and Rory have all gone on to important careers as human rights activists, as has Pat's son, Christopher (who has also had what he views as a somewhat frustrating career as an actor). Of Ted's children, Ted Jr. continues his work with the Marwood Group, advising corporations about health care and financial services. He is also on the board of directors of the American Association of People with Disabilities. His sister, Kara, continues to work for her aunt Jean's Very Special Arts. She is also on the National Advisory Board of the National Organization on Fetal Alcohol Syndrome. Others, including the sons of Eunice and Sargent Shriver, have become advocates for the mentally disabled and have also worked for a number of children's charities.

Mark Shriver, for instance, is managing director of U.S. programs for Save the Children. (Incidentally, Shriver served as a member of the Maryland House of Delegates for two consecutive terms, from 1995 to 2003.) Timothy is chairman and CEO of the Special Olympics. Anthony created Best Buddies International to encourage students to work with mentally retarded children. Bobby is in the film business and has orchestrated many show business–related programs to raise money for charities. Interestingly, he is a Democratic member of the city council in Santa

Monica, California, and has also served as mayor there. At this time, with the retirement of Patrick Kennedy in January 2011, Bobby Shriver is the only member of the Kennedy family in elected office. The Shriver brothers are incredibly close and have never really had the kinds of internal problems experienced by their cousins—Bobby's children, specifically. All, of course, are very close to their sister, Maria.

Some of the third generation of Kennedys have stayed out of the public eye altogether, such as the children of Jean and Stephen Smith and, with the exception of Christopher, Pat Kennedy Lawford's as well. (Amazingly, considering the Palm Beach scandal in which he found himself embroiled ten years earlier, William Kennedy Smith actually considered a run for Congress from the North Chicago district in 2001, but ultimately thought better of it.)

Though not directly related to politics, the work of Ethel's third child, Bobby Kennedy Jr., as an activist certainly cannot be ignored. Oprah Winfrey, who interviewed him in early 2007, calls him "one of the country's most passionate environmental activists." "Our landscapes connect us to our history; they are the source of our character as a people, as well as our health, our safety, and our prosperity," he told Oprah. "Natural resources enrich us economically, yes. But they also enrich us aesthetically and recreationally and culturally and spiritually." As an attorney, Bobby specializes in environmental law, and has also written two books and many articles on ecological issues.

In 1998, Kennedy, Chris Bartle, and John Hoving founded a water company that manufacturers Keeper Springs water, with all of its profits going to the Waterkeeper Alliance. In May 2010, he would be named one of Time.com's "Heroes for the Planet" for his success in helping Riverkeeper to restore the Hudson River. As it would happen, his heroin addiction of the early 1980s turned out to be nothing but an unfortunate footnote in an otherwise truly extraordinary life story.

Would he run for office? "I've got six reasons [I haven't] running around this house [his children]," he says. "But at this point, I would run if there were an office open because I'm so distressed about the kind of country my children will inherit. I've tried to cling to the idea that I could be of public service without compromising my family life. But at this point, I would run. I would run for the Senate or maybe for the governor's office [in New York]."

Maria Shriver

*I*t's safe to say that no member of the Kennedys' third generation is as famous and as high profile as Maria Shriver, the only daughter of Sargent and Eunice Shriver. As a television personality and the former First Lady of California, her face is instantly recognizable to most people. Certainly when she and her husband of twenty-five years, Arnold Schwarzenegger, announceed in May 2011 that they were separating, the story would dominate the news. It took people by surprise; there simply had been no recent rumblings of discontentment in the couple's union.

Shortly before the 2003 gubernatorial election, allegations of sexual misconduct threatened to derail Schwarzenegger's political career. The *Los Angeles Times* published a series of scathing articles in which sixteen women accused him of sexual harassment and humiliation over a thirty-year period. Though he admitted that he'd "behaved badly" in the past, he also said that many of the allegations were not true, "because that's not my behavior." Maria stood by him with unequivocal devotion. She later appeared on her close friend Oprah Winfrey's program and denied that she, like many Kennedy women over the years, "always look[s] the other way." She said, "Well, you know, that ticks me off. I am my own woman. I have not been, quote, 'bred' to look the other way. I look at that man back there in the green room straight on, eyes wide open, and I look at him with an open heart." It should be noted that Maria's mother, Eunice, never had to "look the other way," either. "While Maria may have been exposed to such thinking from the experiences of others in her family—her aunts in particular," noted one good friend of hers, "you have to remember that Sarge was completely devoted to Eunice. *That's* how Maria was raised, *that's* the example that was set for her by her parents. She was also taught that, as a Kennedy-Shriver, loyalty is paramount in a marriage. So, yes, she was loyal to Arnold, even when the rumors upset her terribly."

A week after the split between Shriver and Schwarzenegger was announced, it would also be revealed that the former governor had fathered a child thirteen years earlier with the family's housekeeper, Mildred Patricia Baena, who at the time was earning $1,200 a week. The child, a son, was born on October 2, 1997. Making matters seem some-how worse, if that's even possible, Maria was pregnant at the same time with her and Arnold's son Christopher Sargent, to whom she gave birth on October 12, 1997. It should be stated, though, that Schwarzenegger reportedly did not find out that Baena's child was his until somewhere around the year 2000. He (and presumably Maria) believed the father to be the housekeeper's husband, Rogelio Baena, whose name is on the birth certificate. (Photographs taken at the baby's christening show Maria, Arnold, and their children happily posing with Arnold's mistress, the infant in her arms.) The Baenas separated three weeks after the baby was born; they filed for divorce a decade later. It is said that Schwarzenegger secretly provided support for the child as soon as he learned the truth. The fact that he was able to hold his closely guarded secret while running for public office—twice!—is astonishing considering the close scrutiny to which most public officials are held. Somehow, though, Schwarzeneg-ger was able to keep the secret throughout his campaigns and two terms in office. It was only after leaving office in January 2011 that he finally told Maria the truth. "He stayed quiet all of those years to protect his political career and also, in a sense, to protect his marriage because he knew that Maria had been such an incredible asset to him," said a source close to the former governor. "She had stood behind him, and so publicly. I think he didn't want to make her look like a fool."

Privately, though, it would seem that Maria Shriver had been unhappy for some time in a marriage for which she had sacrificed so much. As a television personality and reporter, she had produced literally hun-dreds of hours of worthwhile programming, the hallmark of which has always been her extreme sensitivity to and understanding of the human condition as well as global concerns and history. Her career was one of her greatest passions. However, it came to an abrupt end in 2004 when Arnold became the thirty-eighth governor of California and she was forced to abandon her own professional goals. To her, it felt like her world was over, as she would recall it. "It all happened so quickly," she recalled. "NBC felt there could be a perception of a conflict of interest between my news job and Arnold's becoming governor. It was uncharted water. The producers said, 'If we put you on the air while Arnold's campaigning, it'll look like we're endorsing him.' A lot of people were uncomfortable with that, so they took me off the air while he was running for office. I thought

I'd return to reporting when the campaign was over. And then he won, and that was that. I realized how much I had identified myself with Maria Shriver, newswoman. When that was gone, I had to really sit back and go, 'Well, actually, who am I today?' That sent me off on a process of really, for the first time in my whole life, looking deep within myself and asking myself, 'Who did I want to be?'"

Shriver attempted to view the surprising turn of events in her life as an opportunity to become involved in many different philanthropic endeavors as California's First Lady, which she eagerly took on, as well as devoting more time to her children. For instance, in October 2009, she launched *The Shriver Report: A Woman's Nation Changes Everything*, a national study that looked at the societal implications of working American women, now making up half of the United States. She also spoke out about her father's Alzheimer's and spearheaded a number of programs to further the nation's understanding of the terrible disease. As she promoted ideals of service and volunteerism in California, she was inexhaustible in her work for the state, conceiving of many statewide programs and heading up numerous community organizations. However, those close to her say that without the television career she had so loved, Maria was never completely satisfied.

"She gave up a lot for Arnold," said one of her intimates. "And, yes, I believe it took a toll on the marriage. It's not that she resented it, but on some level I think she felt it wasn't fair. Then her parents were both ill, and that took a lot out of her—especially Sarge's Alzheimer's. Maria finally had a chance to consider where she was in her own life and she realized that the only thing she and Arnold had in common was their shared history and their children. Maybe that would have been enough, but then at about this same time, she found out about his betrayal with the household staffer. This employee worked in Maria's home for twenty years. Maria was friendly with her, and also with her son. They were at family functions together, holidays and other events. That she'd been betrayed in such a way, well . . . it was as if life just came tumbling down around her. To think that she had given up so much for her husband only to end up in this situation was very upsetting."

The entire Kennedy family would be rattled by the stunning revelation. Maybe Ethel Kennedy best encapsulated the family's feeling upon hearing the upsetting news from one of her children. "Arnold is such a part of the fabric of our lives, I don't know how we can cut him out of the picture," she said sadly. "But I also don't know how we can keep him in it. I keep wondering what Eunice would say. I feel that I should now be that voice of reason for Maria, but I just don't have the words. There was only one Eunice, and God, do we need her now."

Now that Arnold Schwarzenegger's term is over and there is such a sea change under way in her personal life, it is hoped by many that Maria Shriver will find her way back to broadcast journalism. She's a rare breed in a business where tabloid flashiness often trumps real substance.

Today as Maria Shriver grapples with the uncertainty of a future without Arnold Schwarzenegger as her husband, she continues to raise her family in Los Angeles—Katherine, twenty-two, Christina, twenty, Patrick, seventeen, and Christopher, twelve, as of this writing. Maria's friends insist that she is not a naive woman, that she knew very well the man with whom she had spent a quarter of a century. She made a choice a long time ago, say those who know her best, perhaps not to look the other way but definitely to accept her husband's faults, confront him about them when necessary, and then go on with her work and with the raising of her children, all the while hoping for the best. "It hasn't always been easy, especially given that all she wanted was a marriage like that of her parents," said a friend of hers. "To give up, though, and fall victim to the circumstances of what's happened is not the way she was raised. Maria will doubtless go on with her life and career, probably made even stronger by the coming to terms with, and—who knows?—maybe even forgiving, Arnold. She is an incredibly strong woman who will rise above all of this ugliness."

In considering the road ahead for Maria Shriver, the words of her father, Sargent Shriver—when he lost his bid for the Democratic presidential nomination in 1972—come to mind: "We don't know what obstacles will come our way in this life, we only know that they *will* come our way. But we also know that as Shrivers and Kennedys we are genetically built to not only face challenges but to live great and wonderful lives despite them—and maybe even because of them."

Senator Caroline Kennedy?

*T*he years after her brother's death were incredibly difficult for Caroline Bouvier Kennedy Schlossberg as she dealt with the loss of the sibling she had so adored. Immediately following John's death, Caroline retreated to her country home in Sagaponack, New York, and isolated herself, with family members such as Maria Shriver spending as much time there as they could. "I think it's safe to say she had a complete emotional breakdown," said one of her close friends. "She stopped eating, she couldn't sleep. She said that the grief was so overwhelming, there were days when she felt she couldn't breathe. She kept waiting for the phone to ring and it to be John saying, 'Hey, kiddo, what's up?' These were dark days for Caroline. Every little thing reminded her of her brother. It was heartwrenching. She simply could not accept John's death. However, she had long ago accepted that life was not always fair and she knew that she had to go on, if only for the sake of her husband, Ed, and three children, Rose, Tatiana, and John."

During the week, when the kids were in school, Caroline and Ed would reside at their posh Park Avenue co-op apartment. Always the devoted mother, Caroline would walk the girls to nearby Brearley School on Manhattan's Upper East Side every day. Then she and little John would go to St. David's School, the same school his uncle John had attended. She was always there in the morning for breakfasts and at home at the end of the day to greet them. Often the family would eat at their favorite restaurant, Coco Pazzo, on East 74th. "She was very nice, very much a mom the way she dealt with her kids, fussing over them, ordering for them," said Susan Morgan, who worked at the restaurant. "The children were extremely polite. It was a very nice restaurant, and the children seemed right at home, very mannerly. But Caroline, she was very, very private and she had her boundaries. One time, I went over to say how sorry I was about her brother. She didn't say anything. She just looked at me with very sad eyes. Then her husband said, 'Thank you,' and he quickly shook his head at me as if to say, 'Not now.'"

Three months after John's death, Caroline spoke at the twentieth anniversary of the John F. Kennedy Library and Museum. She looked incredibly thin, her shoulder-length strawberry blonde hair stranded with gray. She said that she wanted to salute John, who, as she put it, "brought his own sense of purpose and idealism to the public service, which I wish we can all continue." After her remarks, she hurried backstage and collapsed into the arms of her uncle Teddy, her shoulders heaving, her body racked with wrenching sobs. Later she became angry at herself for the breakdown. "It's not the way I want to handle it," she said.

Though very cordial when in public, privately she is guarded and protective. Many friends of the Kennedys who spoke publicly to reminisce fondly about John after his death found themselves no longer friends of Caroline's. "She cut me and so many others out of her life when she saw us on TV talking about John, sharing our memories," said one good friend. "I love Caroline so much. I'd known her for twenty years. But I guess I should also have known better. She considers it a terrible betrayal when people close to her speak to the media, even if what they have to say is positive. That's how she was raised by her mother. Jackie was exactly the same way."

There would be many more public appearances for Caroline Kennedy over the years—she could always be counted on to present the annual Profile in Courage Awards at the John F. Kennedy Presidential Library and Museum in Boston, for instance. Of course, there were joyous family celebrations too, and some sad Kennedy funerals as well. She also began writing books on civil liberties and even edited a book that featured poems her mother enjoyed, *The Best-Loved Poems of Jacqueline Kennedy Onassis*. She took a job as an advocate and fund-raiser for New York's public schools. In 2000, she appeared onstage at the National Democratic Convention, walking on to the strains of the theme to *Camelot*. "I thank all Americans for making me and John and all of our family a part of your family," she said. "And for helping us dream my father's dream." When she turned fifty, she even appeared on the cover of AARP's magazine. Then, of course, in 2008, she announced her endorsement of Barack Obama for president and played a key role in securing the support of her uncle Ted for Obama as well. Later in the year, she served as cochair of Obama's vice presidential search committee.

A very strange chapter in the life of Caroline Bouvier Kennedy began to unfold at the end of 2008. Now fifty-one, she suddenly seemed poised to become a serious political figure. "She spent a lot of her life balancing public service with obligations to her family," her cousin Robert F. Kennedy Jr. told the Associated Press in December 2008. "Now her children are grown, and she is ready to move onto a bigger stage."

After discussing the matter with Ted, Caroline decided that she wanted to throw her hat into the ring for the senatorial seat once occupied by her uncle Bobby. It was to be vacated by Hillary Clinton now that her confirmation as new secretary of state under President Barack Obama was imminent. A Marist poll of 503 registered voters showed Kennedy and New York attorney general Andrew Cuomo to be the top picks of New Yorkers, each favored by about 25 percent of those surveyed. New York City mayor Michael Bloomberg seemed to support Caroline when he said, quite simply, "Caroline Kennedy can do anything." Barack Obama was said to be supportive as well, and in fact Caroline went on the record as saying he had been "encouraging." It would seem, though, that he had no choice, in that Caroline and Ted had come out so strongly for him in his bid to be the Democratic nominee for president. Ted felt strongly that if Caroline could be appointed now, she would be able to secure the seat in a required 2010 election and then keep it in 2012 when Clinton's term would end. It all seemed to make sense. How fitting would it be that Caroline would start her political career as a senator in her uncle's old seat, and more than fifty years after her father, JFK, was elected to the Senate in 1952?

An intense lobbying effort was quickly under way, with Ted leading the way to convince people with persuasive power over Democratic governor David Paterson, who had the sole responsibility for naming a successor to Clinton's seat. However, there were many problems from the outset where Caroline was concerned. Her interest in politics probably sounded like a good idea when it was proposed, but the actual implementation of it was anything but smooth.

The biggest problem of all was simply this: Caroline Kennedy is not a politician. It was an awkward fit for her. She'd never run for office before and little was known about her or her politics, other than her support for Obama which, in truth, had seemed to come out of nowhere. Gary Ackerman, who represents the 5th Congressional District of New York, put it best, even if somewhat cruelly, when he said that he did not know what credentials Caroline had for the job "except that she has name recognition—but so does J-Lo." Ackerman had a plethora of great lines, such as this one, which he dropped on the television program *Face the Nation:* "One of the things that we have to observe is that DNA in this business can take you just so far. You know, Rembrandt was a great artist. His brother Murray, on the other hand? Murray Rembrandt couldn't paint a house." Maybe the congressman was inelegant in his critique of Caroline, but it made sense. Perhaps Patrick Kennedy had a more level-headed comment when asked by *Newsweek* in 2001 what advice he would give to any of his cousins contemplating running for public office. "Disabuse yourself of the notion that there's this machine out there that just kind of materializes when you say, 'Yes—go!' Growing up watching politics as my cousins and I did, you had this warped sense that that's all you needed to do. That was the way it was for my father's generation."

Caroline's first public appearance was in Syracuse, where she met privately with local politicians and then was trotted out to speak to the media—for about thirty seconds before an aide got her out of there quickly. In Buffalo later that day, she spoke for about two minutes. However, she had so much security and was surrounded by so much media that it was a wasted effort in terms of really getting a look at her, or coming to some understanding of her. "As a mother, as an author, as an education advocate, and from a family that really has spent generations in public service, I feel this commitment," she said while in Rochester. "This is a time when nobody can afford to sit it out, and I feel I have something to offer." She never said, though, what it was she had to offer. Since Paterson was to make his decision in January—perhaps February if it could be put off—Caroline didn't have much time to reveal herself, and she was off to a bad start. Then a series of media interviews in December just made things worse. She was very vague in her answers and was widely criticized for repeatedly saying "um" and "you know." In fact, she became famous for saying "you know" two hundred times in a thirty-minute TV interview. This was odd, because Caroline is ordinarily very articulate. As president of the John F. Kennedy Library Foundation, she'd given countless speeches since her mother and brother died, appearing at all sorts of Kennedy-related functions and acquitting herself quite well onstage. But now it just looked as though she was out of her element. By the time she was interviewed by the *New York Times*, she seemed defensive and snippy, or maybe just plain tired of the questioning. When a reporter from the *Times* asked her to describe the moment she decided she wanted to be a senator, she shot back, "Have you...ever thought about writing for, like, a woman's magazine or something?" To which the reporter countered by asking what she had against women's magazines. "Nothing at all," she responded, "but I thought you were the crack political team here."

Perhaps even more surprising than Caroline Kennedy's decision to try to fill Hillary Clinton's vacated Senate seat was her uncle Ted's encouragement of the idea. Some might argue that he should have known better. After all, he'd been in politics for so many years, he was well aware of what his niece would be up against in terms of the expectations of her, and he also knew and understood her temperament. It's difficult to imagine that he truly believed she was up to the job. Back in 1992 when she turned down an offer to be chairwoman of the Democratic National Convention, he completely understood and said that no one should expect such a thing of her. Nothing really had changed, except perhaps that Ted was facing his own mortality. From discussions with his son Patrick, it had become clear to him that Patrick would not run for reelection to the House of Representatives in 2010. Perhaps Ted realized that with his death, there would not be a Kennedy in the Senate for the first time in fifty years. Bobby Kennedy Jr. had talked for years about possibly filling Hillary's seat one day, but when it came down to it he decided against it. If he'd been interested, there's little doubt that Ted would have encouraged it.

Caroline Bows Out

*B*y 2009, despite the contributions of many of the third generation of Kennedys, it was clear that there wasn't that one powerful leader in the family, the one who would most obviously continue a family tradition into the White House. Ted certainly knew as much, and maybe couldn't be blamed for trying to convince JFK's only daughter, Caroline, to take up the mantle. It probably at least sounded like a good idea. However, once the wheels were set in motion, the idea quickly betrayed certain weaknesses.

One Kennedy family insider recalled a meeting at Caroline Kennedy's home between her, Ted, Ed Schlossberg, and executives from the consulting firm Knickerbocker SKD, a political communications firm.

"What is it you want to say?" one of the executives asked Caroline. "What is your message?"

Caroline, dressed in slim black slacks and a smartly tailored yellow jacket, looked as if she'd drawn a blank. "I just think that a lot can be done, and I can do it," she said, according to one recollection of the conversation. "I just need to figure out the best way to frame it."

"Well," the executive carefully began, "we have to formulate some talking points and be...*specific*."

"Caroline and I will discuss all of this and get back to you," Ted quickly interjected. He was rising to his niece's defense, and she seemed to be appreciative of it, nodding and smiling at him.

Ed Schlossberg just sat in a corner saying nothing. Caroline looked at him, then looked at Ted, then back to Ed. Finally she said, "Let's not get into this now. Uncle Teddy and I will talk about it and we can reconvene at another time."

The meeting was adjourned, but the executives from Knickerbocker SKD were likely left with a few strong notions: Caroline didn't have a clear rationale as to why she wanted the seat; her uncle was pulling for her anyway; and her husband was, to be charitable, ambivalent. The next day, one of the executives called Ted Kennedy to discuss the matter with him. In 2010, he recalled, "My conversation with the senator led me to believe that he felt this thing [Caroline as senator] was very important for the family. He suggested to me that there were very few Kennedys interested in holding office and the Kennedy dynasty was on its way out. He was really pulling for his niece to fill that void. I think it was a desperate attempt. What he said to me was, 'If I knew I was going to live long enough, I could help her so much. But time is running out. I'm not sure how this is going to play out. I wish we'd had this idea many years ago.' It was sad. I hung up feeling very hopeless about it all. It was as if he was trying to preserve something he felt would become obsolete with his passing."

By January 20, Caroline had had enough and decided to pull out of the running, citing "personal reasons," just a day after Hillary Clinton's position with the Obama administration was officially confirmed. Many explanations were put forth as speculation, such as that she was emotionally exhausted by her uncle Ted's illness or, as the *New York Times* reported, there was some question about her taxes and a problem with the payroll of one of her maids. Some felt that she was reluctant to be forthcoming about her finances, estimated by some at more than $400 million. "Perhaps some of that was going on, but the truth is that Caroline just realized that it had been a bad idea, and she wanted out," said one person close to Caroline.

According to a reliable source, Caroline called Ted to tell him that she was afraid she had made a mistake in going after Hillary Clinton's seat. He agreed with her, telling her that given the present climate, there was a good chance she would not get selected, which would prove embarrassing to her and the family. Besides, he now feared that if she did get the job, it would be too overwhelming for her. It was as if he suddenly remembered that she wasn't cut out for politics. "Basically, he didn't want her to further embarrass herself on his account," said the source. "In the end, they said she pulled out for 'personal reasons.' Those 'personal reasons' were simply that she and Ted just decided they'd made a big mistake, that she really was not qualified."

While it would be poetic and fitting to see Caroline hold public office like her father and uncles and some of her cousins, capturing the public's imagination as they had, wishing that it could be her destiny just wasn't enough to make it so. The grace and quiet resolve with which she's led her life in the face of such unimaginable heartbreak is what truly distinguishes her and defines who she is as a woman, not any passing interest she may have had in wanting to be a senator.

No Regrets

*I*n 2003, Sargent Shriver, at age eighty-seven, was diagnosed with Alzheimer's disease. Even though Maria Shriver had referred to her father's disease several times in speeches and interviews over the years, not much is known about its progression in her father's specific case, or how the family dealt with it. It was an intensely personal matter. "It's never easy to look at your parent and realize that he doesn't know who you are," Maria told Diane Sawyer on *Good Morning America* in May 2009. "You have to recalibrate yourself every single time you see your father, and you have to introduce yourself to him." Maria said that when she would walk into Sarge's bedroom, she would try to stay upbeat and greet him by saying, "Hi, how are you doing? I'm your daughter, Maria." Typically, his response would be, "Oh my goodness, you are?" And she would then answer, "Yes, isn't that amazing? I'm *your* daughter." Maria added, "It has taught me to accept a person for who he is in the moment, not for what he used to be or what I want him to be, but to just deal with the person in front of me, and that's a pretty good lesson for life, just in general."

"So be it," Sargent once said when asked about the so-called Kennedy curse. Considering who Sargent had been in his lifetime and his absolute devotion to his Catholicism, there's little doubt but that his faith carried him through. "At the age of ninety-three, my dad still goes to Mass every day," Maria said when she testified before Congress about the difficulties families face when dealing with the disease. "And believe it or not, he still remembers the Hail Mary." For her part, Maria would use her father's terrible illness as a catalyst to make people aware of the ravages of the disease, and also to eliminate the shame associated with it. In May 2009, she was the coexecutive producer of *The Alzheimer's Project*, an HBO documentary series that won two Emmy awards. She also wrote a best-selling children's book about Alzheimer's called *Grandpa, Do You Know Who I Am?*

By 2009, Eunice Kennedy Shriver, who was now eighty-eight, had also been unwell for some time, her body breaking down with the passing of time. The last six years of Eunice's life had been extremely challenging as she dealt with a series of strokes at the same time that she was trying to reconcile herself to her husband's deteriorating condition. Ted and Jean were with her as much as possible, especially given the concerns and demands of Ted's own illness. It was a difficult time for all of the Kennedys as they faced the prospect of possibly losing three of the best of their ranks—Ted, Eunice, and Sarge. "After all we have been through, I don't know, you sort of hope that maybe things might get easier with time," said Jean Kennedy Smith at the time. "They don't, though. You really have to persevere."

Eunice echoed those sentiments to one of her nursing assistants at this time of her life. "Aging can be cruel," she said. "I think now the reason one must be so strong in one's youth is so that it becomes a part of who he or she is as a person, because God knows that when you get older you need all the strength you can muster just to get through it. It is by no means easy." Then, to this aide who was at the time in her late twenties, Eunice said, "I urge you to do what I did with my life. Do not waste a day. Make every day count. Make it important. That's what I did and, as God is my witness, I have not one regret—not a single one."

As her health continued to deteriorate, Eunice became too sick to attend Mass. Therefore, a priest came to her almost every day to perform the Mass in her bedroom. Her son Timothy recalls "at least—I'm not exaggerating—thirty separate images of the Blessed Mother" in his mom's bedroom, "and I mean thirty. I don't mean seven that looks like thirty."

Eunice Kennedy Shriver died on August 11, 2009, at the age of eighty-eight. She was survived by her husband, Sargent, who was ninety-three, her five children—Anthony, Bobby, Mark, Timothy, and Maria—and nineteen grandchildren.

"In the last few years of her life, I found Mummy to be almost more awe-inspiring than in her eighty-five years," her daughter, Maria, said in her moving eulogy of her mom. "She who never sat still was forced to confront stillness, and it was hard for her, but she never complained and she never asked for pity. . . . If you had told me a few years ago that at the end of my mother's life she and I would sit in a room and just be, I would have said you were crazy. If you had told me that at the age of fifty-two, I would finally get up the nerve to crawl into bed with my mother, hold her, and tell her that I love her, I would have said you were nuts. And if you had told me that Mummy and I would write poetry together, I would know for sure you that you'd lost your mind. But all those things really happened, as Mummy learned to let go."

* * *

Sargent Shriver would follow his beloved Eunice in death on January 17, 2011. He would be buried with a rosary in his hands, having never lost his faith, even during the darkest of times.

"Sarge's knowledge of God's love was the structure that supported his public life," Cardinal Donald Wuerl would say at his funeral in Potomac, Maryland. "From this faith, hope, and love flowed his thirst for justice and peace and the courage to speak for those who had no voice. He spoke not from political expediency or correctness, but from an abiding sense of conviction."

President Bill Clinton framed it best that day when, in speaking of Sarge, he asked, "Could anybody be as good as he [Shriver] seemed to be? Every other man in this church feels about two inches tall right now."

But no one could summarize his life better than Sarge himself did, in an interview he gave to the *Chicago Tribune* in July 1987:

"I haven't done everything I've wanted to do with my life. I can't say I've been 100 percent successful. But with respect to the things that count—my marriage, my kids—I've been very, very lucky. I don't know anybody in the world that's been as lucky as I am. Period. Think of anybody you've ever read of in any area, politics, business, government, finance, I don't know a single solitary person—Franklin Roosevelt, Johnson, Kennedy, General DeGaulle, I've known all those people, not one of them, not one has been as lucky as I've been."

Ted—Rest in Peace

*T*wo weeks after the death of Eunice Kennedy Shriver, on August 25, 2009, Ted Kennedy passed away at the age of seventy-seven.

Just a couple days before his death, the senator was still seen around the Cape on a golf cart being driven by Vicki. The two were always amenable to speaking to anyone who approached, as Mabel Simmons learned. She was visiting relatives on the Cape from San Diego. "I had been to the Kennedy compound several times but never had the nerve to actually try to get inside," she recalled. "I would get close and just stand there and hope maybe I would see one of them. One day, I was standing on a street near the home taking pictures of the ocean view when a golf cart approached. I looked and, sure enough, it was Vicki and Ted. It happened to be a very scenic spot, and Vicki stopped the golf cart and, much to my amazement, walked over to me. She said, 'Would you mind taking a picture of me and my husband?' I was so stunned. 'Of course,' I barely managed to say. She handed me the camera and we walked over to the cart and there was Ted sitting there wearing a large straw hat and sunglasses. He looked very weak to me. But his smile was dazzling as he introduced himself and shook my hand. Vicki got back into the cart, they posed and smiled, and I took their picture. Instead of saying, 'Say cheese!' I remember Ted said, 'Say Kennedy!' and we all laughed.

"So, how are you feeling these days, Senator?" Simmons asked Ted.

"The fact that I am out here with my beautiful wife on this gorgeous day is the best medicine in the world," he answered, "so I am doing just fine. Thank you for asking." Mabel asked Vicki if she was taking good care of Ted. Flashing a gorgeous smile, Vicki said, "We take good care of each other." The tourist then told Ted how much of a fan she was of his, how much she admired him and his family. Ted smiled and asked her if she had ever been "down to the house." Of course, she hadn't. "Next time you are in the area, stop by," he said. He told her that if a security guard stopped her, she should tell him "the senator sent you." They then said their goodbyes. "God bless you," Ted said as he and Vicki drove off. That was just three days before Ted died.

"Edward M. Kennedy—the husband, father, grandfather, brother, and uncle we loved so deeply—died late Tuesday night at home in Hyannis Port," said the statement from his family. "We've lost the irreplaceable center of our family and joyous light in our lives, but the inspiration of his faith, optimism, and perseverance will live on in our hearts forever. We thank everyone who gave him care and support over this last year, and everyone who stood with him for so many years in his tireless march for progress toward justice, fairness, and opportunity for all. He loved this country and devoted his life to serving it. He always believed that our best days were still ahead, but it's hard to imagine any of them without him."

"The greatest comfort that I have is that we had those fifteen months," says his wife, Vicki, speaking of the length of time Ted was ill and they had to prepare for his death. "We said everything," she says.

What a career he had in the Senate—forty-six years. He was responsible for almost twenty-five hundred bills, three hundred of which became law. The antiapartheid campaign, the Americans with Disabilities Act, the Family and Medical Leave Act, all that he did in the name of health care reform, and reams of other important legislation speak for his life's work in the Senate. But what also can't be overlooked is the tenacious way he lived his life, refusing to give in to his demons—of which even he had to admit there were many. Somehow, Ted Kennedy always found a way to rebound, even when it looked as if he was truly on the brink of self-destruction. Maybe the great story of Edward Kennedy's life is simply that he was a man who refused to either give in or give up. He always believed in his core that he had important work to do—that his life had real purpose—and that he had to find a way to do it, even during those times when his own human nature presented itself as his biggest distraction, his greatest foe.

When Ted died in 2009, his son Ted Jr., founder and president of the Marwood Group, a firm that advises corporations about health care and financial services, was forty-seven; Kara, who worked as the media director of her aunt Jean's Very Special Arts program, was forty-nine; and Patrick, still a Rhode Island congressman, was forty-two. While Ted and Kara were leading well-adjusted, happy lives, Patrick still faced some significant challenges. In 2006 he was in a car accident that ultimately was the catalyst for another stint in rehab for abuse of sleeping pills. Today, he, like his mother, is sober, but he realizes that the work to stay that way will continue for the rest of his life.

Joan Kennedy was devastated by Ted's death. She'd never stopped loving him, after all. Now all there was left to do was to grieve for her first and, it would seem, only love. Joan attended the Mass at the Big House that was said for Ted right after his passing and prior to the funeral. She wasn't sure that she should be present, however, saying that she didn't want to intrude. "Of course she should be here," Vicki decided, who called Joan and personally invited her. "Ted loved her very much. Her children love her, and they are grieving now as I know Joan is. So this is a time for all of us to be together," she said.

Joan Kennedy's public appearances of late—first at Eunice's funeral in August and then at Ted's—reminded many people who perhaps had long ago forgotten not only her struggles as a Kennedy wife but also her important place in the family's storied history. At one point, Joan was overheard telling President George W. Bush, "I admire your family so much because I know how hard it is staying close to one another when you're a political family." Bush took both of Joan's hands and said, "You are a woman America holds so dear, do you know that?" She just smiled and nodded her appreciation.

The funeral service for Ted Kennedy would be held on August 29 at the Basilica of Our Lady of Perpetual Help in Boston. At the end of the touching memorial service, two tenors and a choir sang, as everyone joined in the chorus of—what else?—"When Irish Eyes Are Smiling." Ted would later be buried at Arlington National Cemetery alongside his brothers Jack and Bobby and his sister-in-law Jackie.

"Of course, Jean was bereft at losing her brother so soon after her sister, but Ethel took it quite, quite hard," said Ethel Kennedy's former assistant, Leah Mason. "Ted had been the rock the family had stood on for so many years. Ethel always felt he was a stabilizing influence on the family, no matter what was going on. They had such a special bond. I mean, who in this world was more loyal to Ted Kennedy than his Ethie? Probably no one."

"I thought for sure I would go before Teddy," Ethel told Leah Mason after the funeral service, according to Mason's memory of the conversation. "I just thought . . . or maybe I *hoped* . . . I don't know." She seemed at a loss for words.

"He's with Jack and Bobby now," Leah Mason said, holding both of Ethel's trembling hands and echoing what Ethel had often said upon the death of a loved one.

"And Grandma and Grandpa, and David and Michael," Ethel added with a sad smile. "You know, I wouldn't have survived one single day after Bobby died if it hadn't been for Teddy," she added. She then reminded Leah that Ted had been with her in the delivery room when she had Rory, who was born after Bobby died. "And from that time on, he never left my side. Not once," Ethel said. "Even through everything that happened with David and then with Michael, never did that man leave my side."

Leah nodded. "And he won't leave your side now, either," she told Ethel. "You can count on that."

Ethel nodded and then embraced her former assistant.

A short time after that conversation, Ethel Kennedy was seen walking along the sandy Cape Cod beach in front of the Kennedy compound, occasionally stopping to enjoy the view as the orange sun melted into the distant horizon, just as Kennedys had been doing for many decades. In years past, as she took her nightly walk and passed the Big House, Ethel would always be sure to look up at one of the windows to Ted's den. There he would be, almost every summer's night, sitting in a chair, peering over his reading glasses as he reviewed paperwork under the warm glow of a single reading lamp. Sometimes he would look down to the beach and notice Ethel standing in place, gazing up at him. He would beam at his sister-in-law, Bobby's still devoted wife, and he would wave at her. Ethel would always smile, knowing in her heart that as long as Ted Kennedy was in that den in that house, all was somehow right with the world.

On this evening, as Ethel walked along the Kennedys' stretch of beach, she looked up at the Big House, her eyes searching out and then finding Ted's den, pretty much out of habit. But the light was out and the room was black, causing her—as she would later tell it—to feel almost overwhelmed by a sense of sadness and grief. But then, as she looked closer, she saw the strangest thing. The shadows of the distant clouds, the colors of the setting sun, and the iridescence of the dazzling sea had somehow conspired to paint a vivid image on glass, a reflection that she could have sworn was the handsome and smiling face of her brother-in-law Ted. She stopped walking and looked closer. "Am I seeing things?" she asked herself, as she would later recall, "or..." She stood in place, squinting at the window, trying to discern whether or not her eighty-one-year-old eyes were deceiving her when, just as magically as it had appeared, it was gone—whatever it was, it was gone. In her heart, "Ethie" knew what it was, though. And she couldn't help but smile.

About a week after the funeral, the family convened once again in the parlor of the Big House for hot coffee and warm memories. "How many years ago was it that we were all in this same room celebrating Jack's election?" Joan asked at one point, according to witnesses. "Remember? We took that family portrait right over there?" she said, pointing to a corner.

"Wow. How long ago *was* that?" Jean asked.

"My gosh! Next year it will be fifty years," Joan said, doing a quick calculation in her head. "I was just twenty-two," she added. "So young to be at the center of all of that history."

"We were all so young," Jean said, now holding Joan's hand. "Do you remember how Jackie looked on that day?" The two women smiled at one another, a wave of nostalgia no doubt washing over them. "In some ways it seems like a lifetime ago," Jean Kennedy Smith concluded, "and in other ways... just yesterday."

CODA

The Kennedys endure as one of the great families of American history, garnering as much curiosity, interest, and attention as ever. While many of its most dynamic personalities are no longer with us and others have withdrawn into private life, the legacy of "Camelot," and of all its tragedy, destiny, and promise, is one all of us share, as Americans, in our own way. It unites us across decades and generations and attracts us as few others have, not simply because of its fame, its "curse," or its scandal; not only because of its beauty or its ugliness, its achievements, or occasional falls from grace. It is a name that spoke to us then, and still does today, because for so long it came to represent our humanity: our flaws, our hopes, our disappointments, our fortitude and fragility, our successes and mistakes.

This family, America's family, at one time or another was the best of us, and the worst of us.

For those of us long fascinated with the legends of our time, eager to know them, to understand them—to break through the wall that so often separates them from the rest of the world—what are we to make of the impact of this family's story on us as individuals and as a nation? As we arrive at the denouement of this epic journey, can we point to one thing in particular that endures as the Kennedy legacy? Is it the Kennedy presidency? Dallas? Sargent and Eunice Shriver? Bobby Kennedy? Chappaquiddick? John F. Kennedy Jr. and Carolyn Bessette? Perhaps the answer lies in the eye of the beholder. Or maybe there is an enduring legacy staring out at us from this story that explains why an entire generation came to love the Kennedy family with such passion and zeal—something that transcends the lure of celebrity, sensation and fame, achievement, mission or purpose. Perhaps it is something far simpler and easier to find, something as foundational and precious for all of us as it has been, and still is, for them.

Perhaps Jackie herself said it best:

"Here we Kennedys are, all these many years later, trying to pick up the pieces of our lives. Trying to survive after Camelot. Clinging to each other with the fear that what little that remains of our kingdom will come crashing down around us, leaving us with nothing but the memory of what was once so great. But the truth is this can never happen. Because the family is the kingdom. And it can never fall."

AFTERWORD

It's fair to say that most, if not all, of the members of the Kennedy family do not take stock in the notion of a so-called Kennedy curse, though the notion has certainly crossed their minds over the years. Joan Kennedy was actually the first family member to verbalize her fears in this regard back in 1965 when her husband, Ted, was almost killed in a plane crash. At the hospital following the accident, Joan asked Jackie if she believed in such a curse. Jackie said she didn't believe in it at all. However, after so many deaths in the family into which she had married—from Joseph Kennedy Jr. to Kathleen Kennedy and, of course, President John Kennedy—Joan wasn't so sure what to believe, and this was before Bobby was assassinated in 1968. Then, in 1969, as stated in the first edition of *After Camelot*, Ted Kennedy was the first to publicly address the idea of a Kennedy curse in his speech to the nation after the Chappaquiddick scandal and the drowning death of Mary Jo Kopechne. Since that time, of course, there have been more Kennedy-related tragedies than almost imaginable—David Kennedy, Michael Kennedy, John Kennedy Jr., Kara Kennedy, all prematurely gone from the family forever, not to mention the perhaps more explicable, but no less sad, deaths by natural, aging-related causes of Eunice Kennedy Shriver, Sarge Shriver, and Ted Kennedy.

Since the first edition of this book was published in April 2012, another Kennedy family member met her fate in a truly tragic way, and that was Mary Richardson Kennedy, the fifty-two-year-old wife of Bobby Jr., who committed suicide in May 2012.

As has long been the case with the sudden death of any Kennedy, little privacy is ever attached to its aftermath. All of the problems of the deceased, many of which had been long concealed from public scrutiny, now become fodder for headlines as journalists scramble to assemble the puzzle pieces of the deceased's life and times in order to address what may have contributed to the death. In the case of Mary Richardson Kennedy, because she wasn't as public a person as her husband, the world was not aware of the very serious challenges she had been facing for decades— problems the family, of course, were well aware of and with which they had been coping for years. Apparently, Mary's dependency on alcohol and drugs, which, from most accounts, was a consequence of the years she had spent battling serious depression, had brought her to a dramatic crossroads in the spring of 2011. It was then, in the midst of an acrimonious divorce from Bobby Jr.—he had filed for divorce in May 2010—that a judge ruled she could see her four children only when all of them were in the presence of the family's housekeeper. Because of an incident that had occurred on Easter Sunday in which Mary was found to be seriously intoxicated in front of the children, it was ruled that Bobby be given full but temporary custody of Conor, 17, Kyra, 16, Fin, 14, and Aidan, 10, until Mary was able to deal with her issues. Mary missed several appointments with a psychologist in early May 2011. When she finally did appear in her doctor's office on May 10, she was left with the impression that, based on her behavior, the judge would likely rule that Bobby be given full custody of the children. It was more than she could handle.

One day in early May 2012, after several days of deep sadness and depression, Mary asked her housekeeper's husband to buy a rope for her, telling him she needed it for a couch she was designing for the family's home in Westchester County, New York. The next day, her housekeeper could not locate her on the premises. After searching to no avail, she became quite alarmed and summoned Bobby, who lived close by. Immediately, he raced over to the house. As he and the housekeeper continued to search the premises, they eventually ended up in the barn, where they found Mary, hanging from a rope. The housekeeper collapsed to the floor in hysterics as Bobby stood, staring at his wife of fifteen years for a few horrified moments before also breaking down into tears. It was later discovered that Mary had searched the Internet in the days before her death for instructions on how to make a proper noose.

After Mary's death, everyone who loved her grappled to come to terms with her suicide, including Kerry Kennedy, Bobby's sister, who had been Mary's roommate at Putney School, a Vermont boarding school, and her best friend. Mary had been the maid of honor at Kerry's marriage to Andrew Cuomo. "She was the kindest woman I had ever met," Kerry wrote in an editorial for *The Huffington Post*. "Everyone loved her who ever came in contact with her. She was an angel, a gift from the Heavens. So, let's not remember her for her despair, but let's take inspiration from her determination to heal the woundedness in herself and in those she loved."

Of course, it was easy for some to blame Kerry's brother Bobby for his wife's death. Kennedy men have a long-standing bad reputation due to the exploits of more than a few of them over the years, and so whenever a Kennedy wife has serious problems the default thinking of much of the media, and the public, is to blame the Kennedy male with whom she is romantically involved. Bobby had, apparently, already moved on to a new relationship with actress Cheryl Hines and, according to Mary's friends and family, every time Mary would see a photograph in the media of Bobby and Cheryl she would sink deeper into despair. Much of the media eagerly portrayed him as a womanizer after Mary's death, and most reports never failed to mention that he was a heroin addict—even though he has been clean and sober since 1980.

In fact, at least based on a sworn affidavit Bobby filed in Westchester County's New York Supreme Court on September 16, 2011, he had been victimized by Mary for many years, to the extent that physical abuse was involved. He testified that early in his marriage to Mary, the two had a blazing argument over his continued friendship with his first wife, Emily, "during which Mary hit me in the face with her fist. She was a trained boxer and I got a shiner. Her engagement ring crushed my tear duct, causing permanent damage." He testified that she asked him to lie to her family about the cause of his black eye.

He also testified to a time in May 2011 when Mary ran over and killed the family's dog in the driveway. She asked the couple's youngest son, Aidan, to call Bobby and give him the news. When he asked the crying child to put his mother on the line—according to Bobby's testimony—Mary demanded that he come to the house and spend the night there in order to help her calm down the children. When he hesitated, she became upset and said that if he didn't recommit to the marriage and call off the divorce, she would kill herself. This had not been the first time she made this threat; however, every time she did so, Bobby took it seriously. He raced to the house. When he got there, he later said, "Mary was intoxicated. I opened the door and she leapt out of her bed and hit me with a roundhouse punch that, had I not blocked it, would have undoubtedly broken my face. Pointing to Aidan, she screamed, 'You told this child you didn't love me?' and hit me again, raining blows down on me as I backed down the hall. She struck me maybe thirty more times or more. I moved slowly backward because she was drunk and unsteady and I didn't want her to tumble over the banister. She screamed at Aidan as she hit me. 'He is a demon. He is a demon. He is the most evil kind of man in the world. Everything he does is evil and a fraud. He is a philanderer, an adulterer, a sex addict.' Aidan was crying. I backed down the back stairs blocking her blows—and dodged out the kitchen door. She pursued me, pummeling and pushing me with her fists all the way."

Bobby Kennedy's sworn declaration with the court provides a harrowing tale of his living with a desperate, often out-of-control woman who had been diagnosed as having borderline personality disorder. He testified that the marriage was long over, but that he was trapped in it; there was no escaping it for him. Every time he made moves toward finally terminating the relationship, Mary would attack him—once in the bathtub with scissors—or threaten to kill herself. He testified that she was also abusive to the two children he'd had with his first wife.

Mary Richardson's family insists that the declaration, which also details run-ins with the police, desperate 911 calls, and many other episodes of emotional desperation, is rife with half-truths and outright lies. Obviously, there are two sides to every story, and, with Mary's death, only Bobby's side can now be told. Even his own sister Kerry painted a different picture of Mary and her relationship with Bobby after her death, though she was careful not to contradict the specifics of any of Bobby's statements. "I have never seen two people more thoroughly enchanted with one another and more completely in love," she wrote in an editorial for *The Huffington Post* after Mary's death. "They brought out the best in one another, and spoke about each other with wonder and awe. And even at the most difficult times, they were still devoted to one another, compassionate, caring, concerned. They had four fabulous children, to whom Mary was absolutely devoted. She took parenting classes to be a better mother, and then started teaching parenting classes herself."

Bobby also stated that he pleaded with Mary's family to hold an intervention. However, Mary's family was angry with him, adhering to their hatred of him and their belief that most of Mary's problems were related to his unfaithful behavior during his marriage to her. On file is a June 17,

2011, e-mail to the family of Mary Richardson written by Bobby, which states: "Mary is a wonderful, generous, kind, and wise person but depression and illness are now killing her. I know you have told me that her frequent suicide threats are not real. I do not believe this is accurate. I see her now sinking into a terrible darkness. She desperately needs a family intervention." The family responded by demanding that Kennedy cease sending e-mails such as that one, lest they be forced to respond to them and "the record that we will be forced to set forth is not one that Bobby will be pleased to have on paper or in electronic form." Based on that exchange, it seems clear that Mary would not be able to get the help she needed unless Bobby and her family were able to reach some sort of accord, and that, at least according to the documents filed with the court, was impossible. It would seem, from all available evidence, that her family loathed him so much they couldn't rise above it and even imagine aligning with him in any way, for any purpose.

Moreover, it also seems that members of Mary's family were emotionally exhausted by years of Mary's broken promises to take better care of herself. Her housekeeper recalled to Laurence Leamer, for his exhaustive report on Mary's death for *The Daily Beast*, the events of Easter Sunday, April 8, 2012, when Mary had custody of the children. The housekeeper says she found Mary passed out, intoxicated, in the kitchen. She says that she called Mary's sisters but that they never showed up. After that, at least according to the housekeeper, Mary told her that her family was very angry with her and didn't even want to speak to her. She then broke down crying, wondering to the housekeeper why she couldn't stop drinking.

When she died, the Richardson family went to the home she had shared with Bobby Kennedy in search of clues as to why she killed herself. When Bobby showed up, some of the Richardsons accused him of being complicit in her death, with Mary's sister Nan screaming at him, "You have killed my sister." (Nan Richardson declined to comment on this allegation).

The death of Mary Richardson Kennedy is a horrifying story on so many levels, illustrating the challenging circumstances that have long played out over the years for women married to Kennedy men. Mary Richardson Kennedy was a striking brunette, tall and willowy, with an effervescent personality that belied the tortured soul beneath the glossy exterior. In that respect, she reminded many people of the lovely blonde Joan Kennedy, also charismatic in the public eye but deeply troubled behind closed doors. Certainly Joan could attest to the difficulties of keeping up the pretense of a happy marriage for public consumption when, at home, everything is falling apart. In the case of Mary Richardson, though, it would seem that her problems ran much deeper than turning to alcohol in order to cope with an unfaithful husband. Mary, who was a successful architect before she married Bobby, suffered from serious psychological problems that were only exacerbated by the slow disintegration of her marriage, by her feelings of betrayal and abandonment, and her desperation over the possibility of losing her children.

"Of course, with any tragedy such as this one, there is a sense that *someone* needs to be held accountable. Why not the husband?" asks one of Bobby's confidantes. "But the question remains: how many years is a spouse expected to be held hostage by a partner's emotional problems. Where do you draw the line? Five years? Ten? Twenty? If we're going to start pointing fingers, I think everyone has to share some blame, including Mary, herself. It's not a popular view to have, and maybe it seems harsh and unkind considering poor Mary's tragic demise. But it's true."

Mary Richardson Kennedy was clearly a very troubled woman. Who's to say what her life would have been like had she never married Bobby Kennedy? Her psychiatric disorders were not solely caused by her marriage. She suffered from anorexia long before she even met Bobby. And people who knew her well insist that the different medications prescribed to her—so many of them, her friends long ago lost count—affected her personality in a negative way.

Maybe her best friend, Kerry Kennedy, put it all in the best possible, most charitable light when she wrote: "Like millions of Americans, Mary suffered from depression. She had it for as long as I knew her, and as it reared up in high school, college and beyond, she fought it back, for a day, a week, a month. These last 6 years or more, she fought it as hard as she knew how. But that disease was not Mary herself. She was deeply Catholic, and she was an angel. And like the archangel Michael, who battled Satan when he tried to take over Heaven, Mary fought back the demons who were trying to invade the Paradise of her very being. She fought with everything she had. And I think God said to her, "Mary, you have been my warrior on the front lines for too long, you have fought valiantly, and now I am bringing you home."

Unfortunately, even after her death, the battles between Mary's family and Bobby continued. For instance, the Richardsons wanted their beloved family member to be buried in a family plot in Vermont. However, Bobby wanted her in a cemetery near the Kennedy compound in Hyannis. His children sided with him, and two of them—Conor and Kyra—testified before a judge to that effect. The judge ruled in their favor, further intensifying the hard feelings between the Richardsons and Bobby Kennedy. In the end, Mary was buried in the St. Francis Xavier Cemetery in Centerville, Massachusetts, outside a circle of shrubs near the gravesites of Sargent and Eunice Shriver. The Richardsons did not attend the services; instead, they had their own for Mary, in Manhattan.

In a final sad twist to this story, seven weeks after Mary Richardson Kennedy was buried, Bobby had the body exhumed and relocated to a different part of the cemetery, seven hundred feet away on a different hilltop. It was explained that Bobby didn't realize how crowded the area was where Mary was originally buried until the day of her funeral, and that he had her moved to an area where there would be room for expansion, where the Kennedys were in negotiation for the purchase of fifty plots. This decision on his part is difficult to reconcile. Why, many have wondered, couldn't he just let Mary rest in peace? As of this writing, there are no other Kennedys buried anywhere near the area of the cemetery where Mary's body was relocated. In fact, there are no other people buried near Mary's plot at all. It would seem that, in death, Mary Richardson Kennedy is still very much alone.

* * *

At about the time that the body of Mary Richardson Kennedy was exhumed and relocated, in July 2012, her close friend, fifty-two-year-old Kerry Kennedy, was arrested after swerving her white 2008 Lexus into a tractor trailer in Westchester County, New York, and then leaving the scene. She later explained to arresting officers that she might possibly have accidentally taken the sleep aid Ambien instead of medication for a thyroid condition before getting behind the wheel. (It's interesting to note that Kerry's cousin former Rep. Patrick Kennedy (D-R.I.) crashed his car in 2006 while taking Ambien.) A Kennedy spokesman quickly denied any wrongdoing, and insisted that blood, urine, and Breathalyzer tests all cleared Kerry.

"I remember getting on the highway, and then I have no memory until

I was stopped at a traffic light and a police officer was at my car door," Kerry later said of the crash while standing in front of the courthouse after her arraignment (where she pleaded not guilty to the misdemeanor charge of DWAI—Driving While Ability Impaired). "I have never had any history of drugs or alcohol abuse." She also stated that a battery of medical tests after the accident "led my doctors to believe that this accident was caused not by a sleeping aid, but by a complex partial seizure.

"I want to apologize to the driver of the truck who I apparently hit and to all those I endangered while driving my car last Friday morning," Kerry Kennedy concluded. "Northern Westchester is my home, and I care deeply about my neighbors and about my community."

The case against Kerry Kennedy is still pending.

* * *

In the fall of 2012, a member of the fourth generation of Kennedys—Conor Kennedy, the son of Bobby and the late Mary Richardson Kennedy—found himself grabbing news headlines because of his romantic pairing with country pop entertainer Taylor Swift, who was twenty-two. At the time, Kennedy had just turned eighteen in August and was, of course, still grieving the death of his mother. Swift purchased a home adjacent to the Kennedy compound on Nantucket Sound at about the same time that she began dating Conor. Originally from Pennsylvania, she moved with her family to Nashville, and she also owns a home in Beverly Hills.

A major recording star who has sold millions of records and won many awards, Taylor Swift is a pop sensation who generates headlines for engaging in even the most mundane of activities, such as clothes shopping. Therefore, a romantic entanglement with the grandson of RFK and Ethel Kennedy was, naturally, going to catch the attention of not only the tabloid media but the mainstream press as well. She had been invited to the Kennedy compound for the 2012 Fourth of July weekend by Rory Kennedy, to whom Taylor had reached out for tickets to see the *Ethel* documentary at Sundance (which Rory had produced about her mother). "She's a great friend of ours," Rory said of Taylor. "We love her."

In August 2012, the budding romance caused a bit of a news stir when Taylor was seen praying with Conor and some other Kennedys at Mary

Richardson Kennedy's gravesite. That same month, more headlines were made when Taylor supposedly "crashed" the wedding of Kyle Kennedy—daughter of the late Michael Kennedy and Victoria Gifford Kennedy—to Liam Kerr. "They texted me an hour before the wedding and asked if they could come," Victoria told the *Boston Herald*. "I responded with a very clear, 'Please do not come.' They came anyway. I personally went up to Ms. Swift, whose entrance distracted the entire event, politely introduced myself to her, and asked her as nicely as I could to leave. It was like talking to a ghost. She seemed to look right past me."

Apparently, Conor had been invited to the wedding but hadn't RSVP'd. When he later texted Victoria Gifford Kennedy to ask if he and his girlfriend could come to the event, Vicki texted back and said "no," because she was afraid that Swift's presence would pull attention from the bride.

In fact, many members of the Kennedy family seemed to approve of Taylor Swift. "She is just spectacular, she is just sensational, she is very kind, and you know what she really is? She's game," said eighty-four-year-old Ethel Kennedy in October 2012 at the 23rd Annual RFK Golf Tournament at the Hyannisport Golf Club (which supports the Robert F. Kennedy Center for Justice and Human Rights). "She had never sailed before, she sailed. She has never gone dragging before, she dragged. [Dragging is searching or sweeping the bottom of a lake with a grappling hook or dragnet.] She played everything that everyone else was doing and she was good at it, and no fuss. I'm happy that we'll be neighbors. I'm thrilled." When asked if her grandson had taken a liking to her, Ethel responded, "Yes! How could you not? I think the world has."

As is usually the case with puppy love, the romance between Conor and Taylor did not last very long; it was over after about three months.

* * *

Ordinarily, Ethel Kennedy would most certainly not have been available to the media for comment about her grandson's infatuation with a pop star. It just so happened that, at the time, she was in the midst of promoting an important project—her daughter Rory's much-anticipated documentary, *Ethel*. Rory's documentary, which she produced and directed about her mother, was a hit at the 2012 Sundance Film Festival and then broadcast on HBO in October of that same year. An interesting, if, arguably, incomplete, examination of the life and times of the Kennedy matriarch, *Ethel* reveals its subject to be honest and forthcoming and even funny, if not always coopera-tive with the filmmaker (even if it was her own daughter).

The reviews for *Ethel* were somewhat mixed. It's worth noting that even the critic for the *Boston Globe*, usually very evenhanded where the Kennedys are concerned, could not resist being cynical. "'Ethel' intro-duces all the siblings at the beginning," wrote Mark Feeney. "It's an amus-ing way to start, and quite practical, too, helping to sort out all those overbites. It does feel a bit 'Brady Bunch,' though. And were there intra-family negotiations as to who got how much screen time?"

The *New York Times* was even harsher. "It is presented as a "private look inside a highly public life"—and it should have been kept private," wrote Alessandra Stanley. "Instead, 'Ethel' is a documentary...that is tone-deaf and maddeningly incomplete. Watching it is a little like read-ing a classified report redacted by Dick Cheney—so much material is blacked out that it's almost impossible to follow.... Most of all the film is a painful reminder that Camelot ended with her husband's death. It's not just that the family's mystique was washed away by too many scandals, exposés and unflattering biographies. The Kennedys were once artful curators of their myth; Rory Kennedy's film suggests that the succeeding generations are spookily oblivious to their own public image."

Given that Ethel Kennedy rarely gives interviews, it's easy to want more from her. However, she is far more open in her daughter's documen-tary than ever before, especially in regard to her memories of her time with Bobby and her recollections, for instance, of his early work investi-gating racketeers or campaigning for his brother Jack. Ethel also recalls the time after the assassination of President Kennedy as being "a tidal wave of grief...everyone was devastated. It was like Daddy [Bobby] had lost both arms." She admitted that she could not reach her husband emo-tionally; he became that disconnected from the family. It was, she said, "six months of just blackness." She added that "he [Bobby] started in little baby steps to come out of it, and I think it was the children who really did it, and you can see it in photographs at the time when he was playing touch football with them."

Ethel's recollection of Bobby's decision to run for presidency is also very compelling, her memory of his decision being based primarily on his unhappiness with the way President Johnson had handled the Vietnam

War. (She also says that by the time Kennedy decided to run, he was "persona non grata" as far as the LBJ White House was concerned.)

Ethel did refuse to talk about the assassination of her husband, which she witnessed in 1968. ("Let's talk about something else," she barely manages to say without breaking down.) She doesn't need to discuss it, though. The expression of heartbreak on her heavily lined face is still so raw these many years later, it's all the viewer needs to fully understand that Ethel Kennedy's grief over the murder of her beloved Bobby is as real and as painful today as it was the very night it happened almost forty-five years ago.

From interviews conducted with her many grown children, the viewer is left with the feeling that each of them is smart, thoughtful, and well spoken and had been taught at a very early age to be engaged in world events and to care about others—and also to be very competitive. One interesting moment occurs when Rory asks if "coming in second was okay," in discussing the family's leisure-time sports competitions. Her brother Douglas responds, "Only if you were the Shrivers."

That Ethel and her children aren't always as candid as one might like is really not much of a surprise if one understands the Kennedy mind-set and the way they have tried to draw, at least whenever possible, a clear demarcation between their private and public lives. Despite its lukewarm reviews, *Ethel* actually brings us closer to the real woman—and also to her children—than we've ever been before. What the viewer gets from Rory's admiring and well-produced documentary is just how strong and determined Ethel Kennedy is and has always been throughout her life. "Nobody gets a free ride," she concludes. "Everybody faces friends who have died or family who have died or who are really sick. So have your wits about you, and dig in and do what you can...because it might not last."

At the same time that the *Ethel* documentary was broadcast, a bizarre legal battle was about to be mounted against the tenth of her eleven children—Douglas Kennedy. Douglas was, earlier in the year, charged with physical harassment and child endangerment, both misdemeanors, stemming from a strange incident that took place on January 7, 2012, at Westchester Hospital in New York. Apparently, Douglas attempted to take his newborn infant son, Anthony Boru Kennedy, for a walk outside the hospital in which the infant was born, saying that he wanted to "get some fresh air" for his son. He was confronted by two nurses who objected to his leaving with the infant, based on hospital regulations. They would later claim that Kennedy became physically abusive toward them during a scuffle, one nurse claiming that Kennedy twisted her arm and the other that he kicked her in the pelvis. When security officers eventually stopped him from leaving the hospital, he maintained that he was only trying to temporarily leave the premises with his baby, and that no father should be barred from doing so by hospital employees. He was charged with the misdemeanor crimes in February.

During the trial in November 2012, prosecutors argued that Douglas Kennedy had recklessly endangered his newborn son. However, Kennedy's lawyers maintained that the nurses completely overreacted to the situation, becoming unnecessarily abrasive. They asserted that Kennedy had been reasonable with them until they tried to block him from an elevator and a stairwell. Kennedy's lawyers also allege that the nurses later attempted to exploit the situation by granting media interviews and then threatening Kennedy with a lawsuit in order to, as the lawyers put it at trial, "line their pockets" with Kennedy money.

The most compelling facet of this is that it was alleged by the prosecution that in the midst of the confrontation with nurses, Kennedy told a security guard, "Do you know who I am?" The implication, of course, is that he carries with him a sense of entitlement that allows him to break the rules without consequence. Whether or not he actually said those words is in dispute. In fact, Douglas Kennedy is a generally soft-spoken, extremely polite family man who is rarely in the news involving any sort of controversy. "If you knew him," said one friend of his, "I mean, really knew him, you would know that he would not have done what he is accused of doing unless he was really pushed to the limits. He's a very protective father when it comes to his children, the way his father was with him and his siblings. I have no doubt that he felt he was not only protecting his child but also his right to take care of the baby as he saw fit."

In November 2012, Douglas Kennedy was acquitted of all charges. Mount Kisco Town Judge John Donohue, who heard the case, ruled that Kennedy's newborn was not in danger and he did not intend to hurt the nurses either. "However, the court is not determining whether the defendant's behavior was wise or prudent," he noted. At a Manhattan news conference, Kennedy's lawyer, Robert Gottlieb, said that Douglas and his wife, Molly, were "thrilled that this nightmare has finally come to an end." He also concluded, "This case from Day One was all about money."

* * *

Doubtless, the most perplexing development to take place since the original publication of *After Camelot* was the October 2012 release of Arnold Schwarzenegger's autobiography, *Total Recall—My Unbelievably True Life Story*, which he wrote with Peter Petre.

Arnold Schwarzenegger's memoir takes the reader from his childhood in Austria during the early days of the Cold War all the way through his years as a world-famous bodybuilder, a famous actor, and, ultimately, the governor of California. The challenge with the publication of this book comes in reconciling that he chose this particular time—at the beginning of very painful divorce proceedings instigated by his wife, Maria Shriver—to write about his affair with the family's live-in housekeeper, Mildred Baena, which led to the illegitimate birth of his son Joseph. It could also be said that his interviews promoting the book, most notably with Lesley Stahl for CBS's *60 Minutes*, actually portrayed him in a more negative light than the work itself, and maybe were even more hurtful to Maria, as well.

Arnold is a man who, by his own admission, has lived his entire life keeping secrets from those he cared most about. For instance, he writes that he planned to keep from Maria the fact that he was going to have open heart surgery in 1997, telling his doctor that he wanted to have the surgery in Mexico and tell his wife—pregnant at the time—that he was going on a vacation there. One can't help wondering if the fact that Mildred Baena was pregnant at the same time had any bearing on this weird plan. (Ultimately, the doctor convinced him to change his mind.) Arnold also writes that even though he had been toying with the idea of running for governor for more than a year, he waited until days before the filing deadline in 2003 to discuss the matter with Maria. Why? Because he "didn't want endless conversation about it at home." When he did tell Maria, she begged him not to run because she has had such heartbreak in her life where politics was concerned, not only based on what happened to her uncles JFK and Bobby but also because of what Sargent Shriver went through in his political career. It was her mother, Eunice, who stepped in and told Maria that if she stopped Arnold from running, he would likely be angry with her for the rest of his life. Therefore, Maria abandoned her career as a television news journalist to support her husband in his endeavor. Then, when allegations surfaced that he had been sexually inappropriate with women over the years, she came to his defense. "You can listen to all of the negativity and you can listen to people who have never met Arnold or who met him for five seconds thirty years ago, or you can listen to me," she said in one speech, vouching for his character. By this time, though she didn't know it, Arnold had already had the affair with the housekeeper. He also writes that he did not tell her that he was planning on running for a second term, leaving her instead to read about it in the newspapers. So, likely, it was not terribly surprising to Maria to discover that he had, for many years, kept the secret of his illegitimate son, born in 1997 around the same time as Christopher, his youngest son with Maria.

The lack of communication in his marriage seems evident when Arnold reveals that Maria asked him if he was the father of Baena's child while in couples' counseling the day after he left office in 2012. Evidently, he thought he was going into therapy with Maria in order to discuss their future after his political career. She had previously asked him in private if the boy was his, and he had lied to her and denied it. Moreover, he suspected—but isn't sure—that Maria had already confirmed the child's true paternity with the housekeeper prior to the therapy session. Finally, in front of the counselor, he had no choice but to admit it. When Maria asked him why he hadn't told her earlier, as he explained to Lesley Stahl, "I told her I didn't know how to tell her without worrying about that it would get out...or whatever." It's not difficult to imagine that another reason was that he was afraid she would leave him while he was still governor, though he said that this wasn't the case—that his only intention was to answer the question, "How do I keep this under wraps?"

Arnold told Stahl that he didn't actually ask Baena if the boy was his; he just started taking care of her and the youngster financially when, at about the age of 7, the child started resembling him. Of course, none of this adds up, as Stahl noted. She asked Arnold how it was explained that money "just started showing up" for Baena. He answered flatly, "I give it to her and she knows what it's about." He admitted to Stahl that having Baena still continue to work for him and Maria was "very difficult, strange and bizarre, but the best way I could handle it." However, it sounds as if he kept Baena in the household just so that he could make sure she wouldn't talk about what was going on, especially when he writes in his book that he wanted to "control the situation." He says, though, that this was not his motivation. In fact, he explains everything away by saying, "That's just the way I operate." It was really, by his own admission, just one lie after another to Maria. At one point in the interview, Stahl looked at Arnold incredulously and—likely echoing what would be the reaction of much of her viewing audience—said, "She gave up her *television* career for you! I mean…*wow!*"

In fact, with the publication of the former governor's book, actress Brigitte Nielsen came forward to claim that she too had a romance with Arnold while he was in a relationship with Shriver, saying, "Maybe I wouldn't have got into it if he said 'I'm going to marry Maria' and this is dead serious, but he didn't, and our affair carried on." Of course, Arnold and Maria were not yet married but, still, it does stretch credulity to think that this kind of behavior did not continue while he was a married man.

Considering her public support of him over the years and her staunch position that he was an honorable husband and father, it somehow seems unconscionable that Arnold would write a book that, basically, demonstrates that he had lied repeatedly to his wife. Why humiliate her any further? Perhaps one of Maria's cousins put it best when he concluded, "I think we can all agree that Sarge and Eunice's only daughter deserved better. Much better."

* * *

It has never been easy for the Kennedys. It seems as if the next family ordeal has always been just around the corner. Is it a curse, though? Perhaps if a person is inclined to believe in such superstitions, enough evidence exists to give the notion some credence. The truth, though, is that the Kennedys are a very large family who have, for the most part, conducted their lives while under heavy public scrutiny with every moment—the celebrated as well as the tragic—magnified and examined by a fascinated public and media. Perhaps Eunice Kennedy Shriver said it best when she told this author in 2002, "I have come to believe that it's not what has happened to our family that has been cursed as much as it's the fact that we have never been able to deal with any of it privately. I'm afraid that there is little dignity to living your life in so public a fashion. However, this burden is one we Kennedys have carried for generations. So, indeed, if there is a curse, and I'm not saying that there is," she hastened to add, "but *if* there is," she concluded, "surely it's that."

Acknowledgments
and Source Notes

ACKNOWLEDGMENTS

THE AUTHOR'S SUPPORT TEAM

A comprehensive book such as *After Camelot* is many years in the making, and during that time its author must depend on a core group of professionals in order to get the job done. As with all of my books, many people became personally invested in this project, from researchers and investigators to copy editors and fact checkers to designers, publicists, and, of course, even attorneys. In my view, it's only when this kind of group effort occurs that a project becomes a truly rewarding working experience. Without others who care, where does a writer find himself? Sitting in an office alone, writing. That's a lonely proposition, but luckily it's never been the road I've had to travel. I have always been surrounded by a dedicated and loyal team of people with whom I could bounce ideas, count on for constructive criticism, talk about storytelling...laugh, cry...whatever it takes to get the job done.

I would first like to acknowledge my colleagues at Grand Central Publishing, my home for the last fourteen years. It's rare these days for an author to remain with the same publisher for such a long time, and when it happens it's usually the result of shared respect and admiration. The fine people at Grand Central have always made it possible for me to do what I must in order to complete a book project, no matter how many years it takes for that to occur. In fact, an author could not ask for a better and more nurturing environment than the one I have been so fortunate to have at Grand Central. None of my books for Grand Central—and this is my sixth, counting back to the days when the company was known as Warner Books—would be possible, though, without the loyal friendship of my publisher, Jamie Raab. She is not only a very smart publisher but a terrific editor as well. And patient, too, as is necessary sometimes when shepherding projects such as this one which take years to come to fruition. I would like to also thank Jamie's very capable assistant, Sharon Krassney, who always goes the extra mile for me.

I was so happy to have worked once again with the very capable Frances Jalet-Miller as my editor on this book. The kind of trust an author and editor share is sacred, and when I learned that Frances would be able to work with me again on this book—as she did with *The Secret Life of Marilyn Monroe*—I was very happy. I would like to thank her for the many hours she invested in this project. We had fun, too!

I would also like to thank my managing editor, Bob Castillo, for his fine work on *After Camelot*. Bob has worked on all of my books since the year 2000 and I love the way we function together. Additionally, I would like to thank Evan Boorstyn in publicity. Thanks to Anne Twomey for her excellent cover design. And I would like to thank Claire Brown in art, Sara Weiss in editorial, and Tom Whatley and Giraud Lorber in production. A special thanks to my copy editor, Roland Ottewell, for a job very well done on yet another one of my books.

I would also like to acknowledge Maureen Mahon Egen, former president of Warner Books, who was my editor on *Jackie, Ethel, Joan: Women of Camelot*. The standard she set with the tone of that book was one I tried to follow in *After Camelot*. I will always be indebted to her.

Thanks to John Pelosi and the staff of Wolf, Effron & Spates for their legal review of this work, which was thorough and much appreciated.

I would have to say that *After Camelot*—my seventeenth book—was my most challenging work, because unlike most of my books, which have been about the life of one person—Diana Ross, Michael Jackson, Elizabeth Taylor, Marilyn Monroe, etc.—this one is about an entire family of complex, fascinating, and sometimes troubled personalities. Though they are a political family, I don't necessarily view this as a political book. My goal with this work was to consider the family dynamics behind the Kennedy image, to come to some understanding of who these people were—are—in relation to one another, and then tell their story in as objective and balanced a way as possible. For me, one of the most interesting aspects about the actual research for this book is that it spanned so many years. Much of the material utilized in this book was gathered in preparation for books I have done over the years that were related to this particular subject matter, such as *Sinatra: A Complete Life*; *Jackie, Ethel,*

Joan: Women of Camelot; and *The Secret Life of Marilyn Monroe*. I have found that, as a biographer, if one sticks around long enough, research from one book to another will usually come in handy once again. To that end, I would like to thank Maryanne Reed for helping me pull taped interviews and transcripts from so many years gone by and with so many people who are now deceased. This was not an easy task, but she did an incredible job and I am indebted to her for it.

I must also acknowledge my domestic agent, Mitch Douglas. Mitch and I have been together for fifteen years—that's a great partnership! He always does his best to make sure my needs as an author are met, and he's a great friend as well. So I want to thank him with all my heart.

Also, I would like to acknowledge my foreign agent, Dorie Simmonds of the Dorie Simmonds Agency in London. Again, we go back fifteen years, at least! Maybe more. I have lost track! Dorie is a terrific agent and also a great friend. It's a pleasure working with her.

I am very fortunate to have been associated with the same private investigator and chief researcher, Cathy Griffin, for more than twenty years. Cathy has worked on every *New York Times* best seller I have ever written—ten at my last count—and has always done an incredible job of not only tracking down people who have never before been interviewed, but also convincing them to talk. This isn't always easy. Cathy conducted scores of interviews for this book with people who have never before told their stories. I want to thank her for always coming through for me, as she certainly did with this new Kennedy family history.

Marcus Edwards also conducted many interviews for this book as well as for *Jackie, Ethel, Joan: Women of Camelot*, and his assistance has always been greatly appreciated. Also, Jayne Edwards-Smith conducted certain interviews and also spent many long hours transcribing tapes, which was an invaluable service to me.

Thank you, also, to Jane Maxwell, a terrific pop culture historian who allowed me to have access to all of her notes and files having to do with the Kennedys.

I would like to thank Juliette Burgonde, Cloe Basiline, Maxime Rhiette, and especially Mary Whitaker in London, who assisted with the U.K. research. As always, Marybeth Evans in London did a terrific job at the Manchester Central Library, reviewing reams of documents for me and pointing me to exactly those I needed for this book. Thanks also to

Suzalie Rose, who did research for me in libraries in Paris. She and Carl Mathers were invaluable to the *After Camelot* project.

I would like to acknowledge the late Kennedy historian Lester David. For a while, we were with the same publisher, Carol Publishing. Mr. David wrote many fine books about the Kennedys and shared with me a good number of very important sources. I would like to thank him for transcripts of his interviews with Joan Kennedy, Ethel Kennedy, Sargent Shriver, David Kennedy, LeMoyne Billings, Jean Kennedy Smith, and Stephen Smith, all of which I utilized in this volume.

Also, I have to acknowledge the late Barbara Gibson, who gave me so many hours of interview time over the years. As Rose Kennedy's personal secretary, she was privy to the inner workings of the Kennedy family, and she shared her memories with me very openly. Also the late Leah Mason, who was one of Ethel Kennedy's assistants, granted me many interviews over the years, and I appreciate her help as well. Moreover, Noelle Bombardier, also one of Ethel Kennedy's assistants, spent many hours with Cathy Griffin going over her memories for this book, and I appreciate her as well.

Thanks to Dale Manesis for all of his help with the vast collection of Kennedy memorabilia that I would never have otherwise had access to.

Thanks also to Dun Gifford, Edward Larrabee Barnes, Jacques Lowe, John Carl Warnecke, Hugh Sidey, Pierre Salinger, Joan Braden, Arthur Schlesinger Jr., Ted Sorenson, Jack Valenti, Roswell Gilpatric, and Senator George Smathers; all are now deceased, but their memories live on in this book.

My personal copy editor James Pinkston has worked with me on my last six books. He reviews absolutely everything I write long before anyone at Grand Central ever sees it—and thank goodness for that! Jim's mandate has to do with accuracy as well as grammar, sentence structure, and storytelling, and when it comes to a book such as *After Camelot* where so many stories intersect, attaining that goal seemed somehow more important than ever. He did a lot more for me on this book than I can even detail here, and his work was amazing. I am indebted to him.

I must also thank the many authors, historians, and researchers in the Boston and Washington areas—too many to note here, but all have received personal letters of gratitude from me—who spent literally years going through all hundreds of archives and manuscripts at the John F.

Kennedy Presidential Library, narrowing them down and then making them available to me for *After Camelot*.

GENERAL RESEARCH

This book would not have been possible without the assistance of so many organizations that provided me with articles, documents, audio interviews, video interviews, transcripts, and other material that was either utilized directly in *After Camelot* or just for purposes of background, including the John Fitzgerald Kennedy Library, the Robert F. Kennedy Library, and the Lyndon Baines Johnson Library. I would like to acknowledge Linda M. Seelke, the Lyndon Baines Johnson Library's archivist, for her dedication to her work and for her assistance to me and my researchers. As well as Ms. Seelke, I would like to thank Harry J. Middleton, director of the library, for his help in many ways, and also for the personal interview he granted to Cathy Griffin on September 28, 1998. My thanks also go to Tina Houston, the supervisory archivist. Also a special thanks to Matthew Hanson, Deirdre Doughty, Mollie McDonnold, and Kate Bronstad. I urge any researcher working on a book involving President Lyndon Johnson even tangentially to contact the Lyndon Baines Johnson Library in Austin, Texas, for they will make your work much easier.

I would also like to thank Lady Bird Johnson's personal assistant, Shirley James.

Thanks to Maryrose Grossman, Nadia Dixson, and Kyoko Yamamoto at the John F. Kennedy Presidential Library.

I would also like to express my gratitude to the following institutions:

American Academy of Dramatic Arts; American Film Institute Library; Associated Press Office (New York); Bancroft Library (University of California, Berkeley); Lincoln Center, New York; *Boston Herald* Archives; Beverly Hills Library; University of California, Los Angeles; Corbis-Gamma/Liaison; Ernest Lehman Collection at USC; Glendale Central Public Library; Hedda Hopper Collection in the Margaret Herrick Library, Academy of Motion Picture Arts and Sciences, Beverly Hills; Lincoln Center Library of the Performing Arts; Kobal Collection; *Los Angeles Times*; Los Angeles Public Library; Margaret Herrick Library, Academy of Motion Picture Arts and Sciences; Museum of Broadcasting,

New York; the former Metro-Goldwyn-Mayer studio archives, now part of the Turner Entertainment Group, Los Angeles; Museum of the Film; National Archives and Library of Congress; New York City Municipal Archives; New York University Library; *New York Daily News*; *New York Post*; *New York Times*; Occidental College, Eagle Rock, California; Philadelphia Public Library; *Philadelphia Inquirer* and *Philadelphia Daily News*; Time-Life Archives and Library, New York; Universal Collection at the University of Southern California; University of Southern California; and, finally, Rex Features.

ORAL HISTORIES

I could not have written *After Camelot* without utilizing the many oral histories provided by the John F. Kennedy Presidential Library. A great deal of material has been archived—hundreds of thousands of pages, in fact—and one has to go through all of it to find the fascinating nuggets. I remember the days when one would have to sit in the library for weeks or months on end looking for just the right oral history—in fact, that was the case with the research for much of this book! But now, amazingly enough, a lot of that material can be found online at http://www.jfklibrary.org.

My thanks to the following staff members of the John F. Kennedy Presidential Library who assisted me and my researchers with oral histories: William Johnson, Ron Whealon, June Payne, Maura Porter, Susan D'Entrement, Kyoko Yamamoto, Allen Goodrich, and James Hill.

Also, I would like to mention David Powers, former special assistant to President John F. Kennedy, the first curator of the JFK Library. Mr. Powers, always the Kennedy loyalist, was extremely reluctant to speak to me for my book *Jackie, Ethel, Joan: Women of Camelot* back in the 1990s. However, he did fill out two lengthy questionnaires, and then finally submitted to a follow-up telephone interview. No mention of the Kennedy Library is complete without a nod to Mr. Powers, who died in April 1998 at the age of eighty-five.

I am also grateful to Marianne Masterson, Leanne Johnson, and Doug Anderson for assisting me in the reading and analyzing of these many transcripts.

It would be impossible—and impractical, given space limitations—to cite paragraph by paragraph how these oral histories were used; they were that important in the general shaping of this work. However, anyone interested in reading the oral histories should avail him- or herself of that opportunity by contacting the John Fitzgerald Kennedy Library in Boston.

Oral histories of the following were in some way utilized in *After Camelot*, whether as quotes or for background purposes:

Joseph Alsop, journalist, author, Kennedy friend and associate; Janet Lee Auchincloss, Jackie's mother; Isaac Avery, White House carpenter; Letitia Baldrige, White House social secretary; Joanne Barhoza, waitress at Kennedy home, Hyannis Port; Albert Wesley "Wes" Barthelmes, press secretary to Robert F. Kennedy; Charles Bartlett, journalist, friend of President Kennedy; Kirk LeMoyne "Lem" Billings, Kennedy family friend and associate; Edmund Pat Brown, governor of California (interview conducted by the Lyndon Baines Johnson Library); Traphes L. Bryant, White House electrician; McGeorge Bundy, special assistant to the president for national security affairs; Kenneth Burke, White House policeman; the Reverend John Cavanaugh, Kennedy family friend, associate, Roman Catholic priest, University of Notre Dame; Peter Cronin, reporter, United Press International; Cardinal Richard Cushing, Roman Catholic archbishop of Boston; Angier Biddle Duke, chief of protocol, White House and State Department; Frederick Dutton, special assistant to President Kennedy; John English, New York political figure, political aide to Robert F. Kennedy (interview conducted for the RFK Oral History Project); Paul B. Fay Jr., friend of President Kennedy and undersecretary of the Navy; Edward Folliard, journalist, *Washington Post*; Elizabeth Gatov (interview conducted by the Women in Politics Oral History Project, University of California, Berkeley); Dun Gifford, legislative assistant to Senator Edward M. Kennedy, national presidential campaign assistant to Robert F. Kennedy, staff member, secretary's office, Department of Housing and Urban Development (interview conducted for the RFK Oral History Project); Roswell Gilpatrick, deputy secretary of defense; John Glenn, Project Mercury astronaut; Josephine Grennan, Irish cousin of John F. Kennedy; Michael Gretchen, West Virginia labor leader; Charles E. Guggenheim, film producer, political media consultant for Robert Kennedy's Senate campaign and presidential campaign, producer of *Robert Kennedy Remembered* (1968) (interview conducted for the RFK Oral History Project); Edwin O. Guthman, editor, *Seattle Times*, director of public information, Department of Justice, press assistant to Robert F. Kennedy; Milton Gwirtzman, presidential adviser, speechwriter, Robert Kennedy's Senate campaign, director of public affairs, Robert Kennedy's presidential campaign, coauthor (with William vanden Heuvel) of *On His Own: RFK, 1964–1968* (interview conducted for the RFK Oral History Project); Andrew J. Hatcher, assistant press secretary to John F. Kennedy; Louella Hennessey, Kennedy family nurse; Jacqueline (Provost) Hirsh, French-language instructor to President Kennedy's children (1966); John Jay Hooker, member, John F. Kennedy's presidential campaign staff; Claude E. Hooten, member, John F. Kennedy's presidential campaign staff; Oscar L. Huber, Roman Catholic priest who administered last rites to President Kennedy in Dallas; Hubert H. Humphrey, vice president of the United States, presidential candidate (interview conducted for the RFK Oral History Project and also by the Lyndon Baines Johnson Library); Rafer Johnson, friend and aide to Robert F. Kennedy (interview conducted for the RFK Oral History Project); Joseph J. Karitas, White House painter; Nicholas Katzenbach (interview conducted for the RFK Oral History Project); Robert Francis Kennedy, brother of President Kennedy, attorney general of the United States, senator from New York; Rose Fitzgerald Kennedy, wife of Joseph P. Kennedy, mother of President Kennedy (interview conducted by the Herbert Hoover Library Foundation); Laura Bergquist Kriebel, journalist, *Look* (interview conducted for the RFK Oral History Project); John H. Knowles, classmate of Robert F. Kennedy, Harvard College, general director, Massachusetts General Hospital (1962–72) (interview conducted for the RFK Oral History Project); Arthur Krock, journalist, *New York Times*, Kennedy family associate; Peter Lawford, actor, brother-in-law of President Kennedy (edited draft transcript); Gould Lincoln, journalist, editor, *Washington Star*; Torbert MacDonald (Hart), roommate of John F. Kennedy at Harvard, representative from Massachusetts; Frank Mankiewicz, press secretary to Robert F. Kennedy (interview conducted for the RFK Oral History Project); Esther Newberg, staff assistant to Robert F. Kennedy (interview conducted for the RFK Oral History Project); Kenneth O'Donnell, special assistant to the president (interview conducted by the Lyndon Baines Johnson Library); Andrew Oehmann, executive assistant to the attorney general (interview conducted for the RFK Oral History Project); Jacqueline Kennedy Onassis (interview conducted by the Lyndon Baines Johnson Library, 1974); Pierre Salinger, press secretary to John F. Kennedy (interview conducted for the RFK Oral History Project); John L. Seigenthaler, reporter, editor, the *Nashville Tennessean*, aide to Robert E Kennedy; Maud Shaw, Kennedy family governess; Eunice Kennedy Shriver, sister of President Kennedy, executive vice president, Joseph P. Kennedy Jr. Foundation; Sargent R. Shriver, director, Businessmen for Kennedy, director, Civil Rights Division, Democratic National Committee, director, Farmers for Kennedy; Hugh Sidey, journalist, *Time, Life*; George Smathers, senator from Florida (interview conducted by the U.S. Senate Historical Office); Theodore C. Sorensen, staff assistant, speechwriter to Senator John F. Kennedy, special counsel to the president; Charles Spalding, Kennedy friend and campaign aide; Stanley Tretick, photographer, United Press International, *Look*; Jack Valenti, special assistant to Lyndon Baines Johnson; Sandy Vanocur, journalist, NBC News (interview conducted for the RFK Oral History Project); Sue Mortensen Vogelsinger, secretary to John F. Kennedy; William Walton, artist, friend of Robert Kennedy, coordinator of Robert Kennedy's 1968 presidential campaign; Ernest Warren, reporter, Associated Press.

PERSONAL PAPERS, ARCHIVES, AND MANUSCRIPTS

Archival materials and manuscripts from the John F. Kennedy Presidential Library relating to the following individuals were used either as source material for this book or for background purposes:

Kirk LeMoyne (Lem) Billings (includes letters from JFK); Clark Clifford, Kennedy family attorney, 1957–61 (includes insightful memos); Barbara J. Coleman, journalist and White House press aide and aide in Robert Kennedy's presidential campaign (papers include miscellaneous correspondence between Jackie Kennedy, Ethel Kennedy, and Eunice Kennedy Shriver); Katherine Evans (including condolence letters and correspondence to Mrs. Robert F. Kennedy, drafts and copies of acknowledgments); Paul B. Fay Jr., personal friend of JFK's and undersecretary of the Navy (includes personal correspondence between Fay and JFK, as well as original manuscript and notes relating to his book *The Pleasure of His Company*); Dun Gifford (including correspondence and campaign materials concerning Joan Kennedy's involvement in Ted Kennedy's senatorial campaigns); Roswell Gilpatrick, deputy secretary of defense, and friend of Jackie Kennedy's; Edward (Ted) Moore Kennedy (Senate files); John Fitzgerald Kennedy Personal Papers; John Fitzgerald Kennedy President's Office Files (the working files of JFK as maintained by his secretary, Evelyn Lincoln; includes correspondence, secretary's files, and special events files through the years of the administration); John Fitzgerald Kennedy White House Social Files (includes papers and records of Jackie Kennedy's and the White House Social Office under the direction of Letitia Baldrige and Pamela Turnure); Robert Francis Kennedy (the author's researcher utilized only the Attorney General Papers 1967–68); Rose Fitzgerald Kennedy (correspondence, family papers, research, background materials, and drafts of her memoir, *Times to Remember*); Evelyn Lincoln, personal secretary to JFK (includes research materials, notes, and other papers pertaining to her book *My Twelve Years with John F. Kennedy*); Frank Mankiewicz; Kenneth O'Donnell, special assistant to JFK (includes correspondence, audiotapes, news clippings, pamphlets, and memorabilia, as well as notes and drafts of "*Johnny, We Hardly Knew Ye*," written with Joe McCarthy); Jacqueline Kennedy Onassis (includes condolence letters, tributes, Mass cards relating to JFK's death; not particularly enlightening but interesting just the same); David Powers (includes copious correspondence, audiotapes, news clippings, and memorabilia); Pierre Salinger, press secretary to JFK (includes correspondence, press briefings, and, most important to my research, press releases and telephone memoranda); Arthur Schlesinger Jr., special assistant to the president (includes correspondence, drafts, and copious research materials, book drafts, and manuscripts for his wonderful books *A Thousand Days* and *Robert Kennedy and His Times*, a treasure trove for any Kennedy historian); Theodore Sorensen, special counsel to the president (includes manuscripts and personal papers, as well as magazine and newspaper articles); Theodore White, journalist and author of *The Making of the President* and other works; the mother lode for any Kennedy historian, including all of White's outlines, notes, drafts, proofs with annotations, correspondence, notes, and transcripts from his interview with Jacqueline Kennedy after JFK's assassination); United States Secret

Service Papers and Files (includes all records of Jackie Kennedy Onassis's activities from 1968 to 1971).

Also utilized: Charles Higham Collection of Papers (Occidental College, Eagle Rock, California); Joseph Kennedy Correspondence (House of Lords Library, London); Peter Lawford Files (Special Collection Division, Hayden Library, Arizona State University, Tempe); Jacqueline Onassis Oral Histories (Lyndon Baines Johnson Library); Secret Service Gate Logs (JFK Library, visits filed chronologically); Sidney Skolsky Papers (Academy of Motion Picture Arts and Sciences); Donald Spoto Papers (Academy of Motion Picture Arts and Sciences); Gloria Swanson Papers (Hoblitzelle Theatre Arts Library, University of Texas, Austin); White House Central Subject Files (JFK Library); White House Files of Chester Clifton Jr. (JFK Library); White House Press Releases (JFK Library); White House Telephone Logs (JFK Library, calls filed chronologically); Zolotow Collection (Humanities Research Center, University of Texas).

ARTS & ENTERTAINMENT

The Arts & Entertainment Network's *Biography* series was invaluable to my research for *After Camelot*, providing me with tapes, transcripts, and other materials.

The following documentaries were reviewed as part of my research: "Chappaquiddick"; "Conspiracies"; "Joseph Kennedy, Sr.: Father of an American Dynasty"; "John F. Kennedy: A Personal Story"; "Ted Kennedy: Tragedy, Scandal and Redemption"; "Magic Moments, Tragic Times: Camelot and Chappaquiddick"; "The Men Who Killed Kennedy"; "Jackie O: In a Class of Her Own" (from which some quotes by John Davis and Pierre Salinger were culled); "Christina Onassis"; "Jacqueline Kennedy Onassis"; "RFK Assassination/'68 Democratic Convention"; "Helen Thomas: The First Lady of the Press"; "Lady Bird Johnson: The Texas Wildflower"; "Lyndon Johnson: Triumph and Tragedy"; "Presidents in Crisis: Johnson Quits and Nixon Resigns"; "Secret Service."

SOURCES AND OTHER NOTES

It is impossible to write accurately about anyone's life without many reliable witnesses to provide a range of different viewpoints. A biography of this kind stands or falls on the cooperation and frankness of those involved in the story. A great number of people went out of their way to assist me over the years. More than five hundred friends, relatives, politicians, journalists, socialites, lawyers, celebrities, Kennedy business executives and former executives, Kennedy family political associates, as well as foes, classmates, teachers, neighbors, friends, newspeople, and archivists were contacted in preparation for this book.

I think it should be obvious to most people that in the research and writing of a book such as *After Camelot*, I and my team carefully reviewed, as secondary sources, the many hundreds of books that have been published over the last fifty years about assorted Kennedy family members, as well as thousands of newspaper and magazine articles written about them. I'm not going to list all of them here, though I will list quite a few. In many cases, though, I will set forth in the following source notes specific books or articles that I relied on and that I believe deserve special acknowledgment.

Also, in writing about a family as beloved and as controversial as the Kennedys, a historian such as myself will encounter many sources who would like to speak, but not for attribution. As I have often stated over the years, it's a personal choice as to whether or not someone wants to be acknowledged as a source for one of my books. After all, it can put a person in a very difficult position with the subject(s) of the book. I have learned over the years that sometimes anonymity is important. Though I would prefer, of course, for all of my sources to be acknowledged by name, it's just not a reasonable or practical expectation. Therefore, whenever a source of mine or of one of my researchers asks for anonymity, I always grant the request. I appreciate and value all of the people from so many walks of life who spoke to me and to my team of researchers for *After Camelot*, whether specifically named in these notes or not.

The following notes and source acknowledgments are by no means comprehensive. Rather, they are intended to give you, the reader, a general overview of my research.

PART ONE. JACKIE

I referred to my interviews with Oleg Cassini, Roswell Gilpatric, Barbara Gibson, Leah Mason, Larry Newman, Sancy Newman, Pierre Salinger, Jacques Lowe, Leo Damore, Liz Carpenter, Helen Thomas, John Davis, Hugh Sidey, Jim Whiting, James Bacon, Nancy Bacon, Marvin Richardson, Morton Downey Jr., Barbara Gibson, David Powers (questionnaire), George Smathers, Letitia Baldrige, Raymond Strait, Jack Valenti, Walter Cronkite, and Stanley Tretick.

The conversation between Ted Kennedy and Senator George Smathers was recreated based on Senator Smathers's memory of it during our interviews in the spring and summer of 1998.

Cathy Griffin interviewed Joe Gargan on March 17, 1999. We also drew from a Q&A submitted and returned from Mr. Gargan that same month.

For this section as well as many others in this book, I drew heavily from my interviews with Joan Braden, originally conducted for *Jackie, Ethel, Joan* in 1998. I also referred to Joan Braden's oral history found in the John Fitzgerald Kennedy Presidential Library as well as many stories for women's magazines about the Kennedys written by Ms. Braden, such as "Joan Kennedy Tells Her Own Story," for *McCall's*, August 1978.

I relied heavily on my interviews with Arturo D'Angelo (May 1, 2009, and June 2, 2010), the attorney representing Creon Broun, Onassis's American money manager. I did speak to Broun, as mentioned in the text, but he wasn't particularly helpful.

Nikos Mastorakis's recollection of the night Onassis welcomed Jackie and Teddy aboard the *Christina* was drawn from an interview with him first published in *Photoplay*, June 1969.

Articles referred to: "The Kennedy Women" by Peter Maas, *Look*, October 11, 1960; "Jacqueline Kennedy," by Mary Van Rensselaer

Thayer, *Ladies' Home Journal*, April 1961; "Jacqueline—What You Don't Know About Our First Lady," by Laura Bergquist, *Look*, July 4, 1961; "Valiant Is the Word for Jackie," by Laura Bergquist, *Look*, January 28, 1964; "The Courtship of Jack and Jackie," by Jim Hoffman, *Photoplay*, March 1964; "How He Really Was," by Jacqueline Kennedy, *Life*, May 29, 1964; "I Should Have Known...," by Jacqueline Kennedy, *Look*, November 17, 1964; "Jackie Kennedy—What the Past Two Years Have Taught Me," by Melisande Meade, *Lady's Circle*, December 1965; "How Jackie Told John-John and Caroline...," by Debbie Sherwood, *Motion Picture*, September 1968; "From Camelot to Elysium" (no author attribution), *Time*, October 25, 1968; "The Old Life for a New Jackie," by Isabel West, *Lady's Circle*, May 1969; "Ethel Relives Wedding Day," *Photoplay*, August 1969; "Assassination Diary," by Michael Beschloss, *Newsweek*, November 13, 1998; "Their History Is Our History," by Michael Beschloss, *Newsweek*, July 1999; "Jackie Style," by Jenny Rubinfeld, *Us Weekly*, April 30, 2001; "Jackie's Style," by Michelle Tauber, *People*, May 7, 2001; "FBI Probing 'Stolen' Jackie Note," Associated Press, September 13, 2006; "A Gift from Long Ago," by Bob Herbert, *New York Times*, November 22, 2010.

I also relied on *Look*'s 1964 One-Year Anniversary of the JFK Assassination.

Volumes referred to: *The Kennedys in Hollywood*, by Lawrence J. Quirck; *The Kennedy Neurosis*, by Nancy Cager Clinch; *The Kennedy White House*, by Carl Sferrazza Anthony; *President Kennedy*, by Richard Reeves; *A Hero for Our Times*, by Ralph G. Martin; *Joseph P. Kennedy: A Life and Times*, by David Koskoff; *Seeds of Destruction*, by Ralph G. Martin; *Hostage to Fortune*, by Amanda Smith; *The Bouviers*, by John H. Davis; *The Death of a President*, by William Manchester; *The Shadow President*, by Burton Hersh; *The Dark Side of Camelot*, by Seymour Hersh; *The Dark Side of Camelot*, by Nelson Thompson; *The Kennedys: America's Emerald Kings*, by Thomas Maier; *The Kennedy Detail*, by Gerald Blaine; *Kathleen Kennedy*, by Lynn McTaggart; *First Ladies*, vol. 2, by Carl Sferrazza Anthony; *John F. Kennedy, President*, by Hugh Sidey; *A Very Personal Presidency*, by Hugh Sidey; *With Kennedy*, by Pierre Salinger; *The Coming of the New Deal*, by Arthur M. Schlesinger; *A Tribute to Jacqueline Kennedy Onassis* (privately printed, by Doubleday, 1995); *In My Own Fashion*, by Oleg Cassini; *A Thousand Days of Magic*, by Oleg Cassini; *Kennedy and the Press*, by Allen H. Lerman and Harold W. Chase;

Counsel to the President, by Clifford Clark; *Of Diamonds and Diplomats*, by Letitia Baldrige; *The Making of the President 1960*, by Theodore White; *Sargent Shriver: A Candid Portrait*, by Robert A. Leston; *Kennedy Justice*, by Victor Navasky; *Those Fabulous Kennedy Women*, by H. A. William Carr; *The Kennedy Family*, by Joseph Dinneen; *The Cape Cod Years of John Fitzgerald Kennedy*, by Leo Damore; *JFK: Reckless Youth*, by Nigel Hamilton; *The Founding Father*, by Richard J. Whalen; *The Power Lovers*, by Myra MacPherson; *A Hero for Our Time*, by Ralph G. Martin; *Ethel*, by Lester David; *Bobby*, by Lester David; *The Consent of the Governed*, by Arthur Krock; *Six Presidents, Too Many Wars*, by Bill Lawrence; *Atget's Gardens*, by William Howard Adams; *Life with Rose Kennedy*, by Barbara Gibson and Caroline Latham; *Rose*, by Gail Cameron; *My Twelve Years with John F. Kennedy*, by Evelyn Lincoln; *An Honorable Profession*, edited by Pierre Salinger, Frank Mankiewicz, Edwin Guthman, and John Seigenthaler; *"Johnny, We Hardly Knew Ye,"* by Kenneth P. O'Donnell and David E. Powers; *One Special Summer*, by Lee Bouvier Radziwill and Jacqueline Bouvier Onassis; *I Was Jacqueline Kennedy's Dressmaker*, by Mini Rhea.

I also relied on my interviews with Mona Latham (May 4, 2009, April 3, 2010, and January 11, 2011), a close friend and business associate of Jackie's business manager, André Benoit Meyer.

I referred to my interview with Olga Price, Jackie's former housekeeper (September 3, 2010).

Of additional interest: A 1963 letter from Jackie Kennedy to Jack Kennedy just a month before he was assassinated is telling in that it illustrates her strong emotion for him. It was written from Greece, where she was vacationing with Aristotle Onassis and other friends after the death of her infant son, Patrick. "I miss you very much," she wrote. "I think how lucky I am to miss you. I know I exaggerate everything, but I feel sorry for everyone else who is married. I realize here so much that [I] am having something you can never have—the absence of tension. I wish so much I could give you that, but I can't. So I give you every day while I think of you. [It is] the only thing I have to give and I hope it matters to you."

A 1965 letter to President Lyndon Johnson demonstrated just how traumatized Jackie was not only by what happened in Dallas but even afterward when, her dress stained with JFK's blood, she witnessed the swearing in of President Johnson on Air Force One. In May 1965, the British memorial to President Kennedy was to be dedicated by Jackie and

Queen Elizabeth II. LBJ felt it would be appropriate for Jackie to travel in a presidential 707. "I thought for two days before writing to you," Jackie said in her March 28 letter to Johnson, "because I did not know if I could steel myself to go in one of those planes again." However, she wrote that she ultimately decided it would be a tribute to President Kennedy if she were to arrive in England that way. "But please do not let it be Air Force One," she wrote, "and please let it be the 707 that looks the least like Air Force One inside."

The note from Jackie to Ethel ("My Ethel, I stayed up...") was put up for auction by Heritage Auction Galleries in 2006. It has since been returned to the Kennedy family.

PART TWO. EUNICE

I referred to my interviews with Helen Thomas, Hugh Sidey, and Sancy Newman.

The conversation the Kennedy women had about Phil Donahue was re-created from the recollection of Joan Braden, as were details of the women's tour of Timberlawn.

Maria Shriver's comments are from the eulogy she gave at her mother's funeral in August 2009. I also drew from informal conversations I had with Maria in April 1994 for this and other sections of the book.

I referred to "A Life of Challenge," by Maxwell Taylor Kennedy, *Inside Borders*, June 1998, and some of the quotes found in other sections of this book are from this article.

I also referred to a tape of CBS News's *60 Minutes* program broadcast on October 19, 1997. Appearing on that show were Robert Kennedy Jr., Kathleen Kennedy Townsend, Kerry Kennedy Cuomo, Christopher Kennedy, and Maxwell Kennedy. (During the broadcast, Robert Kennedy Jr. said he warned his children about the dangers of alcohol, particularly for Kennedys. "I talk to them about my own experience and they're all aware of that," he said in the interview at Hickory Hill, the Kennedy estate in McLean, Virginia. "I tell them that it's in their genes. I feel in many ways that I was born an alcoholic.")

I also consulted an interview with Joseph P. Kennedy in *Time*, July 1960, and an editorial written by Eunice Kennedy Shriver for the

Saturday Evening Post in September 1962. Some of Bobby Shriver's, Timothy Shriver's, and Kathleen Kennedy Townsend's comments here and in other parts of this book are from "The New Kennedys," by Karen Tumulty, *Time*, November 13, 2001.

Volumes consulted: *In the Kennedy Style*, by Letitia Baldrige; *Brothers*, by David Talbot; *A Question of Character*, by Thomas C. Reeves; *Journals, 1952–2000*, by Arthur M. Schlesinger Jr.; *Joseph P. Kennedy Presents: His Hollywood Years*, by Carl Beauchamp; *Sins of the Father*, by Ronald Kessler; *Special Olympics*, by Books LLC; *To Jack with Love: Black Jack Bouvier, a Remembrance*, by Kathleen Bouvier; *The Bouviers*, by John Davis; *The Auchincloss Family*, by Joanna Russell Auchincloss and Caroline Auchincloss; *Our Forebears*, by John Vernon Bouvier Jr. (privately printed); *The Kennedy Legacy*, by Theodore Sorensen; *With Kennedy*, by Pierre Salinger; *Upstairs at the White House*, by J. B. West; *Diamonds and Diplomats*, by Letitia Baldrige; *Power at Play*, by Betty Beale; *Ethel Kennedy and Life at Hickory Hill*, by Leah Mason (unpublished manuscript); *The Other Mrs. Kennedy*, by Jess Oppenheimer; *Ethel*, by David Lester; *The Kennedy Women*, by Laurence Learner; *Jack and Jackie*, by Christopher Andersen; *All Too Human*, by Edward Klein; *The Sins of the Father*, by Ronald Kessler; *Seeds of Destruction*, by Ralph C. Martin; *First Ladies*, by Carl Sferrazza Anthony; *Jacqueline Kennedy*, by Gordon Langley Hall; *The Kennedy White House Parties*, by Ann H. Lincoln; *Jacqueline Kennedy: La Première Dame des Etats-Unis*, by Peter Peterson; *Jackie: The Exploitation of a First Lady*, by Irving Shulman; *Jackie Oh!*, by Kitty Kelley; *The Pleasure of His Company*, by Paul B. Fay Jr.; *The Bouviers*, by John Davis; *Kim Novak: Reluctant Goddess*, by Peter Harry Brown; *Jacqueline Kennedy: Beauty in the White House*, by William Carrl; *Jackie: The Price of the Pedestal*, by Lee Guthrie; *The President's Partner*, by Myra Gutin; *The Kennedy Promise*, by Henry Fairlie.

Of additional interest: I interviewed Eunice Kennedy Shriver in the spring of 2002 for an article I was writing at the time on the Special Olympics for *Redbook*, a women's magazine. I drew from that interview for this part and other sections of this book.

Incidentally, the story never ran because when I submitted it the editors were displeased that it did not contain personal details about her relationships with other Kennedy family members. Looking back on it now, I think I simply didn't have the courage to ask Mrs. Kennedy Shriver the kinds of personal questions the editors felt deserved answers in my story. In my defense, prior to the interview she specifically told me via fax that "no personal questions will be answered." Somehow, I thought that sitting with her face-to-face might give me the courage to tread on terrain she'd deemed off-limits, but, alas, if anything her sheer presence in the room was so overwhelming, I have to admit I was a little intimidated. So I toed the line. As a result, the story was rejected by the magazine.

Six months after I did the interview, I received a telephone call from Mrs. Kennedy Shriver asking for a copy of my story about the Special Olympics. "I somehow seemed to have missed it," she told me. It was then that I had no choice but to tell her that the feature did not run, which was something I have to confess I truly did not want to do. "Well, why is that?" she demanded to know in a clipped tone. Reluctantly, I explained the reason as honestly as I could. "Well, good for you, then!" she said suddenly seeming happy. "I applaud you for your discretion!" She concluded, "Fine, then. Now, goodbye and I hope we meet again one day." And with that, she hung up. She really was quite remarkable.

I also met Sargent Shriver at that time and drew from my conversation with him in this section of the book, as well as in others. It would overstate it to say that I formally interviewed Mr. Shriver. I did not. However, Shriver was such a gregarious person, it was unlikely that one could have a conversation with him and not be left with a wealth of anecdotes— such as the story told here about his conversation with Eunice relating to starting Timberlawn in their own backyard—or as he told me, "I have a story about pretty much everything, don't I?" And that he did!

Also, as part of my research for *Jackie, Ethel, Joan: Women of Camelot,* I attended the Oprah Winfrey taping of "The Young Kennedys" in November 1997 in Chicago, where I had the opportunity to meet Christopher Lawford, Bobby Kennedy Jr., and Kathleen Kennedy Townsend. Some of their quotes in this book are from that show, and also that backstage meeting.

Additionally, in the hope of meeting Rosemary Kennedy, I visited St. Coletta's and the Alverno Nursing Home in 1998 as part of my research for *Jackie, Ethel, Joan: Women of Camelot.* While I was able to have a brief meeting with her, I was not permitted to interview her. However, the staff there were very gracious and provided many of the details found in this section of the book.

PART THREE. SARGE

Interviews referred to: Leah Mason, Frank Mankiewicz, and Pierre Salinger, as well as Cathy Griffin's interviews with Noelle Bombardier. I also referred to my interview with Joan Braden relating to the dinner at Timberlawn during which Jackie discussed Sargent Shriver's appointment by LBJ. I also relied on Cathy Griffin's interview with Donald Dell (June 1998) to re-create the conversation he had with Sargent and Eunice ("The decision is made") relating to Sarge's possibly assisting RFK. Comments by Arthur Schlesinger Jr. are culled from my interviews with him on March 1, 1997, March 28, 2003, and April 18, 2006. I also interviewed Ted Sorensen in May 2008 in conjunction with the publication of his book *Counselor: A Life at the Edge of History*.

Only one serious biography has ever been written about Sargent Shriver, and what a comprehensive and fascinating book it is, and that is *Sarge* by John Stossel. I relied on it for parts of this section of *After Camelot*, and I would recommend it to anyone interested in knowing more about Ambassador Shriver.

My researchers were also able to access the Sargent Shriver Collection at the John Fitzgerald Kennedy Presidential Library in Boston, and we utilized that collection as well.

The late Hugh Sidey was also very helpful in aiding me to understand the complex dynamic between Shriver and the Kennedys, as were Jack Valenti and Senator George Smathers.

I interviewed Frank Mankiewicz, Bobby Kennedy's press secretary, on August 25, 1998, and utilized that interview in the chapter "Bobby Kennedy," as well as in other parts of the book.

I utilized the Arthur Krock Papers (1909–1974) in this section of the book.

I relied on a transcript of a PBS interview with Ted Sorensen, August 29, 1996. I also referred to "Passing the Torch: Kennedy's Touch on Obama's Words," by Susan Donaldson James for ABC News. Moreover, I interviewed Mr. Sorensen in April 1998 for my book *Jackie, Ethel, Joan: Women of Camelot*, and some of his comments from that interview can be found in *After Camelot*. I also referred to the transcript of Mr. Sorensen's speech at the Charleston School of Law on February 23, 2010.

Regarding the Peace Corps, I relied on the Returned Peace Corps Volunteer Collection at the John Fitzgerald Kennedy Presidential Library in Boston.

We pulled all of the Sargent Shriver files from the Lyndon Baines Johnson Library, and referred to many of them for this and other sections of this book. I also referred to numerous audiotapes of conversations LBJ had with Sargent Shriver, which can be found in the National Archives.

Regarding Bobby Kennedy's history, I relied on *Death of a President*, by William Manchester. I also relied on the following articles: "The No. 2 Man in Washington," by Paul O'Neil, *Life*, January 26, 1962; "The Death of Robert Kennedy," by Theodore H. White, *Life*, June 14, 1968.

I referred to Richard B. Stolley's article "Eunice on Sarge and 'the Kennedy People'" in the August 18, 1972, issue of *Life*.

I also reviewed Jackie Kennedy's oral history for the Lyndon Baines Johnson Presidential Library, which she gave on January 11, 1974, from her apartment in Manhattan. She was interviewed by Joe B. Frantz. It's interesting that when asked about the contentious relationship between LBJ and Bobby, Jackie seemed not to know a lot about it. She said that she "was never alone with the two men."

I referred to "LBJ and the Kennedys," by Kenneth O'Donnell, *Life*, August 7, 1970.

For the section "Ted Disappoints," I drew from a confidential source who worked closely with the Shrivers in Paris.

For background on the Special Olympics, I referred to *The Kennedy Family and the Story of Mental Retardation*, by Edward Shorter.

I referred to the following volumes: *The Fitzgeralds and the Kennedys*, by Doris Kearns Goodwin; *A Woman Named Jackie*, by C. David Heymann; *American Legacy: The Story of John and Caroline Kennedy*, by C. David Heymann; *The Uncommon Wisdom of Jacqueline Kennedy Onassis*, edited by Bill Adler; *Point of the Lance*, by Sargent Shriver; *Just Who Will You Be?*, by Maria Shriver; *The Death of the President*, by William Manchester; *The Shadow President*, by Burton Hersh; *The Dark Side of Camelot*, by Seymour Hersh; *The Dark Side of Camelot*, by Nelson Thompson; *The Kennedys: America's Emerald Kings*, by Thomas Maier; *Kennedy and Nixon*, by Christopher Matthews; *Taking Charge: The Johnson White House*, by Michael R. Beschloss; *A White House Diary*, by Lady Bird Johnson; *Changing Habits: A Memoir of the Society of the Sacred Heart*, by V. V. Harrison; *The Society of the Sacred Heart in North America*, by

Louise Callan; *Ethel*, by David Lester; *All Too Human*, by Edward Klein; *Living with the Kennedys*, by Marcia Chellis; *Kennedy Wives, Kennedy Women*, by Nancy Gager; *The Kennedys: An American Drama*, by Peter Collier and David Horowitz; *America's First Ladies*, by Christine Sandler; *Jackie*, by Hedda Lyons Watney; *Torn Lace Curtain*, by Frank Saunders; *JFK: The Man and the Myth*, by Victor Lasky; *My Story*, by Judith Exner, as told to Ovid Demaris; *Bitch*, by Buddy Galon; *The Censorship Papers*, by Gerald Gardner; *The Whole Truth and Nothing But*, by Hedda Hopper and James Brough; *Uncommon Grace*, by J. C. Suares and J. Spencer Beck; *Remembering Jackie*, by *Life* editors; *The Woman in the White House*, by Winzola McLendon; *Ethel Kennedy and Life at Hickory Hill*, by Leah Mason (unpublished manuscript); *Presidential Wives*, by Paul E. Baker.

Of additional interest: I spent considerable time at the Lyndon Baines Johnson Library reviewing their catalog of books, articles, and other materials relating to President Johnson. I also reviewed many taped telephone conversations between LBJ and others, including Jacqueline Kennedy (such as the one cited in the text regarding Johnson's interest in naming her ambassador to Mexico), Ethel Kennedy, Joan Kennedy, Ted Kennedy, Robert Kennedy, Rose Kennedy, Lady Bird Johnson, and many dozens of others. These tapes are also available in the National Archives.

Some who have listened to these tapes feel that Johnson was inappropriately flirtatious where Jackie was concerned, especially in the weeks after the assassination. "You just come over and put your arm around me. That's all you do," he told Jackie when trying to encourage her to visit him at the White House on December 2, 1963. "And when you haven't got anything else to do, let's take a walk. Let's walk around the backyard and just let me tell you how much you mean to all of us...you got the president relying on you," he said. "And this is not the first one you had. They're not many women running around with a good many presidents. So you got the biggest job of your life," he concluded. Jackie laughed. "She ran around with two presidents," she responded. "That's what they'll say about me. Okay. Anytime."

"Give Carolyn and John-John a hug for me," LBJ said to her on December 7, 1963. "Tell them I'd like to be their daddy." Jackie said, "I will."

In fact, Jackie never felt that LBJ was being inappropriate and just chalked his manner up to good ol' Southern charm. As she explained to LBJ in an impassioned letter from the West Indies during the height of her very public disagreement with William Manchester over his book *Death of the President*, "I read in a magazine...that I had objected to your calling me 'honey.' All the rage that I have been trying to suppress and forget down here boiled up again. It is a trivial thing, but so typical of the way that man has twisted everything. The only thing that is nice about it is that it makes you look as kind and solicitous as you always were and are to me....I hope you will call me that ['honey'] again and that you will not become embittered by all this and by all life, really." She continued, "Please forgive me, Mr. President. I know I shall wish I had torn this letter up as soon as I have sent it off, but in some blind way I wished to express to you the fondness I will always feel for you—no matter what happens and no matter how your feelings might change for me."

Also, the Lyndon Baines Johnson Library has in its collection forty years of personal correspondence between Jackie Kennedy and Lady Bird Johnson, which I relied heavily on for many parts of this book. The correspondence is interesting in that some of it reveals a different side of Jackie. At times, she could be incredibly childlike. "After I had done the tree on Christmas eve and everything was so nice and peaceful," she wrote to Lady Bird on December 30, 1965, "I just looked under that tree and thought I would like to open one or two interesting little bundles for myself. Dear Lady Bird, I could not believe my eyes. Those Chinese plates are beyond belief! You think Christmas is for children once you are grown up, but I don't think that's true. Carolyn and John didn't love any present as much as I loved mine! How could you know what I would love more than anything?"

It's also worth noting that even though there was certainly no love lost between Bobby Kennedy and Lyndon Johnson, Lady Bird was hard to resist. Apparently, she managed to sweep Ethel and Eunice off their feet when the two visited the Johnsons in Texas. In an undated letter, Ethel wrote to Lady Bird that she and "Eun" were still "recuperating" from their trip. "I guess we never will get completely over being treated like Kings for five days," she wrote. "It's hard to get back to plain old cabbages. We loved every minute with you and you have my very big thank you for being so friendly and thoughtful and generous. We had a very happy time, and whatever the political consequences, it was great fun." She signed the letter, "much, much love and so many thanks, affectionately, Ethel."

After Bobby was killed in June 1968, Ethel wrote to President Johnson to thank him for all he did for her during her darkest days. "We shall always be grateful to you, Mr. President, for honoring Bobby by attending his funeral," she wrote, "by meeting the train in Washington and by accompanying us to Arlington." She signed the letter, "Love, Ethel."

Also, Max Kennedy's comments (relating to George Wallace) were culled from "A Left Coast Kennedy," by Susan Salter Reynolds, *Los Angeles Times Magazine*, March 14, 1999.

I met Max Kennedy a year earlier at a book party to celebrate the release of his work *Make Gentle the Life of This World: The Vision of Robert F. Kennedy*, a book of quotes his father had loved and an examination of the way RFK had been influenced by the powerful thinkers he so admired. (The title is a quote from the Greek poet Aeschylus, which Bobby Kennedy recited when he broke the news of Martin Luther King Jr.'s death to a crowd in an Indianapolis ghetto.) "I think there's a perception that we Kennedys are opposed to the public having a fuller understanding of who we are, of what makes us tick," Max—who was three and a half when his father was killed—told me. "But it's just not true. Yes, we have been opposed to much of what has been written about us, mostly because of the inaccuracies of the reports and sometimes—such as my aunt Jackie's battle with William Manchester—because it just digs too deep into private thoughts. But we Kennedys understand history and the importance of history. In fact, my mother has been my greatest encourager. She's the one who urged me to read my father's journals, to go through his notes and all of the index cards he had assembled during his life with quotes and other thoughts that had meant so much to him. My uncle Teddy had written a book about his brother called *Words Jack Loved*, and it was always my idea to do sort of the same thing for my father. But it was my mother who pushed the idea along, who felt it was important."

PART FOUR. TED

I would first like to thank author James Spada for providing me with a wealth of material on Ted and Joan Kennedy that he compiled during the process of developing a book about the senator. His in-depth research into the lives and times of Ted and Joan and their family—including his interviews with many of their intimates—proved invaluable to this book, just as it did to *Jackie, Ethel, Joan: Women of Camelot*, and I would like to gratefully acknowledge him.

For this section, I relied heavily on my interview with Leo Damore (June 1994), conducted for my proposal for *Jackie, Ethel, Joan*, then called *The Kennedy Wives*. Damore, who committed suicide a year later, was the author of *Senatorial Privilege*, considered the most reliable book about the Chappaquiddick incident.

I also referred to my interviews with Arthur Schlesinger Jr., Ted Sorensen, Barbara Gibson, Leah Mason, Senator George Smathers, Webster Janssen, Sancy Newman, Roswell Gilpatrick, Dun Gifford, David Burke, and Helen Thomas.

I interviewed Ted Kennedy's assistant Richard Burke on August 23, 1999, and relied on some of his memories for this and other sections of this book.

Cathy Griffin interviewed Joe Gargan for *Jackie, Ethel, Joan* on March 17, 1999, and I followed up with a faxed Q&A that same month, and his memories of the night of the Chappaquiddick accident are culled from those interviews.

I referred to two of Jackie Kennedy Onassis's letters to Joan that, based on their contents, appear to have been written in the summer of 1979. These letters went on auction from Alexander Autographs in February 2007.

Cathy Griffin had several conversations with Helga Wagner and one interview with her on February 20, 2011.

The conversation between Jackie Kennedy Onassis and Roswell Gilpatrick was recreated as per Gilpatrick's memory of it in my interview with him.

I referred to *The Kennedy Case*, by Rita Dallas, for details of Joseph Kennedy's final hours.

I also referred to the transcript of the television broadcast "Chappaquiddick: What Really Happened?" on *Geraldo*, November 9, 1988, with Leo Damore and Leslie Leyland (grand jury foreman).

I interviewed Robert McNamara in June 2008 and utilized some of his memories in this and other sections of the book. Cathy Griffin did a follow-up interview with Mr. McNamara in August 2008.

Articles referred to: "He Now Stands Alone," by Robert E. Thompson, *Sunday Advertiser*, June 9, 1968; "Joan and Ted Kennedy: Their Love

Story," by James Bowser, *TV and Radio Mirror*, October 1968; "An Intimate Portrait of Joan Kennedy," by Barbara Kevles, *Good Housekeeping*, September 1969; "All Quiet on the Kennedy Front in Edgartown," by Homer Bigart, *New York Times*, January 11, 1970; "Joan Kennedy's Story," by Betty Hannah Hoffman, *Ladies' Home Journal*, July 1970; "Paper Claims Ted Danced All Night," UPI, London, November 30, 1970; "Joan and Ted's Tardy Ways Irked Their Herman Hosts," by David Binder, *Stars and Stripes*, April 23, 1971; "Sisters" (Joan and Candy Bennett)," by Mary Fiore, *Ladies' Home Journal*, March 1973; "Joan Had to Learn to Live with Heartache," by Eleanor Roberts, *Herald American*, December 7, 1982; "Prime Time with Joan Kennedy," by Sally Jacobs, *Boston Globe Magazine*, July 9, 2000; "Joan Kennedy Treated for Alcoholism," Associated Press, October 9, 2001.

Volumes referred to: *Ted Kennedy: The Dream That Never Died*, by Edward Klein; *Edward Kennedy: An Intimate Biography*, by Burton Hersh; *Sons and Brothers*, by Richard D. Mahoney; *A Common Good*, by Helen O'Donnell; *Jacqueline Onassis*, by Lester David; *Iron Rose*, by Cindy Adams and Susan Crimp; *JFK: Reckless Youth*, by Nigel Hamilton; *The Bouviers*, by John H. Davis; *Taking Charge: The Johnson White House*, by Michael R. Beschloss; *A White House Diary*, by Lady Bird Johnson; *The Joy of Classical Music: A Guide for You and Your Family*, by Joan Kennedy; *Gloria and Joe: The Star-Crossed Love Affair of Gloria Swanson and Joe Kennedy*, by Axel Madsen; *Swanson on Swanson*, by Gloria Swanson; *JFK: The Presidency of John F. Kennedy*, by Herbert Parmet; *John Kennedy: A Political Profile*, by James MacGregor; *Honey Fitz*, by John Henry Cutler; *John F. Kennedy and American Catholicism*, by Lawrence H. Fuchs; *Rose Kennedy: A Life of Faith, Family, and Tragedy*, by Barbara Gibson and Ted Schwartz; *The Fitzgeralds and the Kennedys: An American Saga*, by Doris Kearns Goodwin; *The Kennedy Women*, by Laurence Leamer; *Times to Remember*, by Rose Fitzgerald Kennedy; *Marilyn: The Last Take*, by Peter Harry Brown and Patte B. Barham; *The Decline and Fall of the Love Goddess*, by Patrick Agan; *The Masters Way to Beauty*, by George Masters; *Marilyn Monroe: An Uncensored Biography*, by Maurice Zolotow; *Marilyn Monroe: Confidential*, by Lena Pepitone; *Robert Kennedy and His Times*, by Arthur M. Schlesinger Jr.; *Jacqueline Kennedy Onassis*, by Lester David.

Of additional interest: I interviewed Mary Jo Kopechne's parents, Gwen and Joseph Kopechne, on April 1, 2000, for the paperback edition of *Jackie, Ethel, Joan: Women of Camelot*. I didn't quote them in *After Camelot* but did use their commentary for background purposes. Interestingly, they told me that they believed Mary Jo was asleep unnoticed in the backseat of the car when it plunged into the river. They believed that Ted Kennedy was in the car with another woman in the front seat at the time of the accident because, they explained, a purse belonging to a guest was found in that seat—and it was not Mary Jo's. (The police theorized that the purse had been left in the car earlier in the day.) They also said that they rejected the idea of an autopsy on Mary Jo because they believed that the primary reason for it would have been to determine if she was pregnant. That said, they did not believe it themselves, and in fact said that she was engaged to marry a man who worked in the Foreign Service, "and she would not have cheated on him with the senator, not ever," said Mrs. Kopechne. "We don't call him Ted Kennedy when we refer to him around the house," Mr. Kopechne told me. "We call him the senator." They didn't sue Kennedy, they said, because they felt "it would be perceived as blood money."

In the end, the Kopechnes told me they received about $150,000 from Kennedy and $50,000 from his insurance carrier. "We should have sued," they said. "It was damn little money for what we went through." They also said they had two meetings with Kennedy after the death of their daughter, "but he had nothing to say," Mrs. Kopechne told me. "He acted as if he didn't know what happened. We just wanted straight answers but we never got them. Then he would call from time to time if he was doing something important like when he was thinking of running for president," she said bitterly, "but we felt that the only reason he stayed in touch was to figure out how angry or hurt we still were and whether or not we planned to say something in the press that would ruin things for him." In the end, Mr. Kopechne told me, "The only thing that we can say is good is that this whole thing kept Ted Kennedy from becoming president. That, to us, was good and right."

PART FIVE. ETHEL

I referred to my interviews with Barbara Gibson, Leah Mason, Thomas Langford, Noelle Bombardier, and John Glenn.

Cathy Griffin interviewed Andy Williams in August 1998, May 2002, and January 2011, and we utilized his memories in this and other sections of this book.

Kathleen Kennedy Townsend's comments are from an interview with Lisa Miller in *Newsweek*, March 2009.

My researcher Monica Pastelle interviewed Christopher Kennedy in December 1997. Also, here and in other parts of this book I drew from Mr. Kennedy's comments in the article "The Kennedy Clan Decides to Cash In on Its Last Big Business," *Wall Street Journal*, January 26, 1998.

Volumes referred to: *The Kennedy Women*, by Laurence Leamer; *The Other Mrs. Kennedy*, by Jerry Oppenheimer; *The Kennedys*, by David Horowitz; *John F. Kennedy: As We Remember Him*, by Rose Kennedy et al.; *The Kennedys: A Time Remembered*, by Jacques Lowe; *John F. Kennedy: The Presidential Portfolio*, by Charles Kenney; *Uncommon Grace*, by J. C. Suares and J. Spencer Beck; *Designing Camelot*, by James A. Abbott and Elaine M. Rice; *A Thousand Days of Magic*, by Oleg Cassini; *Life in Camelot: The Kennedy Years*, edited by Philip B. Kunhardt Jr.; *The Killing of Robert F. Kennedy*, by Dan E. Moldea; *When I Think of Bobby*, by Warren Rogers; *An Honorable Profession*, edited by Pierre Salinger et al.; *Jackie, Bobby, and Manchester*, by Arnold Bennett; *Ethel*, by Lester David; *Robert Kennedy and His Times*, by Arthur M. Schlesinger Jr.

I referred to "The Kennedy of Hickory Hill," by Hays Gory, *Time*, August 25, 1969. (Note: This is Ethel Kennedy's only cover story in *Time*.)

PART SIX. JACKIE, ARI, AND THE LAWFORDS

I referred to my interviews with Arthur M. Schlesinger Jr., Ted Sorensen, Sancy Newman, Noelle Bombardier, and Enrique Fonteyn.

I also utilized Cathy Griffin's interviews with Secret Service agents who worked the Kennedy and Onassis detail, including: Clint Hill (January 4, 1998; March 5, 2010; June 4, 2010; April 3, 2011); Jack Walsh (March 9, 1998); Joseph Paolella (September 11, 1998; September 17, 1998); Anthony Sherman (September 29, 1998); and Larry Newman (September 29, 1998; September 30, 1998; October 7, 1998).

I also drew from a transcript of Clint Hill's interview with Mike Wallace on *The Larry King Show*, March 22, 2006.

As well as Cathy Griffin's interviews with Clint Hill, I had several confidential sources in the Secret Service whom I depended on for material in the chapter "Jackie and the Secret Service." Moreover, the correspondence between Jackie and James J. Rowley, director of the Secret Service, referred to in this section was found in the files of the Lyndon Baines Johnson Library.

I interviewed Secret Service agent Robert Foster in August 1999.

Jackie Kennedy Onassis's letters to Roswell Gilpatrick were made public in February 1970 when they were acquired for auction.

I interviewed Edward Larrabee Barnes on March 2, 1998, and April 7, 1999. The conversations between Barnes, Rose Kennedy, and Jackie Kennedy Onassis were reconstructed based on Barnes's memory of them.

Greta Nilsen's comments are culled from my researcher Maxene Rogers's interview with her, which first appeared in *Photoplay* magazine in September 1970.

I referred to my interviews with Greta Nilsen and Jacques Lowe (December 15, 1998; July 11, 1999; November 7, 1999; October 12, 2000).

I also referred to my interview with Tony Oppedisano, which I conducted on May 23, 2010.

I referred to my interview with Peter Lawford, which I conducted in 1981. I also utilized my interviews with Milt Ebbins, which I conducted for my book *Sinatra: Behind the Legend* in 1996. I also referred to Cathy Griffin's interviews with Jeanne Martin conducted for *Jackie, Ethel, Joan: Women of Camelot.*

I also referred to Cathy's interview with John Davis, September 13, 1998, and her follow-up questions by fax on September 14, 1998.

Cathy Griffin also interviewed Liz Carpenter, executive assistant to President Lyndon Johnson and later press secretary to Lady Bird Johnson, on August 31, 1996 for *Jackie, Ethel, Joan: Women of Camelot*, and we used her memories as background in this and other sections of *After Camelot*. Ms. Griffin also interviewed George Christian, White House press secretary from 1966 to 1969, on September 23, 1998, and we used this interview for background.

I also interviewed White House reporter Helen Thomas for *Jackie, Ethel, Joan: Women of Camelot* on September 25, 1998, and we used that interview for background purposes here as well.

I referred to "For President Kennedy: An Epilogue," by Theodore White, *Life*, December 1963.

Also, my researcher Elizabeth Reeves accessed the papers of Theodore White and we utilized some of his notes in this section.

Articles referred to: "My Twelve Years with Kennedy," by Evelyn Lincoln, *Post*, August 14, 1965; "Bright Light of His Day," by Jackie Kennedy Onassis, *McCall's*, November 1973; "The Dark Side of Camelot," by Kitty Kelley, *People*, February 29, 1988; "Camelot After Dark," by Paula Chin, Joe Treen, and Karen S. Schneider, *People*, May 27, 1991; "Carly Talks Hot About Sex—and Friendship with Jackie O," by Lou Lumenick, *New York Post*, July 5, 1995; "The Exner Files," by Liz Smith, *Vanity Fair*, January 1997; "Book: Camelot a Sex Playpen," by Paul Schwartzman, *New York Daily News*, November 9, 1997; "Smashing Camelot," by Richard Lacayo, *Time*, November 17, 1997; "My Kingdom for a Whore," by Jacob Weisberg, *Manchester Guardian Weekly*, February 8, 1998; "It's Fact! It's Fiction! No Basis for Salacious Tales in 'Jackie After Jack' Many Say," by Paul Schwartzman, *New York Daily News*, February 22, 1998; "The Birth of Cool Politics," by Patrick Goldstein, *Los Angeles Times*, August 13, 2000; "Jackie's Private World," by Deirdre Donahue, *USA Today*, October 16, 2000; "Bobby at the Brink," by Evan Thomas (excerpted from *Robert Kennedy: His Life*), *Newsweek*, August 14, 2000; "A Clash of Camelots," by Sam Kashner, *Vanity Fair*, October 2009.

Volumes referred to: *The Kennedy Women*, by Pearl S. Buck; *The Kennedy Case*, by Rita Dallas with Jeanira Ratcliffe; *Among Those Present*, by Nancy Dickerson; *My Twelve Years with John F. Kennedy*, by Evelyn Lincoln; *The Cape Cod Years of John Fitzgerald Kennedy*, by Leo Damore; *Not in Your Lifetime*, by Anthony Summers; *The Kennedys: A Chronological History*, by Harvey Rachlin; *Nemesis*, by Peter Evans; *Ari: The Life and Times of Aristotle Onassis*, by Peter Evans; *Rose*, by Charles Higham; *In the Kennedy Style*, by Letitia Baldrige; *Designing Camelot: The Kennedy White House Restoration*, by James A. Abbott and Elaine M. Rice; *The Kennedy White House Parties*, by Anne H. Lincoln; *Uncommon Grace*, by J. C. Suarez and J. Spencer Back; *A Woman Named Jackie*, by C. David Heymann; *My Life with Jacqueline Kennedy*, by Mary Barelli Gallagher; *The Other Mrs. Kennedy*, by Jess Oppenheimer; *The Last of the Giants*, by Cyrus Leo Sulzberger; *Joan: The Reluctant Kennedy*, by Lester David; *A*

Tour of the White House with Mrs. John F. Kennedy, by Perry Wolf; *JFK: The Memories*, by Hugh Sidey, Chester Clifton, and Cecil Stoughton; *John F. Kennedy, President*, by Hugh Sidey; *Office Hours: Day and Night*, by Janet Travell; *Upstairs at the White House*, by J. B. West; *The White House Chef Cookbook*, by René Verdon; *Symptoms of Withdrawal*, by Christopher Kennedy Lawford; *Peter Lawford: The Man Who Kept the Secrets*, by James Spada; *The Peter Lawford Story*, by Patricia Seaton Lawford.

I referred to a transcript of President Kennedy's Yale University commencement address, given on June 11, 1962.

Carly Simon's comment about the way Jackie Kennedy Onassis dealt with the unfaithful JFK was published in the article about Simon, "I Never Sang for My Mother," by Marie Brenner, *Vanity Fair*, August 1995.

In writing about Pat Kennedy and Marilyn Monroe, I also relied on research conducted for my book *The Secret Life of Marilyn Monroe*, including my interviews with Patricia Brennan and Bernie Abramson, both of which were conducted in 2008.

I referred to my own extensive research for "Sex, Power, Obsession," a three-part series about Jackie Kennedy Onassis for the *Sunday Mirror*, October 3, 1993.

Of additional interest: I also referred to "JFK Revisited," by Arthur M. Schlesinger Jr., *Cigar Aficionado*, November 1998. "Let us first dispose of Camelot," Schlesinger wrote. "JFK had gone to prep school and college with Alan Jay Lerner, and liked the songs Lerner and Frederick Loewe wrote for the popular 1960 musical. But no one when JFK was alive ever spoke of Washington as Camelot—and if anyone had done so, no one would have been more derisive than JFK. Nor did those of us around him see ourselves for a moment, heaven help us, as knights of the Round Table. Camelot was Jacqueline Kennedy's grieving thought a week after her husband was killed. Later she told John Kenneth Galbraith that she feared the idea had been overdone. For that matter, King Arthur's Camelot was hardy noted for its marital constancy, and the Arthurian saga concluded in betrayal and death."

I interviewed Ben Bradlee in 1995 during his promotional tour for his book *A Good Life: Newspapering and Other Adventures*. One of his comments to me bears repeating here: "I know that it is now common knowledge, supposed historical fact even, that President Kennedy was unfaithful in his marriage. I can tell you that during his administration when I was head of the *Newsweek* bureau on Washington, this wasn't the case. I knew nothing about any of this kind of fooling around, and I think it would have been difficult to keep it a secret if his activities were as consistent and as blatant as reported after his death. Exaggeration is not only possible in this case, I think it is more than likely."

PART SEVEN. SARGENT TRIES YET AGAIN

I referred to my interviews with George Smathers, Pierre Salinger, Hugh Sidey, and Donald Dell (conducted in 1998 for *Jackie, Ethel, Joan: Women of Camelot*). I also had several confidential sources regarding the material found in this section of the book on Sargent Shriver.

Articles referred to: "A Last, Loving Remembrance of JFK," by Jim Bishop, *Good Housekeeping*, March 1964; "Jacqueline Kennedy: The Future of a Noble Lady," by William V. Shannon, *Good Housekeeping*, April 1964; "In Step with Ethel Kennedy," by James Brady, *Parade*, April 3, 1988; "The Dark Side of Camelot," by Kitty Kelley, *People*, February 29, 1988; "Havanas in Camelot," by William Styron, *Vanity Fair*, July 1996; "A Visit to Camelot," by Diana Trilling, *New Yorker*, June 2, 1997; "Smashing Camelot," by Richard Lacayo, *Time*, November 17, 1997; "The Exner Files," by Liz Smith, *Vanity Fair*, January 1997.

I also referred to *Say Good-bye to the President*, 1985 BBC documentary.

PART EIGHT. THE THIRD GENERATION IN TROUBLE

I referred to my interview with Richard Burke, August 23, 1999, as well as my interview with Senator John Tunney in 1998, both *for Jackie, Ethel, Joan: Women of Camelot*.

I referred to Cathy Griffin's interviews with Barbara Gibson on October 1, October 10, November 10, and December 15, 1998. I followed up with Ms. Gibson on March 10, 1999, April 15, 1999, and January 4, 2000.

I referred to Cathy Griffin's interviews with Noelle Bombardier (April 2010) and my interviews with Jacques Lowe (1999).

I interviewed Chuck Spalding in 1996 for my Sinatra biography and used his comments in this and other sections of the book as background.

I used Cathy Griffin's many conversations with Pam Kelley in the spring of 2010 for background purposes only. I also referred to her interview with the *Boston Herald* in 2005.

Volumes referred to: *America's First Families*, by Carl Sferrazza Anthony; *As We Remember Her*, by Carl Sferrazza Anthony; *Happy Times*, by Lee Radziwill; *Remembering Jackie: A Life in Pictures*, by the editors of *Life*; *Sons of Camelot*, by Laurence Leamer; *Torn Lace Curtain*, by Frank Saunders; *The Founding Father*, by Richard Whalen; *The Kennedy Case*, by Rita Dallas and Jeanira Ratcliffe; *Living with the Kennedys*, by Marcia Chellis; *Kennedy*, by Jacques Lowe; *Peter Lawford: The Man Who Kept the Secrets*, by James Spada; *The Peter Lawford Story*, by Patricia Seaton Lawford; *The Kennedy Women*, by Laurence Learner; *Times to Remember*, by Rose Fitzgerald Kennedy; *The Sins of the Father*, by Ronald Kessler; *Seeds of Destruction*, by Ralph G. Martin; *Rose*, by Gail Cameron; *Life with Rose Kennedy*, by Barbara Gibson and Caroline Latham; *Jackie After Jack*, by Christopher Andersen; *Among Those Present*, by Nancy Dickerson; *My Twelve Years with John F. Kennedy*, by Evelyn Lincoln.

Articles referred to: "The Ted Kennedys Conquer Fear," by Maxine Cheshire, *Ladies' Home Journal*, September 1968; "Why Ted Kennedy Can Never Live by the Rules," by Frances Spatz Leighton, *Coronet*, May 1971; "The Ordeal of Teddy Kennedy, Jr.," by Eleanor Roberts, *Boston Sunday Herald Advertiser*, December 2, 1973; "How Caroline Kennedy Plans to Break Out of Her Mother's Jet Set Prison," by Sharon Willson, *Silver Screen*, August 1974; "Teddy Kennedy Jr. Faces a New Test of Faith," by George Carpozi Jr., *Motion Picture*, May 1974; "Two Worlds of a Kennedy," by Susan Deutsch, *People*, October 3, 1983; "Kennedy Linen Hung on the Line," by Paul Taylor, *Washington Post*, September 29, 1985.

I also utilized my research for "Caroline Kennedy," an *Entertainment Tonight* report, by J. Randy Taraborrelli, November 22, 2000.

PART NINE. POOR ARI

I referred to my interview with Stelios Papadimitriou conducted on January 4, 1998, for *Jackie, Ethel, Joan: Women of Camelot*.

I relied on my interview with Tony Oppedisano on May 23, 2011.

Cathy Griffin interviewed Dr. Isadore Rosenfield on August 11, 1998, for *Jackie, Ethel, Joan: Women of Camelot*. I also relied on my interview with Edward Larrabee Barnes and Ms. Griffin's with John Davis.

Volumes referred to: *My Life with Jacqueline Kennedy*, by Mary Barelli Gallagher; *The Other Mrs. Kennedy*, by Jerry Oppenheimer; *Bobby Kennedy*, by Lester David and Irene David; *John F. Kennedy Handbook*, by Gareth Jenkins; *Conversations with Kennedy*, by Benjamin Bradlee; *Quotable Kennedys*, edited by Bill Adler; *My Story*, by Judith Exner; *White House Nanny*, by Maud Shaw; *Onassis*, by Will Frischauer; *The Fabulous Onassis*, by Christian Cafarakis; *The Onassis Women*, by Kiki Feroudi Moutsatsos; *Jacqueline Bouvier Kennedy Onassis: A Life*, by Donald Spoto; *Senatorial Privilege: The Chappaquiddick Cover-up*, by Leo Damore; *Days of Wine, Women and Wrong*, by David Barron; *Ted Kennedy: Triumphs and Tragedies*, by Lester David; *Rose*, by Gail Cameron; *Joan: The Reluctant Kennedy*, by David Lester; *The Kennedy Women*, by Laurence Learner; *Living with the Kennedys*, by Marcia Chellis; *Rose*, by Charles Higham; *Iron Rose*, by Cindy Adams and Susan Crim; *Rose Kennedy*, by Barbara Gibson and Ted Schwartz; *The Kennedy Neurosis*, by Nancy Gager Clinch; *An American Melodrama*, by Godfrey Hodgson and Bruce Page; *Ted and the Kennedy Legend*, by Max Lerner.

Articles referred to: "The Magic and the Myth," by Dr. Joyce Brothers, *Good Housekeeping*, March 1967; "Jackie's Life with Him," by Anna Stravisky, *Motion Picture*, September 1968; "Caroline Kennedy," by Lester David, *Good Housekeeping*, January 1969; "Jackie and Ari," by Greta Nilsen, *Screenland*, October 1970; "The Enemy Within...," by William Honan, *Pageant*, September 1972; "Jackie & Ari Split Rumors," by Liz Smith, *People*, October 14, 1974; "Ethel Kennedy: A Surprisingly Happy Woman," by Stephen Birmingham, *McCall's*, June 1974; "Jackie: Twice Widowed...," by Liz Smith, *People*, March 31, 1975; "Maria Was a Weapon...," by Arianna Stassinopoulos, *People*, March 23, 1981; "Breaking His Silence," by Paul Ciotti, *Los Angeles Times*, June 6, 1988; "Ari's Fate," by Peter Ames Carlin, November 9, 1998; "Callas in Love," by Stelios Galatopoulos, *Vanity Fair*, March 1999.

Jackie's letter to Lady Bird Johnson after the death of President Lyndon Johnson can be found in the Lyndon Baines Johnson Library.

I referred to the extensive research for my television report "The Secret World of Jackie Kennedy," *A Current Affair*, July 16, 1993.

PART TEN. ROSEMARY AND ROSE

I referred to my interview with Sister Joseph Marie conducted on April 1, 2002.

I also referred to my interviews with Barbara Gibson and High Sidey.

Also, I relied on Cathy Griffin's interview with Larry Newman and Sancy Newman.

Volumes referred to: *This Awesome Challenge*, by Michael Amrine; *In Her Sister's Shadow*, by Diana DuBois; *Growing Up Kennedy*, by Harrison Raine and John Quinn; *America's First Ladies*, by Christine Sadler; *With Kennedy*, by Pierre Salinger; *The Kennedy Courage*, by Edward Hymoff and Phil Hirsch; *The Kennedy Women*, by Laurence Leamer; *Sarge: The Life and Times of Sargent Shriver*, by Scott Stossel; *The Kennedys: The Third Generation*, by Barbara Gibson and Ted Schwartz; *Kennedy Wives, Kennedy Women*, by Nancy Gager; *Joan: The Reluctant Kennedy*, by David Lester; *Rose Kennedy and Her Family*, by Barbara Gibson and Ted Schwartz; *Times to Remember*, by Rose Fitzgerald Kennedy; *Ted Kennedy: Profile of a Survivor*, by William H. Honan; *The Joy of Classical Music: A Guide for You and Your Family*, by Joan Kennedy; *The Last Brother*, by Joe McGinniss; *The Senator: My Ten Years with Ted Kennedy*, by Richard E. Burke; *The Kennedy Family*, by Joseph Dineen; *The Next Kennedy*, by Margaret Laing; *Good Ted, Bad Ted*, by Lester David; *The Sins of the Father*, by Ronald Kessler; *The Kennedy Children*, by Bill Adler; *Washington Exposé*, by Jack Anderson; *As We Remember Her*, by Carl Sferrazza Anthony; *The Kennedy Women*, by Pearl S. Buck; *The Onassis Women*, by Kiki Feroudi Moutsatsos; *Cooking for Madam*, by Marta Sgubin; *The Shadow President*, by Burton Hersh.

Some of the quotes from Eunice, Jean, and Patricia Kennedy found here and in other parts of this book are from the article "She Wanted to Inspire Us and She Did," by Dotson Rader, *Parade*, July 22, 1990.

I also referred to A&E *Biography*, "Rose Kennedy."

I referred to my extensive research for "Rose Kennedy: The Family's Power," for *A Current Affair*, November 3, 1992.

Articles referred to: "The Kennedys Gather and Say in Loving Ways, 'Thanks a Lot, Grandma'" (no attribution), *People*, September 22, 1975; "A Kennedy Walks with Memories," by Steve Tinney, Copley News Service, April 20, 1977; "La Vie en Rose" by Carl Sferrazza Anthony, *Fame*, August 1990; "The Stylishness of Her Privacy," by Lance Morrow, *Time*, May 30, 1994; "Rose Kennedy Is Dead at 104," by Rob Speyer and Corky Siemaszko, *New York Daily News*, January 23, 1995; "Rose Kennedy Dies at 104," by Bryna Taubman, *New York Post*, January 23, 1995; "Rose Kennedy, 104, Dies; Matriarch of a Dynasty," by John Goldman, *Los Angeles Times*, January 25, 1995; "Death of a Matriarch," by Elizabeth Gleich, *Time*, February 6, 1995; "TV: In the Service of the President," by Dorothy Rabinowitz, *Wall Street Journal*, December 22, 1997.

I also referred to a tape of *The Joan Rivers Show*, a special program about the Kennedys with John Davis, Cindy Adams, Barbara Gibson, and James Bacon, broadcast on January 11, 1992.

PART ELEVEN. SHRIVER FOR PRESIDENT

I referred to my interviews with High Sidey, Arthur Schlesinger Jr., Barbara Gibson, Senator George Smathers, and Pierre Salinger.

A confidential source relayed the story of Jackie's contentious exchange with Stephen Smith.

Volumes referred to: *Sarge: The Life and Times of Sargent Shriver*, by Scott Stossel; *Jackie O*, by Hedda Lyons Watney; *Jacqueline Kennedy Onassis*, by Lester David; *Robert Kennedy and His Times*, by Arthur M. Schlesinger Jr.; *A Thousand Days*, by Arthur M. Schlesinger Jr.

I also referred to a tape of "The Kennedys in Hollywood" (E!), which includes interviews with Barbara Gibson, Paul Fay, Oleg Cassini, John Davis, and Lynn Franklin (broadcast on August 26, 1998).

PART TWELVE. TED'S 1980 CAMPAIGN

I referred to my interviews with Dun Gifford, Senator John Tunney, Senator George Smathers, Richard Burke, Hugh Sidey, and Barbara Gibson.

Marcia Chellis was interviewed by Cathy Griffin in September 1998. Also, some of her comments elsewhere in this book were drawn from her interview with *People Are Talking*, San Francisco, 1985.

I also referred to Cathy Griffin's interview with Noelle Bombardier.

Volumes referred to: *True Compass*, by Ted Kennedy; *My Life with Joan Kennedy*, by Marcia Chellis; *Jackie: The Exploitation of a First Lady*, by Irving Shulman; *Senatorial Privilege*, by Leo Damore; *John F. Kennedy Jr.*, by J. D. Reed, Kyle Smith, and Jill Smolowe; *The Kennedys: An American Drama*, by Peter Collier and David Horowitz; *Ted Kennedy: Triumphs and Tragedies*, by Lester David; *Joan: The Reluctant Kennedy*, by Lester David; *A Portrait of a President*, by William Manchester; *Jacqueline Bouvier Kennedy*, by Mary Van Rensselaer Thayer; *Good Ted, Bad Ted*, by Lester David; *The Last Lion*, edited by Peter Canellos; *The Kennedy Family and the Story of Mental Retardation*, by Edward Shorter.

Articles referred to: "Joan Kennedy: The Life That Put Her in Silver Hill," by Liz Smith, *People*, June 24, 1974; "Ted Kennedy Whips into Iowa...," by Clare Crawford-Mason, *People*, July 2, 1975; "Watch Them Run: Teddy and the Kennedys," by Dick Schaap, *Look*, March 5, 1979; "Kennedy Women Say OK," Associated Press, *Los Angeles Times*, September 7, 1979; "The Kennedy Challenge," by Frank Merrick, *Time*, November 5, 1979; "Teddy the Underdog Flies into the Main Event," by Myra MacPerson, *Washington Post*, February 10, 1980; "Closing Scenes from a Kennedy Marriage," by Myra MacPherson, *Washington Post*, January 22, 1981; "Ted and Joan Kennedy: Why This Marriage Couldn't Be Saved" (no author attribution), *Ladies' Home Journal*, March 1983; "Joan Kennedy Book and Ethics," by Eunice Kennedy Shriver, *Chicago Tribune*, November 5, 1985.

I referred to a videotape of Ted Kennedy's interview with Roger Mudd.

I referred to Jackie Kennedy Onassis letters to Joan Kennedy written in 1979 that were auctioned by Alexander Autographs of Stamford, Connecticut.

PART THIRTEEN. DAVID'S STORY

Interviews referred to: Richard Burke, John Fitzgerald, Howell Van Gerbig Jr., Terrence Murphy, Leah Mason, Josephine Dampier, Gerald

Beebe, as well as Cathy Griffin's interview with Noelle Bombardier. I interviewed Ed Guthman in January 2006 and used his comments for background purposes here and throughout the book.

Volumes referred to: *The Kennedys: An American Drama*, by Peter Collier and David Horowitz; *Behind Blue Eyes: The Biography of David Anthony Kennedy*, by Grahame Bedford; *The Senator*, by Richard Burke; *JFK: The Man and the Myth*, by Victor Lasky; *RFK*, by Dick Schapp; *The Pleasure of His Company*, by Paul B. Fay Jr.; *Jacqueline Kennedy*, by Deanne and David Heller; *Jackie: A Legend Defined*, edited by Claire G. Osborne; *Teddy Bare*, by Zad Rust; *A Life on the Edge*, by Jim Whitaker; *When I Think of Bobby*, by Warren Rogers; *An Honorable Profession*, edited by Pierre Salinger et al.; *Jackie, Bobby, and Manchester*, by Arnold Bennett; *The Other Mrs. Kennedy*, by Jerry Oppenheimer; *Ethel*, by Lester David; *Robert Kennedy and His Times*, by Arthur M. Schlesinger Jr.

A very important volume relating to Eunice Kennedy Shriver and her work for mental retardation is the previously mentioned *The Kennedy Family and the Story of Mental Retardation*, by Edward Shorter. I referred to this well-researched and reliable book to confirm certain aspects of my research concerning Eunice's disagreements with her siblings over the Joseph P. Kennedy Jr. Foundation. I also referred to voluminous Kennedy notes and minutes of meetings having to do with the Kennedys' interest in mental retardation—all found in the John Fitzgerald Presidential Library archives—and had several confidential sources regarding the Kennedy family's "revolt" against Eunice in the late 1970s and early 1980s.

Articles referred to: "Ethel Kennedy Today," by Adele Whitely Fletcher, *Lady's Circle*, September 1969; "Joan Kennedy Surveys Her Sober Life," by Gail Jennes, *People*, August 7, 1978; "David Kennedy—1955–1984," by Peter Carlson, *People*, May 14, 1984.

PART FOURTEEN. KENNEDY UPHEAVAL

Interviews referred to: Peter Lawford, Milt Ebbins, Bernie Abramson, Patricia Brennan.

Again, in regard to the Kennedy family "revolt," I referred to the minutes of Kennedy Foundation meetings held in 1977 and 1984 as well as additional information provided to me by a confidential source.

Sargent Shriver told me the story of his stomach cancer scare when I met him in 2002.

Volumes referred to: *Symptoms of Withdrawal*, by Christopher Kennedy Lawford; *Peter Lawford: The Man Who Kept the Secrets*, by James Spada; *The Peter Lawford Story*, by Patricia Seaton Lawford; *The Kennedy Family and the Story of Mental Retardation*, by Edward Shorter; *The Founding Father*, by Richard Whalen; *The Remarkable Kennedys*, by Joe McCarthy; *Life with Rose Kennedy*, by Barbara Gibson; *"Johnny, We Hardly Knew Ye,"* by Kenneth P. O'Donnell and David F. Powers with Joe McCarthy; *The Kennedys: An American Drama*, by Peter Collier and David Horowitz; *Times to Remember*, by Rose Fitzgerald Kennedy.

Articles referred to: "Ethel Kennedy and the Arithmetic of Life and Death," by Gail Sheehy, *New York*, June 17, 1968; "The Secrets of Joan Kennedy," *People*, September 23, 1985; *The Ted Kennedy Story* (special tribute magazine), 1970; "An Intimate Visit: Rose Kennedy at 80," by Sylvia Wright, *Life*, July 17, 1970; "Joan Kennedy: The Life That Put Her into Silver Hill," by Liz Smith, *People*, June 24, 1971; "Rose Kennedy at 85," *People*, September 22, 1975; "Joan Kennedy Surveys Her Sober Life," by Gail Jennes, *People*, August 7, 1978; "Joan's Journey," by Myra MacPherson, *Washington Post*, December 14, 1979; "Watch Them Run: Teddy and the Kennedys," by Dick Schaap, *Look*, March 5, 1979; "Is Teddy Ready?," by Clare Crawford-Mason, *People*, July 2, 1979; "Joan Kennedy Silences Reporters," by T. R. Reid, *Washington Post*, January 19, 1980; "Women Stand Up for Joan Kennedy," by Maxine Cheshire, *Washington Post*, October 22, 1980; "Closing Scenes from a Kennedy Marriage," by Myra MacPherson, *Washington Post*, January 22, 1981; "After 24 Years, Joan Kennedy Ends Marriage," by Gail Jennes and Gioia Diliberto, *People*, December 20, 1982; "Ted and Joan: Why This Marriage Couldn't Be Saved" (no author attribution), *Ladies' Home Journal*, March 1983; "Peter Lawford Dies," *Los Angeles Times*, December 26, 1984; "Kennedy Linen Hung on the Line," by Paul Taylor, *Washington Post*, September 29, 1985; "Joan Kennedy: Book Contains Inaccuracies," Associated Press, October 18, 1985; "The Joan Kennedy Book and Ethics," by Eunice Kennedy Shriver, *New York Daily News*, November 4, 1985; "Marcia Chellis," by Cheryl Lavin, *Chicago Tribune*, June 1, 1986; "The Lucky Life of Sargent Shriver," *Chicago Tribune*, July 30, 1987; "The Other Jackie O.," Edward Klein, *Vanity Fair*, August 1989; "How I Got Over: Interview with Joan

Kennedy," by John Stratford, *Star*, August 1, 1989; "La Vie en Rose," by Carl Sferrazza Anthony, *Fame*, August 1990; "Richard Burke: My Ten Year Binge with Teddy," by Frank DiGiacomo and Joanna Molloy, *New York Post*, July 27, 1992; "Chappaquiddick Questions Remain," UPI, July 18, 1994; "Rose Kennedy Dies at 104," by Bryna Taubman, *New York Post*, January 23, 1995; "Farewell Rose," by Bob Speyer and Corky Siemaszko, *Daily News*, January 23, 1995; "Death of a Matriarch," by Elizabeth Gleick, *Time*, February 6, 1995; "Ethel K. Gives Trashman a Trashing," by Gayle Fee and Laura Raposa, *Boston Herald*, July 17, 1997; "Bobby's Kids," by Michael Shnayerson, *Vanity Fair*, August 1997; "A Life of Challenge," by Maxwell Taylor Kennedy, *Inside Borders*, June 1998; "We Happy Few," by Joseph P. Kennedy II, *Esquire*, June 1998; "Sad Tale of an Unraveling Marriage," by Liz Smith, *New York Post*, January 18, 2000.

PART FIFTEEN. CAROLINE, JOHN, AND MAURICE

Interviews referred to: Barbara Gibson, Robert McNamara, Lisa McClintock, Steven Styles, Marian Ronan, Roswell Gilpatric, Stanley Gottwig, Steve Heaslip (June 15, 2010), Joan Braden, Mary Fonteyn, Paul B. Fay Jr., Sancy Newman, Chuck Spalding, Lawrence Alexander, Larry Newman, Joseph Paolella, Joseph Livingston, Ted Livingston, Joe Gargan, Mary Lou McCarthy, Bess Abel, Betty Beale, Oleg Cassini, Paul B. Fay Jr., David Lester, Lem Billings, Morton Downey Jr., Luella Hennessey, Frank Mankiewicz, Jeanne Martin.

Cathy Griffin interviewed Ellis Amburn on May 20, 2010, and though we did not use any of his quotes, we did utilize his memories for background purposes and appreciate his cooperation.

The letters from Lyndon Johnson to John and Caroline Kennedy and from Jackie Kennedy Onassis to Johnson can be found in the Lyndon Baines Johnson Presidential Library.

Volumes referred to: *The Kennedys: Dynasty and Disaster*, by John H. Davis; *John F. Kennedy*, by Hugh Sidey; *The JFK Jr. Scrapbook*, by Stephen Spignesi; *Life with My Sister Madonna*, by Christopher Ciccone; *Madonna: An Intimate Biography*, by J. Randy Taraborrelli.

Articles referred to: "How Caroline and John Remember Their Father," by David E. Powers, *McCall's*, November 1973; "Ted Kennedy's Memories of JFK," by Theodore Sorensen, *McCall's*, November 1973; "Four Generations of Kennedys Together Again," by Jim Nelson, *Star*, July 1995; "Of Movies and Peanut Butter," by Liz Smith, *Los Angeles Times*, November 16, 1995.

PART SIXTEEN. WILLIAM KENNEDY SMITH AND THE PALM BEACH SCANDAL

I referred to my interviews with Dominick Dunne, Barbara Gibson, Senator George Smathers, Siobhan Walsh, Elliot Newman, Steven Silas, Betty LeRoy Thomson, Peter Dilliard, Frank Mankiewicz, Stephen Webb, Inez Foxworthy, Sheridan Bonswell, Patricia Moran, David Powers (questionnaire), and Joe Gargan (questionnaire). Moreover, two Kennedy family attorneys, both of whom have asked for anonymity, painted the story of Ted Kennedy's meeting with Eunice Kennedy Shriver in January 1991.

I also utilized several confidential sources, all of whom are attorneys who worked for the Kennedy family, for this section of the book. I also referred to numerous court transcripts of the trial.

Volumes referred to: *True Compass*, by Ted Kennedy; *Teddy Kennedy: Triumphs and Tragedies*, by Lester David; *Ethel*, by Lester David; *Rose*, by Gail Cameron.

I referred to Oprah Winfrey's interview with Victoria Reggie Kennedy, November 25, 2009.

Of course I referred to numerous published newspaper accounts of the 1991 trial of William Kennedy Smith, more than space would allow me to detail here. I also referred to "Boys' Night Out in Palm Beach," by Michelle Green, *People*, April 22, 1981.

Of additional interest: Patrick Kennedy has acknowledged being treated for cocaine use during his teenage years, and admitted that he abused drugs and alcohol while he was a student at Providence College. He sought treatment for an OxyContin addiction in 2006.

In May 2006, Patrick admitted that he had an addiction to prescription medication and announced he would be readmitting himself to a drug rehab facility at the Mayo Clinic in Minnesota where he has sought treatment for prior addictions. He was released a month later. In June

2009, he again announced that he had "checked into a medical facility for treatment." In a statement to the press, he said his recovery is a "lifelong process" and that he will do whatever it takes to preserve his health. "I have decided to temporarily step away from my normal routine to ensure that I am being as vigilant as possible in my recovery."

Mr. Kennedy has publicly acknowledged suffering from a bipolar condition, as well as from depression. "I myself have suffered from depression," he said during a forum about mental health and senior citizens in March 2000. "I have been treated by psychiatrists. Oh my God, it's out!" he exclaimed, prompting laughter from the crowd. "That's another skeleton in the closet," he continued. "But I'm here to tell you, thank God I got treatment because I wouldn't be as strong as I am today if I didn't get that treatment."

Ted Jr. has publicly acknowledged that he was treated in 1991 for alcohol abuse, at the Institute of Living, a Hartford, Connecticut, alcohol rehab facility. He said he committed himself to his recovery because "continued use of alcohol is impairing my ability to achieve the goals I care about." Kennedy was twenty-nine at the time and had received his master's degree earlier that year from the Yale School of Forestry and Environmental Studies. Said his father, Ted, at the time, "I am very proud of the decision he has made."

PART SEVENTEEN. KENNEDY WIVES—OLD AND NEW

I referred to Cathy Griffin's interviews with Edmund M. Reggie (August 4, 1998), James Cummings, Sheila Rauch Kennedy (June 1998), and my interviews with Patricia Brennan.

I also referred to Joan Kennedy's letter to Cathy Griffin, November 19, 1998: "Thank you for the nice things you have thought about me over the past 40 years since I became Mrs. K," she wrote in part. "Fortunately, I am well and happy in this present stage of my life—the joy of spending a lot of time with my four grandchildren and enjoying my part-time job as Chairperson of Boston's Cultural Council and serving on the Board of Directors of four great Boston institutions. I am blessed with many dear friends whom I have known since my college days, and I still play the piano or narrate with orchestras for a favorite charity."

Volumes referred to: *Shattered Faith: A Woman's Struggle to Stop the Catholic Church from Annulling Her Marriage*, by Sheila Rauch Kennedy; *Living with the Kennedys: The Joan Kennedy Story*, by Marcia Chellis; *The Kennedys: The Third Generation*, by Barbara Gibson and Ted Schwartz; *The Senator*, by Richard E. Burke; *The Magnificient Kennedy Women*, by Stanley P. Friedman; *Jackie: Her Life in Pictures*, by James Spada; *America's First Ladies*, by Christine Sadler; *Kennedy*, by Theodore Sorensen; *Kennedy Weddings*, by Jay Mulvaney; *Kennedy Wives, Kennedy Women*, by Nancy Gager.

Articles referred to: "The Relentless Ordeal of Political Wives" (no author attribution), *Time*, October 7, 1974; "Joan Kennedy's Road Back from Alcoholism," by Dr. Joyce Brothers, *Good Housekeeping*, April 1979; "Kirk Billings, 65, Dies," *New York Times*, May 29, 1981; "White House Families" (no author attribution), *Life*, November 1984; "Joan Kennedy: Book Contains Inaccuracies," Associated Press, October 18, 1985; "Her Cocoon of Values," by Jonathan Alter, *Newsweek*, May 30, 1994; "'Forgotten Kennedy' Ready to Assume the Mantle," by Joe Carroll, *Irish Times/World News*, September 26, 1998.

PART EIGHTEEN. JACKIE: HER FINAL YEARS

I referred to my interviews with Stephen Styles, Joan Braden, Margorie Maitland, Steve Heaslip, Karen Jeffrey (June 13, 2010), Oleg Cassini, and John Carl Warnecke.

I interviewed Marta Sgubin in conjunction to the publication of her book *Cooking for Madam* on October 22, 1998.

There were many sources for the chapter "Vigil," all of whom were present at Jackie's apartment that week and all of whom wish to remain anonymous.

Volumes referred to: *Remembering Jack*, by Jacques Lowe; *Jack and Jackie*, by Christopher Anderson; *Jackie After Jack*, by Christopher Anderson; *All Too Human*, by Edward Klein; *Jackie Oh!*, by Kitty Kelley; *Jackie's Treasures*, by Russell Condon; *Cooking for Madam*, by Marta Sgubin; *Hollywood Is a Four Letter Town*, by James Bacon; *Show Business Laid Bare*, by Earl Wilson; *Sinatra: A Complete Life*, by J. Randy Taraborrelli; *Sinatra: The Man and the Myth*, by Bill Adler; *Where Have You Gone, Joe DiMaggio?*, by Maury Allen; *The Intimate Sex Lives of Famous People*, by Irving Wallace et al.; *RFK*, by C. David Heymann; *Peter Lawford: The Man Who Kept the Secrets*, by James Spada; *The Unabridged Marilyn*, by Randall Riese and Christopher Hitchens; *Crowning Glory*, by Sydney Gudaroff as told to Cathy Griffin; *The Fitzgeralds and the Kennedys: An American Saga*, by Doris Kearns Goodwin; *The Kennedy Men*, by Nellie Bly.

I also referred to "A Fascinating Peek at the Jackie You Never Knew," *National Enquirer*, a June 21, 1994, interview with Marian Ronan, and spoke with the author personally to verify all of her quotes found within it.

The correspondence from Jackie Kennedy Onassis and Caroline Kennedy to Lady Bird Johnson can be found in the archives of the Lyndon Baines Johnson Presidential Library

Articles referred to: "A Working Woman," by Gioia Diliberto, *People*, June 18, 1984; "Jacqueline Kennedy Onassis—1929–1994," *People* tribute issue, summer 1994; "Star Behind the Scenes," by John F. Baker, *Publishers Weekly*, April 19, 1993; "Love Jackie," by Carl Sferrazza Anthony, *American Heritage*, September 1994; "Jackie: By Oleg Cassini," *In Style*, October 1996; "A Great First Lady," by Bill Hoffman, *New York Post*, May 20, 1999; "A 'Who's Who' List of Visitors," by Alex Monsky and John Rogers, *New York Post*, May 20, 1999.

I referred to my extensive research for my broadcast report "Jackie Kennedy Onassis: A Life," for *Hard Copy*, May 6, 1998.

Of additional interest: When Jackie Kennedy Onassis was an editor at Doubleday she was very interested in signing Diana Ross to write her autobiography. Though Diana was flattered, the idea of being so revealing about herself in a book didn't appeal to her at that time. After she declined the offer, I was contracted to write my first book for Doubleday, which was to be called *Diana: A Celebration of Her Life and Career*. Perhaps not surprisingly, when I wrote to Diana Ross—whom I had known for many years—to tell her about my endeavor, she wasn't happy about it. She didn't contact me, though. She went straight to Jackie and asked for a meeting.

Diana and Jackie met at Jackie's office at Doubleday on the morning of February 8, 1983. Diana was joined by Irving "Swifty" Lazar, a high-powered Hollywood literary agent. Two other Doubleday executives were in attendance, one of them being Sam Vaughn, who was Doubleday's president at the time. Diana explained to Jackie and the others that she was opposed to any book being written about her. She said that she had changed her mind and was now interested in writing her own story. She suggested that Doubleday publish her book and cancel mine.

"What kind of book do you have in mind?" Jackie wanted to know, according to the others present.

"It would be an inspirational book," Diana explained. "It would be an autobiography, but with no personal details whatsoever."

When Jackie wanted to know what kind of autobiography has "no personal details whatsoever," Diana explained that she wanted to share her views about life and love, but avoid writing about her firsthand life experiences.

"Well, that's an idea," Jackie offered. She didn't sound very encouraging, though. "Perhaps we can talk about it further." The two women then agreed to schedule a lunch to discuss the matter further.

"But, wait, what about that other book?" Swifty Lazar asked.

"Oh, we'll work something out," Jackie said, turning to Diana. "Don't you worry about it."

In the end, Doubleday decided to reject Diana's idea and instead continue with my book. In the months that followed, I wrote my Diana Ross biography and submitted the manuscript to Doubleday. However, unbeknownst to me, Jackie and Diana had apparently agreed to a secret pact over lunch. Jackie agreed to send my manuscript to Diana for her approval. I don't know for certain that Ms. Ross had a hand in editing it, or that she even received it. I only know that it was sent to her by Jackie Kennedy Onassis and that she had been told she could delete anything from it that she found offensive—this based on correspondence given to me years later when I was researching *Jackie, Ethel, Joan: Women of Camelot*.

At first I was a little dismayed, to say the least. However, my feeling now, more than twenty-five years later, is that Jackie Kennedy Onassis was naturally empathic about Diana Ross's concerns. After all, both were celebrities who well understood image-making. Even though Jackie had told me that she loved knowing the secrets of celebrities, the truth was that she did not want to be responsible for those secrets being revealed. I am reminded of what she and Bobby Kennedy went through with William Manchester over his book *Death of a President*, which Jackie thought was far too revealing and which she fought so hard to censor. It's the nature of most celebrities to at least attempt to control what is known about them—just as it's in the nature of biographers not to let them do it. What's interesting is that Jackie—and eventually her son, John—would also find themselves on the other side of the equation by working in the publishing business.

PART NINETEEN. JOHN AND CAROLYN

I referred to my interviews with Richard Bradley, Stephen Styles, Mary Cullen, Stewart Price, John Perry Barlow (1999), Jacques Lowe, Steve Heaslip, Pierre Salinger, and John Perry Barlow, as well as Cathy Griffin's interviews with Phillip Bloch (May 20, 2010), Gayle Fee (May 22, 2010), and R. Couri Hay (July 2, 2010).

Volumes referred to: *True Compass*, by Edward M. Kennedy; *American Son*, by Richard Blow; *Sweet Caroline*, by Christopher Anderson; *Forever Young*, by William Sylvester Noonan with Robert Huber; *Just Jackie*, by Edward Klein; *John and Caroline: Their Lives in Pictures*, by James Spada.

Articles referred to: "Of Man, Myth and Might-Have-Been's," by Bob Adams, *St. Louis Dispatch*, November 22, 1988; "Lotsa Q, Little A as Kennedys Meet the Press," by George Rush and Joanna Molloy, *Daily News*, November 6, 1996; "Can You Handle the Truth?," by John Kennedy, *George*, March 1998; "Poster Boy for Poster Boy Behavior," (no author attribution), *Spy*, March 1998; "John Jr.—Wearing Success Well," by Katy Kelly, *USA Today*, May 18, 1998; "Hunk's Roving Eye Sparked Park Spat," by Bill Hoffman, *New York Post*, March 2, 1999; "Prince of the City," edited by Maer Roshan, *New York*, August 2, 1999; "Kennedy Expert C. David Heymann—Do His JFK Jr. Stories Hold Up?," by Andrew Goldman, *New York Observer*, August 2, 1999; "The Politics of Personality," by Abigail Pogrebin, *Brill's Content*, March 1999; "JFK Jr.'s Lover Shocks Her Hub Pals," by Gayle Fee and Laura Raposa, *Boston Herald*, January 10, 2000; "Her Mother's Daughter," by Lynn Darling, *Us Weekly*, October 29, 2001; "Crazy for Carolyn," by Tessa Namuth et al., *Newsweek*, October 21, 1996; "Some Press Hounds Heel for Kennedy," by Paul D. Colford, *Los Angeles Times*, November 5, 1996.

I drew from my extensive research for the two-part series I authored,

"The Life and Loves of the Prince of Camelot," *Women's Day*, July 26, 1999.

I drew from John Kennedy Jr.'s comments to me at his press conference to announce *George* magazine in 1994.

I also drew from Larry King's interview with Kennedy, May 22, 1999.

I drew from my research and television report "Madonna's Blond Ambition: JFK Jr.," for the program *Hard Copy*, November 6, 1995.

I drew from my research and television report "JFK Jr.'s Argument with Carolyn," *Day & Date*, March 4, 1996.

PART TWENTY. MICHAEL'S STORY

I referred to my interviews with R. Couri Hay, Andy Williams, Gary Andover, and Brian Holloway.

I referred to numerous press accounts of Michael Kennedy's troubles in the spring of 1997, including "A Betrayal in the Family," by Pam Lambert, *People*, May 12, 1997; and "RFK's Son Accused...," by Tracy Connor, *New York Post*, April 26, 1997.

Articles referred to: "JFK Jr. Surrenders His Single Status," by Karen Thomas, *USA Today*, September 23, 1996; "John-John Is Gone-Gone," by Jeanine Stein, *Los Angeles Times*, September 24, 1996; "Bridal Sweet," by Tom Gliatto, *People*, October 7, 1996; "Kennedy Women Shine Despite Shadow of Kennedy Men," Associated Press, May 11, 1997; "Don't Sit Under the Apple Tree," by John Kennedy, *George*, August 1997; "Michael Kennedy—1958–1997," by Margery Eagen, *Boston Globe*, January 3, 1998; "Kennedy Family, Friends Say Farewell to Michael," by Elizabeth Mehren, *Los Angeles Times*, January 4, 1998; "Ready for Some Football," *New York Daily News*, January 11, 1998; "Tragedy Strikes Again," by Nancy Gibbs, *Time*, January 12, 1998; "The Camelot Curse," by Evan Thomas, *Newsweek*, January 12, 1998; "Kennedy Repercussions," by Jeannie Williams, *USA Today*, January 14, 1998; "Death in Aspen," by Patrick Rogers, *People*, January 19, 1998; "Tragic Michael's Last Angry Spat," by Neal Travis, *New York Post*, March 17, 1998; "For JFK, Jr., Marilyn Isn't Bad Press," by Jeannie Williams, *USA Today*, July 29, 1996; "We Happy Few," by Joseph P. Kennedy II, *Esquire*, June 1998; "JFK Jr.'s Life in Pictures,"

People commemorative issue, summer 1999; "A Letter for the Editor," by the staff of *George, George,* September 1999.

I also referred to the transcripts of "Kennedy Tragedy on the Slopes," *The Geraldo Rivera Show,* January 8, 1998; and "The Deadly Games the Kennedys Play," *The Geraldo Rivera Show,* June 18, 1998.

PART TWENTY-ONE. A PEACEFUL TIME

I referred to my interviews with Leah Mason, and Cathy Griffin's interviews with Andy Williams, Brian Holloway, Tammy Holloway (May 31, 2010), John Glenn, Noelle Bombardier, Mary Cullen, R. Couri Hay, and John Perry Barlow.

Volumes referred to: *Moon River and Me,* by Andy Williams; *RFK,* by C. David Heymann.

Articles referred to: "JFK Jr.'s Galpal Is Beautiful but Headstrong," by Gayle Fee and Laura Raposa, *Boston Herald,* March 11, 1996; "Joan Kennedy Pleads Guilty to DUI," Associated Press, November 7, 2000; "JFK's Galpal Is Burned About Being in Tabloid Hell," by Gayle Fee and Laura Raposa, *Boston Herald,* March 13, 1996.

I also referred to extensive research for my two-part series "Caroline Kennedy," *Woman's Day* (Australia), March 2000.

Of additional interest: Some of the comments by Kerry Kennedy, Rory Kennedy, and Kathleen Kennedy Townsend in this section and in other sections of the book are culled from my conversations with the three of them after a symposium on the legacy of the Kennedy women, part of the International Women's Forum annual conference at the John F. Kennedy Presidential Library on October 4, 1996.

PART TWENTY-TWO. CAMELOT LOSES ITS PRINCE

I referred to my interviews with Virgil McLyn (September 1, 2010), Stephen Styles (May 1, 1998, August 1, 2001), Richard Bradley (June 15, 2010), and Leah Mason. Cathy Griffin interviewed Holly Safford (May 1, 2010, May 11, 2010, July 1, 2010), Bryan Holloway (June 1, 2010), Tammy Holloway (May 31, 2000), Clint Flagg, and John Perry Barlow.

Articles referred to: "The Story of a President and His Son," by Laura Bergquist, *Look*, December 3, 1963; "Joan Kennedy—'Win or Lose, I Win,'" by Myra MacPherson, *McCall's*, June 1980; "Edward Kennedy," by William Greider, *Rolling Stone*, December 1987; "The Family Business," by Julia Lawlor, *USA Weekend*, November 4–6, 1988; "Joan Kennedy's Ode to Joy," by Jeannie Williams, *USA Today*, October 30, 1992; "From Hunk Who Flunked to Media Mogul," by Katy Kelly, *USA Today*, May 18, 1998; "In Search of John-John," by Beauregard Houston-Montgomery, *Playgirl*, June 1998; *Newsweek*'s special issue devoted to Kennedy, "JFK Jr.: His Life and the Kennedy Legacy," July 1999; *Life*'s special edition about JFK Jr., July 1999; "The Boy Under the Desk," by Angie Cannon and David L. Marcus, *U.S. News & World Report*, July 26, 1999; "Time for Joy Ends in Dark Despair," by Maria Alvarez, Jeane MacIntosh, and Andy Geller, *New York Post*, July 18, 1999; "Favorite Son, Forever Fascinating," by Jeannie Williams, *Life*, July 19, 1999; "A Somber Kennedy Farewell," by Elizabeth Mehren, *Los Angeles Times*, July 24, 1999; *Time*'s commemorative issue, July 26, 1999; "The Curse," by Brian Kelly and Kenneth T. Walsh, *U.S. News & World Report*, July 26, 1999; "Kennedys Marked by Success and Tragedy," Associated Press, *USA Today*, July 17, 1999; "Woman Who Won His Heart," by Laura Italiano, *New York Post*, July 18, 1999; "JFK Jr., Wife Likely Dead," by Fred Bayles, *USA Today*, July 19, 1999; "Data Suggests Plane Dived," by Fred Bayles and Alan Levine, *USA Today*, July 20, 1999; "JFK, Jr. to Be Buried at Sea," by Fred Bayles and Andrea Stone, *USA Today*, July 22, 1999; "Ashes of Kennedy Crash Victims Returned to Sea," by Elizabeth Mehren, *Los Angeles Times*, July 23, 1999; "Young Pair Recalled in Simple Mass," by N. R. Kleinfield, *Daily News*, July 24, 1999; "Bessette Sisters Remembered at Memorial in Home Town," Associated Press, July 25, 1999; "JFK Jr.'s Friends Remember How Carolyn Romance Began," by Jeannie Williams, *USA Today*, July 28, 1999; "Remembering John F. Kennedy, Jr." by Richard Reeves, *TV Guide*, July 31–August 6, 1999; "JFK's Final Journey," by Evan Thomas, *Newsweek*, August 2, 1999; *People*'s special issue, August 2 1999; "Love Conquers All" (no author attribution), *People*, August 16, 1999; "Hour of Loss," by Susan Schindehette, *People*, August 9, 1999; "John Kennedy: A Tribute," *George*, October 1999; "JFK Jr. Marriage Died Before Plane Crash," by Annette Witheridge, *New York Post*, November 14, 1999; "John F. Kennedy: A Remembrance," by David Michaelis, *Vanity Fair*, September

1999; "Caroline Without John," by Michelle Green, *Good Housekeeping*, October 1999; "Moving On," by Jill Smolowe, *People*, May 29, 2000; "Final Accounting" (no author attribution), *People*, July 30, 2001; "Are We Still Smitten with Camelot?," by Howard Rosenberg, *Los Angeles Times*, November 3, 2000.

I referred to the following volumes: *American Legacy*, by C. David Heymann; *The Men We Became*, by Robert T. Littell; *The Day John Died*, by Christopher Andersen.

One book that I think deserves special mention is *What Remains*, by Carole Radziwill. It's a lovely and moving book about her relationship with her husband, Anthony Radziwill, and her friendship with John Kennedy Jr. and Carolyn Bessette. I loved it. Ms. Radziwill's quotes in this section are from her TV interviews promoting that work.

I drew from my extensive research for my article "Caroline Kennedy," *Star*, November 15, 1999.

I referred to extensive research for my three-part series "JFK Jr.— Golden Child," *Star*, August 1999.

PART TWENTY-THREE. TRANSITIONS

I referred to my interviews with Senator George Smathers, Pierre Salinger, Patricia Brennan, Joan Braden, Sancy Newman, Luella Hennessey, Leah Mason, Gore Vidal, Anthony Sherman, Betty Beale, Lem Billings, Bess Abel, James Bacon, Letitia Baldrige, Ben Bradlee, George Christian, Leo Damore, John Davis, Joseph Gargan (questionnaire), Jeanne Martin, and Joseph Paolella. I also drew from Cathy Griffin's interviews with Webster Janssen and Karen Jeffrey.

The nun who witnessed the incident in Hyannis when Rosemary Kennedy was momentarily lost asked to not be identified, and her wishes have been respected here. Also, a number of confidential sources were utilized in this section of the book to tell the story of Senator Kennedy's battle with cancer.

Articles referred to: *Teddy: Keeper of the Kennedy Flame*, special magazine, by David Ragan and George Carpozi, August 1968; "An Intimate Portrait of Joan Kennedy," by Barbara Kevles, *Good Housekeeping*, July

1969; "Joan's Journey," by Myra MacPherson, *Washington Post*, December 14, 1979; "The Secrets of Joan Kennedy Come to Market" (no author attribution), *People*, September 23, 1985; "On a Campaign Trail for the Classics," by Robert W. Coffey, *Los Angeles Times*, November 26, 1992; "Bump in the Road, by Bill Hewitt, *People*, September 25, 2000; "Eunice Kennedy Shriver—1921–2009," by Valerie J. Nelson and Elizabeth Mehren, *Los Angeles Times*, August 12, 2009.

I also referred to *Newsweek's* "Special Commemorative Edition: The Last Brother: Edward M. Kennedy, 1932–2009."

Mike Barnicle's comments are from his article "Of Memory and the Sea," *Time*, September 7, 2009. In that same issue of *Time*, I also drew from "The Last Lion," by Ted Sorensen, and "How He Found Himself," by Joe Klein.

I relied on numerous press accounts of Ted Kennedy's endorsement of Barack Obama, too numerous to list here.

Volumes referred to: *The Kennedy Curse*, by Edward Klein; *Living with the Kennedys*, by Marcia Chellis.

I also referred to Vicki Reggie Kennedy's interview with Oprah Winfrey, November 25, 2009.

I also utilized "Ted Kennedy's First Wife Joan Kennedy—Casualty of Camelot," by Susan Dolandson James, ABC News, August 31, 2009.

PART TWENTY-FOUR. LOOKING AHEAD

I referred to my interviews with Susan Morgan, Mabel Simmons, Leah Mason, Peter Dye, Max Block, Nunziata Lisi, Jeanne Martin, Patricia Brennan, Joan Braden, James Bacon, Clint Hill, Gore Vidal, George Masters, Senator George Smathers, Chuck Spalding, Jim Whiting, Ben Bradlee, Morton Downey Jr., Jim Ketchum, and Larry Newman. Also, a number of confidential sources spoke about Caroline Kennedy's senatorial bid.

Articles referred to: "The Lucky Life of Sargent Shriver," by Cheryl Lavin, *Chicago Tribune*, July 30 1987; "Extra! Extra! RFK's Son Douglas Kennedy," by Alex Tresniowski, *People*, July 27, 1998; "Caroline Spends the Anniversary in Private Grief," by Jeannie Williams, *USA Today*, July 20, 1999; "Best Man," by Susan Schindehette, *People*, August 30, 1999;

"My Mother, the Queen of Camelot," by Elizabeth Kastor, *Australian Women's Weekly*, November, 2001; "Caroline Kennedy Busts on *New York Times* Reporter in Interview," Fox News, December 28, 2009; "Caroline Kennedy Tells Daily News: I Wouldn't Be Beholden to Anybody," by Kenneth Lovett, *New York Daily News*, December 27, 2008; "A Final Funeral," by Richard Wolf and Kathy Kiely, *USA Today*, August 28, 2009.

Volumes referred to: *Joan: The Reluctant Kennedy*, by Lester David; *The Kennedy Men*, by Laurence Leamer; *Symptoms of Withdrawal*, by Christopher Kennedy Lawford; *Ten Things I Wish I'd Known*, by Maria Shriver.

I referred to Maria Shriver's interview with Diane Sawyer on *Good Morning America*, May 11, 2009. I also referred to videotapes of Maria Shriver's testimony before Congress about Alzheimer's as well as Ms. Shriver's *The Alzheimer's Project* for HBO and the eulogy for her mother, Eunice Kennedy Shriver.

I referred to the PBS Broadcast *American Experience*, "The Kennedys."

I also referred to "The Kennedys: The Third Generation," *Life* special issue, July 1997.

I referred to my extensive research for my television report "Joan Kennedy," on *Entertainment Tonight*, November 2000.

Of additional interest: Certainly when it comes to broadcast journalism, Maria Shriver has always strived to avoid the sensational and to maintain her integrity at all costs. In two meetings I had with her at NBC in the spring of 1994 relating to a Michael Jackson special she was producing for the program *Dateline* (I am considered by some to be an authority on Jackson's life because of my books about him), her biggest concern was how to portray the beleaguered pop star in a balanced way without overlooking the massive dysfunction of his life. "It's more than just coming from a famous family," she observed in speaking of her views on Jackson. "Each of my cousins who ever had a hard time has his own unique story. It's never just, 'I came from a famous family. Woe is me.' Ultimately, Shriver opted not to produce the story on Jackson. "I have seen in my own family how complicated things can be, and how impossible it is for people on the outside to fully grasp those complexities," she wrote to me in a letter on April 18, 1994. "It's easy to paint people with wide brush strokes, especially on TV when you only have so much time to tell a story. I would rather not tell it at all if I have to tell it in an incomplete way. I have seen too many incomplete stories on my own family to ever want to do the same to someone else." She thanked me for my assistance and wrote, "If at a later date, I decide there is something that can be done in a classy and informative way, I will definitely get back in touch."

I would also like to acknowledge the following people who were interviewed for *After Camelot* and/or *Jackie, Ethel, Joan: Women of Camelot*: Elizabeth Ford, Amanda Fortini, Jon Conley, Mike Hiles, Frank Swertlow, Lou Cataldo, Deborah Perry, Jill Evans, Paul Evans, Kerri Anne Kimball, Kathryn Childers, George Brennan, Matthew Snyder, Maria Keller, Jayne Meadows, Paul Glazer, Corrinna Tomline, Les MacDonald, Stephen Levine, Cynthia Clack, John Green, Tom Barker, John Davis, Ed Lozzi, Gil Garfield, Harry Phillips, Buzz Aldrin, Ivy Harper, Charles Bartlett, Nina Auchincloss Straight, Linda Selke, Harry Middleton, James Bacon, Marcia Chellis, Jim Ketchum, Cindy Adams, Liz Smith, Howell Van Gerbig, and Sheila Gaglan.

Special thanks to Dr. Gerald Aronoff. I'm sorry that the story of his romance with Joan Kennedy did not make the pages of this book strictly because of space considerations, but I appreciate the time he gave us from his busy schedule. It's always the case in a book such as this one, with so many important and historical characters, that not every very good story can be told. The goal is to tell as many as possible, and pick and choose the ones that best illustrate character and personality. I hope my readers agree and think that we—I and my researchers—achieved that goal with *After Camelot*.

PERSONAL ACKNOWLEDGMENTS

My sincere thanks to Jonathan Hahn. Not only is he a brilliant writer and my personal publicist, but he also happens to be my best friend. I thank him for so many years of support in all of my endeavors, both personal and professional.

As I have often stated, without a loyal team of representatives, an author usually finds himself sitting at home writing books no one reads. Therefore, I thank all of those from "Team JRT": attorneys Joel Loquvam and James M. Leonard; CPAs Michael Horowitz and Felinda deYoung, of Horowitz, McMahon and Zarem in Southern California, Inc.

I must thank Jeff Hare, a vice president of DreamWorks, for being such a good and trusted friend.

Andy Steinlen, George Solomon, Andy Hirsch, Jeff Cook, and Frank Bruno have also been great friends, and I would like to acknowledge them as well. In fact, it means the world to me to be blessed with so many good friends, including: Aaron Lawrence, Erik and Connie Rodriguez, George and Vivian Rodriguez, Daniel and Erika Feser, Martha Vamos, David Gunther, Nolan Blackford, Brandon Visco, Brian Schall, Kenny Woods, Phil Farinola, Tolik Kaminsky; Roman D'Angelo, William Rodriguez, Jillian DeVaney, Lisa Young, Michael Bradley, Al Kramer, Richard Tyler Jordan, Steve Ivory, Hazel and Rob Kragulac, Bruce Rheins and Dawn Westlake, Manuel Gallegos, Leslie Miller, Lisa Reiner, Steve Ridgeway, Andy Skurow, Billy Barnes, Scherrie Payne, Freda Payne, Lynda Laurence, Susaye Greene, Barbara Ormsby, John Passantino, Linda DeStefano, Joseph Tumolo, Daniel Tumolo, Charles Casillo, John Carlino, David Spiro, Billy Masters, Mr. and Mrs. Adolph Steinlen, David and Frances Snyder, Abby and Maddy Snyder, Maribeth and Don Rothell, Mary Alvarez, Andy Steinlen, Mark Bringelson, Hope Levy and Tom Lavagnino and little Sam, Patti Torocsik, Sam Munoz, Michelle

Caruso, Leslie Miller, Matthew Barasach, Yvette Jarecki, Scott Allen, Phil Filomowicz, Jonathan Fousek, Felipe Echerri, and Stephen Gregory.

I have always been so blessed to have a family as supportive as mine. My thanks and love go out to: Roslyn and Bill Barnett and Jessica and Zachary, Rocco and Rosemaria Taraborrelli and Rocco and Vincent, and Arnold Taraborrelli. Special thanks to my father, Rocco, who has always been my inspiration. He has encouraged me in ways too numerous to mention. A big smile, also, for Spencer.

It was my mother Rose Marie's idea that I write this book's predecessor, *Jackie, Ethel, Joan: Women of Camelot*, and I know she would have enjoyed this book greatly. We miss her very much.

Finally, I must also acknowledge those readers of mine who have followed my career over the years. I am indebted to each and every reader who has stuck by me over the course of my career. I am eternally grateful to anyone who takes the time to pick up one of my books and read it.

Thank you so much.

J. Randy Taraborrelli
Winter 2011

INDEX